MOON HANDBOOKS
COLORADO

Downtown Telluride

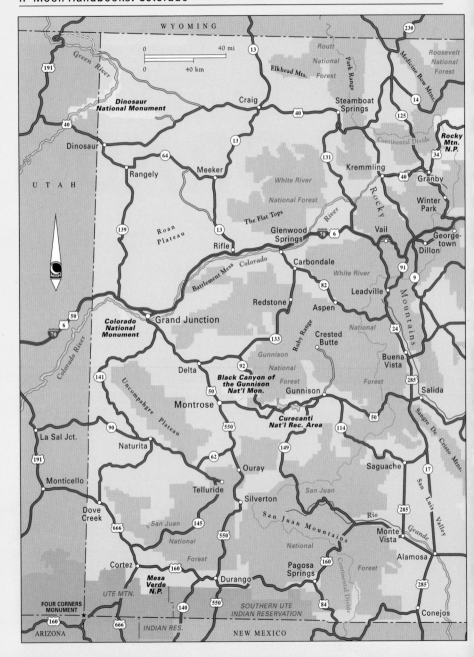

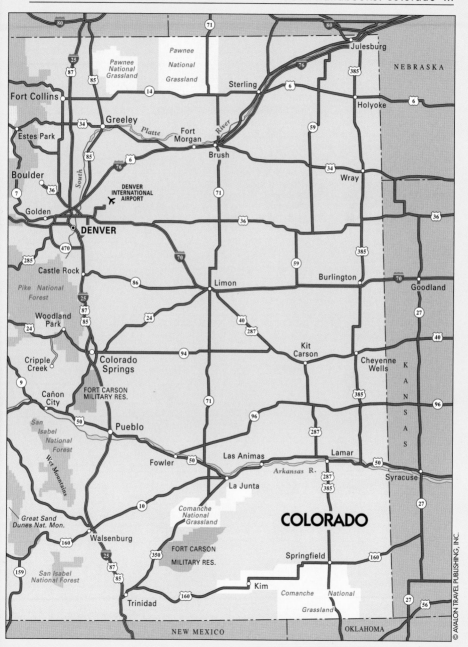

Fish Creek Falls

MOON HANDBOOKS
COLORADO

FIFTH EDITION

STEPHEN METZGER

AVALON
TRAVEL

Moon Handbooks: Colorado
FIFTH EDITION

Stephen Metzger

Published by
Avalon Travel Publishing
5855 Beaudry St.
Emeryville, CA 94608, USA

Please send all comments, corrections,
additions, amendments, and critiques to:

Moon Handbooks: Colorado
AVALON TRAVEL PUBLISHING
5855 BEAUDRY ST.
EMERYVILLE, CA 94608, USA
email: atpfeedback@avalonpub.com
website: www.moon.com

Printing History
1st edition—1992
5th edition—May 2002
5 4 3 2 1

ISBN: 1-56691-389-6
ISSN: 1537-3444

Editor: Karen Gaynor Bleske
Series Manager: Erin Van Rheenen
Graphics Coordinator: Susan Snyder
Production: Alvaro Villanueva, Marcie McKinley
Map Editor: Olivia Solís
Cartographers: Kat Kalamaras, Mike Morgenfeld
Proofreader: Mike Ferguson
Indexer: Emily Lunceford

Front cover photo: © Mary Liz Austin

Distributed by Publishers Group West

Printed in the United States by R.R. Donnelley

ABOUT THE AUTHOR
Stephen Metzger

Stephen Metzger first lit out for Colorado in the winter of 1973, after graduating from high school in Northern California. He had hoped to spend long days skiing on perfect snow under cloudless, Rocky Mountain skies. Instead, he spent long days working as a ski-lift operator for $1.60 an hour. He managed to get a few ski days in, though, if only a run at the end of the day, and on weekends he played pool and drank "Colorado Kool-Aid" at the Gold Pan bar in Breckenridge.

The following summer he returned to California to pursue bachelor's and master's degrees in English. In the early 1980s, after spending a year in Spain teaching English, and writing what he thought was the Great American Novel, he took up skiing again. He spent the mid-80s writing for *Powder* and *Skiing* magazines and other travel publications, while teaching at California State University, Chico.

Travel writing led to his first book, *California Downhill* (Moon), a guide to California ski resorts that appeared on the bookshelves the same year that the West Coast experienced one of the worst droughts in its recorded history. Most ski resorts were open for about an hour and a half that year. Ever the optimist, he signed on to write Moon Handbooks to New Mexico and Colorado. He returns to both states regularly. Two of his favorite places to research in Colorado are Coors Field and the Back Bowls at Vail.

Stephen still teaches English, and is married to Liz, a gorgeous and frighteningly intelligent grant writer and high school English teacher. He serves on the board of directors for a community theatre and plays music and sports with friends. He still skies as often as he can, both in California and Colorado, and usually with his daughters, Gina and Hannah.

For Betsy, whose love and support make life joyous and magical.

Contents

SPECIAL TOPICS

RESOURCES 425

Maps

MAP SYMBOLS

═══ Divided Highway	◉ State Capital	✈ International Airport
═══ Primary Road	○ City/Town	✗ Airfield/Airstrip
═══ Secondary Road	★ Point of Interest	▲ State Park
······· Unpaved Road	• Accommodation	⋀ Campground
—·—· State Boundary	▼ Restaurant/Bar	▲ Mountain
------ Bike Path/Trail	▪ Other Location	\\ Mountain Pass
	⛷ Ski Resort	⚑ Golf Course

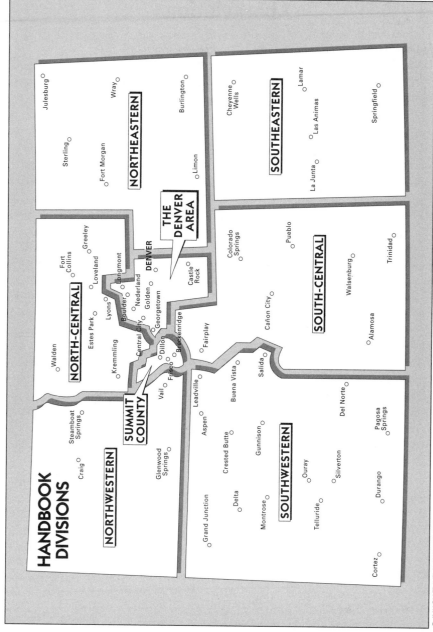

HANDBOOK DIVISIONS

NORTHWESTERN

NORTH-CENTRAL

SUMMIT COUNTY

SOUTHWESTERN

THE DENVER AREA

NORTHEASTERN

SOUTH-CENTRAL

SOUTHEASTERN

Craig
Steamboat Springs
Walden
Fort Collins
Greeley
Loveland
Longmont
Estes Park
Lyons
Nederland
Boulder
Golden
Central City
Georgetown
DENVER
Castle Rock
Kremmling
Dillon
Breckenridge
Vail
Frisco
Fairplay
Glenwood Springs
Leadville
Aspen
Buena Vista
Crested Butte
Salida
Cañon City
Colorado Springs
Pueblo
Delta
Grand Junction
Gunnison
Montrose
Walsenburg
Trinidad
Ouray
Del Norte
Alamosa
Telluride
Silverton
Pagosa Springs
Cortez
Durango
Sterling
Fort Morgan
Julesburg
Wray
Limon
Burlington
La Junta
Cheyenne Wells
Las Animas
Lamar
Springfield

© AVALON TRAVEL PUBLISHING, INC.

Abbreviations

BLM—Bureau of Land Management
DIA—Denver International Airport
elev.—elevation
F—Fahrenheit
I—Interstate

km—kilometers
pop.—population
RV—recreational vehicle
USGS—United States Geological Survey
WPA—Work Projects Administration

Keeping Current

In the 1930s, Scribner's editor Maxwell Perkins visited Ernest Hemingway in the Florida Keys. One day they went fishing together, and Perkins, taken by the beauty of the landscape, asked Hemingway why he had never written about it. "Because I haven't been away from it for 10 years," he answered.

That's the novelist's luxury—to visit a place, reflect on it, and then later describe it, embellishing where necessary. Obviously, guidebook writers can't do that. Readers want to know *exactly* what to expect when they're traveling. So the writer's got to get to work immediately, recording precisely what he or she saw, and the publisher's got to get the book in the stores as soon as possible. Though ostensibly the result is a general accuracy that makes the reader's trip more enjoyable, the fact is—even as we streamline the production process with state-of-the-art electronics—several months might go by between the time I type my last period and you read the first word. And because restaurants come and go, motels and museums raise their prices, and new roads get built, it's possible you'll find something that's not quite current.

But we want to know about it. We're continually working to revise and update these pages, so if you come across an error or omission in *Moon Handbooks: Colorado,* write and let us know. We particularly welcome letters from Coloradans who want to share an insider's view and from travelers who've run into problems other visitors should know about. Also, if you find a map or maps difficult to read, or have a suggestion for a map you think would be helpful, please contact us. Be as specific as you can, and document your sources when possible.

Address all correspondence to:

Moon Handbooks: Colorado
Avalon Travel Publishing
5855 Beaudry Street
Emeryville, CA 94608
email: atpfeedback@avalonpub.com

Introduction

The Land

Laws change; people die; the land remains.
Abraham Lincoln

Comprising more than 100,000 square miles, Colorado is the country's eighth-largest state—twice the size of New York and 10 times as big as New Hampshire. Its landscapes are remarkably diverse; the state stretches from the vast eastern plains to the gently sloping western plateau, and the majestic Rocky Mountains run north to south just west of center. The state's topographical relief is nearly 11,000 feet: from the 3,350-foot-high bed of the lower Arkansas River to 14,433-foot Mt. Elbert. And to the observant traveler, the state is a living, breathing geology lesson, with deep canyons carved by ancient waterways exposing hundreds of thousands of years of the land's settling, uplifting, shifting, and erosion.

A Long, Long Time Ago . . .

During the first part of the Paleozoic era (240 million to 750 million years ago), Colorado was largely flat and entirely submerged beneath the waters of a shallow sea. Toward the end of that era, during the Permian period, mountains began to rise, waters receded, and muddy, sediment-filled rivers wandered about the plains. The remains of the first uplifts can be seen in the bizarre redrock formations at Garden of the Gods in Colorado Springs and at Red Rocks Amphitheater near Denver.

During the Mesozoic era (70 million to 230 million years ago), more mountains rose, and much of the land was lush and marshy. Dinosaurs sloshed through jungles teeming with primitive life-forms. By the end of the era, however, the dinosaurs were gone. In addition, the Gulf of Mexico had crept north to meet the western shores of the Atlantic Ocean, and Colorado was again entirely submerged; the mountains were now underwater reefs.

© STEPHEN METZGER

Clinton Reservoir, north of Leadville

The Cenozoic era (beginning 70 million years ago) brought the beginnings of the landscape we see today. Inland seas had receded, though much of the area remained swampy, and mountains were beginning to take forms we might recognize today. During the Pleistocene epoch, starting less than two million years ago, great glaciers advanced and receded over much of North America. During the most recent ice age, however, between 25,000 and 60,000 years ago, the great continental ice sheet did not creep into Colorado, although smaller glaciers continued to carve away at the Rocky Mountains.

By around 20,000 years ago, the climate had begun to warm, and about that time the first humans probably appeared in Colorado. Nomadic hunters, most likely still en route south after having crossed over the Bering Land Bridge, tracked mastodons, mammoths, ground sloths, and antelope across the Eastern Plains and the western plateau area.

The Eastern Plains

The Eastern Plains of Colorado actually begin as far east as the Dakotas and eastern Kansas and Nebraska—then come to a screeching halt just west of Denver, where the Rockies' Front Range looms sharp and massive. Comprising roughly 40 percent of the state, the plains are marked by vast expanses of low rolling hills and yellow-brown fields of prairie grasses.

Thanks to the development of irrigation systems, these otherwise dry lands are the sites of huge ranches and farms. Herds of cattle graze on sprawling spreads that have been in the same families for a century. Sugar beets, wheat, alfalfa, watermelons, honeydew, and other crops are harvested by hardy farmers who do age-old work with high-tech equipment—cellular phones, computers, and thoroughly modern, air-conditioned tractors.

The Rocky Mountains

The backbone not only of Colorado but of the United States, the Rocky Mountains—and the Continental Divide, which snakes through them—mark the division point of the sources of all North American waterways. Even those who have seen the Rockies before—even those who live in the Rockies and see and feel them daily—cannot help but be awed by their immenseness and majesty. Consider: 54 peaks top 14,000 feet (though none tops 15,000), several roadways wind over 11,000-foot passes, and many towns and communities are nestled in valleys 9,000 feet above sea level. Leadville's elevation is 10,188 feet.

The Rockies' beginnings date from roughly 60 million–70 million years ago, to the Cretaceous period. At that time, tectonic movement and fierce volcanic activity deep within the earth lifted Precambrian layers of rock, creating the wedge-shaped range we see today; the bulkhead-like east side of the Rockies rises abruptly 10,000 feet above the plains, while the west side of the range slopes gently toward the Great Basin. One of the best places to view the eastern escarpment is at the Flatirons, in Boulder, where a sheer cliff face rises so dramatically as to be striking even from the air at 25,000 feet.

No sooner had Mother Nature created the Rockies than she began to wear them down; wind, water, and ice have chiseled relentlessly at the range for 60 million years. Glaciation has had the biggest hand in shaping the Rockies we see today. Off and on between 75,000 years ago and the most recent ice age (10,000 years ago), much of Colorado was covered with large sheets of ice. Slow-moving glaciers carved large valleys, moved huge areas of earth, and created alpine lakes with their meltwater. Small remnants of these glaciers still exist in Colorado's high country; St. Mary's Glacier, near Idaho Springs and Georgetown, is one prime example, but you'll also see numerous tiny unnamed spots of white on the sides (usually north) of towering mountain peaks.

The Western Slope and Plateau Country

The western side of the Rocky Mountains slopes much more gradually than does the steep eastern face, and the area from the Continental Divide west to the Utah border is known generally as the western slope. For more than a hundred years ranchers have taken advantage of this prime land, and hundreds of thousands of cattle graze in these fields from Craig south to Durango. Make no mistake, though: not all of the western slope slopes gently, particularly the towering peaks of the San Juan Mountains around Telluride.

In the northwestern corner of the state, the great plateau is largely shale and underlain with vast fields of coal, oil, and natural gas. Remote river canyons slice deep into the earth. The southwestern corner, meanwhile, particularly the Four Corners area, is a land of redrock canyons and mesas, the dry brown land punctuated by clusters of juniper and piñon.

CLIMATE

In Colorado the joke goes, "If you don't like the weather, just wait 15 minutes." And there's some truth to that, to which anyone who's seen a sunny summer day turn suddenly to rain and thunder can testify. In addition, given the state's dramatic range in geography—from the arid plains to the lush mountain meadows of the Rockies to their windswept peaks—it's difficult to make generalizations.

The Rockies

This is where the weather's the least predictable. Keep in mind that it can get *cold* in the winter. Though it's a dry cold, not nearly as piercing as that damp cold of the coasts, it can still be awfully nasty, especially when the wind blows. Zero-degree temperatures are not at all uncommon in the Colorado Rockies from December to March, and the mercury often drops even lower. Out on the western slope, around Gunnison for example, the wind can whip cold and arctic-like across that high plateau. Sub-zero temperatures are not all that rare.

Anyone traveling in the Rocky Mountains in winter should have plenty of warm clothing. Layering is best: wear a good pair of long underwear (preferably 100 percent polypropylene), a turtleneck, a wool sweater, and a heavy, water-resistant coat, as well as gloves or mittens and a hat. Also, make sure your footwear keeps you not only warm but *dry*. (See Hy-

Summer storms are common on the plains—all of a sudden thunderheads start building, leaves and dust start swirling, and shadows fall across wheatfields.

pothermia under Health and Safety in the On the Road chapter.)

Summer days in the Rockies are often pleasant, into the 80s and even 90s, with the high-elevation sun almost mandating shorts. Remember, though, that afternoon storms are very common, and you should always have warmer clothes and rain gear handy. Also keep in mind that though summer days are warm, night temperatures drop significantly, down into the mid-50s and lower, and if you plan to be outside at night—especially if you're camping—you should have plenty of warm clothing.

The Plains

The climate's not as dramatic out on Colorado's eastern plains as it is in the Rockies. But there are some things to know. First of all, it gets hot, and air-conditioning in your car is more than just awfully nice. Also, summer storms are common; the temperature might be pushing 90°F or even 100°F in midafternoon, when all of a sudden thunderheads start building, leaves and dust start swirling, and shadows fall across wheatfields. In fact, the storms on the plains can be even more threatening than those in the mountains, as they often bring with them high winds and even cyclones, which in the past have even upended cars and mobile homes and flattened office buildings.

Ordinarily, of course, summer storms on the plains aren't that bad. Still, it would be wise to keep rain gear on hand, as well as a coat and a spare pair of shoes. Also, drive especially carefully when that wind whips up and when water pools on the roadways.

Winter on the plains can be harsh. Temperatures dip into the 30s, and biting winds whip across the vast expanses of open fields. Though snow doesn't fall in the amounts it does in the Rockies, it can still pile up in drifts, and sometimes the wind and snow combine in near whiteouts. On the other hand, when the skies are clear and the winds gentle, daytime temperatures can lift into the 60s. In fact, some winter days on the plains are absolutely gorgeous, with views seeming to stretch forever and a cold but tolerable air invigorating you as you draw deep breaths.

Denver

At the western terminus of the Great Plains, Denver, the "Mile-High City," sits snug up against the Front Range of the Rocky Mountains. Summer days are warm but not hot—though occasional heat waves drive temperatures

over 100°F—and they're mostly dry; the city receives less than 15 inches of precipitation a year.

During the winter it can get cold, though it's still quite tolerable. Daytime temperatures are generally in the 40s, though they drop considerably at night, often into the 20s and teens. If you plan to explore Denver between October and April, bring warm clothes. Again, layering is best, starting with wicking long underwear and working out to a good wind- and waterproof coat or jacket.

Flora and Fauna

Colorado's widely varied geography and climate make the state home to a huge range of plant and animal life—from the prairie grasses, yucca, fence lizards, spadefoot toads, and pronghorn of the eastern plains to the aspen, spruce, black bears, bighorn sheep, mountain goats, elk, and moose of the Rocky Mountains. In addition, Colorado is home, either part- or full-time, to many different species of birds—owls, pheasants, grouse, geese, ducks, eagles, turkeys, and hundreds of varieties of small birds. Recent field research also indicates the San Juan Mountains of southern Colorado might be home to a handful of grizzly bears, a species whose remaining numbers are so small that the animals had eluded human contact since the 1930s and were thought to be long gone from the area.

You'll probably see at least a sampling of these critters on your visit, even if you never get out of your car. Though you've got to work awfully hard (and have a good bit of luck thrown in) to see bighorn sheep and mountain goats, chances are pretty good you'll spot elk, deer, pronghorn, and various birds of prey, including hawks and owls.

One of the best places to view wildlife is Rocky Mountain National Park, where elk often graze within yards of the highway (June and July). Once I actually had to stop my car as a big bull elk nonchalantly crossed the road, then turned and gave his adoring harem the come-hither eye. Backcountry hikers and backpackers have the best chance of viewing wildlife in the park, al-

though those simply driving through and stopping at the designated viewing areas will most likely see some form of wildlife, even if it's just ground squirrels. The park is also the best place in the state to see mountain goats and bighorn sheep, though you'll probably need a good pair of binoculars and a perfect sense of timing. These elusive animals stay a bit farther from the road, and if you see them at all, they'll probably appear as nothing more than distant specks of white on a steep cliffside.

Colorado's waters—from the low-lying reservoirs of the eastern plains to the tumbling snow-fed streams of the high mountains—hold many different species of warm- and cold-water fish. Bass, walleye, catfish, bluegill, crappie, and other sunfish are found in the lower lakes, notably John Martin Reservoir near Las Animas and Horsetooth Reservoir near Fort Collins. Trout and kokanee salmon are found in the higher lakes and streams; the most common trout are rainbow and brown, while Mackinaw (lake) trout roam some of the larger, deeper lakes (Grand Lake and Blue Mesa Reservoir, for example).

One of the great joys of visiting Colorado, particularly in the spring and early summer, is seeing the abundant wildflowers that blanket meadows and mountain hillsides. Sheets of bright yellow, blue, and purple contrast dramatically with the backdrops of aspen, fir, and spruce, and with the great granite snowcapped peaks looming in the distance. Especially beautiful is Colorado's state flower, the columbine, a delicate, commonly light blue to purplish flower that grows in damp meadows either singly or in clusters. Though summer visitors are likely to see startling displays of wildflowers throughout the Rockies, here are some areas that have been particularly memorable in my visits: the meadows off Cuchara, Independence, Loveland, and Kebler passes; the sprawling vales of Rocky Mountain National Park; the meadows off Highway 67 between Divide and Cripple Creek; the wetlands near Aspen, particularly along the Roaring Fork River; and leas along Highway 72 between Lyons and Nederland.

Aspen Trees

Colorado's aspens have become almost mythical. During the winter, these beautiful white-barked trees lose their leaves and stand stoically in groves, skinny and dormant contrasting with the evergreens often found in the same forests. In the spring, the trees begin to bud, and the distinctly shaped "quaking" leaves—pale green at first—reappear. In summer, the leaves begin to yellow, and by fall they have turned to stunning electric gold and orange. This is the best time to hike, or drive, into Colorado's aspen forests, though you will not be alone: the vibrant colors attract not only Colorado's color aficionados, but folks from outside the state as well. Tour groups and local boosters have even organized several "color tours" to the various aspen forests.

Bighorn Sheep

One of the other virtual symbols of Colorado is the bighorn sheep. These magnificent beasts, which can weigh up to 350 pounds (and whose horns alone can weigh 35 pounds), are scattered about the state in several specific herds. An arti-

cle in *Colorado Outdoors* (Nov.–Dec., 1991) lists 13 specific "hot spots" where the animals can best be viewed, including: the Georgetown Wildlife Viewing Area in Georgetown; Rocky Mountain National Park; Poudre Canyon, west of Fort Collins; three spots in the Salida-Buena Vista area; and an area on the east side of U.S. 550 between Ridgway and Ouray.

Elk

One of the highlights of a trip to Rocky Mountain National Park is seeing a big bull elk up close, its huge rack seeming to hold up the sky. Though elk, too, are scattered about the state, and there are many places where you can see them, the park is the best. Here, large herds of elk graze in meadows, huge-antlered bulls wander to within yards of the roadway, and during certain times of the year, the crisp darkness is pierced by their bugling—the music of the night.

BOB RACE

bighorn sheep

History

THE FIRST COLORADANS

Although recent finds in Central and South America have contributed to contemporary theories of the New World's first human inhabitants, the discoveries in the North American southwest turned anthropology on its ear by proving humans had come across from Asia at least 10,000 years ago, or 8,000 years earlier than previously thought. In the early 1930s, scientists from the University of Denver determined bones found in northeastern New Mexico were from a post-glacial species of bison, long extinct, and embedded in them were spear points used to kill the animal. Since then, Folsom points, as they have come to be called, have been found throughout the southeastern Colorado plains, as well as on the western slope near Montrose—proof humans wandered in relatively large numbers in the more temperate regions of Colorado 10,000 years ago, hunting giant ground sloths, woolly mammoths, and mastodons.

The Anasazi

The first people to settle in what is now Colorado were the Anasazi (the word is Navajo and probably best translated as "Enemies of Our Ancestors"). As early as A.D. 550, Anasazi of the Basketmaker period had begun migrating north from the Rio Grande area of central New Mexico and were building pit houses in the Four Corners area, particularly around Mesa Verde. Between A.D. 750 and 1100, the Developmental Pueblo period, Anasazi architecture changed from primitive pit houses to above-ground shelters, which were often built in clusters to provide homes and storage for several families. In addition, stone towers 10–15 feet tall were built near these early pueblos, suggesting a need for lookouts. At the same time, they were developing a distinct pottery style, characterized by intricate black designs on a white background, as well as sophisticated water-storage and irrigation systems.

During the Classic Pueblo period, A.D. 1100–1300, the Anasazi further developed their architecture. Some single pueblos contained more than 400 rooms and were four stories tall; some of these pueblo "cities" were home to 5,000 or more people. About A.D. 1150, many of the Anasazi of southwestern Colorado began to move into cliff-side alcoves. Although no one knows the real reason for the move, anthropologists suspect it might have been to secure themselves from enemy attack (although no real evidence of enemies or violence has been found) or to protect themselves from the elements. These cliff dwellings are best seen at Mesa Verde National Park, near Durango.

By 1300, the cliff dwellings, and the free-standing pueblos scattered about the Four Corners area, had all been abandoned. And again, no one knows why. At one time it was thought the Navajos and Apaches arrived from the north and drove them out, although modern thinking is that these tribes didn't show up until about 1450. The most commonly accepted theory today is that the Anasazi overfarmed the little valleys in which they grew their corn, beans, and squash; then they simply headed for greener pastures, most likely filtering southwest back toward the Rio Grande area. It's generally assumed that today's Zuni, Acoma, Taos, Sandia, and other Pueblo peoples are descendants of the Anasazi.

The Shoshone and Algonquin Tribes

Between the time the Anasazi disappeared and the white man arrived, Colorado was home to several tribes, most of whom were from the Shoshone and Algonquin linguistic stocks. The most widely spread and the largest in terms of numbers were the Utes, a Shoshonean mountain-dwelling people who roamed from the eastern mountain passes, which they guarded against the Plains tribes, to the lower reaches of the western slope.

The Plains tribes, primarily Cheyenne, Comanche, Arapahoe, and Kiowa, hunted the great flatlands east of the Rockies. Often at war with each other, they arrived some time after the Utes, probably having been pushed west by other groups. Other tribes of Colorado included Pawnee, Sioux, and Navajo; Blackfoot and Crow hunting parties probably ventured south into the north-central part of the state.

THE ARRIVAL OF THE WHITE MAN

Early Exploration

Most likely the first explorers in Colorado were members of the Francisco Vásquez de Coronado expedition, who might have drifted north from New Mexico in 1541 in their search for the fabled Seven Gold Cities of Cíbola. Unlike in New Mexico, where records indicate Coronado was responsible for the widespread rape and murder of native people, the expedition apparently didn't do much damage in Colorado.

During the early 18th century, Spain and France both sought title to the western plains, and the Spanish, pushing up from New Mexico, began to explore the San Luis Valley area of south-central Colorado. French trappers and traders, meanwhile, pushed west into the mountains. Spain, however, had a stronger hold on the region, and by 1762, France had ceded to Spain all land west of the Mississippi.

In 1776, friars Francisco Antanasio Dominguez and Silvestre Velez de Escalante traveled through southwestern Colorado in search of an overland route that would connect the missions of New Mexico with those of California. The expedition not only provided the first written record of Colorado exploration but also gave the area many of its place names, including the San Juan and Sangre de Cristo mountains and El Rio de las Animas Perdidos en Purgatorio (The River of the Lost Souls in Purgatory).

The Louisiana Purchase

In 1803, two years after Spain had been forced to turn over its hold on northern Colorado to the French, President Thomas Jefferson bought the Louisiana Territory from Napoléon. Though he was ridiculed at the time for squandering $15 million on real estate that was almost wholly un-explored, the Louisiana Purchase doubled the size of the United States and, as every school-child knows, turned out to be a pretty decent deal in the long run.

The First American Explorations

The first American to explore the Colorado area was Zebulon Pike, who pushed into the mountains west of Pueblo and Colorado Springs in 1806. In his journal, Pike described the peak that was named for him as "unscalable."

In 1820, President James Monroe dispatched Major Stephen H. Long to explore the new territory's northern boundary, which had been established a year earlier along the Arkansas River and into the mountains along the Continental Divide. Long's party followed the South Platte River west, then dropped south along the Arkansas, ultimately veering west again near Colorado Springs and venturing as far as Royal Gorge. (One of Long's men, Dr. Edwin James, led the first recorded ascent of Pikes "unscalable" Peak.)

Trappers, Traders, and Colorado Territory

In September 1821, Mexico won its independence from Spain, and almost immediately the United States and Mexico began vigorous trading, with pack trains departing regularly from Missouri for Santa Fe. The Santa Fe Trail, as the route was known, cut across southeastern Colorado and helped further develop this otherwise hostile land. Forts and trading posts were established along the trail, most notably Bent's Fort near Las Animas, providing gathering places for trappers, traders, and mountain men, Americans, French, and Native Americans.

The United States declared war on Mexico on May 13, 1846, and two years later, the Treaty of Guadalupe Hidalgo was signed, which ceded to the United States a large chunk of land running from Texas west to California, including some of southern Colorado. Now, all present-day Colorado belonged to the United States, although a Colorado Territory was still 15 years down the road.

SILVER THREADS AND GOLDEN NEEDLES

"Pikes Peak or Bust"

Gold was discovered in September 1858 on several waterways near what is now Denver, and within weeks a number of buildings had sprung up along area riverbanks, forming the first traces of what would soon develop into the state's largest city. Word of the strike quickly spread to the East Coast, and a flood of prospectors began making their way west. Their motto, after the prominent landmark just to the south, was "Pikes Peak or Bust."

With the onset of winter, little mining could be done, and while the little settlements grew, so did their inhabitants' anticipation of growing rich. With the thaw, though, came the discovery that the strikes weren't nearly as rich as reported. The summer of 1859 saw thousands of disgruntled fortune seekers heading back the way they'd come, often encountering along the way other Pikes Peak or Busters, many of whom were convinced to turn back long before even reaching the mining camps.

COURTESY OF THE COLORADO HISTORICAL SOCIETY

a Ute family

That spring, however, gold was also discovered along Clear Creek in the mountains west of Denver. This time, the strike was for real. Within a matter of days, several mining camps, including Central City, Black Hawk, and Idaho Springs, were teeming with miners. Horace Greeley wrote that at one point 500 men were arriving each day. Over the next few years, dozens of small towns were founded in the nearby mountains, and in 1861, Colorado Territory was officially established.

Early Ranching and Agriculture

During the early days of Colorado Territory, ranchers and farmers began to see the potential of the area's fertile river valleys and vast expanses of grazing lands. The eastern plains and much of the western slope were seen as ideal places to raise wheat, corn, and other crops, and to let cattle and sheep roam.

But Wait, Didn't the Land Still Belong to the Indians?

Absolutely, insofar as Native American philosophy allowed for "ownership" at all. And even though the United States now owned this land on paper, the Indians still considered it theirs.

The 1860s and '70s, then, were years of conflict, and often these conflicts were violent and bloody. In 1864, about 30 miles west of the Kansas border, U.S. soldiers under Colonel John Chivington wiped out a Cheyenne village of as many as 500 people, the majority of whom were women and children. Chivington, who claimed he thought the camped Cheyenne were hostile, was court-martialed for the Sand Creek Massacre but never convicted.

Battles also raged in the northwestern part of Colorado, where ranchers and farmers were intruding upon Northern Utes. In 1879, Indian agent Nathan Meeker, known for his lack of diplomacy, tried to convince the Utes to give up their hunting lifestyles and turn to farming. Meeker was killed after he sent for troops to support his position. The Utes were subsequently vanquished to a reservation in Utah. Ranchers, farmers, and other settlers now had Colorado all to themselves.

COURTESY OF THE COLORADO HISTORICAL SOCIETY

early railroad passengers on Marshall Pass

Makin' Tracks

One of the biggest influences on the development and settling of Colorado was the railroad. In the 1870s, railroad tracks began to be laid across the land, linking isolated towns and communities, mining camps, and supply centers. Almost overnight, the wagon trains and stage coaches were replaced by locomotives, though the only way to get over some of the high mountain passes was still by foot and burro. For the first time, people, cattle, food products, ore, and other items could be transported quickly and reliably across the vast expanses of Colorado Territory. In addition, the new industry brought thousands of jobs to the area, with stations needing to be built about every 100 miles. From Burlington to Grand Junction, from Durango to Julesburg, the railroad significantly changed the landscape of Colorado and the lifestyles of its people.

In 1876, Colorado achieved statehood.

More Gold and Silver

Between 1880 and the turn of the century, the Colorado mountains were swarming with mining camps. From Aspen to Cripple Creek, from Leadville to Telluride, dozens of tiny communities were bursting at the seams with miners, real estate tycoons, newspapermen (sometimes a town of 5,000 would support 10 newspapers), various bunko artists, and women working to service

them. Grand hotels were constructed and lavish parties thrown; elaborate opera houses attracted the biggest names of the day.

After the Gold Rush

And then it all came crashing down. In 1893, silver was devalued, and Colorado's mining camps went into the skids. Mines closed, smelters shut down, and miners hit the road—many of them ending up in Denver where unemployment rates soared. Towns that had once thronged with the newly prosperous were all but deserted. The great hotels and opera houses were boarded up, and banks closed faster than you can say "S and L scandal." Though a handful of towns continued to prosper—Crested Butte, for example, where coal was discovered—Colorado for the most part was in sad shape as the 20th century approached.

THE 20TH CENTURY

The first years of the new century saw great strife between Colorado's mine workers and owners. In Cripple Creek, Victor, and Telluride, particularly, the conflicts were often violent, and on several occasions the National Guard was called in to try to "keep the peace." In 1903 and 1904 miners in Colorado City and Cripple Creek struck to protest a drop in wages, and when "mysterious" explosions in several mine shafts killed a number of workers, labor blamed management and management blamed labor.

In 1914, the United Mine Workers union organized Trinidad-area coal workers, who struck for better wages and working conditions, and in April, after reports of violence in the camps, the Colorado National Guard was sent in. The conflict came to a bloody head on April 20, when several strikers were killed and tent fires killed 13 women and children.

A Short-Lived Prosperity

During World War I, silver prices rose, and many Colorado mines reopened. Though the mining towns saw a general caution instead of the wild abandon of the late 19th century, at least some of the little towns could again keep their heads above water. In addition, prices of farm produce, particularly wheat, skyrocketed, and Colorado farmers enjoyed a new prosperity and status.

Which didn't last long.

The Depression hit Colorado hard. Farmers, ranchers, miners, and businessmen found themselves without work and, oftentimes, without homes. Fortunately, the federal government stepped in where it could, and several major projects, including the development of schools and national forests, as well as highway and irrigation systems, provided workers with jobs and the state with a semblance of stability. In 1935 and '36, Colorado revamped its tax systems, with special sales and service taxes set aside for relief.

Another boon to Colorado's economy was the arrival of the military, which largely came about with the advent of World War II. In addition to the United States Air Force Academy just north of Colorado Springs, several other bases were established in the Denver and Colorado Springs areas.

The Ski Industry

As early as the mid-1930s, downhill skiing was already starting to take hold in some of Colorado's tiny mountain communities. Originally just something to keep locals from getting bored during the long winter months, the sport soon caught on, and folks in the lower-lying areas were making weekend treks to the handful of primitive rope tows.

By the late 1960s and early '70s, skiing had grown up, and Colorado was recognized as one of the best places on earth to strap boards afoot, climb aboard a chairlift, and take off through easy wind and downy flake. In fact, not only had the sport grown up, but it had caught on big time, and new resorts were opening each year, while established resorts were cutting new trails and adding new lifts. In the spring of 1973, the first bore of a tunnel through Loveland Pass was completed, providing Denver-area skiers much easier access to the resorts of Summit County and to Vail, just over the next pass. By the late 1980s, Eisenhower Tunnel's four lanes already seemed too few, and on winter weekends traffic bottlenecked horribly as skiers descended in increasing numbers on the ski towns of Dillon, Breckenridge, and Vail.

Interestingly, the number of Colorado skiers has actually decreased in recent years. The 1999–2000 season saw a drop to 10.8 million

The Colorado Rockies take batting practice at Coors Field.

skier days from the all-time high of 12 million in 1997–98—most likely a reaction to the exorbitant cost of the sport (up to $65 a day for a lift ticket and as much as $800 to $1,000 for a pair of skis and boots). Still, however, there are a whole lot people venturing into what used to be Colorado's backcountry, and we can only hope that common sense, intelligence, and environmental awareness will be the guiding factors in ski-country development.

Recent Developments
In the summer of 1990, Colorado voters approved two measures that effected significant change, in varying ways, upon the state. The first was legalized gambling. Though limited in scope, gambling has been legal in parts of Colorado as of October 1991. Black Hawk, Central City, and Cripple Creek bettors can now play poker, blackjack, and slots ($5 maximum).

On a more positive note, in the same election, voters also approved major-league baseball for Denver. The first two seasons, the Colorado Rockies played in Mile High Stadium (the Denver Broncos' field), but by the 1995 season they had moved into the gorgeous new Coors Field, the building of which has completely transformed the western end of Denver, known as LoDo (Lower Downtown). The empty warehouses and abandoned storefronts dominating the area until as late as 1993 have been replaced, remodeled, and renovated, and now the area is characterized by brewpubs, bookstores, restaurants, antique shops, and espresso bars, and a general sense of vitality and good, safe fun. Evenings before and after games the area around the stadium is teeming with folks taking pride not only in the team and stadium but in a rejuvenated part of Denver as well. Live music wafts from rooftop restaurants and bars, and vendors hawk peanuts to the steady stream of fans passing through en route to the stadium.

The only downside to the upscaling of LoDo has been the skyrocketing of rents in the area; some office workers, tenants, and even homeless people who had found shelter in abandoned warehouses have been displaced, either unable to afford to stick around or hustled along by developers.

Government and Economy

POLITICS
With political roots lying in westward expansionism, frontier justice, and turn-of-the-century unionism, Colorado has long been a fiercely independent state. The state's residents have historically been politically active, engaging in grass-roots organizing and fighting successfully for rights and protections vital to their survival.

Left vs. Right
Until recently, the state was predominantly Democratic, electing Democratic governors, senators, and congressmen. But this seems to be changing. U.S. Senator Ben Nighthorse Campbell—the first Native American senator, elected in 1992—changed his party affiliation from Democrat to Republican midterm. And according to a July 19, 1998, article by David Olinger in *The Denver Post,* the entire state is shifting to the Right, not so much because of folks' changing their allegiances but because of first-time voters and folks moving in from out of state (primarily Texas and southern California) going decidedly Republican. In 1993, Olinger notes, Republicans held a 120,000-voter edge, and since that time Democrats have accounted for only "one-fifth of voters who registered statewide."

In 1992, Colorado's voters passed Amendment 2, the controversial "Anti-Gay Initiative." The law was ultimately thrown out by the courts, which decided homosexuals couldn't be discriminated against after all. But much anti-gay sentiment still exists, particularly in conservative strongholds such as Colorado Springs. Focus on the Family, one Colorado Springs-based conservative organization, founded in 1977, lobbies tirelessly to legally define marriage as:

> *an institution between one man and one woman, [based on its principle that the] institution of marriage was intended by God to be a permanent, lifelong relationship between a man and a woman [and that] the family exists to propagate the race and to provide a safe and secure haven in which to nurture, teach and love the younger generation ... including the unborn.*

Thankfully, the state is as varied politically as it is geographically. Just as Colorado Springs is a conservative stronghold, so is Boulder a bastion of progressive and liberal politics. Known somewhat facetiously as the "People's Republic of Boulder" (as well as "twenty square miles surrounded by reality"), Boulder is refreshingly hip in its lawmaking and social attitudes in general.

Urban vs. Rural

The split between liberal and conservative factions in Colorado is mirrored by a growing division between rural and urban interests. As Colorado government becomes more and more centralized—as Denver continues to develop into an increasingly influential major American city—the small-town and rural folks claim the big-city bureaucrats are seizing too much control. In fact, there is a nearly palpable "us vs. them" competition between the Denver/Front Range (Boulder) population center and much of the rest of the state. In the same *Denver Post* article, Olinger quoted Phillips County (Holyoke) Commissioner Keith Sharp saying, "One size doesn't fit all. What works for the Front Range with all of its growth doesn't work for eastern Colorado." And those sentiments are echoed throughout the state outside the Denver area. Olinger also quotes Steve Sherlock, president of Colorado East Bank and Trust, in Lamar:

> *The problem with the state legislature, with bureaucrats on the Front Range, is they don't think we can manage ourselves.*

ECONOMY

Colorado's economy developed in the 19th century on the backs of the mining, agriculture, and railroad industries. A century later, these industries still contribute to state coffers. Silver, gold, and molybdenum provide paychecks for miners in Summit County, the Four Corners area, and the plains. And vast underground deposits of oil and natural gas lie beneath the western plateau; Chevron runs the largest production oil field in the state near Rangely.

Lives and lifestyles on the eastern plains and western slope of the Rockies still hinge on agriculture. Cattle ranches and fields of alfalfa, melons, corn, and barley dominate the landscape, and folks watch the skies for rain—while they get the latest stock reports on their computers.

Though the railroad industry isn't the economic dynamo it once was, trains still chug between mountain towns, carrying camera-toting tourists from around the world. Railroad museums throughout Colorado document the contributions of the iron horse in state history.

Recent Trends

Manufacturing has become a key player in the state's economy. Though land is growing in value in Colorado, it is still cheap compared to the West Coast; many companies have moved east from California and built plants for the production of computers and other electronic instruments.

And the state's tourism industry has grown phenomenally, today employing nearly 10 percent of the population in one aspect or another. Colorado's ski industry is huge, with new ski resorts in the planning stages and new lifts going in every summer at the existing resorts. And those same ski resorts are increasingly courting summer visitors, offering cheap lodging and package deals to attract mountain bikers, golfers, and sightseers. The flip side to the growth of the tourism industry is that it has the tendency to create wide chasms between those who can afford to cash in on it and those who can't. In Telluride, where an 800-square-foot in-need-of-repair Victorian can fetch up to $700,000, local workers often must live outside of town, where housing is affordable. Boulder holds such a glut of qualified workers that you'll find folks with teaching credentials and Ph.D.s driving airport shuttles while they wait for a chance to work in their field of expertise.

Responding to Colorado's growth, Denver International Airport opened in February 1995, replacing Stapleton Jurassic and making Denver an important midcontinental hub. Note: this edition of *Moon Handbooks: Colorado* went to press just months after the September 11, 2001, terrorist attacks on the World Trade Center and the Pentagon. At that time, all major airlines—including United, based in Denver—were experiencing financial woes due to the recession and terrorism, and had laid off thousands of employees.

The People

In part because Colorado is so strikingly varied—from the ranches of the eastern plains to the mining-villages-turned-ski-towns of the central Rockies, from the tiny streets of Trinidad to the high-rise avenues and lofts of LoDo—its people are a varied lot as well. Though it's difficult to apply generalizations to such a diverse group, you can safely say a few things about Coloradans.

They're highly educated. Colorado boasts the fourth-highest literacy rate in the country.

They love the outdoors. Most towns are within short drives of some of the best outdoor recreation in the country, and outdoor magazines regularly rate Colorado communities—Boulder, Fort Collins, Colorado Springs—among the country's best places to live.

They love professional sports. You'll find insanely rabid fans of the Broncos, Rockies, and Nuggets almost everywhere you go in the state.

Their state—home, a sense of place—is profoundly important to them. Almost everywhere I go in Colorado I find that folks absolutely love where they live and feel a strong bond with the land around them.

They're nervous about newcomers. Many, thinking they live in their own slice of paradise, hate to see it ruined by growth.

They're largely white. Denver's population is roughly 80 percent Caucasian, 12 percent Hispanic, 5 percent African American, and 0.6 percent Native American. (In the southern part of the state, Hispanics and Native Americans make up a much larger proportion of the population.)

For the most part they're tolerant. Though small pockets of anti-immigration, anti-gay, and anti-everything-different sentiments exist, particularly in the more rural areas, most Coloradans appreciate how diversity—in all its forms—contributes to the overall health of a community.

What do they for their livings? They ranch. They manufacture computer chips. They operate ski lifts, they lead white-water raft trips, they wait tables, they invest in real estate, they teach school, they grow apples, alfalfa, and wheat. They fly fighter planes, cut hair, teach snowboarding, mine gold, fight fires, raise hogs, drive trucks, fix broken bones, and sling hash. And many do things other than that for which they are trained—and things that might not be their first career choice—to stay in the state they love.

On the Road

Sightseeing Highlights

The phrase "No visit to Colorado is complete without . . ." probably pops up more than it should in this book. Likewise, when friends ask for help planning itineraries, my list of things I tell them they've *gotta* see and do is probably way too long. But please understand. Not only do I have a passionate love affair with Colorado, but my travels have taken me to so many parts of the state it's difficult even to come up with a Top-10-type list. So ultimately, I suppose, I defer, dear Reader, to you, as you need to make some decisions about what *kind* of trip yours will be: Will you primarily be sightseeing, or will you be enjoying Colorado's myriad recreational activities? Are you more interested in the state's history than in food, wine, and music festivals? Do you want to explore ancient ruins or modern shopping centers? Do you want to see vast meadows blanketed in white, or mountain hillsides ablaze with brilliant golds and deep, fiery reds?

Once you've answered those questions, you can begin looking at what the state has to offer more clearly. And though you certainly can't "do" all of Colorado in a two-week trip, you can tailor your trip to make it as rewarding and fulfilling as possible. Herewith, then, are some of what I think are Colorado's highlights. Rank them as you will.

THINGS TO SEE

Rocky Mountain National Park probably best encapsulates the beauty and intensity of the rest of the state and the Rocky Mountains. Drive through on the above-timberline Trail Ridge Road, or take off with your backpack or cross-country skis into the backcountry. A word of warning: because the park is so accessible, it gets crowded. On long weekends during the summer, traffic on Trail Ridge Road can be virtually bumper to bumper, and if you drive in from the east, through Estes Park, you'll be flagged through town by traffic controllers, doing their best to keep the steady stream of autos, motor homes, and motorcycles moving. At **Mesa Verde National Park** you can explore thousand-year-old Anasazi cliff dwellings, and just outside of Colorado Springs you can drive to the top of 14,110-foot Pikes Peak, the "purple

Highway 62, between Ridgway and Telluride

© STEPHEN METZGER

mountain" to which Katherine Lee Bates referred in *America the Beautiful*. If you're interested in the state's mining history, don't miss **Cripple Creek, Central City, Black Hawk,** and **Leadville,** where you can take mine tours and visit museums displaying the tools and equipment of the 1880s, when these towns were bustling with entrepreneurs and entertainers, prospectors and prostitutes.

If you want to see urban Colorado, you need of course to see **Denver.** From its museums and restaurants to its upscale shopping centers, high-rise hotels, and new airport, Denver is at once thoroughly modern and at the same time a town with a palpable link to its past. If you're around during baseball season, try to take in a **Colorado Rockies** game. Even if you're not a rabid baseball fan, an evening at the park, with the sun setting behind the scoreboard and the Rocky Mountains, is one of the best ways to get a sense of Denver's personality. While in Denver, allow yourself a day to drive up to **Boulder,** an outdoor-oriented university town that seems part Berkeley, part Chamonix, France. Check out the bookstores and street performers on the **Pearl Street Mall** and the coffee shops on **The Hill.**

Another wonderful Colorado town is **Telluride,** though its box-canyon location makes it the kind of town you have to go out of your way to get to (which is part of its charm). Here, Victorian homes cling to hillsides, ski lifts rise just blocks from the main drag through town, and just-passing-through Deadheads share bar space with CEOs.

You might have already formed an opinion about **Aspen,** given its reputation for excellent skiing, expensive lifestyles, and big-bucks resident celebrities. It's a great town, though, and you need neither ski nor be rich to enjoy a visit there—public parks and bike paths allow you to soak in the mountain sunshine, and you can wander the town's little side streets, poke your nose into gift shops, and, weather permitting, grab lunch at any of several outdoor cafés.

Just east of Aspen, **Highway 82** lifts above the treeline to **Independence Pass** (12,095 feet), providing spectacular views before dropping back down again into the gorgeous **Arkansas River Valley.** Several other Colorado mountain passes offer stunning scenery, including Loveland Pass and Berthoud Pass (both over 11,000 feet), Wolf Creek Pass (10,850 feet), Lizard Head Pass (10,222 feet), and Rabbit Ears Pass (9,426 feet). And the entire stretch of **U.S. 550** from Durango to Ouray seems to take your breath at every turn (and there are lots of them).

THINGS TO DO

Though it's natural to want to relax on vacation, you might not want to do too much of that in Colorado—it'd be a shame not to take advantage of the nearly unlimited recreational opportunities the state affords. Colorado's **skiing** is some of the best in the world, with resorts such as Aspen, Vail, Crested Butte, Winter Park, Steamboat Springs, and Telluride drawing visitors from as far away as Europe and Asia. Some of the state's lesser-known resorts, though, also offer skiing that locals will tell you rivals that at the big resorts. Not to let the cat out of the bag here, but A-Basin, Wolf Creek, and Purgatory offer some of the best snow in the Rockies, as well as generally shorter lift lines and an overall more personal and friendly atmosphere than you'll find at some of the larger resorts.

In addition to excellent snow skiing, Colorado also offers first-rate **white-water rafting, mountain biking, fishing, horseback riding, and hiking** for just about every level of participant—first-timer to expert. Plus, visitors to Colorado can take **four-wheel-drive tours** of remote mountain passes and ghost towns, or rent vehicles and head out on their own. You can also take **narrow-gauge–train rides** along steep cliffsides and over harrowing bridges crossing deep gorges.

Finally, there are the **festivals,** scores around the state. To name but a few of the best known: Telluride's bluegrass and film festivals, Boulder's Shakespeare and music festivals, Aspen's food-and-wine and music festivals, Winter Park's American Music festival, and Vail's Winterfaire, as well as golf tournaments, mountain-bike races, and every other imaginable gathering and celebration. (See Calendar in specific chapters for dates and other information.)

A lot to see and do? You bet. And I've only skimmed the surface. My advice: don't try to do it all; you'll only frustrate yourself. Instead, take time to enjoy what you do decide on, and then, as they say in the shoe business, Just do it. Besides, perhaps no visit to Colorado, even a lifelong one, is ever complete.

Recreation

Colorado offers a huge array of outdoor activities. Skiing, biking, fishing, golf, camping, rock climbing, white-water rafting, and kayaking—all are immensely popular. In fact, many folks who've chosen to live here will tell you it's because of the wealth of outdoor recreation. No matter where you are, a lake, stream, golf course, ski slope, hiking trail, or trout stream is nearby.

Skiing and Snowboarding

To many people, of course, skiing and Colorado are virtually synonymous. After all, the state is home to some of the world's best, biggest, and most well-known resorts: Vail, Aspen, Winter Park, Steamboat Springs, Crested Butte, Telluride, Copper Mountain, Breckenridge, and Keystone. In addition, more than a dozen other smaller and lesser-known but equally fine resorts lie within Colorado's borders; among them are Arapahoe Basin, Purgatory, and Wolf Creek, favorites of local powderhounds and bumpshredders, boarders and Telemarkers.

If you're thinking about a ski vacation or snowboard vacation, you couldn't do much better than Colorado. Fly into Denver, take a shuttle to Vail, Winter Park, or any one of the other resorts within 1.5 hours of the airport, and then just spend your time mastering the one mountain; or take a road trip—spread your trip over half a dozen or more resorts. Start at Winter Park, head west to Summit County, then over the pass and on to Vail. Even if you end up as far away as Telluride, you're still less than a day's drive from the airport.

Colorado is also a haven for Nordic skiers. With its thousands of square miles of national forests, as well as many privately run Nordic centers, Colorado welcomes those who'd rather ski quietly off into the woods or crank Telemark turns on a backcountry hillside than stand in lift lines after spending $50-plus for a ticket. Cross-country skiers will find excellent terrain and Nordic centers near most of the major downhill resorts, including Vail, Aspen, and Telluride, while San Juan, Gunnison, San Isabel, and White River National Forests offer exceptional trails, as well as opportunities to explore unmarked backcountry.

For more information on skiing in Colorado, write **Colorado Ski Country USA,** 1560 Broadway, Suite 2000, Denver, CO 80202. You'd also be well advised to check out its website, where you can get information on everything from snow conditions (updated twice daily) to lodging to employment opportunities at all of Colorado's ski resorts. You can also get on both email and snail-mail lists and order vacation guides. To get to the home page, go to www.coloradoski.org.

For information on the 10th Mountain Trail Association's hut-to-hut skiing, phone 970/925-5775. Its website (www.huts.org) has maps, prices, reservation information, and other useful facts, figures, and links.

Ski and snowboard rental prices will vary from resort to resort, as will the degree of hassle of getting equipped. Generally, the cost is approximately $15–20 a day, but will often be paired with discounted lift tickets or as part of an accommodations package. It is recommended you rent your equipment before you arrive at the ski area, even though most of the resorts' rental shops are

If you're thinking about a ski vacation or snowboard vacation, you couldn't do much better than Colorado. Colorado is also a haven for Nordic skiers.

efficient and their employees highly qualified and personable—having your skis when you get there means one fewer obstacle between your car and the chairlift. Also, local shops offer discounts on rentals, and having your own equipment makes it easier to ski several different resorts on the same visit. On the other hand, most ski areas offer packages, particularly to beginners, which include equipment rental, lessons, and lift tickets. Call the individual resorts for information and prices. Rental shops will also often store your ski equipment in the evenings (and your street shoes during the day), minimizing the amount of lugging around you'll have to do, and at the end of your stay, you can simply drop your stuff off and head back to your car.

Prices of lessons vary depending on whether you want to be part of a group or prefer a private lesson; lessons are also more expensive at the higher-end resorts (Aspen, Vail) than at the smaller, family-oriented areas (Purgatory, Ski Cooper). Group lessons usually run $15–40

ON THE ROAD

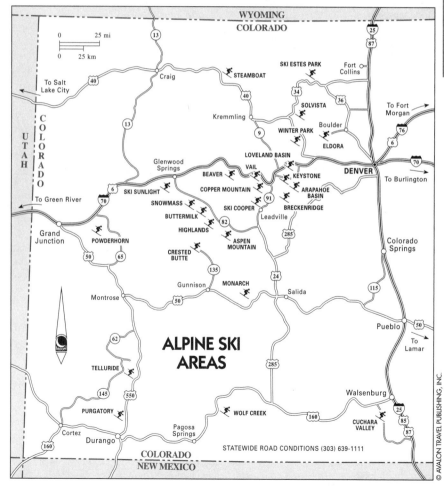

ALPINE SKI AREAS

STATEWIDE ROAD CONDITIONS (303) 639-1111

© AVALON TRAVEL PUBLISHING, INC.

waist-deep powder at Vail

© JEFF AFLECK

for an hour and a half or two (there's generally both a morning and afternoon session). Privates can run $60–90 a hour. Note: though private lessons offer the advantage of one-on-one instruction, and the money can be well spent, groups are often smaller than you'd think—sometimes just two or three students, guaranteeing a lot of individual instruction. The two main factors determining group size are how crowded the resort is and how advanced the group. Generally, if it's a weekday, and the resort's not too crowded, the groups will be small. Also, the more advanced the group, the more likely it is that it will be small. Beginners will want to look into packages that include lessons, lift tickets, and equipment rental, offered by most of the resorts.

Child care is frequently provided, though it is never free. For example, at Vail, all-day, non-ski daycare for children two months to six years old can run in the neighborhood of $55, and it does include lunch. Information has been included on the places where the child care or children's ski school have the best reputations or where folks are most likely to be visiting with kids.

Snowmobiling

Although I can see the thrill of blasting through new-fallen snow at 40-plus mph, the crisp air stinging your face while the sunshine shimmers on distant meadows, it also seems like a loud and obtrusive way to get into the backcountry. If the sport were better regulated, less environmental havoc might be wreaked, though the screaming engines still pierce the sanctity of the forests' natural silences, and exhaust fumes still waft into the air. I recommend cross-country skiing or snowshoeing instead. Sorry.

For information on snowmobiling in Colorado, including safety training and organized tours around the state, plus maps of the state's major snowmobiling areas, write **Colorado Snowmobile Association,** P.O. Box 1260 Grand Lake, CO 80447. It has an exhaustive and nicely linked website (www.sledcity.com/states/colorado/index.cfm), where you can get information on everything from trail conditions and upcoming events to snowmobile parts and accessories, as well as maps. For questions regarding snowmobile registration write the Colorado Division of Parks and Outdoor Recreation, Recreation Unit, 13878

S. U.S. 85, Littleton, CO 80125, or phone 303/791-1920.

Other Winter Activities

In addition to skiing and snowmobiling, winter activities such as tubing, sledding, and tobogganing are very popular in the Colorado mountains, among locals and visitors alike. And there are increasing numbers of places to take part. Though ski areas once turned up their noses at tubes, sleds, and sliding disks (at snowboarders, too, remember?), more and more are realizing they were missing out on potential customers. Many of the resorts now have specially roped-off sections where tubers *only* are allowed; some even provide rentals. One of the best established tubing areas is **Fraser Tubing Hill,** just north of Winter Park (you'll see it on your left off U.S. 40). Cost is around $5; rentals available. For information, phone 970/726-5954.

Still, nothing beats taking off into the woods on your own, whether hauling a sliding disk to a distant hillside or snowshoeing off across a virgin meadow. Colorado is rife with places perfect for such excursions. All the ski towns—especially Aspen, Telluride, Breckenridge, Crested Butte, and Steamboat Springs—offer marked recreation areas and trails. And much of the high backcountry offers opportunities for the more adventurous. Retail ski, hiking, and mountaineering shops can provide maps and information. **A serious caution:** don't take off into the forest unless you know what you're doing, and even then notify someone of where you're going and when you'll be home. Locals love to tell stories of folks who thought they knew their way around the winter outdoors and didn't, and emergency medical personnel can recount tale after tale of backcountry rescues . . . and *near* rescues. Don't let it be you.

Cycling

While touring is enjoying the same renaissance in Colorado that it is in the rest of the country, mountain biking has taken the state by storm. In fact, Crested Butte and Durango are two of the half dozen or so of the sport's true capitals, and both towns not only offer miles and miles of trails and terrain for all levels of ability but also sponsor races, workshops, and various special events throughout the season (generally May through October). In addition, many of Colorado's ski resorts have taken to promoting mountain biking during the summer. At several resorts, including Aspen, Purgatory, Winter Park, and Vail, you can take your bike to the top of the mountain on a ski lift and ride the ski trails back down. Usually sightseeing rides run $10–12, with an additional charge of $5 or $6 for transporting mountain bikes up.

The **International Mountain Biking Association** has an excellent website with links to local chapters and clubs. Check it out at www.imba.com. You can also get information from the association's state representatives. Contact Bill Harris at 970/249-8055 or bharris@gwe.net, or Josh Osterhoudt at 917/522-9083 or Medwheeljo@aol.com.

The following are a sampling of Colorado's many IMBA affiliated clubs: the **Aspen Cycling Club,** Box 4945, Aspen, CO 81612, email ceckart@rof.net; the **Boulder Off Road Alliance,** Box 4954, Boulder, CO 80306, 303/667-2467; **American Cycling Association,** Box 7129, Denver, CO 80207, 303/458-5538, www.americancycling.org; and the **Summit Fat Tire Society,** Box 1296, Frisco, CO 80443, email letsride@oneimage.com.

Hiking, Backpacking, and Camping

With the Rocky Mountains as its centerpiece, Colorado claims some of the best hiking, backpacking, and camping in the United States. From the San Juan Mountains to Rocky Mountain National Park north of Boulder, from Colorado National Monument to Great Sand Dunes National Monument, the state offers wide-ranging types of trail hiking with a variety of lengths and degrees of difficulty. You can take short, naturalist-led day-hikes, or you can hike solo into remote backcountry wilderness areas; you can even organize a group and hike hut-to-hut through one of Colorado's "hut systems."

For information on hiking and backpacking through the 10th Mountain Trail Association's hut-to-hut system, phone 970/925-5775. Its website (www.huts.org) has maps, prices, reservation information, and other useful facts, figures, and links.

In the late 1980s, the Colorado Trail was completed. This 469-mile trail, which stretches from Durango to Denver, offers rich hiking opportunities with specific sections designed for day, overnight, and multiday hikes. Access points and trailheads are scattered along the trail. One of the best sources for information on hiking in Colorado is the **Colorado Mountain Club,** 2530 W. Alameda Ave., Denver, CO 80219, 303/922-8315. Its website (www.cmc.org) offers an excellent overview of the club, with information on hiking, wilderness preservation, and outdoor literature. In addition to publishing a monthly newsletter with articles on climbing and hiking in the state (and beyond), the club sponsors numerous hikes and cross-country ski outings throughout the year.

Colorado's camping opportunities, too, are numerous and varied. Hundreds of public campgrounds are scattered throughout the state in the beautiful San Juan, San Isabel, White River, Pike, Roosevelt, Rio Grande, Grand Mesa, Gunnison, and Arapaho National Forests. In addition, Rocky Mountain National Park offers camping in one of the most scenic wonderlands in the country, while a handful of national monuments and recreation areas, particularly Curecanti, and state parks also offer good camping.

Overnight camping fees at Colorado's National Forest Service campgrounds range $6–13 a night, depending on facilities (running water, showers, etc.), with most of the campgrounds $6–8. Maximum stay is 14 days. For more information on camping in Colorado's national forests, write **U.S. Forest Service,** P.O. Box 25127, Lakewood, CO 80225, or phone 303/275-5350 in Englewood.

Camping in Colorado's 40 state parks will run you $6–7 a night, or $10 for an RV site with an electrical hookup. Note: frequent visitors to the state parks will want to invest $30 in an annual pass, without which you'll be charged an additional $3 entrance fee per day (per vehicle)—10 visits and it's paid off. Phone the **Colorado Division of Parks and Recreation**

at 303/866-3437 for a free camping guide and information on buying an annual pass. Fees at the private campgrounds in Colorado (Good Sam, KOA, etc.) generally run $8–10 a night for tent sites and $12–18 for full hookups; many offer weekly and monthly rates.

Rafting and Kayaking

Colorado is a river rat's paradise. Whether your idea of river running is to float lazily down a wide meandering stream in a rubber raft or to shoot Class IV rapids in a tiny kayak, whether you prefer organized trips and camaraderie or solo excursions and soul searching, Colorado's waterways will satisfy.

Although rivers throughout the state offer good rafting and kayaking, most of the state's river running is concentrated in the Buena Vista-Salida area (Arkansas River), the Four Corners area (Animas and Dolores Rivers), and the northwestern area (Green and Yampa Rivers).

For more information on rafting on Colorado rivers, write **Colorado River Outfitters Association,** P.O. Box 502, Westminster, CO 80030, 303/369-4632. You can also visit the website at www.adventuresports.com/croa/welcome.htm, where you'll find maps, listings of registered guides, and information on how to select the right river trip.

Fishing

While many of Colorado's waterways are tailor-made for rafting, others are trout streams right out of Izaak Walton's *The Compleat Angler* (and some of the rivers are good for both). Unfortunately, mining has destroyed fish habitat in several rivers once rife with trout, though others have been reclaimed, and the Colorado Division of Wildlife, U.S. Fish and Game, and local organizations have successfully reintroduced fish to nearly lost streams.

In addition, sections of several of the state's rivers have special restrictions. Some stretches allow catch-and-release fishing only and/or permit only the use of artificial lures and single barbless hooks. Among the state's most popular streams are the Blue, Roaring Fork, Eagle, Animas, and Gunnison Rivers.

Lake fishermen, too, enjoy Colorado angling. Grand Lake and Blue Mesa Reservoir are stocked regularly with decent-sized fish, and patient and knowledgeable anglers have taken huge Mackinaw from their waters. Reservoirs on the eastern plains offer good warm-water fishing for bass, walleye, catfish, bluegill, and crappie.

Remember, a valid Colorado fishing license is required to fish in all waters except private lakes and a handful of small municipal ponds (usually designated for kids only). Fishing licenses are available at most Colorado sporting-goods stores, as well as directly through the Division of Wildlife. Resident fishing licenses are $20.25. Nonresidents can buy one-day ($5.25), five-day ($18.25), or season licenses ($40.25). For more information on fishing in Colorado, write the **Colorado Division of Wildlife,** 6060 N. Broadway, Denver, CO 80216, or phone 303/297-1192; website wildlife.state.co.us/fishing/index.asp. You can also get information from www.fishcolorado.com, as well as at www.coloradopros.com/colorado fishing.htm, which discusses bag limits, restrictions, and other areas of interest. Another useful information source is **Ufish,** whose website (www.ufish.com.regions/_co.htm) includes information on guides, outfitters, equipment, tournaments, and lodging throughout the state.

Hunting

Hunting licenses are available at sporting-goods stores in Colorado and directly through the Colorado Division of Wildlife. All hunters born in or later than 1949 must have proof of having taken a hunter's-safety course. License fees are significantly higher for nonresidents than for residents (2000 license fees for deer were $20.25 for residents, $150.25 for out-of-staters). For more information on hunting in Colorado, phone the Colorado Division of Wildlife at 303/297-1192, or, for a recorded message specifically about hunting seasons and licenses, 313/291-7529.

A good source of information is the "Hunting Home Page," at wildlife.state.co.us/hunt/index.asp, which provides abundant information on the sport and links to anything related. All resident and nonresident license fees are also detailed at the website www.colorado-go-west.com/fees.html.

Golf

Golf has really taken off in Colorado in the last few years, with large numbers of courses not only in the metro Denver area but scattered

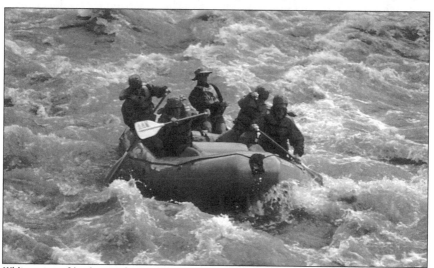

White water rafting is one of Colorado's premier summer attractions.

ON THE ROAD

throughout the state, particularly at the ski areas, where some of the state's best courses unveil themselves when the snow melts. In fact, in the 1990s, more than 60 new courses were built, and by summer 2001 there were well over 200 public and private courses in the state. These vary from nine-hole municipality-run courses to high-profile, nationally known courses, such as the **Broadmoor** in Colorado Springs and **Fox Hollow** in Lakewood (just west of Denver), with green fees ranging from $5 to more than $100 ($125 at the exclusive Tamarron Resort near Durango). In addition, nearly 15 percent of Coloradans golf, with more and more women and minority members (particularly at municipal courses) taking up the sport each year, providing a welcome change from the typically white-male-dominated arena.

> *Aspens provide most of the fall color show, their serrated semi-triangular leaves turning from limpid green to yellow to gold to crimson before falling to the forest floor.*

For travelers, golf can either be something to add to your intinerary or around which to plan your whole trip. Many of the ski resorts, in efforts to keep drawing visitors after the lifts shut down, offer excellent golf-and-lodging packages in the summertime. Even if you're just passing through, a round of golf can offer a chance to be outdoors under that wonderful Colorado sky and in some areas to see foxes, deer, and other wildlife.

Two of the best websites for information on Colorado golfing are www.golfcolorado.com and www.rockiesgolf.com. Both offer maps, course reviews, tips, and links to other useful sites.

Viewing Fall Colors

Though not as well known as those of New England, Colorado's fall colors can be equally dramatic—especially when backdropped by the grandeur of the towering Rocky Mountains and framed by groves of evergreen pines and firs. Aspens provide most of the show, their serrated semi-triangular leaves turning from limpid green to yellow to gold to crimson before falling to the forest floor.

Starting in mid-to-late September and running through October (depending on elevation), the fall colors in Colorado are a seasonal treat that locals like to think they've got for themselves; most of the summer tourists have already headed home and the winter visitors haven't arrived yet. This is one of the best times of the year to visit, especially midweek, when the roads and highways are largely empty of sightseers. Beware, though: the leaves change colors in part because it's getting colder, and nights especially can get awfully cold. Bring warm clothing—including gloves and hats—as evening temperatures often drop into the 40s and 30s as early as mid-October.

For information on fall-color tours, contact the Colorado Tourism Office, 800/COLORADO (265-6723), or on the Web at www.colorado.com. You'll also find names of individual tour providers in the following travel chapters.

Accommodations

Colorado's travelers' accommodations run the full gamut from backcountry campgrounds to plush bed-and-breakfasts, from youth hostels to lavish hotels with valet parking and dining rooms with dress codes. Even the most remote towns usually have a motel or two, and you're rarely far from a national forest campground, where sites run about $7 a night. Colorado's main tourist areas—Denver, Colorado Springs, Summit County, Vail, Aspen, and Durango—have wide ranges of lodging possibilities, including RV campgrounds, luxury hotels, and inexpensive motels. Generally, it's cheaper to stay on the outskirts of town, although you'll sacrifice the convenience of central-location lodging.

Campgrounds

Camping is the least-expensive way to stay in your travels through Colorado, though of course this is recommended for summer travel only (most mountain campgrounds close Oct.–May). With nightly fees ranging from free to about $18 (for some of the more costly RV sites), the state's campgrounds are generally safe, comfortable, and well maintained. Forest Service campgrounds are not generally equipped with flush toilets or showers, though they usually have running water. Camping information is available at the State of Colorado website at www.colorado.com/activities.

Bed-and-Breakfasts

Although generally more expensive than staying in a motel ($75–175 a night), this is one of the best ways to see Colorado. Many of the state's bed-and-breakfasts are situated in turn-of-the-last-century (and older) homes and decorated with authentic Victorian furnishings. In addition, most innkeepers go out of their way to provide personal and intimate service. The only disadvantage of bed-and-breakfasts is that you often must sacrifice a bit of your privacy. Though rooms are usually perfectly private, you may have to share a bath, and often will be eating breakfast in close quarters with—and sometimes at the same table as—the inn's other guests.

Dozens of websites offer information on bed-and-breakfasts in Colorado (many of them are national and international organizations), statewide, regionally, and by municipality. One of the best sites is administered by **International Bed and Breakfast Pages** at www.ibbp.com, which provides information on inns with ratings and reviews from other travelers. You can also get information from **1st Traveler's Choice** at www.virtualcities.com, although keep in mind that the descriptions of the inns were provided by their managers.

Another good source is **Bed and Breakfast Innkeepers of Colorado** at www.innsof colorado.org.

Dude Ranches

Ranch-style accommodations have been a tradition in Colorado since England's Lord Dunraven brought guests from the British Isles to his retreat near Estes Park in the 1870s. Today, there are dude ranches throughout the state, from Durango to Aspen to Steamboat Springs. In addition to offering the proverbial horseback riding, most of the ranches offer a variety of other recreational pursuits as well, including snowmobiling, cross-country skiing, fishing, mountain biking, rafting, and tennis; you can even take part in real ranch-hand chores.

For more information, including a hard-copy directory, on Colorado dude ranches, write **Colorado Dude and Guest Ranch Association,** P.O. Box 2120, Granby, CO 80446, or phone 970/887-3128. Visit the website at www.coloradoranch.com.

Four Distinctive Colorado Hotels

Though there are many excellent hotels in Colorado, particularly in the downtown Denver area, four stand out as places that would make a Colorado vacation especially memorable. **The Broadmoor Hotel** in Colorado Springs was built in the early part of the 20th century and is a sprawling complex actually consisting of three separate hotels, as well as several upscale restaurants, three golf courses, a museum, boutiques, a lake, and an ice-skating arena. One of the classiest and most luxurious hotels in the country, the Broadmoor will take your breath away even if you're prepared to be impressed. Doubles start at around $200, and suites go for more than $1,000.

Downtown Denver's **Brown Palace Hotel** first opened in 1892 and ever since has been accommodating Denver's most discriminating and well-to-do visitors, from Teddy Roosevelt to the Beatles. Rooms for two start at about $200.

The **Far View Lodge** is atop Mesa Verde within a couple of miles of some of the Southwest's most fascinating cliff dwellings. Balconies at each room provide the perfect places to listen to the godly silence and to imagine the juniper- and piñon-studded plateau 1,000 years ago, when the Anasazi were developing their mysterious civilization. Rooms are in the $100 range.

Estes Park's **Stanley Hotel** stands large, white, and sentinel-like on a hillside above town, squaring off with Rocky Mountain National Park. Built in 1909 by F. O. Stanley, who invented the Stanley Steamer, the rustically luxurious Stanley Hotel has hosted many luminaries over the years, including Stephen King, whom the hotel inspired to write *The Shining* (Kubrick and Nicholson hoped to film the movie here but there wasn't enough snow, so the crew moved to the Timberline Lodge on Oregon's Mount Hood).

Though the Stanley ran into trouble in the 1980s and early 1990s, eventually going into bankruptcy, the hotel was acquired in early 2000 by Chesapeake Hotels—which has luxury properties around the country—and the hotel has begun to reclaim the integrity and class for which it was formerly known. Most rooms at the Stanley Hotel range $175–250.

For more information on these hotels, see the Accommodations sections in the corresponding chapters. For information on Colorado's historic inns and hotels, phone 303/546-9040 or go to www.historic-hotels.com/colorado.

A Word about Hotel Rates

The more I travel the more I realize how capricious hotel rates are, how the rate you get depends on so many variables—whether you

phone in your reservation or walk in off the street, whether it's 2 in the afternoon or 10 at night, whether you asked for a "discount" or not. Keep in mind that hotels, and to some degree motels, have widely fluctuating rates, and that above all they don't want empty rooms. True story: I pulled into Fort Collins one afternoon and walked into the lobby of a major hotel chain. Since it was packed with tour groupers, and waiting 10 minutes at the counter got me no closer to a clerk, I walked outside to a pay phone and called the front desk. "Rates are $79 a night," I was told, "but sorry, no rooms available tonight." So I walked next door, where I was told there was one room available, a smoking room. Nope, wouldn't do. So I walked back to the lobby of the first hotel, worked my way to the counter, and asked for a room.

"Yes, we do have a room, sir. For $69."

"Do you offer any corporate discounts?" I asked.

"Let's see . . . Yes, we can give you a room for $59."

Now, this is backward from how it usually works (though it does go to show how arbitrary it can all be). Often you can get a better rate by phone, even if you're calling from just outside the door, as they figure you're not committed

the historic Strater Hotel in Durango

© STEPHEN METZGER

yet, and they *want* you. Once you're in the door they figure you're less likely to go somewhere else.

Another true story: one night in Ratón, New Mexico, I stopped for the night at dusk at a small independent motel. A man in front of me was talking with the desk clerk.

"How much for a room?"

"Do you qualify for any discounts?" the woman asked.

Shrugging and giving her a blank look, he said, "What do you mean?"

"Triple A, corporate, AARP, you know . . . "

"Uh, I guess not . . . "

"Sixty-four dollars for a single."

He said he'd take it, filled out the registration form, and left with his key.

My turn: "Do you have a nonsmoking single available for this evening?"

"Do you qualify for any discounts?"

"Yes, I do."

"Fifty-four dollars for a single."

"I'll take it."

Is there a lesson here? If there is it's that, as I said, rates are not as fixed as you might think. Some things to keep in mind: the later in the day the better your chance of getting a cut rate. The owners want their rooms full, and, if it looks as if they might not be, they'll offer incentives, in the form of a few bucks off the "standard" rate.

(Of course, you also risk not finding a vacancy, and that risk might not be worth it to you.) Also, *ask* about discounts. Most hotels offer at least American Automobile Association, American Association of Retired Persons, and corporate discounts, and you might qualify. Finally, in the case of chain and franchise lodging, I've had better luck phoning the hotel directly than calling the 800 number and talking to an operator who might be booking a room in a town 3,000 miles away from where she's sitting.

Bottom line: phone around, and talk like you do it all the time. You might be surprised at the results.

Hosteling

Although hosteling isn't as popular in Colorado as it is other parts of the country (and world), the state holds a handful of hostels that have been around for a long time, have excellent reputations and loyal followings, and are located near some of the state's main attractions. Among them are the hostels in Crested Butte and Leadville. You can get information on other hostels in the area by phoning the Washington, D.C., offices of **Hostelling International-American Youth Hostels** at 202/783-6161 or 800/444-6111. Internet users can look up **Hostelling International-American Youth Hostels** on the Web at www.hiayh.org.

Entertainment

FESTIVALS AND SPECIAL EVENTS

Colorado festivals vary from huge affairs that attract visitors from around the world to tiny community events that bring out the whole town—maybe a couple of hundred people. No matter where you are in the state, *somebody* is celebrating *something*.

Among the annual highlights:

January: Ullrfest (Breckenridge's three-day winter carnival); National Western Show and Rodeo (Denver's *huge* two-week series of rodeos and stock shows).

February: Winter Carnival (Steamboat Springs).

May: Cinco de Mayo festivals in Denver, Fort Collins, Grand Junction, Pueblo, and Greeley; Kinetic Conveyance Sculpture Race (Boulder's quirky human-powered-vehicle-over-obstacles-course-and-water race).

June: Aspen Music Festival; Aspen Food and Wine Classic; Ute Mountain Roundup (Cortez); International Whitewater and Kayak Races (Durango); Strawberry Days (Grand Junction); Greeley Stampede (rodeo); FibArk Boat Races (Salida); Telluride Bluegrass Festival.

July: Colorado Music Festival (Boulder); Colorado Shakespeare Festival (Boulder).

ON THE ROAD

August: Colorado State Fair (Pueblo).

September: Aspen Filmfest; Meeker Sheepdog Trials; Longs Peak Scottish-Irish Festival (Estes Park).

For information on these and other festivals and events, see the individual travel chapters or contact the **Colorado Tourism Office,** 1625 Broadway, Suite 1700, Denver, CO 80202, 800/COLORADO (265-6723; vacation kit) or 303/832-6171. You can also visit the website at www.colorado.com.

SHOPPING

Something about vacationing and shopping . . . I don't know what it is. Maybe it's the way retailers play on the guilt of visitors, who might have left at home someone who wanted to come along. Or maybe it's the fact that most travelers have a disproportionate amount of in-pocket coin and are more or less in spending modes anyway. Souvenirs, I guess. Mementos of a fun trip. Whatever, traveling and tourism often go hand in glove, even in places where there doesn't seem to be much of a logical connection—ceramic suguaro cacti, which don't grow in Colorado, for sale in Durango, and moccasins from Taos, New Mexico, for sale in Estes Park.

In Colorado, shopping venues vary from tacky gift-and-souvenir shops to upscale boutiques selling thousand-dollar fur coats. In addition, there are the ubiquitous factory-outlet malls, the largest of which is in Dillon/Silverthorne, off I-70 about 70 miles west of Denver (more than 85 stores). In Denver, the main shopping centers of interest to travelers are the 16th Street Mall and the Cherry Creek Mall. Nearby, in Boulder, the Pearl Street Mall offers about 10 blocks of only-in-Boulder shops (e.g., Into the Wind, an "alternative sports shop"; The Lighthouse, a metaphysical bookstore; and The Middle Fish, specializing in "functional art"). Upscale shopping meccas in Colorado include Aspen, Vail, and Telluride, while the greatest concentrations of gift-and-souvenir shops are in Breckenridge, Durango, Estes Park, Steamboat Springs, and Manitou Springs.

Health and Safety

Traveling in Colorado is generally very safe, although you should be aware of several specific diseases and climate-caused maladies that could make your visit far less enjoyable and comfortable than it should be. Understanding these problems, and taking the appropriate precautions, will greatly increase the chances of staying healthy while exploring the state. Much of the following information was taken from the American Medical Association's *Encyclopedia of Medicine.*

Altitude Sickness

Also known as mountain sickness, altitude sickness most commonly affects mountain climbers, hikers, and skiers who ascend too rapidly to heights above 8,000 feet. Caused by a reduction in atmospheric pressure, and a corresponding decrease in oxygen, altitude sickness alters the blood chemistry and affects the nervous system, muscles, heart, and lungs.

Symptoms of altitude sickness include headache, nausea, dizziness, and impaired mental abilities. In severe cases, fluid buildup in the lungs leads to breathlessness, coughing, and a heavy phlegm. Untreated, these symptoms can lead to seizures, hallucinations, and coma. Delays in treatment can even lead to brain damage and death.

The best way to prevent altitude sickness is to ascend *gradually* to elevations above 8,000 feet. Take a day or two for each 2,000–3,000 feet. Victims of altitude sickness should return to lower elevations immediately; carry them if necessary. If available, pure oxygen can be administered (ski patrol usually keeps oxygen tanks handy).

Dehydration

Dehydration is the result of a drop in the body's water level and oftentimes a subsequent drop in the level of salt. Being at higher altitudes can cause an increase in dehydration; symptoms include severe thirst, dry lips, increased heart and breath rate, dizziness, and confusion. Often the skin is dry and stiff; what little urine is passed is dark. When salt loss is heavy, there will also be headaches, cramps, lethargy, and pallor. Severe cases of dehydration can result in coma.

To prevent dehydration, you must replace the three (or more) quarts of water your body loses every 24 hours to perspiration and urination. Even in moderate temperatures and climates, you should be cautious and drink more than you probably think you need; a good rule of thumb is to drink enough water to keep the urine pale. Treatment for dehydration includes fluid and salt replacement—in severe cases intravenously.

Frostbite

Frostbite is the freezing of the skin or underlying tissues, usually of the extremities, as a result of overexposure to cold temperatures. Identifying symptoms include blistering, as well as pale or blue skin that is often stiff or rubbery to the touch. In its most severe form (third-degree, or deep frostbite), the skin turns blue or a blotchy white and the tissue itself feels frozen. The best prevention is to keep the body's core temperature up—dress warmly, ideally in wool or polypropylene layers, and cover exposed areas of skin. Treatments includes warming with your breath and immersing exposed areas in warm water (104–108°F) for up to a half hour. Do not rub or massage the frozen skin, as this could cause further tissue damage. If possible, elevate any frostbitten areas. Do not break blisters.

Giardia

Giardia, or giardiasis, is an infection of the small intestine caused by the single-celled parasite *Giardia lamblia*. Giardia is spread by direct personal contact with another's stool or by contaminated food or water; the latter should be of particular concern to hikers and backpackers. In remote high-country areas clear-running stream water can be contaminated as even wild animals are known to carry the parasite.

Symptoms of giardia usually begin one to three days after the parasite has entered the system and include diarrhea, gas, cramps, loss of appetite, fatigue, and nausea. To avoid contracting giardia, always wash your hands before handling food, and *do not* drink stream or lake water without first boiling or purifying it. Purifying with either iodine (in liquid, tablet, or crystal form) or with a 0.1 micron water filter is sufficient. If using a powdered drink mix to cover the taste of iodine, wait to add it until after the allotted treatment time, as the ascorbic acid (vitamin C) in the mix can interfere with the purification process. Check sporting goods stores and mountaineering shops for water-purification kits.

Hypothermia

Hypothermia occurs when the body temperature drops below 95°F and is caused by prolonged exposure to cold. Most common among elderly and young people, whose bodies are unable to generate enough warmth, hypothermia is characterized by a slowed heart rate, puffiness, pale skin, lethargy, and confusion. In severe cases, breathing is also slow. Taking the proper precautions can go a long way toward prevention; wear warm clothing including gloves and a hat, eat high-carbohydrate foods often, and drink plenty of fluids.

Hypothermia requires immediate medical attention, and victims are often treated in intensive-care units of hospitals and warmed under controlled conditions. While awaiting medical assistance, move the victim to a warm place, remove wet clothing, and replace it with a warm blanket; have another person join and hold the victim beneath the blanket and, if possible, give the victim something warm (not hot) to drink. *Do not* let the victim walk, do not rub the skin or apply direct heat, and do not give the victim alcohol.

Sunburn

Sunburn is most common in fair-skinned people and most likely to occur *at high elevations*, where fewer ultraviolet rays are naturally blocked. Skiers and other winter-sports enthusiasts should be especially careful, as the sun's reflection off the snow doubles the effect of harmful rays, while even a cloudy day allows many of the sun's ultraviolet rays to penetrate.

The two best ways to prevent sunburn are by gradual exposure (increasing each day) and by application of a sunscreen with a high sun-protection factor (SPF). Available at pharmacies, sporting-goods stores, and even grocery stores, sunscreens with a high SPF (15 or higher) should be applied liberally and often. Treatment for sunburn includes the application of any of several available lotions and ointments; particularly effective are those with aloe. Severe cases may require medical treatment.

Ticks

Though ticks can carry Lyme disease and Rocky Mountain spotted fever, these cases are rare, and ticks are more an annoyance than anything. The tiny critters seem to appear out of nowhere; walk into a grassy meadow, especially one that's damp, and it's likely you'll have a hitchhiker. They're easily dealt with at that stage: just pick them off and crush them between your fingernails. If they hit paydirt, though—that is, if they get their barbed lips into your skin and begin to suck blood—they're a little tougher to extract. Contrary to popular belief, you don't have to "unscrew" them. I usually just twist back and forth until they come out. If they've been in long enough to be engorged (at which point they look like gray eggplants and can get as big as a grape), you have to be careful not to squeeze them so hard you pop their bodies. This kills them but will leave a part of the head imbedded in your skin. If this happens, see a doctor, and at the very least keep the spot clean (dose it with hydrogen peroxide) and watch closely for infection.

The best way to avoid ticks is by tucking your shirt into your pants and your pants into your socks and using a DEET-based insect repellent.

One indication of Lyme disease is a tiny ring around the bite area, often described as a "target." Report this immediately to a physician, as the disease is very serious and debilitating.

First-Aid Kits

One night as it was nearing dusk on a remote Forest Service road, I suddenly realized I didn't know exactly where I was nor how long it would take me to find my way back to "civilization." Other than the obvious lesson—travel with maps; know where you are and where you're going—I also realized I wasn't very well prepared on the off chance that I would have to spend the night unexpectedly in the wilderness. I didn't have even a basic first-aid kit in the car. I know, I know . . .

But I do now, and I recommend you carry one as well. Most physicians suggest including at least the following:

a variety of different size bandages
antibacterial ointment
blankets
flares
aspirin or acetomenephin
matches (in a waterproof container)
sunscreen and after-sun lotion
  (aloe cream works well)
lip balm
a multibladed (Swiss Army-type) knife
motion-sickness medication
hydrogen peroxide

Crime and Public Safety

I've talked at length with police officers in major cities, asking them to recommend ways travelers can avoid being victims of crime. Their answers are pretty standard and shouldn't surprise veterans of the road: don't leave valuables in motel or hotel rooms or in plain sight on car seats, etc.; park and walk in well-lighted areas; travel with companions (especially if you're a woman); ask local hotel and motel employees for the safest route to your restaurant; report suspicious activity—in short use common sense.

That good advice is intended primarily for navigating sometimes-seedy urban areas. But as I found out, even the country's rural wilds aren't guaranteed safe. While exploring the stark beauty of Colorado's Four Corners area, alone on a gorgeous summer-stormy day on a remote bluff overlooking McPhee Reservoir near Cortez, I was assaulted myself. Fortunately, it wasn't as bad as it could have been, and though rattled, I was really none the worse for wear. It was, however, a heck of a wake-up call, and it got me wondering to what degree crime has infiltrated the country's wilderness areas.

In fact, there has been a dramatic increase in crime on public lands. Why? In part, of course, it's because of the larger numbers visiting these areas. But it's also a result of federal-level budget cuts, which in turn means less law enforcement. In the late 1990s, according to an article in *Outside Magazine,* there was "about one (law enforcement) officer for every 150,000 acres" of public land.

Crimes on public lands in recent years have included murder, drug growing and trafficking, and theft, as well as less-serious offenses, such as fighting (over the harvesting of extremely valuable mushrooms in Deschutes National Forest in Ore-

gon, for example) and general mischief (bottle throwing, destruction of public property) by rowdy drunks.

And what about assault, and sexual assault? How often does it happen, and nearly happen? How many assaults are not reported and thus can't be factored into the equations? I'm not sure. And I don't think there's any way to find out. I do know this, though: my own private wilderness is no longer what it once was. I will be more cautious on public land, less likely to travel alone. And, sadly, I will raise my two daughters to understand that the wilderness is not only a refuge *from* the dark side of humanity, but also a potential refuge *for* it.

The price, as William Blake would say, of experience.

ON THE ROAD

Information

RESOURCES

Your Colorado vacation will be far more enjoyable if you come prepared. In addition to buying a thorough and entertaining guidebook (which you apparently have already done or are about to do), it's a good idea to send away for any and all information you can get your hands on. One of the best sources for general information is the **Colorado Tourism Office.** Phone 800/COLORADO (265-6723) for a vacation kit or 303/832-6171 to speak with someone in the business office, or go to www.colorado.com. At the **Denver Metro Convention and Visitors Bureau,** 1668 Larimer, 303/892-1112 or 800/645-3446, you can pick up maps, brochures, and other information, and talk with staff members about everything from where to park to where to find a good sushi bar. You can also get information by going to www.denver.citysearch.com.

(See also Internet Resources and Useful Contact Information in the Resources section in the back of the book.)

Colorado Welcome Centers

The Colorado Tourism Board has established official Welcome Centers at most ports of entry.

These are good places to stop in for information on local, regional, and statewide attractions. You'll find Colorado Welcome Centers in **Burlington,** 48265 I-70, **Trinidad,** 309 N. Nevada Ave., **Cortez,** 928 E. Main St., **Fruita,** 340 U.S. 40, and **Dinosaur,** in the center of town on U.S. 40.

Companion Guides

As you'd expect, there are scores of guides to Colorado. Some are thematic; some are regional. Several of these books are excellent and would make ideal companion guides to *Moon Handbooks: Colorado.* Among these are Lee Gregory's *Colorado Scenic Guide* (Johnson Books, Boulder)—two volumes, northern and southern regions. Of particular value here are the dozens of reprinted U.S. Geological Survey topo maps, with hiking trails and 4WD routes, as well as the wealth of statistics and facts (including best time of day to take photos). Another good book is Warren Ohlrich's *Aspen-Snowmass Guide to Outdoor Activities* (Warren Ohlrich, Aspen). With more than two dozen activities, from Telemark skiing to tennis, from dogsledding to kayaking, this book provides lots of useful firsthand information and tips, as well as listings of shops and agencies specializing in each activity.

For general guides, you'd be hard-pressed to find a book more intriguing than the Work Projects Administration's *Colorado: A Guide to the Highest State.* First published in 1941, this fascinating book is part of the famous series that put some of the country's best writers to work during the lean times of the Depression. The book, available now in used and rare-book stores (and reissued in 1987 by the University Press of Kansas as *The WPA Guide to 1930s Colorado),* includes minutely detailed tours of main routes and back roads, in addition to thorough discussions of the state's history, economy, geography, and population.

(For a comprehensive list of other books about Colorado, see Suggested Reading in the Resources section at the back of the book.)

FACTS FOR THE TRAVELER

Setting Your Watch

Colorado is on mountain standard time, one hour later than the West Coast and two hours earlier than the East Coast.

Business Hours

Where possible, I've tried to give specific hours of operation of restaurants, museums, and other attractions. But these schedules change frequently, especially in resort towns, where the capriciousness of business makes for capricious business hours. Restaurants—even long-standing ones—are particularly notorious for opening with new hours when a new tourist season arrives. So call ahead if you have any doubt whatsoever. You don't want to go out of your way to a restaurant or museum I've recommended only to find it closed.

Keep in mind that most businesses are closed on major holidays—Christmas, New Year's Day, Easter—and that restaurants usually close at least one day a week, often Monday and/or Sunday.

Alcohol Laws

Alcoholic beverages are sold in Colorado in package stores between the hours of 7 A.M. and midnight Monday–Saturday. Alcohol is sold in restaurants and bars between 7 A.M. and 2 A.M. Monday–Saturday and on Sunday 8 A.M.–midnight.

Transportation

Although several companies offer tours of Colorado—from cliff dwellings to Pikes Peak—and most of the major tourist areas provide excellent public transportation, you're better off with your own rig. Unless you plan to stay in one specific area for your entire visit (which can work very well, especially if all you plan to do is ski), you're probably going to want to get out and do a little exploring. Remember that it's a long way between places you'll want to see, and you'll enjoy the luxury of capricious stops—whether for rest, water, or to explore a mining town or recreation area that's not on your itinerary.

Colorado by Air

The new Denver International Airport (DIA), the first major U.S. airport built in 20 years, opened in the winter of 1995, nearly two years behind schedule. The project, ambitious by any standard, was fraught with problems from early in the planning stages to well after planes were coming and going—from engineering glitches that led to luggage leaping from carousels to lawsuits among contractors; embarrassing to both Coloradans and the airline industry, these problems got worldwide press as international travelers waited to see how the new airport would turn out.

Chief complaints consisted of noise restrictions being violated, and takeoff and landing patterns sprawling over far more airspace than had been promised in contracts. Indeed, residents of the Front Range, from as far away as Ward and Boulder, complained that planes were flying directly over their homes and decibel levels were not only unbearable but in violation of ordinances. In addition, United Airlines, as virtually the only carrier servicing DIA, had jacked prices so high travelers were simply not

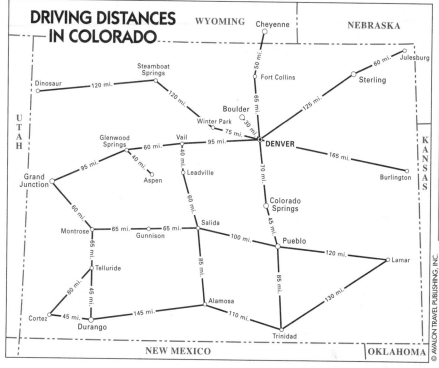

DRIVING DISTANCES IN COLORADO

WYOMING   Cheyenne   NEBRASKA

Dinosaur — 120 mi. — Steamboat Springs

120 mi.

Fort Collins — 50 mi.

65 mi.

Julesburg — 60 mi. — Sterling

125 mi.

Boulder

Winter Park — 30 mi.

75 mi.

UTAH

Glenwood Springs — 60 mi. — Vail — 95 mi. — DENVER

40 mi.

40 mi.

Aspen

Leadville

95 mi.

Grand Junction

60 mi.

60 mi.

165 mi. — Burlington

KANSAS

Colorado Springs

70 mi.

Montrose — 65 mi. — Gunnison — 65 mi. — Salida

65 mi.

100 mi. — Pueblo

45 mi.

Telluride

85 mi.

120 mi. — Lamar

80 mi.

45 mi.

85 mi.

Alamosa

Cortez — 45 mi. — Durango — 145 mi.

110 mi.

130 mi.

Trinidad

NEW MEXICO

OKLAHOMA

ON THE ROAD

© AVALON TRAVEL PUBLISHING, INC.

using the airport in the numbers expected. By midsummer, Denver air traffic was down 6 percent, yet that at Colorado Springs was up a whopping 67 percent; Denverites were driving the 1.5 hours to Colorado Springs to save themselves bucks on airfare.

But things have smoothed themselves out considerably, with more airlines servicing DIA, and the engineering problems all seem to be history. In fact, you'll probably be impressed with DIA's "user friendliness," from the design of the terminals to the light railroad whisking you underground from one end to the other. Plus, DIA has made access to other parts of Colorado—particularly the resorts—much easier, with regular connecting flights to smaller Colorado towns, including Aspen, Telluride, Montrose, Durango, and Fort Collins. Keep in mind that DIA is about 20 miles east of downtown and that it'll take you between 30 and 45 minutes to drive the distance.

If you want to forgo DIA altogether, some of the resorts, including Aspen, Telluride, Crested Butte, and Steamboat Springs, offer direct flights from several U.S. cities, such as Phoenix, Chicago, Los Angeles, and Dallas-Fort Worth. There are also large jet airports in Grand Junction and Colorado Springs. Contact your travel agent or look on the Web for specific information about flight schedules and rates.

Although you might be able to step off your plane and arrange a rental car, you're much better off making reservations, not only to guarantee you'll get the vehicle you want but to make your airport getaway smoother and quicker. You'll find rental cars available at Colorado's airports. In addition to the standard chains (Avis, Hertz, etc.), several "rent-a-wreck" companies offer discount rates, and a handful of outfits specialize in "snow-ready" vehicles (four-wheel- and front-wheel-drive with ski racks).

Colorado Springs Airport also has connections to most major U.S. cities. Flying into this smaller airport offers not only convenience and simplicity but better proximity to the southern part of the state, should that be your destination.

Information on DIA is available at 800/AIR-2-DEN (247-2336) or www.flydenver.com. The main phone number for Colorado Springs Airport is 719/550-1900.

By Rail

Colorado's history is defined in large part by the development of the railroad, and by rail is still an excellent way to get here and to see the state. One of **Amtrak**'s major east-west routes cuts across the northern part of Colorado, with stops in Glenwood Springs, Fraser (near Winter Park), and Denver.

The **Ski Train** runs weekends during the ski season between Denver's Union Station and Winter Park. Round-trip tickets start at $25, and the two-hour trip, which dives under the Continental Divide through Moffat Tunnel, guarantees passengers won't have to fight the oftentimes thick I-70 and Berthoud Pass traffic. For information, phone 303/296-I-SKI (296-4754). (Also see Transportation under Winter Park.)

In addition, several of Colorado's historic towns have begun tourist-oriented train tours. The best-known of these is the **Durango and Silverton Narrow Gauge Railroad,** which hauls more than 200,000 passengers a year between the two mountain towns. Rates start at about $50 for the eight-hour trip. For more information, phone 303/247-2733. (Also see Durango and Silverton Narrow Gauge Railroad under Silverton in the Southwestern Colorado chapter.)

Driving in Colorado

Driving in Colorado can be tricky. Even in the summer, when the roads are generally dry and free of snow, you should be very careful. Some of the mountain passes are extremely high and steep, with dramatic switchbacks requiring greatly reduced speed. Make sure your brakes are in good working order.

WINTER DRIVING TIPS

• Pay attention to highway rules and regulations, including closures and chain requirements; they're meant for your safety.

• Make sure your brakes are in good working order and your tires have plenty of tread.

• Make sure your cooling system has been properly winterized.

• Check your windshield wipers and wiper fluid; wiper fluid with antifreeze in it is available at auto-parts stores and gas stations.

• Always carry chains.

• Do not brake or turn the steering wheel suddenly.

• If you rent a car, rent a 4WD vehicle if you can (they're significantly more expensive than 2WD models). If you're on a 2WD budget, at least request front-wheel-drive, which offers far greater traction than rear-wheel-drive.

• Drive slowly, and always stay in control; remember that your car's stopping distance is greater when the road is wet, snowy, and/or icy.

• Stop if you begin to lose control or confidence.

• Keep seatbelts fastened at all times (common sense as well as Colorado state law).

In the winter, snow drifts across roadways, making visibility difficult, and even when the roads are dry, extreme caution must be taken. When the roads get snowy and wet, it's even more dangerous, and drivers without experience in snow driving should consider waiting until the routes have been cleared. Snowplows usually begin clearing interstates and other major arteries as soon as the snow starts to pile up, and these routes are rarely closed very long. Lesser-traveled routes, lower on the priority list, take longer to get cleared. In the spring, melted snow from warm daytime temperatures often trickles across roadways. During the night, this water freezes, resulting in hard-to-see sheets of ice on the road; these spots are even more slick and dangerous than patches of snow.

For recorded information on road conditions, phone 303/639-1111. You can also get road-condition information at www.cotrip.org.

The speed limit on Colorado interstates is generally 70 mph, though lower limits are sometimes marked. On U.S. and state highways, the speed limit is 55 or 60 mph. Seat belts are required for driver and front-seat passenger, as well as for passengers 4–16 years of age in back seats. Child seats are required until the child is at least four years old *and* weighs 40 pounds.

Motorcycle helmets are not required.

Colorado by Bus

Greyhound, 800/231-2222, offers service between most cities. Local bus lines, including those in Denver/Boulder, Colorado Springs, and Pueblo, can get you around town. Almost all the tourist towns, from Breckenridge and Vail to Crested Butte and Durango, have excellent shuttle buses that are free or next to it. Organized bus tours, meanwhile, will give you the overview ("On your right is Coors Field . . ."), but you won't likely be able to experience Colorado or Coloradans close up.

Northwestern Colorado

The huge northwestern corner of Colorado—comprising Moffat, Routt, Eagle, Rio Blanco, and Garfield Counties—is a relatively sparsely populated section of the state, where the highways stretch for miles and miles between tiny little towns. About two-thirds high plateau (the west side) and one-third Rockies' Front Range, northwestern Colorado offers a remarkable variation in scenery. From the barren brown oil shale of the Dinosaur National Monument area to the lush green mountains of White River and Routt National Forests, this area is a startling study in contrasts.

Two of the three main east-west routes into the state pass through northwestern Colorado: I-70, which snakes along the Colorado River from the Utah border, then rises over Vail and Loveland Passes; and U.S. 40, which barrels out of northern Utah making a beeline for Steamboat Springs before being turned south by the Rockies' spine, the Continental Divide. Eventually, just east of Loveland Pass, the two routes join forces and assault Denver in tandem.

Northwestern Colorado is best known today for two things: oil and recreation. The western plateau is thick with fossil fuel, and the world's sixth-largest oil field is just outside Rangely. The eastern side of the plateau area—especially around Craig, Meeker, and (appropriately) Rifle—is very popular with hunters, and the mountains, from Steamboat down to Vail, are world famous for their skiing. In addition, the huge expanses of the forest draw campers, backpackers, rafters, mountain bikers, and anglers to the high mountains when the snow melts.

Steamboat from US-40

East along I-70

Interstate 70 veers north from Grand Junction, follows the Colorado River, and gradually yet persistently rises into the heart of Colorado and the Rocky Mountains. En route it passes through or provides access to some of the state's most popular attractions: Aspen, Vail, Summit County, Georgetown and Idaho Springs, and Denver.

Between the Utah border and Glenwood Springs, the largest town between Grand Junction and Vail, the freeway is mostly wide open and flat, passing occasionally through deep canyons carved by the Colorado River. In Glenwood Springs, the valley grows narrow, the canyons often pinching tightly together (see Glenwood Canyon under Glenwood Springs and Vicinity, below). You can find plenty of inexpensive lodging in Glenwood; this is also where you'll turn south to catch U.S. 82 to Aspen or U.S. 133 to Telluride.

Between Glenwood Springs and Vail, the interstate bypasses a number of small towns—Eagle, Edwards, Avon—which also offer lodging and services. At Avon you enter the Vail Valley, a resort region devoted largely to skiing. Three ski areas, Arrowhead, Beaver Creek, and Vail, attract skiers by the thousands (Vail's uphill capacity is 36,000 per hour), not only from Denver, a hundred miles to the east, but from the East Coast and around the world. Because of the area's popularity, as well as I-70's importance to cross-country traffic, the road is kept plowed, and even during the severest of storms delays will be few and short-lived (but carry chains anyway!).

PARACHUTE

About an hour northeast of Grand Junction, Parachute is a little bitty town where you can rest up, gas up, and pick up road pops and other supplies for the cooler. A small picnic area at the turnoff offers a welcome respite for the road weary, who'll also find a booth with tourist information (maps, brochures, etc.) and the Thunder River Trading Post, where you can buy souvenirs, gifts, postcards, T-shirts, and other knickknacks. In addition to the minimarts and

other small businesses you can see from the road, a City Market (no salad bar or deli) is up on the hill in the Battlement Mesa development (follow the signs).

If you're too tired to drive on, here you can pull off the road to catch some shut-eye, the better to face the road that lies ahead. A **Super 8 Motel,** 970/285-7936, is just north of the freeway exit at 252 Green Street.

RIFLE

Rifle is about 63 miles northeast of Grand Junction at the junction of I-70 and Highway 13 north, which shoots straight up to Meeker (40 miles) along the base of the White River Plateau. Long a shopping center and meeting place for area ranchers, Rifle is also a base for folks heading into the mountains of White River National Forest, just north of town; in the late summer and fall, the area is particularly popular among deer and elk hunters.

According to legend, the town's name came about inadvertently when a mapmaker from an early surveying party left his rifle leaning against a tree, headed back to camp, then suddenly realized his mistake. He grabbed the map he was working on and scribbled the word "rifle" to

---

NORTHWESTERN COLORADO HIGHLIGHTS

Dinosaur National Monument: sightseeing, camping, museums

Steamboat Springs: snow skiing, fishing, rafting, hiking, Winter Carnival, Cowboy Roundup Days

Vail: skiing, shopping, cycling, sightseeing, 10th Mountain Hut and Trail System

Glenwood Springs: Frontier Historical Museum, Doc Holliday's Grave, hot springs, Vapor Caves, skiing, fishing

White River and Routt National Forests: camping and cross-country skiing

NORTHWESTERN

NORTHWESTERN COLORADO

WYOMING

UTAH

To I-80

To Salt Lake City

To Green River

Roosevelt National Forest

Rocky Mtn. N.P.

Lake Granby

Granby

Arapaho National Forest

To Denver

Frisco

Dixie

Leadville

To Salida

Walden

Routt National Forest

Continental Divide

Kremmling

Rocky Mountains

Vail

Continental

Mt. Zirkel (12,180 ft.)

Rabbit Ears Pass (9,426 ft.)

Steamboat Springs

Hahns Peak

Routt National Forest

Toponas

Wolcott

Eagle

White River National Forest

Aspen

White River National Forest

Sheep Mtn. (12,241 ft.)

The Flat Tops

National Forest

Glenwood Springs

Carbondale

White River

Craig

Meeker

Rio Blanco

Rifle

Roan Plateau

De Beque

Grand Junction

Danforth Hills

Cathedral Bluffs

Battlement Mesa

Colorado River

Rangely

Dinosaur

Maybell

Yampa

Little Snake River

Green River

Dinosaur National Monument

20 mi

20 km

0

0

© AVALON TRAVEL PUBLISHING, INC.

indicate where the tree was. Later, "rifle" being a prominent word on the only map of the area, folks naturally took to calling the town Rifle. And if you believe that. . . .

For more information on Rifle and the surrounding area, contact the Rifle Area Chamber of Commerce at 970/625-2085.

Rifle Creek Museum

This small museum displays frontier gear (saddles, snowshoes, traps, etc.) as well as early farming and medical equipment and domestic utensils. Downtown at 337 East Ave., the museum is open May through October Mon.–Fri. 10 A.M.–4 P.M. For further information, or to arrange tours, phone 970/625-4862.

Rifle Gap Falls and Lake State Recreation Area

This is where locals go to cool off during the hot summer months, for fishing, swimming, sailing, windsurfing, water-skiing, and even spelunking. Camp beside the Rifle Gap Reservoir, and fish for brown and rainbow trout and smallmouth bass, as well as walleye and other panfish.

Rifle Falls is a broad 50-foot-high waterfall on East Rifle Creek, at the base of which is lush foliage and a series of caves. The caves are large, save for a few narrow crawlways, and perfect for novice explorers.

The lake and falls are about 15 miles north of Rifle. Take Highway 13 north about five miles, and turn right on Highway 325. Cost to get into Rifle Falls is $3 per vehicle; additional cost for camping. For further information, phone 970/625-1607.

Accommodations

Rifle offers several clean and easy-to-get-to places to bed down for the night. The **Rusty Cannon**

Motel, 970/625-4004, and the **Red River Inn,** 970/625-3050, are both right off the interstate and offer doubles in the $60 range.

Food and Drink

Not a whole lot to choose from here, though you really can't go wrong at **Audry's Cafe,** 117 4th (at Railroad), 970/625-1311. It's a true down-home restaurant where the waitresses call you (and each other) "Hon." It serves breakfast, lunch, and dinner Mon.–Sat. at very reasonable prices. Pick up road snacks and picnic fixin's at the **City Market,** 1320 Railroad.

Services

The offices of the **Rifle Police Department** are at 202 Railroad Ave., 970/625-2331. Phone the **Garfield County Sheriff** at 970/625-1899. Rifle's small **Clagett Memorial Hospital** is at 701 E. 5th Ave., 970/625-1510. Larger medical facilities are in Glenwood Springs, about 25 miles west, at **Valley View Hospital,** 970/945-6535. Rifle's **post office** is at 330 Railroad Ave., 970/625-1070. Get **maps** and **Forest Service information** at the White River National Forest District Office, 94 County Rd. 244, 970/625-2371.

Drop off most recyclables at the **City Market** at 1320 Railroad Avenue.

Information

The **Rifle Visitor Information Center** is at the rest area at the I-70 exit (200 Lions Park Circle). You'll find information here not only about local attractions, accommodations, and recreation opportunities, but also about much of the White River National Forest and Glenwood Springs-Aspen areas. You can also write P.O. Box 809, Rifle, CO 81650, or phone 970/625-2085.

Glenwood Springs and Vicinity

One of Colorado's most historically and geologically fascinating towns, Glenwood Springs is the site of what it claims is the world's largest natural hot springs pool. Actually comprising two pools—the larger 405 by 100 feet and containing more than a million gallons of water—Glenwood Hot Springs has been attracting travelers for centuries, from nomadic Ute, Comanche, Cheyenne, and Arapahoe peoples who believed in the waters' spiritual healing powers to modern-day après-skiers who believe simply in its powers to ease aching muscles.

A gateway to the best ski areas in the state, Glenwood Springs (pop. 7,500; elev. 5,764 feet) has a small ski resort (Sunlight Mountain Resort) right in its backyard and is the last decent-sized town you pass through heading east on I-70 before you get into the heart of the Rockies and Colorado's real winter sports arenas: Vail and the ski mecca of Summit County. In addition, Glenwood Springs is at the junction with U.S. 82, the only road into Aspen in the winter (when the highway southeast of Aspen is closed over Independence Pass). In fact, not only do a large number of Aspen-area workers live in Glenwood Springs (where housing's much less expensive) and commute the 40 miles every day to the ski town, but many people who live in Aspen drive regularly into Glenwood Springs to do their shopping; from razor blades to dog food to fresh produce, everyday necessities are far cheaper in Glenwood Springs than in Aspen.

All of which should tell the savvy winter tourist something: if you want to ski Aspen, and you want to save some money, think about staying in Glenwood Springs. Though you'd be hard-pressed to find a room in Aspen for much under $80 or $90 a night, Glenwood has several motels where clean rooms start at around $35, as well as a hostel where you can get a bed for about $12. That's a savings of close to $400 a week—which could almost buy you and a date a nice dinner out in Aspen.

HISTORY

Known for centuries to Utes, who, protective of their sacred waters, fought to keep the Cheyenne and Comanche away, Glenwood Springs was first discovered by whites in 1860, when Captain Richard Sopris took sick while exploring the Eagle River Valley and was brought to the waters by the Utes. In the 1870s, the discovery of silver in Leadville brought about a population boom and a flurry of mining-camp construction in the mountains east of Glenwood. Leadville's John Landis arrived at Yampah springs in 1880 and, in true colonial fashion, claimed it for his own.

By the mid-1880s, the Native Americans had been mostly displaced, and white settlers had taken control of much of the fertile Roaring Fork River Valley. In 1885, Walter Devereux, an Aspen miner and engineer, bought the hot springs, incorporated Glenwood Springs, and began to solicit tourism and investment. By the latter part of the 1880s, Glenwood Springs was a rip-roaring town whose nearly two dozen saloons were well known to many of the hard-living miners, ranchers, cowboys, merchants, and lawmen who opened up the West.

the Glenwood Springs Historical Museum

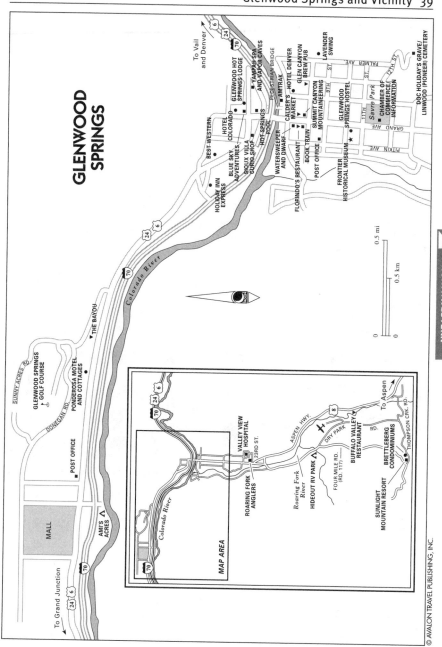

GLENWOOD SPRINGS

To Vail and Denver

GLENWOOD HOT SPRINGS LODGE
YAMPAH SPA AND VAPOR CAVES
PEDESTRIAN BRIDGE
LAVENDER SWING
AMTRAK
HOTEL DENVER
GLEN CANYON BREW PUB
CALDER'S
HOTEL COLORADO
BEST WESTERN
HOT SPRINGS POOL
MARKET
SUMMIT CANYON MOUNTAINEERING
BLUE SKY ADVENTURES
SIOUX VILLA CURIO SHOP
WATERSWEEPER AND DWARF
FLORINDO'S RESTAURANT
GLENWOOD SPRINGS HOSTEL
Sayre Park
CHAMBER OF COMMERCE INFORMATION
BOOK TRAIN
POST OFFICE
FRONTIER HISTORICAL MUSEUM
DOC HOLIDAY'S GRAVE/ LINWOOD (PIONEER) CEMETERY
PALMER AVE.
GRAND AVE.
PIKIN AVE.
9TH ST.
11TH
14TH ST.

HOLIDAY INN EXPRESS

THE BAYOU

Colorado River

SUNNY ACRES RD.
GLENWOOD SPRINGS GOLF COURSE
PONDEROSA MOTEL AND COTTAGES
DONEGAN RD.
POST OFFICE
MALL
AMI'S ACRES
To Grand Junction

0   0.5 mi
0   0.5 km

N
NORTHWESTERN

MAP AREA

VALLEY VIEW HOSPITAL
23RD ST.
ROARING FORK ANGLERS
Roaring Fork River
HIDEOUT RV PARK
ASPEN HWY.
DRY PARK
To Aspen
FOUR MILE RD. (RD. 117)
BUFFALO VALLEY RESTAURANT
RD.
BRETTLEBERG CONDOMINIUMS
THOMPSON CRK. RD.
SUNLIGHT MOUNTAIN RESORT
Colorado River

© AVALON TRAVEL PUBLISHING, INC.

The Denver and Rio Grande Railroad pushed through Glenwood Springs in 1887. A year later, thanks largely to the labor of local prison inmates who worked to break up the rock-hard ground and divert water from the Colorado River, old Yampah springs had been converted into a concrete pool, with an adjacent bathhouse, hotel, and casino.

In 1893, the Hotel Colorado was completed, and the area soon became a popular resort destination for some of the more monied eastern families, including Vanderbilts and Astors. Partly because of the influence of this upscale clientele, and because of the importance of the horse to Glenwood's development, polo became a celebrated local pastime, and Glenwood teams won national championships in the early part of the 20th century (trophies are on display in the Frontier Historical Museum).

The mid-20th century was essentially a slow time for Glenwood Springs, as other mountain towns began to draw crowds; however, with the boom in the ski industry (and in the health and fitness industries), in addition to an increased in-terest in local history and heritage, things in Glenwood Springs began to pick up. By the 1970s and '80s, the public was rediscovering the hot springs, realizing the important part this little town played in the development of the state, and taking advantage of its proximity to Aspen and the other nearby ski resorts.

SIGHTS AND PARKS
Frontier Historical Museum
Founded in 1963 by the Glenwood Springs Historical Society, this small museum—originally a home built in 1905 by a local doctor—features a replica of a coal mine, a collection of pioneer-era toys, dolls, and clothing, as well as Native American artifacts and historical maps and photos of Glenwood Springs and the surrounding areas.

Hours are Mon.–Sat. 11 A.M.–4 P.M. (Monday, Thursday, Friday only, 1–4 P.M., in winter). Admission is $3 (no charge for kids under 11). Guided group tours are available by appointment. For more information, write Glenwood

Hot Springs Lodge and Pool in Glenwood Springs

Springs Historical Museum, 1001 Colorado Ave., Glenwood Springs, CO 81601, or phone 970/945-4448.

Doc Holliday's Grave, Linwood Cemetery

An easy half-mile trail leads from Cemetery Road (off Bennett Avenue) to Linwood Cemetery, where Doc Holliday—the famous Wild West gambler and roustabout—is reportedly buried: although a gravestone with his name and the inscription "died in bed" stands in the cemetery, some claim he was buried in an unmarked grave in town. Kid Curry, a member of Butch Cassidy's Hole-in-the-Wall gang, is also buried at Linwood.

In the winter, the trail is perfect for a short Nordic ski excursion.

Glenwood Hot Springs Pool

Advertising itself in the early part of last century as a "Health and Pleasure Resort," serving both "invalids and tourists," this gigantic hot springs has actually been serving travelers for hundreds of years. Utes, who called them Yampah (or "Big Medicine") springs, used the pools, as did early white settlers and several U.S. presidents, including Teddy Roosevelt.

The pools are completely refilled about every eight hours by the 3.5 million gallons of 124-degree water that flows from the springs daily—perfect for basking in after a day on the slopes or an afternoon chasing trout in the Colorado or Roaring Fork River. A daily pass is $8.75 for adults ($5.75 for kids 3–12). There's also a weight and exercise room and a water slide. Suits and towels can be rented for a nominal fee. The pool is open daily 7:30 A.M.–10 P.M. (9 A.M.–10 P.M. in the winter). For information, write Hot Springs Lodge and Pool, P.O. Box 308, Glenwood Springs, CO 81602, or phone 970/945-6571 or 800/623-3400 (toll free from Denver), or 800/537-SWIM (537-7946—toll free from the rest of Colorado). You can also get information at www.hotspringspool.com.

Yampah Spa and Vapor Caves

Three caves, heated by mineral hot springs to 115°F and approximately 100 percent humidity, are open to the public seven days a week. At one time part of the Utes' Yampah springs (along with the hot springs pools), the caves are now privately owned. In addition to a cleansing sweat in the caves, you can get a variety of health ministrations: massages, facials, cranial-sacral therapy, Reiki therapy, reflexology, and earwax removal. Afterward, you can relax in the solarium or on the sundeck with a glass of natural juice. Prices start at $8.75 (for a cave visit) and run to about $100 (for the full treatment—massage, foot reflex, facial).

The Vapor Caves are open seven days a week 9 A.M.–9 P.M. For more information, phone 970/945-0667, or write 709 E. 6th St., Glenwood Springs, CO 81601.

City Park

Glenwood Spring's Sayre's Park is right on the main drag (U.S. 82/Grand Avenue) about a half mile south of downtown and has picnic facilities, tennis and basketball courts, and spacious lawns.

RECREATION
Skiing

One of Colorado's smaller ski resorts, but a favorite among locals who want to avoid the crowds and pretentiousness of the larger areas, **Sunlight Mountain Resort** offers both downhill and cross-country skiing about 10 miles from Glenwood Springs (free shuttles run regularly between town and the resort). With a 2,010-foot vertical drop, Sunlight's 470 acres of trails and runs, serviced by four lifts, are 20 percent novice, 55 percent intermediate, and 25 percent advanced.

Lodging, equipment rental, lessons (downhill, cross-country, Telemark, and snowboarding), and day care are all available at Sunlight, as are package deals with local hotels and motels and with the Hot Springs Lodge (for an after-ski soak). For more information, write Sunlight Mountain Resort, 10901 County Rd. 117, Glenwood Springs, CO 81601, or phone 970/945-7491 or 800/445-7931. For central reservations and lodging, phone 800/445-7931. Information is also available on the Web at www.sunlightmtn.com.

Southwest of Glenwood Springs off Highway 82, **Spring Gulch** is a Nordic area with 10 miles of trails operated by the Mount Sopris Nordic Council. Skiing is free. For maps and information, check ski shops in the Glenwood Springs-Carbondale-Aspen area. You can also get information on cross-country skiing in the Glenwood Springs area by calling the Glenwood Group of the Colorado Mountain Club at 970/945-1238; the club has regular cross-country outings and encourages the public to come along.

Golf

Glenwood Springs Golf Course is a nine-hole public course north of the frontage road in west Glenwood Springs. For tee times or further information, phone 970/945-7086.

Hiking

Virtually surrounded by mountains and national forest lands, Glenwood Springs offers the hiker and backpacker hundreds of miles of trails to explore. Just a few miles east of town, **No Name Trail** and **Hanging Lake Trail** are good day hikes. In town, the **Boy Scout Trail** takes hikers from the top of 8th Street to the base of Lookout Mountain—3.5 miles, approximately two hours. Bring water. **Red Mountain Trail** will take you from the end of West 9th Street to the site of Glenwood's first ski area, where the lift towers are still standing. The hikes from Cemetery Road to Linwood Cemetery and from the Vapor Caves to the Colorado River are both easy, scenic, and enjoyable.

For maps and more information, contact the Glenwood Springs Chamber of Commerce (1102 Grand Ave., 970/945-6589) or the White River National Forest headquarters (900 Grand Ave., P.O. Box 948, 970/945-2521). You can also get USGS maps and tips on hiking and backpacking in the area at **Summit Canyon Mountaineering,** 732 Grand Ave., 970/945-6994. Summit Canyon Mountaineering is also in Grand Junction, 461 Main St., 970/243-2347.

Hunting and Fishing

Come winter, you'll likely hear longtime Glenwoodians talking about how full their freezers are. "Didn't think I was gonna get my elk this year, but I finally did, just before the season closed." Deer, too, are popular prey of local (and visiting) hunters, though they know the 150 pounds of meat a decent-sized mulie provides is nothing next to what a big bull elk can—upward of 400 pounds. Good fishing abounds in the Glenwood Springs area, too—rainbows and brown trout in the Colorado River west of town, and brookies and rainbows in the small lakes in the surrounding mountains. For tips on local fishing, stop by **Roaring Fork Anglers,** 2114 Grand Ave., or phone 970/945-0180.

Rafting

On the confluence of the Roaring Fork and Colorado Rivers, Glenwood Springs is a rafter's paradise, and companies based throughout the area offer a variety of trips, from short, two-hour jaunts to three-day excursions. **Blue Sky Adventures,** 319 6th St., 970/945-6605, offers a short range of trips starting at about $25 (adult) for a two-hour tour of Glenwood Canyon. Look for the vans and the rafts on trailers between the Hotel Colorado and The Hot Springs Lodge. (Note: Blue Sky also operates **Canyon Bikes,** with rentals, guided tours, and shuttle service; you can also book rafting/biking packages.)

Among several other companies that book raft trips on the Roaring Fork and Colorado Rivers are **Rock Gardens Rafting,** 1309 County Rd. 129, 970/945-6737; and **Whitewater Rafting,** at Exit 114 on I-70, 970/945-8477.

TOURS

The Glenwood Springs Chamber of Commerce (see Information, below) has outlined a historic walking tour of downtown Glenwood Springs. Included are the stone bathhouse at the hot springs pool, the vapor caves, the Hotel Colorado, the Glenwood Barber Shop (the only remaining part of the Hotel Glenwood, built before the turn of the 20th century and mostly destroyed by fire in 1945), and more than three dozen other buildings of historical significance—homes, banks, and retail stores. The chamber can provide you with a map.

Crystal River Jeep Tours, 116 E. Main St., Marble, CO 81623, 970/963-1991, offers trips to the Yule Marble Quarry, Crystal City, and Lead King Basin.

ACCOMMODATIONS

Glenwood Springs isn't as well known or developed as Aspen or Vail, which means you can stay here relatively inexpensively. But be forewarned: the little town still fills up. Last time I passed through, I had to make about six phone calls (a week before my visit) to find an available room. I wouldn't recommend pulling into town looking to find a place to stay the night, especially during the ski season and in the summer.

Under $50

The **Glenwood Springs Hostel,** 1021 Grand Ave., 970/945-8545 or 800/9-HOSTEL (946-7835), is walking distance from the hot springs. The hostel offers discounts on ski tickets and rentals, discounts at Yampah Vapor Caves, free pickup from the bus and train depots (with notice), laundry and kitchen facilities, and a record library for use by guests. Dorm rooms and individual rooms are available.

$50–100

The **Glenwood Hot Springs Lodge,** in downtown Glenwood, just across I-70 from the hot springs, 970/945-6571 or 800/537-SWIM (537-7946—in Colorado only), offers discounts for the pool and fitness facilities at the springs. The **Ponderosa Motel and Cottages** in West Glenwood at 51793 U.S. Highways 6 and 24, 970/945-5058, has rooms and cabins (from small efficiencies to large A-frames). You can also get rooms at the **Holiday Inn Express,** 501 W. 1st St., 970/945-8551; and at **The Antlers Best Western,** 171 W. 6th St., 970/945-8535.

$100–150

Looking for a taste of history? Check out the **Hotel Colorado,** 526 Pine, 970/945-6511 or, toll-free from Denver, 800/623-3400. Dating from the early 1890s, this Colorado classic has hosted such luminaries as Teddy Roosevelt,

William Taft, Molly Brown, and the Mayo brothers (of the Mayo Clinic), who came to Glenwood Springs for the healing powers of the waters. Photos of famous guests line the walls of the hotel's lobby. Now renovated—the hotel was converted to a military hospital in the 1940s—the old stone building today offers travelers spacious rooms on gorgeously maintained grounds overlooking the town and river.

Also of historic significance, the **Hotel Denver,** 402 7th St., 970/945-6565, was built just after the turn of the 20th century and offers some of the nicest rooms in town.

If you're going to be skiing at Sunlight Mountain Resort, you'd be hard-pressed to do better than the **Brettelberg Condominiums,** 970/945-7421 or 800/634-0481. More a 1940s-style ski lodge than a modern-day condo complex, the Brettelberg is right on the slopes, actually uphill from the base lodge—the ultimate in "ski in and ski out." For more information, write Brettelberg Condominiums, 11101 County Rd. 117, Glenwood Springs, CO 81601.

Bed-and-Breakfast

The **Lavender Swing,** 802 Palmer, 970/945-8289, is a bed-and-breakfast in an elegant Victorian dating from 1903. Three rooms are available (one with two beds), each with a private bath. Rooms run about $90.

Camping and RVing

Campgrounds are scattered throughout the White River National Forest, large units of which surround the Glenwood Springs area. **Deep Lake** and **Coffee Pot Spring** have free camping at moderately improved sites (pit toilets, no showers—drinking water at Coffee Pot Spring only). For more information, phone the Eagle District Office of the Forest Service at 970/328-6388; for maps of White River National Forest, stop by forest headquarters at 900 Grand Avenue.

RV and tent camping are available at **Hideout Cabins and Campground,** 970/945-5621, about two miles up the road toward Sunlight Mountain Resort (1293 County Rd. 117), and at **Ami's Acres Campground,** 970/945-5340, off I-70 at Exit 114. A **KOA** campground, 970/984-2240, in

New Castle, 11 miles west of Glenwood Springs on I-70 (581 County Rd. 241), has tent sites, full-hookup RV sites, and cabins, as well as hot showers, laundry facilities, and a small store. Take Exit 105 from I-70, and follow the signs to East Elk Creek Road. Two miles east of Glenwood Springs, **Rock Gardens Camping and Rafting,** 970/945-6737, offers tent and RV sites as well as half- and full-day raft trips.

FOOD

The Devereux Room at the **Hotel Colorado,** 970/945-6511, serves breakfast (pancakes, omelettes, etc.), lunch (fish and chips, sandwiches, salads), and dinner (veal, chicken, beef, and Southwestern food) at moderate prices. You can also get coffee and pastries to go at **The Legends Espresso and Juice Bar,** in the lobby of the Hotel Colorado. For a light, continental-style breakfast, try **Calder's Market,** at 8th and Grand in downtown Glenwood, 970/945-2055—espressos and pastries with sidewalk seating, weather permitting.

Florindo's, 721 Grand, 970/945-1245, focuses on homemade southern-Italian cuisine and has a reputation for quality food and service. Veal, seafood, and pasta entrées run $12–18. It's open for lunch Mon.–Fri. 11:30 A.M.–3:30 P.M. and for dinner Mon.–Sat. 5–10 P.M.

Glenwood's step onto the brew-pub bandwagon is **Glenwood Canyon Brewing Company,** 402 7th St. (floor level of the Hotel Denver), 970/945-1276. Serving traditional brew-pub fare—pastas, burgers, salads, fish and chips—this place is particularly lively on Friday afternoons, when locals stop by the bar on their way home from work and on Saturday and Sunday afternoon, especially if a Rockies' or Broncos' game is on one of the several televisions.

You might also want to check out **Buffalo Valley Restaurant,** 3637 U.S. Hwy. 82, 1.5 miles south of Glenwood, 970/945-5297, for down-home Western grub—buffalo steaks, ribs, barbecue chicken, plus pastas and a salad bar. Live dance music on weekends.

For "Food so good you'll slap yo mama," served by a "well trained . . . and slightly warped staff," try **The Bayou,** on the frontage road in West Glenwood, 970/945-1047. During ski season, get a free cup of gumbo by showing your lift ticket or ski rental receipt, and a free cocktail if you've got a cast from a ski injury. Entrées are in the $8–18 range.

About five miles south of town on Highway 82 (to Aspen) is the **Sopris Restaurant and Lounge,** 970/945-7771. One of the nicer eateries in the area, the Sopris is popular with everyone from local ranchers and outfitters to Aspen luminaries, who rave about the eclectic menu—from American-standard beef dishes to daily continental specials—and extensive wine list. Entrées run $12–22. Open daily.

ENTERTAINMENT AND EVENTS

Though there's undoubtedly more going on up the road in Aspen, Glenwood Springs does offer its share of nightlife. **Buffalo Valley Inn,** 1.5 miles up the road toward Aspen, 970/945-5297, has a large dance floor, with live music on weekends. In addition, the lounge at the **Sopris Restaurant,** 7215 U.S. Hwy. 82, 970/945-7771, regularly features live listening and dancing music. For current information on what's going on where, pick up a free copy of *Mountain Leisure,* published every Friday by the *Glenwood Post* and distributed in racks around town. You'll find listings of art, recreation, and nightlife happenings, as well as reviews and theater schedules.

Calendar

Glenwood's biggest annual event is the popular **Strawberry Days** in mid-June. Dating from 1863, this is the oldest town festival in Colorado (canceled only during the food and gasoline rationing of World War II) and features foot and bicycle races, Pony Express rides, a parade, arts-and-crafts fair, beauty pageant *(de gustibus non est disputandum . . .),* live country-and-western music, and free strawberries and ice cream.

The **International Folk Festival and Oktoberfest** in the fall in downtown's Sayre Park offers food, drink, and entertainment from around the world. And every summer for 10 weeks, the city offers **Summer of Jazz** in Two Rivers Park on

Wednesday nights. Concerts are by big-name acts and are free, though donations are solicited during intermissions.

For exact dates, times, and locations, as well as for more information on other Glenwood Springs events, contact the chamber of commerce (see Information, below).

SHOPPING

In downtown Glenwood Springs you'll find a handful of souvenir and curio shops, as well as some stores carrying quality arts and crafts. The **Watersweeper and the Dwarf,** 717 Grand Ave., 970/945-2000, carries handcrafted pieces carved, sculpted, assembled, and molded from silver, gold, clay, glass, and other odds and ends. **Sioux Villa Curio,** 970/945-6134, one block west of the hot springs pool on 6th Street, sells souvenirs and knickknacks, including moccasins, "authentic" Black Hills gold jewelry, and postcards. The Glenwood Springs Mall in west Glenwood has a **JCPenney, Kmart,** and more than two dozen smaller stores selling everything from hats and shoes to jewelry and pets.

SERVICES

The **Glenwood Springs Police Department** is at 823 Blake Ave., 970/945-8566. Phone the **State Patrol** at 970/945-6198 (24-hour emergency line). Glenwood's **Valley View Hospital** is at 6535 Blake Ave., 970/945-6535. The main **post office** is at 113 9th St., 970/945-5611.

Recycling

Glenwood Springs operates two recycling centers, both of which will take aluminum and glass. Locations are 1600 Grand Ave. and the **Wal-Mart** at 3010 Blake. Recycle aluminum only at the **City Market,** 1410 Grand Ave., and **Safeway,** 2001 Grand Avenue.

INFORMATION

Stop by or write the **Glenwood Springs Chamber Resort Association** at 1102 Grand Ave., Glenwood Springs, CO 81601, 970/945-6589.

You'll find plenty of information on area history, recreation, dining, and lodging, as well as maps and schedules for the Ride Glenwood Springs shuttle (see below). Another excellent source of information is the **Glenwood Post,** the area's (small) daily newspaper, available in racks around town for $.40. You'll also find information on Glenwood Springs at www.glenwoodguide.com, where there are lots of links to other sites of interest to visitors.

For information on the **White River National Forest,** contact either the forest headquarters, 900 Grand Ave., P.O. Box 948, Glenwood Springs, CO 81602, 970/945-2521; or the Eagle District Office, 125 W. 5th St., P.O. Box 720, Eagle, CO 81631, 970/328-6388.

The **Book Train** magazine and bookstore, 723 Grand Ave., 970/945-7045, has an excellent selection of books on Colorado and the Southwest, as well as other travel books (including those Cadillacs of travel guides, Moon Handbooks). The Glenwood Springs branch of the **Garfield County Library** is at 413 9th St., 970/945-5958. The Colorado **Mountain College Library** is at the college at 3000 County Rd. 114, 970/945-7481.

The **Frontier Historical Museum** has a gift shop with books on the area's history, as well as videos for rent. In addition, the museum's archives are available (by appointment only) for more extensive research. Phone 970/945-4448 or 970/945-8465.

For **road and weather information,** phone 970/945-2221.

TRANSPORTATION

Glenwood Springs's **Amtrak** station, 970/945-9563, is directly across the freeway from the hot springs pool (accessible via footbridge). The **Greyhound-Trailways** bus depot is at 118 W. 6th St., 970/945-8501. **Ride Glenwood Springs** is a shuttle that operates daily, with service to motels, restaurants, the hot springs, pool, and the mall.

Aspen's airport, 40 miles southeast of Glenwood Springs, is serviced by **Continental Express,** 970/925-3350, and **United Express,**

970/925-3400. You can rent cars at the Aspen airport (see Aspen under Southwestern Colorado). **Colorado Mountain Express,** 800/525-6363, offers service between Glenwood Springs and Aspen and Denver.

GLENWOOD SPRINGS TO VAIL

It'd be tough to find a stretch of American interstate prettier than that running east from Glenwood Springs to Vail, over Vail Pass, through Summit County, over (or under, via tunnel) Loveland Pass, and into Denver. From Glenwood to Vail, it's about 75 miles and when the road is clear takes less than 1.5 hours. Allow more time during winter storms (a main east-west artery, this is one of the first roads to be plowed, yet snow can still pile up, making it slick and dangerous).

A half hour out of Glenwood Springs, you're approaching the soul of Colorado ski country. The Rockies' sharp peaks loom in front of you; the road grows steeper, the air thinner; condominium complexes begin to proliferate and sprawl at freeway exits. Lift towers, chairs, and clearcuts punctuate the hillsides. Finally, you roll into the Vail Valley, site of one of the world's premier ski resorts and summer vacation areas.

Glenwood Canyon

Just a few miles east of Glenwood Springs, you enter Glenwood Canyon, the most scenic stretch

of the Utah-to-Kansas freeway. Here, I-70 snakes through a 15-mile-long crevice carved by the Colorado River, bridging it and flirting with its steep, rocky banks. In some places, the canyon walls are 2,000 feet high.

An important artery for travelers since 1887, when the Denver and Rio Grande Railroad first laid tracks along the river, Glenwood Canyon has seen several generations of roadways. The recently completed Glenwood Canyon Highway, in planning since the mid-1970s and under construction throughout the '80s and early '90s, makes every attempt to wed modern transportation needs with the environmental considerations dire to such a sensitive area. While the road was being built, workers had to conform to strict ecological guidelines and were under the constant scrutiny of environmentalists.

The completed stretch of highway, which includes more than 40 bridges (totaling over six miles), used 30 million pounds of structural steel, 30 million pounds of reinforcing steel, and 400,000 cubic yards of concrete.

Four rest areas along this short stretch of road offer access to hiking trails into White River National Forest, as well as to the recreation/bike path (wheelchair accessible) that follows the entire course of the highway through the canyon. One of them, Grizzly Creek Rest Area, also has a launch for kayaks, rafts, and other small boats.

Vail and Beaver Creek

Nestled in the Gore Creek Valley between the Gore and Sawatch mountain ranges, Vail has earned a reputation as one of the finest ski areas in the world. Just 100 miles west of Denver via I-70, Vail attracts not only hundreds of thousands of skiers each year, but also more and more summer visitors, who descend on the little community of Vail Village (permanent pop. 5,000; elev. 8,150) to take part in the virtually limitless recreational opportunities—golfing, tennis, cycling, fishing, horseback riding, and rafting—as well as to wander through the town's cobblestone streets and Tyrolean-style buildings.

Vail, like Aspen, is almost always associated with money. This is one of the playgrounds of the East Coast rich, and hotel rooms can run $300 a night; you can't very well vacation here if you've got to keep a close eye on finances.

Then there's Beaver Creek, Vail's even richer neighbor, where summer homes run into the millions and a suite in a luxury hotel can cost up to $600. People who can afford to stay here don't even blink at the thought of spending $60 for a ski-lift ticket (prices are the same at both Vail and Beaver Creek, both of which are owned and operated by Vail Resorts).

But don't let it intimidate you. Even though, as F. Scott Fitzgerald once said to Ernest Hemingway, "The rich aren't like you and me," and they do own much of the Vail area, they don't own all of it. And there are ways for a working person to enjoy a visit without going hopelessly into debt. In fact, one of the best parts of visiting Vail is simply wandering around, browsing in the wide range of specialty shops, and strolling along the bike and walking path between the town and the base of the lifts.

History

Compared to Telluride, Breckenridge, Aspen, and many other Colorado ski towns, Vail is a relative newcomer, not even four decades old. The area was probably explored to some degree as early as 1850, when Irishman Sir George Gore (whose surname is unfortunately fitting) and a huge hunting party went on a blood-lusty trophy tour of Colorado and southern Wyoming. In 1873, the Hayden Survey Party passed through the valley, with photographer William Henry Jackson lugging 100 pounds of equipment up Notch Mountain to take his now-famous photo of Mount of the Holy Cross. The near-perfect cross in the photo, first displayed at the Philadelphia Centennial Exhibition of 1876, has inspired thousands of pilgrims to the area.

It wasn't until the middle of the next century, though, that the Vail Valley saw any real settlement. In 1942, 15,000 troops from the Army's 10th Mountain Division were stationed in the mountains south of Vail. Many of these men—trained in backcountry winter survival, including getting around on skis—saw action in Italy's Po River Valley and Apennine Mountains. After the war, a handful of them, led by Peter Seibert, who had been wounded in Italy, returned to the area and began developing their own ski area. Vail saw its first lift-borne skiers on December 15, 1962. By the winter of 1965, a small village had begun to develop, with several restaurants, saloons, hotels, and a

Although the rich do own much of the Vail area, they don't own all of it. And there are ways for a working person to enjoy a visit without going hopelessly into debt.

medical clinic. The town was incorporated that year.

In the mid-1970s, Vail began to make itself known as one of Colorado's best ski areas, its "Back Bowls" earning the respect of the most discriminating skiers in the country. In 1974, Gerald Ford, who had owned a home in Vail since the mid-1960s, became president of the United States after Richard Nixon's resignation. Photos of Ford at his "Western White House" graced the pages of newspapers throughout the world.

Work on Vail's sister resort, Beaver Creek, was begun by Vail Associates in the late 1970s; it had originally been part of a plan to bid for the 1976 Winter Olympics (defeated by Colorado voters). By the early '80s the two ski areas had developed a reputation not only for some of the best snow in the Rockies, but for some of the best "show." Vail and big money became almost synonymous, and the perception, not wholly inaccurate if obviously stereotypical, of the Vail visitor was one of furs, fancy German cars, expensive state-of-the-art ski equipment, and a foreign accent, either European or Texan.

Also during the early '80s, Vail and Beaver Creek began to expand from primarily winter playgrounds to year-round resorts. More golf courses were built, gondolas and chairlifts were made available to sightseers and mountain bikers, and the village began to sponsor hot-air balloon rallies, tennis tournaments, and concerts, from chamber music to rock 'n' roll. During the summer of 1988, Vail Ski Area's Back Bowls were further developed, more than doubling the amount of skiable terrain on the mountain.

Colorado Ski Museum and Ski Hall of Fame

Offering an overview of the history of skiing around the world, with an emphasis on Colorado, this small museum features excellent exhibits, including lots of wonderful historical photos and examples of century-old equipment.

Check out skis used by early Colorado miners in the 1880s, early "beartrap" bindings, the first buckle boots and metal-edged skis, the infamous K2 Cheeseburger Deluxes, and skis used by recent Olympic-medal winners, as well as equipment once belonging to Gerald Ford. You can also learn more about the Army's 10th Mountain Division and view some of its equipment—tents, skis, white camouflage parkas, etc.

The Colorado Ski Museum, 231 S. Frontage Rd. E, is open Tues.–Sun. 10 A.M.–6 P.M. Admission is $1. For further information, phone 970/476-1876.

Betty Ford Alpine Gardens

With more than 2,000 varieties of plants from alpine and subalpine elevations around the world, a 120-foot waterfall, and an Asian meditation garden, this park offers a cool and quiet respite from the hustle and bustle of Vail's shops, restaurants, and general high-energy lifestyle. The gardens, 520 S. Frontage Rd. in Ford Park, are open dawn to dusk, from snowmelt to snowfall. Admission is free, with donations encouraged. For further information, phone 970/476-0103.

PARKS AND RECREATION

Recreation is what Vail's all about. Folks come from all over the world to vacation here, to ski the vast expanses of the Back Bowls, to hit golf balls into the 8,000-foot-high, thin mountain air, to toss caddis flies at native rainbow trout. Or just to relax. What better place to hide behind a pair of Foster Grants and a Stephen King novel than beside a pool or at a sidewalk café in Vail Village?

WINTER SPORTS

Vail was founded on downhill skiing, and even as the resort has diversified, downhill skiing remains its primary draw. From mid-November through April, weather permitting, Vail's parking lots are packed with ski-racked 4WD rigs, its streets bustling with ski-booted shoppers, its restaurants and hotels packed to the gills with skiers of all abilities, from complete novices to cer-

tified powderhounds and boarders just off the half pipe. In the winter, just about everything in the Vail Valley revolves around snow skiing and boarding.

Vail

This gigantic ski resort offers 5,290 acres of wide open skiing terrain with enough of every level to go around: 18 percent beginner, 29 percent advanced, and 53 percent expert. The largest single-mountain ski area in the United States, Vail has a 3,450-foot vertical drop, 33 lifts, 193 runs, some of which are more than four miles long, a super pipe, snowboard zones, NASTAR course, and snow-play area, for tubing, snowshoeing, and laser tag. Its total uphill capacity is 50,000 skiers per hour.

Of course, as one of Colorado's premier ski resorts, and certainly its most accessible, the place can get crowded, especially on weekends. Just over 100 miles from Denver, Vail is close enough even for day-trippers. Still, though, thanks particularly to the new Back Bowls and high-speed chairs, the mobs are handled relatively graceful-

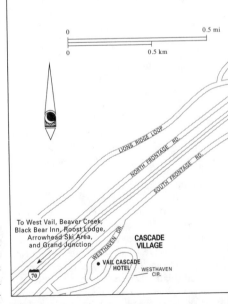

ly, and you should be able to find a fairly un-crowded slope to crank some turns (though if you'd rather strut your stuff for the masses, there's plenty of opportunity for that too).

Like a luxury hotel, Vail is exclusive in both feel and actual cost, and folks on budgets will have a tough time here: a single day's lift ticket will set you back over $60 (though seniors 70 and older and kids four and younger ski free, and you can get multiple-day discounts). Still, it's a great splurge, and every serious skier should try to make it to Vail at least once.

Vail has a full-service ski school, including programs for kids (three and older; nonski programs for kids two months to six years), racers, snowboarders, Telemarkers, and cross-country skiers. Vail also offers NASTAR recreational racing.

For more information on skiing Vail, write Vail Resorts, P.O. Box 7, Vail, CO 81658, 970/476-5601. For information about children's ski programs, phone 970/479-2044; adult ski school, 970/476-3239 or 800/354-5630; cross-country and Telemark, 970/845-5313. For in-formation on **snow conditions,** phone 970/476-4888 or 800/985-9843. For information on NASTAR racing, phone 970/476-5601, ext. 4050. Get a snow report at www.vail.snow.com. The address for the resort's main website is www.vail.com.

Beaver Creek

Vail's little sister, Beaver Creek first opened in the winter of 1980–81. Ten miles west of Vail, Beaver Creek's 1,625 acres are serviced by 13 lifts providing access to 146 trails. Total vertical drop is a respectable 4,040 feet; uphill capacity is 24,739 skiers per hour.

Beaver Creek was originally designed with the 1976 Olympics in mind. It offers a wide range of skiing for all ability levels, with about 40 percent of the mountain designated inter-mediate. The resort offers a children's ski school (for kids three and older), a nonski program for kids two months to six years, as well as a full range of adult instructional programs, includ-ing snowboarding, cross-country skiing, and Telemarking.

NORTHWESTERN

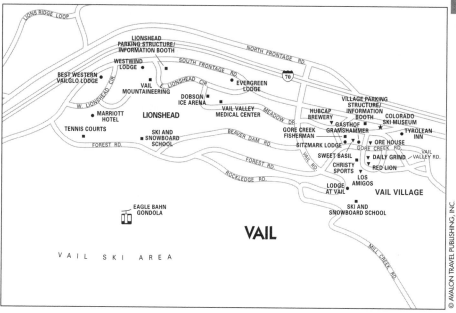

For further information about skiing Beaver Creek, write Vail Resorts, P.O. Box 7, Vail, CO 81658, 970/949-5750. For information about the nursery and children's ski school, phone 970/845-5464; adult ski school, 970/845-5300; cross-country ski school, 970/845-5313. For **snow conditions,** phone 970/476-4888 or 800/622-3131, or go to www.beavercreek.snow.com. The resort's main website is www.beavercreek.com.

Cross-Country Skiing

In addition to the designated cross-country trail systems operated by Vail Resorts (Golden Peak Center in Vail and McCoy Park at Beaver Creek), the Vail Valley and surrounding area offers some exceptional opportunities for Nordic skiers of all abilities. You can get out and cruise groomed trails for an hour, or you can head out into serious backcountry, staying in designated huts for a week or longer.

In winter, the golf course becomes the **Vail Nordic Center,** 1778 Vail Valley Rd., 970/479-2291, run by the Vail Recreation District. The center offers 33 km of free groomed trails (both skating and classic track). Equipment rentals are available, and the interpretive staff from Vail Nature Center offers guided snowshoe tours. The Nordic Center is open daily 9 A.M.–5 P.M. from around Thanksgiving to March, depending on snow cover.

For more information on cross-country skiing in the Vail Valley, contact one of the offices of **White River National Forest.** The Holy Cross Ranger District Office is at 401 Main St. in Minturn, 970/827-5715. The national forest's headquarters is at 900 Grand Ave., P.O. Box 948, Glenwood Springs, CO 81602, 970/945-2521.

You can also get information from most of the retail ski and board shops in the area, including **Vail Mountaineering** in Lionshead, 970/476-4223; **Cascade Sports,** 1300 Westhaven Dr., 970/476-0186; and **Christy Sports,** 293 Bridge St., 970/476-2244.

10th Mountain Hut and Trail System

Named for the 15,000 U.S. Army troops who trained in the 1940s at Camp Hale in the moun-

Snowboarding gets more popular each year at Colorado ski resorts.

© STEPHEN METZGER

tains south of Vail, this network of backcountry trails and huts—situated between 9,700 and 11,700 feet—offers the ultimate Nordic skiing experience. The trail system itself is immense, 300 miles long and linking the towns of Aspen, Leadville, Copper Mountain, and Vail. It would take most of a season to bag the whole thing. And the "huts"? Well, they're not huts as *I* would use the word. Chalets, maybe. Chateaus.

10th Mountain System skiers can either head out on their own or go with guides. The huts, most of which sleep 16, run about $25–35 per person per night (bring your own food). Guides offer three- to eight-day trips, with rates starting at about $70 a day (food and other necessities provided). Though not for the first-timer, most parts of the trail system are suitable for low-intermediate skiers. For further information or reservations (the huts are always booked up), contact the 10th Mountain Trail Association, 1280 Ute Ave., Aspen, CO 81611, 970/925-5775.

The best way to learn more about the huts or to make reservations is to visit the website at www.huts.org, where you can also get information about and make reservations for other hut systems in the state.

Other Winter Activities

Don't think skiing is the only winter activity for Vail Valley visitors. If you're not into strapping boards afoot, there's still plenty to do. The **John Dobson Ice Arena,** 321 E. Lionshead Circle, 970/479-2271, is open to the public daily. Skate rentals available.

If you want to get into the backcountry but don't feel like huffing and puffing your way through drifts of snow, you can take a **Snowcat Tour.** You can arrange tours through the **Vail/Beaver Creek Activities Desk,** 970/476-9090.

Another popular winter activity is **snowmobiling.** Tours and rentals are offered by several companies, including **Nova Guides,** 970/949-4232, and **Piney River Ranch,** 970/476-3941.

WHEN THE SNOW MELTS

Cycling

One of the first things a summer visitor to Vail will notice is the proliferation of bicyclists. And why not? Not only is this a community where health and fitness are paramount, but cycling is an excellent way to stay in shape for skiing. In addition, the area is ideally suited to cycling, with excellent paved bike paths and hundreds of miles of backcountry trails beckoning mountain bikers. Also, many of the ski shops change their tune in the summer, renting out bikes instead of skis.

From Gore Creek Campground five miles east of Vail to West Vail Village, this is a perfect valley to explore by bike. Try the mostly flat "recreation path" that winds between the shopping area and the base of the lifts. For something a bit more demanding, head east from the village to the Vail Pass bike path, which you can take all the way into Frisco. Not for the weak of heart, the path tops out at 10,600 feet. If you're up to it, though, you'll find the scenery well worth the effort.

Mountain bikers have most of White River National Forest at their disposal. Maps and information are available from the Forest Service.

For the truly ambitious, the **10th Mountain Hut and Trail System** has recently expanded its winter operations to include backcountry bi-

cycle tours. All told, the trail network is 300 miles long, linking Aspen, Leadville, Vail, and several other mountain resort communities. Rent a bunk in one of the 10 huts, which sleep up to 16, for about $30 a night. For information and reservations, contact the 10th Mountain Trail Association, 1280 Ute Ave., Aspen, CO 81611, 970/925-5775, or visit its website at www.huts.org

Many Vail sporting goods stores and ski shops rent bikes. Hourly rates usually run $8–10, half day $12–20, and full day $20–30. Among the shops providing gear, rentals, maps, and other information: **Vail Bike Tech** at the base of the gondola, 970/476-5995, and **Christy Sports,** 293 Bridge St., 970/476-2244.

Golf

The popularity of golfing in Vail shouldn't surprise anyone. After all, this is a town built on a foundation of skiing, and the two sports share some significant similarities, not the least of which are the costs to participate and the resulting generally upscale, monied participants. Also, just as Vail is a premier ski area in anyone's view, the golf courses here are some of the finest in the West, offering challenges, great scenery, and stimulating mountain air.

Vail Golf Course is an 18-hole public course and the oldest in the valley. The course, 1778 Vail Valley Dr., sponsors several tournaments throughout the season, including the Jerry Ford Invitational (helmets optional). Phone 970/476-1330 for information and tee times. Green fees are $70 for 18 holes in the peak season (June–Sept.). The fanciest course in the area is the Robert Trent Jones–designed **Beaver Creek Golf Course,** 970/949-7123. Green fees for the 6,400-yard par-70 course are in the $110 range (including cart), with discounts offered in May. **Eagle-Vail Golf Course,** 970/949-5267, is a relatively modest course with considerably lower green fees but considerably less golf (about $80 for nine holes). The course is about 10 miles west of Vail in Avon. **Sonnenalp Golf Course,** 970/926-3533, is about 15 miles west of Vail at Edwards. Rated by *Golf Digest* as one of the top 50 courses in the country, the course is one of the

NORTHWESTERN

first in the area to open each year, with green fees running about $90.

Among the most recent additions to the Vail-area golf scene is the 18-hole **Club at Cordillera Valley Course,** 970/926-5950, which opened in 1997. The **Club at Cordillera Mountain Course,** 970/926-5100, opened in 1994. Both are just west of Vail Valley in Eagle.

You'll also find several fine golf courses just over Vail Pass in Summit County.

Hiking and Backpacking

Surrounded by national forest lands, the Vail Valley offers nearly unlimited hiking and back-packing opportunities, from short day-hikes to serious backcountry excursions. For maps, information, and advice, stop by the **Holy Cross Ranger District Office,** 401 Main St., Minturn, or phone 970/827-5715. You can also get information from **White River National Forest Headquarters,** 900 Grand Ave., P.O. Box 948, Glenwood Springs, CO 81602, 970/945-2521. Local bookstores and mountaineering shops carry books and hiking guides that discuss specific routes in detail. The following descriptions provide an idea of the range of hikes available.

One of the shortest but still visually rewarding hikes is the two-miler to **Booth Falls,** a 60-foot waterfall that's the highlight of a series of cascades on Booth Creek. The hike is only moderately demanding. From Vail Village, go east, crossing over to the frontage road on the north side of I-70, and continue to Booth Falls Road.

At the other end of the spectrum is the climb to the top of **Mount of the Holy Cross**—about 12 miles round-trip. At just over 14,000 feet, the peak offers excellent views of the surrounding mountains.

Camping

White River National Forest also offers superb camping, with scores of campgrounds scattered throughout the forest's two million-plus acres. In addition, backcountry camping is available in the Holy Cross and Eagles Nest wilderness areas.

Forest Service campgrounds in or near the Vail Valley include **Gore Creek Campground,** five miles east of Vail (take Exit 180 from I-70), as well as **Tigiwon, Half Moon,** and **Gold Park** campgrounds, all south of Vail via U.S. 24 to Leadville. Contact the Forest Service (see Hiking

© STEPHEN METZGER

A summer visitor takes a stroll across a pedestrian bridge over Gore Creek in Vail.

and Backpacking above) for information and reservations.

Fishing

Along with biking and golfing, fishing is one of the sports that truly characterizes summer in Vail. In the very center of Vail Village you'll probably see anglers practicing their casts by tossing fly lines out over the pools of **Gore Creek.** Though fishing can actually be respectable right in town, if you'd rather not fish near boutiques, head upstream to Gore Creek Campground and beyond.

Another popular stream is the **Eagle River,** the South Fork of which parallels U.S. 24 south of town. When fishing in streams, particularly, be sure to be aware of local restrictions; many stretches of trouty water are designated artificial bait and/or single barbless hooks only.

Local lakes that regularly offer good fishing include **Homestake Reservoir** (take U.S. 24 south three miles south of Redcliff, and turn west on Homestake Road), and **Black Lakes** at Vail Pass (lots of traffic, but regularly stocked).

For information and gear, stop in at **Gore Creek Fisherman,** 183 E. Gore Creek Dr., 970/476-3296, where you can also arrange guided tours through **Vail Fishing Guides,** 970/653-4334 or 800/461-5267.

Rafting

One of the best ways to stay cool when the summer sun pierces that thin mountain air, rafting is growing more and more popular in the Vail Valley. Several outfitters offer trips on local waters (the Eagle River), as well as rivers in other parts of the state (the Arkansas and Colorado). Among the local companies offering half- and full-day tours are **Lakota River Guides,** 970/476-7238; **Nova Guides,** 970/949-4232; and **Timberline Tours,** 970/476-1414.

Ballooning

Though not as popular as in Aspen, where the wider valley is more conducive to expansive views and meandering flights, hot-air ballooning is still a way to see Vail from a unique vantage point. For information and reservations, contact **Camelot Balloons** 970/926-2435 or

800/785-4743. Prices run about $150 for a half-hour to hour-long ride.

Horseback Riding

For those who want to see the backcountry without having to tax the ol' heart and soles, horseback is a great alternative. Local outfitters offer a range of rides—from easy, one-hour trips on virtually catatonic critters to more demanding, multiday adventures on properly spirited steeds. Try **Piney River Ranch,** 970/476-3941, where rates start at about $25 an hour and range to over $300 for overnight rides with fly-fishing along the way.

Tennis

Many of Vail's condominium complexes have their own tennis courts. Public courts are available at **Booth Creek, Gold Peak, Ford Park,** and **Lionshead.** For more information, phone the **Vail Metropolitan Recreation District** at 970/479-2296. You can also play at the **Avon Municipal Courts** in Avon, 10 miles west of Vail, 970/949-4280.

Chairlift Rides

Vail Resorts offers both chairlift and gondola rides from shortly after ski season ends into the early fall. For nonskiers, especially, who aren't used to this kind of transportation and the scenery it affords, this can be a wonderful way to see a different side of Vail. The 15-minute gondola ride from Vail's Lionshead to Eagles Nest guarantees stunning panoramas. At the top you can grab a barbecue lunch, take some photos, and climb back in the gondola for the ride back down, or you can hike back to the base on marked trails. Tickets cost about $22 for adults, $10 for kids under seven (seniors 70 and older ride free). Beaver Creek also offers chairlift rides, somewhat scaled down but more reasonably priced; rates are about $10 for adults, $6 for kids under 12. For more information, phone Vail Resorts at 970/476-5601, ext. 3071.

Llama Trekking

Paragon Guides offers three- and four-day llama treks into the Holy Cross Wilderness. Costs are about $200 a day for adults, $100 a day for kids under 10. Phone 970/926-5299.

Take Me out to the Ball Game

In a town where it seems you're constantly forking out dough to buy, rent, reserve, and tip, it's nice to know there are still some things to do that are absolutely free. Watching a local softball game is one of the most relaxing ways to spend a couple of hours on a weekend afternoon or weekday evening. Grab a lawn chair and set up on the bank above the fields, which are just off the south frontage road in Vail—you can't miss 'em.

Vail Nature Center

In East Vail off Vail Valley Drive (just east of Ford Amphitheater; park across the road at the soccer field, then walk down toward Gore Creek), 970/479-2291, this small center/museum features exhibits on the valley's natural history. Open daily 9 A.M.–4 P.M. in summer. In winter, the staff moves out to the Nordic Center at the golf course and offers guided interpretive snowshoe tours. Visit the website at www.vailrec.com for information on special events and weekly activities.

Parks

You'll find several parks throughout the Vail Valley, most of them perfect for a picnic or to park the bike and take a snooze in the shade of a poplar. A **children's playground** in Vail is directly behind the softball fields and adjacent to Gore Creek.

ACCOMMODATIONS

Vail is a decidedly upscale ski area, defined in large part by its luxury accommodations—most of which are within a ski pole's toss of the slopes. Keep in mind that this is the playground of the rich and famous, and that you won't have much luck finding bargain-rate lodging. But if you're talking Vail, you're already talking major financial commitment, and if you're gonna pamper yourself, why not go whole hog? Especially if it's for a honeymoon, a special week away from the kids, or that once-in-a-lifetime vacation you've always dreamed about.

On the other hand, if you strictly want the ski experience, and want to cut corners everywhere else, there are possibilities. You'll find less expensive lodging in Eagle (see below) about 30 miles west of Vail, and there are still a handful of relatively inexpensive motels in Frisco and Dillon (see Summit County), over Vail Pass about 25 miles east.

Remember, too, rates are significantly lower in the off-season (late spring, summer, and fall). Though Vail is growing rapidly as a year-round resort area, winter is still high season. Many of the lodges offer relatively attractive low-season rates with special incentives, such as golf, biking, tennis, and sightseeing packages. Keep in mind the prices given below should be used for comparison only, and that the *huge* range accounts for seasonal adjustments. The low prices will generally be effective mid-April through mid-November, high prices during the ski season's peak times (Christmas and Easter holidays). Remember, too, most visitors do opt for multiday stays (most often a "ski week," Mon.–Sun.), when the price *per night* isn't quite so unnerving.

For further information on lodging in Vail, contact the Vail Resorts-affiliated **Vail/Beaver Creek Reservations,** P.O. Box 7, Vail, CO 81658, 800/622-3131. You can also get information on lodging from the **Vail Valley Tourism and Convention Bureau,** 970/476-1000, or 800/525-3875, which can also provide information on air and ground transportation, packages (skiing, golf, etc.), and convention and group facilities. You can also get lodging information from the **Vail Valley Chamber of Commerce,** whose website at www.vailvalleychamber.com is both exhaustive and very user-friendly.

Under $50

Ha!

$50–100

Well, maybe. If you plan to visit during low season (mid-April through mid-June), you just might get lucky. Both the **Evergreen Lodge,** 250 S. Frontage Rd. W, 970/476-7810, and the **Sitzmark Lodge,** 183 Gore Creek Dr., 970/

476-5001, are long-standing inns with excellent reputations. They both offer discounted rates during the slower times of the year, but bump back up to the $200-plus range in high season.

$100–150

If you can afford this much, you'll increase your chances of finding a room in Vail, though you'll still be in budget digs by Vail standards (though very nice). The **Best Western Vailglo Lodge,** 701 W. Lionshead Circle, 970/476-5506, has been accommodating Vail skiers and other visitors for decades. Rooms are large and clean, and the location is extremely convenient. Mid-season, doubles are right about $150. You might also find rooms in this range at the **Roost Lodge,** 1783 N. Frontage Rd. W, 970/476-5451.

$150–250

Now you're beginning to venture into everyday, run-of-the-mill Vail lodging rates. Among the recommended accommodations here is the classic **Vail Cascade Hotel,** at 1300 Westhaven Dr. in Vail Village, 970/476-7111. Offering every imaginable amenity—ski and golf packages, exercise facilities, luxury dining rooms, and kitchens, not to mention its convenient location—the Vail Cascade is without doubt among the creamiest of a very creamy crop. Another popular high-end Vail inn is **The Lodge at Vail,** 174 E. Gore Creek Dr., 970/476-5011.

$250 and Up

If money is no object, or you're ready to be pampered, you've come to the right place. In addition to many lodges at Vail, the following at Beaver Creek offer opportunities to be pampered. The **Inn at Beaver Creek,** 10 Elk Track Ln. (at Village), 970/845-7800, is unquestionably one of the nicest hotels in the state. Also upscale and elegant is the **Hyatt-Regency Resort and Spa at Beaver Creek,** 136 E. Thomas, 970/949-1234.

Bed-and-Breakfasts

Because Vail Valley is narrow and development within it therefore concentrated, and all of the buildings are relatively new, you won't find small back-street bed-and-breakfasts in old Victorians

like you do in Breckenridge and Aspen. Still, some of the inns are moving in that direction, offering either continental or full breakfasts with a night's stay. Two miles west of Lionshead, the **Black Bear Inn of Vail,** 970/476-1304, offers 12 rooms with private baths ($120–225, including full breakfast). The **Eagle River Inn,** 145 Main St., Minturn, 970/827-5761 or 800/344-1750, is an adobe Southwestern-style lodge offering a healthful breakfast of yogurt, granola, and fruit. Built in 1894, the Eagle River is decorated with Indian rugs and pottery; each of the 12 rooms has a private bath.

For a Real Splurge

If you're looking for totally distinctive deluxe digs, **Trapper's Cabin** may be the answer. Operated by Vail Resorts, this 3,000-square-foot inn, at 9,500 feet between Beaver Creek and Arrowhead, can indulge most every whim—its solitude enhanced by the lack of telephones, televisions, and radios. Use the cabin as a base to explore the mountains by foot, horseback, or cross-country skis. In the evenings dine on elk steak, pheasant breast, duck, or salmon.

Summer 2001 rates were $500 per person per night (four-person minimum), and winter 2002 rates were $850 per person per night (four-person minimum). For information and reservations, phone 970/845-5990 or 888/485-4317.

Camping and RVing

The Vail Valley is in the thick of the White River National Forest, and most of the campgrounds in the area are small, Forest Service-administered areas. Some private RV campgrounds can be found nearby, including **Eagle River Village** in Edwards (about 16 miles west of Vail), 970/926-3754, where sites are available by the month only (about $500). For information on national forest campgrounds contact the Forest Service (see Camping and Hiking and Backpacking above).

FOOD

Dining is a big part of the Vail experience. The valley has a number of first-class continental-style restaurants, and Vail Village seems to consist of about one-third eateries, serving everything from pastries to chimichangas to stir-fry. The socializing at many of them is as crucial as the actual eating.

Thankfully, many of the restaurants in Vail post their menus outside, so you can scope out the offerings and prices. Indeed, one of the best parts about a morning's shopping stroll through the village is scanning the various menus and deciding where to have lunch. If the basil-chicken special doesn't grab you, see what's cooking next door. You can also peruse the *Vail Valley Dining Guide,* published annually by the Vail Valley chapter of the Colorado Restaurant Association. The guide holds full and partial menus from many area eateries.

Your Wake-up Call

Offering a wide range of imported and gourmet coffees, the **Daily Grind,** 288 Bridge St., 970/476-5856, also serves freshly baked croissants, muffins, bagels, and other pastries daily from 7:30 A.M. Weather permitting, you can sit at a table on the patio and watch the rest of Bridge Street come to life as you sip your coffee and read the paper.

Restaurants

A long-running favorite—especially with those out for a romantic rendezvous—is **Sweet Basil,** 193 E. Gore Creek Dr., 970/476-0125. Entrées, including seafood pastas, chicken, and beef, are in the $20–30 range. The **Tyrolean Inn,** 400 E. Meadow Dr., 970/476-2204, is another favorite for wild game, as well as pasta, seafood, and lamb; entrées run $20–35.

For more moderately priced meals, try the **Ore House,** 228 Bridge St., 970/476-5100, for steaks, chicken, seafood, salad bar ($10–20), or Vail's entry in the microbrewery market, the **Hubcap Brewery and Kitchen,** in Vail Village, 970/476-5757, where traditional brewpub fare (burgers, pot pies, fish and chips) runs $8–12.

For Mexican food, try **Los Amigos,** 476 Bridge St., 970/476-5847, where burritos, fajitas, and fish and shrimp tacos are $8–14.

ENTERTAINMENT

You shouldn't have too much trouble finding something to do in Vail once the lifts shut down (or it's too dark to find your errant golf ball). Many of the restaurants in the village feature live music, ranging from acoustic folk to electric rock 'n' roll. For starters, check out **Pepi's,** 970/476-5626, and the **Red Lion,** 970/476-7676, two definitive Vail après-ski hangouts. The **Hubcap Brewery** also regularly books live music. The *Vail Daily* is the best source for checking out who's playing what kind of music where and when.

CALENDAR

Since the early 1980s, when Vail began seriously to court year-round visitors, its schedule of events has been booked. Indeed, there's a festival, concert, gallery opening, bike or ski race, or tennis or golf tournament almost every weekend. Highlights include **Winterfaire,** an annual winter carnival with dog-sled races, ice sculpture, and music; **VailAmerica Days,** a huge Fourth of July celebration, with fireworks, music, arts and crafts, barbecues; the **Bravo! Colorado Music Festival,** a classical concert series that runs through July and August; and the **Jerry Ford Invitational Golf Tournament,** in late July. In addition, there's the annual **BobFest** in Avon in late May, celebrating "Bob," the "ultimate OK guy." Activities include a Bob-B-Que, and Bobbing for apples. For complete information, phone 970/476-1000 or 970/476-9090. You should also watch for the *Vail Daily,* available in newspaper racks throughout Eagle County; the paper contains a calendar of weekly events, as well as movie and concert listings.

SHOPPING

Any structure in Vail that's not a restaurant or ski shop is most likely a boutique, gift shop, or gallery. And a fun part of visiting Vail is wandering around the shops. You'll find everything from souvenir and knickknack shops to places selling furs that cost more than your Ford. Also *lots* of jewelry (especially Native American) and T-shirt shops.

In addition to the standard gift shops you'd expect in a resort town, Vail has plenty of specialty stores, with something for every interest—shops selling gifts imported from Alaska, fly-fishing gear, and one devoted entirely to Scottish terriers (and their owners). Even if you're not looking to buy, these stores can be fun to poke your head into, and you should allow at least one afternoon to "do" shopping in Vail Village.

SERVICES

The offices of the **Vail Police Department** are at 75 S. Frontage Rd.; phone 970/479-2200. Phone the **Eagle County Sheriff** at 970/949-5620, and the **State Patrol** at 970/328-6343. The full-sevice **Vail Valley Medical Center,** 970/476-2451 or 970/476-8085 (in emergencies), is in Vail Village at 181 W. Meadow Drive. Vail's main **post office** is at 111 S. Frontage Rd., 970/476-5217.

Recycling

Recycle aluminum, glass, newspaper, and plastic at **We Recycle,** 111 S. Frontage Rd., Vail, and in Eagle at **Beasely's Food Town,** 212 E. Chambers Road. The **Safeway** in Vail takes aluminum only.

INFORMATION

First-time visitors to Vail should stop at the tourist information center on South Frontage Road in Vail. Signs to it are posted at freeway exits. The center is staffed with friendly people who can answer just about any question you might have, and you'll also find lots of brochures with information on dining, lodging, shopping, and all manner of recreational activities.

You can also get information from the following centers: **Vail Resorts** P.O. Box 7, Vail, CO 81658, 970/476-5601; **Vail Valley Tourism and Convention Bureau,** 100 E. Meadow Dr., Vail, CO 81657, 970/476-1000 or 800/525-3875; **Lionshead Visitor Center,** 970/479-1391; and **Vail Village Visitor Center,** 970/479-1394. The **Activities Desk of Vail and Beaver Creek,** 970/476-9090, can provide information on the area's myriad

activities, from hot-air ballooning to chairlift rides to golf. For **road and weather information,** phone 970/328-6345. For **ski conditions,** phone 970/476-4888. Check out Vail Resorts' website at www.vail.com. You can also get information from the website administered by the chamber of commerce: www.vailvalleychamber.com.

TRANSPORTATION
Getting There

Vail is one of Colorado's most accessible resorts, as well as one of the easiest to get around in once you're here. The valley is 110 miles west of Denver, which is serviced by most major airlines. If you fly into Denver International Airport, you can either rent a car there and drive out (less than two hours when the roads are clear) or take a shuttle bus. See the Denver chapter for names and phone numbers of Denver auto-rental agencies, most of which specialize in "winterized" cars (front-wheel- and four-wheel-drive, ski racks).

Colorado Mountain Express, 800/525-6363, and **Timberline Express,** 800/288-1375, both offer reliable and affordable transportation between Vail and Denver International Airport (about $60 one-way for adults).

You can also fly directly to Eagle County Airport (in Eagle, about 30 miles west of Vail; both of the above-listed shuttle services provide transportation from Eagle County Airport to Vail). Phone **American Airlines** at 800/433-7300; **Delta,** 800/221-1212; **Northwest,** 800/225-2525; or **United** at 800/241-6522.

Getting around the Valley

Getting around once you're in Vail is so easy a car could actually get in the way. Besides, parking, especially in the winter, can be a pain in the neck. **Free shuttles** run daily through the valley, the first bus firing up at 7 A.M. and the last one shutting down at 1:30 A.M. (a bit earlier in the summer and fall); buses run every 10 minutes. For taxi service, phone **Vail Valley Taxi,** at 970/476-TAXI (476-8294).

Free parking is provided except during the ski season, with lots conveniently located and well marked.

U.S. 40—Utah Border to Steamboat Springs

From the Colorado-Utah border to Steamboat Springs is about a 125-mile drive, flat and open with not much traffic. Not a whole lot to look at the first two-thirds of the way, the barren landscape is characterized by miles and miles of flatland, mottled dirty green by the endless sagebrush. Beyond these horizons, though, the Yampa and Green Rivers, as well as the Little Snake, carve deep canyons into the plateau.

This is where the land's true colors are seen. Here the canyon walls form tiered mosaics of countless shades of red, ever changing with the angles of the flirting sun. And on the canyon floors, rivers—churning white, brown, then sleeping in still green pools—continue to carve into the stone. Beneath it all are the still darker pools of fossil fuels—oil and coal, as well as natural gas. In Craig, toward the eastern edge of the plateau, smoke and steam rise from the 15-story-high chimneys of the state's largest coal-fired electrical plant, which processes coal from several nearby mines.

In Craig, the plateau tilts, and the highway slowly begins its apparent assault on the Rockies' western slope. This 45-mile stretch follows the course of the Yampa River, winding through the valley, the country growing prettier by the meter. By the time you're face to face with Steamboat Ski Area's Mt. Werner and beginning to climb up Rabbit Ears Pass, you're into the Colorado you'll recognize from postcards and calendars—clear mountain streams and green meadows, with a backdrop of snowy, sawtoothed mountain peaks.

DINOSAUR

Three miles east of the Utah border, the town of Dinosaur is little more than a minimart, a café, a couple of dinky old motels, and a Colorado Welcome Center. The main drag through town (U.S. 40) is Brontosaurus Boulevard, and most other streets are named after dinosaurs as well—Plateosaurus Place, Brachtosaurus Bypass, Stegosaurus Freeway, even Triceratops Terrace. The little community was known as Artesia until

1965, when it changed its name to reflect its proximity to Dinosaur National Monument.

A **Colorado Welcome Center,** 970/374-2205, open 8 A.M.–6 P.M. May 1–Oct. 31, has lots of information on things to do and see in the area and throughout Colorado. It is in the center of town on U.S. 40, with friendly and helpful staff, free coffee, and restrooms.

Accommodations and Camping

If you're heading east, there's not a whole lot along the 90 miles of U.S. 40 between here and Craig, and if it's getting late you might want to take advantage of Dinosaur's limited lodging options. You can get inexpensive, no-frills digs at the **Hi-Vu Motel,** 122 E. Brontosaurus, 970/374-2267, or the **Terrace Motel,** 312 E. Brontosaurus, 970/374-2241. RV camp sites are available at **Blue Mountain Village RV Park,** 970/374-2747; plan to roll out your awning, 'cause there's not a shade tree in sight.

Information

For more information on Dinosaur and the area, write Town of Dinosaur, P.O. Box 238, Dinosaur, CO 81610. You can also get information on Dinosaur from the Moffat County Tourism Association, 360 Victory Way, Craig, CO 81625, 970/824-5689 or 800/644-4405. The website address is www.colorado-go-west.com.

DINOSAUR NATIONAL MONUMENT

One of the most remote national monuments in the country, Dinosaur National Monument sprawls over 325 square miles of barren and rugged badlands. It straddles the Colorado-Utah border, its distinctly triangular, three-toed shape vaguely resembling a giant dinosaur footprint. A fascinating testimony to the huge reptiles that sloshed through this part of Colorado 140 million years ago, Dinosaur National Monument is also evidence of the great powers of nature: the Yampa and Green Rivers have sliced far into

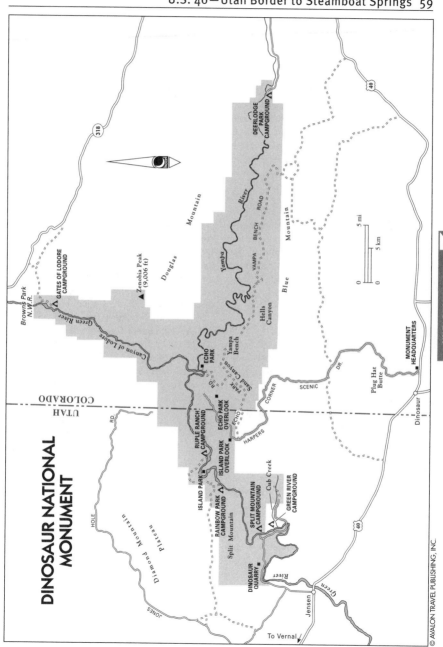

NORTHWESTERN

© AVALON TRAVEL PUBLISHING, INC.

the plateau, leaving narrow 3,000-foot-deep canyons, whose sheer cliffs ensure darkness even at midday.

Though paleontologists had known for years that northwestern Colorado once teemed with dinosaurs of every size and shape, it wasn't until 1909 that Earl Douglass discovered eight brontosaurus tailbones, apparently undisturbed even after millions of years. The find led to several others nearby, including complete skeletons. In 1915, the site was designated a national monument, and in 1938 the monument was expanded to include the Green and Yampa River canyons.

Dinosaur National Monument is not only unique for the sheer numbers of bones and fossils discovered here (350 tons of bones have been sent to museums), but also for the number that remain. At the Dinosaur Quarry building, you can view huge femurs, toes, and vertebrae in states of partial excavation, and watch scientists chipping away at the surrounding rock to better display them.

Monument Headquarters and Visitors Center

The visitor center on the Colorado side is a mile east of the town of Dinosaur. From here, a 31-mile road leads into the monument, past several scenic overlooks. It dead-ends at Harpers Corner, where you can view the canyons formed by the Yampa and Green Rivers.

The center is open daily 8 A.M.–4:30 P.M. June–Aug., and Mon.–Fri. the rest of the year. It stocks lots of books, guides, brochures, and other information, and rangers are available to answer your questions. You can also watch a short video about the monument. Phone 970/374-3000.

Dinosaur Quarry

This is the only place in the monument to view dinosaur fossils and bones. On the Utah side of the monument, the quarry has a visitor center (open daily 8 A.M.–4:30 P.M.; till 7 P.M. in summer) where you'll get a feel for the variety of life that once thrived here, from prehistoric turtles to brontosauruses. In the summer, a shuttle runs daily from the main parking area to the quarry; take your own rig the rest of the way.

The quarry is seven miles north of Jenson, Utah, on U.S. 149.

Camping

Two developed campgrounds lie within the monument, **Split Mountain** and **Green River** (both accessible from the Utah entrance only). Both can accommodate RVs, although neither hookups nor dump stations are available. You can also camp at any of the five free primitive grounds, three of which are in Colorado. **Echo Park Campground,** in the heart of the park 40 miles from Monument Headquarters, offers excellent views of the river and canyons, as well as river access. A ranger station is open summers only. Take Harpers Corner Road north from the visitor center and turn east on Echo Park Road. **Deerlodge Park Campground** is at the monument's east end and can be reached by turning north on Road 14 at Elk Springs, about 35 miles east of Monument Headquarters. There are no designated sites or drinking water; a ranger station is open summers only, as is the campground.

Gates of Lodore Campground is at the far north end of the park and has a ranger station open year-round and drinking water available summers only. From the headquarters, take U.S. 40 east for 60 miles to Maybell; then take U.S. 318 another 50 miles west to the campground.

Hiking

You'll find several nature trails in the park, most of which are accessible only from the Utah side. On the Colorado side, you'll find trailheads at Harpers Corner and Gates of Lodore Campground, both leading to stunning gorge views. A half-mile marked trail loops out from Plug Hat Butte picnic area, four miles north of the visitor center (not yet technically in the park).

Information

For more information on Dinosaur National Monument, write Park Headquarters, P.O. Box 210, Dinosaur, CO 81610, or phone 970/374-3000. Be sure to ask for a copy of *Echoes, A Guide to Dinosaur National Monument*, which provides detailed information on hiking, backpacking, camping, rafting, and fishing in the park, as well as maps and lists of books for further reading. Phone the Dinosaur Quarry Visitors Center (Utah) at 801/789-2115. You can also get information by writing **Dinosaurland Travel Board,** 235 E. Main St., Vernal, UT 84078, 801/789-6932 or 800/477-5558.

Moon Handbooks: Utah provides detailed descriptions of the monument's geology, history, and recreational opportunities, and it also discusses practicalities (accommodations, etc.) in nearby Utah towns. The book is available from Avalon Travel Publishing, 5855 Beaudry St., Emeryville, CA 94608, 510/595-3664, as well as from your local bookstore and Amazon.com.

BROWNS PARK NATIONAL WILDLIFE REFUGE

Situated on the Green River north of Dinosaur National Monument, this 6,000-acre marshland is an excellent (if remote) place to see a variety of wildlife in its natural habitat. A nesting area for thousands of migratory waterfowl, including mallards, teal, canvasbacks, and Canada geese, the region is also home to huge numbers of partridge, grouse, wading birds, and hawks, as well as deer and antelope. It is also offers excellent trout fishing.

The refuge is off Highway 318 about 10 miles east of the Utah border and is open year-round, with two primitive (no water) campgrounds. For further information, write Browns Park National Wildlife Refuge, Greystone Route, Maybell, CO 81640, or phone 970/365-3613.

RANGELY

A small plateau town that owes its existence almost entirely to the oil and ranching industries, Rangely (pop. 3,000; elev. 5,280 feet), is home to the sixth-largest oil field in the country. Its surrounding landscape, flat and sagey and bleak, dominated by pumpjacks chain-link fenced and nodding round the clock, Rangely is 20 miles southeast of Dinosaur via Highway 64.

The town dates from 1880, when it was established as a Ute trading post. In the mid-1880s, ranchers began driving huge herds of cattle to the area, and in 1912 the first shipments of sheep arrived. The first signs of oil were probably seen in 1900, when a local rancher noticed a vague slick on the White River, and the first crude, shallow wells were dug in 1903.

In 1933, the California Company, a subsidiary of Standard Oil, drilled 6,000 feet into the ground and discovered a huge oil deposit, although the well was plugged right away. World War II increased the demand for oil, though, and in 1943, the well was unplugged. By late 1945, 56 wells were in operation.

Today, Rangely is surrounded by Chevron's Weber Sand Unit Oil Field, the largest production field in Colorado, and though some might be offended by the industry's impact on the landscape, Rangely has recently benefited in other ways from the oilers' presence: the oil companies have made financial retributions, and oil money has gone to build Elk Park, which given the size of the town is one of the nicest in the state, as well as a beautiful hillside rec center.

Rangely Outdoor Museum

This museum complex focuses on three periods of Rangely-area history: prehistory and Native American (until 1833), pioneer and ranching

A pumpjack nods just outside downtown Rangely.

© STEPHEN METZGER

NORTHWESTERN

(1833–1946), and energy development (1946–present).The museum offers interesting displays of local rocks, minerals, and Indian artifacts, as well as pioneer clothing and other domestic items. Chevron has an exhibit explaining drilling techniques and technology. Admission is free (donations encouraged). The museum is just east of town on East Main (look for the sign just past the college). Hours are Fri.–Sun. 10 A.M.–4 P.M. April–October. For more information, write Rangely Museum Society, Box 131, Rangely, CO 81648, or phone 970/675-2612.

Elk Park

This huge town park with rolling lawns (big enough to warrant "no golfing" signs) has picnic tables and barbecue grills, basketball and volleyball courts, and a softball field. Take Stanolind three blocks south of Main.

Rangely's **Recreation Center,** on the hill above the park, features a large indoor swimming pool, weight room, racquetball courts, pool, and Ping-Pong table, in addition to jogging and biking trails and an ice-skating rink. Take Stanolind south past Elk Park to the top of the hill—the address is 611 S. Stanolind. For hours, phone the center at 970/675-8211.

Kenny Reservoir

Five miles east of Rangely on Highway 64, this small lake offers a cool break from the dry plateau surrounding it—fishing, boating, water-skiing, and swimming—and public restrooms. For information, contact Water Users Association Number One, 2252 E. Main St., Rangely, CO 81648, 970/675-5055

Petroglyph Tours

The **Rangely Museum Society,** in conjunction with the town of Rangely and Colorado Northwestern Community College, has designated three short self-guided driving tours from which you can view a variety of prehistoric rock art at nearby **Pintado Canyon Historic District.** Petroglyphs include drawings of buffalo, sheep, and deer, as well as many abstract forms and some vaguely resembling humans. The work is from both the Fremont Culture (A.D. 650–1150) and the Ute tribe (A.D. 1200–1880). Recently a series of prehistoric astronomical sites has been discovered. To get to Canyon Pintado, take Highway 64 east 18 miles from Rangely, then Highway 139 about eight miles south; the area is well marked. Tour maps and information are available from the Rangely Outdoor Museum and from the Rangely Chamber of Commerce, 209 E. Main Street.

Accommodations and Food

The **Budget Host Inn,** 117. S. Grand, 970/675-8461, is a favorite of oil-rig crews, who sometimes book half a dozen or more rooms for weeks at a time. The motel is one block off the main drag on the west end of town. The newest and largest motel in town is the 32-room **4-Queens,** 260 E. Main St., 970/675-5035. Both offer doubles in the $50 range. You can camp down in the shade of the cottonwoods at **Rangely Camper Park,** 940 E. Rangely Ave., 970/675-8211, for about $12 a night; there's also a nice lawn and small kids' play area. The campground is just east of town.

Pretty slim pickin's in terms of food—only a couple of small markets and a very small handful of small restaurants. Try **Magalino's Family Restaurant,** 124 W. Main, 970/675-2321, a long-time local favorite. Entrées are in the $7–15 range.

Services and Information

For more information, write the **Rangely Area Chamber of Commerce,** 209 E. Main, Rangely, CO 81648, 970/675-5290. The chamber's website is www.rangely.com; email for information at info@rangely.com.

Recycle at **Town of Rangely Recycling Program,** 214 E. Main, or 825 E. Main. Phone 970/675-2413.

Craig

Seat of Moffat County, the northwesternmost county in the state, Craig (pop. 9,500; elev. 6,190 feet) lies on the Yampa River 42 miles west of Steamboat Springs and 200 miles west of Denver. Rich in natural resources, particularly coal, oil, natural gas, and uranium, Craig is also rich in prehistory and history, with dinosaur fossils, Native American petroglyphs, and remnants of the Old West all within short drives of town. Craig is also a hub of ranching and agricultural activity, particularly sheep, cattle, and wheat.

We approached Craig from the west on a late January afternoon after spending the previous night in Salt Lake City. The high plains were dotted with snow, ice formed along the edges of streams, and the sagebrush looked brittle in the cold. The sun dropping behind us hung shadows across the land. Suddenly out of nowhere a deer darted into the road in front of us. A big mulie buck. Wild-eyed and frightened. *I've really messed up this time,* he must have been thinking. Fortunately I slammed on the brakes, the car swerved dramatically, and he had time to bound to the shoulder, then into the brush, where he quickly, magically, dissolved into sage and shadows.

No fool, I took this as advice to slow down (not to mention to plan to get my brakes adjusted). And once I did that, and our goal was no longer simply to make Craig before dark, we began to see what was really out there: deer. Dozens of them. Alone, in pairs, threes, and in herds of six, eight, and more. At every turn, over every rise. I'd never seen so many deer in one stretch. Between Elk Springs and Lay, a distance of about 40 miles, we must have seen more than 200 deer, all within 50 yards of the highway. Who knows how many thousands grazed in the brush beyond our small theater?

As you approach Craig, though, the prevalence of Moffat County wildlife might take a backseat to the airborne residue (a towering, thunderheadlike stack of steam) of Colorado's largest coal-fired electrical generating plant,

which processes coal from nearby Trapper Mine, as well as from the Colowyo Mine, 27 miles southwest. Providing the power for the lights, stoves, refrigerators, televisions, VCRs, and microwaves of much of northwestern Colorado, the plant also provides work and a solid economic base for Craig and the surrounding area. In fact, the plant provides weekly paychecks for 1,200 people.

History

Craig was founded in 1888, seven years after the first homesteader, William Rose, arrived and built a small cabin along Fortification Creek. Though originally called Rose, the community took its current name from the Reverend Bayard Craig, who, along with W. H. Tucker, arrived in 1887 from Glenwood Springs and helped finance and lay out the town. Within a few years, a hotel and saloon had been built, and in 1891 Clarence Bronaugh founded the town's first newspaper, the *Pentagraph.*

On Valentine's eve 1897, most of downtown Craig was destroyed by fire. Originating in the town hall, where there was to be a dance and party the next night, the blaze burned out of control up Yampa Avenue. Though devastated by their loss, the citizens of Craig quickly went about rebuilding their town, and within a year most of the buildings had been reconstructed (many with brick this time).

SIGHTS

Museum of Northwest Colorado

In the former Armory at 590 Yampa, this museum documents the history of Craig, Moffat County, and in fact much of the northern plateau. Displays cover early native populations, cowboys and gunfighters, mining, ranching, and farming, and local flora and fauna. The museum is open Mon.–Sat. 8:30 A.M.–5 P.M. Memorial Day through Labor Day; the rest of the year it opens at 10 A.M. For more information, phone 970/824-6360.

Marcia Railway Car

Built for $25,568 in 1906 for David Moffat (the Denver railroad tycoon), this elegant coach once accommodated 12 passengers and two servants. Hauled by winch along specially built tracks to its present site, the Marcia (named for Moffat's daughter) is 68 feet long, 12 feet wide, and features an ornate interior, with African mahogany with oak inlay, two heating systems, and three ice boxes, as well as a kitchen, observation room, and combination dining/sitting/sleeping room. The car is on Victory Way near Craig City Park. Free tours are offered during the office hours of the Craig Chamber of Commerce, Mon.–Fri. 9 A.M.–5 P.M., 970/824-5689 or 800/864-4405.

Sandrocks Nature Trail and Petroglyphs

Sheer sandstone cliffs overlooking the town of Craig, a marked nature trail, and carvings from ancient Anasazi to more recent Shoshone—this nice little side trip will help you better appreciate Moffat County's heritage and natural history. A joint project of Craig-area 4-H'ers, city council members, nearby homeowners, and faculty and staff from Colorado State University, the trail was dedicated in August 1988. In addition to carvings of hands, paws, lightning bolts, horses, and other animals—perhaps symbolic, perhaps simply the recording of daily events—you can also view areas where Native Americans sharpened axes and made arrows and arrowheads. Various plants and bushes—prickly pear, Indian rice grass, and rabbit brush—are identified to help you better appreciate other high-desert exploring you may do. Take 9th Street to Alta Vista Drive, and go west.

Colorado-Ute Power Station

The largest coal-fired plant in the state, this power station generates 1,264 megawatts of power and pays enormous amounts of taxes to Moffat County. In the softly rolling hills of the high plateau 3.5 miles southwest of Craig, the 25-story main building spews columns of smoke and steam far into the Colorado sky. Meeting or surpassing all environmental guidelines and restrictions, the plant is primarily emitting steam (after electrostatic precipitators have removed 99.6 percent of particulate matter from the burning coal).

Free tours of the plant are offered by appointment. For information, contact the Craig Chamber of Commerce, 970/824-5689, or phone the plant at 970/824-4411. You can also get information by contacting the Communications Group, Colorado-Ute Electric Association, P.O. Box 1149, Montrose, CO 81402, 970/249-4501.

PARKS AND RECREATION

Town Parks

At the corner of 6th and Rose Streets, Craig's city park has two swimming pools, tennis and volleyball courts, a playground, and picnic facilities. **Loudy Simpson Park,** where South Ranney crosses the Yampa River, offers fishing, picnicking, a nature trail, jogging paths, a launch area for canoes and rafts, and ice skating.

Elkhead Reservoir

This narrow lake on Elkhead Creek nine miles northeast of Craig is a favorite among sports enthusiasts and folks looking to escape the oftentimes harsh high plains summers. Fishing, boating, water-skiing, and picnicking are all available.

Take U.S. 40 east to County Road 29 and go north to the reservoir.

For New Wavers Only

To paraphrase Brian Wilson, "Catch a wave and you're sitting on top of the plains." The public swimming facilities at Craig's city park include an adjacent "wave pool," with 180,000 gallons of churning white water. In addition to swimming laps in the six-lane, 25-meter Olympic pool, you can frolic in Craig's answer to a surfin' safari. You'll find it at 605 Washington. For hours and prices, phone the **Craig Parks and Recreation Department** at 970/824-3015.

Golf

The **Yampa Valley Golf Course,** 970/824-3673, is an 18-hole public course along the Yampa River two miles south of town. Phone for tee times and information. Take Ranney Street south to County Road 394.

Hiking

The BLM administers 1.5 million acres of public land in Moffat County. Six miles north of Craig, Cedar Mountain rises 1,000 feet above "plain-level" and offers good hiking and sightseeing opportunities. Take County Road 7 from Craig.

You'll also find hiking trails along the Yampa River at Loudy Simpson Park, off South Ranney Street, and at Sandstone Cliffs (see above). For more information, contact the Craig office of the BLM at 455 Emerson, 970/824-8261, or the Forest Service District Office at 356 Ranney, 970/824-9438.

Hunting and Fishing

Moffat County is prime hunting and fishing country, home of deer, elk, trout, and other game. The Yampa and Green Rivers are well known for good trout fishing, and good-sized northern pike are pulled from Elkhead Reservoir. For tips on hot local hunting and fishing spots, as well as for licenses and supplies, stop in at **Craig Sports,** 124 W. Victory Way, 970/824-4044. **Outdoor Connections,** 34 E. Victory Way, 970/824-5510, also carries equipment and licenses. The BLM (455 Emerson, 970/824-8261) and Forest Service (356 Ranney, 970/824-9458) offices in Craig can provide maps and further information.

Rafting

The Yampa is a popular rafting and canoeing river. You can put in at Loudy Simpson Park or at the Yampa Valley Golf Course. Both private and public lands flank the 50-mile stretch of raftable water; don't trespass on private property (camping is allowed on public lands).

Tours

The Craig Chamber of Commerce has designed several short self-guiding tours of downtown and the surrounding area. The attractions (and excitement levels) vary widely, from the scintillating pass by Craig High School (on Tour number 1) to a stop at **Lay Valley Bison Ranch,** where you can pick up a buffalo steak to take home and throw on the barbie. For more information, contact the chamber, 360 E. Victory Way, 970/824-5689.

Helicopter tours over the western Rockies are offered through Yampa Valley Regional Airport; phone 970/276-3723.

PRACTICALITIES

Accommodations

Of the dozen or so motels in Craig, most are on the main drag (U.S. 40) through town and very easy to find. The rates at the following are all in the $50–100 range. At the west end of town at the junction of U.S. 40 and Highway 13 is a **Holiday Inn,** 300 S. Hwy. 13, 970/824-4000, where there's a good-sized indoor pool, jacuzzi, and a children's play area, with toys to ride and climb on. At the same junction you'll find **Craig TraveLodge,** 2960 U.S. Hwy. 40, 970/824-7066, and **Super 8,** 200 S. Hwy. 13, 970/824-3471. The **Best Western Inn of Craig** is at 755 E. Victory (U.S. 40), 970/824-8101.

Freeman Campground, about 20 miles north of Craig, has 17 sites, pit toilets, nature trails, and fishing on Freeman Reservoir. Go 13 miles north on Highway 13, then nine miles northeast on Forest Service Road 113 (dirt). The **Craig KOA/Rocky Mountain Campground,** about two miles east of Craig on U.S. 40, 970/824-5105 or 800/562-5095, has 108 RV sites, 13 tent sites, laundry facilities, a pool, small store, playground, and dump station.

Food

Two restaurants at the Holiday Inn, the **Paradise Grill** and **Cassidy's Bar and Grill,** 970/824-9455, serve breakfast, lunch, and dinner daily. Dinner entrées include salads, chicken, steaks, seafood. Entrées run $8–18.

For good Chinese food, try the **Galaxy Restaurant,** 524 Yampa, 970/824-8164, and for steaks **Beef and Pepper's,** 1111 Victory, 970/824-0369, which specializes in hot sauces that you can have bottled up to go. A Safeway and City Market are on Victory Way.

Shopping

"The shopping hub of Northwestern Colorado," according to the chamber of commerce, Craig has two malls (Centennial and Country) and a downtown shopping center. Included among the de rigueur mall stores are a Kmart (2355 W. Victory Way) and a JCPenney and Anthony's (1111 W. Victory).

Calendar

Craig's **Fall-Color Festival** (mid-September) features a parade, fiddle competition, square dancing, and a pancake breakfast. Firework displays are held on the Fourth of July. Contact the chamber of commerce for exact dates, times, places, and further information.

Services

The offices of the **Craig Police Department** are at 300 W. 4th St., 970/824-8111. Phone the **Moffat County Sheriff** at 970/824-4495. **State Patrol** offices are at 280 S. Ranney, 970/824-6501. Craig's **Memorial Hospital,** 970/824-9411, has 24-hour emergency service, as does **Routt Memorial Hospital,** 970/879-1322, 40 miles east in Steamboat Springs. Craig's main **post office** is at 556 Pershing, 970/824-5795.

Recycle aluminum and glass at **Axis,** 802 E. 2nd St., and at the **City Market,** 505 W. Victory.

Information

For more information on Craig and Moffat County, write the **Moffat County Visitor Center/Craig Chamber of Commerce,** 360 E. Victory Way, Craig, CO 81625, or phone 970/824-5689. Visit the website at www.craig-chamber.com, or email for information at craigco@craig-chamber.com. The **Moffat County Library** is at 570 Green St.; for hours, phone 970/824-5116. Craig's newspaper, the *Colorado Daily Press,* is published five days a week and runs stories of local and statewide interest. For subscription information, write P.O. Box 5, Craig, CO 81626, or phone 970/824-2600.

For more information on outdoor recreation in the area, contact the **Bureau of Land Management,** 455 Emerson, Craig, CO 81625, 970/824-8261, or the Rabbit Ears District Office of **Routt National Forest,** 356 Ranney, Craig, CO 81625, 970/824-9438.

For **road and weather information,** phone 970/824-4765.

Transportation

Continental Express, 970/879-2468, offers passenger service to Yampa Valley Regional Airport (in Hayden, about 20 miles east of Craig) and to Steamboat Springs (40 miles east). The **Greyhound-Trailways** terminal is at 470 Russell; phone 970/824-5161.

Meeker and Vicinity

Highway 13 drops south out of Craig, follows the course of the Yampa River for 10 miles or so before the river doglegs to the west, then flirts for a few miles with the western border of White River National Forest. Pagoda Peak (elev. 11,120 feet) and Mt. Marvin (elev. 12,045 feet) tower to the east. Be sure to gas up in Craig, as no services are available along the 50-mile stretch to Meeker.

Meeker itself (pop. 2,300; elev. 6,249 feet) is about midway between U.S. 40 and I-70 at the western base of the White River Plateau. A quiet and picturesque little town with a strong sense of community and civic pride, Meeker is a favorite among fishers and hunters, especially the latter, who during the fall fill up the town's scattering of lodges and motels, which remain fully booked throughout hunting season.

History

Meeker takes its name from Nathan C. Meeker, an Indian agent prominent in Colorado affairs. In September 1879, three years after Colorado achieved statehood, Meeker and 10 of his employees were killed by Utes in what has come to be known as the Meeker Massacre.

Meeker had been appointed to his post at the White River Agency in the spring of the previous

© STEPHEN METZGER

White River Museum is located in a 19th-century U.S. Army cabin.

year. Apparently not much of a diplomat, Meeker presently set about trying to domesticate the Utes, to convert them from a nomadic, hunting people, which they had been for centuries, into a sedentary aggregation of agriculturists.

The Utes resisted. Accustomed to ritual and grace, they couldn't understand Meeker's lack of civility and decorum. In addition, they were already angry at the government, not only for its attempts to yoke them onto the reservation but for not living up to earlier promises of money and supplies. When Meeker plowed an irrigation channel through an Indian horse-race track and then plowed under some of their best pastureland, they'd had enough.

Hearing war drums echoing down the canyons, Meeker sent for troops. Seeing the troops approach, the Utes got even angrier. They attacked the soldiers, and then the agency. Meeker and most of his men were killed, his wife, daughter, and other women taken hostage. A month later, the hostages were released when the Utes and the government negotiated a peace pact, a condition of which was the northern Utes' banishment to a Utah reservation.

After the massacre, the U.S. government established a fort where downtown Meeker now stands. In 1883, it sold the buildings to settlers arriving in the area. Three log cabins, once used as barracks, today house the White River Museum. The massacre site can be viewed from Highway 64 about four miles west of town. Look for the marker.

White River Museum

In an old log cabin built by soldiers who had come after Meeker's massacre, this museum features five rooms of exhibits, including lots of pioneer artifacts (eyeglasses, sewing machine, tack, guns), Native American artifacts, and a wagon Teddy Roosevelt took from town to the hunting grounds. There are also lots of historical photos, including several of an 1896 bank robbery. Evidently, a group that had been holed up with Butch Cassidy and his gang swept into Meeker, not expecting much violent resistance from the townspeople. Photos show the dead would-be robbers. Nice.

The White River Museum, at 565 Park behind the courthouse, is open Mon.–Sat. 9 A.M.–5 P.M., May 1–Nov. 15. Limited hours the rest of the year; call for times at 970/878-9982. You can also arrange special tours. No admission fee; donations accepted.

White River National Forest

The northern unit (Blanco District) of the White River National Forest, once a prime hunting ground of the Utes, sprawls to the mountains east of Meeker. Gorgeous country, with several peaks topping 12,000 feet, the forest offers virtually unlimited recreational opportunities. Especially popular are hunting, fishing, and camping; the area's also famous for excellent backpacking, cross-country skiing, snowmobiling, and other activities. Take County Road 8 east from Meeker.

Fishing

Excellent stream and lake fishing, and trophy-sized brown, rainbow, brook, and cutthroat trout, lure fishermen to the White River area east of Meeker. (In fact, large trout have been caught on the White River within Meeker's city limits.)

Twenty miles east of town is **Lake Avery,** where fishing is good in summer and winter (ice fishermen do *very* well). Another 30 miles into the park is **Trappers Lake,** which, although remote, still gets lots of traffic. The best way to catch fish here is by boat (no motors allowed), which you can rent at **Trappers Lake Lodge,** 970/878-3336.

Be sure to check local regulations, as some restrictions apply.

Camping

You'll find several excellent Forest Service campgrounds in White River National Forest east of Meeker, including **North Fork Campground,** right on County Road 8 (one mile into the forest, 45 units). Also easily accessible and nearby are **South Fork Campground, Marvine Campground,** and **Himes Peak Campground.** There are four separate campgrounds at Trappers Lake, with a total of nearly 60 sites.

Walking Tour

The Meeker Chamber of Commerce has designed a short self-guided walking tour of the historic downtown area. Included are the Meeker Hotel, the White River Museum, St. James Episcopal Church (built in 1889), and several pre-1900 residences. The tour is described in detail in the chamber's *Visitor Information Guide* (see Information, below).

Accommodations

Because Meeker draws such crowds during the hunting season, plan to make reservations for an autumn stay well in advance. The **Meeker Hotel,** 560 Main, 970/878-5255 or 800/847-6470, is on the National Register of Historic Places and has nicely appointed rooms in the $50–100 range. Even if you don't plan to stay here, poke your head in. The place hasn't changed all that much since Teddy Roosevelt stayed here on a bear-hunting trip. It's right downtown across from the county courthouse. You can also get rooms and nice, clean cabins at the **Rustic Lodge,** 173 Market, 970/878-3136, **Valley Motel,** 723 Market, 970/878-3656, and **White River Inn,** 970/878-5031. All are in the $50–100 range.

Trappers Lake Lodge, 970/878-3336, offers definitively rustic cabins—stoves for heating, no plumbing. Common shower and bathroom area. The lodge also offers pack trips, guided fishing, and canoe, rowboat, and horse rentals. Write 7700 Trappers Lake Rd., Meeker, CO 81641. Cabins for four run about $125.

Two campgrounds lie two miles west of Meeker at the junction of Highways 64 and 13. **Rimrock Campground,** 970/878-4486, is strictly for "passing through," with basic sites right next to the road. **Stage Coach Park and RV Campground,** 39084 Hwy. 13, 970/878-4450, offers a bit more privacy, with sites nestled down off the road among the cottonwoods.

Food

The Bakery, 265 6th St., 970/878-5500, fax 970/878-3309, serves a variety of homemade breads, pastries and cookies, as well as gourmet coffees, teas and herb teas, and soft drinks.

The **Sleepy Cat Restaurant,** 970/878-4413, 20 miles east of town on County Road 8, is a more than 50-year-old Meeker tradition. A classic hunting lodge, its walls lined with trophies, the restaurant is a Meeker favorite, also popular among visiting hunters and anglers and local ranchers. The Sleepy Cat specializes in various beef entrées, but it also offers chicken, seafood, and a salad bar. Entrées run $10–26. Open for dinner 5–10 P.M. daily.

Calendar

Meeker's **Range Call Parade, Rodeo, and Pageant,** on the Fourth of July weekend, was begun in 1885 and is the oldest rodeo in the nation. In addition to providing lots of food, music, and rodeo competition, the pageant offers a re-enactment of the Meeker Massacre, with locals acting out the attack, kidnapping, and murders.

The **Meeker Classic Sheep Dog Trials** are held the second weekend in September. The trials attract upward of 75 competitors and 2,000 spectators, who not only enjoy watching some of the finest dogs and best trainers in the West, but who also get to listen to traditional Irish music and take part in other festivities.

Services

The offices of the **Meeker Police Department** are at 236 7th St., 970/878-5555. Phone the **State Patrol** at 970/675-8311. **Pioneers Hospital** is at 785 Cleveland (turn north on 3rd), 970/878-5047 (in emergencies, 970/878-5700). The Meeker **post office** is at 656 6th St., 970/878-5830.

Recycle at **Gofer Foods,** 812 Market St., 970/878-4492.

Information

An excellent source for local information is the chamber of commerce-published ***Meeker and White River Country Visitor Information Guide.*** Copies are available at the chamber offices on the corner of Highway 13 (West Market) and 7th. Write Meeker Chamber of Commerce, Box 869, Meeker, CO 81641, or phone 970/878-5510. Excellent information is also available on the Web at www.meekerchamber.com. The Meeker **public library** is at 200 Main St., 970/878-5911.

For information on **White River National Forest,** stop in at the ranger station at 361 7th St., 970/878-4039.

NORTHWESTERN

Steamboat Springs and Vicinity

Best known for the ski resort that was built here in 1963, Steamboat Springs, seat of Routt County, is a small town (pop. 7,400; elev. 6,695 feet) surrounded by towering mountains and verdant river valleys. With an economy based largely on ranching (sheep and cattle), farming (hay, wheat, oats, barley), and tourism, Steamboat Springs offers a true taste of the Old West—where real cowboys still ride the real range—while at the same time luring upscale travelers in search of an escape from glitzy resort trappings.

HISTORY

Though Steamboat Springs's high-rise hotels and sprawling condominiums attest to the town's membership in the club of modern resorts, the area has actually been a playground of sorts for

600 years. As early as the 1300s, Utes spent their summers here, hunting buffalo and other large game, and, most likely, taking advantage of the 100-plus-degree hot springs in the Yampa River Valley. The name "Steamboat Springs," in fact, comes from one of the hot springs: a party of 19th-century trappers heard the waters rumbling and bubbling and thought a steamboat was approaching from downriver.

In 1868, the United States government took claim to the Utes' summer home, yet the Indians resisted relinquishing their land. Between 1868 and 1880, when the Utes were finally forced onto a reservation in Utah, several skirmishes took place between various tribes and white settlers, including the Meeker Massacre of 1879.

The Yampa River Valley's first white settler of record was James Crawford, a Missourian, who homesteaded here in 1875, though his first home was an abandoned log building, suggesting someone had passed through earlier and had stayed long enough to need solid shelter. Evidently respectful of the Utes and their hunting grounds, Crawford became friends with them, and they left him alone while they attacked other settlements in the area, as well as other settlers passing through. Meanwhile, the Yampa Valley was becoming increasingly well known for its high-quality native hay, and in the early 1880s, once the Utes had been vanquished from the valley for good, the region began to see a large influx of farmers and ranchers.

In 1885, Crawford, having obtained financial backing from Boulder businessmen J. P. Maxwell and Andrew Mackay, formed the Steamboat Springs Townsite Company, laid out the streets of the small town, and sold lots. By 1888, the number of buildings in Steamboat Springs had grown from half a dozen to nearly 50. Also germane to the town's early development was the introduction of Steamboat's first newspaper, the *Steamboat Pilot,* which was first printed (on a second-hand foot-powered press hauled over from Boulder) on July 31, 1885.

Also at this time, as farmers and ranchers were establishing themselves in the fertile Yampa Valley, a mine at the base of Hahn's Peak, 30 miles to the north, was drawing miners from throughout the area. This further added to Routt County's population, and though some of these miners were transient and would eventually move on (particularly when the Hahn's Peak mine played out in the early 1890s), some would stay in the area permanently.

Still another crucial stage in Steamboat's de-velopment was the arrival of the railroad. The talk of the town since the turn of the century, the railroad to Steamboat was completed on December 13, 1908, and the first passenger train chugged into town a month later on the evening of January 19. The *Steamboat Pilot* reported the event the next day: "Steamboat's long-looked-for day has come. . . . Over 75 Steamboat people, including the band, met the train [about eight miles south of town] and rode down, while hundreds more were at the Steamboat Station to cheer it when it arrived."

In 1913, Norwegian cross-country and ski-jumping champion Carl Howelsen arrived in

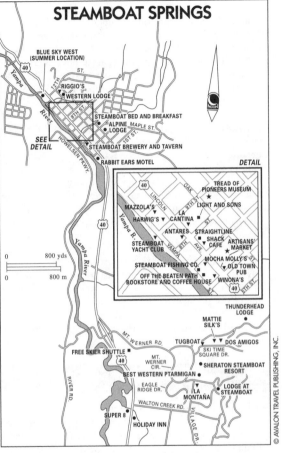

Steamboat and, in 1914, organized the town's first Winter Carnival. Howelsen so impressed locals with his jumping hill and 110-foot leap that many were inspired to try ski jumping themselves. Local lore has it that some of the jumpers at the first carnival landed in a herd of startled elk grazing nearby.

By 1940, downhill skiing had become popular among Steamboaters, and in 1943 it was added to the curriculum of the local school. In 1963, Steamboat Ski Area was officially opened for business on Storm Peak three miles south of town. A year later, when one of the town's early Winter Olympians, Buddy Werner, was killed in an avalanche in Switzerland, the peak's name was changed to Mt. Werner. Over the last 40 years, the Steamboat Ski Area has grown dramatically. Lifts and a gondola now spoke out over four different mountains, and the base facilities include everything from a golf course (for summer visitors) to bars, restaurants, condominiums, and a fleet of shuttle buses.

SKIING AND OTHER WINTER SPORTS

This is a town that bills itself "Ski Town, USA," and most everything here revolves around the fact that the area's meadows, mountains, and moraines are blanketed with snow from November to May. The town's main attraction is the world-class alpine ski resort three miles from downtown.

Steamboat Ski Area

With 3,668 vertical feet of skiing, more than 140 runs on 3,000 acres, an uphill capacity of nearly 30,000 skiers an hour, World Cup races, more than 300 inches of snowfall per year, and internationally acclaimed tree and powder skiing, this is without doubt one of the best ski areas in the West (many say in the world). In fact, *Mountain Sports and Living* magazine's annual readers' poll regularly rates it in the country's top 10, and it earned the number-five spot in 1998.

In a sport growing more pretentious and exclusive by the season—a sport of doctors, lawyers, and accountants, turbo Saabs, Volvos, and

BMWs—Steamboat is a breath of fresh air. Drawing largely on its Old West heritage, as well as on the real-life Old West town down the road, Steamboat has managed to maintain its integrity and charm—even in the path of an advancing epidemic of condos, high-rises, and boutiques. Oh, there are still boutiques, and ferny bars, and more real estate and property-management companies than you can shake a ski pole at. But still, it all feels more real here than in some of the Rockies' other big resorts.

And it's probably because most everything else here really does take a back seat to skiing and boarding. It's a big mountain, and some people come an awfully long way to explore—and, perhaps, master—it. So by day's end, they don't have much energy for shopping. They want to relax, maybe take a hot tub or sauna, and get some food in their bellies for strength for the next day; hardcores with energy left at the end of the day can boogie to live music at several clubs—both on the mountain and in town.

So, what about that mountain? Well, for starters, it's got a wide variety of terrain for all ability levels, although it's best suited to the intermediate-to-advanced skier, with 56 percent of its runs designated intermediate (31 percent are advanced and 13 percent are beginner). Spread over four different mountains and rising to 10,385 feet, Steamboat's 2,900 acres of runs and off-piste skiing are serviced by 20 lifts, including an eight-passenger gondola and 17 chairlifts—a quad, seven triples, and nine doubles (which Steamboat returnees claim keep lift lines minimal).

Don't be deceived by what you can see of Steamboat from the base of the mountain. Though it looks big enough, there's lots more. In fact, the majority of the runs and lifts are beyond that first 1,000-foot vertical rise. Experts and advanced skiers and boarders will want to check out the runs off Storm Peak, Sundown, and Priest Creek chair, while Burgess Creek, Sunshine, and Thunderhead offer intermediates a chance to explore and work on their form.

If you can remember back to the 1974 Winter Olympics, or if you read the skiing magazines at all during the late '60s and early '70s, the

© STEPHEN METZGER

NORTHWESTERN

Steamboat village, at the base of the ski lifts

name Billy Kidd should ring a bell. Perhaps you even have an image of him in your head: the archetypal all-American cowboy-skier, boyish tanned face grinning beneath the brim of his 10-gallon Stetson. Well, Kidd's still around. He's the Director of Skiing at Steamboat, and he's out on the slopes almost every day. And Kidd's not the only Olympian to have cut his ski teeth in the gates of Steamboat. As of 1990, Steamboat had produced 34 winter Olympic athletes, more than any other town in the United States.

The marketing department of Steamboat Springs Ski Resort will gladly send you more information—from maps of the mountain to complete listings of nearby lodges. Write 2305 Mt. Werner Circle, Steamboat Springs, CO 80487, or phone 970/879-6111. For **Steamboat Central Reservations and Lodging,** phone 800/922-2722. For snow conditions, phone 970/879-7300. Check out the resort's website at www.steamboat.com.

Howelsen Hill

Named for Carl Howelsen, who at Steamboat's 1914 Winter Carnival jumped 110 feet on skis, this is one of the oldest ski areas in the country.

Open seven days a week (night skiing Tues.–Fri. 6–9 P.M.), Howelsen Hill, owned and operated by the city of Steamboat Springs, has a 440-foot vertical rise and 30 acres of skiable terrain serviced by two surface lifts.

Best known for its five jumping ramps (20, 30, 50, 70, and 90 meters), Howelsen is the training grounds for the U.S. Ski Jumping Team, and it has been the "home field" of many world-class jumpers. Remember "Eddie the Eagle," England's entry in the 1988 Olympic Ski Jumping Competition? Even the Eagle jumped here, having stopped here that year en route to Banff.

The Winter Sports Club, based at Howelsen, offers instruction in downhill, cross-country, and freestyle skiing. There's also an ice-skating rink at the complex, which is downtown at the south end of the 5th Street Bridge. For more information on Howelsen Hill, phone the Steamboat Springs Parks and Recreation Department at 970/879-4300, or contact the chamber of commerce at 970/897-0880.

Backcountry Powder Skiing

For hard-core backcountry skiers and powder-hounds whose idea of graffiti is a series of figure eights in a remote bowl, **Steamboat Powder Cats** will take you by snowcat up into virgin powder—for both day-trips and overnight excursions. Single-day outings begin at around $200 per person. Phone 970/879-5188 or 800/288-0543.

Cross-Country Skiing

Though better known for its downhill skiing, the Steamboat area also offers excellent opportunities for cross-country skiers—on groomed trails as well as in the backcountry. The **Steamboat Ski Touring Center,** based at the Sheraton Golf Course, has 28 miles of trails winding out over the links and along nearby Fish Creek. The center caters to the broadest range of Nordic skiers—from the most cavalier recreational skier to the serious Nordic—and offers rentals, lessons, and backcountry tours. For more information, write Steamboat Ski Touring Center, P.O. Box 772297, Steamboat Springs, CO 80477, or phone 970/879-8180.

You'll also find cross-country trails at **Rabbit Ears Pass,** about 10 miles southeast of Steamboat Springs on U.S. 40, as well as at **Clark Store,** 970/879-3849, 20 miles north of Steamboat on Elk River Road (County Road 129). Just off Elk River Road, **Seedhouse Road** offers ungroomed trails along the Elk River; and **Howelsen Hill** (see above) offers rentals, equipment, and trails.

In addition, **Mountain Recreation Company,** in Hahn's Peak Village, 970/871-1495, website www.mountainrec.com, offers lessons, rentals, tours, and access to a number of nearby inns and lodging, including a number of guest ranches in and around Steamboat that offer cross-country skiing. Among them: **Hahn's Peak Guest Ranch,** 970/879-8638; **Vista Verde Guest and Ski Touring Ranch,** 970/879-3858; and **Dutch Creek Guest Ranch,** 970/879-8519.

For maps and information on ski touring in Routt National Forest, contact the Hahn's Peak District Office, 970/879-1870, or the Supervisor's Office at 29587 W. U.S. 40 in Steamboat, 970/879-1722.

Other Winter Sports

Those averse to strapping skis afoot have several other options when it comes to winter recreation in Steamboat. Howelsen Hill Ski Complex also offers bobsledding and ice skating. Snowshoeing trips are available through **Blue Sky West,** 970/871-4260 or 800/288-0543. The various other activity and reservations centers, as well as the chamber of commerce, have complete listings and schedules. (See Recreation Information and Tours, below.)

WHEN THE SNOW MELTS

Don't worry—Ski Town, USA doesn't board up its windows once the chairlifts shut down and wildflowers begin pushing up through the meadows' snowcovers. Quite the contrary. In fact, folks looking for outdoor diversions in the warmer months actually have more to choose from than their winter counterparts do. Golf, for example. Tennis. Cycling (both touring and mountain biking). Rafting. Hiking, backpacking, camping, and fishing. And don't forget hot-air ballooning and horseback riding. You'd have to have the imagination of a hitchin' post not to be able to find something to do in Steamboat once you've put your skis and snowshoes in storage.

Tread of Pioneers Museum

In a gorgeous Victorian home built in 1908, this museum displays the history of Steamboat Springs and Routt County beginning with the Utes and finishing with the story of the ski resort. Exhibits include Native American pottery, ranching and farming implements, medical gear, musical instruments (including a square grand piano shipped from New York in the mid-19th century), firearms, children's dolls and toys, and the evolution of ski equipment. Videos include footage of early skiing in the area, including jumping off Howelsen Hill and tag-team jorring races (skiers were pulled, water-ski-style behind horses) down U.S. 40 in the early part of the last century. The museum is at 800 Oak (corner of 8th Street). Open daily 11 A.M.–5 P.M. Admission is $1. For information, phone 970/879-2214.

Steamboat Lake State Park

Twenty-five miles north of Steamboat Springs on County Road 129, this state park on Steamboat and Pearl Lakes offers camping, boating, fishing, water-skiing, hiking, and, in winter, snowmobiling. Pit toilets and running water are available. Phone 970/879-3922 for more information.

Stagecoach State Recreation Area

South of Steamboat Springs off U.S. 40, this recreation area at Stagecoach Reservoir has hiking trails, tent and RV camping facilities, fishing for rainbow and cutthroat trout, and a boat ramp. During the winter, Stagecoach is a popular snowmobiling and cross-country skiing site. For more information, write the Colorado Division of Parks and Outdoor Recreation, 1313 Sherman St., Room 618, Denver, CO 80203, 970/866-3437.

Golf

Steamboat has three golf courses. The 18-hole **Sheraton Steamboat Golf Club,** at the base of Mt. Werner, is a high-class course designed by Robert Trent Jones. It's affiliated with the Sheraton Hotel; Sheraton guests get discounts on the expensive-anyway green fees. Carts are required, Cadillacs or better recommended. Phone 970/879-2220 for a tee time, prices, and more information. You can also get information by phoning 800/848-8878.

Haymaker Golf Course, in the Yampa River Valley at the junction of U.S. 40 and Highway 131 three miles east of town, is another high-end course. Unlike the Sheraton, Haymaker is not surrounded by condos and hotels and offers gorgeously unobstructed high-mountain vistas. This new public course was designated "Best New Course" by *Golf Digest* in 1998. Phone 800/494-1818 or 970/870-1846. **Steamboat Golf Club,** at the west end of town off U.S. 40, is the town's pleb course, with the attendant retrenched prices and lack of ostentation. Phone 970/879-4295.

Hiking and Backpacking

Routt National Forest, which sprawls from Steamboat Springs north across the Wyoming border and south nearly to Kremmling (another unit lies east of Kremmling in eastern Rio Blanco and Garfield Counties), is an Eden of hiking and backpacking trails and backcountry. Part of this million-plus-acre national forest, the Mt. Zirkel Wilderness Area, about 25 miles north of Steamboat Springs in the gorgeous Park Range, offers lots of backcountry to explore. Take Elk River Road/County Road 129 north to Seedhouse Road, where you'll find one of several trailheads leading into the wilderness area.

The Forest Service supervisor's office in Steamboat Springs, 29587 U.S. 40, 970/879-1722, and the Hahn's Peak District Office, 57 10th St., 970/879-1870, can provide maps and information.

One of the more popular short hikes for Steamboat visitors is to **Fish Creek Falls,** a 283-foot waterfall just minutes from town. The quarter-mile trail (restrooms, picnic, and wheelchair-accessible facilities provided) leads to a viewing area, then on to a second waterfall (not nearly as swamped with visitors), and eventually to Dumont Lake, about 11 miles from the trailhead. Take Fish Creek Falls Road south from downtown. **Note:** the four-mile road is paved halfway; the second half is a fairly deeply rutted dirt road.

Fishing

The lakes and streams in the Steamboat area offer a wide range of fishing possibilities—from easy-to-fool, recently stocked hatchery fish the size of a large pencil to wily four-pound natives that can tell an artificial fly from the real McCoy at 50 feet. Dumont Lake, on Rabbit Ears Pass 25 miles south of Steamboat via U.S. 40, is stocked regularly with catchable-sized rainbow trout, as is Steamboat Lake, about 30 miles north of Steamboat off County Road 129. The Elk and Yampa Rivers also offer good fishing. For information, licenses, gear, and guided fishing tours, stop by **Steamboat Fishing Company,** 635 Lincoln Ave., 970/879-6552; or **Straightline Sports,** 744 Lincoln Ave., 970/879-7568. You can also arrange guided tours through **Blue Sky West,** 970/871-4260.

For more information on fishing in Routt County, contact the Steamboat Springs Chamber Resort Association, 970/879-0880 or 800/332-3204 (from in Colorado).

Rafting and Kayaking

As you'd expect in a town on two decent-sized rivers, as well as near so many smaller streams, Steamboat is a paradise for river rats, especially those who can settle for water a tad less violent than, say, the Andes' Apurimac. You can put in at a variety of spots along the river, although you need to be careful not to trespass on the private property that flanks much of both rivers.

Blue Sky West, downtown, 970/871-4260, offers a wide range of float trips, from mild to wild. You can also book trips with **High Ad-**ventures/**Bucking Rainbow Outfitters,** 970/879-8747 or 888/810-8747.

Ballooning

Though not cheap, hot-air balloon rides are getting more and more popular each year, with several companies in Steamboat offering quarter-, half-, and full-hour rides daily. **Balloons over Steamboat,** 970/879-3298, and **Pegasus Balloon Tours,** 970/879-9191, offer various promotional come-ons (free champagne and transportation, senior and group discounts, personalized flights, etc.) to offset the cost of a bird's-eye view of Steamboat in the quietude of the wind-borne schooner.

Horseback Riding

It should come as no suprise in a town such as Steamboat Springs—whose Western heritage oozes from every barn wall, saloon door, and Stetson hat—that riding is big here. You may find yourself downtown trying on some après-ski boots while across the store some cowpoke with a wad of chew in his lip is eyeing saddles and tack. And though there are some dude ranches in the area, most of the cowboys in Routt County are for real. This is an area that grew up with horses. And horses still work here.

They're also for hire. A stirrupful of outfits in and around Steamboat have horses for rent, as well as guides that will lead tours, instructors who will give lessons, and, if you'd rather ride behind than on a horse, sleighs, coaches, and carts are available to make you feel equestrian without risking a bruised posterior. Some of the services provide meals with the trips.

Try **Del's Triangle 3 Ranch,** 970/879-3495; or **Steamboat Stables/Sombrero Ranch,** 970/879-2306.

Recreation Information

For more information on what to do in the Steamboat-Routt County area, contact the **Steamboat Springs Chamber Resort Association,** 970/879-0880 or 800/922-2722, website www.steamboat-chamber.com.

© STEPHEN METZGER

Take a short hike to Fish Creek Falls, just outside Steamboat Springs.

NORTHWESTERN

ACCOMMODATIONS

You won't have an easy time if you go looking for cheap digs in Steamboat Springs—particularly in winter, when some of the best snow in the country has blanketed the runs of Mt. Werner and Sunshine Peak. As in many resort towns, especially those as isolated as Steamboat is, travelers here are more or less at the mercy of the innkeepers and whatever prices they want to charge.

You can save some money, though, by staying in nearby towns. Skiers who don't mind driving 45–60 minutes can get rooms for substantially less in Craig, for example, where rooms at the Holiday Inn may run $40–80 a night less than at the Holiday Inn in Steamboat. In addition, reservations aren't nearly as crucial if you go outside Steamboat. In town, many rooms are reserved up to a year ahead of time, and in a season of decent snowfall, Steamboat will have fewer rooms available than there were in Bethlehem. Ultimately, you just have to ask (and answer) yourself if the trade-off's worth it. Is what you save by staying 45 miles away worth what you'd gain by staying slopeside, or at least within walking distance to a shuttle stop? Is saving $50 a day on lodging worth missing out on the experience of hanging out after skiing in one of the West's great winter sports towns?

The newcomer to Steamboat, especially one who's bought into the resort's claim to being a down-to-earth ski town, will most likely be surprised at the number of high-rise hotels and condominiums sprouting from Steamboat Village and the base of the lifts. The ultimate in convenience for the skier who likes to ski right to her doormat, these rooms provide that fine feeling of knowing that when you step out of your skis you're home. No need to worry about finding your car in the parking lot, checking shuttle departure times; no need to fear getting caught in après-ski traffic. In fact, before other skiers have even secured their skis atop their cars, you can be soaking away the day's aches in a hot, swirling jacuzzi as you pull on a cold one. Not a bad way to close the curtain on the day.

Most Steamboat inns offer ski-and-lodging package deals, which include lift tickets, and sometimes shuttle transportation, meals, equipment, and other enticements; many offer multibedroom units with complete cooking facilities.

$50–100

You definitely won't find anything less than $50 in Steamboat, unless you run across a lodge or inn that's running some kind of off-season promotion—off-season generally being those times between ski season and the heart of summer, April and May, September to mid-November. And even in the $50–100 range, you're not going to find much.

Following are among Steamboat's smaller motels where you'll probably find the best rates and at the same time reliably clean rooms and dependable service: the **Alpiner Lodge**, 424 Lincoln, 970/879-1430; the **Rabbit Ears Motel**, 201 Lincoln, 970/879-1150; and the **Super 8 Motel**, 3195 S. Lincoln.

$100–150

Once you move into this range, you increase your chances of being close to the mountain, and of course, the lodges themselves will be a bit nicer. A long-standing tradition with ski-in/ski-out convenience is the **Best Western Ptarmigan Inn**, 2304 Apres Ski Way, 970/879-1730 or 800/538-7519. Another nice place is the **Thunderhead Lodge and Condominiums,** 1965 Times Square, 970/879-9000 or 800/525-5502, where you can get a small room for two or a multilevel suite for eight or more. Steamboat's **Holiday Inn**, 3190 S. Lincoln, 970/879-2250 or 800/HOLIDAY (465-4329), is just east of town near the road to the ski area.

The **Steamboat Bed and Breakfast,** 422 Pine, 970/879-5724, offers seven rooms in a rebuilt 19th-century church.

$150–250

Among the most elegant and convenient ski-area lodges is the **Sheraton at Steamboat Resort,** 2200 Village Inn Ct., 970/879-2220. With an on-site restaurant and rental facilities, you'll never have to leave—golf and ski packages are available. The **Sky Valley Lodge,** 31490 E. U.S. Hwy. 40, 970/879-7749, is a resort property about eight miles east of town offering convention facilities, tennis courts, and deluxe lodging—with shuttles to the ski area in winter.

Lodging Information

For more information on the more than 50 hotels, motels, and condominiums in Steamboat, as well as complete lists of lodging packages, phone Steamboat Springs Chamber Resort Association's **Steamboat Central Reservations** at 970/879-0740 or 800/922-2722. Remember, too, that during the height of the ski season you're going to need reservations well in advance—though if you find yourself strapped and desperately needing a Steamboat fix within the month, you might call around to see if there've been any cancellations. You can also get lodging information (and make reservations) on the Resort Association's Internet site: www.steamboat-chamber.com.

Camping and RVing

A number of campgrounds are available in and around Steamboat Springs, including three open year-round with RV facilities. **Ski Town KOA campground,** 970/879-0273, on the Yampa River about two miles west of town on U.S. 40, has 100 RV sites (tent camping on about a quarter of them) and cabins with nightly, weekly, and monthly rates; shuttle service available. **Fish Creek Campground,** 970/879-5476, 1.5 miles east of Steamboat on Fish Creek, has 15 tent and 30 RV sites, laundry facilities, and a rec room. **Steamboat Lake State Park** (see above), 25 miles north of Steamboat, has 200 tent and RV sites on Pearl Lake. For information and reservations, phone 970/879-3922.

In addition, several Forest Service campgrounds are scattered throughout the area. **Meadows Campground,** 15 miles southeast of Steamboat; **Dumont Lake,** 10 miles east of Meadows (watch for the sign); and **Summit Lake Campground** (no drinking water), about 15 miles northeast of town (take Strawberry Park Road to Forest Service Road 60), all have tent and

RV sites and pit toilets. Phone the Hahn's Peak District Office of the Forest Service at 970/879-1870 for more information.

FOOD

Good Morning!

A handful of excellent Steamboat breakfast places guarantee a jump-started morning. For a light breakfast—muffins, grain cereals, and excellent espresso drinks—try **Off the Beaten Path Bookstore and Coffeehouse,** downtown at 56 7th St., 970/879-6830. Another excellent option is right around the corner at **Mocha Molly's Coffee Saloon,** 635 Lincoln, 970/879-0587. This cozy little shop has couches, easy chairs, board games, and books and magazines, and offers egg dishes in addition to muffins and other pastries. Both Off the Beaten Path and Mocha Molly's are open at 7 A.M. daily.

If you're up for a little heartier breakfast, try **Winona's,** 617 Lincoln, 970/879-2483, where you'll find homemade granola, pancakes with fruit, and egg dishes. It's open every day at 7 A.M. The **Shack Cafe,** 740 Lincoln, 970/897-9975, is a local favorite, featuring waffles, *huevos rancheros,* and omelettes. The Shack is open at 6 A.M. weekdays and 6:30 A.M. weekends.

Up at the ski area, try **The Tugboat,** right at the base of the lifts at 1860 Ski Time Square Dr., 970/879-7070.

Steamboat Traditions

Steamboat abounds in good places to eat, and just about everyone has a favorite restaurant. For Mexican food, try **Dos Amigos,** 1910 Mt. Werner Rd. in Ski Time Square, 970/879-4270, which serves excellent fajitas, burritos, chimichangas, and assorted *especiales* running $10–14. **La Montaña,** 2500 Village Way, 970/879-5800, is another favorite, though a bit pricier, with Mexican and Tex-Mex entrées including chili, fajitas, and enchiladas at $10–24. Also good for Mexican is **Cantina,** 818 Lincoln, 970/879-0826, serving enchiladas, burritos, and tacos ($8–12), with your choice of red, green, or cheese sauces. Lots of domestic and Mexican beers are available to wash down those nachos (no bangers to complement the Watneys and Guinness on tap, though). For dessert, try the flan, cheesecake, or sopaipillas.

Mattie Silk's, in Ski Time Square, 970/879-2441, serves seafood, beef, veal, duck, lamb, and pasta dishes for $16–25; check out the huge selection of imported beers. It's open daily for dinner. **Mazzola's,** 440 S. Lincoln (between the lifts and downtown), 970/879-2405, is open for lunch and dinner seven days a week. Specialties include pizzas, calzones, lasagna, pastas, and a salad bar; prices range from about $8 for an Italian meatball sandwich to $18 for the Seafood Medley, various shellfish served in a white sauce over linguine. Another classic is the **Old Town Pub,** downtown at 600 Lincoln, 970/879-2101. Dinners include burgers, chicken, steak, and seafood ($8–21); open daily for lunch and dinner.

For excellent Italian food, **Riggio's,** 1106 Lincoln, 970/879-9010, is tough to beat. Choose from a wide range of authentic pasta dishes or one of the entrées, including saltimbocca and *vitello.* Entrées run $10–22. With a reputation for excellent "new American cuisine," **Antares Restaurant,** 57 1/2 8th St., 970/879-9939, serves a range of salads, grilled foods, and pastas, including a game hen on tomato-and-basil pasta. Entrées run $12–24. The **Steamboat Brewery and Tavern,** downtown at 5th and Lincoln, 970/879-2233, is a lively pub serving burgers, pizzas, salads, and seafood, all of which you can wash down with a homemade beer (maybe the Powder Keg Porter?). Dinners range $7–18. It's open daily for lunch and dinner.

Harwig's, 911 Lincoln, 970/879-1980, serves a wide array of multicultural dishes, including jambalaya, Thai chicken curry, and Southwestern chicken, plus steaks, pastas, and seafood, for $8–15. The **Steamboat Yacht Club,** 811 Yampa, 970/879-4774, serves high-end ($10–32) dinners, including elk, lamb, and seafood at tables overlooking the Yampa River and Howelsen Ski Hill. When the weather is nice you can sit out on the deck. It's open for lunch and dinner daily.

Sleigh-Ride Dinners

Departing from the top of the gondola Thursday, Friday, and Saturday nights, mid-December to April 1, **Ragnar's** offers elegant European-style cuisine, live music, and the thrill of an after-dark sleigh ride midmountain at Steamboat Ski Resort. (Sleigh-ride lunches are offered daily.) Child care is available. Call for reservations and prices, 970/871-5151.

ENTERTAINMENT

Many of Steamboat's clubs, restaurants, and hotels offer a variety of après-ski entertainment. For current listings, pick up a copy of *Steamboat Today,* published daily and available free throughout the area. In addition, the *Steamboat Whistle,* published weekly and also free, lists current happenings, theater showings, gallery openings, etc.

The **Old Town Pub,** 600 Lincoln, 970/879-2101, has live music Sunday and Monday nights, and a big-screen television showing skiing and other sporting events most of the rest of the time. The **Tugboat,** 970/879-7070, in Ski Time Square regularly features live music.

CALENDAR

There's something going on in Steamboat almost every weekend—from on-skis torchlight parades and ski races to local theater productions and rodeos. One of the highlights is the 80-year-old weeklong **Winter Carnival,** which takes place in early February each year. Among the events are ice-sculpture competitions, ski jumping, hockey games, and a parade on skis. A local tradition, the festival is marked by a general sense of revelry and nuttiness. For more information, phone 970/879-0695 or 970/879-0880.

In early June, you can join the runners (and walkers) in the Steamboat Marathon (actually a 10-K course), and a month later, the Fourth of July weekend is **Cowboy Roundup Days,** a potpourri of fireworks, community barbecues, a Rocky Mountain Oyster Fry, and a Cowboy Poetry and Storytelling Jamboree.

Strings in the Mountains is a six-week music festival at the base of the ski lifts offering a range of chamber and other classical music, with musicians from around the world, most days of the week, plus lectures and other activities. Friday is "Different Tempo" night, when you can hear anything from gospel to bluegrass to jazz.

Rainbow Weekend, at the end of July, is an annual hot-air balloon festival, including arts-and-crafts booths, live music, and food.

For exact dates and more information on these events and many more, phone the **Steamboat Springs Chamber Resort Association** at 970/879-0880. When staying in Steamboat, check out the community calendars in the daily paper *Steamboat Today* and in the weekly *Steamboat Whistle.*

SHOPPING

Though Steamboat's a mecca for lovers of the outdoors, the town and village do offer a variety of gift shops and boutiques as well. While the rest of your party skis, golfs, fishes, balloons, or otherwise explores the area's copious mountains, parks, forests, and lakes, you can venture into the town's world of boutiques, gift shops, galleries, and, alas, tourist traps.

If you drive to Steamboat, you can't miss the zillions of billboards advertising **F. M. Light and Sons,** and most likely you'll be a bit curious. Go ahead and check it out; it's definitely a one-of-a-kind store. Originally a Western-wear and supply shop dating to the early part of the 20th century, Light's now carries a huge array of apparel—from lizard-skin cowboy boots to Marlboro-man ponchos, from after-ski boots to I-Heart-Steamboat sweatshirts. You'll also find postcards and other knickknacks. The shop's at 830 Lincoln, 970/879-1822.

You'll also find a dozen or so galleries in the Steamboat area, both in town and at the village. The **Artisans' Market of Steamboat,** 626 Lincoln, 970/879-7512, is a local artists' cooperative, selling the work of a variety of Steamboat and Routt County artists. Open daily 9:30 A.M.–8:30 P.M.

SERVICES

The **Steamboat Springs Police Department** is at 840 Yampa St.; call 970/849-1144. Phone the **Routt County Sheriff** at 970/849-1090. **State Patrol** offices are at 29587 W. U.S. Hwy. 40, 970/879-4306. Steamboat's **Routt Memorial Hospital** is at 80 Park Ave., 970/879-1322. The central **post office** is on the east end of town at 200 Lincoln Ave., 970/879-0363.

Recycling

Recycle aluminum and glass in Steamboat Springs at the **City Market,** 1825 Central Park Avenue. Phone the City of Steamboat **recycling information line** at 970/879-2060.

INFORMATION

The **Steamboat Springs Chamber Resort Association** is a professional and aggressive group, and a card or phone call will get you on its mailing list, which in turn will get you generous amounts of information (brochures, maps, advertising leaflets, relocation info, etc.). Write P.O. Box 774408, Steamboat Springs, CO 80477, or phone 970/879-0880 or 800/922-2722. The Internet address, which can provide you with lodging, dining, and activities information, is www.steamboat-chamber.com.

The **Bud Werner Memorial Library** (Steamboat's public library) is at 1289 Lincoln Ave., 970/879-0240; special events are sponsored year-round, including children's storytelling.

For maps and information on hiking, snowmobiling, cross-country skiing, and otherwise exploring Steamboat's backcountry, write the district office of the **Routt National Forest,** 57 10th St., Steamboat Springs, CO 80477, or phone 970/879-1870.

For **road and weather information,** phone 970/879-1260. For **Steamboat ski conditions,** phone 970/879-7300.

TRANSPORTATION

Getting around Steamboat, particularly in the wintertime when the shuttles are running full tilt, is relatively easy, as is getting there. Several major airlines, including **American, United,** and **Northwest,** fly nonstop to Steamboat from cities on both coasts (Los Angeles, San Diego,

New York) and in between (Phoenix, Chicago, Dallas, Denver). Check with your travel agent for fares. You might want to fly into Denver instead, as it's considerably cheaper than flying directly into Steamboat, and then either rent your own rig or take a shuttle to the ski area (see below).

Once you arrive in Steamboat, whether you're staying downtown or in the village, you don't really need a car to get around. **Steamboat Springs Transit,** 970/879-5585, has several regular routes around the village, as well as one that runs into town. The "Red Line" and the "Green Line" circle through the condo complexes and will drop you off at the ski area in the morning and virtually at your doorstep at the end of the day. For you night owls, the last bus leaves the village for downtown at 2:03 A.M. (an hour earlier on Sunday). Phone for more information and for nonski-season schedules.

Alpine Taxi-Limo, 970/879-8294 or 800/343-RIDE (343-7433), offers standard taxi service as well as charters between Steamboat and Denver International Airport, mountain tours, and shuttles between Steamboat lodges and Yampa Valley Airport. **Storm Mountain Express,** 970/879-1963, offers upscale, "executive" limo and van service between the resort and airports.

Rent cars in Steamboat (Yampa Valley Aiport) from **Budget,** 970/276-3612; **Dollar,** 970/276-3702; or **Hertz,** 970/276-3304. You can also rent cars at Denver International Airport from all major companies, most of which offer special ski vehicles—4WD, ski racks, etc.

SOUTH TO I-70

U.S. 40 south to the junction with I-70 near Georgetown is absolutely stunning for its variety of breathtaking scenery. Just south of Steamboat, you arc to the east and begin the climb up and over the Continental Divide at Rabbit Ears Pass (elev. 9,426 feet). Just a few miles later, though, the highway dips south again and back onto the western side of the divide at Muddy Pass (8,722 feet). Then the road drops into the Blue River Valley and into Kremmling, where you can either continue due south to Dillon via Highway 9 and Green Mountain Reservoir or bank east to Granby. At the southwestern corner of Rocky Mountain National Park, Granby offers access to U.S. 34 through the park to Estes Park (the road is closed in the winter). Continuing on U.S. 40 south from Granby takes you through the high windswept Fraser River Valley, surrounded by the towering mountains of the deep heart of the Rockies, and into Winter Park. Just past Winter Park, U.S. 40 begins a nasty series of switchbacks, winding and snaking its way up and over Berthoud Pass (11,307 feet). Views along this stretch are unsurpassed (just make sure your brakes are in good working order). From the junction of U.S. 40 and I-70 it's less than an hour's drive to Denver.

North-Central Colorado

Stretching from the Great Plains west to the Continental Divide and from Winter Park north to the Wyoming border, north-central Colorado displays the state's fascinating geological diversity in all its grandness and at its most breathtaking. Here you'll find scores of peaks topping 12,000 feet and several over 14,000, as well as great expanses of prairie grasslands; narrow one-way mountain passes and long, straight stretches of uninteresting interstate; cold, crisp glacier-carved alpine lakes and the muddy South Platte River, which James Michener's *Centennial* narrator described as "the most miserable river in the west."

In addition, north-central Colorado is home to some of the state's best recreation opportunities, from backpacking in Rocky Mountain National Park to windsurfing on Horsetooth Reservoir, from skiing at Winter Park to fishing in Grand Lake or the Cache La Poudre River. In fact, the area offers an amazing amount of public land ideal for exploring by foot, mountain bike, horseback, or cross-country skis—Roosevelt, Routt, and Arapaho National Forests, along with Colorado State Forest, combine to occupy about half of north-central Colorado's total area.

The showpiece of north-central Colorado is Rocky Mountain National Park. Accessible from U.S. 34 either from the east or west (although the road through the park is closed in winter), this 265,200-acre year-round wonderland attracts nearly three million visitors a year. The park features more than 350 miles of hiking trails, excellent opportunities to view Colorado wildlife, including bighorn sheep, elk, and deer, and some of the absolutely most spectacular scenery on the planet—alpine meadows blanketed with wildflowers, massive granite peaks white with year-round snow, and lush valleys vibrantly green from summer rains.

Stanley Hotel, Estes Park

NORTH-CENTRAL COLORADO

© AVALON TRAVEL PUBLISHING, INC.

The two largest communities in north-central Colorado are Greeley and Fort Collins, both about an hour's drive north of Denver. Fort Collins is home to the 20,000-student Colorado State University, best known for its agriculture programs. Kept vital by its youthful population, Fort Collins is committed to preserving its past, with several historical museums and the renovated Old Town shopping area.

Greeley is a ranching and farming area and the central subject of *Centennial*. In the book, Michener describes it as "nothing less than the soul of America . . . as seen in microcosm."

Which could also be said about the whole of north-central Colorado. From its geology and history to its economy and industry, the area is like a living textbook in American studies.

Winter Park

Over Berthoud Pass

The drive up and over Berthoud Pass from I-70 to Winter Park is one of the most spectacular in the state. Cutting through sheer canyons and switching back up from the valley floor, finally rising above the timberline and across the Continental Divide, the road affords stunning panoramas of purple mountains and sawtoothed peaks that appear to stretch forever.

At the summit is a plaque marking the Continental Divide. A handful of tables perched precariously on the cliffside let you picnic with a view to the north of Winter Park and on to Rocky Mountain National Park. And if the elevation makes you queasy and you're not sure you can trust your stomach, you can also wait till you get to the bottom, where Midland Picnic Area (in the Arapaho National Forest) will welcome your safe descent.

At the foot of Berthoud Pass at the south end of the gorgeous Fraser River Valley, Winter Park (pop. 600; elev. 9,000 feet) is a small community devoted almost entirely to tourism and recreation. From Thanksgiving to mid-April, the town is swollen with winter sports enthusiasts of every stripe, while summer brings a proliferation of warm-weather-sports fans, from mountain bikers to trout anglers.

Virtually inseparable from the Winter Park Ski Area, founded in 1940 and whose runs drop almost to the little town's main drag, Winter Park offers an ideal blend of old-ski-town charm and the latest in high-tech equipment and deluxe lodging. You can stay in a cozy inn or a luxury hotel, take a backwoods sleigh ride or zoom to the

top of the mountain via five high-speed detachable quad chairlifts.

Surrounded by towering mountains and Arapaho National Forest, Winter Park sits at the southern end of the beautiful Middle Park region of the Rockies. Winter Park also provides access to the Fraser River Valley, the resort town of Grand Lake, and the western entrance to Rocky Mountain National Park. In fact, the Denver-to-Denver circle—through Winter Park, Rocky Mountain National Park, Estes Park, Lyons, and Boulder—is one of most breathtaking scenic drives in the country. (Note: the road through Rocky Mountain National Park is closed in the winter.) U.S. 40 through Winter Park is also the best way to get to Steamboat Springs from Denver.

HISTORY

The Fraser River Valley was first settled in the mid-1800s, although the area had been explored earlier in the century, and hunters and fur trappers frequented the valley in the 1820s and '30s. The valley's first post office was established in Fraser in 1850, and by the 1870s there were enough settlers in the area that local Native Americans were beginning to feel intruded upon. By 1883, the Utes had been relocated to a reservation in Utah after the Meeker Massacre.

Winter Park began to come into its own in 1927 with the completion of the $18 million, seven-mile Moffat Tunnel, which bore through the Continental Divide and linked Denver and the Fraser Valley. The tunnel was named for

NORTH-CENTRAL COLORADO HIGHLIGHTS

Rocky Mountain National Park: sightseeing, camping, hiking, cross-country skiing

Estes Park: hiking and mountain biking in Roosevelt National Forest, cross-country skiing, fishing the Colorado, Arkansas, and Cache La Poudre Rivers, museums, shopping, Stanley Hotel (majestic, turn-of-the-20th-century hotel), Long's Peak Scottish Festival

Winter Park: skiing and hiking in Arapaho National Forest, 660 miles of mountain-bike trails, American Music Festival, Rocky Mountain Wine and Food Festival, Famous Flame Thrower High Altitude Chili Cook-off

Poudre Canyon: sightseeing, fishing, camping

Grand Lake: entry to Rocky Mountain National Park, fishing, camping, hiking, and skiing in Arapaho National Recreation Area, Indian Parks Wilderness Area

Fort Collins: Anheuser-Busch Brewery, Horsetooth Reservoir, hut-to-hut Nordic skiing along the Never Summer Nordic Yurt System, renovated old-town area, shopping, dining, college-town nightlife, Colorado Brewfest, Balloon Festival

Greeley: Fort Vasquez, University of Northern Colorado, Denver Broncos' summer training camp, summer festivals and fairs, museums, shopping, dining (best Rocky Mountain oysters in the state)

David H. Moffat, a Denver banker who had worked for nearly a quarter century to run the Denver and Pacific Northwestern Railroad through the mountains to provide safer and more reliable passage between Denver and Salt Lake City. The tunnel's western terminus is adjacent to the community of Winter Park, which was originally known as West Portal.

In 1937, the Forest Service built an 800-foot rope tow at Berthoud Pass, and by the end of the decade, 50,000 skiers a year were descending on the little ski resort. Because the area and skiing were growing so popular with Denverites, the city sought a way to open a municipal "winter park" of its own. West Portal was the perfect locale, and Winter Park Ski Area, under management of the City of Denver, first opened on Jan. 28, 1940. Lift tickets that day were $1.

The city ran into difficulties, however, trying to maintain a park on the other side of the Continental Divide, and during the late 1940s, Winter Park fell into disrepair. Sensing the first wave of Colorado's midcentury ski boom, Denver realized it had the opportunity to take part—if it could make Winter Park a viable resort. In 1950, city officials created the Winter Park Recreational Association (WPRA), a 15-member board of trustees that would work independently of the city and run operations at Winter Park. The nonprofit corporation quickly got to work improving

the ski area, beginning with a surface lift. The $167,000 project, financed by the City of Denver, increased uphill capacity to 1,600 skiers per hour. Since then, the WPRA has remained nonprofit and self-supporting, successfully managing one of Colorado's best ski areas. The 1991 ski season brought $5.3 million in improvements—including construction of a high-speed quad chair, increased snowmaking capabilities, and the remodeling of on-mountain eating facilities.

SIGHTS

Cozens' Ranch House Museum on U.S. 40 just north of town on the Fraser-Winter Park line was the site of a stage stop and post office dating from 1876. Check out the room commemorating "Doc Suzie," Grand County's first woman doctor, who moved to the area from Cripple Creek in 1907, practiced until 1941, and died in 1960 at age 90. The museum is open Mon.–Sat. 10 A.M.–5 P.M. and Sunday noon–5 P.M., with limited hours during the winter. Admission is $3 for adults, with discounts for seniors and kids. For more information, phone 970/726-5488.

WINTER SPORTS

Winter Park's accessibility to Denver, just 70 miles away via I-70 and U.S. 40 (broad and well maintained, if a bit steep and harrowing in places), makes it a natural for day-trippers looking for the heart of the snow country. Denver alpine skiers, cross-country skiers, snowboarders, and Telemarkers flock to Winter Park when the snow flies, knowing they can get a good day's skiing in and still be home in time for dinner. In addition, families, honeymooners, and college students from all over the country come to Winter Park for their vacations—by train, plane, and automobile—with the knowledge they'll find some of the state's best skiing here, as well as one of the West's friendliest mountain towns. And nonskiers know there's a lot to do here besides ski. Though the community's too small to offer a whole lot in the way of nightlife and other entertainment, the area affords a wide range of other winter recreational opportunities, from ice skating to moonlight sleigh rides.

Skiing and Snowboarding

Regularly ranked by discriminating skiers as one of the North America's top-50 ski resorts, **Winter Park Ski Area** has earned a solid reputation as one of the state's best family ski areas, with terrain suitable for every ability level, from snowplower to backcountry bowler. In addition, the resort is held in high esteem worldwide for its commitment to skiers with disabilities—amputees, paraplegics, and the blind. Those who haven't visited Winter Park recently will be impressed with the brand-new Zephyr Mountain Lodge (2000-2001 ski season), which offers 220 ski-in/ski-out condo units at the base of the lifts.

Winter Park Ski Area sprawls across three separate mountain ridges connected by a sophisticated network of lifts and runs. Combined, Winter Park, Mary Jane, and Vasquez Ridge offer 23 lifts on 2,886 acres of terrain with an uphill capacity of more than 30,000 skiers an hour. The longest run is more than five miles, and the total vertical is 3,060 feet.

Winter Park and Vasquez Ridge offer the most skiing for intermediate-range skiers, while Mary Jane has the more demanding runs. In

Winter Park Ski Area is held in high esteem worldwide for its commitment to skiers with disabilities— amputees, paraplegics, and the blind.

fact, about 50 percent of Mary Jane's runs are designated advanced or expert, and the steep bump runs here are among the nastiest in the state. Only 6 percent of Mary Jane is designated for beginning skiers.

The true pride of Winter Park, though, is the **National Sports Center for the Disabled.** Founded by Hal O'Leary in the winter of 1969–70, the program started out small. Its goal was to teach children with cancer and leg amputations to ski. Since then, the program has grown to embrace people with more than 40 disabilities and provides instruction and adaptive equipment to more than 17,000 skiers a year. From single-track skiers (single amputees skiing with outriggers, crutches with short skis on the end) and blind skiers (who follow instructors or partners with bells) to sit skiers (double amputees or paraplegics, who ski in "sleds"), Winter Park's slopes are covered with folks who manage to all but leave their disabilities behind. Don't be surprised to see a single-track skier zip by you demonstrating more élan and control than you can muster on your very best day.

The National Sports Center for the Disabled also offers a number of competitions for disabled skiers, and it has recently expanded to offer an array of summer programs, including mountain biking, hiking, and white-water rafting.

Winter Park Ski Area has a full range of instructional programs for skiers of all abilities and offers complete rental and equipment-repair services. For more information on ticket prices, hours of operation, or instruction, phone 970/726-5514. For **snow conditions,** phone 303/572-SNOW (572-7669). Write the ski area at P.O. Box 36, Winter Park, CO 80482, and look at its website at www.winterpark-resort.com. For central reservations and lodging, phone 800/977-2754.

Cross-Country Skiing

The Winter Park-Fraser Valley areas offer nearly unlimited opportunities for the cross-country

looking east at the Continental Divide from Winter Park

© STEPHEN METZGER

skier, thanks to the surrounding Arapaho National Forest. Whether you like to follow old logging roads or break your own trails, you won't be disappointed. For maps and information on exploring Arapaho National Forest on Nordic skis, contact the district office in Granby at 62429 U.S. Hwy. 40, 970/887-3331 (or 970/887-3165 for a recorded message).

In addition, the area has a number of groomed public trail systems. **Devil's Thumb Ranch Resort** offers 90-plus km of trails in the quiet backcountry in the woods along the Fraser River. The resort is east of Fraser at 3530 County Rd. 83. For information, phone 970/726-5632 or write P.O. Box 750, Tabernash, CO 80478. Check out the website at www.rkymtnhi.com/devthumb/home or email the resort at devthumb@rkymtnhi.com.

You'll also find excellent groomed cross-country trails at **Snow Mountain Ranch's YMCA Nordic Center** about 15 miles north of Winter Park off U.S. 40. It has 100 km of trails on 4,600 acres of woodsy backcountry, with three km lighted for night skiing. Visit website www.ymcarockies.org or phone 970/726-4628 for information.

Snowmobiling

The broad Fraser Valley and sprawling expanses of Arapaho National Forest make the area a natural for exploring by snowmobile; several outfits offer rentals and tours. **Trailblazer Snowmobile Tours,** 800/669-0134, provides a range of tours. Write Box 3437, Winter Park, CO 80482, or visit website www.columbine.com.

Snowcat Tours

You can tour the Winter Park Ski Area by snowcat, with machines leaving the base of the lifts three times daily. For reservations and information, phone the resort at 970/726-5514.

Totally Tubular

Snow tubing is a Winter Park tradition. One of the best tubing hills in the Rockies is just north of town on U.S. 40 (you'll see it off to your left). Link 'em together to make tube trains, or go solo. Go head, feet, or butt first. Just dress warm—the wind can *really* whip across that meadow. For rates and information, phone the **Fraser Tubing Hill** at 970/726-5954.

O'er the Fields We Go

In contrast to the gift shops and high-tech lifts, a horse-drawn sleigh will take you out into the quiet moonlit woods for a short scenic tour or a romantic dinner. Among the companies that have been offering the service to the Winter Park area for many years are: **Dashing Thru the Snow Sleigh Rides,** 1400 County Rd. 5, Fraser, CO 80442, 970/726-5376; **Dinner at the Barn Sleighrides,** 970/726-4923; and **Devil's Thumb Ranch Resort,** 970/726-5632. It's not the cheapest way to spend an evening (about $50 adult, $40 child), but it's ideal for a special celebration.

Ice Skating

You'll find ice-skating rinks at **Fraser Valley Elementary School** in Fraser, **Beaver Village Resort** in Winter Park, 970/726-5741 or 800/666-0281, and **Snow Mountain Ranch—YMCA of the Rockies** north of town, 970/726-4628 or, from Denver, 303/443-4743. For more information on ice skating in the Winter Park-Fraser Valley area, contact the Winter Park Recreational Association at 970/726-5514.

Mush, Puppies

To see the Fraser Valley Iditarod-style, check out **Dog Sled Rides of Winter Park,** 970/726-TEAM (726-8326), which has been featured in numerous TV programs, magazines, and newspapers. The tour is nine miles long and lasts one hour and 45 minutes. Call for rates.

WHEN THE SNOW MELTS

Don't let the name deceive you. Though best known as one of the state's winter-sports paradises, Winter Park is a year-round resort. When skis get hung in racks, out come the mountain bikes, fishing poles, rafts, backpacks, and saddles and tack. Cross-country ski trails become havens for mountain bikers, and ski lifts are open to sightseers.

Mountain Biking

This is without doubt the Fraser Valley area's latest rage, and indications are the sport is here to stay. The old logging trails of Arapaho National Forest offer enough miles of spleen-shaking backcountry riding to keep you rock-hopping all summer, maybe without ever going down the same path twice.

Winter Park's **Fat Tire Society** (FATS) has developed a 660-mile trail system named "best mountain biking system in Colorado" by *Rocky Mountain Sports* magazine, and the Winter Park Chamber of Commerce publishes a mountain-biking map available at the chamber and at sports

© STEPHEN METZGER

Tubing at the Fraser Tubing Hill is a Winter Park tradition.

shops around the valley. In addition, several companies offer rentals and guided tours. **Mad Adventures,** 970/726-5290 or 800/451-4884, accommodates beginning to advanced riders, with instruction, "Jeep Up/Bike Down" trips, and single-track tours. You can rent bikes and equipment, and get expert advice, at **Sport-Stalker** in Cooper Creek Square, 970/726-8873, and at **Winter Park Ski & Sports Shop** at Club Meadowridge, 800/222-7547.

Golf

The Fraser Valley's public 18-hole **Pole Creek Golf Course** is 10 miles west of Winter Park. The 6,230-yard Pole Creek remains on *Golf Digest* magazine's list of top 50 American courses. The course hosts several tournaments annually, including the famous **Bert and Ernie Classic** in September. For information and tee times, phone 970/726-8847.

Grand Lake Golf Course is 40 minutes north of Winter Park on the east side of Rocky Mountain National Park. Views from this 18-hole course are some of the best anywhere. Phone 970/627-8008.

Hiking

You'll find lots of excellent hiking opportunities in the Winter Park area. Hiking's best in the morning, as the sky often clouds up in the afternoon, and hard rains are quite common. **Byer's Peak** (elev. 12,804 feet) towers west of the Fraser Valley and offers a short (just under three miles) but rugged trail to the top. Panoramas are excellent. Go west from U.S. 40 in Fraser.

For information on hiking in Arapaho National Forest, stop in at the information center at the Sulphur District Office in Granby, or phone 970/887-3331. For maps, equipment (to rent or buy), and advice, stop by **Black Dog Mountaineering,** in downtown Winter Park, 970/726-4412.

Fishing

The Fraser Valley-Grand County area offers a wide range of mountain fishing for trout and kokanee salmon. Free fishing is provided for kids in the small roadside ponds between Winter Park

and Fraser; the lakes are stocked regularly by the local chapter of the Lions Club. More serious (and older) lake anglers should head up to the Three Lakes Area near Granby and the town of Grand Lake. **Grand Lake, Shadow Mountain Reservoir,** and **Lake Granby** are home to some good-sized rainbow, cutthroat, lake (Mackinaw), and brown trout, as well as landlocked kokanee. Fishing is best from a boat, but shore anglers have done well too.

Stream fishermen will want to try the **Colorado River** and **Fraser River.** The Fraser flows through Winter Park and offers decent fishing (planters) near the ski area, while a stretch just north of town is designated a Wild Trout Area (be sure to check local fishing restrictions). For information, tackle, and licenses, stop by **Nelson's Fly and Tackle Shop,** north of Winter Park in Tabernash along U.S. 40, 970/726-8558.

Rafting

With the North Platte, Colorado, and Arkansas Rivers all tumbling through the mountains in Grand County, you can bet there's plenty of rafting action. In Winter Park, several companies offer a variety of trips, from mellow floats to serious white water. Try **Mad Adventures,** 970/726-5290 or 800/451-4844; or Red Tail Rafting, 888/733-3599.

Horseback Riding

Monarch Stables & Wagon Rides, 970/726-5376, offers guided rides from its base in Fraser (1400 County Rd. 5), while **Sombrero Ranch Stables** in Grand Lake, 970/627-3514, books tours and pack trips and rents horses by the hour.

Chairlift Rides

For spectacular views of the surrounding scenery, it's tough to beat an off-season chairlift ride. **Winter Park Ski Area,** 970/726-5514, runs lifts during the summer for sightseeing.

Alpine Slide

Winter Park's Alpine slide (the longest in Colorado) gives summer visitors a chance to crank turns on the slopes in a completely different fashion, though the ride to the top is the same (via chairlift). At the base of the ski hill, the half-mile, 30-turn slide is open June to mid-August and costs about $5 a ride (multiride discounts are available). Children must be least 45 inches tall. Phone Winter Park Resort at 970/726-5514 for more information.

ACCOMMODATIONS

Much less developed than some of Colorado's major destination ski resorts, Winter Park nonetheless offers the visitor a wide range of lodging options—from an American Youth Hostel to conventional motels to upscale condos with all the bells and whistles. **Note:** it's necessary to make reservations in winter and highly suggested the rest of the year. Also, prices here should be used for comparison; rates often vary significantly from summer to winter. For information on more than 50 lodging options—from motels to bed-and-breakfasts—in the Fraser Valley, contact **Winter Park Central Reservations** at P.O. Box 36, Winter Park, CO 80482, 800/729-5839. You can also visit the website at www.skiwinterpark.com.

$50–100

Frankly, you'll be fortunate to find lodging for under $100 a night in Winter Park, except between seasons (ski and summer). Following, however, are a handful of places offering among the least expensive and reliably clean and convenient rooms.

A favorite among families, the **Snow Mountain Ranch—YMCA of the Rockies,** 970/726-4628, offers a variety of lodging options, from individual cabins (sleeping up to 12) to rooms in the central lodge ranging $25–250 a night. Kids and their parents love it here, as there's always something to do: go hiking or cross-country skiing (with a lodge guide), play in the indoor pool, or even lose yourself in the lodge library. Just south of Granby at 1344 County Rd. 53 off U.S. 40, Snow Mountain is a nonprofit operation that's been in business for more than 20 years. (YMCA of the Rockies also operates **Estes Park Center**—see Estes Park.) For a brochure

with complete information, write P.O. Box 169, Winter Park, CO 80482.

The **Olympia Motor Lodge,** 800/548-1992, the **Sundowner Motel,** 800/521-8279, and the **Super 8,** 800/541-6130, are all right downtown and offer easy access to the ski slopes and other attractions (including the town shuttle).

One of the best deals in town is the **Arapahoe Ski Lodge,** 970/726-8222 or 800/338-2698, a classic '40s-era ski lodge downtown (also on the shuttle line), where lodging rates (14 rooms) include breakfast and dinner. You can also get lodging for under $100 at **Devil's Thumb Ranch Resort,** 800/933-4339, where a room with a shared bath will run you about $70 (also see below).

$100–150

Again, rates will vary, depending on season, but you should be able to find several lodging options in this price range. A long-standing Winter Park tradition is the **Gasthaus Eichler,** 970/726-5133 or 800/543-3899, downtown at 78786 U.S. Hwy. 40. The 15 rooms are upstairs from the restaurant of the same name, and lodging is available with or without meals included in the rates.

One of Winter Park's nicest and most convenient condo complexes is the **Iron Horse Resort Retreat,** 970/726-8851 or 800/621-8190, at the base of the lifts between Winter Park and Mary Jane. Depending on the number in your party, and the time of year, this complex can actually be quite affordable. Ski and golf packages are available, offsetting the prices of rooms.

For bed-and-breakfast accommodations, try the **Pines Inn of Winter Park,** 1120 County Rd. 716, 970/726-5416 or 800/824-9127, 600 yards from the base of the lifts. Six of the eight rooms have private baths (two rooms have whirlpools), and there's a spa for the proverbial after-ski soak. One of the area's newer bed-and-breakfasts is the **Whistle Stop Bed and Breakfast,** 888-TAWANDA (829-2632), where there are four rooms, two with private bath, and rates run right around $100 a night. It's near the shuttle and the ski-train depot. Write Box 418, Winter Park, CO 80482.

$150–250 (and up)

Devil's Thumb Ranch Resort, 970/726-5632 or 800/525-3304 (outside Colorado), in a huge meadow three miles north of Fraser, is first a cross-country ski lodge, but it's also a perfect base for a mountain-biking, hiking, fishing, or just an I-need-to-get-away-from-the-rush vacation. The rustic restaurant overlooking the meadow is open to nonguests as well. Simple cabins run $160–$170, while cabins complete with kitchens and dining and living rooms run up to $350 a night.

For total luxury in backwoods lodging, check out the **C Lazy U Guest Ranch,** 970/887-3344, "the country's only five-star dude ranch." A year-round resort offering cross-country skiing, snowmobiling, tennis, fishing, horseback rides, cross-country skiing, and many other activities, the C Lazy U is one of the best places around to be pampered. Rates are luxury-level but include three gourmet meals a day. For complete information, write P.O. Box 378B, Granby, CO 80446.

Camping

Several campgrounds—those operated by the Forest Service, as well as privately run camps—are scattered in and around Winter Park. **Robbers Roost** is a small Forest Service campground at the north base of Berthoud Pass, just before the turnoff to Mary Jane Ski Area. A few miles farther north, almost right downtown, **Idlewild Campground** also offers Forest Service-run sites. For information, contact the Winter Park Chamber of Commerce, 970/726-4118, or the Forest Service District Office in Granby, 970/887-3331.

FOOD

Start Me Up

One of Winter Park's favorite breakfast spots, in business since the mid-1970s, is **The Kitchen,** 970/726-9940, at 78542 U.S. Hwy. 40 on the north end of town, where locals and visitors alike go for the homemade food. Favorites include breakfast burritos and French toast, a house specialty. For fresh-roasted and specialty coffees and a wide assortment of baked goods, try the **Rocky Mountain Roastery and Coffee Company** in Fraser, 970/726-4400.

Lunch and Dinner

Deno's Mountain Bistro, 970/726-5332, downtown on U.S. 40, is part sports bar and part restaurant and has a wide range of food, from chicken-wing appetizers to burgers, fish and chips, steaks, and Cajun dishes. Prices run $5–20 for dinner. Deno's has several television monitors, as well as an excellent beer selection, making it one of the best places in town to catch a game.

A veritable Winter Park institution, **Gasthaus Eichler,** 78786 U.S. Hwy. 40, 970/726-5133, serves lunch and dinner daily. For lunch try the bratwurst, the quiche of the day, or a salad ($5–8). Dinners include German specialties as well as beef, veal, and seafood and run to $30 (lobster tail). At **Hernando's Pizza and Pasta Pub,** 970/726-5409, pizzas range $8–16, and pasta dinners (spaghetti, ravioli, lasagna, etc.) are around $8. Hernando's is just north of town on U.S. 40. The **Crooked Creek Saloon** in Fraser, 970/726-9250, has a reputation for excellent burgers, salads, and sandwiches.

ENTERTAINMENT

You're much more likely to find night-owl action in Winter Park in the winter, when skiers are looking for places to boogie after a day on the slopes, than in summer, when the clubs are generally open only on weekends. If you like things a bit slower and quieter, though, Winter Park's bars can be downright nice in the summer—you won't have to elbow your way through a crowd to order a beer or a plate of nachos. **The Slope,** 970/726-5727, just north of the base of the lifts, and the **Crooked Creek Saloon** in Fraser, 970/726-9250, both book live music, and Crooked Creek also has pool tables and darts. At **Rome on the Range,** 970/726-1111, downtown on U.S. 40, you can play pool, dance to live music, and even take a line-dancing lesson.

CALENDAR

From first snow till the lifts shut down, and again from early June through August, Winter Park sponsors a wide range of events, from ski races and mountain-bike hill climbs to art shows and concerts.

Among Winter Park's annual highlights: the **First Interstate Bank Cup** features professional ski races in late January, with excellent opportunities to see top competitors. The **High Country Stampede,** Saturdays in July and August, is Fraser Valley's popular rodeo, attracting top professional and amateur riders from around the country.

A Winter Park classic is the **American Music Festival** in mid-July. The stage is set up at the base of the Winter Park Ski Area, and the audience lines the gentle lower slopes; there ain't a bad seat in the house. Lineups feature mostly American music, with a contemporary country bent. Past acts have included Bonnie Raitt, John Prine, Hootie and the Blowfish, Mother Hips, and Leon Russell.

Winter Park's late-July **Alpine Art Affair,** first held in 1975, features more than 100 juried artists from throughout the western United States, as well as food booths and music. In mid-August, the **Rocky Mountain Wine and Food Festival** offers winetasting and seminars, with more than 200 wines and champagnes, as well as gourmet meals prepared by the **Colorado Chefs de Cuisine**—a benefit for the National Sports Center for the Disabled. Also in the food category, the **Famous Flamethrower High Altitude Chili Cook-off** in early September is a high-spirited competition between local chefs vying to represent the Rocky Mountain region in the world chili cook-off.

On Christmas Eve, watch the beautiful **Torchlight Parade** wind its way down the runs of Winter Park Ski Area.

For more information or exact dates, contact the **Winter Park Recreational Association,** 970/726-5514, or the **Winter Park/Fraser Valley Chamber of Commerce,** 800/903-7275.

SHOPPING

Though you won't find the busy shopping village of a Vail or Aspen, a number of stores carry gifts, souvenirs, and other items. The main drag through town is rife with ski and sports shops, which often unload the previous season's gear and clothing during the summer at "sidewalk" sales. This can be a good time to pick up a pair of ski boots or a parka for a very good price.

© STEPHEN METZGER

NORTH-CENTRAL

The best way to get to Winter Park from downtown Denver in the winter is on the Winter Park Ski Train.

Winter Park's Children's Center is one of the best ski-area facilities in the country.

SERVICES

Most Winter Park services, including the police and sheriff departments, are based in Hot Sulphur Springs, about 10 miles west of Granby on U.S. 40. **Police department** offices are at 670 Spring Rd., 970/726-5666. The offices of the **Grand County Sheriff** are at 308 Byers; 970/726-5666. **Winter Park Medical Center,** 970/726-9616, is in downtown Winter Park, and **7-Mile Clinic,** 970/726-8066, is at the base of the lifts of Winter Park Ski Area. The Winter Park **post office** is at 78876 U.S. Hwy. 40, 970/726-5495.

Child Care

Winter Park is one of the country's best family ski areas, so it should come as no surprise that children's facilities on the mountain are very highly regarded. A recent article in *Skiing* magazine lauded the resort's **Children's Center,** the oldest in Colorado, giving high praise to the facility's expert and kid-sensitive staff, and to its efficient organization.

The center divides kids into four groups (age three to kindergarten, first to third grade, fourth

grade to age 12, and ages 13–16). While the little ones are playing games that acquaint them with the snow, the older ones can ski at their own pace with instructors. The center, operating out of a multistory 32,000-square-foot building, also provides day care for children ages two months to five years. For more information or to make reservations, phone 970/726-5514, ext. 337.

Recycling

Drop off most recyclables at **Grand Recycles** at the firehouse on U.S. 40 in Fraser. The Safeway in Fraser (on U.S. 40) takes aluminum.

INFORMATION

The **Winter Park/Fraser Valley Chamber of Commerce** has a new visitor center open seven days a week. This is an excellent source of information on everything from what to do to where to stay in the area. The office is in town on U.S. 40 (east side of the road); write P.O. Box 3236, Winter Park, CO 80482, or call 800/903-7275. From among the many brochures, maps, and activity guides, be sure to pick up the Grand County *Exploration Guide,* a listing of more than 100 historical and geographical places of interest in the county, as well as a copy of *Trails* (*Tracks* in winter), which lists local events. You can also visit the website at www.winterpark-info.com. Contact **Winter Park Central Reservations** at P.O. Box 36, Winter Park, CO 80482, 800/729-5839.

For **weather information,** tune your radio to AM 930. If you're padding around in the morning waiting for your coffee to brew, tune your television to channel 5 for news about what's going on in the area.

Get **road and weather information** by calling 970/725-3334.

TRANSPORTATION

Winter Park is only 67 miles from Denver and very easy to get to, despite the taxing drive over Berthoud Pass. **Home James Transportation Service,** 800/359-7536, offers door-to-door round-trip (and one-way) shuttle service between Denver and Winter Park (and on to lodges farther north and to Grand Lake). One-way between Denver International and Winter Park is about $40. (For information on car rentals at Denver International Airport, see Colorado by Air in the Introduction.) You can rent a car in Winter Park by calling Winter Park Central Reservations at 800/729-5839.

Without doubt, though, the best way to get to Winter Park is by train. **Amtrak** deposits 30,000 skiers a year at the Winter Park Ski Area station in nearby Fraser. For information, phone 970/726-8816 or 800/USA-RAIL (872-7245). From downtown Denver (the depot is at the west end of the 16th Street Mall), take the **Winter Park Ski Train,** which has been taking skiers to the slopes for more than 50 years, literally to the base of the lifts. (In 1998, service expanded to include summer as well.) The two-hour ride takes you through 29 tunnels and drops you off 100 yards from the lifts. For rates, information and reservations, phone 303/296-ISKI (296-4754).

North of Winter Park

U.S. 40 continues north into the heart of Middle Park, following the Fraser River to Granby and then doglegging west toward Hot Sulphur Springs and Kremmling. Just past Granby is the junction with U.S. 34, which continues north past Lake Granby, Shadow Mountain Reservoir, and the town of Grand Lake, before lifting east into Rocky Mountain National Park and over the Continental Divide (closed in winter).

The scenery throughout this area is stupendous, characterized by long broad mountain valleys surrounded by rugged, sawtoothed peaks, many of which are over 12,000 feet high. Towering just east of the town of Grand Lake is Longs Peak, at 14,256 feet one of the highest mountains in the state. To the north is Mt. Richthofen (elev. 12,940 feet), and to the west is Park View Mountain (elev. 12,296 feet).

GRANBY

Granby (pop. 1,200; elev. 7,600 feet) is a small ranching and farming center in the Fraser River Valley about 20 miles north of Winter Park. Once known especially for its mountain lettuce, Granby served as a railroad shipping point for vegetables, cattle, and timber. Many of the valley's older ranches have been converted to guest ranches (see Accommodations under Winter Park), and the town now relies heavily on the tourism industry—skiing in the winter, hunting, fishing, mountain biking, and sightseeing in the summer and fall. Granby's Fourth of July fireworks show is the biggest in the state, usually drawing around 75,000 visitors.

SolVista Golf and Ski Ranch

One of Colorado's youngest and smallest ski areas, this resort opened as Silver Creek Ski Resort in 1982 as a primarily beginner and intermediate mountain catering to families and other folks wanting to get away from the crowds. Never really making much of a name for itself, the resort suffered for a couple of decades before changing ownership and opening in 2001 as SolVista. The resort, as its name implies, is marketing itself as a year-round playground for golfers and skiers.

At the ski area, four lifts service just over 200 acres of skiable terrain with a 970-foot vertical drop. The terrain is rated 20 percent beginner, 50 percent intermediate, and 20 percent advanced, though most sources indicate a certain degree of "slope inflation." (Even the advanced skiing isn't all that challenging at SolVista.)

Though a relative newcomer to Colorado skiing, SolVista has already established a reputation as a good cross-country area. Nordic skiers can both explore the groomed trails and ride the lifts on the mountain.

The public golf course is brand new, the first nine holes opening in June 2001. The back nine—which will complete the 7,200-yard, par-72 course—was scheduled to open in the summer of 2002.

Most lodging at SolVista includes ski or golf packages. For information, contact **SolVista Reservation and Travel** at 800/757-7669. See the website at www.silvercreek-resort.com.

Accommodations

The **El Monte Motel,** 970/887-3348, is just south of town on U.S. 40. A handful of small motels right in town on U.S. 40 offer clean quiet rooms. They include the **Littletree Inn Motel,** 970/887-2551, and the **Blue Spruce Motel,** 970/887-3300. Rooms for two at these three lodges will run $50–70.

Services

The offices of the local **police department** are west of town in Hot Sulphur Springs, 970/887-3866. Phone the **State Patrol** at 970/725-3393. **St. Anthony Hospital Systems Emergency Medical Center** is at 62801 U.S. Hwy. 40 in Granby, 970/887-2117. The **post office** is at 54 Zero St., 970/887-3612.

Information

The **Granby Chamber of Commerce** operates a tourist information booth on the north end of town next to the Blue Spruce Motel. Stop in for maps, activity guides, and dining and lodging brochures, and more information on area guest ranches. You can also write P.O. Box 35, Granby, CO 80046, or phone 970/887-2311 or 800/325-1661.

West of Granby

U.S. 40 arcs west just outside Granby, following the course of the Fraser River to its confluence with the Colorado at Kremmling. The road is flanked by Routt (north) and Arapaho (south) National Forests, and it passes through the little historical town of Hot Sulphur Springs. In Kremmling, you can either continue north to Steamboat Springs, or turn south onto Highway 9, which follows the Blue River into Summit County, past Green Mountain Reservoir, continuing to Dillon, Frisco, and Breckenridge.

HOT SULPHUR SPRINGS

Seat of Grand County, Hot Sulphur Springs (pop. 400; elev. 7,655 feet) was named for the nearby springs thought by Native Americans to have medicinal powers. According to legend, a Ute chief, whose tribe had left him to die, appealed to his gods for power. The chief built fires below the bubbling waters, bathed and drank in them, was healed, and rejoined the tribe.

Today, Hot Sulphur Springs is the site of the district offices of the Arapaho National Forest, as well as of several local agencies, including police, sheriff, and state patrol. For more information on Hot Sulphur Springs, write **Grand Lake Chamber of Commerce,** P.O. Box 57, Grand Lake, CO 80447, or phone 970/627-3402.

Grand County Museum

Housed in the Hot Sulphur Schoolhouse (1924), this museum exhibits a wide array of historical items, including 8,500-year-old Native American artifacts, pioneer firearms, clothing, utensils, and snow gear (snowshoes, etc.), as well as historical photos. Also here are a blacksmith shop, jail, the original county courthouse, a display commemorating pioneer women and their role in the settling of the area, a 1905 BLM ranger station, and a one-room school.

The museum, 110 E. Byers, is open daily 10 A.M.–5 P.M. and Sunday noon–5 P.M., Memorial Day through October 1, and Wed.–Fri. 11 A.M.–4 P.M. and Sunday noon–4 P.M. the rest of the year. Admission is $4 for adults, with discounts for kids and seniors. For more information, phone 970/725-3939.

Accommodations

You'll find inexpensive (under $50) no-frills doubles in Granby at the **Canyon Motel,** 970/725-3395 or 888/489-3719, and at the **Ute Trail Motel,** 970/725-0123 or 800/506-0099. Both are on U.S. 40 in town.

KREMMLING

On the western side of the Middle Park area at the junction of Highway 9 and U.S. 40, Kremmling offers access to a wide range of recreational pursuits. Borders of Arapaho, Routt, and White River National Forests are all within 20 miles of Kremmling, and the nearby waters—the Blue, Fraser, and Colorado Rivers all pass through Kremmling—are favorites among kayakers and canoers; there's a put-in one mile south of town on Highway 9.

You'll find a **visitor information center** on U.S. 40 on the west end of town (corner of Park and Center), and a park with picnic tables and playground equipment. **Kremmling RV Park,** 970/724-9593, is east of town on U.S. 40 (2200 Central).

For more information on the area, contact the **Kremmling Chamber of Commerce** at 970/724-3472.

North of Kremmling

U.S. 40 continues north from Kremmling over Muddy and Rabbit Ears Passes to Steamboat Springs, and then beelines west across the high plateau toward Dinosaur and the Utah border. Just a couple of miles beyond Muddy Pass you can catch Highway 14 north to Walden, the isolated seat of isolated Jackson County. From Walden it's only another 20 miles to the Wyoming border, and then 50 miles to Laramie.

WALDEN AND NORTH PARK

The North Park/Jackson County area is a high, intermontane glacial basin and the location of the headwaters of the North Platte River. The basin is rimmed by stunning mountain peaks, some rising to nearly 13,000 feet. Long a favorite hunting ground of the Utes, North Park hosts abundant wildlife, although its harsh winters force many of the critters to lower elevations.

Jackson County's economy relies largely on ranching and farming, although the area is being discovered by outdoor enthusiasts who appreciate its backpacking, hiking, fishing, camping, and cross-country skiing opportunities. Walden's **North Park Pioneer Museum** displays the basin's history, from the days of early settlement through Walden's founding in 1890 and into modern times. Admission to the museum is free, but hours of operation are irregular. Phone 970/723-8371 or 970/723-4212.

In Walden you'll find a number of motels and bed-and-breakfast inns, as well as campgrounds and restaurants. The **North Park Motel,** 625 Main (Walden), 970/723-4271, is open year-round and has 20 units, some with kitchenettes. The phone number for the **North Park KOA Campground** is 970/723-4310.

For more information on this remote but gorgeous area, contact the **North Park Tourism Information Center** (at the Town Hall), P.O. Box 489TB, Walden, CO 80480, 970/723-4344, or the **North Park Chamber of Commerce,** P.O. Box 227, Walden, CO 80480, 970/723-4600. The chamber's offices are at 491 Main.

NORTH-CENTRAL

Grand Lake and Vicinity

Grand Lake (pop. 380; elev. 8,369 feet) is a small summer resort village on the north shore of Grand Lake, the largest natural lake in Colorado. Situated on the western border of Rocky Mountain National Park, the town is a popular stop for tourists heading both into and out of the park. The town itself also attracts its own share of summer visitors, most of whom come to fish and explore the waters and shores of the three nearby lakes, camp in the area's many campgrounds, or hole up in the lodges, guest ranches, and summer homes in town, lakeside, and hidden among the valley's woods and rolling hills. In the summer, the town's population swells to more than 3,000. In the winter, things die down considerably, though hardcore outdoorsfolks still prowl the Grand Lake area. Snowmobiling, cross-country skiing, and ice fishing are popular wintertime activities.

Downtown Grand Lake is defined pretty much by the main drag, Grand Avenue, which parallels the lake's north shore, and a couple of cross streets that provide access to the water. The downtown section of Grand Avenue comprises three blocks of gift shops, cafés, saloons, Western-art galleries, and Indian pottery and jewelry stores. There's also the proverbial miniature golf, as well as the obligatory proliferation of T-shirt and souvenir shops. As a resort town, though, Grand Lake doesn't feel *quite* as touristy and gimmicky as other Western resort towns do. This is perhaps because of its isolation and its link to Rocky Mountain National Park—one of the most rugged backcountry parks in the nation.

History

Although many of Colorado's resort areas were Native American playgrounds or hunting grounds long before white settlers showed up, the Utes avoided this lake, which they called "Spirit Lake," and the surrounding area. According to legend, a Ute village once stood on the shores of Grand Lake, but it was wiped out by invading Cheyenne and Arapahoes who had come to the area to hunt. Ute men were killed, women and children set adrift on a raft as a storm approached. When the raft reached the lake's deep waters, it capsized. Utes believed the mists rising from Grand Lake's surface were the spirits of the drowned villagers.

Grand Lake began to develop as a resort area in the late 19th century. Gold had been discovered nearby, and the community started out as a supply stop for prospectors heading into the high country. In the early 1900s, well-to-do Western families began building summer homes around the lake (which explains the large expanses of private property in the area), and in 1905, the Grand Lake Yacht Club was founded. Rocky Mountain National Park was dedicated in 1915, and Grand Lake, on the park's western border, once again became a supply point—this time for motorists heading up to camp in the park or to cross over into Estes Park via Trail Ridge Road.

In the early 1950s, Colorado completed its Big Thompson Water Project, an irrigation system providing water to the farms and ranches on the state's eastern plains. In addition to a 13-mile tunnel through the mountains, the project involved a series of reservoirs, including Lake Granby and Shadow Mountain Reservoir. By midcentury, the area was attracting anglers, boaters, and other summer recreation enthusiasts to its three lakes and to the many resort lodges scattered about its woodsy shores.

Kauffman House Museum

Built in 1892, the Kauffman House was one of Grand Lake's first resort hotels, hosting visitors from around the country for nearly 30 years. In 1921, Ezra Kauffman, the log hotel's builder and owner, died, though his wife and family continued to operate it every summer until the end of World War II. The Kauffman House has been restored and is open to the public for tours (summer only), exhibiting artifacts from Grand County's pioneer days.

The Kauffman House is at 407 Pitkin. For hours, phone 970/627-3351, or contact the

Grand Lake Area Chamber of Chamber of Commerce at 970/627-3402 or 800/531-1019.

PARKS AND RECREATION

Rocky Mountain National Park

This is one of the most spectacular national parks in the country, with breathtaking vistas from virtually every point on the main road, and hundreds of miles of backcountry climbing, hiking, and camping. Encompassing more than 265,000 acres, Rocky Mountain National Park is one of the country's true wonders and a must for any traveler who wants to see Colorado at its grandest, and nature at its most spellbinding and wondrous.

Trail Ridge Road, which winds up into the park out of Grand Lake, across the Continental Divide, and down the park's eastern slope to Estes Park, is one of the most scenic drives in the state, offering above-timberline vistas of the Rockies' grandest peaks, more than 70 of which are higher than 12,000 feet. The drive also affords chances to view and photograph a wide array of high-mountain wildlife, including mountain goats, bighorn sheep, elk, moose, black bears, and smaller animals.

view of the west side of Rocky Mountain National Park

Visitors who get away from the roads, though, are the ones who see the park at its best. The park offers nearly unlimited hiking, ranging from short, marked nature trails to extended excursions into the park's most remote areas. Visitor centers at both the park's east and west entrances provide complete information on the park, including history, wildlife, and ecology, as well as hiking, camping, sightseeing, and photography opportunities. The **Kawuneeche Visitors Center** is on the west side of the park just outside the town of Grand Lake. There you'll find books, tape tours, maps, wildlife displays, and rangers to answer any questions you might have. Cost is $15 per car to drive through the park.

For general information on Rocky Mountain National Park, phone 970/586-1206. For a regularly updated recorded message, phone 970/586-1333. (For more detail on the park, see the Rocky Mountain National Park section, below.)

Arapaho National Recreation Area

Adjacent to Rocky Mountain National Park's southwestern boundary, Arapaho National Recreation Area covers 36,000 acres surrounding Lake Granby and a number of smaller lakes. Popular particularly among anglers, the area offers several campgrounds and picnic areas with boat ramps and shoreline access.

One of the nicer campgrounds is **Willow Creek Campground** at Willow Creek Reservoir. Three miles down a well-maintained dirt road, the campground has both RV and walk-in tent sites, and a picnic area and launching ramp. To get there, turn west off U.S. 34 between Granby and Lake Granby (it's well marked). You'll also find picnic areas on the north and south shores of Lake Granby (watch for the signs).

For more information on Arapaho National Recreation Area, phone the Sulphur District Office of Arapaho National Forest in Granby at 970/887-3331.

Indian Peaks Wilderness Area

Bordered on the west by Arapaho National Recreation Area, on the north by Rocky Mountain National Park, and on the east by the Continental

Divide, this triangle-shaped wilderness is very popular with backcountry hikers, backpackers, fishermen, and hunters. Overnight permits are required and usually need to be reserved well in advance. For information, contact the **Sulphur District Office** of Arapaho National Forest in Granby at 970/887-3331.

Fishing

Fishing is one of Grand Lake's main draws. The three lakes, Grand, Lake Granby, and Shadow Mountain Reservoir, hold monster trout and kokanee salmon. Mackinaw (lake) trout running 20–25 pounds are not uncommon (though experienced trout fishermen will tell you that lake trout don't put up nearly the fight that smaller rainbow and cutthroat will, and the latter fish are much more fun to catch).

Because of the amount of private property surrounding the lakes, you're better off in a boat. In addition to the several public launching ramps, you can rent boats from a number of marinas, including **Boater's Choice**, 1246 Lake Ave., 970/627-9273, or **Trail Ridge Marina**, 970/627-3586. **Monarch Guides**, 970/653-4210 or 800/882-3445, offers a range of guided trips on nearby waters—from a "Twilight Bite" trip to four-day floats, and custom excursions.

For tips, tackle, and licenses, stop by **Grand Lake Pharmacy** in downtown Grand Lake, 970/627-3465, **Lakeview General Store** on U.S. 34 in Grand Lake, 970/627-3479, or, along the way, at **Budget Tackle** in Granby or **Nelson's Fly and Tackle Shop** in Tabernash.

Boating

Sailing, windsurfing, and water-skiing are popular on all three lakes, particularly Grand, and public ramps are scattered about the shorelines. At **Boater's Choice**, 11246 Lake Ave., 970/627-9273, you can rent a range of different boats, including paddleboats, by the hour or for half-day or full-day outings. You can also rent boats, or take a tour of the lake, at **Spirit Lake Marina**, 1030 Lake Ave., 970/627-8158, and **Grand Lake Marina**, 1246 Lake Ave., 970/627-3401.

Rafting

White-water rafting is very popular in the Grand Lake area, with many companies offering half-, full-, and multiday trips on nearby rivers, particularly the Colorado. **Monarch Guides River Adventures**, 970/653-4210 or 800/882-3445, is a friendly and professional outfit with offices at 1028 Grand in downtown Grand Lake. Monarch also offers fishing trips (see above).

Golf

Grand Lake Golf Course is an 18-hole course whose greens are carved among tall pines at 8,420 feet. Turn west from U.S. 40 onto County Road 48 just north of the turnoff to Grand Lake. For information and tee times, phone 970/627-8008.

Camping

Surrounded by national forest, park, recreation, and wilderness areas, Grand Lake offers an abundance of camping opportunities, from RV camping (see Camping and RVing, below) to remote and rugged hike-in-only sites. Keep in mind that even though the area is indeed remote, it gets a lot of traffic, and reservations are a good idea. For information or to make reservations to camp in Arapaho National Forest, contact the Sulphur District Office in Granby at 970/887-3331. Contact Rocky Mountain National Park at 16018 U.S. Hwy. 34, Grand Lake, CO 80447, 970/627-3471.

In Arapaho National Recreation Area (see above), there are campgrounds at Willow Creek Reservoir, Meadow Creek Reservoir, and the north and east shores of Lake Granby.

Hiking

Grand Lake itself is literally a trailhead for some of the best hiking in the state. Indian Peaks

lake trout

BOB RACE

NORTH-CENTRAL

Wilderness Area, east of Lake Granby and south of Rocky Mountain National Forest, offers dozens of miles of marked trails. You can walk along lake shoreline, or hike up into the steep backcountry. Topo maps are available from the Forest Service, 970/887-3331, and Grand County has published an excellent recreation guide with maps and contact telephone numbers. Pick up a map at any of the Grand County chambers of commerce or visitor centers, or phone the Forest Service.

Cycling

The Grand Lake Metropolitan Recreation District, in conjunction with Arapaho National Forest and local businesses, has published a mountain-biking map of the Grand Lake area. The excellent guide, which implores riders to "tread lightly," lists more than two dozen different trails (from two to 15 miles long) around the lakes and into the heart of the national forest. Included are degrees of difficulty, lengths, vertical rises, and other useful information. To get a copy of the guide, or for more information, phone the Grand Lake Metropolitan Recreation District at 970/627-8328 or Arapaho National Forest at 970/887-3331.

Horseback Riding

This is a very popular way to explore Arapaho National Forest, Indian Peaks Wilderness Area, and Rocky Mountain National Park. Many of the guest ranches have their own stables and provide both rentals and tours. **Sombrero Ranch,** 970/627-3514, near the turnoff to Grand Lake, offers a range of services, from hourly rentals and evening steak-fry rides to weeklong pack trips. For information on these stables, as well as on other Sombrero Ranches around the state, check out www.sombrero.com.

Cross-Country Skiing

The Three Lakes area is a natural for cross-country skiing, with miles and miles of trails for all ability levels wandering through mountain meadows and deep into steep woods. The **Grand Lake Touring Center** operates at Grand Lake Golf Course with 25 km of track and skating trails.

The center's ski shop offers equipment rentals and lessons; phone 970/627-8008. You can also get information on cross-country skiing by writing the **Grand Lake Metropolitan Recreation District,** P.O. Box 590, Grand Lake, CO 80447.

You'll also find excellent Nordic skiing northwest of Grand Lake in Rocky Mountain National Park. Pick up the free booklet, *Ski Touring in Rocky Mountain National Park,* at the Kawuneeche Visitors Center just north of Grand Lake.

Snowmobiling

Increasing each year in popularity, snowmobiling is a favorite activity of locals and visitors alike. Within minutes/miles of town, snowmobilers can be cruising above the timberline—engines shattering the blissful silence and stillness of the backcountry—where views of the valley below and the sprawling mountains are said to be extraordinary.

The Grand Lake Metropolitan Recreation District publishes the *Grand Lake Snowmobile Trail Map,* which describes nearly 20 different routes. This excellent guide provides directions to trailheads, lengths, specific precautions, and other indispensable information. Write P.O. Box 690, Grand Lake, CO 80447, or phone 970/627-8008.

Rent snowmobiles from **Grand Lake Motor Sports,** 10438 U.S. Hwy. 34, 970/627-3806; **Spirit Lake Rentals,** 970/627-9288; and **On the Trail Snowmobile Rentals,** 970/627-0171.

Other Winter Activities

In addition to offering cross-country skiing and snowmobiling, the Grand Lake area is a favorite of ice fishing enthusiasts and snowshoers. Lake Granby, Grand Lake, and Shadow Mountain Reservoir are all open to ice fishing, and competitions are held annually. For information and equipment stop in at **Lakeview General Store, Grand Lake Pharmacy, Budget Tackle** (in Granby), or **Nelson Fly and Tackle** (in Tabernash). Many of the area's summer hiking trails are ideal for snowshoeing. Pick up maps from the Forest Service or the Grand Lake Chamber of Commerce.

ACCOMMODATIONS

$50–100

The **Bighorn Lodge,** 613 Grand Ave., 970/627-8101 or 800/621-5923, is a modern and very comfortable motel just a couple of blocks from the center of town. Also right downtown is **The Inn at Grand Lake,** 1103 Grand Ave., 970/627-9234 or 800/722-2585.

The **Grand Lake Lodge,** 970/627-3967, sits on the hillside above Grand Lake and affords a gorgeous view of the lake and mountains. The lodge was established in 1920 and is a National Historic Landmark that retains an early-20th-century feel. Cabins scattered about the secluded property start at about $75 a night (for two) and go up to $150 (will sleep six). Roll-away beds are also available for $10. The family-friendly lodge has no TVs, telephones, or radios. Check out the lodge on the website: www.grandlakelodge.com. The **Spirit Lake Lodge,** in town at 829 Grand Ave., 970/627-3344, has one- and two-bedroom units (some with kitchenettes).

Camping and RVing

Shadow Mountain Marina RV Park, 12394 U.S. Hwy. 40, 970/627-9971, which offers full-service RV camping as well as tent camping, is right on the lake. You can also camp at **Winding River Resort Village,** 970/627-3215, where you'll find 150 sites with horseback rides, volleyball, and other activities.

FOOD

A popular breakfast spot for locals and tourists alike is the **Chuckhole Cafe,** 1119 Grand Ave., 970/627-3509, where you can get get omelettes, deep-dish pies, and other fare. Open daily.

A personal favorite is **EG's Garden Grill,** 1000 Grande Ave., 970/627-8404, which serves soups, salads, burgers, and pizzas ($5–8), as well as pastas, trout, and ribs ($8–12). Patio dining available. For Mexican food, try the **Mountain Inn,** 612 Grand Ave., 970/627-3385, serving good and inexpensive *comida.*

In addition, you'll find several boardwalk delis and hamburger stands on Grand Avenue and picnic tables (many near the water) throughout the Grand Lake area. The city park on the boardwalk also has picnic tables and a playground.

ENTERTAINMENT

An evening stroll along the Grand Avenue boardwalk will lead you naturally to the live music, as you hear rock 'n' roll and country wafting through open doors. **EG's Garden Grill,** 1000 Grand Ave., 970/627-8404, regularly features live acoustic music, while **Grumpy's,** 913 Grand Ave., 970/627-3149, offers a bit louder and rowdier fare.

CALENDAR

Every January, Grand Lake hosts its **Winter Carnival,** and in mid-February there's a popular Nordic ski race (10K and 20K). Warm-weather events include Fourth of July fireworks, a parade and buffalo barbecue (late July), the **Lipton Cup Sailing Regatta** (early August), and a couple of golf tournaments (mid-August and early September). For more information, contact the Grand Lake Chamber of Commerce (see Information, below).

SHOPPING

Gift shops, souvenir stores, and art galleries line the two or three blocks that make up downtown Grand Lake Village. Though it's not exactly a shopper's mecca, you can pick up T-shirts and other knickknacks, as well as some quality jewelry and pottery.

SERVICES

Offices of the **Grand Lake Police Department** are at 308 Byers in Hot Sulphur Springs; the local phone number is 970/627-3322. The nearest medical facility is **Timberline Medical Center** at 6281 U.S. Hwy. 40, about a mile from Silver Creek, 970/887-2503. The **post office** in Grand Lake is at 520 Center, 970/627-3340.

Recycling

You can drop off most recyclables at **Grand Recycles** in downtown Grand Lake. For information, phone 970/726-8435.

INFORMATION

An excellent source of information is the **chamber of commerce/tourist information center** on U.S. 34 at the turnoff to downtown Grand Lake. Staff will answer questions about Grand Lake, Grand County, and Rocky Mountain National Park, and you can also pick up helpful brochures and activity guides. Be sure to pick up Grand County's *Sports and Recreation Map,* which has maps of all the nearby communities, as well as various recreation trails (hiking, cross-country skiing, four-wheeling, etc.). You can write the chamber at P.O. Box 57, Grand Lake, CO 80447-0057, or call 970/627-3402 or 970/627-3372. For a vacation planner, phone 800/531-1019. You can also visit the chamber's website at www.grandlakecolorado.com.

Get information on Rocky Mountain National Park from the administrative offices at 16018 U.S. Hwy. 34, or phone 970/586-1206.

Estes Park and Vicinity

Estes Park (pop. 3,200; elev. 7,522 feet) is a resort town at the eastern gate to Rocky Mountain National Park. Surrounded by some of the most gorgeous country in the Rockies, Estes Park is a popular base camp for folks heading up into the high country by tour bus, auto, or hiking boot.

Because Rocky Mountain National Park sees fewer than 5 percent of its visitors in the winter, Estes Park is naturally a summer-oriented town, and many of its lodges, galleries, shops, and other attractions are open only in the warmer months, usually May through September. During those months, though, the town swells with tourists. Sidewalks swarm with souvenir hunters; traffic through town is often bumper to bumper and directed by traffic police; restaurants and cafés are packed; the town's motels and the valley's many lodges and guest ranches are fully booked; even the backcountry trails and campgrounds can get crowded.

Come winter, though, and the closing of Trail Ridge Road (U.S. 34) through the park, most tourists head for more temperate climes, and Estes Park becomes a quiet, laid-back little mountain town. Some lodge owners and gallery operators themselves leave. Other locals, however, know this is the best time to be in the area. Rocky Mountain National Park offers excellent cross-country skiing and snowshoeing, and there's no denying that the Rockies shrouded in snow are at their most visually arresting and spiritually wondrous.

HISTORY

The lush, sprawling mountain valley that is Estes Park was named for cattle rancher Joel Estes, who arrived here with his family in 1859. Though the area, fertile and bountiful, had probably been a hunting ground for nomadic bands of Ute and Arapahoe tribes, the Estes family found few signs of villages or other settlements.

The winter of 1866 was an unusually harsh one, and Estes herded up his clan and cattle and hit the road, heading for warmer climates. The following year, Griffith J. Evans acquired the property and built a handful of cabins that he rented out to travelers, many of whom used the valley as a base camp for ascents of nearby Longs Peak and explorations into what would become Rocky Mountain National Park. One of the area's first visitors was Albert Bierstadt, and travelers familiar with the painter's work will no doubt recognize the inspirations for some of his huge oils.

Another one of Evans's early guests was English nobleman Lord Dunraven. So impressed with the area was Dunraven that he sought to acquire the valley for himself and turn it into a hunting refuge for his fellow aristocrats. However, settlement and land ownership in the valley

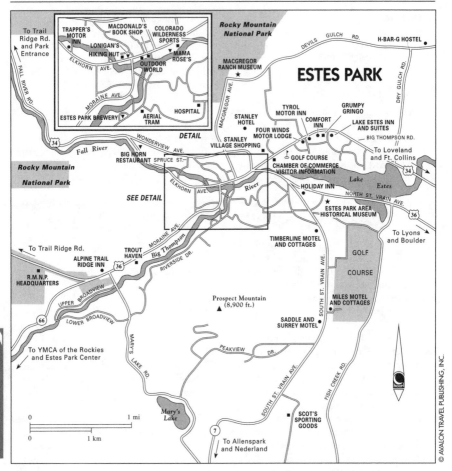

was controlled by the Homestead Law, which allowed only 160 acres of land per person. Quite used to having his own way, Dunraven circumvented the law, engineering a classic land-grab scheme. He had the deeds to all the 160-acre parcels in the valley transferred to "loafers and drifters," and, apparently, to some folks residing in local cemeteries. Dunraven then "bought" the land from its new owners, offering the live ones piddling amounts of cash or, in the cases of the dead ones, simply taking possession of the property. It was then just a matter of paying the government a small transfer fee and registering

what he called the "English Company," a corporation established in England as the Estes Park Company, Ltd.

In 1907, Dunraven sold out to F. O. Stanley and B. D. Sanborn, who split the valley between them. Stanley immediately went to work building the Stanley Hotel and Stanley Manor House. The hotel opened in 1909 and the Manor House the following year.

Stanley, who had invented the Stanley Steamer, ran a line from the closest railroad terminal, 25 miles away in Lyons, to the hotel, and soon began attracting visitors from around the country. With the success of the hotel, a number of other lodges and cabins were built, and Estes Park began to establish a reputation as a premier resort area. In 1915, Rocky Mountain National Park was born, securing Estes Park as a major tourist destination.

SIGHTS
Estes Park Area Historical Museum
This museum displays Estes Valley's history from its first settlers, Joel Estes and family, through the founding of Rocky Mountain National Park and the incorporation of the village of Estes Park. Exhibits and buildings include the original headquarters of Rocky Mountain National Park, a Stanley Steamer, and lots of pioneer artifacts and historical photos. May–Sept., the museum is open Mon.–Sat. 10 A.M.–5 P.M. and Sunday 1–5 P.M.; limited hours the rest of the year. Admission is $2 ($10 will get any size family in).

The Estes Park Area Historical Museum is at 200 4th Street. For more information or to arrange tours, phone 970/586-6256.

MacGregor Ranch Museum and Education Center
The MacGregor is a working ranch commemorating the Alexander Q. MacGregor family, one of the valley's largest and most influential ranching families, and displaying life in Estes Park from the 1870s through the mid-20th century. Exhibits include historical photos and documentation of MacGregor's staunch opposition to Lord Dunraven's land company, as well as family domestic items, including furniture and silver. Cowhands use century-old equipment to display early ranching techniques.

The museum is at the foot of Twin Owls on Devil's Gulch Road about a mile north of Estes Park. Admission is free, donations encouraged. Hours are Tues.–Fri. 10 A.M.–4 P.M., Memorial Day through Labor Day. For more information, phone 970/586-3749.

Enos Mills Cabin
The "Father of Rocky Mountain National Park," Enos Mills was a naturalist, writer, and photog-

rapher who homesteaded in Estes Park in the late 19th century. Mills's small cabin, which he built in 1885 at the base of Twin Sisters Mountain, today operates as a nature center and museum. Docents offer tours of the house, where Mills's books, photos, and other memorabilia are displayed, and nature trails lead out into the 200-acre property. Copies of his books and photographs are sold in the museum's gift shop.

The Enos Mills Cabin is just south of Estes Park on Highway 7. Admission is free. Open Tues.–Sun. 11 A.M.–4 P.M., Memorial Day through Labor Day; by appointment the rest of the year. For more information, phone 970/586-4706 or 970/586-1016.

Lulu Dorsey Museum
At the YMCA of the Rockies, Estes Park Center is a hands-on museum displaying antique children's toys and musical instruments, as well as domestic items of historical interest and historical photos, particularly in relation to the founding of the YMCA of the Rockies (see Lodges and Cabins under Accommodations, below).

The Dorsey Museum is on the grounds of the YMCA at 2515 Tunnel Rd.; open Mon.–Sat. 9 A.M.–4 P.M. and Sunday noon–4 P.M., Memorial Day through Labor Day. Hours the rest of the year are Mon–Sat. 9 A.M.–4 P.M. Admission is free, though a donation of $1 is encouraged. For more information, phone 970/586-3341.

Stanley Hotel
Tours of the Stanley Hotel are regularly scheduled during summer and are available by appointment the rest of the year. Cost is $5. Sign up in the lobby of the hotel. (See also Accommodations, below.)

PARKS AND RECREATION
Rocky Mountain National Park
This is Estes Park's main draw. Every year thousands of tourists use the little village—and its numerous ranches and motels—as a headquarters for exploring the park. (See Rocky Mountain National Park below for complete description.)

NORTH-CENTRAL

Bicycling

This area's ideal for mountain biking, and Roosevelt National Forest's 800,000 acres of public land sprawl east of town, providing lots of excellent trails and logging roads (no off-road riding is permitted in Rocky Mountain National Park).

Some of the area's better rides include Crossier Mountain, near Glen Haven, seven miles north of town; Pole Hill, three miles east of town on U.S. 36; and Pearson and Johnny Parks, south of town on Highway 7.

For maps and more information on cycling in the Estes Park area, stop by the Estes Park Ranger Station at 161 2nd St., 970/586-3440, or write Roosevelt National Forest, 240 W. Prospect, Fort Collins, CO 80526, 970/498-1100.

For guided bicycle tours of Rocky Mountain National Park, contact **Colorado Bicycling Adventures,** 184 E. Elkhorn Ave., 970/586-4241, website www.colorado bicycling.com.

Golf

The Estes Valley Recreation and Park District maintains two golf courses. The 18-hole **Estes Park Golf Course,** which dates from 1912, is one of the oldest courses in the state. At 1080 S. Saint Vrain, the course sprawls through woods at nearly 8,000 feet above sea level. Green fees are about $35. For tee times and information, phone 970/586-8146. **Lake Estes Executive Golf Course** is a nine-hole course along the banks of the Thompson River, 690 Big Thompson Ave., 970/586-8176. Green fees are about $12.

Hiking

The Estes Park area is a heaven on earth for hikers, abounding in nature trails to walk, woods to explore, and peaks to climb. The best hiking is in Rocky Mountain National Park, which offers scores of trails with a full range of lengths and difficulty levels. (See complete section on Rocky Mountain National Park, below.) In addition, Roosevelt National Forest offers excellent backcountry hiking. Topo maps and information on hiking in the national forest are available from the main office at 240 W. Prospect, Fort Collins, CO 80526, 970/498-1100, or locally at 161

2nd St., 970/586-3440. You can also get information, as well as quality equipment, from **Outdoor World,** 156 E. Elkhorn, 970/586-2114.

The **Colorado Mountain Club** has been sponsoring hikes in the Estes Park area since before World War I, and runs about 2,000 outings a year. Free literature about the club, including information on hikes, meeting places, degrees of difficulty, etc., is available by phoning 970/586-6623. You can also get information from its Denver office, 2530 W. Alameda Ave., Denver, CO 80219, 970/922-8315. The Colorado Mountain Club publishes a monthly newsletter, *Trail and Timberline,* which lists upcoming outings, reviews books on mountains and mountaineering, and tackles sensitive environmental issues.

If you're surfing the Web, you might check out the website for **Mike's Hikes** at www.mtnds.com/hikes/main.asp. This is a fun, lighthearted site that provides information on various hikes and trails in Rocky Mountain National Park and also offers opportunity for hiker feedback and communication.

Fishing

Fishing in the Estes Park area varies from pay-by-the-inch trout farms where no license is required to remote backcountry lakes and streams where wily native trout elude all but the most skilled and patient angler. And of course the scenic rewards of hiking into an isolated lake in Rocky Mountain National Park, even if you get skunked, are far greater for most people than hauling hatchery lunkers from highway-side lagoons.

If you're looking for guarantees, though, you have at least a couple of options. **Trout Haven,** about a mile west of Estes Park on U.S. 36, 970/586-2955, and **Rock 'n' River Trout Farm,** about 15 miles southeast of town on U.S. 36, stock their ponds with rainbows up to 26 inches. Open daily till dusk April 1 through mid-October.

For anglers looking for more of a challenge, the Big Thompson River east of Estes Park offers good trout fishing and decent-size fish. Some stretches are designated artificial lures and flies only. (Always double-check local restrictions.) You can also fish (and picnic) just below the dam at the east end of Lake Estes. An excellent source of information and equipment is **Scot's Sporting Goods,** 2325 Spruce Ave., 970/586-2877.

For information on fishing in Roosevelt National Forest, stop by the district office at 161 2nd St., 970/586-3440. For guided fly-fishing trips in the area, contact **Renegade Outfitters,** 303/404-0333. It specializes in trips in Rocky Mountain National Park, and it provides all equipment and supplies.

Rafting

As in most mountain resort towns, white-water rafting is big here, and several companies offer a range of trips down local rivers. Adult rates for half-day trips usually run between $30 and $40, and full-day trips between $50 and $60. You can arrange trips with **Rapid Transit Rafting,** P.O. Box 4095, Estes Park, CO 80517, 970/586-8852 or 800/367-8523; **Mad Adventures,** 970/726-5290 or 800/451-4844; and **Colorado Wilderness Sports,** 358 E. Elkhorn, 970/586-6548 or 800/504-6642.

Horseback Riding

This is a popular way to explore both Rocky Mountain National Park and Roosevelt National Forest, and several outfitters in the area offer tours and rentals. **Hi Country Stables,** with two centers within the boundaries of Rocky Mountain National Park, runs a range of tours into some of the park's most scenic spots, including Bierstadt and Bear Lakes. Rates range from about $35 for a two-hour ride to $80 for eight hours. Phone 970/586-2327. **Sombrero Ranch** offers several types of rides, from one-hour to several-day pack trips, and pancake breakfast and evening chuckwagon rides. For information and reservations, phone 970/586-4577. **Elkhorn Stables** also offers rides, ranging from one to eight hours, some with meals. Phone 970/586-5225.

Tram Rides

For a bird's-eye view of the Estes Park Valley, and of towering Longs Peak and other Rocky Mountain National Park peaks, take the 12-passenger aerial tram to the summit of Prospect Mountain (elev. 8,800 feet). Check out the gift shop and snack bar at the top; open daily mid-May through mid-September, 9 A.M.–6:30 P.M. Fare is $10 for adults, with discounts for kids and seniors. The base of the tram and ticket office are at 420 E. Riverside Drive. For rates and more information, phone 970/586-3675.

Cross-Country Skiing

Most visitors to Estes Park come to hike the nearby trails and explore Rocky Mountain National Park backcountry under a warm summer sun. Yet some of those very same trails and woods also offer excellent opportunities for Nordic skiers. The best cross-country skiing is in the park (see Rocky Mountain National Park, below), although Roosevelt National Forest also has hundreds of square miles of picture-book Nordic terrain. Get maps and information from the Forest Service District Office at 161 2nd St., 970/586-3440; rent equipment and get expert advice from **Colorado Wilderness Sports,** 358 E. Elkhorn, 970/586-6548. Another excellent source of information on cross-country skiing in the area is the **Colorado Mountain Club,** 970/586-6623, which sponsors 2,000 hiking and cross-country skiing trips a year and publishes literature on trails and specific areas.

ACCOMMODATIONS

If you're new to Estes Park, you'll be amazed at the number of inns, lodges, motels, cabins, hotels, and combinations thereof. With its ideal location adjacent to Rocky Mountain National Park, Estes Park has zillions of rooms and campsites available for passers-through, as well as for travelers who want to use the town as a base to do some exploring in the area. For complete listings of available lodging, contact the Estes Park Chamber of Commerce, which publishes several accommodations guides to the area. Its toll-free telephone number is 800/44-ESTES (443-7837).

Stanley Hotel

Of the first-class lodges in the Rockies, the Stanley Hotel, 970/586-3371 or 800/ROCKIES (762-5437), is without doubt one of the most elegant and glorious. Standing high on the hillside, castlelike, and looking out over the town, the valley, and west toward the towering Rockies, the Stanley seems to cast a cynical eye over the rest of Estes Park and some of its more touristy trappings and Johnny-come-lately attendants. First opened in 1909, after three years' construction, the Stanley was the brainchild of F. O. Stanley, whose guests arrived at the lodge via Stanley Steamer, which he invented. At the time, the Stanley was known as one of the most luxurious hotels in the West, and in addition to its fancy furnishings offered guests a golf course, stables, bowling, billiards, and theater.

Though some people claim the hotel was used in the Stanley Kubrick film *The Shining,* anyone who's seen both the movie and the hotel can tell you this isn't true. It is true, however, that the hotel inspired one of its guests, Stephen King, to write the novel upon which the film was based. The filming crew, faced with a lack of snow at the Stanley, shot the movie at the Timberline Lodge on Oregon's Mt. Hood. It's also true that a 1996 made-for-television miniseries, *The Shining,* was filmed at the Stanley, although the crew had to truck snow in from Nederland (after which, of course, it snowed heavily).

During the late 1980s and early 1990s, the Stanley ran into tough times, with the owner finally filing Chapter 11. In May of 1995, the hotel was acquired by the Grand Heritage Hotel chain, whose luxury hotels are scattered about the globe—San Francisco, Paris, London—and the late 1990s saw the Grand Heritage mount an aggressive campaign to restore both the hotel and its reputation, beginning with $3 million in renovations. Then, in early 2000, the lodge was sold to the Chesapeake Hotel chain, which has continued the effort to restore dignity to the old hotel. Doubles run about $250–300 in high season, $160–220 in low.

Under $50

The **H-Bar-G Hostel,** 970/586-3688, is a member of the American Youth Hostel system and provides the least expensive lodging in the area ($8 for members, slightly more for nonmembers). Open summers only, the H-Bar-G is just north of Estes Park with a variety of hiking trails leading from the property into Roosevelt National Forest. In addition, the hostel has tennis and volleyball courts and a game room. Write: H-Bar-G Ranch Hostel, 3500 H-Bar-G Rd., Estes Park.

$50–100

You'll find bizillions of motels in Estes Park, though that shouldn't keep you from making reservations, especially in the height of the summer. Competition keeps the rates, well, competitive; doubles for all of the following lodgings run from around $80 to a little over $100.

Try the **Trappers Motor Inn,** 553 W. Elkhorn, 970/586-2833; the **Alpine Trail Ridge Inn,** 927 Moraine Ave., 970/586-4585 or 800/233-5023 (some with kitchens); **Lake Estes Inn and Suites,** 1040 Big Thompson Ave., 970/586-3386; the **Tyrol Motor Inn,** 1240 Big Thompson, 970/586-3382; the **Four Winds Motor Lodge,** 1120 Big Thompson, 970/586-3313; or the **Saddle and Surrey Motel,** 1341 S. St. Vrain, 970/586-3326.

$100–150

One of the most unusual lodges in the area is **Estes Park Center, YMCA of the Rockies,** 970/586-3341 or 800/228-3947 (in Colorado). Like its sister, Snow Mountain Resort (see Winter Park, above), this is a sprawling, self-contained resort complex offering a huge range of lodging options, facilities, and amenities. Situated on 1,400 acres adjacent to Rocky Mountain National Park, the Estes Park Center has furnished two- and four-bedroom cabins as well as a variety of lodge-style rooms. Activities include hiking, horseback riding, tennis, cross-country skiing, and snow tubing. Perfect for families, the lodge has lots of kid-oriented programs, as well as its own library, museum, grocery store, and gift shop. Rates range $50–125 for rooms in the lodge and $70–250 for cabins. For reservations, write YMCA of the Rockies, Estes Park, CO 80511-2550.

Last time I passed through Estes Park, I stayed at the **Miles Motel and Cottages,** 1250 S. St. Vrain, 970/586-3185, and was impressed with the convenient location and the gracious hosts—the property also has a swimming pool and a large four-bedroom, two-bath cabin that sleeps 10.

The **Deer Crest,** a mile west of town at 1200 Fall River Rd. (U.S. 34), 970/586-2324 or 800/331-2324, has rooms and cottages on the Fall River.

The **Holiday Inn, 101 S. St. Vrain (at the junction of U.S. 36 and Highway 7),** 970/586-2332, offers meeting and convention facilities.

Camping and RVing

Estes Park is surrounded by public campgrounds, administered either by the National Park Service or the Forest Service. **Olive Ridge Campground** is in Roosevelt National Forest about eight miles south of Estes Park on Highway 7 (see Rocky Mountain National Park, below, for camping information).

Privately administered RV campgrounds, generally open May–Sept., include a **KOA,** two miles east of town on U.S. 34, 970/586-2888; **Park Place Camping Resort,** six miles southeast of Estes Park on U.S. 36 (also cabins), 970/586-4230; **National Park Campground and Resort,** right at the park's Fall River entrance, 970/586-4563; and **Estes Park Campground,** about five miles southwest of Estes Park on Highway 66, 970/586-4188.

Campers will want to keep in mind that **public showers** are available at Dad's Maytag Laundry, 970/586-9847, in the Upper Stanley Village Center.

FOOD

A resort town catering to free-spending passersthrough, Estes Park is packed with cafés and restaurants. A local breakfast favorite, **Bighorn Restaurant,** 401 W. Elkhorn, 970/586-2792, is open daily at 6 A.M. and serves breakfast burritos, omelettes, pancakes, and egg dishes. The outdoor seating, weather permitting, is especially pleasant. The **Notchtop Natural Foods Cafe,** in the Stanley Village Shopping Center (459 E. Wonderview), 970/586-0272, specializes in health-oriented breakfasts, including fat-free muffins, veggie omelettes, and "tofu scramble." It's also got excellent espresso

drinks and a cozy atmosphere, with board games and several different newspapers available for customers.

Another local favorite is the **Estes Park Brewery,** 470 Prospect (turn left onto Moraine as you're heading west on U.S. 34), 970/586-5421. Free samples of the beer, plus beer to go, as well as sandwiches, burgers, and salads are served upstairs above the brewery.

For excellent margaritas and first-rate, inexpensive Mexican food, try **Grumpy Gringo,** 1560 Big Thompson/Hwy. 36, 970/586-7705, a favorite among locals and tourists alike. Dinner will run you $6–12.

A nice Italian restaurant, with outdoor seating when weather permits, is **Mama Rose's,** 338 E. Elkhorn, 970/586-3330. Here classic Italian entrées run $9–14, while pasta dishes run about $7–9. Another favorite for Italian food is the **Dunraven Inn,** 2470 Hwy. 66, 970/586-6409, which calls itself the "Rome of the Rockies." About seven miles south of town at 4900 S. Hwy. 7, the **Baldpate Inn,** 970/586-6151, has a reputation for excellent food, particularly the soup-and-salad buffet and homemade breads and pies. The Baldpate also offers bed-and-breakfast accommodations.

If you're looking for picnic fixin's before heading up into Rocky Mountain National Park, stop at the **Safeway** on the hill above downtown, where you'll find a deli and salad bar.

ENTERTAINMENT

Lonigan's, 110 W. Elkhorn, 970/586-4346, features live music off and on through the week, with acoustic music on Tuesday and Friday and Saturday evenings devoted to rock 'n' roll, blues, and dancing.

The **Stanley Hotel,** 970/586-3371, offers a wide range of music, including a summer music festival and Friday-night big-band dancing. For a classic Colorado chuck-wagon supper served with Western music and cowboy comedy, try the **Lazy B Ranch,** 1915 Dry Gulch Rd., 970/586-5371. Dinner and show will run you about $15—less for kids and seniors. Call for schedule and reservations.

Serenading the Mountains

If you feel like some lung exercise, head downtown to the park (at West Elk and Park), where on weekend summer evenings (Thurs.–Sun. at 7:30 and 8:30 P.M.) you can join a sing-along with other visitors from around the world.

CALENDAR

Estes Park has a rather idiosyncratic lineup of annual events, varying from the proverbial fireworks-over-the-lake on the Fourth of July to a wild Celtic celebration. Though there are a handful of wintertime affairs, including the **Estes Park Snow Festival** in late March, things don't really kick off until early June, when Trail Ridge Road through Rocky Mountain National Park traditionally opens. The Stanley Hotel hosts a variety of music throughout the summer, most notably the classical **Summer Concert Series;** phone 970/586-3371 for information. The YMCA of the Rockies sponsors its **Summerfest Concert Series,** with music varying from classical to jazz to bluegrass; phone 970/586-3341.

Fall's highlight is the two-day Celtic fair in September. Officially known as the **Longs Peak Scottish Fair,** it usually draws 20,000 people and features a parade (with more than two dozen bagpipe bands), athletic competitions (including the hammer and tree-trunk tosses), and a general craziness that usually lasts into the wee hours. For complete information, phone 970/586-6308. For more information on Estes Park's wide range of annual events, phone the chamber of commerce at 800/44-ESTES (443-7837).

SHOPPING

Estes Park has one of the state's largest concentrations of gift shops and galleries, selling gifts and souvenirs varying from hopelessly tacky to museum quality. You'll find lots of Native American art, photos and renderings in various other media of Rocky Mountain National Park, as well as Christmas stores, boutiques, and jewelers. Part of the fun is simply wandering around the village, poking your head into the various shops.

A handful of the galleries are particularly worth checking out. The **Art Center,** in the lower level of Stanley Village, features a wide range of quality art, with exhibits changing monthly. The center also offers classes and demonstrations. The **Ricker-Bartlett Casting Studios and Museum,** two miles east of town on U.S. 34, is the world's largest pewter-casting studio. Pieces from the studio have been presented to several U.S. presidents, and some are in the Smithsonian Institution. Among the displays is a 300-square-foot re-creation of an American small town at the turn of the 20th century. Phone 970/586-2030 or 800/373-9837 for complete information.

The **Charles Eagle Plume Gallery and Museum of Native American Arts,** 10 miles south of Estes Park at 9843 Hwy. 7, has been around since 1917 and has a huge collection of baskets, jewelry, rugs, and other art and artifacts on display and for sale. Charles Eagle Plume, the shop's owner and curator, graduated from the University of Colorado in 1932 and was active in Native American rights for the better part of the 20th century. Eagle Plume has been awarded an honorary Doctorate of Humanities from the University of Colorado. The museum and gallery are open summers only. Phone 970/747-2861 for more information.

The **Fine Arts Guild of the Rockies** publishes the *Estes Park Gallery Guide,* which lists about 20 galleries and shops in town. Write the guild at P.O. Box 1165, Estes Park, CO 80517, or phone the chamber of commerce at 970/586-4431 or 800/44-ESTES (443-7837).

SERVICES

The offices of the **Estes Park Police Department** are at 170 MacGregor; phone 970/586-5331. Phone the **Larimer County Sheriff** at 970/586-9511 and the **State Patrol** at 970/484-4020 (Fort Collins). **Estes Park Medical Center** is at 555 Prospect, 970/586-2317. The **post office** is at 215 W. Riverside, 970/586-8177.

Recycling

The transfer station for **Estes Park Recycling Center** is on Elm Road and will take aluminum, glass, and newspaper. For information, phone 970/586-3772.

INFORMATION

An excellent place to begin your visit to Estes Park is at the chamber of commerce's **visitor information center,** at 500 Big Thompson Avenue. You'll find tons of info on Estes, the surrounding area, and Rocky Mountain National Park. You can also write the chamber at P.O. Box 3050, Estes Park, CO 80517, or call 970/586-4431 or 800/443-7837. The **public library** is at 225 E. Elkhorn, 970/586-8116. **MacDonald Book Shop,** 152 E. Elkhorn, 970/586-3450, has a good selection of books on Rocky Mountain National Park, the Estes Park area, and Colorado.

Several websites have been set up to help folks plan their vacations here. You can find them by doing a search for Estes Park Colorado, or go to www.estesparkresort.com, which I found to be the most useful and thorough.

For information on Rocky Mountain National Park, phone the headquarters at 970/586-1206.

For **road and weather information** phone 970/586-4000.

TRANSPORTATION

Estes Park is situated at the junctions of U.S. 34 and U.S. 36 and Highway 7, making it approachable from the south, east, and west (except during the winter, when U.S. 34 to the west, through Rocky Mountain National Park, is closed). **Estes Park Shuttle and Mountain Tours,** 970/586-5151, offers daily service between Estes Park and Denver International Airport; round-trip fares run about $70.

SOUTH OF ESTES PARK

Highway 7 drops south out of Estes Park, paralleling the eastern border of Rocky Mountain National Park for about 18 miles. Affording excellent views, both of the park (particularly Longs Peak) and of the valley to the east, the route has several places worth stopping along the way. The stretch from Estes Park south to Central City, which includes Highways 7, 72 through Nederland, and 119, has been designated the **Peak to Peak Highway** and offers breathtaking vistas and panoramas around virtually every turn.

About five miles out of Estes Park is **Lilly Lake Picnic Area,** a day-use-only area administered by Roosevelt National Forest. In addition to picnicking, you can explore the shores of this lovely little alpine lake via a number of hiking trails that begin near the parking lot.

A couple of miles south of Lilly Lake is **Twin Sisters Trailhead,** which leads to Twin Sisters Peak (elev. 11,248 feet) in a small isolated unit of Rocky Mountain National Park east of the highway.

Longs Peak Campground (in Rocky Mountain National Park) is about nine miles south of Estes Park. The campground is designated for tents only. Between Longs Peak Campground and Allenspark (about seven miles), you'll find several Rocky Mountain National Park trailheads, including access to Wild Basin. A mile north of Allenspark is Roosevelt National Forest's **Olive Ridge Campground** (56 sites, pit toilets, no showers).

Allenspark and Ferncliff are two quaint little towns just off the highway at the southeastern edge of Rocky Mountain National Park. The **Allenspark Lodge Bed and Breakfast,** 303/747-2552, is a rustic old inn that would be perfect for one of those occasionally mandatory getaways when you just want to shut out the world and not let *anyone* know where you are. It has 13 rooms and one small apartment— $65–135.

Four miles south of Allenspark the road arcs east, and you can either continue to Lyons or catch Highway 72 south for Nederland, where you can shoot into Boulder the back way.

Rocky Mountain National Park

Without doubt one of the most gorgeous and breathtaking of Colorado's natural wonders, Rocky Mountain National Park includes more than 265,000 acres of towering peaks, rolling alpine meadows, pristine lakes, and dense forests of aspen, fir, spruce, and pine. A paradise for hikers, backpackers, mountain climbers, and sightseers, the park attracts nearly three million visitors a year, the greatest percentage of whom come between May and October as the main road through the park (see Driving through the Park, below) is closed in winter.

A microcosm of the greater Rocky Mountains' geology, Rocky Mountain National Park is like a giant wedge of cheese, gently sloping up from the west, then dropping dramatically at the Front Range to the flatlands below. Within the boundaries of the park are more than 75 peaks towering 12,000 feet or more above sea level, including several over 13,000. The highest point in the park is Longs Peak, at 14,255 feet. Trail Ridge Road, the main road through the park, passes through 12,000-foot-high meadows, with wildflowers and grasses waving softly in mountain breezes. Five small alpine glaciers, vestiges of the great ice floes that carved valleys and lakes from the heaving mountains, remain within the park's boundaries.

Not surprisingly, the park is full of wildlife: bighorn sheep, mountain goats, elk, deer, bear, and many smaller animals, from marmots and beavers to coyotes and mountain lions. Thankfully, no hunting is allowed.

History

Rocky Mountain National Park's history dates from just after the turn of the 20th century, when naturalist, writer, and photographer Enos Mills, who had been living in a small cabin just outside Estes, began a campaign to protect the land. Although Mills soon had enough support to convince the federal government to set aside some land, the first designation was as a national forest. But conservationists were not yet satisfied. A small but vocal group, led by the newly founded Colorado Mountain Club, sought national park status, against the wishes of the Forest Service and landowners.

The group, led by Mills, and the club, got its way. In January 1915 the land was officially designated Rocky Mountain National Park.

One of the park's most influential administrators was its third superintendent, Roger Toll, who took office in 1920. Toll, an avid mountain climber and preservationist, made first ascents of many of the park's peaks and wrote the park's first climbing guide, *Mountaineering in Rocky Mountain National Park* (Department of the Interior), as well as the classic *The Mountain Peaks of Colorado* (Colorado Mountain Club). Toll also oversaw construction of Bear Lake Road (1920), Trail Ridge Road (1932), and many of the park's first trails, which opened up much of the backcountry to visitors. Toll served until 1936, when he was killed in a car crash en route to Mexico to consult with U.S. and Mexican authorities about establishing game preserves along the border. In 1940, the name of Ute Horn was changed to Mt. Toll, and in 1941, the Toll Memorial was erected on Sundance Mountain near Trail Ridge Road.

VISITOR CENTERS

There are excellent visitor centers at both the east and west entrances to Rocky Mountain National Park, as well as at the summit of Trail Ridge Road. You'll find a wide range of books, maps, and brochures, as well as staff members to answer all questions. The **Park Headquarters/Beaver Meadows Visitors Center** is on U.S. 36 just west of Estes Park, 970/586-1206. Also on the Estes Park side is the **Moraine Park Museum,** 970/586-3777, where you can study the park's geology, history, and wildlife, and take a hike on a half-mile, self-guided nature trail. The museum is open mid-May to September.

The **Kawuneeche Visitors Center,** 970/627-3471, is on the park's west side just north of Grand Lake. The **Alpine Visitors Center,**

© STEPHEN METZGER

Rocky Mountain National Park's Trail Ridge Road rises well above the treeline on its 12,183-foot summit.

970/586-4927, is near the top of Trail Ridge Road at Fall River Pass (elev. 11,796 feet) in the heart of the park. You'll find exhibits about the surrounding alpine tundra, plus other park information. Closed in winter.

DRIVING THROUGH THE PARK

The main road through Rocky Mountain National Park is **Trail Ridge Road,** a 48-mile stretch of highway that offers some of the most spectacular scenery on the planet. Its summit at 12,183 feet, Trail Ridge Road lifts past the treeline and meanders along the ridgetop through meadows of alpine tundra. Allow three to four hours, as along the way you'll want to get out of your car to take pictures or simply appreciate the scenery. There are also several short hikes to scenic overlooks.

Old Fall River Road is the original road through the park. Completed in 1920, the one-way (east-to-west) 11-mile gravel road parallels

The main road through Rocky Mountain National Park is Trail Ridge Road, a 48-mile stretch of highway that offers some of the most spectacular scenery on the planet.

Trail Ridge Road from Endovalley to the Alpine Visitors Center. Don't expect the sweeping panoramas you get on Trail Ridge. Motor homes longer than 25 feet and trailers are not allowed.

Bear Lake Road leads from the Moraine Park Museum to Bear Lake, where a number of trails lead to waterfalls and other lakes. The road is paved and gets a lot of traffic, and the parking lot at the lake is usually full in the summer in midday. To avoid parking hassles, you can take a Park Service shuttle from Glacier Basin Campground, about three miles past the museum (watch for the signs).

At the visitor centers you can pick up cassette tapes with recorded information on the drive through the park. The narrator points out areas of geological and historical interest, and also discusses regional wildlife and Native American legends. Tapes cost about $12 and include maps. They're available at the park visitor centers, as well as at gift shops in Estes Park.

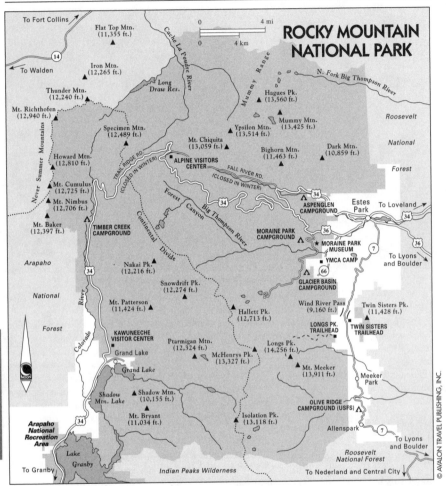

ROCKY MOUNTAIN NATIONAL PARK

To Fort Collins

Flat Top Mtn.
(11,355 ft.)

14

To Walden

Iron Mtn.
(12,265 ft.)

Thunder Mtn.
(12,240 ft.)

Mt. Richthofen
(12,940 ft.)

Long
Draw Res.

Cache La Poudre River

Mummy Range

N. Fork Big Thompson River

Roosevelt

Hagues Pk.
(13,560 ft.)

Mummy Mtn.
(13,425 ft.)

National

Ypsilon Mtn.
(13,514 ft.)

Specimen Mtn.
(12,489 ft.)

Mt. Chiquita
(13,059 ft.)

Bighorn Mtn.
(11,463 ft.)

Dark Mtn.
(10,859 ft.)

Forest

Howard Mtn.
(12,810 ft.)

ALPINE VISITORS CENTER

TRAIL RIDGE RD. (CLOSED IN WINTER)

FALL RIVER RD.
(CLOSED IN WINTER)

34

34

Mt. Cumulus
(12,725 ft.)

Mt. Nimbus
(12,706 ft.)

Mt. Baker
(12,397 ft.)

TIMBER CREEK CAMPGROUND

Forest Canyon

Big Thompson River

Continental Divide

ASPENGLEN CAMPGROUND

Estes Park

To Loveland

34

To Lyons and Boulder

36

36

MORAINE PARK CAMPGROUND

MORAINE PARK MUSEUM

YMCA CAMP

7

Arapaho

National

Forest

Nakai Pk.
(12,216 ft.)

Snowdrift Pk.
(12,274 ft.)

Mt. Patterson
(11,424 ft.)

Hallett Pk.
(12,713 ft.)

66

GLACIER BASIN CAMPGROUND

Wind River Pass
(9,160 ft.)

Twin Sisters Pk.
(11,428 ft.)

LONGS PK. TRAILHEAD

TWIN SISTERS TRAILHEAD

34

River

KAWUNEECHE VISITOR CENTER

Grand Lake

Ptarmigan Mtn.
(12,324 ft.)

McHenrys Pk.
(13,327 ft.)

Longs Pk.
(14,256 ft.)

Mt. Meeker
(13,911 ft.)

Meeker Park

Colorado

Grand Lake

Shadow Mtn. Lake

Shadow Mtn.
(10,155 ft.)

Mt. Bryant
(11,034 ft.)

Isolation Pk.
(13,118 ft.)

OLIVE RIDGE CAMPGROUND (USFS)

Allenspark

7

To Lyons and Boulder

Arapaho National Recreation Area

34

Lake Granby

To Granby

Indian Peaks Wilderness

Roosevelt National Forest

To Nederland and Central City

HIKING AND BACKPACKING

You could spend a lifetime exploring the trails and backcountry of Rocky Mountain National Park (and some folks have). More than 350 miles of marked trails weave in and out of forests and meadows, up mountainsides, and along meandering streams. They vary from short paths between parking lots and scenic overlooks to trails that cross the park from one side to the other, *over* the Continental Divide. Your best bet is to stop in at one of the visitor centers to check out the several available hiking guides. They vary from the brief Park Service-published brochure to full-blown books with maps, charts, descriptions, difficulty levels, and any information you could possibly need. A popular (very!) short hike is the half-miler around **Bear Lake.** Take Bear Lake Road to the trailhead. In addition to the short Bear Lake Trail, several other hikes of varying lengths and degrees of difficulty begin here.

The **Sprague Lake Five Senses Trail** is specifically designed with disabled visitors in mind; the half-mile trail is level, wide enough to accommodate wheelchairs, and encourages appreciation of the park, and nature, through all five senses. Take Bear Lake Road about three miles past the Moraine Park Museum.

Just west of the Fall River Entrance Station (on U.S. 34), you'll find a turnoff to Aspenglen Campground. Several trails wander through this lush valley and along the Fall River (this is before the road begins to climb to Trail Ridge). Hiking and nature trails are also at all the visitor centers.

At the other end of the spectrum are the **Longs Peak trails.** The highest peak in the park (elev. 14,255 feet), Longs can be reached by at least two routes. The most popular is the main trail from the Longs Peak trailhead, south of Estes Park just off Highway 7. The 16-mile round-trip is for experienced hikers only, although no climbing equipment is generally needed in July and August; allow about 12 hours. **Note:** the Park Service recommends getting an early start and being on your way down by early afternoon to avoid the almost-every-afternoon summer storms.

Remember, too, that hiking in Rocky Mountain National Park is serious business, and even though you don't need a permit for a day hike, you should always let someone else know where you're going and when you expect to return. Backcountry hiking is limited to seven nights June–Sept. (15 nights the rest of the year). Camp in designated areas only, unless authorized by permit, available at the visitor centers, 970/586-1242.

Camping

Rocky Mountain National Park has five campgrounds. **Longs Peak, Moraine Park, Glacier Basin,** and **Aspenglen** are out of Estes Park on the east side of Fall River Pass; **Timber Creek Campground** is on the west side, out of Grand Lake. Not one of the campgrounds has electrical outlets or water or sewer connections, and all are full by noon (earlier in June, July, and August). Longs Peak Campground is designated tents only, and stays are limited to three days. You can camp up to seven days at the others.

Permits to camp in the backcountry are available at the visitor centers. Be sure to read regulations carefully and to follow them closely. They're designed for your safety and the health of the park. For more information, phone park headquarters at 970/586-1206.

CROSS-COUNTRY SKIING

The lower valleys of Rocky Mountain National Park are perfect for exploring on cross-country skis, and roads to several of the lower trailheads are plowed throughout the winter. Moraine Park, Longs Peak, and Timber Creek campgrounds are open year-round, providing access to a wide range of excellent trails and woodsy backcountry. There are also trails at Glacier Basin Campground and at Bear Lake.

For more information on cross-country skiing in Rocky Mountain National Park, stop by **Colorado Wilderness Sports,** 358 E. Elkhorn in Estes Park, 970/586-6548. You can also get information from the **Colorado Mountain Club,** 970/586-6623. The club, founded in 1912 as an offshoot of the Colorado Mountain Climbing Club (itself founded in 1896), sponsors a wide range of trips into the park each season.

INFORMATION

For more information, write Rocky Mountain National Park, Estes Park, CO 80517. You can also phone 970/586-1206 (headquarters), 970/586-1333 (recorded information), or 970/586-1242 (backcountry office).

In your car, tune your radio to AM 1610 for recorded visitor information.

Greeley and Vicinity

Near the confluence of the Cache La Poudre and South Platte Rivers about 60 miles north of Denver, Greeley (pop. 78,000; elev. 4,663 feet) is a proud and civic-minded community whose roots are in cattle ranching and agriculture. Weld County, of which Greeley is the seat, comprises two million acres and ranks fourth in the nation and first in the state in the value of its agricultural products, primarily corn, wheat, and alfalfa.

Greeley is home to the University of Northern Colorado as well as the summer training camp of the Denver Broncos. Several Fortune 500 companies, including Hewlett-Packard and Eastman Kodak, have facilities nearby. Greeley's size and western plains location ensure a laid-back, small-town lifestyle and a relatively mild climate. At the same time, it's just an hour from Denver nightlife or the rugged backcountry of Rocky Mountain National Park.

In 1989, Greeley scored a major coup. In May of that year it was selected as one of the 10 All-American Cities by the National Civic League of Chicago. Focusing primarily on the candidates' senses of community, the program seeks "to encourage and recognize civic excellence." Among the 10 judging criteria are citizen participation, community leadership, government performance, volunteerism, and civic education.

Walking the streets of Greeley, you can see it. There's a genuine wholesomeness and classic Western friendliness here. And there's also a clear sense that folks who live here are proud of themselves and their community, and that they wouldn't live anywhere else.

History

Greeley was named for *New York Tribune* editor Horace Greeley, who visited Colorado Territory in 1859 and returned with his exhortation, "Go West, young man, and grow with the country." Impressed by the land's immense potential for farming, Greeley, along with his agriculture editor, Nathan Meeker, campaigned to establish a utopian community in Colorado based on religion, temperance, and cooperative farming. According to the WPA's 1930 Colorado guidebook, Meeker circulated flyers and advertised in eastern papers, emphasizing that "the idle, immoral, intemperate, or inefficient need not apply." In 1869, Meeker bought 12,000 acres of land on the banks of the Cache La Poudre River in the South Platte Valley, with provisional title to another 60,000. The following year he led a group of 50 New England families to the site, traveling from Cheyenne on the newly completed Denver Pacific Railroad. There the group established the Union Colony, each member paying $5 to belong and $150 for no more than 160 acres of land. A 100-by-150-foot townsite was also laid out.

Work began immediately on housing and irrigation ditches, though one of the first construction projects on the agenda was a church, in which services were held within two weeks of the colonists' arrival. One of the new community's commandments was, "Thou shalt not sell liquid damnation within the lines of Union Colony."

By the mid-1870s, homes, stores, and office buildings had been built, and water was being run into the fields to irrigate tomatoes, potatoes, melons, cucumbers, and fruit trees. In October of that year, Horace Greeley visited for the first time the town that had taken his name.

In 1877, Greeley was designated seat of old Weld County, which included almost all of what is now northeastern Colorado, including Logan, Washington, Morgan, Sedgwick, Phillips, and Yuma Counties. Weld County, named for Lewis Leyard Weld, whom Abraham Lincoln appointed Colorado Territory's first Secretary in 1861, was reduced to its present size in 1899.

During the last quarter of the 19th century and into the 20th, Greeley began to grow proportionately more potatoes, and "Greeley Spuds" earned a national reputation. In addition, the

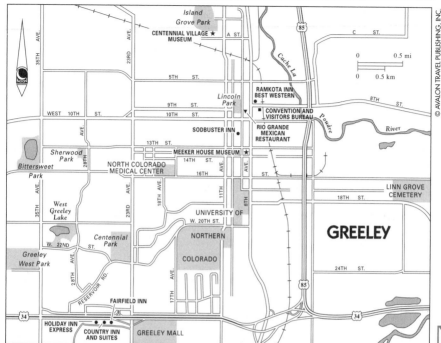

surrounding area began to develop as a ranching center, with huge herds of beef cattle blanketing the plains. In 1890, Greeley citizens matched $10,000 in state funding to establish the University of Northern Colorado, which opened its doors in 1899.

Shortly after the turn of the century, farmers in Weld and other Platte River Valley counties began to contract with sugar companies to grow sugar beets. Sugar factories were built in Greeley and other nearby towns. From the early 1900s through the 1930s, the area attracted large numbers of immigrants, who came to work in the newly built factories and in the productive fields, as well as to take advantage of homesteading opportunities. According to *Greeley Style Magazine*, many current residents' German, Russian, Japanese, and Hispanic roots date from early 20th-century recruiting.

Greeley remained true to the vision of its founding fathers for its first 100 years, and it wasn't until 1969 that the sale of liquor was allowed within the city limits. In the 1980s, James Michener lived in Greeley while he researched and wrote *Centennial*, his fictional account of the history of the town and area. Anyone looking to learn more about Greeley and Weld County would do well by Michener's novel.

SIGHTS
Meeker House Museum
Listed on the National Register of Historic Places, this was the home of Greeley founder Nathan Meeker, who built the two-story house in 1870. The museum offers docent-led tours of the building and offers an opportunity to view some of Meeker's personal belongings and furniture, as well as other artifacts collected from the area.

The Meeker Museum is at 1324 9th Avenue. Memorial Day through Labor Day, the museum is open Tues.–Sat. 10 A.M.–5 P.M., and the rest of the year it's open Tues.–Sat.

10 A.M.–3 P.M. Free admission; donations accepted. For more information, phone 970/350-9221 or 970/350-9220.

Centennial Village Museum

This multistructure museum complex occupies five acres and offers an interpretive history of Greeley and Weld County from 1860 to 1920. Exhibits and buildings include an 1863 log courthouse, an 1872 cottage, and a turn-of-the-century church and one-room schoolhouse, as well as displays emphasizing the importance of agriculture, such as a granary and an early 20th-century sugar beet shanty. Guided tours take about an hour. At the small gift shop you can buy souvenirs, books on local history, and homemade candy.

The Centennial Village Museum, 1475 A St., is open mid-April through mid-October. Call for hours. Admission is $3.50—discounts for kids and seniors—which includes entrance to the Meeker House Museum (see above). For more information, phone 970/350-9224 or 970/350-9220.

Greeley Municipal Museum

A gallery and research center, this museum exhibits traveling displays and stores archives on the history of Greeley and Weld County. In addition, the museum houses the Colorado Collection: rare, out-of-print, and contemporary books and journals on all aspects of the state. The museum is at 919 7th St. and is open Tues.–Sat. 10 A.M.–4 P.M. Admission is free, tours available. For more information, phone 970/350-9220.

Fort Vasquez

On U.S. 85 in Platteville, about 18 miles south of Greeley, this National Historical Society site is a WPA-constructed model of the original Fort Vasquez, which was built in 1835. Originally established as a trading post where mountain men and Plains tribes swapped furs, weapons, and tools, the Fort Vasquez enterprise was a relatively short-lived one. Today the visitor center next to the fort offers an overview of early 19th-century South Platte Valley fur trade. In addition to viewing the

displays in the visitor center, you can also tour the fort itself.

Fort Vasquez is open to visitors Memorial Day through Labor Day, Mon.–Sat. 9:30 A.M.–4:30 P.M. and Sunday 1–4:30 P.M. Admission is free. For more information, phone 970/785-2832.

PARKS AND RECREATION
City Parks

Greeley's got more than two dozen city parks scattered within its boundaries. **Lincoln Park,** across the street from the downtown mall, has lush lawns and shade trees and is perfect for picnicking. Another nice city park is **Bittersweet Park,** at 16th Street and 35th Avenue, which has lawns, shade, and playground equipment. For more information on Greeley's city parks, contact the **Parks and Recreation Department,** 651 10th Ave., 970/350-9400.

Golf

Greeley's **Highland Hills Municipal Golf Course** is on the west side of town off 20th Street (2200 Clubhouse Dr.). For information and tee times, phone 970/330-7327. The **Eaton Country Club,** in Eaton about 10 miles north of Greeley on U.S. 85, is an 18-hole "championship course" with a restaurant and banquet room. Phone 970/454-2106.

ACCOMMODATIONS
$50–100

The **Best Western Ramkota Inn and Conference Center,** 970/353-8444, is right downtown kitty-corner from the Greeley Mall and has nearly 150 rooms. On the south side of town, at 29th Street and U.S. 34, are several chain hotels, including the **Fairfield Inn by Marriot,** 2401 W. 29th St., 970/339-5030; and a **Holiday Inn Express,** 2563 W. 29th St., 970/330-7495. The **Sodbuster Inn Bed and Breakfast,** 1221 9th, 970/392-1221 or 888/300-1221, is a newly built (1997) lodge designed to look like the historic structures that surround it. Ten rooms are available, all with private baths, some with jetted tubs.

Greeley Campground and RV Park, 970/353-6476, a mile east of town on U.S. 34, has 95 sites on 10 acres.

FOOD

Bruce's

Call them what you will, bull fries, prairie oysters, swinging steaks, or the more popular Rocky Mountain oysters, but the best, well, bull testicles around are (reportedly!) served at Bruce's, west of Greeley in Severance. Sliced thin, breaded, and deep-fried, Bruce's fries are very popular—folks go nuts for 'em. In fact, Bruce's owners Ruth and Betty Schott sell between 20 and 25 tons of the things a year and have been known to let patrons think they were eating "headless and tailless shrimp." A *Rocky Mountain News* article once quoted Schott as saying, "I always tell people to come to Severance and have a ball." Travelers watching their weight or red-meat intake might want to try the turkey variety.

Like something out of *Thelma and Louise,* Bruce's doubles as a Western bar and has been open since 1958. Regular customers include members of the Denver Broncos, whose summer training camp is in Greeley. The exterior walls of the restaurant are adorned with murals of bulls holding picket signs reading "Unfair" and "Very Unfair." Inside is a painting of a rather startled and angry-looking bull experiencing "the procedure." Saturday nights, locals come to dance and drink beer. You can also get a freshly shot goose cleaned for $6.

To get there, take U.S. 85 north about 10 miles to Eaton, and go west another nine miles. Phone 970/686-2320.

Other Greeley Food

If you don't have the stomach for Rocky Mountain oysters, or you don't feel like driving up to Severance, you'll find plenty of more conventional cuisine in Greeley—lots of fast-food places, franchises (Red Lobster, Golden Corral), and other restaurants. For Mexican food and a margarita to wash it down, try **Rio Grande Restaurant,** 825 9th St., 970/304-9292, a wonderful cantina with patio seating on the mall downtown just off Lincoln Park. Entrées run $6–10.

ENTERTAINMENT

With the 10,000-student University of Northern Colorado (UNC) in town, Greeley offers more in the way of entertainment than the many other plains communities that roll up the sidewalk when the sun goes down. In addition to clubs that book live dance music—from bluegrass to rock 'n' roll—Greeley also has a philharmonic orchestra, chamber orchestra, and a number of community theater groups, including **Greeley Civic Theater** and **Encore Theater,** as well as the **Children's Theater of Gridley.** A good bet for finding out what and who's playing when is *Greeley Style Magazine,* published by the chamber of commerce and available at its offices and around town. You can also get a copy by writing P.O. Box 5195, Greeley, CO 80631-0195.

There's also always a lot going on over at UNC, from dance to jazz to opera. UNC's **Little Theater of the Rockies** has been producing plays since 1934. For information and schedules regarding UNC performances, write Little Theater of the Rockies, College of Performing and Visual Arts, University of Northern Colorado, Greeley, CO 80639, or phone 970/351-2200.

CALENDAR

Semana Latina (Latin Week) in early May is a weeklong celebration of the area's Hispanic heritage. Festivities include music, dance, and poetry readings, and exhibits demonstrate contributions to politics, education, and other aspects of Greeley and Weld County life. The event is designed to highlight Cinco de Mayo. For more information, contact the Greeley Cultural Affairs Office, 919 7th St., Greeley, CO 80631, 970/353-6123.

One of Greeley's most popular annual events is the **Greeley Independence Stampede,** running from late June through the Fourth of July. The eight-day celebration features rodeos, barbecues, lots of live music, and a Fourth of July parade, culminating with an evening of fireworks displays. For information, phone 970/356-BULL (356-2855). The **Weld County Fair** in August provides a forum for local farmers and ranchers to display their prize crops and critters, as well as for local bakers, canners, and sewing hobbyists to compete for best pies, peaches, and quilts. Contact the Weld County Extension Office, 970/356-4000.

For more information or for a complete calendar of events, contact the convention and visitors bureau, 970/352-3566 or 800/449-3866.

SHOPPING

Greeley's downtown mall is a very pleasant retail shopping area, with a full range of shops and boutiques, including newsstands and bookstores, as well as cafés, benches, and shade trees. Ideally situated across the street from Lincoln Park, the mall offers an excellent opportunity to stroll about to get a feel for Greeley and its people.

The Greeley Mall is a generic mall at the U.S. 34 bypass and 23rd Avenue. You'll find what you'd expect: Sears, JCPenney, Joslin's, etc.

SERVICES

Phone the **Greeley Police** at 970/350-9605, the **Weld County Sheriff** at 970/356-4000. **North Colorado Medical Center** is at 1801 16th St., 970/352-4121. The Greeley **post office** is at 925 11th Ave., 970/353-0398.

Recycling

You can drop off most recyclables in Greeley at the **King Soopers** store at 2712 11th Ave., or at **Greeley-Weld Recycle,** 310 8th St. and 2699 47th Avenue. For more information, phone 970/352-8312.

INFORMATION

The **Greeley Convention and Visitors Bureau** publishes several guides and directories you'll probably find very useful. Stop by its offices at 902 7th Ave., or phone 970/352-3566 or 800/449-3866. Be sure to ask for a copy of

Greeley Style Magazine, which runs stories on Greeley and Weld County history, reviews restaurants, and profiles local businesspeople. For subscription information, write P.O. Box 5195, Greeley, CO 80631. The bureau's website, www.greeleycvb.com, provides information on lodging, dining, day trips, and relocation, as well as updated material on special events.

The **Greeley Municipal Museum** contains the Colorado Collection: new, rare, and out-of-print books on the area and state. The museum is at 919 7th St. and is open Tues.–Sat. 9 A.M.–5 P.M., 970/350-9220. The **UNC Book Store** is on campus in the University Center at 2045 10th Ave., 970/351-2136. You can also get information on Greeley, Weld County, and Colorado at the Greeley **public library,** 917 7th Street.

TRANSPORTATION

The **Greeley/Weld County Airport** is at 600 Crosier Ave., 970/356-9141. Rent cars from most national agencies, plus **Econo Rent-A-Car,** 1030 7th Ave., 970/351-6969, and **Hertz Local Edition Car Rental,** 711 11th St., 970/336-0998. For taxi service, phone **Shamrock Yellow Cab** at 970/352-3000.

Public transportation is available on Greeley's "The Bus," which has routes throughout town. For schedule information, phone 970/350-9BUS (350-9287).

NORTH OF GREELEY

U.S. 85 continues north from Greeley, paralleling I-25 all the way to Cheyenne. Between Nunn and Rockport, a distance of about 20 miles, the highway skirts the western edge of the 193,060-acre **Pawnee National Grassland.** The area is open to the public and offers the amateur geologist a fascinating case study. (For a description of the region, see The I-76–South Platte Corridor in the following chapter.) You can get information and maps from the Grasslands headquarters, in Greeley at 660 O St., 970/353-5004.

Fort Collins and Vicinity

Fort Collins (pop. 100,000; elev. 5,004 feet) is a gem of a small town with just the right blend of youthful edge and classic Americana. Stroll downtown and you'll meet tattooed and hemp-necklaced skateboarders drinking espressos, Lycra-clad twentysomethings nursing smoothies or microbrews, business folks and professors planning seminars and conferences, and graying big-belt-buckled ranchers in town to pick up John Deere parts or to get their boots resoled. All of them with an almost palpable sense of civic pride. Understandably—Fort Collins is a Boulder without the pretension and self-importance, a Denver without the skyscrapers, smog, crowds, and crime. Thanks to its location, 60 miles north of Denver on the Cache La Poudre River, just east of sprawling Roosevelt National Forest, Fort Collins offers plenty of outdoor-recreation opportunities. And it's a college town, with all the vibrant entertainment and intellectual life that status brings; what better way to wind up a day on the trails or on the lake than by quaffing a locally made ale and digging a local blues band's rendition of "Good Mornin', Little School Girl"?

Though the Fort Collins-area economy has traditionally relied on ranching and farming for its stability, recent years have brought an influx of modern industry, with several large companies, including Hewlett-Packard and NCR, building plants nearby. In addition, Colorado State University has a growing reputation as a center for high-caliber research and has been instrumental in linking academia and agriculture. The result has been an increase in the efficiency and productivity of local farmers and a state-of-the-art agricultural technology that Fort Collins proudly exports. About 20,000 students attend the university, which is the city's largest employer (nearly 8,000).

Fort Collins's plains location guarantees a fairly moderate climate (local boosters claim the sun shines 300 days a year), yet the city is close enough to the Front Range of the Rockies to allow for day-trips to some of the state's best hiking, backpacking, mountain biking, skiing, and other sports. One of the highlights of the downtown area is the renovated Old Town, a couple of square blocks where you can visit boutiques and bookstores, gift shops and galleries, and pubs and restaurants with fountain-side outdoor seating perfect for people-watching. Cart vendors also sell a variety of items, from tie-dyed T-shirts and novelty sunglasses to frozen yogurt and bratwurst.

HISTORY

As one of the last stops for fur trappers heading west into the rugged Rocky Mountains, the prairie lands surrounding what is now Fort Collins, as well as the various local waterways and routes leading into the high country, were well known by early-19th-century mountain men and the Native Americans with whom they traded and sometimes fought. In fact, the Cache La Poudre River, which runs north of town, takes its name from the French trappers who, to lighten their loads before heading up into the snow, often stashed their powder barrels in the lower river basin.

The Colorado gold rushes of the mid-1800s brought the first real settlers to the Fort Collins area—many of them frustrated miners who hadn't hit pay dirt in the mountains. In 1862, Camp Collins (named for U.S. Cavalry Lieutenant Colonel William O. Collins) was established to protect traders traveling the Overland Trail, which passed about five miles north of present-day Fort Collins. On June 9, 1864, the camp was wiped out by flood, and three months later a new post (Fort Collins) was established downstream. During the 1870s and '80s, a series of irrigation canals was built in the area, allowing for much more efficient farming—primarily wheat, oats, and barley—and establishing the economic base that still exists. By 1872, Fort Collins could claim a hotel, general store, and post office.

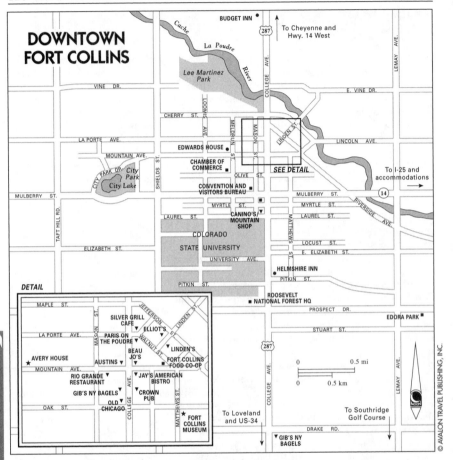

DOWNTOWN
FORT COLLINS

In 1876, the town was hit by a horde of grasshoppers, which, along with the failure of Fort Collins's first bank, almost destroyed it. In fact it might have, were it not for the Colorado Central Railroad, which arrived the following year. In 1879, the first building of what would become Colorado State University was constructed—on land donated by the townspeople—and the Agricultural College of Colorado opened its doors for the first time in September of that year.

By the end of the 19th century, local farmers had begun to harvest sugar beets and alfalfa, and in the early 1900s the area was also prime

cattle- and sheep-raising country. In 1910 the population of the town was over 8,000; by that time, however, Fort Collins's population had divided itself into two disparate camps, the "wets" and the "drys," the infamous Blue Laws having been enacted in 1896 (Fort Collins remained "dry" until 1969).

The addition of a college to Fort Collins proved fortuitous, as students and professors worked together on projects that greatly improved farming conditions and the quality of the crops. Eventually, the school began to earn a reputation as a frontrunner among the nation's agricultural colleges and began to attract students from beyond the nearby fields. Colorado State University, as it came to be known, was largely responsible for the town's increase in population, which doubled in the 1950s and '60s.

During the 1970s, the people of Fort Collins began to realize the importance of their own past (the Fort Collins Historical Society was founded in 1974), and by the 1980s the town was at work restoring itself: Old Town Square was an early '80s project that sought at once to recognize the town's history and to attract shoppers and tourists by restoring the downtown area.

SIGHTS

Fort Collins Museum

Specializing in historical artifacts pertinent to the settling of the Fort Collins area, the Fort Collins Museum also curates a handful of the area's original buildings, which have been moved to the Library Park site just off College Avenue. A log cabin built by fur trapper Antoine Janis and purportedly one of the oldest buildings in the state, a stone cabin from the 1860s, and a schoolhouse built in 1884 have all been dismantled and moved to the park. The museum also houses an excellent selection of Folsom points found north of town in the 1920s and '30s.

The museum sits on a city block surrounded by lawn and shade trees, with picnic tables and a playground—the perfect post-museum-tour picnic site.

The Fort Collins Museum, 200 Matthews St. (two blocks east of College), is open Tues.–Sat. 10 A.M.–5 P.M. and Sunday noon–5 P.M. Admission is free, donations gladly accepted to help maintain exhibits. For more information, phone 970/221-6738.

Avery House

Listed on the National Register of Historic Places, the sandstone Avery House was built in 1879 by Franklin C. Avery, a Fort Collins architect and banker. His descendants lived in the house until 1962, when it was obtained by the city, restored, and turned into a museum. The house contains original Avery-family furniture and decorations, in addition to other authentic period pieces.

The Avery House is at 328 W. Mountain and is open Sunday and Wednesday 1–3 P.M. and by appointment. For more information, or to book tours, phone 970/221-0533.

Fort Collins Municipal Railway

Take a trolley ride down Mountain Street from City Park to Howes Street (1.5 miles) in a restored 1919 Birney streetcar, reportedly the only one in operation in the western United States. Cost for the ride is $1 for adults, $.75 for seniors, $.50 for kids 12 and under. Open weekends and holidays May–September. Phone 970/482-8246.

Historical Walking Tours

The Fort Collins Convention and Visitors Bureau has designed a 22-site walking tour of some landmarks of historical Fort Collins. Included are the Avery House, several of the first Colorado State University buildings, and an early church, drugstore, and hotel. For a list of the sites and addresses, contact the convention and visitors bureau.

Anheuser-Busch Brewery

Free tours of the state's fastest brewery (not to be confused with its largest, the Coors plant in Golden, or its best, the Wynkoop in Denver) are offered at this facility year-round. (Smaller-quantity and home brewers scorn both speed and size; how much beer you make and how fast you make it are generally in inverse proportion to the quality of the resulting brew.) In addition to viewing the brewing and packaging processes, visitors also get to see the Budweiser Clydesdales and taste some beer before browsing in the gift shop (natch!).

A relative newcomer to Colorado brewing, having opened for production in 1988, the Bud brewery is open to visitors daily 9:30 A.M.–5 P.M. June–Aug., 10 A.M.–4 P.M. in September, and Mon–Thur. 10 A.M.–4 P.M. Oct.–May. To get there, take I-25 north from town to Mountain Vista Drive (Exit 271), and turn right onto Busch Drive. For more information, phone 970/490-4691.

© STEPHEN METZGER

Fort Collins Museum is just two blocks away from Old Town.

NORTH-CENTRAL

PARKS AND RECREATION

Fort Collins's location at the foot of the Rockies and virtually in the shadow of Rocky Mountain National Park guarantees plenty of year-round outdoor activity for residents and passers-through. Not to be overlooked, though, are the great numbers of recreational possibilities outside the park and mountains—from fishing in nearby lakes and streams to cycling, hiking, and golf in the warmer months to cross-country skiing in the winter.

City Parks

Fort Collins has several large city parks and many smaller neighborhood parks. **City Park,** 1500 W. Mulberry, has lots of lawns for tossing Frisbees or napping, picnic facilities, a fitness course, and fishing (at the small lake). For tennis or horseshoes, try **Edora Park,** 1420 E. Stuart, where you'll also find a public swimming pool and ice-skating rink. **Lee Martinez Park,** 600 N. Sherwood, features picnic facilities, tennis courts, and softball fields. You can also visit Martinez Park's 12-acre farm and experience first-hand the responsibilities of raising animals and harvest-

ing crops (kids can pet the animals). For information, phone 970/221-6665.

For more information on Fort Collins city parks, phone the **Parks and Recreation Department** (north of town) at 707/221-6660.

Horsetooth Reservoir

Horsetooth Reservoir is a popular recreational area just southwest of Fort Collins. The 4,000 acres of water and its rocky shoreline attract lots of outdoor enthusiasts, particularly in the warmer months when folks flock to the water to escape the heat. **Horsetooth Mountain Park** borders the lake and offers fishing (for bass, trout, and landlocked salmon), water-skiing, windsurfing, picnicking, horseback riding, mountain biking, and backcountry camping. For information, contact the **Larimer County Parks Department** at 970/226-4517.

Lory State Park is on the northwest shore of Horsetooth Reservoir. In addition to hiking and mountain biking on the park's two-dozen-plus miles of trails, you can explore the area on horseback. At **Double Diamond Stables** you can rent horses for two-hour rides (starting at 9 A.M.), and one-hour rides (noon, 2 P.M., and 4 P.M.

Open Thurs.–Tues. May–September. For information, write 710 Lodgepole, Bellvue, CO, or phone 970/224-4200. Lory State Park also offers fishing and bird-watching and is a favorite place to check out the wildflowers in spring and early summer. For more on Lory State Park, contact the **Colorado Division of Parks and Outdoor Recreation,** 3842 S. Mason, Fort Collins, CO 80525, 970/226-6641.

To get to Horsetooth, head west from downtown to Overland Trail; then take County Road 42C (which runs into Overland between Prospect and Drake). You can also get there by heading west on U.S. 287 through Laporte and turning west at the Bellvue exit.

Colorado State Forest

About 70 miles west of Fort Collins via U.S. 287 and Highway 14 (and 10,276-foot Cameron Pass), Colorado State Forest offers excellent hiking and backpacking, as well as camping, fishing, and sightseeing. Write Colorado State Forest, Star Route Box 91, Walden, CO 80480, or phone 970/723-8366.

Cycling

Any self-respecting college town's got to have its share of bike paths and mountain-bike trails, where students can go to alleviate post-exam stress (or avoid thinking about an exam on the horizon). No exception, Fort Collins has nearly 60 miles of city bikeways, and the city is dedicated to making cycling safe and convenient. The *Tour de Fort Bike Guide* is a city map that designates a variety of interconnecting routes, including some set aside for pedestrians and cyclists only. The guides are available at local bike shops, as well as from the chamber of commerce and the convention and visitors bureau.

Local mountain bikers like to head into Roosevelt National Forest or Colorado State Forest, west of town via Highway 14. For maps and information on biking in the national forest, stop by its headquarters at 240 W. Prospect, or phone 970/498-1100. State forest information is available from the main office in Walden; phone 970/723-8366.

For bicycle rentals and equipment, as well as for tips and advice, stop by **Lee's Cyclery,** 202 W. Laurel, 970/482-6006.

The **Never Summer Nordic Yurt System** is a hut-to-hut cross-country skiing system open in the summer to mountain bikers. There are three yurts (small cabins that sleep six) and an interconnecting series of trails. The area is in Colorado State Forest about 70 miles west of Fort Collins (east of Walden). For reservations and more information, write P.O. Box 1983, Fort Collins, CO 80522, or phone 970/482-9411, or visit the website at www.neversummer nordic.com.

Closer to town, **Horsetooth Reservoir** offers a decent amount and range of off-road cycling on 2,100 acres of public land (county maintained). Small entrance fee.

Golf

The city of Fort Collins maintains three municipal golf courses, and there are a handful of private courses in the area. **City Park Nine** is a nine-hole course at City Park (411 S. Bryan). For information and tee times, phone 970/221-6650. The other two city courses are **Collindale Golf Course,** 1441 E. Horsetooth, 970/221-6651, and **Southridge Greens,** 5750 S. Lemay, 970/226-2828, both 18-hole courses. Green fees at all three are $13 for nine holes, $21 for 18 holes.

Hiking

Fort Collins is close to some of the state's best hiking areas. Rocky Mountain National Park and Roosevelt National Forest offer hundreds of miles of trails to wander, woods to explore, and peaks to bag.

The **Colorado Mountain Club,** based in Estes Park, hosts day and overnight trips into the backcountry. Phone its main office at 970/586-6623; for the name and number of the current Fort Collins Outing Chairman, phone the Denver office at 303/922-8315. You can get schedule and other information on Fort Collins-area hikes at the club's extensive website at www.members.aol.com/FortCMC.

For geologist-led tours of the nearby mountains, contact **Geo Outdoor Adventures** at

970/484-3834 or 800/949-0004; or write 1201 Buttonwood Dr., Fort Collins, CO 80525.

The **Mountain Shop,** 632 S. Mason, 970/493-5720, is an excellent source for expert advice and quality equipment; it also carries maps and rents gear.

Fishing

Several of the lakes in the Fort Collins area offer good fishing for bass, crappie, walleye, and other warm-water species. At Horsetooth Reservoir, you can cast for warm-water fish as well as trout and kokanee salmon; the reservoir is especially well regarded for its large lake trout. There are public boat launches and marinas at Horsetooth, though fishing can be productive from the shore. Kids might enjoy fishing for panfish at the small lake at City Park.

For information on fly-fishing—or to book guided trips—stop by **St. Peter's Fly Shop,** 202 Remington St., 970/498-8968, or **Rocky Mountain Fly Shop,** 124 E. Monroe Dr., 970/223-7735.

If you'd rather not take chances of getting skunked (or if you don't want to buy a license), **Frank's Trout Pond,** 2912 W. Mulberry, 970/482-5102, is stocked with hungry fish you pay for by the inch. (See also West of Fort Collins, below.)

Rafting

Several companies in Fort Collins and the surrounding area offer white-water rafting trips on the Cache La Poudre, Arkansas, and Green Rivers. Phone **A-1 Wildwater,** 970/224-3379, and **Wanderlust Adventures,** 970/484-1219.

Cross-Country Skiing

Excellent cross-country skiing opportunities await the Fort Collins-area three-pinner—from the woods of Roosevelt National Forest to the valleys of Rocky Mountain National Park, and a lot closer to town as well, including the trails around Horsetooth Reservoir.

The **Never Summer Nordic Yurt System** offers hut-to-hut Nordic skiing in Colorado State Forest. Sleeping six people each, the three yurts are connected by an intricate series of back-country trails. For reservations and more information, visit the website at www.neversummernordic.com, write P.O. Box 1254, Fort Collins, CO 80522, or phone 970/484-3903.

The best source for information on Nordic skiing around Fort Collins is **The Mountain Shop,** 632 S. Mason, 970/493-5270. In addition to providing advice, rental gear, and maps, the store also stocks quality equipment and clothing.

You can also get information and maps from Roosevelt National Forest Headquarters, 240 W. Prospect, Fort Collins, CO 80526, 970/498-1100.

ACCOMMODATIONS

Fort Collins has been hammered in the last eight or 10 years by the major chain motels, all of which are generally clean and quiet. At press time, my favorite inn in town, the Helmshire, 1204 S. College, was in the process of being sold. I hope the new owners maintain the little hotel's charm and elegance. You might try phoning 970/493-4683; if that doesn't work try phoning information and asking for a new listing.

Under $50

Among the least expensive rooms in town are those at the **Budget Host Inn,** 1513 N. College, 970/484-0870. The **Motel 6** is at 3900 Mulberry, 970/482-6466.

$50–100

For bed-and-breakfast accommodations, try **Edwards House Bed & Breakfast,** 402 W. Mountain Ave. (one block from Old Town), 970/493-9191 or 800/281-9190. All rooms have fireplaces; some have spas. The convention and visitors bureau can provide a full list of the dozen or so others scattered about town and nearby.

The following are among Fort Collins's better franchise hotels/motels: **Best Western Kiva Inn,** 1638 E. Mulberry St., 970/484-2444 or 888/299-5482; **Best Western University Inn,** 914 S. College Ave., 970/484-1984 or 800/528-1234; **Holiday Inn I-25,** 3836 E. Mulberry St., 970/484-4660 or 800-HOLIDAY (465-4329);

Holiday Inn University Park, 425 W. Prospect Rd., 970/482-2626 or 800/HOLI-DAY (465-4329).

Camping and RVing

The **Fort Collins KOA** campground, 970/493-9758, is about 10 miles northwest of town on U.S. 287. **Heron Lake RV Park,** 1910 N. Taft Hill Rd., 877/254-4063, has 175 sites on 35 landscaped acres.

FOOD

Breakfast

For breakfast, it's tough to find a place with a better reputation than the **Silver Grill Café,** 218 Walnut, 970/484-4656. Serving the residents of Fort Collins since the 1930s, the Silver Grill specializes in gargantuan cinnamon rolls, and it dishes up other standard American fare as well. Another place worth checking out is **The Egg and I,** 1112 Oakridge Dr., 970/223-8022, which regularly garners rave reviews among local breakfast aficionados.

For the best bagels in town, try **Gib's NY Bagels & Deli,** 107 S. College Ave., 970/472-4020. Gib's also has locations at 2531 S. Shields St., 970/224-5946; 2722 S. College Ave., 970/282-1190; and 1112 Oakridge Dr., 970/223-5253. Meanwhile, the younger, body-pierced-in-weird-places crowd might prefer **Paris on the Poudre Coffee House,** in Old Town at 255 Linden, 970/498-0705, where mellow dogs lie waiting patiently for their rasta mastas.

Lunch and Dinner

If you're looking for a lunch spot with lots of local flavor, stop in at **Coopersmith's Brew Pub,** 970/498-0483, in Old Town Square. Quaff a beer (Scottish Ale, India Pale, or Oatmeal Stout) while you munch on bangers and mash, fish and chips, bratwurst, or a burger with artichoke hearts, scallions, and sour cream. Coopersmith's also serves stir fry, steaks, salads, and homemade desserts; lunches and dinners run $6–14. Open Mon.–Sat. 11 A.M.–2 A.M. and Sunday 11 A.M.–midnight. Also at Old Town Square is **Jay's American Bistro,** 151 S. College, 970/483-1876, where you can get everything from crab cakes to pastas to wild game. Entrées run $12–24. Open weekdays for lunch, daily except Sunday for dinner. Nearby, **Austin's American Grill,**

A kayaker works the Cache La Poudre River outside of Fort Collins.

110 W. Mountain (corner of College), 970/224-9973, serves excellent salads, burgers, and sandwiches, as well as steak and chicken dinners for $6–15. Open daily for lunch and dinner.

One of Fort Collins's hot spots for south-of-the-border fare is **Rio Grande Mexican Restaurant,** 149 W. Mountain, 970/224-5428, which serves traditional Mexican food and Tex-Mex. Dinners run $6–9; lunch specials are $4–6. Locals claim the margaritas here are the best in town, if not the country—limit, three to a customer. Open daily for lunch and dinner. (The Rio Grande has a sister restaurant in Boulder just below the Pearl Street Mall.)

Another standby is **Old Chicago,** 147 S. College, 970/482-8599, serving pizza, pastas, salads, more than 125 types of beer, and offering patio dining. Open for daily for lunch and dinner. Prices range $6–14.

Also popular for Italian food is **Canino's,** 613 S. College, 970/493-7205. A longtime family-owned favorite, Canino's offers takeout and delivery as well.

If you start feeling guilty after gorging yourself on pub fare, pasta, *burritos de pollo,* and local brew, and you're looking for something healthful to pack for the road, stop in at **Fort Collins Food Co-op,** 250 E. Mountain (just around the corner from Old Town Square), 970/484-7448. The little shop carries organically grown fruits and vegetables, in addition to juices, nuts, breads, and other goods.

For the best Rocky Mountain oysters in the state, check out **Bruce's** in Severance, near Greeley (see above) just southeast of Fort Collins.

ENTERTAINMENT

Any college town has got to have places where folks can let loose on weekends, and Fort Collins doesn't disappoint. On just about any given night you're likely to hear everything from bluegrass to jazz to headbanging rock 'n' roll, and many of the clubs are right downtown. Among those consistently offering live music are the **Aggie Theater,** 204 S. College, 970/407-1322; **Bar Bazaar,** 215 Walnut, 970/493-4497; the **Crown Pub,** 134 S. College, 970/484-5929; **Elliot's Martini**

Bar, 234 Linden, 970/472-9802; and **Linden's Brewing Co.,** 214 Linden, 970/482-9291, where you can watch (or join in) open jazz jam sessions on Wednesday night.

To catch a game (or 10), check out the **Sports-Caster Bar and Grill,** 165 E. Boardwalk Dr. (near College and Boardwalk), 970/223-3553, where at least one of the 50 televisions will be tuned to your event. Open daily 11 A.M.–2 P.M.

For up-to-date information on clubs and other entertainment, check out *The Scene,* a free monthly distributed around town in racks, hotel lobbies, and cafés (or at www.scenecolorado.com). Also, take a look at the entertainment section of the *Fort Collins Coloradoan,* the local daily ($.35 in racks).

CALENDAR

An event or festival of one kind or another happens almost every weekend in Fort Collins, either at the university or downtown. Highlights include the **Colorado Brewers' Festival** in late June, where you can sample the pilsners and porters of Colorado's many microbreweries, munch from a wide range of food booths, and listen to a variety of ethnic music. On the **Fourth of July** there's a fair with food, music, and fireworks at City Park, and in mid-September balloons from the Fort Collins **Balloon Festival** fill the sky. The **Octoberfest,** during the first week of October, features street dancing, traditional food and drink, and a general sense of revelry and carrying on.

For a complete calendar of Fort Collins's annual events, contact the chamber of commerce or convention and visitors bureau. (See Information, below.)

SHOPPING

Old Town Square, in one of Fort Collins's original financial centers, is one of the town's true delights. Built in the early 1980s, with a fountain to keep it cool and several cafés with patio seating, the little shopping mall offers several different retail shops, galleries, as well as cart vendors selling T-shirts, jewelry, and souvenirs. **Children's**

Mercantile has tons of kids' games, toys, and an exceptional selection of books. **Colorado Classics** carries menswear and specializes in Western duds, particularly Pendleton shirts. **Trimble Court Artisans** and **Walnut Street Gallery** are worth poking your head into if you're interested in prints, posters, and art by local craftspeople.

Farmers Market

Every Wednesday 3–6 P.M., local farmers (and remember, this is one of the agricultural capitals of the state) sell their freshly picked wares in the parking lot at the corner of College Avenue and History Cabin.

SERVICES

The offices of the **Fort Collins Police Department** are at 300 Laporte, 970/221-6540. Phone the **Larimer County Sheriff** at 970/221-7000; offices are at 200 W. Oak. **State Patrol** offices are at 2412 E. Mulberry, 970/484-4020. **Poudre Valley Hospital,** 970/482-4111 or 800/284-5241, is at 1024 S. Lemay Avenue.

Fort Collins's main **post office** is in the Federal Building, 970/482-2837.

Recycling

The **King Soopers** stores at 1015 Taft Hill Rd. and 2325 S. College take aluminum, glass, newspaper, and plastics.

INFORMATION

The offices of the **Fort Collins Convention and Visitors Bureau,** are at 3745 E. Prospect Rd. #200, 800/274-FORT (274-3678) or 970/491-3388, where you'll also find the Fort Collins Information Center; the folks here are always good for information on things to do and see (and where to spend your money) in the area. They've also got one of the best visitor websites in the state: www.ftcollins.com.

The **Fort Collins Chamber of Commerce,** 225 S. Meldrun, 970/482-3746, is across College Avenue from Old Town Square. Be sure to pick up a copy of *The Guide to Fort Collins,* which contains listings of parks, restaurants, nightclubs, and

shopping centers, and other attractions. The Fort Collins **public library** is at 201 Peterson, 970/221-6740. **Stone Lion Books,** 970/493-0030, in Old Town Square, has a wide selection of books on local and state history, as well as on recreation.

The local daily is the *Fort Collins Coloradoan,* a Gannett paper. For subscription information, phone 970/224-7730.

TRANSPORTATION

Airport Express, 970/482-0505, has shuttle service between Denver International Airport and Fort Collins (as well as between Fort Collins and Cheyenne and Fort Collins and Laramie). Round-trip between DIA and Fort Collins is about $35. Fort Collins's public transportation **Transfort** has routes throughout town; phone 970/221-6620 for rates and route information. For taxi service, phone **Shamrock Yellow Cab** at 970/224-2222.

Rent cars in Fort Collins from all the major rental-car companies, as well as from **Advantage Rent-A-Car,** 2539 S. College, Suite 2, 970/224-2211.

WEST OF FORT COLLINS

U.S. 287 continues north through Fort Collins for a couple of miles, hooks to the west, then meanders north again, crossing the border into Wyoming and rolling into Laramie.

Fourteen miles northwest of Fort Collins, you can catch Highway 14 west through the Poudre River Canyon, Roosevelt National Forest, and Colorado State Forest, eventually arriving in the small town of Walden. This is a wonderfully scenic route, taking you along the shores of the Cache La Poudre, past some excellent fishing spots, camping and picnic areas, through the Medicine Bow Mountains, and over Cameron Pass (elev. 10,276 feet) near the northwest corner of Rocky Mountain National Park. Along the 80-mile stretch from Laporte to Gould are numerous Forest Service access roads leading to more campgrounds. Be sure to check local fishing regulations with the Colorado Division of

Wildlife, 303/297-1192, or local sporting goods stores as some stretches of the Cache La Poudre have special restrictions.

Forest Service campgrounds along Highway 14 include **Ansel Watrous,** 18 miles west of Laporte (open all year, pit toilets, no showers); **Kelly Flats,** 30 miles west (open mid-May to mid-November, pit toilets, no showers); and **Chambers Lake** (60 miles west, open June–Oct., pit toilets, no showers). In addition, camping is available in the **Red Feather Lakes** area northwest of Fort Collins, where a series of lakes offers good trout fishing just north of the Poudre River Canyon. Be sure to check local regulations; some of the waters have special restrictions. To get there, turn north onto Feather Lakes Road at Rustic.

For information on lodging and camping in the Feather Lakes Area, write **Poudre River–Red Feather Lakes Tourist Council,** P.O. Box 505, Red Feather Lakes, CO 80545, or phone 800/462-5870. For information on the other Forest Service campgrounds accessible from Highway 14, contact the offices of **Roosevelt National Forest,** 240 W. Prospect Rd., Fort Collins.

Northeastern Colorado

This is not the Colorado most imagine when they think of the state. It's not John Denver's "Rocky Mountain High" or Boulder's progressive politics and New Ageism; nor is it Cripple Creek's Victorian shops or Colorado Springs's mountain vistas. Yet this Colorado offers the traveler something just as much a part of the state's soul and heartland: the plains, where people have been farming, ranching, and drawing their livelihoods from the soil and the sky for generations. It's a place where bumper stickers advise you to Eat Beef, where acres of sugar beets and alfalfa stretch as far as you can see, where folks haul ass on long, straight unpaved back roads in pickups and Cadillacs, like characters out of Larry McMurtry novels. It's a place where you can get not only a sense of rural Colorado and

hard-working Coloradans but a very real taste of something that is truly and uniquely American as well.

Just listen to the names of some of the towns out here: Yuma, Burlington, Holyoke, Sedgwick, Heartstrong, Haxtun, Crook—most of them blink-and-you'll-miss-it burgs where things are so slow and the citizenry so insulated that if you do slow down you're likely to be given the once-over by just about everyone you pass on the street, from the kid in the high-school letter jacket and his young adoring girlfriend to the retired rancher in his pickup. That's not to say the people out here aren't friendly. On the contrary, they welcome passers-through, and they'll usually go out of their way to help

Old Town Museum in Burlington

NORTHEASTERN COLORADO HIGHLIGHTS

Fort Morgan: museum, Pawnee National Grassland, Pawnee Buttes
Sterling: Overland Trail Museum, parks, boating, fishing, Sugar Beet Days
Tamarack Ranch State Wildlife Area (Crook): 7,000-acre refuge
Limon: Twilight Train rides
Burlington: museum and Kit Carson County Carousel (National Historic Register)

you find a restaurant or coffee shop, campground, park, or picnic area. In fact, get a local talking about his town—or, more accurately, his county—and you'll have a tough time getting him to stop. These are proud people, and they love their county fairs, livestock shows, and harvest festivals.

Long before the white man arrived here, these grasslands had been home to roaming bands of Cheyenne and Arapahoe, who hunted the prairie's great herds of buffalo. As early as the 1820s, though, traders and trappers began infringing on Native American lands, working the South Platte area (which parallels present-day I-76 from Julesburg to Fort Morgan, then veers northwest to Greeley) for beaver pelts and building a series of forts and trading posts. Like the buffalo, though, which within a few years would be all but extinct on the American plains, the beaver, which had once been abundant in the South Platte, were quickly too few to be very profitable. By the 1850s, interest in trapping along the South Platte was dying out.

Toward the end of the 1850s, however, gold was discovered at Pikes Peak and Cherry Creek (near what is now Englewood, a suburb of Denver), and prospectors began streaming across Colorado, many of them below the South Platte corridor. In 1860, Julesburg became a stop on the short-lived Pony Express Trail, and though that enterprise only lasted a year, when the Union

Just take the time to drive through the grasslands, imagining a time when the country wasn't in such a hurry.

Pacific Railroad arrived in Julesburg in 1867, the sleepy little hamlet was transformed almost overnight: its dance halls and saloons, prostitutes and gamblers earned it the nickname "the wickedest little town in the West." (Actually, the present town of Julesburg is not in the same place as the Julesburg of the 1860s; there were, in fact, four separate Julesburgs, the current one having been founded in 1881.)

During the early 20th century, the South Platte Valley became prized for its sugar beets, and although other crops—including alfalfa, wheat, and other grains—are grown out on these plains, it's the beets that have been sweetening the local economy ever since. Several northeastern Colorado towns, including Haxtun, Sterling, Merino, and Atwood, have relied heavily over the years on the annual beet harvest (beginning in October) for their economic survival. And even the towns whose economies are primarily livestock-related also rely on the beets; ranchers in Fort Morgan, for example, fatten sheep on beet pulp.

Traveling through northeastern Colorado today, whether by interstate or back road (the latter is advised), is in a way like stepping back in time. The pace in these little towns is a lot slower than it is in Denver, Colorado Springs, or Boulder. The stockyards are much the same as they were a hundred years ago, though ranching has changed considerably. Today, ranchers buy and sell by computer and telephone (don't be surprised to see them sitting in coffee shops or behind the wheels of their pickups, talking into cellular phones), though the weather, with its ability to capriciously determine fates, still dominates conversation.

But don't write northeastern Colorado off as strictly a bunch of lazy cowtowns. Even if you're just passing through on your way to Vail, take the time to get off the main highways. Check out the Fort Morgan Museum, with its Glenn Miller display (Miller grew up in Fort Morgan), the Overland Trail Museum in Sterling, or the Kit Carson County Carousel

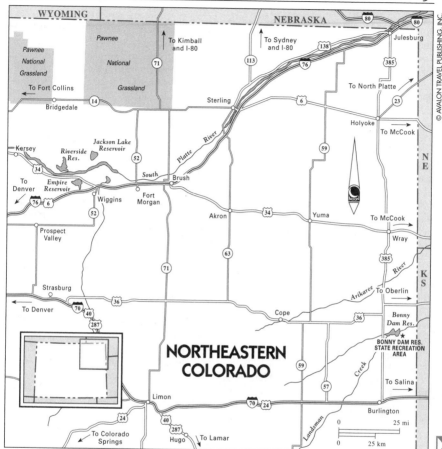

NORTHEASTERN COLORADO

(a hand-carved merry-go-round built in 1905 and designated a National Historic Landmark). Or just take the time to drive through the grasslands, imagining a time when the country wasn't in such a hurry.

Northeastern Colorado Information

You'll find a **Northeast Colorado Gateway Information Center** at the Julesburg exit off I-76. Pick up brochures and publications promoting areas of historical and recreational interest, as well as information on lodging, dining, and sightseeing throughout the northeastern part of the state.

The **Northeast Colorado Visitor Information Center** is just east of downtown Sterling between I-76 and the Platte River (take the Sterling exit). Farther south in Burlington, check out the **State of Colorado Welcome Center,** where you can get information on northeastern Colorado as well as on the rest of the state. Be sure to pick up a copy of the *Northeast Colorado Travel Guide,* which discusses the area's history, highlights specific areas of interest, and suggests several different tours. The publication is available at visitor centers, as well as at the Logan County and Sterling chambers of commerce. You can also get a copy, and more information, by writing

NORTHEASTERN

Northeast Colorado Travel Region, 451 14th St., Burlington, CO 80807, or by phoning 800/777-9075.

Further Reading

James Michener's typically sprawling historical novel *Centennial* explores in great depth and de-tail the history of this part of Colorado, as well as the area just to the west. As in most Michener novels, in which the setting becomes a central character, the plains play a pivotal part. Locals claim the town in which most of the book takes place was based on Greeley, Colorado (see North-Central Colorado).

The I-76–South Platte Corridor

Interstate 76 angles from Denver up to a point about as close to the precise northeastern corner of Colorado as you can get. The drive northeast from Denver to Julesburg, just two miles from the Nebraska border, is a little more than 200 miles and it's flat, fast, and arrow straight. Without stopping, it will take less than four hours. Along the way, though, are a handful of museums and other diversions that are well worth exploring if you've got the time. The Overland Trail Museum in Sterling, for example, with its displays from the 19th century, will give you a better sense of the area's history and of its land and people. Another good way to appreciate the region is to stay off the interstate entirely: a series of two-lane highways parallels both the South Platte and I-76, from Fort Morgan to Julesburg, passing through several tiny farming and ranching towns and communities along the way. The little general stores and watering holes provide great opportunities to experience local color.

FORT MORGAN AND VICINITY

Fort Morgan (pop. 9,100; elev. 4,330 feet) is the seat of Morgan County, one of the smallest (1,296 square miles) but most agriculturally rich counties in the state. Producing a wide variety of crops, including sugar beets, wheat, beans, al-falfa, onions, barley, and potatoes, Morgan County relies on Fort Morgan as a shipping and distribution hub. The area is also known for its beef, sheep, and dairy ranches.

Founded in 1864 as a military post to protect gold rushers and other travelers on the Overland Trail, Fort Morgan was originally called Camp Tyler, then Camp Wardell. The town assumed its present name in 1866 in honor of Colonel C. A. Morgan, the post's first commanding officer. The town today is one of quiet tree-lined streets, many with beautiful, well-maintained homes and large lush yards. Fort Morgan is also the hometown of Glenn Miller (see below) and Philip K. Dick, the well-known science-fiction writer and author of the short story on which the film *Total Recall* was based. Dick is buried in the Fort Morgan cemetery.

Fort Morgan Museum

Depicting Morgan County from the first no-madic bands of hunters up to bandleader Glenn Miller, who grew up here, this small museum displays artifacts and photos that testify to the area's varied history. Particularly worth checking out is the Koehler Site display, which explains the 1980 discovery at a nearby landfill of a pre-historic campsite. Also on display are Plains tribe moccasins, belts, and pipes, as well as an exhibit devoted to Miller, with many intriguing photos of him as a teenager and young man (Miller graduated from Fort Morgan High School in 1921), as well as a re-created soda fountain from the old Hillrose Drugstore, and a room reserved for traveling exhibits (usually with Western themes, from Navajo blankets to Charles Russell's paintings).

Museum hours are Mon.–Fri. 10 A.M.–5 P.M., Tues.–Thurs. evenings 6–8 P.M., and Sat-urday 11 A.M.–5 P.M. Admission is free, with donations encouraged. The Fort Morgan Mu-seum is at 414 Main Street, also the site of the city library. For more information, phone 970/867-6331.

Riverside Park and Canfield Recreation Area

This large and beautiful city park just off the freeway (Exit 80) tempts the weary road warrior with shaded lawns, picnic tables, restrooms, volleyball, basketball, and tennis courts, horseshoe pits, and (for winter travelers) an ice-skating rink, as well as tons of playground equipment. The park is a perfect stop for a quick leg-stretch or maybe even a long afternoon nap under a shade tree. In addition, the park offers free overnight camping and has a swimming pool that's free and open to the public.

Pawnee National Grassland and Pawnee Buttes

The two separate units of Pawnee National Grassland sprawl on the plains of northern Weld County, north of Greeley and Fort Morgan. Desolate, dry, and sparsely populated, the grasslands don't offer the traveler much in the way of views, especially when compared to the eastern slope of the Rockies looming just to the west. There are two startling exceptions, though, to all this flatness: Pawnee Buttes.

Rising over 250 feet above the plain, the two buttes, composed of sedimentary rock protected by a layer of hard sandstone, have resisted the forces that have eroded the surrounding area. Of great interest to paleontologists and anthropologists, the buttes have yielded several prehistoric animals, including *Alticamelus,* a giraffelike camel, and *Amphycyon,* a large animal that would appear today part dog and part bear, as well as an abundance of Native American artifacts (the area was once the hunting grounds of the Pawnee).

The Pawnee National Grassland and Buttes are open to the public, though getting to the Buttes does require some back-roading. The dirt road leading to them is fine for passenger cars, but it gets thick with mud when rainstorms hit. For more information and specific directions, see Lee Gregory's excellent book, *Colorado Scenic Guide, Northern Region.* You can also get more information, including maps, from the Pawnee National Grassland Office of the Forest Service, in Greeley at 660 O St., 970/353-5004.

Golf

The **Fort Morgan Municipal Golf Course,** 970/867-5990, is adjacent to the Fort Morgan Country Club, 17856 County Rd. T, and is open to the public.

Accommodations

You can get good clean rooms right downtown at the **Park Terrace Best Western,** 725 Main St., 970/867-8256, as well as the **Fort Morgan Super 8 Motel,** 1220 Main St., 970/867-9443; the **Central Motel,** 201 W. Platte Ave., 970/867-2401; the **Quality Inn,** 14378 U.S. Hwy. 34, 970/867-8208; and the **Days Inn,** 1150 Main, 970/542-0844. All will run about $50–75.

If you've got the time and the inclination to get off the beaten path and see this part of the country close up, check out the **Elk Echo Ranch Bed and Breakfast.** Included: homemade pie, full breakfast, and backcountry tours ("elk tours") of the southern edge of Pawnee National Grasslands. About $100 for two. Dinners optional: elk steak, grilled salmon, pheasant, etc. For information on rates and tours, write Elk Echo Ranch, Stoneham, CO 80754, or phone 970/735-2426, or visit the website at www.elkecho.com

Food

You'll find the requisite fast-food and franchise restaurants in Fort Morgan, including Pizza Hut, Kentucky Fried Chicken, and Hardee's. In addition, the Best Western Park Terrace motel has a dining room. For good and relatively inexpensive Italian food, check out **Cable's Italian Grille,** 431 Main St., 970/867-6144. A favorite for steak and seafood is **Country Steak Out,** 19592 E. 8th Ave., 970/867-7887, where an all-you-can-eat lunch buffet is available on Tuesday and Sunday.

Services

Fort Morgan Police can be reached at 970/867-5678. The offices of the **Morgan County Sheriff** are at 400 Warner, 970/867-2461. Reach the **State Patrol** at 970/867-6657. **Colorado Plains Medical Center** is at 1000 Lincoln,

NORTHEASTERN

970/867-3391. The central **post office** in Fort Morgan is at 300 State, 970/867-7111.

The **Safeway,** 620 W. Platte, recycles aluminum. For more information on recycling in the Fort Morgan area, phone **All Trash Recycling** at 970/867-6196.

Information

The Fort Morgan **public library,** 970/867-9456, is next door to the Fort Morgan Museum at 414 Main Street. For more information on Fort Morgan and Morgan County, phone the **Fort Morgan Chamber of Commerce,** 970/867-6702 or 800/354-8660, or write 300 Main St., P.O. Box 971, Fort Morgan, CO 80701. Be sure to check out the chamber's website at www.fortmorgan chamber.org. A pleasant surprise awaits, if you're "In the mood. . . ." For **road and weather information,** call 970/522-4848.

STERLING

The largest town in the ranching and farming country of the northeastern corner of Colorado, Sterling (pop. 1,200; elev. 3,945 feet), seat of Logan County, is a quiet little community with towering shade trees and old homes with long front porches. Only the southwestern end of town has been invaded by the proverbial Wal-Mart, Kmart, and Taco John's and other fast-food franchises. Its economy supported by cattle, sugar beets, corn, and alfalfa, Sterling hosts several agricultural and livestock festivals each year; the whole town'll turn out for a 4-H show or the annual alfalfa festival.

Calling itself the "City of Living Trees," Sterling is particularly proud of the dozen or so sculptures scattered around town, carved "on location" by Brad Rhea out of, well, living trees. These include *Skygrazers,* a herd of giraffes stretching skyward; *The Dreamer,* a clown; *Minute Man;* and *The Golfer,* the latter standing, of course, at the Sterling Country Club.

In 1871, railroad surveyor David Leavitt passed through the area and was impressed enough with the valley to return the following year to begin ranching. The town of Sterling was founded a decade later in 1881, and origi-

nally settled by pioneers from Mississippi and Tennessee. The little town's riverside location led to rapid growth, and throughout the early- and mid-20th century, it served as a hub for area beet farmers. Today, many of Sterling's buildings, including the Logan County Courthouse, are on the National Register of Historic Places. Sterling's Northeastern Junior College, founded in 1941, offers a wide variety of fully accredited two-year programs in several different fields, including agriculture, humanities, business, sciences, and social sciences. For information on admissions or visiting the college, phone 970/522-6600, ext. 651.

Overland Trail Museum

One of the best small-town museums in the state, the Overland Trail Museum features excellent displays of Native American clothing, tools, and weapons, pioneer clothing and domestic utensils, a grand piano shipped from Mississippi to Sterling in 1889, and, out back, a reconstructed blacksmith's shop with tools and items typically made by a smithy (horseshoes, spades, plow hardware, etc.). Also out back is an old schoolhouse used these days as a summer school by Sterling teachers and students, who dress as pioneers. Be sure to spend a few minutes looking over the native grasses display between the parking lot and front door. A nice shaded picnic area is next to the museum.

The Overland Trail Museum is at Exit 125 off I-76. It's open April 1–Oct. 30, Mon.–Sat. 9 A.M.–5 P.M. and Sunday and holidays 10 A.M.–5 P.M.; the rest of the year Tues.–Sat. 10 A.M.–4 P.M. Call 970/522-3895. Admission is free.

Parks and Recreation

Columbine Park, on U.S. 6 between South 3rd Avenue and Division Avenue, is huge, shady, and lawny, with picnic tables, swings, and other playground equipment, as well as two of the "Living Tree" sculptures. **Pioneer Park,** two miles west of downtown on Main Street, offers horseshoe pits, tennis courts, a merry-go-round, a series of nature trails among 14 acres, and campsites. For more information, contact the **Sterling Recreation De-**

partment, 421 N. 1st St., 970/522-9700. You can phone the offices of Pioneer Park at 970/522-0441.

North Sterling Reservoir, as well as nearby Jumbo and Prewitt Reservoirs, offers fishing for catfish, bass, walleye, and other warm-water fish. Even if you're not into water-skiing, boating, or fishing, take a drive out to the lake in the evening. It's quiet out here, except for the sound of an occasional fish rising, and the prairie seems to stretch endlessly, to the horizon and into the past—it's easy to forget the 21st century and imagine yourself a westbound pioneer, one of the first settlers crossing the Great Plains.

Sterling also has four golf courses, including the public **Riverview,** 970/522-3035, and the private **Sterling Country Club,** 970/522-5523. For swimming, racquetball, and other indoor sports (the pool is indoor, with a $5 fee for non-residents), check out the **Sterling Recreation Center,** 808 Elm, 970/522-7882.

Accommodations

Several motels cluster near the I-76/U.S. 6 junction just east of downtown Sterling. The most upscale of them are the **Best Western Sundowner,**

one of Brad Rhea's "Living Tree" sculptures

970/522-6265 or 800/528-1234, and the **Ramada Inn,** 970/522-2625. There's also a **Days Inn** at 12881 U.S. Hwy. 6, 970/526-2195.

Buffalo Hills Camper Park, 970/522-2233, has tent and RV sites, a laundromat, recreation room, and heated pool. Camping is also available at **North Sterling Reservoir.** Two separate campgrounds (Chimney View, no electrical hookups; Elks Campground, electrical hookups available) offer a total of 141 sites. Rates are $12. Phone 800/678-2267 for information or reservations.

Food

A favorite hangout for local ranchers and merchants, the **J and L Café,** 423 N. 3rd, 970/522-3625, has been serving meals for nearly 60 years. A classic small-town café—its atmosphere defined by cigarette smoke and formica—the J and L serves breakfast, the meal it's best known for, all day. Steak and eggs, German sausages, and hot cakes, rolls, and other standard fare run $2–6. For lunch, try **Fergie's West Inn Pub,** 324 W. Main, 970/522-4220, a small bar and restaurant specializing in sandwiches (Italian subs and barbecued beef), soups, and nachos. It's open Mon.–Sat. 3 P.M.–2 A.M. While you're waiting, amuse yourself with the *Far Side* cartoons on the back of the menu.

There are also full-service restaurants at the **Ramada Inn,** 970/522-2625, and the **Best Western Sundowner Inn,** 970/522-6265.

Calendar

Among Sterling's annual events are the **Northeastern Junior College Rodeo** in May, **Hay Days** in June, the **Heritage Festival** July 4, the **Logan County Fair** in August, and **Sugar Beet Days** the third weekend in September. For specific dates, contact the **Logan County Chamber of Commerce,** 970/522-5070 or 800/544-8609, or the Northeastern Colorado Visitor Information Center at 800/544-8609.

Services

Phone the **Sterling Police** at 970/522-3512, the **Logan County Sheriff** at 970/522-1373, and the **State Patrol** at 970/522-4693 (Fort Morgan). **Sterling Regional MedCenter** is at

The Northeast Colorado Information Center in Sterling is a good source for advice and literature on the area.

615 Fairhurst, 970/522-0122. A larger facility, **Fort Morgan Community Hospital,** is in Fort Morgan at 1000 Lincoln, 970/867-3391. The main **post office** is at 306 Poplar, 970/522-1105.

Recycle aluminum at **Pioneer Distributing,** 915 State St., 970/522-0706. **Disposal Services,** 18211 Iris Dr., recycles aluminum and newspapers.

Information

The independently published *Journal-Advocate,* 970/522-1990, is Sterling's daily newspaper, a good source to get a feel of the town, as well as to find out about what's going on in the area, from movies to alfalfa fairs. Published weekday afternoons and Saturday morning, the paper is available in racks around town.

You'll find the **Northeast Colorado Information Center** just east of town between I-76 and the South Platte (across the street from the Overland Trail Museum). Pick up brochures and other information on Sterling, Logan County, and much of the northeastern corner of the state. Phone at 970/522-7649 or write P.O. Box 1683, Sterling, CO 80751.

The **Logan County Chamber of Commerce** is in Sterling at 109 N. Front St.; phone 970/522-5070 or 800/544-8609, or write P.O. Box 1683, Sterling, CO 80751.

The Sterling **public library,** 970/522-2023, is at the corner of 5th and Walnut. For **road and weather information,** phone 970/522-4848.

JULESBURG

If you're heading east on I-76, Julesburg will be the last you'll see of Colorado before lifting up over the border into Nebraska (two miles from town). At various times over the history of the region, the name Julesburg was given to three different communities in the same vicinity. It was finally affixed to the present townsite in 1881, when the town was founded as a division point on the main line of the Union Pacific Cutoff to Denver. Today, Julesburg is one of the area's major agricultural shipping stations.

One of Colorado's eight state welcome centers is in Julesburg at Exit 180, the junction of I-76 and U.S. 385. Information is available here on Julesburg, northeastern Colorado, and the rest of the state.

The **Fort Sedgwick Depot Museum,** 202 W. 1st St., 970/474-2264, is open from the week before Memorial Day through the week after Labor Day and exhibits prehistoric and Native American artifacts, pioneer gear (from bullets and casings found at battle sites to hat pins and carriages), and historical photos. Hours are Mon.–Sat. 9:30 A.M.–4:30 P.M. and Sunday 12:30–4:30 P.M. Tours are also offered by appointment; phone 970/474-3682. Admission is $1 for adults, $.50 for kids under 12. A nice picnic area is right next door.

Lodging is available at the **Platte Valley Inn Motel,** 15225 U.S. Hwy. 385, 970/474-3336, for under $50 for two. A full-service restaurant is on-site.

OTHER PLATTE RIVER CORRIDOR TOWNS

If you take U.S. 6 from Fort Morgan up to Sterling and then continue on U.S. 138 to Julesburg, you'll pass through a handful of intriguing little towns, including Merino, Atwood, Iliff, Proctor, Sedgwick, and Crook. If you want to get even more off the beaten path, you can explore Highway 113 north (where you'll find the little town of Peetz, just a few miles from the Nebraska border), or U.S. 6 east (where you'll pass through Fleming and Haxtun before arriving in Holyoke, the seat of Phillips County).

For specific information on any of these towns, call or write the **Centennial Country** branch of the Colorado Tourism Board, P.O. Box 1683, Sterling, CO 80751, 800/544-8609.

Atwood

Just southeast of Atwood is the **Summit Springs Battlefield,** site of the last major battle between the United States Cavalry and the indigenous Plains people. On July 11, 1869, Cheyenne Chief Tall Bull and his warriors were attacked by eight companies of the Fifth Cavalry and 150 Pawnee scouts—the Cheyennes, in a last desperate attempt to fend off the encroaching whites, had kidnapped two white women on a "rampage" through Kansas. Fifty-two Cheyennes, including Tall Bull, were killed in the battle, and the soldiers took 12 Indian prisoners. According to reports, one of the kidnapped women was rescued, though the other died, having been tomahawked before the battle began.

Peetz

Just south of the Nebraska border on Highway 113, Peetz is a tiny community made up largely of ranchers and farmers who are descendants of the area's original white settlers. Though this part of Colorado is mostly flat prairie, grasslands seeming to roll oceanlike forever toward all horizons, the plain is broken up, and quite dramatically, about 15 miles west of Peetz. There, the plain breaks, and the Chimney Canyons rise, their mesa-tops towering 250 feet above the prairie in stark contrast to their flat surroundings. To get there from Peetz, take County Road 74 west to County Road 37, then County Road 37 south to I-70 and go west again.

First settled in 1885 by homesteaders Peter Peetz and Nick Treinan, the town has a reputation for mischief that's belied by today's quiet community. Local legend has it that early 20th-century residents, particularly those living in the area during Prohibition, were a fiercely independent folk who did not take kindly to the restrictions the feds attempted to levy on their lifestyles. Some say there was a "still over every hill." There's even a story of one woman who supposedly took out the backseat of her Model T, which she then filled with her homemade potables, making housecalls along the area's dusty country back roads. In keeping with the town's bibulous tradition, the **Hot Spot,** 970/334-2265, is a watering hole popular among locals throughout the county.

Crook

Best known in the area for the **Tamarack Ranch State Wildlife Area,** a hunting and bird- and wildlife-watching refuge on 7,000 acres of river-bottom land, Crook is another small ranching and farming community in the fertile Platte River valley. Two Overland Trail stage stops, Spring Hill and Lillian Springs stations, both designated with historical markers, are just outside Crook on the Tamarack Ranch. For more information on the Tamarack Ranch State Wildlife Area, phone 970/886-2992.

The town was named for General George F. Crook, to whom Geronimo surrendered in New Mexico in 1866. The **Crook Museum,** 970/886-3301, at the end of 4th Street, displays pioneer artifacts, local brands and tack, and a gorgeous 19th-century rosewood piano originally sold for $.50. It's open Sunday 2–4 P.M., Memorial Day to Labor Day, and by appointment.

East to Nebraska

ALONG U.S. 34

Brush

Ten miles from Fort Morgan, where U.S. 34 forks off I-76 and shoots due east into the heart of the plains, Brush is a small plains town that has historically been dependent on agriculture and the local beef industry. Huge ranches and muddy stockyards packed with lowing cattle punctuate the surrounding prairie, and billboards claim Nothing Satisfies Like Beef. Ranchers in dusty Ford pickups, often with Queensland blue heelers or border collies in the back, zoom down highways and bump over rutted dirt back roads.

Named for Jared L. Brush, one of northeastern Colorado's pioneer cattlemen, Brush also relies heavily on agriculture, particularly sugar beets. The town itself is one of quiet streets shaded by huge numbers of fir, pine, and cedar trees, obviously not indigenous to the area and looking a bit incongruous against the prairie backdrop. You'll find camping with electrical hookups for RVs at **Brush City Campground** (take Clayton Street four blocks south of U.S. 34), as well as shaded lawns, picnic tables, playground equipment, a pool, showers, and restrooms. The first night's free, $10 a night thereafter. Brush's **Best Western Inn** is at 1208 N. Colorado, 970/842-5146 (about $65 a night). Down the street is a new **Microtel Inn,** 975 N. Colorado, 970/842-4241 (also about $65).

For more information on Brush, write the **Brush Area Chamber of Commerce,** 301 Box 363, Brush, CO 80723, or phone 970/842-5001.

Akron

About midway between Brush and Yuma, Akron has been a division point on the Burlington Railroad since 1882, when it was the only townsite on the line. Akron is the seat of Washington County. You'll find a picnic area with barbecue grills and restrooms at the corner of U.S. 34 and Custer. Lodging is available at the **Crestwood Manor Motel,** 970/345-2231, and at the **4 B's Motel,** 970/345-2028.

The **Gin Jer Snap Ranch,** 26252 County Rd. 35, offers chuck-wagon suppers, which include live entertainment and horse-drawn hay-wagon rides. Bed-and-breakfast accommodations are also available. For information or reservations, phone 970/345-2955 or 877/777-9095.

Yuma

Incorporated in 1887, Yuma is on the western edge of Yuma County, where the local economies are chiefly dependent on agriculture and ranching; Yuma County grows more corn than any other county in the state. Other crops include oats, winter rye, wheat, pinto beans, soybeans, sunflowers, and alfalfa. At one time, Yuma was known for the Federal Agricultural Experiment Station here, which developed new methods of soil conservation. Tourist information is available at the **Yuma Chamber of Commerce,** 413 S. Main St., 970/848-2704. The **Yuma Historical Society Museum,** at the corner of Highway 59 and East 3rd Avenue, is open weekends only.

Wray

Seat of Yuma County, Wray is like an oasis on the prairie flatlands: it's got actual hills, shaded with indigenous trees, and the North Fork of the Republican River tumbles through town. The **Wray Museum,** 205 E. 3rd St., 970/332-5063, displays Native American arrowheads, barbed wire, local brands, a 1907 switchboard, dolls, and military uniforms and weapons. The museum is open year-round, Tues.–Sat. 10 A.M.–5 P.M. Admission is $1.

Free tent camping is available at West City Park on U.S. 34 on the west end of town, where you'll also find a picnic area with barbecue grills, a playground, and restrooms. The only motels in Wray are the **Butte Motel,** 970/332-4828; the **Traveler's Inn,** 970/332-4848 (generally rented out by the month to construction workers, etc.), on U.S. 34 in town; and the **Sandhiller Motel and Restaurant,** 411 N.W. Railway, 970/332-4134.

Bob's Pizza Plus, 313 W. 2nd, 970/332-3177, serves sandwiches, lasagna, stews, and chili for $3–6, and pizzas for $5–15. There's a **Safeway** on the east end of town.

For more information on Wray, call the **Wray Chamber of Commerce** at 970/332-3484.

ALONG U.S. 6
Fleming
Sitting 20 miles east of Sterling on U.S. 6, Fleming was first settled in the 1880s and incorporated in 1917. Another agriculture-dependent small town, Fleming relies heavily on wheat, alfalfa, and corn. The town has two small museums of interest to passers-through. The **Fleming Heritage Museum and Park,** 970/265-2591, at the old Burlington Northern Train Depot, displays items of local historical interest (the park has restrooms, playground equipment, and picnic shelters). **Al's Country and Western Museum** has antique wagons, surreys, carriages, and automobiles. Ask locals for information on and directions to some of the area's first homesites: a rock house, "soddies"

(early sod houses), and two homes ordered pre-cut from an early 20th-century Sears-Roebuck catalog.

Holyoke
Holyoke, at the junction of U.S. 6 and U.S. 385, is a small town of beautiful brick homes with nicely maintained yards. Very young mothers push strollers along the sidewalks of sleepy, shady streets. *It's a Wonderful Life* could have been filmed here.

Just 15 miles from the Nebraska border, Holyoke, seat of Phillips County, is a hub for area ranchers and farmers; the main crops are alfafa, wheat, and corn. Passers-through will find two nice parks, one on the north end of town (on U.S. 385), with a picnic area and kids' playground; the other, on the town's south end (also on U.S. 385), is a bit bigger and also has tennis and basketball courts, and a swimming pool. You can get lodging at the **Cedar Motel,** 970/854-2525. For more information on Holyoke, write the chamber-operated **Information Center,** 100 Emerson, Holyoke, CO 80734, or phone 970/854-3517.

East on I-70

LIMON
Limon (rhymes with "rhymin'") lies in the heart of Colorado's "outback" about midway between the Rockies' Front Range and the Kansas border. If you're westbound on I-70, you can either continue on the interstate at Limon (pop. 1,800; elev. 5,360 feet) where it veers north toward Denver (about 75 miles), or you can catch U.S. 24 and drop southwest to Colorado Springs (also about 75 miles).

Ordinarily a typically quiet little plains community, Limon, and the surrounding area, is subject to severe summer weather, most notably thunderstorms that sometimes cause great damage. Case in point: on June 6, 1990, the skies over Colorado's plains began to darken and churn—not particularly unusual for that time of the year—and a series of tornadoes was re-

ported touching down in remote plains locations. What was unusual that night, though, was that the winds didn't settle down; they got angrier, and one of the tornadoes happened to choose to twist, moving slowly and forcefully, right through the middle of downtown Limon, demonically, like some hell-born evil bent on destruction, spitting hail and turning almost everything that had been Limon to rubble.

When the tornado was gone, so was most of the town: homes had been slashed apart (70 mobile homes were destroyed). Town Hall totaled. Retail stores and banks leveled, or pummeled beyond recognition (23 businesses were destroyed). Cars upended, lifted clear off the ground, and dumped like toys in heaps. Crops and fields ruined (agricultural damage was estimated to be well over $1 million). Total damage: over $20 million.

As you'd expect in a small farming community such as Limon, the townspeople banded together, offering moral, emotional, and financial help to each other. The Salvation Army and the American Red Cross also helped out, as did Colorado grocery stores (including Albertson's, King Soopers, and Safeway) and other businesses, and Limon has mostly recovered. In fact, within weeks, most businesses (especially those on the edges of town, where the damage wasn't so severe) were back to normal operations. By late spring 1991, even most of downtown had been rebuilt, and in June the governor came to dedicate "New" Limon.

Limon Heritage Museum and Railroad Park

In the original Limon depot of the Union Pacific Railroad, this small museum displays a wide range of artifacts relating to local history, including three box cars, an 18-foot-tall replica of a Cheyenne teepee, more than 30 cowboy saddles, and a reconstructed one-room schoolhouse. The museum, at the corner of East Avenue and 1st Street, is open June–Aug., Mon.–Sat. 1–8 P.M. Admission is free. Phone 719/775-2373 for more information.

Practicalities

Passers-through looking for lodging in Limon have several options, including the independently owned **Silver Spur Motel,** 514 Main St., 719/775-2807; the **Preferred Motor Inn,** 148 Main St., 719/775-2385; **Midwest Country Inn,** 719/775-2373. All about $50–65. The **Comfort Inn,** 719/775-2752, is at 2255 9th St., and has a full-service restaurant, indoor pool, and exercise room.

For more information on points of interest, events, and services in the Limon area, stop by the **Limon Chamber of Commerce** at 1062 Main St., or write P.O. Box 101, Limon, CO 80828. Phone the chamber at 719/775-9418.

BURLINGTON

Thirteen miles from the Kansas border, Burlington (pop. 3,000; elev. 4,160 feet) is home to a historic carousel still offering rides to the public, and Old Town, a reconstructed frontier town featuring a museum and 20 historic buildings (some are restorations, some are new). Seat of Kit Carson County, Burlington was once the largest grain-shipping point between Omaha and Denver. If you're arriving from the east, be sure to stop at the **State Welcome Center** just off the interstate, where you can get brochures and information on the Burlington/Kit Carson County area, as well as on the rest of Colorado.

Kit Carson County Carousel

Built in 1905 by the Philadelphia Toboggan Company for Denver's Elitch Gardens (where it operated until sold to Kit Carson County in 1928), the carousel is a National Historic Landmark. Among the 46 hand-carved animals on whose backs you can ride are horses, giraffes, zebras, camels, goats, and a "hippocampus" (seahorse), all of which parade in lines of three to the robust and throaty music of a Wurlitzer Monster Military Band Organ, built in 1909. The details on the animals, including tigers' snarling mouths, lions' saddles adorned with cherubs, and a snake crawling up a giraffe's neck, are exquisite.

The Kit Carson County Carousel is open from Memorial Day to Labor Day 1–8 P.M. at the Burlington Fairgrounds. A ride will set you back all of a quarter. For information, phone 719/825-0828.

Old Town Museum

With melodrama, cancan girls, gunfights, and hayrides, as well as a saloon, drugstore, blacksmith shop, and bank, Burlington's Old Town Museum offers an attractive break from the tedium of long-haul cross-plains travel. (You can also take a wagon ride from Old Town to the Kit Carson County Carousel.)

Old Town Museum is open Memorial Day through Labor Day, daily 9 A.M.–6 P.M.; the rest of the year, 9 A.M.–5 P.M. Admission is $6 adults, $5 for seniors, $4 ages 12–18, and $2 ages 3–11. For information, phone 719/346-7382 or 800/288-1334. Signs throughout town will direct you there.

Bonny State Recreation Area

About 22 miles north of Burlington off U.S. 385, this 7,000-acre park offers picnicking, camping, fishing, bird-watching, and boating. Four different campgrounds (with 200 sites) vary from rather primitive (pit toilets) to more developed (flush toilets, showers, and laundry facilities). Camping is free on weekdays; a small fee is charged on weekends. At the Bonny Marina, 970/354-7306, you can rent boats and buy fishing tackle, licenses, and groceries.

For more information on Bonny State Recreation Area, write P.O. Box 78-A, Idalia, CO 80735, or phone the Bonny Marina. You can also get information from the Colorado Division of Parks and Recreation, 1313 Sherman St. #618, Denver, CO 80203.

Accommodations

You'll find a handful of motels just off the interstate in Burlington. **Sloan's Motel,** 1901 Rose, 719/346-5333 or 800/362-0464, offers about the least inexpensive lodging in town—29 clean rooms running about $40 for two people. At the **Comfort Inn,** 282 S. Lincoln, 719/346-5555, and **Western Motor Inn,** 222 Rose Ave., 719/346-7676, doubles are $50–100.

Services

The **Burlington Police Department** is at 1394 Webster, 719/346-8353. The offices of the **State Police** are at 179 Webster, 719/346-5430. **Kit Carson County Memorial Hospital** is at 286 16th St., 719/346-5311. The main **post office** is at 259 14th St., 719/346-8964.

Information

For more information on Burlington and Kit Carson County, contact the **Burlington Chamber of Commerce,** 415 15th St., Burlington, CO 80807, 719/346-8070. The **public library** is at 321 14th St., 719/346-8109.

Southeastern Colorado

At first glance, southeastern Colorado may appear much like the northeastern corner of the state. Both comprise vast prairie land stretching from the Rockies' Front Range to the state's eastern border. And both are primarily agricultural regions, divided by important waterways that start in the Rockies and eventually reach the Missouri-Mississippi River system and the Gulf of Mexico. A closer inspection, however, will reveal significant differences in the two eastern corners of Colorado—in their histories, people, and even in the geology and the composition of the prairie itself.

If you come into southeastern Colorado from the north, you'll note gradual changes in the flora of the plains. Its makeup shifts from waving wheat fields and rolling grasslands to deserty stretches of yucca and sage, and the hills are dotted with juniper and piñon. This is the southwestern United States, and it looks a whole lot more like New Mexico than it does Kansas.

In addition, as you get farther south into Colorado, you'll find the proportion of people of Spanish descent increases dramatically. This is reflected in the region's place names (the towns of La Junta, Las Animas, Granada, and Campo, as well as Baca and Otero Counties) and its cooking (you tend to see more authentic Mexican restaurants out this way than you do burger shacks). Why the change in demographics? Is it simply because you're that much closer to Mexico? In part, yes. But the reason's also historical: from the early 1820s until the late 1870s, the

Kit Carson Museum in Las Animas

Santa Fe Trail cut across this part of Colorado, linking Santa Fe, New Mexico—then old Mexico's major northern trade center—with Independence, Missouri. Goods, and people, were transported along the rutted dirt highway, creating a natural amalgamation of cultures.

Settlement of southeastern Colorado began in the late 1820s, when traders Ceran St. Vrain and Charles and William Bent built a trading post along the Santa Fe Trail between what are now the cities of La Junta and Las Animas. A major hub of trading activity—for mountain men, Cheyennes, and Mexican and American troops—the outpost at one time employed more than 100 men. The fort was abandoned in 1852, although it has since been reconstructed and is an excellent stop for modern travelers interested in the history of the West (see Bent's Old Fort National Historic Site under Las Animas, below).

The railroad arrived in southeastern Colorado in the 1870s, and during the 1880s the area was prime cattle-grazing country, with huge herds of longhorns roaming freely. It was largely this cattle-ization and railroad-ization of eastern Colorado that marked the end of the area as a wilderness populated by the great indigenous animals: bison and bears fell victim to sharpshooters, government, and bounty hunters. In his excellent book *Grizzly Years,* Doug Peacock writes:

It was the livestock industry that finished off the grizzly [bear] in the more arid states. The principal reason given for killing grizzlies was protection of livestock. But few bears actually preyed on domestic animals, though the reprisals were always unrelenting and unforgiving. Bears were shot on sight out of ignorance, irrational hatred, and because of illusions about what constituted duty or sport.

By the early 20th century, the great cattle roundups had gone the way of the bison, wolf, grizzly, and Indian. Ranchers and farmers had turned to poultry, lamb, dairy cattle, and irrigated crops, particularly melons and sugar beets.

Holly, after the sugar company of the same name, and Sugar City are both in this part of the state.

In many ways, southeastern Colorado has not changed much since its conversion from cattle-grazing country to agriculture. Melons and sugar beets are still primary crops, and the little towns and farming communities, miles and miles from the state's sprawling metropolitan centers and chic resort areas, remain slow paced, close-knit, and timelessly and essentially yoked to the earth and their own landscape.

Travelers in southeastern Colorado, though not afforded the mountain vistas and cultural centers of other parts of the state, can take advantage of several museums, including the restored Bent's Fort and a fascinating Native American museum in La Junta. In addition, motorists can follow the route of the Old Santa Fe Trail, from Holly, near the Kansas border, to Trinidad, where the route drops into New Mexico. Campers and fishermen and women can explore the Arkansas River, as well as John Martin Reservoir, where the river is dammed, about midway between Las Animas and Lamar.

Before You Go

If you're coming into the area from the south, stop in Trinidad at the state welcome and tourist center, where you'll find information not only on southeastern Colorado but on the rest of the state. Pick up brochures on everything from historical sites to recreation. There's also a welcome center in Burlington that provides lots of information on eastern Colorado. For information on specific towns and areas in southeastern Colorado, contact the local chambers of commerce, whose phone numbers and addresses follow.

SOUTHEASTERN COLORADO HIGHLIGHTS

Bent's Old Fort: "living" museum in Santa Fe Trail fort dating from 1830s

La Junta: Native American and historical museums

John Martin Reservoir: fishing and camping

Arkansas River Corridor and U.S. 50

Dropping out of the Rocky Mountains west of Pueblo and slicing across the southeastern Colorado plains to the Kansas border, the 2,000-mile Arkansas River, which drains nearly 190,000 square miles, is the greatest tributary of the Missouri-Mississippi River system. U.S. 50 follows this main artery of southeastern Colorado, passing through a number of small towns and communities, including Holly, about 4.5 miles from the border, Lamar, Las Animas, and La Junta: U.S. 50 and the Arkansas continue to run parallel west through Pueblo, Cañon City, and Salida, where the river drops from its headwaters near Leadville.

LAMAR

Named for L. Q. C. Lamar, President Cleveland's Secretary of the Interior, Lamar (pop. 9,500; elev. 3,500 feet) still feels like the rowdy cowboy town it was during the late 19th and early 20th centuries. As late as 1928, four bank robbers rode into Lamar, held up the First National Bank (shooting the president and his son and kidnapping an employee, who was also eventually shot), and escaped with nearly a quarter of a million dollars.

Today Lamar is the seat of Prowers County, as well as home to Lamar Community College. In the fall, the town, which calls itself the "Goose Hunting Capital of the World," fills up with bird hunters, who pour into town by the barrel, fill up most of the motels, and spend their days working the sprawling fields and wetlands.

Big Timbers Museum

Admission is free to this pioneer museum, named for a stretch of the Animas River where William Bent and company had camps during the height of their trading empire (see Bent's Old Fort National Historic Site, below). In addition to historical photos, you'll find an array of domestic tools and equipment, as well as clothing from the mid-19th century. The museum is open daily

1:30–4:30 P.M. It's at 7515 U.S. Hwy. 50 just north of Lamar. Phone 719/336-2472 for more information.

Accommodations, Food, and Camping

The nicest lodging in town is the Cow Palace Inn Best Western, 1301 N. Main, 719/336-7753. You'll find inexpensive rooms at the El Mar Budget Host Motel, 1210 S. Main, 719/336-4331.

The dining room at the Cow Palace Inn has good food (burgers, chicken, beef, salads) at reasonable prices ($6–13). Ranchers 24-Hour Family Restaurant, 719/336-3445, at the Lamar Truck Plaza, three miles west of town at the junction of U.S. 50 and U.S. 287, serves BIG truckers' breakfasts for $3–6 and sandwiches and burgers for $4–8. There's also a soup and salad bar.

The Lamar KOA campground, 719/336-7625, is about five miles west of town on U.S. 50. Hud's Campground, 719/829-4344, about 15 miles west of Lamar, has nice RV sites in the shade of cottonwoods and a small grocery store.

Services

The offices of the Lamar Police Department are at 505 Main St., 719/336-4341. Reach the Prowers County Sheriff at 719/336-5234 and the State Patrol at 719/336-7403. Prowers Medical Center is at 2101 S. Memorial Drive, 719/336-4343. The central post office is at 300 S. 5th St., 719/336-4421.

Recycle aluminum at the Safeway, 405 E. Olive St., and aluminum and glass at the Lamar Area Hospice, 1001 S. Main.

Information

The Lamar Chamber of Commerce is downtown at 109-A E. Beech St, 719/336-4379. The public library is at 104 E. Parmenter, 719/336-4632. Tourist information is also available from the KOA campground west of town.

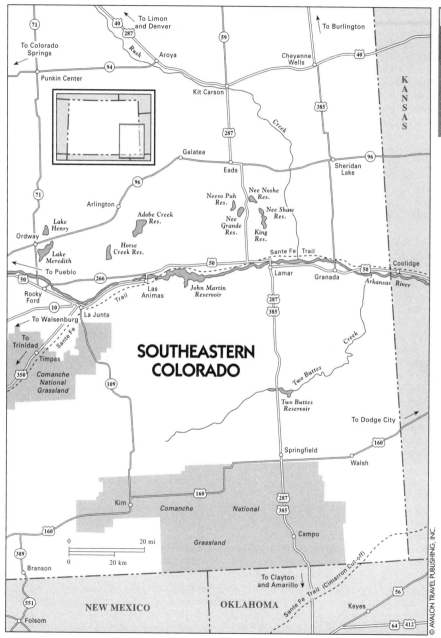

LAS ANIMAS

U.S. 50 beelines due west for 30 miles from Lamar to Las Animas, following the courses of the Arkansas River, the Santa Fe Trail, and the Atchison, Topeka, and Santa Fe Railroad. Not a whole lot to look at along here—mostly dry, brown, and flat—though you can pull off at John Martin Reservoir to camp or do some warm-water fishing. Also watch along the highway for communities of prairie dogs.

Las Animas (pop. 2,800; elev. 3,900 feet) was founded in 1869 at the confluence of the Arkansas and Purgatoire Rivers and near the site of Fort Lyon, a U.S. Army post built in 1860 to house cavalry troops and to protect Santa Fe Trail travelers. Between the mid-1870s and about 1915, the Las Animas area was the scene of huge cattle roundups, though the region has long been rich in agriculture as well. As early as 1866, Thomas O. Boggs and John Prowers were experimenting with irrigated crops on a farm two miles south of present-day Las Animas. Boggsville, as the community came to be known, eventually became a regional center for cattle, sheep, and a variety of crops, and it was the first seat of Bent County. Kit Carson died in 1868 in a cabin in Las Animas and was buried near Bent's Fort with his third wife, Maria Josefa Jaramillo, though their remains were later moved to Taos, New Mexico. The abandoned Boggsville was acquired in 1985 by the Pioneer Historical Society of Bent County, which is in the process of restoring the community.

Kit Carson Museum

If you think this place is odd to look at, with the word "MUSEUM" spelled out in letters atop tall poles like an advertisement for some tacky motel, get a load of the building's history. Built of adobe in 1940, it originally housed German prisoners of war captured in North Africa. After the war, it was home to Jamaican field workers, and later it became a home for widows and the poor. Don't expect upscale displays here with high-tech dioramas and fancy collections. This is a pioneer museum pure and simple. Wander

through the historical displays of the main building—Native American artifacts, early farming equipment, domestic gear. Then wander out back to the several historical buildings that have been moved onto the site: the first Las Animas jail, built in 1882; the original Bent County Jail; an 1860s log stage station, originally standing between Bent's Fort and Pueblo; a one-room school; a blacksmith shop; and a carriage house. Be sure to check out the replica of the gallows in the field across the street from the museum.

Kit Carson Museum is open daily 1 P.M.–5 P.M. Memorial Day through Labor Day and is on 9th Street near the junction of U.S. 50 and Highway 101. Watch for the sign (you can't miss it). For more information, phone the museum at 719/456-2005.

John Martin Reservoir and Lake Hasty

About 15 miles east of Las Animas, this large reservoir and smaller, nearby lake offer a variety of water sports, as well as sightseeing, picnicking, and camping, with lots of very nice campsites right on the water. Originally part of a federal flood-control and irrigation project, the dam was completed in 1946. It's more than two miles long and rises more than 100 feet above the river; the spillway is more than 1,000 feet long. Seventy-five-acre Lake Hasty is immediately downstream and was formed when earth was moved to build the dam.

Stop in at the visitor center in the Project Office, where you can pick up maps and other information. Tours can also be arranged by calling in advance. For information, or to book tours, phone 719/336-3476, or write John Martin Reservoir Resident Office, U.S. Army Corps of Engineers, Star Route, Hasty, CO 81044.

Bent's Old Fort National Historical Site

Anyone with even a moderate interest in history will find this fort absolutely fascinating, definitely one of the highlights of a visit to this part of the state. Completed in 1833, the adobe fort was for nearly 20 years a critical trading hub—the most important stop between Independence, Missouri,

© STEPHEN METZGER

Don't miss Bent's Old Fort National Historical Site between Las Animas and La Junta.

and Santa Fe, New Mexico—where Native Americans, mountain men, U.S. Army troops, and Mexican soldiers gathered to swap furs, manufactured goods, and tales of life in the rugged West as they swigged the notorious Taos Lightning.

The trading company was the brainchild of two brothers, Charles and William Bent, along with Ceran St. Vrain, the three of whom had left St. Louis to make their fortunes in fur trading. William Bent, historians tell us, was unusually sensitive to the Native Americans, whose lands their trading empire encompassed (Southern Cheyenne, Arapahoe, Ute, Northern Apache, Kiowa, and Comanche). The business-savvy William went to great lengths to ensure the post saw large numbers of traders; he encouraged rival tribes to make peace with each other, and in 1837 he even married a Cheyenne woman, apparently to look better in the eyes of potential native traders.

By the late 1840s, Santa Fe Trail trade was already on the wane—due to the Mexican-American War, increasing native uprisings, Charles's death in Taos, St. Vrain's departure, and finally, in 1849, cholera, which decimated the tribes upon which William relied for trade.

Bent's Old Fort has been restored to approximate its 1830s prime, and it's one of the best examples in the West of a "living museum." A costumed guide takes visitors through the fort's many rooms—blacksmith's shop, military and trappers' quarters, billiard room, and warehouse—while employees, also in costume, quietly go about their work, as though it were a century and a half earlier. Be sure to check out the orientation film before going through the fort (if only to hear the attempt at a French accent by whoever's doing the voice of Ceran St. Vrain).

The fort is open daily 8 A.M.–5:30 P.M., Memorial Day through Labor Day, and 9 A.M.–4 P.M. the rest of the year. Closed New Year's Day, Thanksgiving, and Christmas. Admission is free during the nonsummer months, although you can arrange a guided tour for $2. Admission during the summer is $2. To get there, take Highway 194 or U.S. 50 west from Las Animas, or U.S. 50 east from La Junta, and watch for the signs. A 200-yard paved walkway leads from the parking lot to the fort; rides are provided for visitors with disabilities. For more information, phone 719/383-5010, or write 35110 U.S. Hwy. 194 E, La Junta, CO 81050-9523.

Accommodations and Food

In addition to a handful of independently run motels in Las Animas, you can get rooms at the **Best Western Bent's Fort Inn,** 10950 U.S. Hwy. 50, 719/456-0011. The **Troll Haus Restaurant,** 604 Locust, 719/456-0062, is a local favorite. It's open weekends only, Fri.–Sat. 5:30-8:30 P.M., Sunday 10:30 A.M.–2 P.M.

Services

The **Las Animas Police Department** is at 326 Prowers Ct., 719/456-1313. Contact the **Bent County Sheriff** at 719/456-1363 and the **State Patrol** at 719/384-2562 (La Junta). The nearest hospital is the **Arkansas Valley Regional Medical Clinic** in La Junta at 1100 Carson Dr.; phone 719/456-2088 from Las Animas, 719/384-5412 from La Junta. The Las Animas **post office** is at 513 W. 6th St., 719/456-0310.

Recycle aluminum and glass in La Junta at **Greenstreet Distributing Company,** 706 E. 1st St. (call ahead: 719/384-8761), or at **Safeway,** 315 W. 2nd Street.

Information

For more information on the Las Animas area, write **Las Animas/Bent County Chamber of Commerce,** 332 Ambassador Thompson Blvd., Las Animas, CO 81054, or phone 719/336-3476. In town, stop by the Las Animas **public library** at 308 W. 5th St., 719/456-0111.

LA JUNTA

Seat of Otero County, La Junta (Spanish for "The Junction," though mispronounced La-HUNT-a) is about 20 miles west of Las Animas at the junction of the old Navajo and Santa Fe Trails. At La Junta (pop. 7,600; elev. 4,050), U.S. 350, following the Santa Fe Trail, splits off U.S. 50 and drops through the Comanche National Grassland to Trinidad. La Junta is also at the junction of the Santa Fe Railroad's main line and its Denver branch, and so has long been an important shipping town. It was founded in 1875 and originally called Otero, after Spanish settler Miguel Otero.

One of the prettier towns on the southeastern plains, La Junta is characterized by huge hillside homes and nicely kept lawns and gardens. Its city park is perfect for a picnic and/or an afternoon snooze.

Koshare Indian Museum

It might be tempting to zip through La Junta without stopping, but it'd be a shame to miss this wonderful museum. Among the highlights are Crow, Cree, Shoshone, and Flathead buckskin clothing, moccasins, and hide paintings, in addition to Zuni pottery, Hopi, Zuni, and Navajo silver, Hopi kachina, and Hupa baskets. There's also a full-size model of a kiva, where a local Boy Scout troop performs authentic Native American dances Saturday evening in the summer and during holidays (the group started in the 1930s and has earned a national reputation for itself, performing around the country). A gift shop sells quality Native American artwork, as well as souvenirs and knickknacks.

The museum is open 10 A.M.–5 P.M.; call for times of dances. Admission is $2 for adults, with discounts for seniors and kids. It's on the Otero Junior College campus. Take Santa Fe Avenue south to 18th Street (Santa Fe is interrupted by the city park; circle around it). Small entrance fee. For more information, phone 719/384-4411, or write 115 W. 18th St., P.O. Box 580, La Junta, CO 81050.

Otero Museum

This pioneer museum, in a turn-of-the-20th-century building listed on the National Register of Historic Places, displays artifacts from the area's history, emphasizing the arrival of the railroad and the development of agriculture. Exhibits include grocery items (the building was originally a grocery store), farming and ranching tools and equipment, and even a mid-19th-century stagecoach.

The museum, at 2nd and Anderson, is open Mon.–Sat. 1–5 P.M. June through September, as well as by appointment. Phone 719/384-7500 for more information or to arrange a tour.

City Park

Just north of the Koshare Museum and Otero Junior College is a large city park with hilly lawns, shade, picnic tables, and a large pond.

Accommodations and Food

You'll find a handful of motels and inns in La Junta, most running about $60 for two. I'd start at the **Super 8,** U.S. Hwy. 50 W, 719/384-4408, or the **Quality Inn,** 1325 E. 3rd St., 719/384-2571. The **La Junta Budget Inn** is at 110 E 1st St., 719/384-2504.

Predictably, La Junta holds many good Mexican restaurants. Try **El Azteca,** 710 W. 3rd St., 719/384-4215, or **Felicia's,** 27948 Frontage Rd., 719/384-4814.

Services

You can reach the **La Junta Police** at 719/384-2525, the **Otero County Sheriff** at 719/384-5941, and the **Colorado State Patrol** at 719/384-8981. La Junta's **Arkansas Valley Regional Medical Center** is at 1100 Carson Ave., 719/384-5412. The main **post office** is at 4th and Colorado, 719/384-5944.

Recycle aluminum and glass at **Colorado Beverage,** 706 E. 1st St., 719/384-8761 (call ahead), and aluminum at **Safeway,** 315 W. 2nd Street.

Information

La Junta's **Woodruff Memorial Library** is at 522 Colorado Ave., 719/384-4612. The **La Junta Chamber of Commerce** may be found at 110 Santa Fe Ave., 719/384-7411. Check the **Book Stop,** 318 Santa Fe, 719/384-8839, for books of local interest.

WEST OF LA JUNTA

If you've been out poking around on the eastern plains for a while you're probably growing weary of all the flat, barren landscapes. Driving west out of La Junta, then, offers cheap thrills in the form of a bona fide view of mountains. Whether you take U.S. 50 to Pueblo, Highway 10 to Walsenburg, or U.S. 350 to Trinidad, somewhere about a half hour out of La Junta (sooner on clear days) you see them: the Rockies, looming snowcapped in the distance. Truly a sight for sore eyes.

The 65-mile stretch of U.S. 50 from La Junta to Pueblo takes you through a handful of small farming towns and communities, including Swink, Rocky Ford, Manzanola, Fowler, and Avondale. Pueblo sits at the foot of the Front Range, and from there it's just a half hour or so before you're winding up into some serious mountains.

Rocky Ford

This little agricultural community, about 15 miles west of La Junta, is known nationwide for its melons. The Rocky Ford cantaloupe, particularly, but locally grown watermelons as well, attract buyers from throughout the country. Each summer, in mid-August, Rocky Ford hosts the Arkansas Valley Fair, which celebrates the region's multicultural heritage and agricultural harvests.

Information

For more information on Rocky Ford or the Arkansas Valley Fair, write the **Rocky Ford Chamber of Commerce,** 105 N. Main St., Rocky Ford, CO 81067, or phone 719/254-7483.

La Junta to Walsenburg and Trinidad

From La Junta to Walsenburg it's about 75 miles, the drive straight and unbroken, with little to amuse, save for two exciting crosses over county lines. Best, then, simply to get on with it.

La Junta to Trinidad is about an 80-mile drive, U.S. 350 following the Santa Fe Trail southwest and then dropping nearly due south at Trinidad and the junction with I-25. From there it's just 90 miles to Ratón Pass and the New Mexico border. In fact, along this stretch of U.S. 350 the landscape begins to look even more southwestern, the brown bluffs and mesas dotted with yucca and cane cholla. Then, just about 15 miles out of Trinidad, the flora turns dramatically green, the valleys lush and fertile. Readers heading to New Mexico and heartbroken about having to glovebox the witty traveling companion that has guided them thus far, or those simply intrigued with the mystery and seductiveness of that wonderful state, might consider investing 17 bucks in the critically acclaimed *Moon Handbooks: New Mexico,* by yours truly (and humbly); it's available at your local bookstore.

South-Central Colorado

The diversity of south-central Colorado makes it in a very real sense a microcosm of the rest of the state. This one region, stretching north from the New Mexico border to Colorado Springs and Fairplay and west from the Great Plains to the towering Rocky Mountains, offers fascinating lessons in the state's geology, history, and demographics, as well as myriad sightseeing and recreation opportunities.

South-central Colorado is split lengthwise by I-25, which crosses over from New Mexico at Ratón Pass, then follows the plains' western edge north through Trinidad, Pueblo, and Colorado Springs, and continues through Denver and up into northern Wyoming. U.S. 50 bisects I-25 at Pueblo, cutting east to west across south-central Colorado from the plains up into the foothills of the Cañon City area and then on to Salida, Gunnison, Grand Junction, and west to California. Just north of the New Mexico border, between Del Norte and the Sangre de Cristo Mountains, is the San Luis Valley, a 50- by 125-mile pocket of austere beauty surrounded by mountains—the San Juans, Sangre de Cristos, La Garitas, and Conejos-Brazos.

This was the first part of Colorado to be explored by nonnative peoples. Perhaps as early as the mid-16th century, Spanish expeditions were pushing up from the south. San Luis, a small community a half hour from the New Mexico border at the junction of Highway 159 and Highway 142, is the oldest town in the state. Because the Spanish were the first to explore and settle this area, it still maintains its Hispanic heritage—evident in its architecture, cooking, folk art, and the surnames of a large proportion of the people.

© STEPHEN METZGER

Garden of the Gods

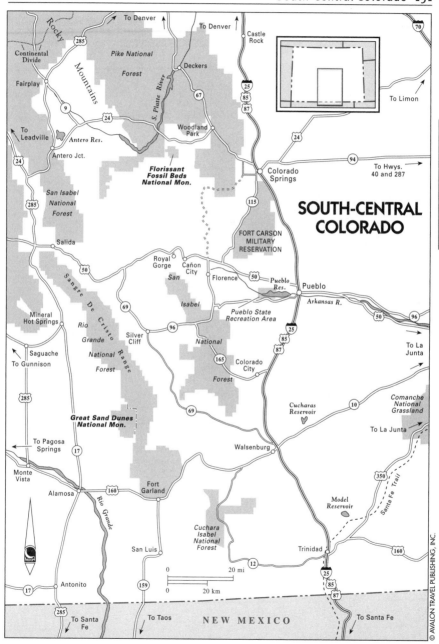

SOUTH-CENTRAL

To Denver
To Denver
Castle Rock
Rocky Mountains
Continental Divide
285
Pike National
Forest
Deckers
70
Fairplay
S. Platte River
67
25
85
87
To Limon
9
24
Woodland Park
Antero Res.
To Leadville
24
Antero Jct.
24
94
To Hwys. 40 and 287
Florissant Fossil Beds National Mon.
Colorado Springs

San Isabel National Forest
115

285
FORT CARSON MILITARY RESERVATION

SOUTH-CENTRAL COLORADO

Salida
50
Royal Gorge
Cañon City
San
Florence
50
Pueblo Res.
Pueblo
Sangre De Cristo Range
69
Isabel
Arkansas R.
96
Pueblo State Recreation Area
50
96
Mineral Hot Springs
Rio Grande
96
National
25
85
87
To La Junta
Saguache
To Gunnison
Silver Cliff
National
165
Colorado City
285
Forest
Forest
Comanche National Grassland
Great Sand Dunes National Mon.
69
Cucharas Reservoir
10
To La Junta
To Pagosa Springs
17
Walsenburg
Monte Vista
160
350
Santa Fe Trail
Alamosa
Rio Grande
Fort Garland
Model Reservoir
Cuchara Isabel National Forest
San Luis
Trinidad
160
12
0   20 mi
0   20 km
Antonito
17
159
25
85
87
To Santa Fe
To Taos
NEW MEXICO
To Santa Fe

© AVALON TRAVEL PUBLISHING, INC.

SOUTH-CENTRAL COLORADO HIGHLIGHTS

Trinidad: museums, the Bloom Mansion, Sangre de Cristo Mountains, fishing, camping

Highway 12, Trinidad to Walsenburg: San Isabel National Forest, Monument Lake, wildflowers in the Cuchara Valley, Spanish Peaks, fishing, camping, skiing

Great Sand Dunes National Monument: sightseeing, camping

Pueblo: Rosemount House Museum, Mineral Palace Park, city zoo, Colorado State Fair, fishing, camping, sightseeing

Cañon City: Colorado Territorial Prison Museum and Park, museums, sightseeing, whitewater rafting

Royal Gorge: sightseeing, tram rides, camping

Cripple Creek: Narrow Gauge Railroad, Mollie Kathleen Mine Tour, sightseeing, museums, gambling, shopping

Colorado Springs: museums, U.S. Olympic Sports Complex, Will Rogers Shrine of the Sun, ProRodeo Hall of Fame, Broadmoor Hotel

Bishop Castle (Westcliffe): modern stone castle

Pikes Peak: Pikes Peak Highway, cog railway, hiking

Manitou Spings: historical tours, museums, Garden of the Gods (National Natural Landmark)

In the mid-19th century, south-central Colorado was the scene of important mining activity. The mines of Cripple Creek, in the high mountains west of Colorado Springs, produced millions of dollars in gold and silver and made fortunes for their owners, who built palatial homes, opera houses, and resorts in Denver and Colorado Springs.

Today south-central Colorado offers the traveler lots to see and do. Drive to the top of Pikes Peak. Visit the United States Air Force Academy or ProRodeo Hall of Fame in Colorado Springs. Explore the old mining towns of Victor and Cripple Creek, or a stretch of the Old Santa Fe Trail. Camp in the gorgeous San Isabel and Pike National Forests. Take a narrow-gauge train over into New Mexico. Wander into the tallest sand dunes in the country. Or just enjoy some of the prettiest scenery in the state.

Before You Go

If you're coming in from the south, stop at the **Colorado Welcome Center** in Trinidad, 309 N. Nevada Ave., 719/846-9512. You'll find a friendly staff and lots of information and brochures on things to do and see in the area, as well as in the rest of the state. The center, open daily 8 A.M.–6 P.M., also provides information about lodging and camping. Be sure to pick up a copy of *Spirit: The Magazine of Southern Colorado.*

Trinidad

Situated just east of the Sangre de Cristo ("Blood of Christ") Mountains and 20 miles from the New Mexico border, Trinidad (pop. 9,500; elev. 6,025 feet), seat of Las Animas County, maintains a strong sense of its Spanish heritage. Its narrow, hilly brick streets, stone churches, and mellow, Old World pace, as well as the nearby place names (Segundo, Aguilar, Isabel, Cuchara, La Veta) indicate the town's ties to the Spanish colonial era and, later, to the period when the surrounding area was part of the Territory of New Mexico.

The hub of several highways, Trinidad is a funny town to drive in, as I-25, U.S. 160 and U.S. 350, and Highways 12 and 239, not to mention the railroad, all convene near the river, winding linguine-like before heading out again in their different directions. The downtown area, Corazón de Trinidad (Heart of Trinidad), is an excellent spot to spend a few hours poking around and getting a feel for a part of the state that's very different from the resort towns and sprawling urban centers to the north. Also, take a few minutes to drive up into the hills on Trinidad's east side above the Pioneer Museum; the brick streets are truly unique and add a distinct flavor to the little town.

Trinidad maintains a strong sense of its Spanish heritage in its narrow, hilly brick streets, stone churches, mellow, Old World pace, and nearby place names.

Trinidad, a Cut Above

Little-known Trinidad fact: this tiny town, out in the middle of the proverbial nowhere, has been dubbed the "sex-change capital of the world." According to a 1998 episode of *60 Minutes,* and to an Associated Press story from the May 29, 1998, *San Francisco Chronicle,* Trinidad's Dr. Stanley Biber has performed more than 3,500 "gender-reassignment" surgeries (on both men and women) since the late 1960s. Though not part of Trinidad's public-relations campaign, Dr. Biber's work doesn't seem to faze Trinidadians, who, in fact, seem grateful for the revenue generated by the $10,000 operations and other pa-

tient spending. The patients, too, are grateful, having come from all over the world to take what they call "the road to Trinidad."

HISTORY

The Trinidad area, including the Sangre de Cristos and the Purgatoire River Valley, was long a hunting and ceremonial ground for various Indian tribes, and though the town was never actually attacked, early European settlers were accustomed to threats by Ute war parties. Long before the Comanches, Utes, and other groups arrived, prehistoric people lived in caves and crude shelters in the nearby hills.

Shortly after 1598, when Juan de Oñate arrived in the Santa Fe area from Spain, he led a group north into the Purgatoire River Valley. During the next two centuries, Spanish priests, explorers, and soldiers continued to probe the area north of Santa Fe, and between 1822 and the late 1870s, Trinidad was the last stop on the Santa Fe Trail before Ratón Pass and the drop into Santa Fe.

On May 13, 1847, the United States declared war on Mexico, and a month later, Stephen Watts Kearny, after passing through what is now Trinidad, arrived in Santa Fe and took control of that town without resistance. In 1859, New Mexican Gabriel Gutierrez came north to Trinidad to herd sheep, and his cabin was the first building of record.

Gradually, Trinidad saw more and more settlers, at first mostly from the south. Soon, though, people began to arrive from the north, and for a time the rambunctious town seemed to symbolize the larger frictions between the United States and Mexico; fights between the two groups were commonplace. On Christmas Day, 1867, nearly a thousand people took part in a rumble of sorts, which resulted in several deaths and could be brought under control only

SOUTH-CENTRAL

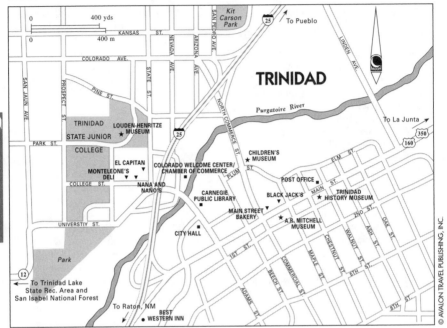

© AVALON TRAVEL PUBLISHING, INC.

by the U.S. cavalry, who declared martial law. That year also saw the opening of Trinidad's first coal mine.

The arrival of the railroad in the late 1870s helped encourage cattle ranchers to come to the area, boosting the local economy; the town was incorporated in 1877. On April 20, 1914, striking coal workers, with support from the United Mine Workers, battled U.S. militiamen, who had been called in to keep the peace. During the ensuing gunfight, which took place about 12 miles north of Trinidad, six coal miners were shot, and 11 children and two women were killed when the tent in which they were hiding burned. (If you find this period of history interesting or are intrigued by the early American labor movement, see John Sayles's excellent film *Matewan,* which, based on a true story and set in West Virginia, examines the deplorable working conditions in the mines and the resistance labor organizers met when they tried to improve them.)

The United Mine Workers of America erected a monument near the Ludlow exit north of

Trinidad in recognition of those killed. In June 1990, the 100th anniversary of the founding of the UMWA, labor leaders from around the country gathered at the site of the monument to commemorate the massacre.

MUSEUMS
Trinidad History Museum

This three-museum complex occupies the 300 block of East Main Street. A small entrance fee gets you a guided tour of all three buildings.

The **Baca House,** made of adobe and dating from 1869, is the oldest still-standing building in Trinidad. Built by Pennsylvanian John S. Hough and sold a year later to Felipe Baca, a Spanish sheep rancher, shipping tycoon, and politician, the house has been redecorated with period furnishings.

The 13-room **Bloom House** is reportedly the state's best example of Second Empire French architecture; it was built in 1882 for cattle rancher and banker Frank L. Bloom. All of the furnishings in the mansion are either originals or exact duplicates. Bloom House highlights include elaborate draperies and wallpapers and a Victorian garden, complete with waterfall.

Occupying what were once the stables and servants' quarters for the Baca House, Trinidad's **Pioneer Museum** displays an array of artifacts from the Santa Fe Trail and from Trinidad's past, including Indian arrowheads, carriages, guns, and historical photos.

The museum complex is open 10 A.M.–4 P.M. daily May 1–Sept. 30, and by appointment the rest of the year. Admission is $5, with discounts offered to kids and senior citizens. For information on all three museums, write 300 E. Main St., Trinidad, CO 81082, or phone 719/846-7217.

Louden-Henritze Archaeology Museum

Housed in the library of Trinidad State Junior College, this small museum features dioramas of nearby Trinchera Cave, which was occupied thousands of years ago by nomadic hunters. The museum also displays arrowheads, fossils, and samples of local gems and minerals. Some of the artifacts come from a 1962 excavation of hundreds of sites now deep beneath the waters of Trinidad Reservoir.

The museum is open daily Mon.–Fri. 10 A.M.–4 P.M., in December by appointment only. Admission is free. For more information, phone 719/846-5508.

Trinidad Children's Museum

In an old firehouse that was also the town's first city hall and jail, this is a museum full of hands-on displays, including a firecart, fire engine, and primitive alarm system.

The museum, at 314 N. Commercial St., is open June–Aug., Mon.–Fri. noon–4 P.M. Admission is free. For more information, or to book tours, phone 719/846-7721 or 719/846-8418.

A. R. Mitchell Memorial Museum and Gallery

Famous for his Western paintings and the scores of covers he did for Western dime novels, Arthur Roy Mitchell died in 1977. The Trinidad gallery

displays about 200 of his original oils, in addition to work by other Western-style painters, including Harvey Dunn and Grant Reynard. The museum also exhibits a collection of Spanish folk art, and a gift shop sells jewelry, paintings, cards, and souvenirs. Admission to the museum, at 150 E. Main, is $2 for adults. Hours are Mon.–Sat. 10 A.M.–4 P.M., mid-April through September. For more information, phone 719/846-4224.

PARKS AND RECREATION

City Parks

Kit Carson Park, northwest of the downtown area at San Pedro Street and Kansas Avenue, has picnic facilities, lawns, shade trees, and a playground, as well as a turn-of-the-century bandstand and a statue of Carson. **Central Park,** west of I-25 at Stonewall and San Juan, has softball fields, a small lake, picnic tables, a playground, and a jogging trail. **Southside Park,** on Benshoar Drive, has a jogging trail, horseshoe pits, softball fields, picnic tables, and a playground. For more information, phone the Trinidad Community Center at 719/846-4454.

Trinidad Lake State Recreation Area

This 2,300-acre park, with a 900-acre lake, about four miles west of Trinidad on Highway 12, offers a wide range of recreational activities, including hiking, fishing, boating, picnicking, swimming, and camping (tenting and RVing). You'll find 62 campsites, running water, flush toilets, and hot showers, as well as laundry facilities and RV dump stations. Fish for rainbow and brown trout, largemouth bass, channel catfish, bluegill, walleye, and crappie. Two short nature trails (Carpios Ridge Trail, one mile, and Levsa Canyon Trail, 1.5 miles) have been laid out for hikers.

For more information on Trinidad Lake State Recreation Area, write 32610 Hwy. 12, Trinidad, CO 81082, or phone 719/846-6951. Call to reserve campsites or group picnic areas. You can also get information from the **Colorado Division of Parks and Outdoor Recreation,** Department of Natural Resources, 1313

Sherman #618, Denver, CO 80203, 303/866-3437.

Highway 12 and San Isabel National Forest

Highway 12, which winds west out of Trinidad, up into the gorgeous Sangre de Cristo Mountains of San Isabel National Forest, over 9,941-foot Cucharas Pass, then back down through La Veta and into Walsenburg, offers excellent camping (three Forest Service campgrounds lie just east of Cucharas Pass) and fishing opportunities, as well as spectacular sightseeing. (The 82-mile drive is discussed in detail under North to Walsenburg via Highway 12, below.) Monument Lake Resort, about 35 miles west of Trinidad, is owned by the city. For further information on San Isabel National Forest, write 1920 Valley Dr., Pueblo, CO 81008, or phone 719/545-8737.

Golf

The **Trinidad Municipal Golf Course,** 719/846-4015, just south of town, is a nine-hole course open year-round and sponsor of various local tournaments.

PRACTICALITIES

Accommodations

Though Trinidad's a rather small town, room rates are higher than you might expect, in part because there's little else available nearby. Supply and demand, you know. Last time I passed through, it was a Tuesday evening, and I couldn't find anything for under $70. The following lodges should have doubles priced between $70 and $90: the **Days Inn,** 702 W. Main (just off I-25 at Exit 13B), 719/846-2271; **Best Western Trinidad Inn,** 900 W. Adams (Exit 13A), 719/846-2215; and the **Super 8,** 124 Freeman Rd. (Exit 15), 719/846-8280.

Twelve miles from downtown, the **Chicosa Canyon Bed and Breakfast,** 719/846-6199, has three guest rooms and a separate cabin renting for $90–130. The rustic decor and secluded location make it an ideal getaway from

city strife; it even has boarding facilities and encouragess you to bring your horse(s) along. Check out www.bbonline.com/co/chicosa.

Food

For starters, try the **Main Street Bakery & Café,** 121 W. Main St., 719/846-8779, open Mon.–Sat. at 6 A.M. I had a great Mexican dinner at **El Capitan,** 321 State St., 719/846-9903—entrées run $6–12. A long-standing favorite for Italian food is **Nana and Nano's Pasta House,** 415 University St., 719/846-2697 ($7–14), over on the west side of town en route to Trinidad Lake. Right next door, **Monteleone's Deli** sells homemade Italian sandwiches (meatball, Italian sausage, etc.). You might also try **Black Jack's Saloon & Steakhouse,** 225 W. Main St., 719/846-9501, open 4 P.M.–11 P.M. Let me know how it is.

Calendar

Each June (usually around the second weekend), Trinidad sponsors the **Santa Fe Trail Festival,** featuring arts-and-crafts shows, costume competitions, and lots of food and live entertainment. There's also a staged melodrama. For information and exact dates, contact the chamber of commerce, 309 Nevada St., 719/846-9285.

Services

The offices of the **Trinidad Police Department,** 719/846-4441, and the **Las Animas County Sheriff,** 719/846-2211, are downtown next to city hall on North Animas. Reach the **Colorado State Patrol** in Trinidad at 719/846-2227. **Mt. San Rafael Hospital** is at 410 Benedicta, 719/846-9213. The main **post office** is at 301 E. Main, 719/846-6871.

Recycle aluminum at the **Las Animas County Rehabilitation Center,** 1205 Congress Dr., and at **Safeway,** 457 W. Main.

Information

At the **Colorado Welcome Center** in Trinidad, you can pick up information on recreation, dining, and lodging, as well as maps of the area and a self-guided historical walking tour.

Write the **Trinidad Chamber of Commerce** at 309 Nevada St., Trinidad, CO 81082, or phone 719/846-9285.

Trinidad's historical **Carnegie Public Library** is at 202 N. Animas, 719/846-6841. Pick up Trinidad's daily newspaper, the *Chronicle-News,* 719/846-3311, for listings of current events and other happenings.

For **road conditions,** phone 719/846-9262.

Transportation

Although Trinidad's a weird town to drive in, with all the different highways converging, the downtown area is pretty square and easy to walk. To make it even easier to get around, the city offers the **Trinidad Trolley,** with stops at parks and historical sites. Departures are hourly from the parking lot next to the city hall (summer only).

North to Walsenburg via Highway 12

Though this route will take you at least 1.5 hours out of your way (I-25 to Walsenburg takes 40 minutes, max), this scenic byway, one of the prettiest in the state, is definitely worth the extra time. The highway first drops southwest out of Trinidad, passes Trinidad Lake State Recreation Area and the historical mining town of Cokedale, winds through the lush Purgatoire River Valley, then begins to climb into the high mountains, offering breathtaking vistas along the way. You'll pass through a number of tiny resort communities, San Isabel National Forest, over 9,941-foot Cucharas Pass, and past several pristine alpine lakes near, or above, timberline. Linguists take note: occasionally in the Purgatoire River Valley, you'll see the word "Picketwire" in place names. This is an Anglo bastardization of "Purgatoire," French for purgatory.

TRINIDAD TO LA VETA

Cokedale

Now a National Historic District, Cokedale was founded in 1906 by the American Refining and Smelting Company. Though the community bustled with work and workers during the early part of the last century, when coke from the town's ovens was shipped to Leadville, today the town's all but abandoned. Dirt streets wind past dilapidated houses—some still occupied—which cling to the hillside in last-gasp efforts to remain standing.

Segundo

About 10 miles past Cokedale, the tiny town of Segundo is little more than a gas station, small

market, and deli (Ringo's). Years ago, citizens of Spanish descent painted the doors and window frames of Segundo homes and businesses bright blue to keep the devil away.

Stonewall

Named for the gigantic granite stone wall you can see through the trees on the west side of the highway, this town was established by Juan Gutierrez (nephew of Gabriel Gutierrez, one of Trinidad's founding fathers) in the late 1860s. Long a resort community for fishermen, as well as for people simply wanting to escape the heat of the lowlands, Stonewall still offers a couple of inns tucked away in a beautiful valley setting, highlighted by the rushing river, green meadows, and tall pines and cottonwoods. The **Picketwire Lodge,** 7600 Hwy. 12, 719/868-2265, has rooms with kitchens and is open year-round for hunting, fishing, and cross-country skiing. Accommodations—in motel rooms or cabins—run $42–104 for two. A small on-site store sells groceries and fishing licenses and equipment.

Monument Lake

With a large granite stone sticking straight up out of its deep blue waters, Monument Lake is a perfect place to stop and picnic and set up camp for a couple of days. **Monument Lake Resort and Campground,** 719/868-2226 or 800/845-8006, owned and operated by the city of Trinidad, offers a full range of accommodations (summers only), from tent and RV sites to cabins and luxury rooms in the adobe lodge; there is also a full-service restaurant, lounge, and gift shop. Tent sites run about $10, RV sites $17.50, cabins and rooms $65–85 for two. Write Star Route 1, Box 81A, Trinidad, CO 81091, for more information.

Cucharas Pass

The views from this pass are stunning. In the early summer, columbines sheet the steep meadows, and the mountainsides are mottled green with aspen, fir, spruce, and pine. Several of the lakes along the road offer excellent fishing, although you should check the restrictions—some allow flies or artificial lures only. Just north of the pass is a turnoff to a rocky dirt road leading to three Forest Service campgrounds (pit toilets only, no showers). The first, **Cucharas Pass** (22 sites), is a half mile from the highway; **Blue Lake** (15 sites) is four miles; and **Bear Lake** (14 sites) is five.

Spanish Peaks, 719/742-3392, is a private campground also on the north side of the pass, with nicely sheltered tent and RV sites ($10 and $15, including showers).

Cuchara

Cuchara is a century-old resort between the gorgeous Cucharas Pass and the lush Cuchara Valley. With a boardwalk, saloon, gift shops, and a "trading post," as well as a disproportionate number of real-estate offices, the little village is making a brave attempt to make it in the fickle world of year-round resorts. It's always been primarily a summer destination, but a ski area up the road has been on-again, off-again under several different owners since 1981. It's now on-again, though sale negotiations were again under way at press time.

Cuchara Mountain Resort covers 230 acres with five lifts, 28 runs, snowboarding and tubing areas, and a vertical drop of 1,562 feet. For information, contact Cuchara Mountain Resort, 946 Panadero Ave., Cuchara, CO 81055, 888/282-4272, website www.cuchara.com.

Lodging options in Cuchara include **Rivers Edge Bed & Breakfast,** 90 E. Cuchara Ave., 719/742-5169, where rooms go for $125 (two people) and suites are $250 (up to eight people); and the **Cuchara Inn,** 73 Cuchara Ave.,

719/742-3685 (about $150 for four people). For information on lodging at the Cuchara Mountain Resort (ski area), write 946 Panadero Ave., Cuchara, CO 81055, or phone 719/282-4272.

For more information on Cuchara and the surrounding area, check out www.cucharaco.com.

Cuchara Valley

Just past Cuchara, Highway 12 drops out of the high mountains and begins its gentle roll through the Cuchara Valley back toward I-25 and the western edge of the plains. During the summer, the valley meadows are ablaze with wildflowers—especially impressive are June's wild irises and July's columbines. This verdant valley offers spectacular views of the Spanish Peaks, or Las Cumbres Españolas, which have been landmarks for travelers for hundreds of years. To the Native Americans, the mountains were known as Huajotolla (which I've seen translated both as "the Twins" and as "the Breasts of the World"), and as early as 1654 New Mexico governor Diego de Vargas reported having spotted them on a trip north from Santa Fe. The mountains, rising 13,610 and 12,669 feet, have also been called Dos Hermanos ("Two Brothers"), the Mexican Mountains, and Twin Peaks.

LA VETA

This kick-back little resort town and artists' community sits in the shadow of the Spanish Peaks and on the banks of the slowly tumbling Cucharas River. Founded in the mid-19th century, La Veta ("The Vein") served as a trading center for about a hundred years. Today, La Veta caters to folks looking to escape lowland heat and urban craziness, whether they come to rejuvenate for a weekend or to relocate for a lifetime. Passersthrough can stop in at the town's impressive historical museum, play a round of golf at the club, or camp at one of the many nearby campgrounds.

Fort Francisco Museum

Built in 1862 by Colonel John M. Francisco and Judge Henry Daigre, both to serve as a trade center and to protect local settlers from Indian attacks, this was the first structure in the Cuchara Valley. In 1871, the area's first post office opened at the fort. When the railroad arrived in the valley in the late 1870s, and the depot was built a few blocks north, the community's merchants and traders all but abandoned this once-thriving hub.

In 1957, the Huerfano County Historical Society obtained the fort and shortly thereafter opened it as a museum. Many of the buildings and furnishings are original, and descendants of local settlers have donated artifacts of historical interest. Exhibits include the old saloon (which over the years also served as a pool hall, restaurant, post office, roller rink, and general store), barbershop, one-room school, blacksmith shop, and mining museum. The museum, open Memorial Day through the first weekend in October Mon.–Sat. 10 A.M.–4 P.M. and Sunday 1 P.M.–4 P.M., has an excellent collection of historical letters and documents, including Kit Carson's will. Admission is $2. A gift shop sells souvenirs, cards, and locally made crafts. It's right downtown on the west side of the road. For more information, contact the La Veta/Cuchara Valley Chamber of Commerce, P.O. Box 32, La Veta, CO 81055, 719/742-3676.

The Gallery

Established in 1975, La Veta's Friends of the Arts Guild displays and sells work by local artists. The Gallery, on West Ryus, was built in 1983. In addition to exhibiting artwork, the building also serves as a classroom and meeting place for guild members who are spread throughout the area. Ordinarily, the Gallery displays the work of more than two dozen artists, with media varying from charcoal and pencil drawings to weaving, woodwork, and stained glass. For information and business hours, contact the La Veta/Cuchara Valley Chamber of Commerce, P.O. Box 32, La Veta, CO 81055, 719/742-3676.

Golf

La Veta's **Grandote Peaks Golf and Country Club** is an 18-hole course designed by famous

golfer Tom Wieskopf. One of the state's newer golf courses, Grandote (gran-DOH-tay) hosts a number of tournaments throughout the summer and fall. For information on green fees and tee times, phone 719/742-3391.

Accommodations and Food

La Veta offers a range of accommodations options, from RV campgrounds to bed-and-breakfasts. The **Hunter House Bed and Breakfast,** 115 W. Grand Ave., 719/742-5577, offers three rooms (all with shared bath) and full breakfasts in a comfortable, down-home setting (rooms start at $65). The brand new Santa Fe-style adobe **Inn at the Spanish Peaks**, 310 E. Francisco St., 719/742-5313, also has three rooms (suites), running $95–125.

Circle the Wagons RV Park, 719/742-3233, offers RV sites, rates for which can include a variety of square-dancing packages.

If you happen to be in the area on a Tuesday, Thursday, or Sunday morning, don't miss the **Ryus Avenue Bakery,** 129 Ryus, 719/742-3830, where you can get delicious fresh-baked breads, rolls, and other goodies. The **Covered Wagon,** 205 S. Main, 719/742-5280, serves a variety of beefy entrées, fowl, salads, etc. If you're looking for a place to grab a hot dog, some fries, and a cold one, try the **La Veta Sports Pub and Grub,** 923 S. Oak, 719/742-3093, open Sun.–Thurs. 11 A.M.–midnight and Friday and Saturday 11 A.M.–2 A.M.

Information

The **La Veta/Cuchara Valley Chamber of Commerce,** P.O. Box 32, La Veta, CO 81055, 719/742-3676, has assembled a thorough package of tourist information, including a *La Veta/Cuchara Tour Map and Guide,* which features hot springs, hiking trails, geological highlights, and other points of interest in the area. The chamber can also provide a complete list of restaurants, retailers, accommodations, and other information services.

The best website for information on La Veta is at www.lavetacolorado.com.

West on U.S. 160

U.S. 160 runs west out of Walsenburg, over North La Veta Pass (elev. 9,413 feet), and then cuts across northern Costilla County, through Fort Garland, Blanca, and into Alamosa. The 75-mile stretch follows pretty closely the Denver and Rio Grande Western Railroad route.

This southern prairie pocket of Colorado, roughly 125 miles north to south and 50 miles across, is the San Luis Valley, long a hunting area for Utes and Comanches. One of the first parts of Colorado to be explored by the Spanish, as early as 1761, the San Luis Valley still claims a great many Hispanic citizens, many of whom are descendants of original mid-18th-century Mexican land-grant settlers.

As you approach Fort Garland, watch the mountains to the north. Four "14ers" are clustered within a few miles of each other: Mt. Lindsey (14,042 feet), Little Bear Peak (14,037 feet), Blanca Peak (14,345 feet), and Ellingwood Point (14,042 feet).

FORT GARLAND

The first U.S. outpost in the San Luis Valley was Fort Massachusetts, built in 1852 about five miles northeast of Fort Garland. The fort saw active duty for only six years, as it was built on swampland, and the army had trouble providing fresh drinking water for the troops. Fort Garland, named for Brigadier General John Garland, was built in 1858, when Fort Massachusetts was abandoned. For 25 years, Fort Garland served both to protect settlers from Utes, who were attempting to save their land and herds, and also to provide a social and trading center in an otherwise lonely and barren region. Kit Carson was assigned to the fort 1866–67; it was his last military post.

Sixteen miles south of Fort Garland on Highway 159 is the little town of San Luis, the oldest community in the state.

Fort Garland Museum

Reconstructed to provide visitors with a genuine sense of life on the lonesome frontier in the mid-

19th century, the old fort displays a wide range of Native American, Mexican, and Anglo historical artifacts, including original military uniforms and weaponry. There's also a sampling of Hispanic folk art from the area.

The museum, at the junction of U.S. 160 and Highway 159, is open 9 A.M.–5 P.M. daily April–Labor Day, with limited hours the rest of the year. Admission is $3, with discounts for kids and seniors. For more information, write P.O. Box 368, Fort Garland, CO 81133, or phone 719/379-3512.

ALAMOSA

Alamosa (pop. 9,500; elev. 7,544 feet) is the largest town in the San Luis Valley. It's also the closest town to Great Sand Dunes National Monument. Long a hub town and shipping center, particularly for potatoes, the San Luis Valley's principal crop, Alamosa ("Cottonwood Grove") today is the seat of Alamosa County, as well as home to Adams State College, a four-year state university.

History

In 1878, Alamosa's founding father, A. C. Hunt, president of the Denver and Rio Grande Construction Company, loaded flatcars with stores, churches, and houses and moved them from Garland City—which until then had been the railroad's terminus—and plunked them down at the site of the new one. Voilà. Alamosa.

A rambunctious town from the get-go, early Alamosa saw more than its share of ramblers, gamblers, and frontier crazies, particularly the notoriously rowdy railroad construction workers. Lynchings are said to have been commonplace, with one particular riverside cottonwood designated the "hangin' tree."

Later, things mellowed out some, and Alamosa became a central shipping point for San Luis potatoes, as well as wheat, oats, alfalfa, lettuce, cauliflower, and peas, which were commonly fed to hogs, another Alamosa-area export.

Great Sand Dunes National Monument

Created by winds blowing Rio Grande–eroded particles of valley floor east across the San Luis Valley and up against the Sangre de Cristo range, these sand dunes, which reach heights of 700 feet, are the tallest in the country. A true geological oddity, the 39 square miles of dunes stand in stark contrast to both the snowcapped mountains behind them and the desert valley at their base.

Great Sand Dunes National Monument offers year-round camping (both in developed and in primitive backcountry areas), picnicking, and hiking, as well as a chance simply to goof around in this huge and most unlikely of sandboxes. Most of the dune area is off-limits to motorized vehicles, a short hike from the parking lot, one mile past the visitor center, will take you into sand completely undisturbed by anything save the wind and the handful of small critters that make their homes there.

The visitor center, open daily 9 A.M.–5 P.M. (and sometimes longer in the summer), has brochures, maps, books, wildlife and geology displays, explanatory videos, a touch screen, and a self-guided nature trail, as well as rangers to answer your questions. Admission is $3 for adults, kids under 17 free.

To get to Great Sand Dunes National Monument, take U.S. 160 16 miles east from Alamosa and then Highway 150 20 miles north. You can also go north 14 miles from Alamosa on Highway 17 and turn east on County Lane 6 one mile north of Mosca. For more information, phone 719/378-2312.

City Park

Alamosa's **Cole Park** is at the east end of town on the banks of the upper Rio Grande. You'll find huge lawns, cottonwoods for shade, and picnic tables—all just yards from the Alamosa Chamber of Commerce tourist information center, in the depot building.

Golf

There are several golf courses within driving range of Alamosa. Among them: **Cattails Golf Course,** 719/589-9515, just north of downtown on State Street on the Rio Grande; and **Great Sand Dunes Country Club and Resort,**

Sand dunes created from particles blowing up from the Rio Grande stand in contrast to the towering Sangre de Cristo mountain range.

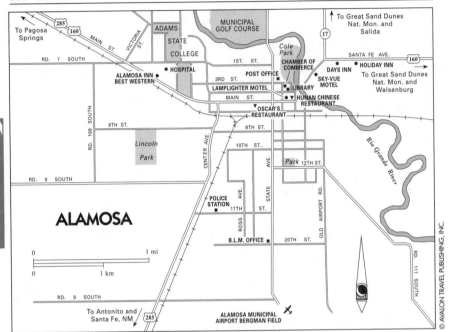

719/378-2357, about seven miles south of Great Sand Dunes National Monument.

Where Are We, the Everglades?

No, but you're near Colorado's next best thing, the **San Luis Valley Alligator Farm.** That's right, in geothermal ponds (87°F) 80 alligators nap, yawn, and grin for visitors. In addition, the habitat area offers fishing, hiking, and picnicking, plus a gift shop where you can pick up smoked fish and, ahem, alligator meat. It's open daily 7 A.M.–7 P.M. June–Aug. and 10 A.M.–3 P.M. Sept.–May. Admission is $3 for adults, $2 for kids 6–12. For more information, phone 719/378-2612.

Accommodations

Not a whole lot to choose from here, but since you're most likely not on your honeymoon you shouldn't be too disappointed. The following all offer doubles in the $50–100 range: **Sky-Vue Motel,** 250 Broadway, on the east end of town, 719/589-4945; **Alamosa Inn Best Western,** 1919 Main, 719/589-2567; the **Lamplighter,** 425 Main, 719/589-6636; **Days Inn,** 719/589-9037; and **Holiday Inn,** 719/589-5833. (The Days Inn and Holiday Inn are both on U.S. 160 on the east side of town, just east of the junction with Highway 17.)

Camping and RVing

KOA, 719/589-9757, is on U.S. 160 as you pull into town from the east—tent and RV sites available. You can also camp at Great Sand Dunes National Monument, about 35 miles northeast of Alamosa; **Great Sand Dunes Oasis and RV Park,** three miles south of the visitor center on CO 150, 719/378-2222, has more than 100 tent and RV sites, and a few cabins.

Food

Passers-through can fill up ice chests at the City Market and Safeway in Alamosa (west side of town, U.S. 160). If you'd rather sit down and eat than buy picnic fixin's, **Oscar's,** right downtown at 710 Main, 719/589-9320, serves Mexican lunches and dinners daily 11 A.M.–8:30 P.M. For Asian food, try **Hunan Chinese Restaurant** at 419 Main, 719/589-9002—serving Hunan, Szechuan, and Cantonese dishes for lunch and dinner daily. **Clancy's,** in the Holiday Inn, 333 Santa Fe, 719/589-5833, is open daily for breakfast, lunch, and dinner.

Services

The offices of the **Alamosa Police Department** are at 425 4th St., 719/589-2548 (tel. 719/589-5807 in emergencies). Phone the **Alamosa County Sheriff** at 719/589-6608 (719/589-5807 in emergencies). The **State Patrol** offices are at 1205 West Ave., 719/589-2503. The **San Luis Valley Regional Medical Center** is in Alamosa at 106 Blanca Ave., 719/589-2511; branch clinics are in La Jara, 719/589-3000, and in Monte Vista, 719/589-3658.

Alamosa's **post office** is behind the chamber of commerce at 505 3rd St., 719/589-4908.

Information

At Cole Park, along the Rio Grande just off U.S. 160 on the east side of town, the **Alamosa County Chamber of Commerce** has lots of brochures, maps, and other information on Alamosa and the San Luis Valley. Write Alamosa Chamber of Commerce, Cole Park, Alamosa, CO 81101, or phone 719/589-4840 or 800/BLU-SKYS (258-7597). For maps and information on the San Luis Valley, write the **Bureau of Land Management,** 1921 State Ave., Alamosa, CO 81101; or phone 719/589-4975.

Alamosa's daily newspaper is the *Valley Courier,* which serves the San Luis Valley. For information or subscriptions, write P.O. Box 1099, Alamosa, CO 81101, or phone 719/589-2553 or 719/359-0742.

For **road and weather information,** phone 719/589-9024.

Transportation

Alamosa lies at the junctions of U.S. 160 running east to west, U.S. 285 running north to south, and Highway 17, which runs north from Cone-

jos (northbound termination point of the Cumbres-Toltec Railroad), through Alamosa, and north toward Salida.

Air transportation is provided by **United Express,** 719/589-3804 or 800/241-6522, which offers flights between Denver International and San Luis Valley Airport (tel. 719/589-2593).

Tours

You can arrange two-hour 4WD tours of the Great Sand Dunes area through **Great Sand Dunes Oasis and RV Park,** 719/378-2222. May through September, tours are offered at 10 A.M. and 2 P.M. Phone for rates and reservations.

MONTE VISTA

Monte Vista is a small shipping and agricultural center on the western side of the San Luis Valley. The town is a gateway to Rio Grande and San Juan National Forests, which sprawl to the north and west, and to Wolf Creek Pass, about 60 miles west on U.S. 160. Monte Vista's annual Ski-Hi Stampede (late July) is Colorado's oldest rodeo.

Accommodations

The Monte Villa Historic Inn, 925 1st Ave., 719/852-5166, is a unique, 40-room stone lodge built in 1929. The inn also has a dining room, coffee shop, and lounge. You can also get rooms at the **Movie Manor Inn Best Western,** 2830 W. Hwy. 160 (two miles west of town), 719/852-5921, where a room for two ($50–100) includes admission to the drive-in movie theater next door.

Information

A small visitor center on U.S. 160 on the east side of town has information on Monte Vista and the surrounding San Luis Valley.

For information on Monte Vista, write the chamber of commerce at 1035 Park Ave., Monte Vista, CO 81144, or phone 719/852-2731 or 800/562-7085. Good information is also available at its website: www.monte-vista.org.

South to Antonito and New Mexico

From Alamosa, it's only a half-hour drive south on U.S. 285 to Antonito and the northern terminus of the Cumbres and Toltec Scenic Railroad, and from there it's just five miles to the New Mexico border. A fairly straight shot this, beelining down along the western side of the San Luis Valley.

A mile north of La Jara, or about 14 miles out of Alamosa, you'll find the **Conejos Peak Ranger Station** for the Rio Grande National Forest, where you can get maps and information on camping in the forest (which stretches to the west from Del Norte nearly to Silverton). At the junction of Highway 142, about seven miles past La Jara, you can turn east to Manassa, birthplace of Jack Dempsey, the "Manassa Mauler," and visit the **Jack Dempsey Museum.** Though Dempsey left the tiny town as a young teenager to fight in the mining camps to the north, and by 1950 was famous worldwide as one of the greatest heavyweight boxers of all time, he kept in close contact with his friends and family in Manassa until he died in 1983. The museum, downtown, displays boxing artifacts and photos of young Jack and his family. For hours and more information, write P.O. Box 130, Manassa, CO 81141.

From Manassa, continue east to San Luis, one of the oldest towns in Colorado. Founded in 1851 by Spanish settlers, the town has remained largely isolated, and its citizenry is still almost entirely Hispanic.

For more information on San Luis, write the **San Luis Visitor Center,** P.O. Box 307, San Luis, CO 81152, or phone 719/672-4441.

Antonito

The northern terminus of the **Cumbres and Toltec Scenic Railroad,** Antonito is little more than a train depot and a couple of motels and small cafés. Beginning in Chama, New Mexico, the 1880-vintage railroad winds 64 miles through some of the most beautiful country in the Rockies—through tunnels and pristine vales, and across high trestles over deep mountain gorges—crisscrossing the border several times. The summit is 10,022-foot Cumbres Pass, where the Spanish first entered Colorado.

From Antonito to Chama is a full-day ride, and you can return by van. Another option is to stop at Osier, the halfway point, for lunch, and to return to Antonito. Either way it's one full day. Fare from Antonito to Chama, including return by van, is about $60 for adults, $30 for kids. Osier-to-Antonito round-trip fares are about $35. Reservations are highly recommended. For more information, contact Cumbres and Toltec Scenic Railroad, P.O. Box 668, Antonito, CO 81120, 719/376-5483, or P.O. Box 789, Chama, NM 87520, 505/756-2151.

You can get lodging in Antonito at the **Narrow Gauge Railroad Inn,** 719/376-5441 ($50–100).

The **Antonito Tourist Information Center and Chamber of Commerce** is at the south end of town across from the railroad tracks. Write to P.O. Box 427, Antonito, CO 81120, or phone 719/376-2277 or 800/835-1098.

Walsenburg and Vicinity

About 17 miles separates La Veta and Walsenburg (pop. 6,200; elev. 6,186 feet), and Highway 12 joins U.S. 160 about 12 miles west of town. Predictably, it gets flatter and drier as you drop back onto the prairie. About five miles west of Walsenburg, you'll pass Martin and Horseshoe Lakes and Lathrop State Park, where you'll find facilities for camping, boating, fishing, swimming, and other activities (see below).

Founded by Spanish farmers in the mid-19th century as Plaza de los Leones, Walsenburg was renamed in the 1870s for Fred Walsen, one of the town's early merchants. Today it's a true hub town, at the junction of I-25, U.S. 160 and U.S. 85, and Highway 10.

Lathrop State Park

With a commanding view of Spanish Peaks in the distance, this recreation area offers a watery and scenic respite from the heat of the plains. Whether it's water-skiing, sailing, windsurfing, fishing (for trout, bass, catfish, walleye, bluegill, and crappie), swimming, camping, picnicking, golfing, or just plain sightseeing, the two lakes and surrounding area offer a bit of relaxation for just about everyone. The two campgrounds, **Piñon** and **Yucca,** offer a total of nearly 100 campsites, and much of the park is wheelchair-accessible.

Even if you're just passing through, you might want to stop at the visitor center, where nature trails help you identify local flora and you can pick up maps, books, area guides, and postcards. For more information, write Lathrop State Park, 70 County Rd., Walsenburg, CO 81089, or call 719/738-2376. For information on the golf course, phone 719/738-2730.

City Park

You'll find a nice, lawny, shady park as you come into town from the west. The park has a public pool, picnic facilities, and playground equipment.

Accommodations

You can get nice rooms (under $50) in town at the **Anchor Motel,** 1001 S. Main, 719/738-2800. The **Best Western Rambler,** 719/738-1121, is on the north end of town (Exit 52 from I-25). Rooms run $50–100 and are very clean and comfortable, though you're just a bit too far from downtown (a couple of miles) to walk. Campers can pull in at **Lathrop State Park** (see above) or **Dakota Campground,** north of town on Pueblo Road/U.S. 85–87, 719/738-9912. A **Day's Inn** lies five miles north of Walsenburg just off I-25, 719/738-2167; rates are $50–100. A handful of other motels lie at the north end of Walsen Avenue on the way to I-25.

Food

The **Alpine Rose Café,** downtown on Main Street, 719/738-1157, is a classic small-town eatery, offering breakfast, lunch, and dinner at reasonable prices. For Mexican food, try **Corine's,** 822 Main St., 719/738-1231. Not exactly food to write home about, but you can wash it down with a couple of cold *cervezas* and leave mostly *satisfecho*. Burritos and other entrées are $6–8.

Services

You'll find the **Walsenburg Police Department** at 202 W. 6th St., 719/738-1044. The **Huerfano County Sheriff** is at 112 W. 5th St., 719/738-1600. The **State Patrol** offices are at 500 S. Albert, 719/738-1600. The **Huerfano Medical Center,** 719/738-5100, is five miles west of Walsenburg on U.S. 160. The main **post office** is at 204 E. 6th, 719/738-2100.

Recycle aluminum at the **Walsenburg City Hall** at 525 Albert.

Information

The **Huerfano County Chamber of Commerce** provides extensive information on Walsenburg, Huerfano County, and the surrounding area, including local histories and

SOUTH-CENTRAL

© AVALON TRAVEL PUBLISHING, INC.

dining, lodging, and recreation guides, as well as helpful information if you're thinking of relocating. Write to the chamber at 400 Main St., Walsenburg, CO 81089, or phone 719/738-1065. If you're in town, stop by the offices (closed weekends) in the train depot on Main Street between 4th and 5th. The Walsenburg **public library** is at 323 Main St., 719/738-2774. The local paper is the *Huerfano World,* 111 W. 7th, 719/738-1720.

North from Walsenburg

The 50-mile, less-than-an-hour stretch of I-25 from Walsenburg to Pueblo is largely nondescript, save for the impressive views of the Wet Mountains, a Rockies' subrange standing massive and snowcapped to the west. Two miles north of Walsenburg, Highway 69 shoots northwest off the interstate, follows the Huerfano River to Gardner, snakes between the two largest units of San Isabel National Forest, passes through the beautiful Wet Mountain Valley and Westcliffe, then intersects with U.S. 50 west of Cañon City and Royal Gorge. To the west, just south of Westcliffe, you'll be able to see five mountain peaks topping 14,000 feet. Known collectively as the Crestone Needle Peaks, they include Kit Carson Mountain (14,165 feet), Crestone Peak (14,294 feet), Crestone Needle (14,191 feet), Challenger Peak (14,080 feet), and Humboldt Peak (14,064 feet). At both Westcliffe and Hillside you can turn west off Highway 69 to campgrounds in San Isabel National Forest.

WESTCLIFFE

At the junction of Highway 69 and Highway 96 and nestled between the Wet and Sangre de Cristo Mountains, Westcliffe is the seat of Custer County, long one of Colorado's important ranching regions. Westcliffe was founded in 1885 by transplanted Englishman Dr. J. W. Bell, who named it after Westcliffe-on-the-Sea, where he was born. Today Westcliffe and its sister city, Silver Cliff (once a booming silver town a mile east), are bases for hikers, backpackers, anglers, cross-country skiers, climbers, and hunters heading either west or east up into the mountains. It's also one of the prettiest spots on the planet, nestled in a lush and verdant valley between the towering Sangre de Cristos to the west and Wet Mountains to the east.

Bishop Castle

A legitimate candidate for *Ripley's Believe It Or Not!*, this is one of the state's most unlikely attractions—a three-story (and growing!) medieval stone castle, complete with buttresses and ornamental iron. The obsession of one man, Jim Bishop, who has been building it at a rate of 1,000 stones a year since 1969, the as-yet-uncompleted castle stands 160 feet tall and will, when completed, also have a moat and drawbridge.

Bishop Castle, which stands partially hidden among the mountain pines and firs, is about 28 miles southeast of Westcliffe and open to the public free of charge. Take Highway 96 east, turn south on Highway 165, and watch for the signs. For more information, write Bishop Castle, HCR 75, Box 179, Rye, CO 81069. Phone 719/564-4366. To preview some photos before your visit, check out the following website: www.lost.strange.com/mark/castle.

Practicalities

Lodging is available in Westcliffe at **Westcliffe Inn,** 719/783-9275; **Antler Motel,** 719/783-9305; and **Alpine Lodge,** 719/783-2660. (All around $50.)

Karen's Gourmet Coffee Cafe, 104 Main St., 719/783-2313, houses an espresso coffeehouse (serving breakfast and lunch) and a small store where you can get fishing gear, licenses, sundries, and USGS maps.

For more information on lodging, dining, camping, etc. in the Custer County area, contact the **Custer County Chamber of Commerce,** P.O. Box 81, Westcliffe, CO 81252, 719/783-9163.

SOUTH-CENTRAL

Pueblo and Vicinity

Pueblo (pop. 102,000; elev. 4,690 feet) sits right on the edge of the Great Plains. Just a couple of miles west of town, the Rockies begin their gradual yet unrelenting ascent from foothills to deep forested mountains. Short drives west from Pueblo take you into some of Colorado's most scenic and historically significant areas; you'll even find a well-maintained back road leading to the high mining country around Cripple Creek and Victor (see West to Cañon City, below).

HISTORY

Long a popular hunting ground for bands of plains and mountain native tribes, particularly Comanche, Kiowa, Arapahoe, Cheyenne, and Ute, the Pueblo area was first explored by Europeans in the mid-17th century, when Spaniards from Santa Fe came looking for gold and convertible pagans, and to investigate rumors that the French were beginning to colonize the area. The first recorded accounts of actual encampments at the site of present-day Pueblo are from 1706, when a group from Santa Fe rested here briefly on their quest for escaped Native American slaves. During the next century, the area was explored by trappers, soldiers, prospectors, and Spanish priests.

In 1806, Lieutenant Zebulon Pike erected Pueblo's first structure—a five-foot-high log shelter in which his party camped for a week—and in 1822, Major Jacob Fowler and a small party of trappers and traders built a three-room log house on the banks of the Arkansas River. Twenty years later, James Beckwourth and his party built a small trading post, attracting to the site a couple of dozen settlers, whom Beckwourth put to work building a small adobe fortress, which he dubbed Fort Pueblo.

Between 1842 and 1854, Pueblo attracted a wide range of settlers, from a splinter group of a westbound Mormon party to Indian agents, trappers, traders, and rambunctious pioneers. One of the most famous traders to pass through Pueblo was Richens Lacy "Uncle Dick" Wooten, who

would later make a fortune building a 27-mile road over Ratón Pass into New Mexico, erecting a tollgate, and charging every trader, trapper, soldier, and outlaw who passed through. In 1854, a year after he had driven 9,000 head of sheep from New Mexico to California, Wooten settled briefly in Pueblo. At Christmas that year, the inhabitants of the fort, against Wooten's advice, invited local Utes to join in their celebrations. The Utes, taking advantage of the Puebloans' drunkenness, massacred all of them save for three children and one man. By 1855, Pueblo was all but abandoned, former traders avoiding it, believing it haunted by the ghosts of the Christmas massacre.

Pueblo City was actually established in 1860. By 1863, the town had its own post office and by 1868 its first newspaper. The town was incorporated in 1870. Two years later the narrow-gauge Denver and Rio Grande Railroad arrived, and four years after that the rails of the Atchison, Topeka, and Santa Fe Railroad were laid to Pueblo. The late 19th century saw the development of Pueblo as an industrial area, with the construction of several smelters, and in the early 20th century a number of steel mills were built.

One of the city's most painful memories can still be recalled by Pueblo old-timers: on July 3, 1921, the Arkansas River overflowed its banks, submerging the downtown area under more than 10 feet of water. Hundreds of homes and businesses were washed away, destroyed, or damaged, and scores of people were killed. Two years later the capricious river was rerouted, domesticated with concrete channels and levees.

Today, Pueblo is on the heels of much of the rest of Colorado in its move to clean up its neighborhoods and downtown historical district. Many of the old buildings have been converted to gift shops and cafés, and homes are getting facelifts and paint jobs. And though parts of town still appear run down, in many ways Pueblo is a very pleasant little city, with quiet tree-lined streets, stunning Victorian

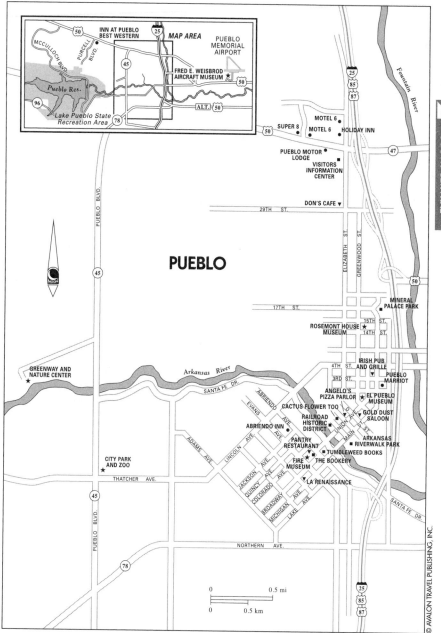

PUEBLO

MAP AREA

PUEBLO MEMORIAL AIRPORT

INN AT PUEBLO BEST WESTERN

FRED E. WEISBROD AIRCRAFT MUSEUM ★

MCCULLOCH BLVD.

PURCELL BLVD.

Pueblo Res.

Lake Pueblo State Recreation Area

MOTEL 6

MOTEL 6

HOLIDAY INN

SUPER 8

PUEBLO MOTOR LODGE

VISITORS INFORMATION CENTER

DON'S CAFE ▼

29TH ST.

ELIZABETH ST.

GREENWOOD ST.

17TH ST.

MINERAL PALACE PARK

ROSEMONT HOUSE MUSEUM ★

15TH ST.

14TH ST.

GREENWAY AND NATURE CENTER ★

Arkansas River

SANTA FE DR.

4TH ST.

3RD ST.

IRISH PUB AND GRILLE ▼

PUEBLO MARRIOT

ANGELO'S PIZZA PARLOR

EL PUEBLO MUSEUM ★

CACTUS FLOWER TOO

GOLD DUST SALOON

RAILROAD HISTORIC DISTRICT

ABRIENDO INN

PANTRY RESTAURANT

ARKANSAS RIVERWALK PARK

TUMBLEWEED BOOKS

FIRE MUSEUM

THE BOOKERY

CITY PARK AND ZOO

ADAMS AVE.

LINCOLN AVE.

EVANS AVE.

ABRIENDO AVE.

UNION AVE.

D AVE.

MAIN ST.

B ST.

JACKSON AVE.

QUINCY AVE.

COLORADO AVE.

BROADWAY AVE.

MICHIGAN AVE.

LAKE AVE.

LA RENAISSANCE

THATCHER AVE.

NORTHERN AVE.

PUEBLO BLVD.

Fountain River

Arkansas River

SANTA FE DR.

0   0.5 mi

0   0.5 km

© AVALON TRAVEL PUBLISHING, INC.

N

NOON

homes, and a population that's quite happy here, thank you, and wouldn't live anywhere else.

MUSEUMS
Rosemount House Museum

This gorgeous 37-room Victorian was built in 1893 for banker and merchant John A. Thatcher, who amassed his fortunes in mining, ranching, and farming. The 24,000-square-foot house is constructed of pink rhyolite stone and features extensive marble and silverplate tile, elaborate gold, silver, and brass lighting fixtures, and an oak dining table that seats 36. The house cost $60,000 to build.

Tours of the home, at 419 W. 14th St., are offered during the summer every half hour, Tues.–Sat. 10 A.M.–3:30 P.M. and Sunday 2–3:30; the rest of the year tours are Tues.–Sat. 1–3:30 P.M. and Sunday 2–3:30. It's closed in January. Admission is $5 for adults, $4 for seniors, $3 for ages 13–18, and $2 for ages 6–12. For information, phone 719/545-5290.

El Pueblo Museum

Operated by the Colorado Historical Society, this museum displays the history and culture of Pueblo and Pueblo County. Included are permanent exhibits (Native Americana, the contributions of iron and steel to the area, and a section of the town's "hanging tree," a 388-year-old cottonwood cut down in 1883 to make way for Union Street) and traveling displays. The museum occupies the site of a trading post built in 1842.

El Pueblo Museum, 324 W. 1st St., is open Mon.–Sat. 10 A.M.–4:30 P.M. Admission is $3 for adults and $2.50 for kids and seniors. You can also arrange group tours. For more information, or to book tours, phone 719/583-0453.

Fred E. Weisbrod Aircraft Museum

At the airport east of town, this outdoor museum lets you wander among a wide array of once-important aircrafts, including a Lockheed F-80 fighter plane, a B-29 (with original crew members listed on a display stand), an F-101 Voodoo, a Douglas C-47 Skytrain, and the B-47E "Might in Flight." Statistics, including passenger or load

capacity, crew, special uses, etc., about each craft are displayed on plaques. It's open daily 9 A.M. to sunset, 719/948-9219; admission is free.

International B-24 Memorial Museum

Across the street from the Aircraft Museum, the B-24 Museum is dedicated to the crews of World War II B-24 Liberators. Exhibited here are historical photos, uniforms, documents, and other artifacts. It's open Mon.–Fri. 10 A.M.–4 P.M. and Saturday 10 A.M.–3 P.M.; admission is free. For information, phone 719/948-9219.

Hose Company #3 Fire Museum

This museum at 114 Broadway displays historical fire-fighting gear, including an 1881 hand-drawn fire-hose cart, a fire truck from 1917, a collection of helmets from around the world, as well as ladders, nozzles, rescue equipment, and historical photos. It's open by reservation only; admission is free. For more information, phone 719/544-4548, or write P.O. Box 4127, Pueblo, CO 81004.

Historical Walking Tours

Local historical groups have developed self-guided walking tours of two Pueblo districts. The **Union Avenue District** tour includes homes and businesses in the Union and Grand Avenue areas, many dating from the 1880s. Some 40 buildings are listed on the National Register of Historic Places. The **Mesa Junction** tour, on the other side of the Arkansas River, explores the 1880s shopping area where two trolley lines met.

Maps and more information on the tours, as well as detailed discussions of the buildings, are available from the Pueblo Chamber of Commerce (see Information, below).

Historic Arkansas Riverwalk Park

One of Pueblo's most ambitious and exciting community projects, this 26-acre $50 million San Antonio-like river mall completely transformed the downtown area when it was completed in the fall of 2000. It includes bike pathways and pedestrian walkways, paddle-boat rentals, and beautifully landscaped gardens and wildlife-viewing areas. Ultimately, it will feature shops, restaurants, and entertainment venues. Beginning with nothing less than the rerouting of the Arkansas River—ironically, back to the course it took naturally before the 1920s, when it was diverted to avoid flooding—the multistage project has been the talk of the town for the last four or five years. Local businesspeople are counting on Riverwalk's ultimately becoming a tourist destination itself. For information, write Arkansas Riverwalk, 200 W. 1st St., Pueblo, CO 81003, or phone 719/595-0242.

Sangre de Cristo Arts and Conference Center

This two-building complex at 210 N. Santa Fe, with four art galleries, a 500-seat theater, and a hands-on children's museum, attracts upward of 200,000 visitors a year. The galleries feature both permanent and traveling displays, and the center offers dance and music workshops, as well as a summer concert series. There's also a gift shop.

The center's art galleries are open Mon.–Sat. 11 A.M.–4 P.M. The children's museum is open Mon.–Sat. 11 A.M.–5 P.M. For information, or to arrange free tours, phone 719/543-0130.

PARKS AND RECREATION
Lake Pueblo State Recreation Area

Pueblo Reservoir offers a variety of water sports, including sailing, windsurfing, fishing, and swimming (permitted only in the Rock Canyon Swim Area), in addition to camping, horseback riding, hiking, wildlife viewing, and sightseeing. Though its 60-mile shoreline is mostly barren, surrounded by treeless bluffs and rocky cliffs, the lake still affords a stark, high-plains sort of beauty, especially against the massive Rockies in whose shadow it lies.

First open in the early 1970s, the recreation area has several different campgrounds, with hot water, flush toilets, and RV hookups—nearly 300 campsites all told. Fish for trout, black bass, crappie, and bluegill, from the shore or boat, or hoist a sail and run on the wind. You can also tour the fish hatchery. To

get there, take U.S. 50 west and watch for the signs. For information, write 640 Pueblo Reservoir Rd., Pueblo, CO 81004, or phone 719/561-9320.

Greenway and Nature Center

Situated on the Arkansas River below the Pueblo Reservoir Dam, the center offers picnicking, fishing (from a large deck out over the river), volleyball courts, and raft, kayak, and canoe put-ins. Cyclists will enjoy the 20 miles of bike trails, while hikers can follow the short nature trail (wheelchair-accessible). Canoes and bikes are available to rent.

Above the greenway is a small nature center displaying much of the flora and fauna found in the area, and the nearby Raptor Rehabilitation Center cares for injured hawks, owls, falcons, and eagles, with the hope of returning them to the wild. The Nature Center, 719/545-2414, is open daily 9 A.M.–5 P.M., and the Raptor Rehabilitation Center, 719/545-7117, is open daily 11 A.M.–4 P.M. To get there, take U.S. 50 west to Pueblo Boulevard/Highway 45, turn south, and follow the signs.

City Park and Zoo

This is a very popular weekend destination for locals and passers-through. Highlights include a carousel built at the turn of the 20th century (moved to its present site in 1940), a small lake (open for fishing only to kids 15 and under and people with disabilities), and a train that loops you out around the lake. The park also has other amusement-park rides, playground equipment, tennis courts, a softball field, golf course, and picnic facilities.

The **Pueblo Zoo,** adjacent to the park, houses more than 70 kinds of animals, including Bengal tigers, camels, American bison, and an Andean condor, as well as the state's largest herpatology display. The zoo is open in the summer 10 A.M.–5 P.M. and the rest of the year 9 A.M.–4 P.M. Admission to the zoo is $4 for adults, with discounts for kids and seniors. To get there from U.S. 50, take Pueblo Boulevard south to Goodnight. From downtown, take 4th Street west to Pueblo Boulevard, then go north to Goodnight. Phone 719/561-9664 or visit pueblozoo.org.

Mineral Palace Park

This huge city park, with gorgeous gardens, lawns, and tall shade trees, is frequently the site of weddings. A perfect place to picnic after wandering around Pueblo, the park also has a public swimming pool and exercise course. From downtown, take Santa Fe or Main north; from Elizabeth or Greenwood, turn east on 17th.

Golf

Pueblo's municipal golf course is the **City Park Golf Course,** 3900 Thatcher Avenue. The two separate courses comprise a 27-hole facility. For information and tee times, phone 719/561-4946. Other area courses include the **Desert Hawk at Pueblo West,** eight miles west of town off U.S. 50 in the Pueblo West development, 719/547-2280; **Walking Stick,** 4301 Walking Stick Blvd., 719/584-3400; and the **Hollydot Course,** 25 miles south of Pueblo on I-25 (Exit 74), 719/676-3340.

Cycling

The Pueblo area has miles and miles of biking trails. For maps, contact the chamber of commerce or the **Pueblo Parks and Recreation Department,** 800 Goodnight Ave., Pueblo, CO 81005, 719/566-1745. For maps of cycling trails in Pueblo, Colorado Springs, Cañon City, and Trinidad, write **Colorado Division of Parks and Outdoor Recreation,** 1313 Sherman St., Denver, CO 80203, or phone 303/866-3437.

ACCOMMODATIONS

In the mid- to late 1990s, Pueblo got absolutely hammered by the franchise inns. Look up on the hill to the west as you come in from the north, and you'll see them. Of course, this phenomenon is not limited to Pueblo. It's a trend around the country, perhaps hastening the demise of small-town America; as more and more franchise motels (and restaurants) open up at freeway off-ramps, passers-through have fewer and fewer reasons to go downtown.

Bed-and-Breakfast

The **Abriendo Inn,** 300 W. Abriendo, 719/544-2703, in the elegant and beautifully restored 1906 home of brewing magnate Martin Walter, is one of the classiest and most comfortable bed-and-breakfasts around. Hostess Kerrelyn Trent serves up huge and delicious homemade breakfasts, the menu changing daily. If your timing's right, there just might be some bearclaws or poppyseed cake waiting for you in the sunny dining room. The inn has 10 rooms, including three top-floor units with whirlpool tubs. Rates run $75–125.

Motels: Under $50

Tom Bodet's got two lights on at the junction of U.S. 50 and I-25: you'll find one **Motel 6** at 4103 N. Elizabeth, 719/543-6221, and another one around the corner at 960 U.S. Hwy. 50, 719/543-8900. Take Exit 101 from the interstate.

Motels and Hotels: $50–100

Also at Exit 101 (junction of I-25 and U.S. 50), you'll find a **Super 8,** 1100 U.S. Hwy. 50 W, 719/545-4104; **Holiday Inn,** 4001 N. Elizabeth, 719/543-8050; and the **Pueblo Marriot,** downtown at 110 W. 1st, 719/542-3200. The **Inn at Pueblo West Best Western** is eight miles west of town on U.S. 50, 719/547-2111.

Camping and RVing

In addition to the campgrounds at **Lake Pueblo State Recreation Area** (see above), the Pueblo KOA campground, 719/542-2273 or 800/562-7453, is five miles north of town off I-25 (take Exit 108). RV sites are $18–24.

FOOD

Along with the revitalization of downtown, Pueblo is experiencing a renaissance of sorts in dining. In the last few years, several good and well-priced places have opened, many of them in restored historic buildings. If you want a real taste of Pueblo, dine in the downtown area; if you're just hungry and don't mind cookie-cutter chains, head to the fast- and not-so-fast food places on the north end of town.

First Things First

A popular morning hangout among the Abriendo-area business crowd, the **Pantry Restaurant,** 109 E. Abriendo, 719/543-8072, is a down-home and home-style restaurant with complete breakfasts running $4–8. It's a great place to linger over a cup of joe and the morning paper.

A Pueblo Classic

One of my favorite restaurants in the whole state is the **Irish Brew Pub and Grille,** 108 W. 3rd in downtown Pueblo, 719/542-9974. This comfortable little place serves inexpensive and delicious Italian entrées (hey, corned beef and cabbage gets old after a while), chicken, steak, and seafood—not to mention beaver and alligator sausage. It's also got the only on-site-brewed beer in town and a *great* jukebox. Dinners run $5–12.

Mexican Food

As you'd expect, Pueblo has lots of excellent Mexican restaurants, varying from neighborhood holes in the wall to upscale dining rooms. A sure bet is **El Valle Mexican Restaurant,** 208 W. Northern, 719/564-9983, a family-run joint in business since 1937. You can get shrimp, pork, chicken, avocado, and beef burritos for about $6; a bowl of *menudo* is $3.25. For dessert, try the *conchas—sopaipillas* stuffed with apple, pineapple, or cherry. Open for lunch and dinner Fri.–Tuesday. El Valle is on Central Avenue near the junction with I-25. From the freeway, take the Central Avenue exit and go north one block. Another Mexican favorite is **Nacho's,** 409 N. Santa Fe, 719/544-0733. Complete dinners and combinations run $5–10.

A bit more upscale, in fact, described by a local as a "California-style Mexican restaurant—you know, great atmosphere, lots of lettuce, fruit, stuff like that . . . ," the **Cactus Flower,** 2149 Jerry Murphy Rd., 719/545-8218, serves blue-corn enchiladas, *pollo* dishes, as well as *carne asada,* crab chimichangas, and *pescado Veracruz* for $8–13. A second restaurant, **Cactus Flower, Too,** 310 S. Victoria, 719/583-1111, in the Union Avenue Historic District is popular among tourists and local business folk alike.

Other Pueblo Restaurants

A long-standing Pueblo favorite is **Ianne's Whisky Ridge,** 4333 Thatcher, 719/564-8551, where you can get excellent pastas, seafood, veal, and beef. Open daily for lunch and dinner. **The Gold Dust Saloon,** 130 S. Union (Historical District), 719/545-0741, is a cozy neighborhood sports bar and saloon serving dynamite burgers and fries with which to chase your beer.

La Renaissance, 218 E. Routt Ave., 719/543-6367, is one of Pueblo's more upscale restaurants, serving prime rib, baby-back ribs, and seafood (about $12–30) in a church dating from 1888. Open Tues.–Fri. for lunch, Tues.–Sat. for dinner.

ENTERTAINMENT

Bars

Downtown Pueblo is a strange blend of modern-looking office buildings and neighborhood taverns, from biker bars to sports pubs. Some of the downtown joints feature live music on weekends. The **Rendezvous Restaurant,** 218 W. 2nd, 719/542-2247, has live music—often jazz—on Friday nights. In addition, the lounges of many of the franchise inns on the north end of town feature live music.

The Gold Dust Saloon, 130 S. Union, 719/545-0741, is a friendly little place where you can munch popcorn or peanuts while tossing darts or catching a game on one of the several television screens.

CALENDAR

Pueblo's big annual event is the **Colorado State Fair.** In addition to offering the standard rides, livestock shows, and booths where you can win a mirror etched with a likeness of Elvis or of a large-breasted woman on a Harley, this huge and highly anticipated fair also features big-name entertainment. Headliners at recent fairs include Bob Dylan and Wayne Newton, and other acts included Waylon Jennings, Kenny Rogers, and Los Lobos.

SOUTH-CENTRAL

Held in late August, the Colorado State Fair attracts thousands of people from all over the Southwest. For information, phone 719/561-8484 or 800/444-FAIR (444-3427).

Pueblo also hosts a number of other events during the course of the year, from arts-and-crafts and home-and-garden shows to rodeos and concerts. For information on what's going on in Pueblo, check the *Pueblo Chieftain,* or phone the city Events Line (weekly listing) at 719/542-1776, or the Community Calendar (coming events) at 719/542-1704.

SHOPPING

Downtown Areas

Combine your shopping with historical tours at three downtown shopping areas, **Mesa Junction, Downtown,** and **Union Avenue Historic District.** You'll find gift shops, bookstores, boutiques, and other specialty shops in restored 19th-century buildings. You'll also find restaurants and neighborhood pubs for refreshment.

Pueblo Mall

The Pueblo Mall, at I-25 and U.S. 47 East, has (surprise!) a JCPenney, Mervyn's, Ward's, Joslin's, 10 shoe stores, seven jewelers, and a whole lot of other stores. A slew of strip malls is near the corner of Pueblo and Northern—Kmart, Wal-Mart, SuperCuts, fast-food franchises, etc.

SERVICES

The offices of the **Pueblo Police Department** are at 130 Central, 719/549-1200. The **Pueblo County Sheriff** is at 909 Court, 719/546-1123. Phone the **Colorado State Patrol** in emergencies at 719/544-2424 (546-5465 in nonemergencies). **Parkview Episcopal Medical Center** is at 400 W. 16th (Exit 99B off I-25), 719/584-4000. **St. Mary-Corwin Regional Medical Center** is at 1008 Minnequa (Exit 96 off I-25), 719/560-4000. The main **post office** is at 421 Main St., and there's also one at 6th and Central.

Recycling

Recycle aluminum, glass, newspapers, and plastic at the **King Soopers** stores: 3050 W. Northern and 102 W. 29th. Recycle aluminum at the **Safeway:** 1322 E. 8th St., 617 W. 29th St., and 1231 S. Prairie.

INFORMATION

Chamber of Commerce and Tourist Information

Contact the Pueblo **Chamber of Commerce** at 302 N. Santa Fe, Pueblo, CO 81003, 719/542-1704. The **Visitor Information Center** in the Kmart parking lot at U.S. 50 West and Elizabeth Street (from I-25, take Exit 101), 719/543-1742, is an excellent place to begin your visit. You'll find a friendly staff, plus lots of brochures and other information on what to do and where to stay in the area. For electronic information on Pueblo, visit the chamber's website at www.pueblo.org/visitorsguide. The offices of the **Parks and Recreation Department** are at 800 Goodnight Ave., 719/566-1745. Offices for Pike and San Isabel National Forests are at 1920 Valley Dr., 719/545-8737.

For **road and weather information,** phone 719/545-8520.

Bookstores and Libraries

The **Bookery,** 129 E. Abriendo, 719/544-1135, has a good selection of books on Colorado—history, travel, etc. For used books and rare books, check out **Tumbleweed Books,** 687 S. Union, 719/544-3420, which specializes in, among other subjects, Western Americana. A **Waldenbooks** is in the Pueblo Mall.

The main branch of the **Pueblo Library District** is at 100 E. Abriendo, 719/543-9600. Branches are also at 1515 Bonforte, 719/544-5040, and 2525 S. Pueblo, 719/564-8382.

The independently published *Pueblo Chieftain,* first printed in 1868, comes out Mon.–Sat. and is available in racks around town. Its offices are at 825 W. 6th Street. Write P.O. Box 4040, Pueblo, CO 81003, or phone 719/544-3520.

TRANSPORTATION

Pueblo is an easy town to get around in, though it does get a bit messy downtown, where streets change names and loop around each other. It helps to remember when driving that the main north-south arteries are Elizabeth, Greenwood, Abriendo, Santa Fe, and, on the west side, Prairie and Pueblo. East-west thoroughfares are Northern, 4th Street (which, heading west, turns into Lincoln, which turns into Thatcher), Midtown, 29th Street, and U.S. 50. Remember, too, that the numbered *streets* run east to west and the numbered *avenues* run north to south.

Pueblo Airport is served by **United Express,** 719/948-4423 or 800/241-6522. **Greyhound-Trailways** has passenger service to Pueblo, 719/544-6295.

WEST TO CAÑON CITY

On the north side of Pueblo, U.S. 50 rises out of the plains and into the scrubby Rocky foothills, loosely following the courses of the Arkansas River and the Atchison, Topeka, and Santa Fe Railroad. Eight miles out of Pueblo, you'll pass the planned community of Pueblo West, a sprawling development of newer homes, many owned by retirees. You can turn south here, wind your way through Pueblo West and down to Lake Pueblo State Recreation Area (see above), where you'll find boating, camping, and fishing opportunities. Thirty miles out of Pueblo, Highway 115 tees into the highway, dropping back to the northeast to Colorado Springs, and following the western boundary of Fort Carson en route. Turn south at this junction onto Colorado 115 to **Florence,** site of the oldest continually producing oil well in the world. Long an important oil and coal town (Petroleum Avenue is one of the main north-south streets), Florence (pop. 3,000) today is the seat of Fremont County. The **Price Pioneer Museum** on the corner of Pikes Peak and Front Street displays mining and domestic artifacts. It's open June through mid-September. You'll find a city park and public swimming pool on Pikes Peak between 3rd and 4th. For information about Florence, write **Florence Chamber of Commerce,** Rialto Theatre Building, P.O. Box 145, Florence, CO 81226, or phone 719/784-3544.

Four miles past the junction with 115, you can turn north onto **Phantom Canyon Road,** which follows the old Denver and Rio Grande Railroad line up into the historic mining towns of Victor and Cripple Creek. A seldom-used route, this well-maintained dirt road takes you gradually up into the high mountains, offering some excellent scenery along the way. From this turnoff it's about eight miles to Cañon City.

Cañon City

Cañon City (pop. 25,000; elev. 5,332 feet) is a gateway to some excellent recreational and sightseeing opportunities. It's surrounded by thousands of square miles of national forest land (for camping, hiking, and cross-country skiing), and it's close to the 1,000-foot-deep, eight-mile-long Royal Gorge and some of Colorado's favorite stretches of white water. Not really sure how to define itself, Cañon City is at once both proud of its fascinating history and scenic wonders and at the same time somehow determined to exploit them in silly and embarrassing ways.

HISTORY

With its mild climate and proximity to so much natural bounty, the Cañon City area was a favorite hunting ground and base camp of Utes long before the first white settlers showed up. The first nonnatives to explore the area were most likely Zebulon Pike and his party, who camped here in December 1806 (although he mistook the Arkansas River for Texas's Red River). The next half century or so, though, the area remained solely Ute land, and it wasn't until 1859 that the first miners started to arrive.

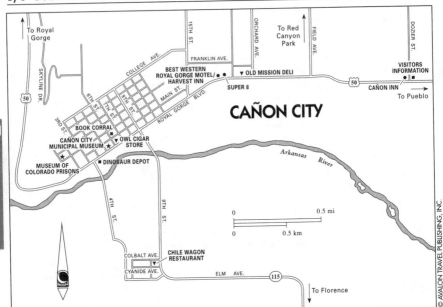

To Royal Gorge

SKYLINE DR.

50

3RD ST.
6TH ST.
7TH ST.
8TH ST.
9TH ST.

COLLEGE AVE.

15TH ST.

FRANKLIN AVE.

BEST WESTERN
ROYAL GORGE MOTEL/
HARVEST INN

MAIN ST.

ROYAL GORGE BLVD.

ORCHARD AVE.

▼ OLD MISSION DELI

To Red Canyon Park

FIELD AVE.

SUPER 8

DOZIER ST.

VISITORS
INFORMATION

50

CAÑON INN

To Pueblo

CAÑON CITY

BOOK CORRAL

CAÑON CITY
MUNICIPAL MUSEUM ★   ▪ OWL CIGAR
                        STORE

★ MUSEUM OF
COLORADO PRISONS

▪ DINOSAUR DEPOT

Arkansas River

4TH ST.

9TH ST.

0   0.5 mi
0   0.5 km

COLBALT AVE.

CYANIDE AVE.

CHILE WAGON
RESTAURANT

ELM   AVE.

115

To Florence

MOON

© AVALON TRAVEL PUBLISHING, INC.

The early town's economy was a hybrid, derived from both mining (gold and silver) and agriculture (fruits and vegetables). Writer Joaquin Miller was one of Cañon City's first administrators, serving as mayor, judge, and minister.

In 1868, Colorado Territory gave Cañon City a choice. It could be the site of either the state university or the state penitentiary. Cañon City chose the latter, figuring attendance would be better at prison than at school. The university, of course, went to Boulder. And, as the University of Colorado has largely given definition to the city of Boulder since then, so has Colorado State Penitentiary defined Cañon City. Today, the Department of Corrections is Fremont County's largest employer, and the townspeople thank the prison system for the stability it provides.

In the late 1870s, as the West's railroads competed for rights to key routes, Cañon City, because of its choice location—near the mouth of Royal Gorge, a crucial passage west—became an unwitting participant in the fray. The Denver and Rio Grande and the Santa Fe Railroads went to court over the rights to the canyon, with the

rights ultimately awarded to the Denver and Rio Grande. The Santa Fe had to run its line south from Pueblo and then west from Ratón.

In 1908, Cañon City acquired Royal Gorge Park, and in 1929, a suspension bridge, still the highest in the world (1,053 feet), was built across it. Since then, Cañon City has appealed to tourism, attracting upward of a half million visitors a year, who, in addition to being awed by the bridge, also appreciate the canyon's sheer beauty, the aerial tramway across, and the railroad rising 1,500 feet from the river to the canyon's rim.

SIGHTS

Museum of Colorado Prisons

A genuinely unique and perversely intriguing experience, a tour of this museum offers a realistic view of the 120-year history of Colorado State Penitentiary. Originally a single, two-story stone structure, the prison saw 77 executions (45 by hanging, 32 by gas) and a number of escapes and riots; the bloody aftermath of one of which has been re-created with broken cell doors and blood on floors. A fascinating collection of historical photos includes shots of Alferd Packer (who served 15 years for cannibalism), John Dockerty (Colorado's first convicted abortionist), and Anton Wood (at 11, the state's youngest prisoner of record—sentenced to 25 years for murdering a neighbor in a dispute over a watch). The grisliest photos are of the hanging of one George Witherall.

The Museum of Colorado Prisons and Park, at 1st and Macon, is open daily 8:30 A.M.–6 P.M. in summer; shorter hours the rest of the year. Admission for adults is $5, $4 for seniors, and $3 for kids 6–12. For more information, phone 719/269-3015.

Cañon City Municipal Museum

Housed in a complex that includes the second floor of the Cañon City municipal building, as well as two historic buildings behind the city hall, this museum displays a wide range of items from the Fremont County area's history. Included are rocks and minerals from the

© STEPHEN METZGER

The Museum of Colorado Prisons offers an uncomfortably realistic view of the history of Colorado prisons and prisoners.

region, the mounted heads of the last of the area's buffalos (shot by poachers in 1897), Ute artifacts, replicas of a saloon and blacksmith shop, as well as antique furniture and clothing and other personal belongings and domestic items.

The museum, at Royal Gorge Boulevard and 6th Street, is open May–Sept. Tues.–Sun. 10 A.M.–4 P.M.; the rest of the year it's open Tues.–Sat. 10 A.M.–4 P.M. Admission is $1.50 for adults, $1 for kids 6–12. For information, phone 719/276-5279.

Royal Gorge

An internationally famous geological landmark, Royal Gorge is a 1,000-foot-deep cleft in the plateau above the Arkansas River. Eight miles west of Cañon City, the canyon is spanned by Royal Gorge Bridge, which locals claim is the highest suspension bridge in the world. Attractions at the gorge include sightseeing, horseback riding, railway tours, an aerial tram, and theme parks. Note: the bridge is too narrow to allow for passage by motor homes, trailers, and large vans. (See below for more information.)

Royal Gorge Route Railway

The new (summer 1999) Royal Gorge Route takes visitors on a diesel train from Cañon City down into Royal Gorge to Parkdale and back. The 24-mile, roughly 90-minute trip departs from Dinosaur Depot at 330 Royal Gorge Blvd. three times daily (9 A.M., noon, and 3 P.M.) and costs $26.95 for adults and $16.50 for kids. Seasonal operation—May through mid-October only. For more information, phone 800/RAILS-4U (724-5748) or 303/569-2403 or check out the website at www.royalgorgeroute.com.

Dinosaur Depot

This museum/lab is housed inside a 1930s Cañon City firehouse and focuses on educating the public about local prehistory while scientists continue to excavate a 150-million-year-old stegosaurus skeleton, part of what curators call the "largest Jurassic graveyard in the world." Hours are Mon.–Sat. 9 A.M.–5 P.M. June–Aug. and Tues.–Sat. 10 A.M.–4 P.M. the rest of the year.

PARKS AND RECREATION

Surrounded by lush national forests, steep mountains, and countless lakes, streams, and rivers, Cañon City is an outdoor-lover's paradise. Particularly popular is river rafting, with several guide services offering half- and full-day trips on the Arkansas and other area rivers. Of course, the scenery, too, is wonderful, and the area offers excellent sightseeing opportunities.

City Parks

Twelve miles north of Cañon City is 500-acre city-owned **Red Canyon Park,** characterized by its bizarre redrock formations. It offers sightseeing, hiking trails, and picnic facilities. Take Field Avenue north from town.

Temple Canyon Park, also owned by Cañon City, offers picnicking, hiking, and sightseeing as well. A natural amphitheater along one of the hiking trails is reportedly an ancient Ute ceremonial site. Take 1st Street south from town.

Hiking and Biking

The Cañon City area abounds in hiking and biking trails, and the city, in conjunction with the Forest Service, publishes a map with a dozen different routes. Pick up maps at the visitor information center in Centennial Park off U.S. 50 on the west side of town, and at bike shops in town, including **Bike Depot,** 212 S. 4th St., 719/276-0777.

White-Water Rafting

The section of the Arkansas River between Cañon City and Salida is a favorite among river rats, and even those new to the sport can get in on the fun. Half- and full-day trips can be arranged. You'll have no problem finding an outfitter/guide, as the countryside, particularly right at Royal Gorge, is studded with billboards advertising the services. Rafting companies include **American Adventure Expeditions,** 719/539-4680 or 800/288-0675, and **Colorado White-water,** 719/275-0534. Prices usually start at about $50 per person (half day).

An excellent place from which to view rafters is an over-the-water observation deck at **Five Points Arkansas Headwaters Recreation Area,** about eight miles west of Royal Gorge; public restrooms and picnic tables are available.

For a complete list of Cañon City-area rafting companies (with links to the outfitters' own websites), visit www.canoncitycolorado.com/rafting.

Scenic Drives

Eight miles east of Cañon City is the junction with **Phantom Canyon Road,** where you can turn north and drive into Victor and Cripple Creek the back way. The twisting, turning, well-maintained 35-mile dirt-and-gravel road, which follows the old Denver and Rio Grande Railroad line, is not recommended for large (over 35 feet) RVs. Three-mile **Skyline Drive,** built in 1906 with convict labor and stones from every state in the union, takes you 800 feet above the town. The one-way road begins just west of Cañon City on U.S. 50; follow the signs.

Camping

With San Isabel National Forest to the south and southwest, and Pike National Forest to the west and north, Cañon City offers almost unlimited camping possibilities (in addition to the RV camping at Royal Gorge—see that section, below). For maps and information, stop by the Forest Service office in town at 300 Dozier, 719/275-4119, or the BLM office at 3170 E. Main, 719/275-0631.

Golf

The private **Shadow Hills Golf Club** is open to nonmembers with some restrictions. Built shortly after World War II, the course has long been a local favorite. Take 4th Street south from town; phone 719/275-0603 for tee times and information.

Horseback Riding

This is another activity popular in the Cañon City-Royal Gorge area, with several companies offering rentals and rides. Among them: **Royal Gorge Frontier Town and Railway,** 719/275-5149; and **Lazy-J Resort,** 719/942-4274, headquartered in Coaldale, about 35 miles west of Cañon City on U.S. 50.

ACCOMMODATIONS

The nicest among the many motels in Cañon City are the **Best Western Royal Gorge Motel,** 1925 Fremont, 719/275-3377, and the **Cañon Inn,** at U.S. 50 and Dozier, 719/275-8676. The **Super 8,** is at 209 N. 19th, 719/275-8687. Doubles at all three will run $50–100.

In addition to the RV campgrounds at Royal Gorge (see that section, below), you can also camp at **RV Station and Campground,** in town at 3120 E. Main, 719/275-4576. Much more isolated, in fact pretty much out in the proverbial middle of nowhere, **Indian Springs Ranch Campground,** 719/372-3907, is at the end of a four-mile dirt road that forks off Phantom Canyon Road east of Cañon City (no vehicles over 25 feet).

FOOD

You'll find lots of fast-food franchises in Cañon City, a number of good mom-and-pop places, plus restaurants in many of the larger motels and hotels. The **Harvest Inn,** in the Best Western Royal Gorge Motel, 1925 Fremont, 719/275-1299, serves excellent traditional American breakfasts. Open daily, with breakfast items running $3–8.

For the best burgers ($4–6) in town, try the **Owl Cigar Store,** 626 Main, 719/275-9946. The popular establishment—if you get there right at noon, you won't find a seat—has a full bar, pool tables, and a friendly atmosphere, reminiscent of a 1950s malt shop. Open Mon.–Sat. 8 A.M.–8 P.M.

For excellent Mexican food, try **Old Mission Deli,** 1905 Fremont, 719/275-6780, where specialties include burritos, chimichangas, *aztecas,* and authentic homestyle green chile, running $5–8. Open for lunch and dinner daily. Also good for Mexican food is the **Chile Wagon Restaurant,** at the "rather unappetizing address" of 807 Cyanide Ave., 719/275-4885—$4–7.

For picnic packin', there's a **City Market** on U.S. 50 on the east end of town.

SERVICES

The offices of the **Cañon City Police Department** are at 816 Royal Gorge Blvd., 719/275-8638. Phone the **Fremont County Sheriff** at 719/275-2000 or 719/275-1553. The **Colorado State Patrol** can be reached at 719/275-0015 or 719/275-1558. Cañon City's **St. Thomas More Hospital** is at 1019 Sheridan, 719/275-3381. The main **post office** is at 505 Macon, 719/275-6877.

Recycling

Recycle aluminum and glass at the **City Market** on the east end of town off U.S. 50. Recycle aluminum, cardboard, glass, newspapers, tin, and more at **Recycling Opportunities,** in the Alco Parking lot, Saturday 10 A.M.–4 P.M., and at **Florence Super Foods,** (in Florence) Tuesday noon–4 P.M.

INFORMATION

You'll find a tourist information booth just off U.S. 50 on each end of town. Pick up information on lodging, recreation, and other attractions. You can also get information from the **Cañon City Chamber of Commerce,** 403 Royal Gorge. Write P.O. Box 749, Cañon City, CO 81215, or phone 719/275-2331. The chamber's website, www.canoncitycolorado.com, has lots of information about the area, as well as links to sites that will let you book tours (of Royal Gorge, for example) and reserve rooms in town.

To learn more about the history of the town and surrounding area, visit the **Local History Center,** 719/269-9020, which collects newspapers (from 1860); historical periodicals, journals, and photographs; oral histories and transcripts; and maps and extensive prison records and publications. It's downstairs in the **Cañon City Public Library,** 516 Macon, open Mon.–Fri. noon–5 P.M. and Saturday 10:30 A.M.–2 P.M.

The Book Corral, 621 Main, 719/275-8923, carries an excellent selection of books about Colorado, from histories to recreational and backcountry guides. The local newspaper, the ***Daily***

Record, comes out weekday afternoons and Saturday morning. Watch for the weekly insert "This Week in the Royal Gorge Region," which lists current events and highlights particular points of interest. For information, phone 719/275-7565.

For information on the Pike or San Isabel National Forests, contact the district offices at 300 Dozier, Cañon City, CO 81212, 719/274-4119. Or write the central offices at 1920 Valley Dr., Pueblo, CO 81008, 719/545-8737. The local office of the BLM is at 3170 E. Main, 719/275-0631.

For **road and weather conditions,** phone 719/545-8520.

Royal Gorge

A bizarre blend of absolutely stunning scenery and god-awful promotion and exploitation, Royal Gorge can be enjoyed on a number of levels, and for a range of prices. If you've got the time and money (about $40), you can take in the entire experience: take the aerial tram, the Scenic Railway, the train to the bottom, and/or a helicopter tour (added cost); view a "25-minute sight and sound extravaganza" in the Royal Gorge "Plaza Theatre"; buy some deer food "for a buck" from the human-type beings dressed as a chipmunk and a miner; stay at "Yogi Bear's Jellystone Park RV Camp and Resort" (I'm not kidding).

Or . . .

Drive up to the tollgate, turn around, park, and walk over through the piñons to the cliffside (protected with chain-link fence), and take a look. For free. A free picnic area is just east of the tollgate. The problem is, you may have already been turned off by the tackiness of it all, the way the natural beauty has been subjugated, hidden away behind the waterslide and the billboards advertising "buffalo burgers" and "Pepsi, the Official Soft Drink of Royal Gorge." What's truly stunning is that nature still manages, somehow, to awe and inspire despite it all. But just think what it must have been like in the days B.C. (Before Commercialism).

Royal Gorge Bridge and Park
Encompassing the Royal Gorge Bridge, an aerial tram, and an incline railway, Royal Gorge Park provides a variety of ways to view and experience the canyon. Said to be the highest suspension bridge in the world (1,053 feet), the bridge is too narrow for trailers, motor homes, and campers—drivers and passengers must park and walk or take the park's trolley. The $37.95 admission includes bridge, tram, and railway passes, as well as entrance to a carousel and theater, where a video shows a history of the bridge's construction. The park is open year-round. For more information, write P.O. Box 549 AAA, Cañon City, CO 81215, or phone 719/275-7507.

Buckskin Joe Frontier Town and Scenic Railway
This theme park next to Royal Gorge offers gold panning, gunfights, horseback riding, a horse-drawn carriage, country music, and the Royal Gorge Scenic Railway, which will take you the three miles from the park to the gorge. Hours are 8 A.M.–8 P.M. Memorial Day through Labor Day; 9 A.M.–6:30 P.M. from Labor Day through early October. Admission to the park is $8 for adults, $6 for kids 4–11. Additional charges for the railway ($7 adults, $6 kids) and carriage rides ($3). For more information, phone 719/275-5149.

Accommodations
Although a number of private RV campgrounds at Royal Gorge vie for your patronage, you can camp free at what's probably the nicest area anyway. **Cañon City Campground** is a sprawling area with isolated sites (no water) off the turnoff from U.S. 50 and the tollgate about a mile down a well-maintained dirt road. Among the private campgrounds near Royal Gorge (east side of the canyon): **Royal View RV Campground,** 719/275-1900, and **Yogi Bear Jellystone Park RV Camp and Resort,** 719/275-2128.

the suspension bridge over 1,053-foot deep Royal Gorge

SOUTH-CENTRAL

Food

The **Grandview Steakhouse,** at the U.S. 50 turnoff to Royal Gorge, 719/269-3594, serves steaks, seafood, and pastas. Open for lunch and dinner daily, Memorial Day through Labor Day; weekends only the rest of the year. Entrées run $9–16. There's also a restaurant at Royal Gorge Frontier Town Railway and a cafeteria and a beer and pizza garden inside the tollgate at Royal Gorge Bridge.

Information

For more information on Royal Gorge, write P.O. Box 549, Cañon City, CO 81212-0549, or phone 719/275-7507 or 888/333-5597. The Royal Gorge website has additional information, as well as online tickets. You can also get information from the **Cañon City Chamber of Commerce,** Box Bin 749, Cañon City, CO 81215-0749, 719/275-2331.

Colorado Springs

Snug up against the Rocky Mountains' forested eastern slope, with Pikes Peak rising towerfully just a few miles to the west, Colorado Springs (pop. 291,000; elev. 6,035 feet) is one of the state's more popular tourist destinations. With a huge variety of historical, recreational, and geological attractions, Colorado Springs could keep a traveler charmed for weeks.

A planned community dating from the late 1880s, Colorado Springs still reflects its original design—the downtown streets are wide, the sidewalks broad, and lush parks dot the city. You'll find a scattering of outdoor cafés, buildings that have been remodeled but not overly gentrified, and small shops. The centerpiece of the downtown area is Acacia Park, a lovely central park and plaza that looks like something out of *The Music Man* or a Norman Rockwell painting. The park had gone to seed (locals dubbed it "Needle Park"), but it has been "reclaimed," and on summer evenings these days is full of families, young couples, and old-timers. Some sit on benches enjoying ice cream cones from Michelle's across the street; others pack the shuffleboard courts or just idly watch the wonderfully summer-paced competition.

HISTORY

Between modern downtown Colorado Springs and Manitou Springs is Colorado City, or "Old Town." Founded in 1858 as "El Paso" (the site was chosen for its location at the base of popular Ute Pass Trail) by a group of Kansas miners, the town changed its name to El Dorado City just a year later, when a second group of Kansans laid out streets and housing sites. By the late 1850s the community was known as Colorado City, and by the early '60s it had 300 homes and cabins; for a few short years Colorado City was the territorial capital.

In 1871, William J. Palmer, a Denver and Rio Grande Western Railroad baron and former Civil War general, bought 10,000 acres of land east of Colorado City and went about designing what he foresaw as a thoroughly modern and "upright" community, complete with schools, parks, and churches. Calling his new town Fountain Colony, Palmer discouraged industry of all kinds, as well as saloons and gambling houses, which he believed were better left to the still-wild-and-woolly Colorado City. In fact, the new town was so bent on maintaining a "temperate" community that all city deeds had specific contracts disallowing the manufacture and sale of alcoholic beverages. Colorado Springs remained "dry" until the repeal of the 18th Amendment in 1933.

Little London

Although one of Colorado Springs's original aims was to set itself apart from rowdy Manitou Springs, a road between the two communities was built within a year of the construction of Palmer's first buildings. Soon visitors, drawn to Colorado Springs by the railroad companies' boasts of pure, medicinal mineral waters and a dry and healthful year-round climate, were regularly making the short trek to Manitou. Meanwhile, Colorado Springs grew from its original buildings—a post office, hotel, and railroad office—to a bustling resort community with elegant mansions, polo and cricket fields, and golf courses. So popular was Palmer's Colorado Springs with easterners and Europeans, who gave it a decidedly cosmopolitan flair, that Palmer's resort city earned itself the nickname "Little London." During these same years, several sanatoriums were built to accommodate the increasing numbers of tuberculosis patients moving to the area. Evidence of Colorado Springs's TB days can be seen today in the huge porches on hillside houses, as well as in the immense number of towering trees, originally planted to increase the city's air quality.

Like many Colorado cities and towns, early Colorado Springs was shaped to a large degree by the railroad (or, more precisely, the railroads). In the mid-1880s, the Colorado Midland Railroad ran a line west from Colorado Springs to facilitate ore transportation from the thriving mountain camps, and four years later, the city was designated as the far-western stop on the Chicago, Rock Island, and Pacific Railway. In 1890, a cog railway was built to the top of Pikes Peak (see Pikes Peak Area, below).

The Town Hits Pay Dirt

The development of Colorado Springs ground to a near standstill in the early 1890s when the silver market went bust; at the same time, the once-thriving Colorado City all but shut down. A few years later, however, things picked up again when the mines of Cripple Creek began producing vast quantities of gold. By the end of the century, Colorado Springs, as well as Colorado City, was back on its feet.

Colorado Springs continued to grow as a resort town, attracting large numbers of wealthy investors and vacationers. In addition, many of the miners who had struck it rich in the Rocky Mountain mines moved to the young town, built huge homes, and established an upscale social order, the remains of which can still be seen today in their palaces around the Broadmoor Hotel (see Accommodations below) and in the almost Old World-like separation of the people who live in them from the working class. From 1900 to 1910, Colorado Springs's per-capita wealth was the highest in the country.

Meanwhile, Colorado City, whose economy relied largely on wages and on those who did the grunt work for the mine owners, ran into hard times when the mines played out. By the 1920s, most of the community's mills had been shut down and its saloon doors boarded up.

During the early 1940s, Colorado Springs began to take on the shape it has today, as military presence grew more and more part of the city's personality. In 1942, Fort Carson (originally called Camp Carson) was built to the

So popular was Colorado Springs with easterners and Europeans, who gave it a decidedly cosmopolitan flair, that the resort city earned itself the nickname "Little London."

south, and a few years later Peterson Air Force Base and the North American Aerospace Defense Command were part of the city's landscape. Work on the United States Air Force Academy, today the state's third most popular tourist attraction (see Vicinity of Colorado Springs, below), began in 1954.

Modern Colorado Springs

The 1970s and '80s saw a huge boost in Colorado Springs's appeal to tourism. Many of Colorado City's and Manitou Springs's old buildings were converted to specialty shops, and the area's many geological wonders—from Royal Gorge and Pikes Peak to Garden of the Gods and Cave of the Winds—began to solicit visitors with more aggressive pitches, from elaborately slick brochures to monstrously hideous billboards that often screened off and scarred the mountains' otherwise scenic landscapes.

By the late '80s and the beginning of the 20th century's last decade, Colorado Springs had taken on the feel of so many of the country's larger urban centers. Though the mountains keep the town from sprawling very much to the west, and the downtown area is nicely preserved, the east side has fallen victim to suburban blight, with miles and miles of housing developments, all looking very much alike, seeming to roll forever toward the plains. In addition, the mid- to late 1990s saw the city creeping southward as well. New housing now flanks much of Highway 115 south of town, many of the homes scrunched onto the tiniest of lots to make room for more.

Colorado Springs is also headquarters of Focus on the Family, the creation of James Dobson, who claims to have "biblical and empirical insights" that will help people "discover the founder of homes and the creator of families: Jesus Christ," ignoring the fact that "nontraditional" and/or non-Christian families can be just as viable and can contribute just as much to society as "traditional families."

SOUTH-CENTRAL

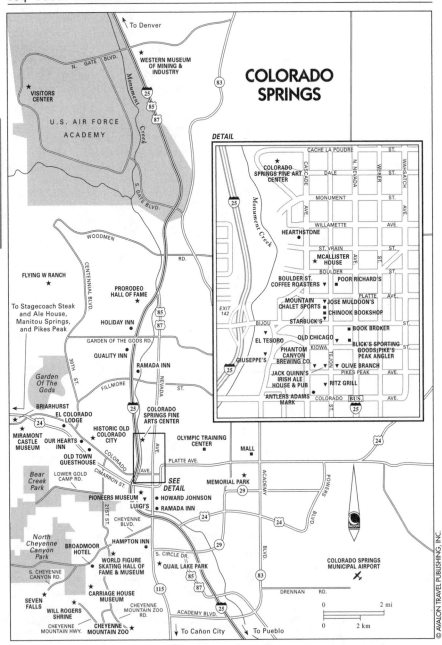

COLORADO SPRINGS

To Denver

WESTERN MUSEUM OF MINING & INDUSTRY

VISITORS CENTER

U.S. AIR FORCE ACADEMY

N. GATE BLVD.

Monument Creek

S. GATE BLVD.

WOODMEN RD.

CENTENNIAL BLVD

FLYING W RANCH

PRORODEO HALL OF FAME

HOLIDAY INN

To Stagecoach Steak and Ale House, Manitou Springs, and Pikes Peak

GARDEN OF THE GODS RD.

QUALITY INN

RAMADA INN

30TH ST.

NEVADA ST.

Garden Of The Gods

FILLMORE

BRIARHURST

EL COLORADO LODGE

MIRAMONT CASTLE MUSEUM

OUR HEARTS INN

HISTORIC OLD COLORADO CITY

COLORADO SPRINGS FINE ARTS CENTER

OLD TOWN GUESTHOUSE

COLORADO AVE.

OLYMPIC TRAINING CENTER

PLATTE AVE.

MALL

Bear Creek Park

LOWER GOLD CAMP RD.

CIMARRON ST.

SEE DETAIL

MEMORIAL PARK

ACADEMY BLVD

POWERS BLVD

PIONEERS MUSEUM

LUIGI'S

HOWARD JOHNSON

RAMADA INN

North Cheyenne Canyon Park

21ST ST.

CHEYENNE BLVD.

HAMPTON INN

BROADMOOR HOTEL

WORLD FIGURE SKATING HALL OF FAME & MUSEUM

S. CIRCLE DR.

QUAIL LAKE PARK

BLVD.

COLORADO SPRINGS MUNICIPAL AIRPORT

S. CHEYENNE CANYON RD.

CARRIAGE HOUSE MUSEUM

SEVEN FALLS

WILL ROGERS SHRINE

CHEYENNE MOUNTAIN HWY.

CHEYENNE MOUNTAIN ZOO

CHEYENNE MOUNTAIN ZOO RD.

ACADEMY BLVD.

DRENNAN RD.

To Cañon City

To Pueblo

0   2 mi
0   2 km

DETAIL

CACHE LA POUDRE ST.

COLORADO SPRINGS FINE ART CENTER

CASCADE AVE.

DALE

N. NEVADA

WEBER

WAHSATCH AVE.

MONUMENT ST.

WILLAMETTE AVE.

HEARTHSTONE

ST. VRAIN ST.

MCALLISTER HOUSE

BOULDER ST.

Monument Creek

BOULDER ST. COFFEE ROASTERS

POOR RICHARD'S

PLATTE AVE.

MOUNTAIN CHALET SPORTS

JOSE MULDOON'S

CHINOOK BOOKSHOP

STARBUCK'S

BIJOU ST.

BOOK BROKER

OLD CHICAGO

EL TESORO

BLICK'S SPORTING GOODS/PIKE'S PEAK ANGLER

PHANTOM CANYON BREWING CO.

KIOWA

LEON

GIUSEPPE'S

OLIVE BRANCH

PIKES PEAK AVE.

JACK QUINN'S IRISH ALE HOUSE & PUB

RITZ GRILL

ANTLERS ADAMS MARK

COLORADO ST.

BUS. 25

AVE.

EXIT 142

EXIT 83

© AVALON TRAVEL PUBLISHING, INC.

SIGHTS

Pioneers Museum

Don't let the name mislead you: the Pioneers Museum, though basically historical in concept, displays a wide range of artifacts from the Pikes Peak area. The museum's highlights are temporary exhibits (often on loan from places such as the Smithsonian), as well as several permanent displays: Pikes Peak Natives, for example, which includes Paleo-Indian and more modern Native American cultures; and a look at the area's medical history, with an emphasis on tuberculosis—patients and cures. A gift shop stocks an excellent selection of books. Also unique to this museum is its location in the old El Paso County Courthouse, which opened in 1903, was restored in 1972, and was dedicated as Pioneers Museum in 1979. Today the exhibits are in the original courtrooms; mock trials, open to the public, are held from time to time.

The Pioneers Museum, at 215 S. Tejon St., is open Tues.–Sat. 10 A.M.–5 P.M. and Sunday 1–5 P.M. Admission is free. For more information, phone 719/385-5990.

McAllister House Museum

Built in 1873 by Henry McAllister, one of General Palmer's protégés and an early civic leader, this was one of early Colorado Springs's first landmarks and showplaces. Listed on the National Register of Historic Places, the house had three white marble mantelpieces, shipped from Philadelphia, as well as running water. The home has been restored to its original elegance and appointed with authentic Victorian furnishings and decorations.

Today the McAllister House, at 423 N. Cascade (on the east side of the street; park in the alley), is open for tours and viewing. The museum is open year-round Thurs.–Sat. 10 A.M.–4 P.M. Admission is $4 for adults, $3 for seniors and students. For more information, phone 719/635-7925.

Carriage House Museum

This is a real sleeper—not many people even know about it. But right across Lake Circle from the main building of the Broadmoor Hotel, this little museum displays the carriage (and other vehicle) collection of Spencer Penrose, who built the Broadmoor Hotel in 1918. In perfect condition, all 33 of them, they include a one-horse *carromat* and *caliza* (from the Philippines), an 1890 opera bus (for two or four horses), an Abbott Downing and Company Concord Coach, built in 1850 and shipped around the Horn to be used for mail service in Mendocino County, California. There's also a beautiful 1928 Cadillac and an antique gun collection, including several examples of dueling pistols. A bonus is the two friendly and knowledgeable gentlemen who tend the museum. As classy as the carriages themselves.

The museum is open Mon.–Sat. 10 A.M.–5 P.M. Admission is free, though donations are accepted. Phone 719/634-5353.

Colorado Springs Fine Arts Center

With both rotating and permanent exhibits, this museum displays a wide array of 19th-century, modern, and postmodern art. The Charles Russell Room contains sketches and letters by the artist, as well as original manuscript pages from his autobiography. The museum also houses pieces by Georgia O'Keeffe, Peter Hurd, and Edward Hopper.

The museum, at 30 W. Dale (one block off North Cascade), is open Tues.–Fri. 9 A.M.–5 P.M., Saturday 10 A.M.–5 P.M., and Sunday 1–5 P.M. Admission is $4 for adults, $2.50 for seniors and students—free on Saturday. For more information, phone 719/634-5581.

U.S. Olympic Training Center

Colorado Springs is one of the most outdoors- and sports-oriented areas in the country, so it's no surprise that the city is home to this 36-acre training complex, which also serves as headquarters for the U.S. Olympic Committee. Stop by to watch athletes working out (the thin air at 6,000 feet is ideal for training)—at everything from fencing to gymnastics to volleyball. Guided 90-minute tours take you through the facilities, beginning with a 90-minute film on the Olympics. There's also a gift and souvenir shop.

SOUTH-CENTRAL

The complex, at 1750 E. Boulder, is open year-round, Mon.–Sat. 9 A.M.–5 P.M. and Sunday 10 A.M.–4 P.M. Tours start on the hour. Admission is free. Phone the visitor center at 719/578-4644 or 888/OLY-TOUR (659-8687). You can also get information at www.usolympicteam.com.

World Figure Skating Hall of Fame and Museum

A true special-interest museum, this complex commemorates the history of ice-skating and honors famous skaters such as Sonja Henie and Peggy Fleming (who hails from Colorado Springs and the rink at the Broadmoor Hotel). Besides costumes, medals, and trophies, the museum also houses a library of ice-skating books and what it claims is the world's largest collection of ice-skating art.

Year-round hours are Mon.–Sat. 10 A.M.–4 P.M. Admission is $3, $2 for kids and seniors. It's near the Broadmoor Hotel at 20 1st Street. For information, phone 719/635-5200.

Cheyenne Mountain Zoo

Perched on the hillside above the Broadmoor complex and southern Colorado Springs, this small zoo features about 800 animals in a natural setting lush with flora. Wind your way from cage to cage along narrow pathways overgrown

© STEPHEN METZGER

Not known for their sense of humor, giraffes just can't keep tongue in cheek.

with tall bushes. Highlights: gorgeous snow leopards, giraffes that eat out of your hand, and a monkey house.

Of course, a zoo is a zoo, and particularly on hot days one tends to wonder at the absurdity of locking wild animals in cages hundreds of times smaller than what they'd ordinarily need to sustain themselves. But given that, this zoo tends to be environmentally responsible, with attention drawn to the plights of endangered species (many of which are represented here), as well as scheduled workshops for local school groups.

Zoo hours are 9 A.M.–6 P.M. Memorial Day through Labor Day and 9 A.M.–5 P.M. the rest of the year. The admission ($10 adult, $9 senior, and $5 child) also gets you into the Will Rogers Shrine (see below). To get to the zoo, take Lake Avenue from South Nevada (Highway 115), and follow the signs. The route is well marked. For information, phone 719/633-9925.

Will Rogers Shrine of the Sun

Even if you're not necessarily interested in Will Rogers, a drive up to this shrine is well worth your time. Clinging to the steep mountainside above southern Colorado Springs, the stone tower, made of indigenous gray-pink granite, offers excellent views of the city, particularly of the Broadmoor area (from here, you can really see the property's sprawling majesty).

Begun in 1934 and dedicated to the entertainer in September 1937, the shrine was commissioned by Spencer Penrose, who owned the Broadmoor Hotel. When Penrose's friend Will Rogers died in 1935, Penrose decided to name the tower in his honor. (One story, perhaps apocryphal, is that Penrose—not known for his modesty—originally intended to honor himself with the shrine.)

Today, a tape of a Will Rogers monologue plays continually, and the interior of the tower is decorated with lots of photos of Rogers, including the plane crash that took his life, as well as with painted murals depicting Colorado's history. The shrine is open to the pub-

© STEPHEN METZGER

The Will Rogers Shrine of the Sun offers excellent views of Colorado Springs.

lic daily 9 A.M.–5 P.M. from Memorial Day through Labor Day, and 9 A.M.–4 P.M. the rest of the year. Follow Mirada Road through Cheyenne Mountain Zoo (see above), admission to which includes entrance to the shrine.

Seven Falls

This is a beautiful series of seven waterfalls cascading into a tiny pool. If you've been faithful to your stair machine, or are in moderately good shape, you can climb the *steep* steps to the tops of the two viewing platforms. The first clings to the canyon's side across from the falls (a snack bar and gift shop are at the top); the second climbs the granite alongside the falls themselves and takes you to a trail that follows the meandering upper creek back into the woods. Native American dances are performed at the falls' base several times daily.

The site is open 8:30 A.M.–10:30 P.M., mid-May through early September and 9 A.M.–4:15 P.M. the rest of the year. Admission is $8.50 for adults, $6 for seniors, and $5.50 for kids 6–12. Take Cheyenne Boulevard and watch for the signs. For information, phone 719/632-0765.

PARKS AND RECREATION

Near some of the finest outdoor recreation areas in the country, Colorado Springs is a natural for just about any sport or activity you can name (well, maybe not *surfing*...). And the folks who live here take advantage of it. They're an outdoorsy bunch—runners, skiers, hikers, climbers, cyclers, golfers, all enjoying that crisp mountain air and fabulous scenery.

Several city-maintained parks are scattered around town, offering grass, shade, and picnicking. **Memorial Park** is near downtown Colorado Springs (at Pikes Peak and Union) and has a public swimming pool, tennis courts, picnic facilities, huge lawns, shade trees, and a small lake. **Quail Lake Park,** just east of Nevada Avenue/Highway 115 on Cheyenne Mountain Road, is a very nice little community park with lush lawns, picnic tables, grills, hiking and biking trails, boating and fishing, and a wonderful kids' playground. **North Cheyenne Canyon Park,** on the west side of town at the end of Cheyenne Canyon Road, offers hiking trails, guided nature walks, and interpretive programs, as well as rock-climbing and picnicking. For information, phone

719/634-9320 or 719/578-6640. At **Bear Creek Regional Park,** 245 Bear Creek Rd., you can hike the five miles of nature trails, join in a guided walk, or explore the **Bear Creek Nature Center.** For more information, phone 719/520-6387.

Golf

Colorado Springs has several excellent golf courses, public and private. The courses at the **Broadmoor Hotel** complex, 719/634-7711, attract some of the best (and wealthiest) golfers in the country. It's open to members and hotel guests only. The 18-hole Robert Trent Jones course at the **U.S. Air Force Academy** is open to military personnel only (including retirees). Phone 719/472-3456 for information and tee times. **Country Club of Colorado** is at 125 E Clubhouse Dr., 719/583-4095.

If you've got neither the bucks nor the connections to play a private course, don't be putt off: the city has places for plebes too. **Pine Creek Golf Club,** 9850 Divot Dr., 719/594-9999, is an 18-hole public course open year-round, as are the **Patty Jewett Golf Course,** 900 E. Espanola, 719/578-6825, and **Valley-Hi Golf Course,** 610 S. Chelton Rd., 719/578-6926.

Hiking

Hiking and backpacking opportunities in the Colorado Springs area vary from nature walks at the city parks (see above) to full-bore excursions into serious backcountry and treks to the top of Pikes Peak. The most popular route up Pikes Peak is **Barr Trail,** which begins above the hydroelectric plant in Manitou Springs off Ruxton Avenue. You'll find overnight shelters along the 13-mile (one way) trail at the 6.8-mile (Barr Camp Cabins) and 8.5-mile (Timberline A-frame) points. For information on camping, phone the Pike National Forest office at 719/636-1602. **North Cheyenne Canyon Trail** will take you on an easy 10-mile (round-trip) day hike with good views of Colorado Springs and the mountains. Look for the trailhead just past the entrance to North Cheyenne Canyon at the end of Cheyenne Canyon Road.

For more information on hiking and backpacking in the Colorado Springs area, write the **El Paso County Parks and Recreation Department** at 1045 W. Rio Grande, Colorado Springs, CO, or phone 719/520-6375.

Cycling

As in the rest of the country, bicycling is enjoying a renaissance in Colorado Springs. This is in large part because of the overnight explosion in the popularity of mountain biking, though the interest in touring has also been rekindled. The city has published a wonderful map, *Pikes Peak Area Trails Map and Recreation Guide,* available at bike shops, outdoor shops, and the Colorado Springs Convention and Visitors center. For information on mountain biking and touring in the area, stop by **Mountain Chalet Sports,** 226 N. Tejon, 719/633-0732, or **Old Town Bike Shop,** 426 S. Tejon, 719/475-8589.

Climbing

The steep sandstone spires and cliffs of the **Garden of the Gods** (see below) attract highly skilled rock climbers, as well as photographers and others awed by these athletes' arachnid abilities to cling to vertical surfaces. Climbers must register at the visitor center before heading up.

Mountain Chalet Sports, 226 N. Tejon in Colorado Springs, 719/633-0732, carries climbing equipment, maps, and local guidebooks, and also rents gear.

Horseback Riding

Those disinclined to climb their way around Garden of the Gods or to wind around the paved roadways with the summer tourist hordes can rent horses by the hour at **Academy Riding Stables,** 719/633-5667. Rates are $20 an hour ($35 for two), and reservations are recommended.

Skiing

Colorado Springs is close enough to the state's major resorts that (weather permitting) serious shredders can head up for the day and be stepping into skis at, say, Monarch or A-Basin when the lifts open.

Cross-country skiers need not go all the way to Summit County to find some good fluff, as some excellent trails await in nearby **Pike National**

Forest. For cross-country rentals, as well as advice on where to head, stop by **Mountain Chalet Sports,** 226 N. Tejon, 719/633-0732, or **Christy Sports,** 1808 N. Academy Blvd., 719/636-3355.

TOURS

Gray Line, 719/633-1181, offers tours to Pikes Peak, Royal Gorge, and other area attractions, including Seven Falls and Cave of the Winds. Gray Line also offers white-water rafting trips.

Group tours of the area can be arranged through **Falcon Tours and Motorcoaches,** 719/495-1653.

ACCOMMODATIONS

Colorado Springs's lodging runs the gamut from cookie-cutter franchise motels to bed-and-breakfasts to one of the nicest hotels in the country (see Broadmoor, below). If you're looking to be out and about exploring the area and don't need anything more than four walls, a bed, and a bathroom, then a Motel 6, Super 8, or other chain inn should do the trick. If you'd rather experience some local color, one of the historic bed-and-breakfasts might be a better call. If cost is not a consideration or you're just ready for a big splurge, then you could do no better than the Broadmoor. In fact, even if you don't stay at the Broadmoor, you ought to head up and have a look-see.

Under $50

Limited possibilities here, but you might be able to sneak in for under $50. Try the **Motel 6,** 3228 N. Chestnut (Exit 145 from I-25), 719/520-5400, or the **Stagecoach Motel,** 1647 S. Nevada Ave., 719/633-3894.

$50–100

You're much more likely to find lodging in this range, though you're still at the low end by Colorado Springs's standards. The following inns offer doubles in this range: the **Super 8—Garden of the Gods,** 4604 Rusina Rd. (Exit 146 from I-25), 719/594-0964; **Howard Johnson Express Inn,** 1231 S. Nevada Ave., 719/634-

1545; and the **Ramada Inn,** 1703 S. Nevada Ave., 719/632-7077.

$100–150

You'll find some excellent bed-and-breakfasts in this category, including one of the nicest and best known in the state, **The Hearthstone,** 506 N. Cascade, 719/473-4413. Remodeled from two side-by-side Victorians, now joined by what was originally a carriage house, the Hearthstone has 25 different rooms, each beautifully decorated in a specific theme and most with private baths. The smallest room, "The Dormer," has no bath, while "The Fireside" has a fireplace and its own private porch.

The **Holden House,** 1102 W. Pikes Peak Ave., 719/471-3980, is another elegantly restored Victorian (built in 1902). Named for historically important Colorado towns (Cripple Creek, Silverton), the Holden House's rooms are decorated with authentic furnishings from Colorado's past.

One of the area's newest inns, and certainly one of its nicest, is the **Old Town GuestHouse,** 115 S. 26th (Old Colorado City), 719/632-9194. Built in 1997, specifically as a bed-and-breakfast, the Old Town features elegant rooms with a historical feel yet with completely modern amenities, including computer-data ports, VCRs (for the 200-plus movies available in the lobby), and refrigerators. The inn—which also has a corporate meeting facility in the basement—is walking distance to the Old Colorado City shops and restaurants, and at the same time offers easy access to both the Manitou Springs area and to central Colorado Springs, without the hustle-bustle traffic of downtown. (The rainbow decal on the door was a pleasant surprise here in a town well known for its right-wing politics—Colorado Springs spawned the ill-fated anti-gay Amendment 2.)

Another fine bed-and-breakfast is **Our Hearts Inn,** 2215 W. Colorado Ave., 719/473-8684 or 800/533-7095, with three rooms in a turn-of-the-century Victorian and one cottage.

Both the Old Town Guesthouse and Our Hearts Inn are members of **Authentic Inns of the Pikes Peak Region,** just one of several bed-and-breakfast associations in the area that provide

© STEPHEN METZGER

The Broadmoor is one of the classiest lodges in the West.

information on amenities and availability. Phone 888/892-2237 or check out its website at www.bbonline.com/co/pikespeak.

In Manitou Springs, the **Rockledge Country Inn,** 328 El Paso, 719/685-4515, offers seven rooms in a remodeled 9,000-square-foot greenstone-and-stucco home originally built in 1912. The gorgeous grounds include sprawling terraced gardens, while the interior is furnished largely with antiques, including an 1875 Steinway piano. Also in Manitou, the **Frontier's Rest Bed and Breakfast Inn,** 341 Ruxton, 719/685-0588, has four Western-themed rooms, all with private baths.

A complete list of the area's plethora of bed-and-breakfast inns is available at the Colorado Springs Convention and Visitors Bureau website at www.coloradosprings-travel.com.

For hotel accommodations in this price category, try the **Doubletree,** 1775 E. Cheyenne (Exit 138 from I-25), 719/576-8900, or **Embassy Suites Hotel,** 7290 Commerce Center, (Exit 149 from I-25), 719/599-9100.

$150–250 and up

Without doubt one of the grandest of all hotels west of the Mississippi, **The Broadmoor,** 719/634-7711, will take your breath away even if you've prepared yourself to be impressed. Built in 1918, and added onto and renovated several times over the years, the 30-building complex—looking more like an Italian villa than an American hotel—sprawls beautifully at the foot of the Rocky Mountains.

Of course, none of the 700 rooms here is cheap, but for those rare occasions when you really want to toss caution to the wind, The Broadmoor offers you first class all the way. Lodging plans range from no-frills digs to packages that include meals, champagne, golf, skiing, and tours of the area.

To get there, take Nevada Avenue south from downtown, and turn right on Lake Avenue (you'll see the signs). Check out the website at www.broadmoor.com.

Another Colorado Springs institution is **The Antlers Adams Mark,** 4 S. Cascade Ave., 719/473-5600, originally built in 1883 by William Palmer and for many years a rival to the Broadmoor. Recently bought and completely remodeled by the Doubletree chain and then sold to Adams Mark, the hotel offers luxurious rooms and downtown convenience.

Camping and RVing

You'll find virtually limitless camping opportunities in **Pike National Forest** west of Colorado Springs, from improved areas with running water to backcountry sites where no one else may have ever camped. For maps and information on Pike National Forest, stop by the district ranger office at 601 S. Weber, or phone 719/636-1602. Another great source is **Mountain Chalet Sports,** 226 N. Tejon, 719/633-0732, where you can pick up books and maps and talk to experts on camping and exploring the Colorado backcountry. Another good source for gear and information is **Blick's Sporting Goods,** 119 N. Tejon, 719/636-3348. Inside Blick's, **Pikes Peak Angler** provides tips and information on area fishing, especially fly-fishing.

There's also lots of RV camping in the Colorado Springs area. Situated on 1,000 isolated acres four miles south of town on Highway 115, **Golden Eagle Ranch RV Park,** 719/576-0450, has 500 RV campsites. It's also right next to the May Museum of Natural History (see Vicinity of Colorado Springs, below). **Garden of the Gods Campground,** 719/475-9450, is adjacent to Garden of the Gods in Manitou and has 300 RV sites, as well as tent sites and cabins. You'll find bus and trolley service to Manitou Springs and lots of social events (barbecues, watermelon feeds, Sunday pancake brunches). You'll also find several RV campgrounds west of Colorado Springs on U.S. 24 (between Green Mountain Falls and Woodland Park).

FOOD

Get up and Go

Thankfully, Colorado Springs has jumped on the espresso bandwagon, and while looking for gourmet coffee in the Springs was once like looking for burgers in a Zen monastery, these days it's a lot easier. In fact, downtown is home to more than a handful of excellent espresso-and-baked-goods shops, where you can linger over the morning's paper or your itinerary of the day's events. **Boulder Street Coffee Roasters** is right downtown at 322 Tejon, 719/577-4291 (open at 6:30 A.M. daily), while **Starbucks,** 719/447-0680, is just a block south at the corner of Tejon and Bijou. Both, as well as the several other coffee shops downtown, have tables outside, and if Pikes Peak weren't looming just to the west you might think you were in North Beach.

If it's a late start you're getting, try the traditional Irish breakfast at **Jack Quinn's Irish Ale House and Pub,** 21 S. Tejon, 719/385-0766—about $8 for eggs, pudding, rashers, potatoes, and toast. Open at 11 A.M. daily.

Across the street, the **Olive Branch,** 23 S. Tejon, 719/475-1199, specializes in less artery-clogging breakfasts, including vegetarian dishes, moderately priced. Open daily, also for lunch and dinner.

Downtown Colorado Springs Restaurants

A favorite among both locals and passers-through, particularly families, is **Giuseppe's Old Depot,** 10 Sierra Madre, 719/635-3111, serving good solid Italian food at reasonable prices—in the Old Depot (just a couple of blocks from downtown), where trains roar by regularly just outside the back door (ask for a window table to get the best view of the tracks). Specializing in pasta dishes (the lasagna is superb), sandwiches, and pizzas, as well as prime rib, steaks, and seafood, Giuseppe's also has a soup and salad bar and desserts (if you're not yet dragging your caboose). Entrées run about $6–15. From downtown, go about three blocks west—it's between the train tracks and old Engine 168, the power that pulled the first passenger train from Denver to Ogden, Utah, on May 21, 1883. Open daily for lunch and dinner. **Luigi's,** 947 S. Tejon, 719/632-7339, is a family-owned Colorado Springs tradition (since 1958), where you can get chicken, veal, pastas, and pizzas for $8–20. Open for dinner Tues.–Sunday.

Another favorite for Italian food is **Old Chicago,** downtown at 118 N. Tejon, 719/634-8812, serving excellent pasta dishes, deep-dish pizzas, and Italian sandwiches ($8–14). The place does tend to get a bit crowded, especially on Friday evenings, when the downtown business crowd flocks in to wind down, but waiting for a table here is half the fun. The bar features more than

100 different kinds of beer from around the world, as well as a couple of television sets usually tuned to the seasonally appropriate sport. Old Chicago also offers takeout.

Speaking of beer and fun, if these two concepts interest you, don't miss the **Phantom Canyon Brewing Company,** 2 E. Pikes Peak Ave. (corner of Cascade), 719/635-2800, where you can wash down excellent sandwiches, pastas, salads, and traditional pub fare such as shepherd's pie and fish and chips with some of Colorado's best microbrewery ales, beers, and stouts, as well as novelties, such as raspberry ale. A very popular local hangout. Lunch entrées run $5–8; dinner $8–14. Open for lunch and dinner daily, with brunch served starting at 9 A.M. Sunday.

At 222 N. Tejon is another hoppin' place, **Jose Muldoon's,** 719/636-2312, serving steaks, seafood, chicken, and Mexican and New Mexican food for $6–12. The **Ritz Grill,** 15 S. Tejon, 719/635-8484, serves pastas, fish, and stir-fry for $8–18, as well as soups, sandwiches, and salads for lunch, $4–8. Open for lunch and dinner daily.

Highly regarded by locals for Mexican and New Mexican food is **El Tesoro** ("the treasure"), 10 N. Sierra Madre (right next door to Giuseppe's), 719/471-0106. Here you can get blue-corn enchiladas, *chile verde,* and some of the best margaritas in town; dinners run $6–16.

For a taste of Ireland, try **Jack Quinn's Irish Ale House and Pub,** 21 S. Tejon, 719/385-0766, which was literally imported—lamp by lamp, table by table—from the old country. Entrées—corned beef and cabbage, of course, as well as sandwiches, stews, and fish and chips—are $6–9. You can sit at the bar, a table in the main dining area, or in one of several booths that actually close off behind fine woodwork and stained glass. Open daily till 10 P.M.

Dining at The Broadmoor

As a resort town founded primarily by big money, Colorado Springs claims its share of upscale restaurants, most notably those in The Broadmoor hotel. In fact, The Broadmoor complex includes eight separate restaurants, varying from casual (relatively speaking) dining rooms off the golf course to those in the main buildings, with dress codes and don't-ask-the-prices menus.

The Broadmoor's classiest, fanciest, and most expensive restaurant is **Charles Court,** 719/577-5774, in the west lobby. The **Penrose Room,** 719/577-5773, in Broadmoor South, specializes in continental cuisine. Both require coats and ties for men and dresses or skirts for women. The **Tavern,** 719/634-7711, in the Broadmoor Main, serves excellent food—steaks, prime rib, and seafood, as well as daily specials—at more affordable prices (dinners run about $13–26). Live music nightly.

For more information on dining at The Broadmoor, phone 719/577-5252 or 800/634-7711.

Food in Old Colorado City

For one of the best breakfasts around, check out **La Baguette,** 2417 W. Colorado Ave., 719/577-4818, which serves espresso coffees and a variety of tasty pastries, as well as croissant sandwiches and other fare.

A Colorado Springs tradition and favorite for Mexican food is **Henri's,** 2427 W. Colorado, 719/634-9031, serving stuffed sopaipillas, shrimp, *chiles rellenos,* and other dinners ($7–9), as well as à la carte tacos, tostadas, etc. Dinners run $6–14. For one of the best burgers in town, try the loud and rowdy **Meadow Muffins,** 2432 W. Colorado, 719/633-0583, where the decor alone—the walls are hung with old carriages, animal heads, boats, and cannons—is worth a visit. Burgers, sandwiches, and salads are $4–7. Open for lunch and dinner daily, from 11 A.M.

ENTERTAINMENT

Colorado Springs is a big enough city that you're likely to find live music and other entertainment just about every night of the week, varying from lounge music to comedy to hardcore rock 'n' roll. Check the *Gazette-Telegraph,* Colorado Springs's daily newspaper, for listings of who's playing where and when. Friday's edition carries the "Scene" supplement, geared specifically to entertainment. Also check the weekly *Independent.*

Clubs

A great place to go with family and friends is the **Golden Bee,** in the International Center at the Broadmoor. Gather round a table, order a yard-long schooner of beer, pass around the house songbooks, and join the crowd accompanying the tavern's pianist.

To quaff a few with the downtown locals, stop by **Old Chicago,** 118 N. Tejon, 719/634-8812, or **Jose Muldoon's,** 222 N. Tejon, 719/636-2312, especially on a Friday around happy hour. At the **Phantom Canyon Brewing Company,** 2 E. Pikes Peak Ave., 719/635-2800, you can shoot a game of pool while you down a cold on-site-brewed beer and dig the tunes on the city's best jukebox. There's also live music or a DJ at **Meadow Muffins,** 2432 W. Colorado (Old Colorado City), 719/633-0583. For boot scootin' (lessons available), check out **Cowboys,** 3910 Pioneer Park, 719/596-1212, regularly named "best country-western club in town by the *Gazette-Telegraph.* The club's open Wed.–Sunday.

Take Me Out to the Ball Game

As anyone who's been to a minor league baseball game knows, these games have a charm and attraction all their own. You don't have to fight crowds, all the seats are good (and cheap!), the young players, while working hard to make it to the Bigs, are having great fun, and the fans are absolutely *rabid.* The Colorado Skysox are the AAA team of the Colorado Rockies and play 72 games in the Springs. Take in an afternoon or evening game and watch these young players on their way up (and some on their way down . . .). All seats are less than $10. For information and tickets, phone 719/597-1449.

CALENDAR

From chili cook-offs to rodeos, auto races, and arts-and-crafts festivals, there's something going on nearly every weekend in Colorado Springs. The town's biggies are the **Air Force Academy Graduation,** in late May; the **Fourth of July Celebration and Fireworks;** the **Pikes Peak Auto Hill Climb,** in July (past winners include Bobby and Al Unser and Mario Andretti); **Pikes**

Peak or Bust Rodeo, in mid-August; and the **International Balloon Classic,** Labor Day Weekend. Watch the *Gazette-Telegraph* for listings of events. You can also get up-to-date information by phoning the convention and visitors bureau's **FunFone Events Line,** 719/635-1723.

SHOPPING

Colorado Springs–area shopping is essentially clustered in three areas: downtown Colorado Springs, Colorado City, and Manitou Springs. Downtown in the Springs, you'll find everything from upscale gift shops and boutiques to Western traditions—hardware stores, shoe stores, and uniform stores. Be sure to allow some time to explore Old Colorado City, a National Historic District between the 2400 and 2700 blocks of Colorado Avenue (west of downtown). Lots of boutiques, art galleries, and cafés are housed in 1860s-era buildings that once served as supply stores and saloons for Cripple Creek miners. Check out **Michael Garman Galleries,** 2418 W. Colorado Ave., 719/471-1600, for miniature figurines and dioramas of street scenes. Equally impressive is **Simpich Character Dolls,** 2413 W. Colorado Ave., 719/636-3272, where you can get (or just look at) exquisitely detailed, handmade ceramic and fabric miniature dolls, with an emphasis on Christmas figures. The dolls come to life in the **Simpich Marionette Theatre,** where past productions include *A Christmas Carol, Heidi,* and *Beauty and the Beast.* Phone the theater at 719/636-3539 for more information.

You'll also want to spend some time exploring the boutiques, galleries, and arcades in Manitou Springs. Shops vary from some rather tacky rubber-tomahawk "trading posts" to legitimate and classy galleries and boutiques selling quality jewelry, pottery, and other crafts and artwork. When you're done shopping, or just need a break, there are lots of sidewalk cafés, as well as vendors selling soft drinks and saltwater taffy.

Colorado Springs's main mall is at 24th and Academy and includes a Mervyn's, JCPenney, and scores of the other traditional mall shops—Victoria's Secret, Eddie Bauer, B. Dalton, and Foot Locker.

SOUTH-CENTRAL

SERVICES

In emergencies in Colorado Springs, always dial **911.** For nonemergencies, phone the **Colorado Springs Police** at 719/635-6611; the **El Paso County Sheriff** at 719/390-5555; and the **Colorado State Patrol** at 719/635-3581.

Colorado Springs's **Memorial Hospital** is at 1400 E. Boulder, 719/475-5000. The **Penrose-St. Francis Healthcare System** maintains three separate facilities: Penrose Community Hospital, 3205 N. Academy, 719/591-3000; Penrose Hospital, 2215 N. Cascade, 719/630-5000; and St. Francis Hospital, 825 E. Pikes Peak, 719/636-8800. For information, phone its **Healthline** at 719/630-5555.

The downtown branch of the **post office** is at 210 E. Pikes Peak; phone 719/570-5343. For information, or for locations of other branches, phone 719/570-5339.

Recycling

Colorado Springs is a relatively big city, and there are scores of places to recycle just about anything you've managed to collect on your trip. Recycle aluminum, glass, newspapers, and plastic containers at all Colorado Springs **King Soopers,** including those at the following sites: 1750 W. Uintah, 2720 Palmer Park, 6930 N. Academy, and the corner of Hancock and Academy. You can also recycle aluminum, glass, and newspaper, at two **Recycle America** locations (419 E. Vermijo and 1965 Commercial), as well as at **Springs Recycling,** 3436 W. Colorado Avenue. Colorado Springs **Safeways** will recycle aluminum and grocery bags.

For more information on where to recycle in the Colorado Springs area, contact **Waste Management of Colorado Springs,** 719/632-8877.

INFORMATION

For more information about Colorado Springs and the Pikes Peak-Manitou Springs area, contact the **Colorado Springs Convention and Visitors Bureau,** 719/635-7506 or 877/745-3773. The bureau's offices are downtown at 104 S. Cascade (free parking at entrance on Colorado Avenue and camper parking one block west). Stop in to pick up brochures on area attractions, as well as dining, lodging, and events guides; particularly useful is the free Colorado Springs *Official Visitors Guide.* The bureau's website, www.coloradospringstravel .com, is one of the most sophisticated, thorough, and user-friendly in the state. Write the **Colorado Springs Chamber of Commerce** at Drawer B, Colorado Springs, CO 80901, or phone 719/635-1551. Its online business directory is at www.introcoloradosprings.com.

The information center for the **Pikes Peak Library District** is at 5550 N. Union Blvd., 719/531-6333. The district's downtown branch is the **Penrose Public Library,** 719/473-2080, at Kiowa and Cascade.

One of the area's best bookstores is **The Chinook Bookshop,** downtown at 210 N. Tejon, 719/635-1195. It stocks an excellent selection of books (travel, recreation, histories, etc.) on the Colorado Springs area, as well as on the rest of Colorado and the West, including a large section of Native American works. For used books, check out **Poor Richard's,** 320 N. Tejon, 719/578-0012, where you'll also find a café and espresso bar. Another excellent used bookstore is **The Book Broker,** 119 Bijou, 719/635-4514. And, naturally, Colorado Springs has been **Barnes and Nobled:** 795 Citadel Dr. (at Citadel Mall), 719/637-8282.

Colorado Springs's daily newspaper is the *Gazette-Telegraph.* For subscription information, phone 719/632-5511 or write P.O. Box 1779, Colorado Springs, CO 80901. The city's weekly alternative, *The Colorado Springs Independent* is a refreshing change from the *Gazette-Telegraph,* with profiles of locals, restaurant reviews, and stories with environmental-libertarian perspectives.

For information on **road and weather conditions,** phone 719/635-7623.

Further Reading

One of the best histories of the area is Marshall Sprague's *Newport of the Rockies.* Available in most Colorado Springs–area bookstores, this book documents the city from its beginnings under General William Palmer, through its popularity with health- and cure-seekers, particularly tuberculosis patients, and into the later 20th century. Sprague's

Money Mountain, the Story of Cripple Creek Gold will also interest travelers who want to learn about the area's past. Sprague writes as though he were telling you yarns as you sat around a campfire at the base of Pikes Peak.

TRANSPORTATION

Getting There

Colorado Springs Airport is a small, user-friendly facility that has seen huge increases in customers since Denver International Airport (DIA) opened in early 1995. With United's virtual monopoly at DIA, as well as DIA's distance from downtown, many Denver-area travelers are finding it's both cheaper and easier to drive to Colorado Springs, which is served by several major carriers, including **American Airlines, America West, Continental, Mesa, Northwest,** and **TWA. Colorado Springs Airport Shuttle Services** 719/578-5232, offers regular shuttles from the airport to Colorado Springs hotels and private residences. Colorado Springs's bus terminal is at 327 S. Weber; phone **Greyhound-Trailways** at 719/636-1505 or 800/527-1566.

Automobile rentals are available both downtown and at the airport. Rent from **Avis,** 719/596-2751; **Budget,** 719/574-7400; **Dol-**lar, 719/637-2620; **Hertz,** 719/596-1863; and **Thrifty,** 719/390-9800. Phone **Yellow Cab** at 719/634-5000.

Getting Around

Getting around in Colorado Springs is not difficult. **Colorado Springs Transit** buses serve most of the metropolitan area. For route information, phone 719/475-9733.

When driving, remember the major north-south arteries are I-25, Highway 115, Academy/Highway 83, Wahsatch, Nevada, Tejon, and Cascade; major east-west arteries include Fountain, U.S. 24/Platte, Colorado (which connects Colorado Springs and Manitou Springs and becomes Pikes Peak Boulevard east of U.S. 24), Constitution, Fillmore, and Austin Bluffs Parkway. It's helpful, too, to keep a bit of history in mind: Queen Palmer, wife of founding father General William Palmer, named Colorado Springs's original north-south streets, or those parallel with the Rockies, after other mountain ranges (Cascade, Sierra Madre, Wahsatch) and east-west streets after rivers (Cimarron, Cuchara, Rio Grande, Las Animas, Colorado, Platte, Willamette). Finally, remember that Pikes Peak and the Rocky Mountains are always to the *west*—you couldn't ask for a better landmark.

Vicinity of Colorado Springs

In addition to the many things to do and see in town, the surrounding area has a wide range of other attractions, from museums, railways, and shopping areas to mountains, forests, and redrock canyons—enough to keep the budding naturalist exploring happily for weeks on end. Whether your bent is to watch white-capped cadets marching in formation at the U.S. Air Force Academy or to hike to the top of Pikes Peak and take in the incredible vistas, you're sure to find plenty to do.

SIGHTS

United States Air Force Academy

One of Colorado Springs's main tourist attractions, this 18,000-acre officer-training campus is impressive (even if you're not a military buff) for its military importance, its intriguing architecture and layout, and the gorgeous grounds, rife with wild game, in the forests at the foot of the Rocky Mountains.

Though much of the campus is off-limits to visitors, you can take a self-guided driving tour through the grounds, with a number of stops along the way. The huge visitor center, open daily 9 A.M.–5 P.M. (till 6 P.M. Memorial Day through Labor Day), has displays on the academy's beginnings (founded in 1954), a map with pins showing hometowns of current cadets, textual and photo exhibits of the school's educational programs, the requisite display showing how being a cadet "builds character," and a gift shop,

© STEPHEN METZGER

B-52 bomber displayed on the campus of the U.S. Air Force Academy.

where you can get Air Force sweatshirts and other souvenirs. Regularly scheduled guided tours are offered free of charge. Admission to the visitor center is also free.

To get there, take Exit 156B from I-25 to the academy's north entrance, and follow the signs. At the gate, you'll be given a map to help guide you through the grounds and to the visitor center and other parts of the campus open to tourists, including the chapel, planetarium, parade ground, and nature trail.

For more information, write **Visitor Services Division,** Directorate of Public Affairs, HQ USAFA/PAV, USAF Academy, CO 80840-5151; or phone 719/593-8840.

ProRodeo Hall of Fame and Museum

Even if you didn't grow up ropin' and ridin', and even if the closest you've come to a rodeo is the pages of a Larry McMurtry novel, you'll still get a boot out of this museum.

Displays include works by Gary Morton, of New Mexico's Bell Ranch (paintings), who's also a cowboy ("I'll keep on ridin' for my pleasure and paintin' the cowboy's domain"); a memorial to Casey Tibbs, with memorial by Charlie Daniels (his gold record for "Simple Man" and a poem, "Casey's Last Ride" dedicated to Tibbs);

and lots of great photos, including shots of clowns *working* (saving bronc riders in BIG trouble), trophies, silver spurs, gold buckles, and beautifully tooled saddles.

The museum, north of town at Exit 147 off I-25, is open daily 9 A.M.–5 P.M. Admission is $6 for adults; discounts for seniors, kids, and groups. For information, phone 719/528-4764.

Western Museum of Mining and Industry

A nonprofit and low-key outfit, this is one of Colorado Springs's true gems, one that avoids the touristy trappings of some of the other attractions. Tours begin with a short slide show (sponsored in part by the National Endowment for the Humanities) on the history of Western mining, and then you're taken through displays of various steam engines (which your tour guide will fire up), and even to a sluice box (where you'll learn how to pan for gold). In all, there are over 15,000 square feet of exhibits in several different buildings. An 8,000-volume library is open to museum members and students (by appointment only).

Admission, including the tour, is $6 for adults, $5 for seniors and students, and $3 for kids 5–12. Group rates (the museum is a natural for field trips!) are available. Hours are Mon.–Sat. 9 A.M.–4 P.M.

Take Exit 156A (Gleneagle Drive) from I-25 and follow the signs (east side of the highway). For more information, phone 719/488-0880.

John May Museum of Natural History and the Space Museum

A couple of the area's quirkiest museums, these two display the lifetime collections of artifacts owned by John May. The Museum of Natural History actually specializes in entomology, as you would have guessed from seeing the giant beetle at the turnoff. But even for nonbug fans, this is some interesting stuff—butterflies, moths, spiders, and beetles of every imaginable size, shape, color, and attitude, all well displayed and safely dead, thank you. Check out the 20-inch-long Karabidionaustrala monster from New Guinea (something like a giant praying mantis), the megasoma beetle from South America (just smaller than a Volkswagen), a Peruvian tarantula scarfing a hummingbird, and foot-long Venezuelan centipedes.

There's also a small gift store, where you can pick up an odd assortment of souvenirs—how 'bout a shiny gold black widow lapel pin?

The Space Museum, off in the woods 100 feet or so from the bug museum, is even more peculiar—but for entirely different reasons. First of all, it's in an old musky-smelling house trailer, with

© STEPHEN METZGER

Lasting eight seconds is easy if you're cast in bronze.

warped paneling, and then there are the displays—model airplanes and photos and maps, most of which look like they were picked up in dime stores and in gift shops at other museums. There's also an early-flight exhibit, and a display, with news clippings and photos, of the American space program.

Again, a quirky little place, where a sense of humor will get you a long way. Entrance fee to both museums is $4.50, $3.50 for seniors and $2.50 for kids 6–12. Open May–Sept. 9 A.M.–7 P.M. To get there, take Highway 115 south of town, past Fort Carson, and watch for the giant beetle on the west side of the road. The Golden Eagle Ranch RV Park is adjacent to the museum and administered by the same people (see Accommodations under Colorado Springs, above). For more information, phone 719/576-0450.

PIKES PEAK AREA

Of course, the main attraction here is Pikes Peak itself, the flagship of the Front Range. First spotted in 1806 by Zebulon Pike, the mountain had been known to the Utes for years as "The Long One." In the 1850s, the mountain was a welcome sight to westbound gold seekers, whose covered wagons often bore their motto, "Pikes Peak or bust." Pikes Peak was also the "purple mountain . . . above the fruited plains" to which Katherine Lee Bates was referring when she wrote *America the Beautiful.* Each summer in July, top race-car drivers from around the world compete in the Pikes Peak Hill Climb, or the "Race to the Sky." There's also an annual footrace to the top.

Pikes Peak Highway

In 1916, a road was cut to the top of Pikes Peak, and for the next 20 years was maintained with funds collected at the tollgate ($2 per car), providing a popular, if somewhat nerve-rattling, manner in which to test the guts, and brakes, of early motorcars. Between 1936 and 1948, the Forest Service took over the highway's operations and allowed free passage, although since it collected no funds to maintain the road, it quickly fell into a state of decline. The City of Colorado

Springs took over the highway in 1948 and has been managing it since.

Pikes Peak Highway is open daily April–Oct. (weather permitting). The nearly 20-mile (one-way) route, which rises about 7,000 feet, is paved the first third of the way, and is gravel-dirt the rest. Allow at least two hours round-trip. At the 13-mile point is the **Glen Cove Inn,** where you'll find a snack bar, souvenirs, and restrooms. The road quickly gets steep, zigzagging dramatically up the mountainside, past the treeline, then rolling out onto some positively lunar landscape. Watch for bighorn sheep, deer, and marmot, as well as figure eights made by skiers. The views along the way, of Denver, the San Juans, the plains, are stunning.

At the top is the **Summit House,** a second gift shop, and a doughnut shop and snack bar. If you plan to get out, bring a sweater: it may be warm down in Colorado Springs, but it'll be *cold* up top, most likely with a biting wind.

The toll is $10 per person or $35 per car, and all proceeds go to road maintenance. The tollgate is open 7 A.M.–7 P.M. Memorial Day through Labor Day and 9 A.M.–3 P.M. the rest of the year. Be sure to get a map and information brochure,

and pay attention to its driving tips. To get there, take U.S. 24 west from Manitou Springs to Cascade Road and watch for the signs. For more information and road conditions, phone 719/684-9383.

Hiking Trails

The in-shape and adventurous can hike to the summit of Pikes Peak, something Zebulon Pike wrote would never be possible. Many hikers take Barr Trail (named for Fred Barr, the trail's designer) and allow two days to make the 26-mile round-trip. You can spend the night at either of two camps about halfway up from the trailhead (see Hiking under Colorado Springs, above). For maps and more information, stop by the office of Pike National Forest, 601 S. Weber St., or phone 719/636-1602.

Pikes Peak Cog Railway

If you don't trust your rig, or your nerves, you can instead get to the top of Pikes Peak by rail. The seven-mile ride offers equally stunning views and takes just over three hours round-trip (the old Swiss-made trains chug s-l-o-w-l-y up the 26 percent grade). The train runs mid-April through

looking down on Pikes Peak Highway from the summit

mid-October, leaving about every 1.5 hours—varying with the season—departing from Manitou Springs. At the top is a snack bar and gift shop. Cost is about $25 for adults and $13 for kids 5–11; no charge for kids under five if they're held on laps.

To get to the depot, take Manitou Avenue to Ruxton, go left, and watch for the signs. For information, write Manitou and Pikes Peak Railway, P.O. Box 351, Manitou Springs, CO 80829, or phone 719/685-5401.

North Pole/Santa's Workshop

In a beautiful mountain setting at the foot of Pikes Peak, this amusement park offers a variety of rides, shows, and other diversions for kids from one to 92. You can pet Santa's reindeer and other animals, see toys being made for Christmas delivery, ride the antique carousel, take a train ride, and then stop for a milk shake or hot chocolate in the ice-cream parlor.

The North Pole is open mid-May through Christmas Eve, with varying hours. Closed the rest of the year. Admission is $11.50, with discounts for kids and seniors. Phone 719/684-9432.

Pikes Peak Information

For more information on Pikes Peak-area attractions, contact the **Pikes Peak Country Attractions Association,** 354 Manitou Ave., Manitou Springs, CO 80829, 800/525-2250, or the **Colorado Springs Convention and Visitors Bureau,** 104 S. Cascade, Colorado Springs, CO 80903, 719/635-7506. For online information, visit www.coloradosprings-travel.com.

MANITOU SPRINGS

About 10 miles west of Colorado Springs on U.S. 24, Manitou Springs was named for the two dozen mineral springs that have been attracting health seekers for centuries. Long before white settlers arrived in the mid-19th century, Native American hunting parties visited the springs when passing through the area. In the 1860s and '70s, miners heading into or out of the Cripple Creek area would stop here. Many of

them eventually settled, turning Manitou into a sort of frontier resort.

Manitou Springs today is part artists' community, part resort, and part tourist trap—a blend of galleries, gift shops, quiet city parks, tastefully remodeled Queen Anne homes, and Coney Island-type arcades. A National Historic District, Manitou Springs offers a wide range of history-oriented attractions, from turn-of-the-last-century stone castles and old stagecoach stops to "trading posts," wax museums, and reproductions of Anasazi cliff dwellings.

Garden of the Gods

One of the most popular attractions in the Colorado Springs area, Garden of the Gods is a geologic oddity of bizarre red Morrison sandstone rock formations, some angry, jagged, and jutting, others softly and sensuously eroded. American novelist and campaigner for social justice Helen Hunt Jackson described the gardens in the 1880s as:

colossal monstrosities looking like elephants, like gargoyles, like giants . . . all motionless and silent, with a strange look of having been stopped and held back in the very climax of some supernatural catastrophe.

Dedicated in 1909, this city park is not only a geologist's dream come true, but it's also a hiker's, horseback-rider's, and climber's paradise. And—here's the best part—this 1,350-acre registered National Natural Landmark is absolutely *free.* That's an oddity in itself in a region where it's routine to shell out 20 bucks so the family can view paraffin approximations of American historical figures waxing nostalgic under museum lights.

The lunarlike landscape of the Garden of the Gods began to take shape 300 million years ago, long before the Rockies pushed up to their modern (in geological terms) elevation and eminence. Some of the spires you see standing above the garden floor—the tallest of which is 300 feet—have withstood the eroding powers of wind and rain that long.

A series of loop roads will take you out into the gardens (past several picnic areas), and even if you don't get out and do much exploring, you ought to stop in at the relatively new **visitor center** (opened in May 1995). You'll find a variety of geology, history, and wildlife displays there, as well as a small theater where an excellent multimedia show ($1.50) explains the geology of the region. You can also sign up for guided nature walks. Rock climbers must register with rangers here. The Garden of the Gods Trading Post is the largest gift shop in the Pikes Peak area and sells a range of artwork, jewelry, and souvenirs, including work by highly regarded Native American artists such as R. C. Gorman.

Garden of the Gods is open year-round. Hours are 5 A.M.–11 P.M. May–Oct.; and 6 A.M.–9 P.M. Nov.–April. Admission is free. The visitor center is open June–Aug. 8 A.M.–8 P.M., and 9 A.M.–5 P.M. the rest of the year. Admission is $2. To get there, take U.S. 24 from Colorado Springs to Manitou Springs, turn north on Ridge Road, and follow the signs. You can also get there by taking Garden of the Gods Road off I-25 to 31st Street and following the signs. For more information on Garden of the Gods, write 1401 Recreation Way, Colorado Springs, CO 80905, or phone 719/578-6640. Call the Trading Post at 719/685-9045 or 800/874-4515.

Glen Eyrie

This sprawling estate and castle, listed on the National Register of Historic Places, was built in 1904 by Colorado Springs's founding father William Palmer for his wife, Queen. The property includes stables, lagoons, a schoolhouse, and a dairy, as well as the castle itself, decorated with furnishings from Europe and heated by 24 fireplaces, many of which were also brought from abroad—one was carved by Benedictine monks in the late Middle Ages.

Tours of Glen Eyrie, which begin at 11 A.M. and at 1 P.M., take approximately 60 minutes and cost $5, less for kids and seniors (no charge for ages 12 and younger). Reservations are highly recommended.

For information and reservations, phone 719/634-0808 or 800/944-4536. To get there, take Garden of the Gods Road west from I-25,

and turn left on 30th Street, or take 30th or 31st north from Colorado Avenue in Manitou. Glen Eyrie is just north of Garden of the Gods.

Miramont Castle Museum

If Garden of the Gods is Manitou Springs's geologic oddity, then Miramont Castle is its architectural one. Dating from just before the turn of the last century, this four-story, 14,000-square-foot structure, with its two-foot-thick stone walls, looks like it's part medieval castle, part Swiss chalet, and part San Francisco Victorian. In fact, the castle's original design drew on nine distinct architectural styles.

Commissioned in 1895 by Father Jean Baptiste Francolon, an ailing but wealthy French priest who came to Manitou with his mother for the mineral springs, the castle has 46 rooms varying from open and airy sitting rooms to small and dark bedrooms barely bigger than closets. After the priest died, the castle served as a sanatorium and later as an apartment building. It was put on the National Register of Historic Places in 1977.

Today, the castle is open to the public. Some of the rooms have been restored to approximate their original flavor, while others house various displays—a doll museum, railroad museum, and a miniature reproduction of turn-of-the-20th-century Colorado Springs, complete with an in-progress baseball game. The castle also has a restaurant and hosts weddings and other groups and parties.

Summer hours are daily 10 A.M.–5 P.M. (the restaurant is open 11 A.M.–3 P.M. by reservation only), with shortened hours the rest of the year. Admission fee to the castle is $4 for adults, $3.50 for seniors, and $1 for kids 6–11. For more information, or to book tours, phone 719/685-1011. You can also write Miramont Castle, 9 Capitol Hill Ave., Manitou Springs, CO 80829. To get there, take Manitou Avenue west to Ruxton, turn left, and then go right on Capitol Hill Road.

Cave of the Winds

A strange blend of nature at its most impressive and commercialism at its most shameless, Cave of the Winds is a mile-deep cavern, tours of which are so orchestrated and slick that you feel more like you're at Universal Studios than deep underground. Look beyond the fancy lights and talking rocks, though, as well as the corny group photo and the push to buy a print at tour's end ($5), and you'll find the cave quite fascinating. Discovered in 1880 by children who were playing nearby, the cave is named for the sound the wind makes as it whistles through the subterranean tunnels.

Of particular interest is the nature display, where area birds and minerals are identified, and kids can use blocks to make wolf, deer, raccoon, coyote, and other animal tracks in the sand. The gift and souvenir shop sells the standard key chains, mugs, T-shirts, and Native American jewelry; there's also a snack bar. A second tour, the Wild Winds Tour, is available to visitors who want to go beyond where most visitors get and to do some genuine spelunking (reservations, old clothes, flashlight, and another $35 required). There's also a special "lantern tour" available for an added cost.

Cost for the regular tour is $15 for adults, $8 for kids 6–15 (tours last 45 minutes). Hours are 9 A.M.–9 P.M., mid-May through Labor Day, and 9 A.M.–5 P.M. the rest of the year (last tour a half hour before closing). Take U.S. 24 west and watch for the signs. For more information, phone 719/685-5444.

Cliff Dwellings Museum

Not to be mistaken for the real McCoys—in New Mexico, Arizona, and southwestern Colorado—these cliff dwellings were built here in 1906, 600 years after the last Anasazi packed his spare loincloth into his Samsonite, checked out of his room, and climbed down off Mesa Verde. Actually a decent facsimile, the dwellings were made of rocks hauled from the Four Corners area with the best of intentions—to preserve the remains of a culture that was disappearing as fast as its people once did. Regular dances by Plains (?) Native Americans suggest a possible nomination for an Unclear-on-Concept Award.

In addition to the dwellings, there's a small museum, where you can get a sense of 13th-cen-

tury pueblo life, as well as of the dwellings' construction, by viewing dioramas and Anasazi and Mogollon pottery and other artifacts.

Open daily 9 A.M. and closing at 8 P.M. June–Aug.—closing earlier the rest of the year. Admission is $7 adults, $6 seniors, $5 kids. For information, phone 719/685-5242.

Ghost Town Museum

Though a bit on the gimmicky side, Ghost Town offers a wide array of authentic historical artifacts and knickknacks, arranged to simulate an American frontier town. There's a general store, with candy jars, hog tonic, hats, corsets, and washbowls, a barbershop, jail, post office, bank, and a stagecoach that ran between Denver and Cheyenne in 1868. You can also view Roosevelt's 1942 bullet-proof Lincoln limousine (and wonder what the hell it's doing here), as well as the proverbial two-headed calf. Exit, of course, through the "Trading Post" (read, gift shop).

Summer hours are weekdays 9 A.M.–6 P.M. and Sunday noon–6 P.M. Labor Day through Memorial Day, hours are 10 A.M.–5 P.M. and Sunday noon–5 P.M. Admission is $5 for adults, $2.50 for kids 6–16. To get there, turn south on 21st Street from U.S. 24 west. For more information, phone 719/634-0696.

Pikes Peak Auto Hill Climb Museum

This small museum displays race cars and motorcycles that have raced in the annual Fourth of July Pikes Peak Hill Climb since the 1920s. The brief tour, which takes you from the first cars (a 1920 Lexington, a 1936 Coniff Special) to very recent high-tech jobs (including several that were built and raced by Bobby Unser), winds up at a small sitting room where you can see video footage (ESPN) of recent races. A small gift shop sells hats, jackets, banners, and other race mementos. The museum is at 135 Manitou Ave. in Manitou Springs. Open daily 9 A.M.–5 P.M. Admission is $5 adults, $4 seniors. For more information, phone 719/685-4400.

Van Briggles Art Pottery

Billed as an art studio offering free instructive tours, Van Briggles has been in business since

1899, and the uniquely gorgeous pottery is one of the prides of Manitou. Paris-taught founder Artus Van Briggle was world-famous and he won numerous awards for his work, many of which are on display in the studio.

Maybe I'm naive to the ways of the business world, but I was expecting more from my visit than a sales pitch. Most of the five-minute "free tour" is spent watching a potter at work on a wheel while your tour guide explains the process of "throwing"—the whole thing really just a gimmick to get you into the "showroom" and the clutches of too many eager salespeople. Too bad, because the work is beautiful, and it'd be nice to be able to enjoy it without feeling pressured.

The studio, at the corner of Colorado Avenue and 21st Street, is open Mon.–Sat. 8:30 A.M.–5 P.M., with the last tour leaving at 4:30. For more information, phone 719/633-7729.

Flying W Ranch

The Flying W is a working cattle ranch where you can get an authentic chuck-wagon dinner before settlin' in for a Western stage show featuring The Flying W Wranglers, a Western band that plays swing, gospel, and country favorites and dishes a healthy portion of cornpone humor. The dinner, which includes baked beans, beef, homemade biscuits, and apple sauce (delicious!), and show are offered rain or shine (indoors if it's wet, outdoors otherwise) at long picnic-style tables, where you can get a chance to meet and talk with some of the 1,400 guests the Flying W serves nightly. While you wait for the dinner and show, you can wander around the grounds, which include a reconstruction of 19th-century old-West town, with a blacksmith shop (watch the smith at work between 6 P.M. and 7 P.M. daily), jail, and other outbuildings/gift shops, selling everything from old-West cookbooks to Western wear to Native American jewelry (our favorite item was the book of John Wayne paper dolls at the bookstore). Reservations are required for dinner, seatings for which are nightly May–September. Call for rest-of-the-year hours of operation. Cost for dinner and show is $14–19 for adults, $9 for kids. Phone 719/598-4000 or 800/232-

3599. To get there from I-25, take Garden of the Gods Road west to 30th Street, turn right, and then go left on Flying W Ranch Road. From Manitou, take 30th Street north past Garden of the Gods to Flying W Ranch Road.

Manitou Springs–Area Lodging

The adobe **El Colorado Lodge,** 719/685-5485 or 800/442-4884, is a unique and rustically handsome motel just east of Manitou Springs. Also in Manitou are the **Super 8–Garden of the Gods,** 229 Manitou Ave., 719/685-5898; **Garden of the Gods Motel,** 2922 W. Colorado Ave., 719/636-5271; and the **Apache Court Motel,** 3401 W. Pikes Ave., 719/471-9440. All are in the $50–100 range for doubles.

Two Sisters Inn Bed and Breakfast, 10 Otoe Pl., 719/685-9684 or 800/274-7466, was built in 1919 and is a half block from the center of town. Stay in one of the five bedrooms in the main house or in the separate cottage ($70–115).

Manitou Springs–Area Dining

Manitou Springs is home to several excellent restaurants, and a good number of small cafés, many with sidewalk seating. **The Stagecoach Steak and Ale House,** 702 Manitou Ave., 719/685-9400, occupies an 1880s-era stagecoach stop that was also a summer home for novelist Helen Hunt Jackson. The Stagecoach specializes in salads, soups, and quiches, and also serves steak, chicken, and seafood entrées running $13–18. The **Briarhurst Manor,** 404 Manitou, 719/685-1864, is a high-end dinner restaurant ($13–40 for entrées) housed in a stone mansion built in 1878 and serving continental cuisine cooked with organically home-grown herbs, fruits, and vegetables, and home-smoked meats and fish. Open daily till midnight. The **Keg Lounge,** 730 Manitou, 719/685-9531, offers excellent beef, chicken, seafood, and rib entrées for $10–20. Open for lunch and dinner daily.

If you're out wandering around in Manitou Springs and feel like snacking but aren't in the mood for the cotton candy, fudge, and caramel corn the arcades are pushing, check out **Market La Rue Too** just off the main drag at 102

Canyon. This unpretentious little grocery store sells organically grown produce, natural sodas, and other healthful treats.

Manitou Springs Information

Contact the **Pikes Peak Country Attractions Association,** 354 Manitou Ave., Manitou Springs, CO 80829, 800/525-2250, or the **Colorado Springs Convention and Visitors Bureau,** 104 S. Cascade, Colorado Springs, CO 80903, 719/635-7506. For online information, visit www.coloradosprings-travel.com.

West of Colorado Springs

U.S. 24 west from Colorado Springs rises quickly into beautiful mountain country, skirts the northeast flank of Pikes Peak, and passes through the southern section of Pike National Forest. About midway between Colorado Springs and Woodland Park, you'll pass turnoffs to Cascade, Chipeta Park, and Green Mountain Falls—small resort communities nestled at the base of Pikes Peak.

Cascade was founded in 1886 by transplanted Kansans, who built a number of small cottages along Fountain Creek. Among those who spent summers here was Indiana lawyer John Milton Hay, assistant secretary to President Lincoln. Hay wrote much of his 10-volume *Abraham Lincoln: A Life History* in Cascade, as well as his *Pike County Ballads.* Chipeta Park was named after Ute Chief Ouray's wife, Chipeta.

In **Green Mountain Falls,** you'll find a nice shady picnic area just off the highway, as well as a public swimming pool and a small lake with a tiny island and gazebo. The **Falls Motel,** 719/684-9745, is right on the lake, and many of the rooms have kitchens ($50–100). **The Pantry,** 6980 Lake St., 719/684-9018, gets rave reviews from locals, who claim it's one of the best restaurants on the Front Range. Folks from Colorado Springs drive up here for dinner, enjoying tables right by the lake. Also open daily for breakfast and dinner.

In Woodland Park, you can either turn north onto Highway 67, which will take you up through the national forest to the little fishing/resort village of Deckers, or you can stay on U.S. 24, which continues west over Ute and Wilkerson Passes, to Buena Vista and Leadville. Seven miles past Woodland Park is the turnoff to Cripple Creek, an important Western historical site and one of Colorado's most popular tourist attractions.

Highway 67 south to Cripple Creek is one of the highlights of exploring this part of the state. Winding up through Pike National Forest, along aspen- and spruce-sided mountains, and through a rickety, log-lined one-way tunnel, the 20-mile stretch offers more great views per mile than many of even the most famously scenic of Colorado highways. It's also one of the state's least nerve-wracking high-mountain passes, the road unfolding gently across above-timberline alpine meadows—you half expect to hear distant singing, and then to see the Von Trapp family appearing blonde and knickered over a windswept knoll.

WOODLAND PARK

Woodland Park (pop. 4,800; elev. 8,500 feet) is an attractive, vital, and rapidly growing mountain community just 20 miles west of Colorado Springs. With its crisp mountain air and omnipresent view of Pikes Peak, Woodland Park attracts many Colorado Springs workers who find the under-half-an-hour commute a fair price to pay for the slower and more healthful mountain lifestyle. The town was founded in the early 1880s, and until the early 20th century was an important lumber supply center, serving both Cripple Creek and Colorado Springs.

Accommodations

You can get good inexpensive ($50–100) rooms at **The Lofthouse,** 719/687-9187, at 222 E. Henrietta on the hillside above the downtown area. The rooms, some of which have kitchenettes, are smoky, well stocked with murder mysteries, and feel like the kind of places where Officers Gannon and Friday might stay while investigating some insidious crime. A reader sent me a brochure for the **Woodland Inn Bed and Breakfast**, 159 Trull Rd., 719/687-8209 or 800/226-9565, which she highly recommends. Sitting on 12 woodsy acres, the inn offers four rooms ($100–150).

Food

Locals rave about the **Ute Inn**, 719/687-1465, across from Bergstrom Park at 204 W. U.S. Hwy. 24. It's the area's oldest food and alcohol establishment and also occupies a historical building, providing a healthy dose of Rocky Mountain local color at its friendliest.

Information

For more information on Woodland Park and the surrounding area, stop by the **chamber of commerce** at the junction of U.S. 24 and Highway 67 north. You can also write P.O. Box 9022, Woodland Park, CO 80866, or phone 719/687-9885 or 800/551-7886. You can also get information from the chamber's website at www.woodlandparkchamber.com.

CRIPPLE CREEK

To get a proper perspective on Cripple Creek's importance to the state, as well as to the history of the West, consider: between 1891 and 1916, Cripple Creek produced $340 million worth of gold. By 1952, 625 tons, or 20 million ounces, of the stuff had been taken from Cripple Creek mines for a total value of over $413 million (figured at the long-running midcentury rate of $20.67 an ounce). Cripple Creek produced twice as much gold as California's famed Mother Lode, and nearly $100 million more than Nevada's Comstock produced in gold and silver combined. Alaska's and the Yukon's gold camps—Klondike, Fairbanks, Nome—pale in comparison to Cripple Creek's. In fact, no single geological deposit on earth has produced as much gold as Cripple Creek.

According to Colorado Springs historian Marshall Sprague, Cripple Creek's population increased from 15 to 50,000 between 1891 and 1900, its monthly payroll from $50 to $1 million. During the same period, the town's annual production went from "$2,000 worth of calves to $20 million worth of gold bricks." Among those who cashed in on Cripple Creek's boom was Winfield Scott Stratton, who left his $3-a-day carpentry job in Colorado Springs, staked a claim in Cripple, and later sold his mine for $10 million. According to the WPA guide to Colorado, just after the turn of the century, Cripple Creek had 41 assay offices, 91 lawyers, 88 doctors, 70 saloons, and 14 newspapers.

Today, Cripple Creek is a major tourist destination, many of the old buildings having been converted to boutiques, restaurants, and gift and specialty shops. Walking Cripple Creek's main drag, and touring mines where huge fortunes were made, you can easily imagine how it must have been a century ago, when the camp was roaring with gambling saloons, bars, and brothels, and the very existence of every citizen and visitor—from wealthy mine owner to exploited mine worker, from postal clerk to pickpocket—was inextricably linked to the goldfields. In fact, seeing Cripple Creek—a small town so germane to the development of the state—crystalizes one's understanding and appreciation of Colorado.

In part because here you can also see close up the ugly side of it all.

In addition to bringing wealth and prosperity to Colorado, mining—and its myopic policymakers—also caused great environmental harm. One need not look awfully hard to see the scars and ugly mine dumps that remain on the bare mountainsides surrounding the little town. Look a little more closely, or talk to people who live in the area, and you'll come to know mining's more subtle and perhaps longer-ranging consequences: the contamination of soils and waters from gold mining processes. In short, there's a much bigger lesson in a visit to Cripple Creek. As Sprague wrote in 1952:

Cripple's story . . . is a capsule history of the United States from country bumpkin to world power.

He might add today that its subsequent fall—marked by depression, environmental destruction, desperate appeal to tourism through commercial exploitation, and, finally, in a last-ditch effort to prop itself back up, legalized gambling—resembles the recent sad stumble this country's taken.

Today during the summer, Cripple Creek's sidewalks are packed with visitors clinging to shopping bags, and its side streets are lined with motor homes with out-of-state plates and every imaginable brand of sport utility vehicle piled high with ice chests, tents, lawn chairs, and tricycles—while the casinos bulge with folks pulling slot-machine handles, marking keno cards, and watching dealers draw to 21.

History

During the 1860s and early '70s, the valley in which Cripple Creek lies was known as Poverty Gulch, through which meandered a small stream. Actually the crater of a long-extinct volcano, the valley was blessed with sides steep enough to contain cattle, and the first settlers in the area were ranchers, one of whom was Levi Welty, who, according to a perhaps apocryphal story, gave the town its name.

One day Welty and his three sons were building a cabin in the valley when they lost their grip on a heavy log, which rolled into one of the boys. In the commotion, Levi Welty's shotgun discharged, injuring his hand and frightening a pet calf grazing nearby. The calf tried to jump the stream, but stumbled and broke its leg. His son, his hand, and his calf all injured, Levi later supposedly lamented, "Well boys, this sure is some cripple creek!"

One of the valley's more colorful characters was Bob ("Crazy Bob") Womack, a cowboy who had come to Colorado from Kentucky and taken over the Welty ranch. Apparently rarely sober—which is probably why his claims of gold in the

Cripple Creek produced twice as much gold as California's famed Mother Lode, and nearly $100 million more than Nevada's Comstock produced in gold and silver combined. Alaska's and the Yukon's gold camps pale in comparison to Cripple Creek's. In fact, no single geological deposit on earth has produced as much gold as Cripple Creek.

area were not taken seriously—Womack in 1886 did finally manage to haul some gold out of a Poverty Gulch mine, the El Paso. Womack sent specimens to an assayer's office in old Colorado City, where it was found to be of high quality. On a Christmas morning years later, after watching tiny Poverty Gulch transform into the bustling Cripple Creek Mining District, Bobby Womack would stand on a street corner in Cripple Creek, drunk and holding the $500 for which he had sold his share of the mine the night before. There, in the cold of that wintry morning, Womack handed out a one-dollar bill to each child who passed by, until a long line formed and Womack realized he was giving money to adults. At that point, an embittered Womack slugged the next person in line, who slugged back, knocking Womack to the ground. Womack was taken home by the deputy sheriff and the next day left Cripple Creek, never to return. The El Paso would go on to produce gold worth over $5 million.

By 1896, 10,000 people were living in Cripple Creek, and the little town's reputation for wild times and wilder women, particularly those employed at the "pleasure palaces," was well known throughout the country. On a Saturday afternoon in late April of that year, a couple fighting in their apartment above the Central Dance Hall knocked over a lighted gasoline stove, igniting a fire in the building that quickly spread up and across the street. The fire, which lasted only three hours but which was abetted by stiff breezes, destroyed 40 homes, the Cripple Creek Mining Exchange, the First National Bank, the post office, and several "one-girl cribs," including "The Library" and "Old Faithful." By the time it was over, 1,500 people were homeless.

A determined and not easily daunted lot, Cripple Creek residents quickly set about rebuilding their town. The Cripple Creek *Times* moved into a new office and put out a paper the very next day; carpenters began construction on new buildings; and many of the dance halls, some partly burned, were once again raucous and rolling.

For three days.

On Wednesday another fire broke out. This one, buffeted by even stronger winds, destroyed 10 saloons and numerous other homes, stores, and businesses. Many people were seriously injured, including six firemen hurt when a boiler exploded, and 5,000 people were left without homes. Still, the cloud of fires had its silver lining: the phoenix that rose from the ashes was largely brick and built to last. Cripple Creek was less a mining camp now, bastion of rascals and con artists, and much more a legitimate town, an alliance of businesspeople and civic leaders.

Which isn't to say Cripple Creek became an instant model of righteousness. Indeed, though the town did take more pride in itself, the lowlife faction was decidedly still extant. Just before the turn of the century, the murder rate rose from one to eight a month.

In the early 1900s, labor-management relations in Cripple Creek began to grow strained. Workers' attempts to unionize were violently resisted. According to some reports, as many as 500 laborers simply "disappeared" from Cripple Creek's streets.

By 1915, the price of gold had fallen, and Cripple Creek's mines were mostly played out. In 1920, fewer than 10 percent of the district's mines were in operation. Still, ore continued to be taken from the hillsides, though by midcentury most of the remaining mines were owned by large conglomerates. The days of individual ownership—the days of Womack, Stratton, and the rest—were long gone. In the 1970s and 1980s, Cripple Creek began to appeal to tourism. Mine tours were offered, artisans opened shop in some of the old buildings, and boutiques and gift shops appeared in others. Town boosters hoped the tourist dollar would facilitate a second boom for the little mountain town.

Then, in the late summer of 1990, holding what it hoped was one last wild card up its sleeve, Cripple Creek looked its tourists in the eye and upped the ante. Cripple Creek, along with Central City and Black Hawk, legalized gambling. Though limited in scope, especially compared to the virtually-anything-goes wagering you'll find in Nevada, gambling is now a major part of Cripple Creek's personality, with many of the old buildings having been converted to casinos. In addition, the community has built a new minimall, and larger grocery stores have sprung up to accommodate the increase in visitors.

Cripple Creek District Museum

With a large collection of mining artifacts, including equipment and tools, ore samples, mine models, and a reconstructed assay office, this small museum offers an opportunity to see what made Cripple Creek tick between 1890 and the early 20th century. Also on display are domestic items and Victorian-era clothing. The museum is open daily 10 A.M.–5 P.M. June–Sept., and weekends noon–4 P.M. the rest of the year. Admission is $2.50 for adults and $.50 for kids. Follow the signs to the top of Bennett Avenue (east end). For more information, phone 719/689-2634.

Historical Tours

The Cripple Creek Chamber of Commerce designed a self-guided historical tour of the Cripple Creek Mining District, including the town of Victor (see that section, below). The 18-mile (round-trip) auto tour takes about 45 minutes. For a map and guide, stop by the office at 107 E. Eaton. **Ghost Town Tours** offers guided trips through the area. Legitimate historians (not college kids doing summer work), the guides provide in-depth explanations of the mining district and the various mines. The 1.5-hour tours, beginning at the Mollie Kathleen Mine (see below), are offered three or four times a day, depending on demand, usually at 11 A.M., 1 P.M., 3 P.M., and 5 P.M.; $11 for adults. When you're finished, stick around for the 30-minute "Story of Cripple Creek" video. For more information, phone 719/689-2466.

Mollie Kathleen Mine Tour

In continuous operation between 1892 and 1961, "the Mollie" now offers miner-led tours

1,000 feet into its recesses. View the equipment miners used to extract the gold and convey it to the surface; listen to stories and explanations of how the shafts were dynamited. Take a look at what real gold looks like before it finds it way to earrings and necklaces. Learn what to look for should you find yourself getting "the fever."

Tours of the Mollie Kathleen begin every 20 minutes 9 A.M.–5 P.M., May–October. Admission is $11 for adults, $5 for kids. Take Bennett Drive east, turn north on Highway 67, and follow the signs. For more information, phone 719/689-2466.

Cripple Creek and Victor Narrow Gauge Railroad

This four-mile run from Cripple Creek to Anaconda provides an authentic way to get a sense of the mining district's past (at one time 56 ore-laden trains left Cripple Creek daily). The coal-burning steam engine hauls you out past several abandoned mines (and the attendant dumps and junk piles), and offers views of many historical sites, including Bobby Womack's "Poverty Gulch." Trains run daily 10 A.M.–5 P.M. Memorial Day through mid-October, departing from the Cripple District Museum; the trip takes 45 minutes. Cost is $8.75 for adults, $7 for seniors, and $4.75 for kids. For more information, phone 719/689-2640.

Imperial Hotel Melodrama

Established in 1948, this old-time theater group is one of the most famous in the country, having been written up in *Time, The New York Times,* and many other publications. It is also the oldest in continuous operation. Season is mid-June through Labor Day. Call for show times and ticket prices. It's in the Imperial Hotel and Casino, 123 N. 3rd St.; for reservations or more information, phone 719/689-7777 or 800/235-2922.

Shopping

Downtown Cripple Creek consists of several blocks of turn-of-the-20th-century (and earlier) buildings, and though most have been converted to casinos and restaurants, others house boutiques, gift shops, and souvenir shacks. Which means, of course, there's no shortage of places to pick up T-shirts, mugs, hats, and key chains. For higher quality gifts and artwork, check out

© STEPHEN METZGER

shops and hotels in downtown Cripple Creek

Jahn's Jewelry, 253 E. Bennett, 719/689-2949. Also fun is **Rocky Mountain Canary General Store,** 246 E. Bennett, 719/689-2496.

Scenic Drives

If you're in Cripple Creek, you've taken at least one scenic drive: there's no way to get here without passing through some of the state's most beautiful country. If you've come in from the north and are looking for an alternative route out, you have several (well-maintained gravel) options. **Phantom Canyon Road** runs south out of Cripple Creek through Victor and down toward Cañon City. **Gold Camp Road** follows the old rail line between Cripple Creek and Colorado Springs. Both of these offer gorgeous views and exceedingly light traffic.

Accommodations

For a real taste of historic Cripple Creek, try the **Imperial Hotel,** 123 N. 3rd St., 719/689-7777. Built in 1896, it's the only one of Cripple Creek's original hotels still standing ($100–150). The Imperial also hosts melodrama theater during the summer (see above). A new **Holiday Inn Express,** 601 Galina, 719/689-2600, has been built on the hill above town ($100–150). You can also get lodging at **Cripple Creek Motel,** 201 Bison, 719/689-2491 ($50–100); **Gold Rush Hotel and Casino,** 209 E. Bennett, 719/689-2646 or 800/235-8239 ($50–100); **Midnight Rose Hotel and Casino,** 256 E. Bennett, 719/689-2865, which also has a kids' arcade ($150–250); and **Palace Hotel and Casino,** 2nd and Bennett, 719/689-2992 ($50–100).

For bed-and-breakfast accommodations, try the two-bedroom, 1890s-era **Iron Gate Inn,** 204 N. 2nd St., 719/229-6554 or 719/689-0302 ($100–150). Another bed-and-breakfast that comes highly recommended is the **Cherub House,** 415 Main St., 719/689-0526 ($100–150).

Two miles northeast of town, **Cripple Creek Gold Campground,** 12654 Hwy. 67, 719/689-2342, offers very nice secluded campsites, for both tents and RVs. A couple of hundred yards down the road at the junction of Highway 67 and County Road 81 is a **KOA** campground, 719/689-3376, with 60 RV sites and 20 tent sites.

Food

You'll find on-site restaurants at most of the hotel/casinos, including the **Gold Rush,** 209 E. Bennett, 719/689-2646; **Bronco Billie's,** 233 E. Bennett, 719/689-2142 (which also has a sports bar); and the **Midnight Rose,** 256 E. Bennett, 719/689-2865. The **Imperial Hotel and Casino,** 123 N. 3rd, 719/689-7777, has a long-standing tradition of excellent dinners, with specialties including beef, seafood, and chicken ($8–18). **Goldie's,** upstairs in Johnny Nolon's Saloon, serves sandwiches, steak, and salads (prime-rib special, $4.99), and it also has a selection of locally brewed beers and ales on tap.

Note: many of the casinos have excellent food and even better prices. Remember, however, a casino's prime directive: to get folks in the door. Your $1.99 burger can quickly turn into 10 or 20 bucks if you stop at the slot machines or the blackjack tables. I stopped in at Johnny Nolon's recently for a salad and a beer that ended up costing me about $25 (shouldn't have doubled down on that pair of fives . . .).

Services

The offices of the **Cripple Creek Police Department** are in the city hall building on East Bennett, 719/689-2655. Phone the **Teller County Sheriff** at 719/689-2644. The **post office** is at the corner of 2nd Street and Masonic, 719/689-2423.

Information

The **Cripple Creek Chamber of Commerce** provides extensive visitors packages, with complete information on attractions, lodging, dining, etc. Write P.O. Box 650, Cripple Creek, CO 80813, or phone 719/689-2169 or 800/526-8777. In town, stop by its offices at 337 E. Bennett. Visit the website at www.cripple-creek.co.us.

Cripple Creek's **Franklin-Ferguson Memorial Library** is on the northwest side of town at the corner of B Street and Galena, 719/689-2800.

VICTOR

The second-largest city in the Cripple Creek Mining District, Victor was once home to 18,000 people. Lowell Thomas spent a good part of his youth here, jump-starting his journalism career by delivering newspapers in the town's red-light district. Jack Dempsey once trained and fought in the city hall building. Today fewer than 300 people live in Victor.

History

Though through the years Victor and Cripple Creek have been rival cities, Victor was largely to thank not only for helping put out Cripple's 1896 fires but also for sending men and supplies and for helping shelter the 6,000-plus residents the fires left homeless. Victor's streets are said to be literally "paved with gold": in the district's early days only the highest-grade ore was trucked out, the low grade used for road surfacing.

In 1893, after mine owners attempted to reduce the district's $3-a-day wage, 800 Cripple Creek and Victor members of the Western Federation of Miners went on strike. Arbitration, and the National Guard, kept things from getting out of hand, and the workers' wages remained unchanged. In 1903, some of the mines began shipping ore to a nonunion mine in Colorado City, and Cripple Creek and Victor members of the WFM struck in sympathy. Tension escalated, with many miners refusing to work while others broke the strike and kept working. In September, the militia was called in, and by December the entire Cripple Creek Mining District was under martial law.

In early 1904, there was both a "mysterious" mine explosion and a mine "accident" involving a broken cable hoist. Many men were killed, management claiming the mines had been sabotaged and workers claiming management was attempting to discredit the union. Two more men were killed when rioting broke out in the streets of Victor. Eventually, troops were again called in, and union members unconvinced it would be in their best interest to leave of their own accord were escorted down off the mountain. The Cripple Creek Mining District's chapter of the WFM was effectively dismantled.

Victor today is a crumbling remnant of its once-booming self. Though a couple of hundred of the old red-brick buildings still stand, they lean tiredly and wistfully into the hillside. Still, Victor has its own special draw, in part its refreshing lack of tacky souvenir shops. Walking the steep streets of Victor one can, perhaps more easily than in Cripple Creek, imagine ghosts of Victorian-era miners lurking in doorways and dissolving before the future's great wash.

Lowell Thomas Museum

This is at once both a monument to Victor's history and to the early life of Lowell Thomas, who moved here with his family just after the turn of the 20th century. Thomas delivered the *The Denver Post* and the *Victor Daily Record* in the area, worked in the mines in 1911, and for a short time was editor of the *Victor Daily News*. He left Victor in 1912.

In addition to old miners' gear, a fire truck, slot machine, mail-order catalogs, quilts, dolls, clocks, typewriters, and historical photos, the museum displays Lowell Thomas memorabilia, including various editions of the many books he wrote. Some of the rooms have been reconstructed to approximate the Thomas family's home.

The Lowell Thomas Museum in Victor offers illuminating glimpses into frontier Colorado.

At press time, the museum was closed for remodeling but was to open again in the summer of 2002. For hours and more information, phone the Cripple Creek Chamber of Commerce at 719/689-2169.

UTE PASS WEST TO FAIRPLAY

Ute Pass (elev. 9,165 feet) has long been an important gateway between the central Rockies and the eastern foothills. Until 1859, when whites came looking for gold, the pass was a stronghold of the Utes, who took advantage of its narrowness and steep granite walls to keep the Plains tribes at bay. Even into the early 20th century, Utes maintained small fortresses in the area. Today, U.S. 24 climbs out of Divide, over the pass, winds through a broad alpine valley, through the tiny towns of Florissant and Lake George, and then climbs again, over Wilkerson Pass (elev. 9,507 feet), before dropping into the South Park basin. There, the highway crosses Highway 9, which shoots north through the basin to Fairplay (18 miles) or south to meet U.S. 50 between Cañon City and Royal Gorge (50 miles).

Florissant Fossil Beds National Monument

Just three miles south of Florissant lies this natural paradise for the budding paleontologist. Between 26 and 38 million years ago, the area was lush waterland, with palm trees, towering redwoods, and tall birches and willows lining the shores of Lake Florissant. There were also thousands of species of insects. Toward the end of that period, volcanoes began spewing ash and lava into the air, which settled onto the thriving ecosystem, preserving it and providing for visitors today one of the world's most extensive fossil records.

Visiting Florissant Fossil Beds is a good way to get an overview of what life in Colorado was like during the Oligocene period. The visitor center has excellent fossil displays and books, and it also offers guided walks out into the fossils. In addition, you can take a self-guided tour on a series of hiking trails, ranging from one-half to four miles long, where you can view petrified redwood trees (some estimated to have been

350 feet tall) and other 35-million-year-old specimens.

It's open Memorial Day through Labor Day, daily 8 A.M.–7 P.M.; the rest of the year, daily 8 A.M.–4:30 P.M. Admission is $2 per person or $4 per family. For more information, write P.O. Box 185, Florissant, CO 80816, or phone 719/748-3253.

Lake George

This small town is little more than a roadside market and a couple of RV campgrounds: **Stage Stop Campground,** 719/748-3393, and **Lake George Cabins and RV Park,** 719/748-3822. Just past Lake George is the turnoff to Pike National Forest's **Round Mountain Campground,** where you'll find a couple of dozen sites nicely set back in the aspens and ponderosas (pump water and pit toilets only).

Forest Service Information

You'll find a district office for Pike National Forest at Wilkerson Pass. Stop in for information on camping and other activities in the area, as well as for maps.

FAIRPLAY

Though not as well known as Cripple Creek or Leadville, Fairplay, too, was once a thriving mining town. Named by prospectors who'd been run out of Tarryall, another gold camp, about 20 miles east, Fairplay (pop. 500; elev. 10,000 feet) is the seat of Park County and the largest community in South Park. From Fairplay, you can continue north on Highway 9 to Summit County (about 35 miles to Frisco), turn south on U.S. 285 to Buena Vista (35 miles), or head back to Denver on U.S. 285 (85 miles). All routes guarantee breathtaking scenery—high mountain passes and lush forests.

South Park City Museum

Comprising 30 different buildings, this museum is a model of a Victorian-era town, with artifacts from throughout the state. Included are a general store, assay office, drugstore, saloon, and brewery, all furnished with authentic period artifacts. Open daily 9 A.M.–5 P.M. mid-May through mid-October. Admission is $5. For more information, phone 719/836-2387.

Recreation

The **Fairplay Nordic Center,** 719/836-2658, offers 20 km of groomed cross-country-ski trails with views of the South Park area. Instruction and rentals available. To get there take North 4th Street to Bogue and turn left. The center is about two miles outside of town. Write P.O. Box 701, Fairplay, CO 80440.

Ten miles south of Fairplay is the **Middle Fork of the South Platte River,** a designated Gold Medal trout stream known for its 20-inch (and larger) fish.

Accommodations

Two historic hotels in the Fairplay area offer accommodations and dining in genuine Victorian-era settings. The **Fairplay Hotel,** 500 Main St., 719/836-2565, offers 22 rooms and suites with private baths and also has a dining room and saloon (right at $50). The **Hand Hotel Bed and Breakfast,** 531 Front St., 719/836-3595, has 11 bed-and-breakfast rooms—each decorated in a different historical or local theme ($50–70).

Information

For more information on activities in the Fairplay area, as well as on lodging and dining, contact the **Park County Tourism Office,** P.O. Box 220, Fairplay, CO 80440, 719/836-4279.

SOUTH-CENTRAL

Southwestern Colorado

Most folks who know Colorado have soft spots in their hearts for the southwestern corner of the state. They know this area offers as much scenic beauty, history, culture, and recreation as any similar-sized area in the country—perhaps more. From the towering peaks of the San Juan Mountains to the deep gorges of Black Canyon of the Gunnison, from the sharp Continental Divide to the gently falling western slope, from the high lakes of Grand Mesa to the western reaches of the San Luis Valley, and from the cliff dwellings at Mesa Verde National Park to the trendy boutiques in Aspen, southwestern Colorado offers enough to see and do to keep you here for weeks on end, or for a lifetime, to which many transplanted locals will testify.

The first thing that'll most likely strike you is the pure scenic wonder of the area. Drive in from the south, over Wolf Creek Pass, or down out of Carbondale, through the Crystal River Valley. Head north from Durango over the "Million Dollar Highway" to Silverton and Ouray, or explore the Maroon Lakes area just outside Aspen. Out here, even cynics shake their heads and mutter things about "God's Country."

The history, rich with railroads and mining, is fascinating as well. Drive up to Leadville and take a tour of the famous Matchless Mine. Ride an 1880s coal-powered narrow-gauge train from Durango to Silverton. Stay in a historic hotel in Telluride or Aspen, or toss back a shot and a beer at a 19th-century bar in Crested Butte.

And then check out the culture: 1,000-year-old Anasazi ruins, and museums and heritage centers in the Four Corners area; film, jazz, rock, and bluegrass festivals in Telluride; film, classical music, and wine and food festivals in Aspen. Plus scores of

Winter casts a stark silence over meadows and mountains just outside the town of Ridgeway.

STEPHEN METZGER

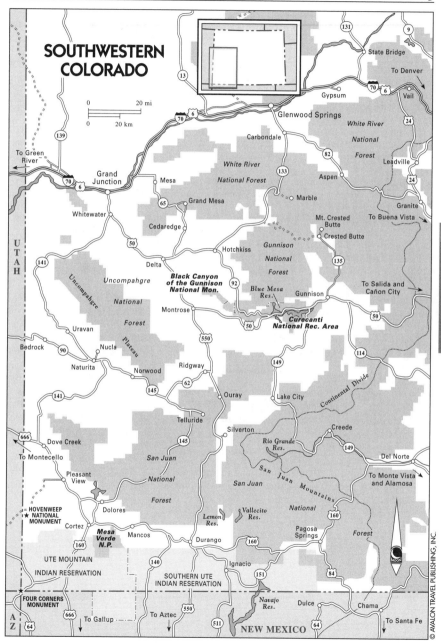

SOUTHWESTERN
COLORADO

0   20 mi
0   20 km

To Green
River

To Denver

State Bridge

Gypsum

Glenwood Springs

White River

National

Forest

Leadville

Carbondale

White River

National Forest

Aspen

Marble

Granite

To Buena Vista

Grand
Junction

Mesa

Grand Mesa

Whitewater

Cedaredge

Mt. Crested
Butte

Crested Butte

U
T
A
H

Uncompahgre

Uncompahgre

National

Forest

Delta

Hotchkiss

Black Canyon
of the Gunnison
National Mon.

Gunnison

National

Forest

Blue Mesa
Res.

Gunnison

To Salida and
Cañon City

Montrose

Curecanti
National Rec. Area

Uravan

Plateau

Bedrock

Nucla

Naturita

Norwood

Ridgway

Ouray

Lake City

Continental Divide

Telluride

Silverton

Creede

Rio Grande
Res.

Del Norte

Dove Creek

To Montecello

San Juan

National

San Juan

San Juan Mountains

National

To Monte Vista
and Alamosa

Pleasant
View

Forest

Vallecito
Res.

Forest

HOVENWEEP
NATIONAL
MONUMENT

Dolores

Lemon
Res.

Pagosa
Springs

Cortez

Mesa
Verde
N.P.

Mancos

Durango

UTE MOUNTAIN

INDIAN RESERVATION

Ignacio

FOUR CORNERS
MONUMENT

SOUTHERN UTE
INDIAN RESERVATION

A
Z

To Gallup

To Aztec

Navajo
Res.

Dulce

Chama

To Santa Fe

NEW MEXICO

SOUTHWESTERN

© AVALON TRAVEL PUBLISHING, INC.

SOUTHWESTERN COLORADO HIGHLIGHTS

Grand Junction: Colorado National Monument, museums, mountain biking, camping, fishing, and other recreation

Aspen: downhill skiing on Buttermilk Mountain, Snowmass, Aspen Mountain and Aspen Highlands, hut-to-hut Nordic skiing on the 10th Mountain Trail Association Hut System, dogsledding, fishing along the Roaring Fork River, hiking in the White River National Forest, festivals such as Winteröl, and the Aspen-Snowmass Food and Wine Classic

Leadville: mining tours on the Leadville, Colorado, and Southern Railroad, hiking up Mt. Elbert (state's highest peak), museums, camping, fishing, skiing, Oro City Festival

Salida/Buena Vista: rafting on the Arkansas River, museums, camping, hot springs, Aspen-Salida Music Festival

Crested Butte/Gunnison: alpine skiing at Mt. Crested Butte, fishing in the Taylor, East, and Gunnison Rivers, 4WD tours, biking, hiking, camping, American Indian Cultural Festival, Fat Tire Week, Festival of the Arts

Ouray/Silverton/Durango: Durango-Silverton Narrow Gauge Railroad, hiking, mountain biking in the San Juan National Forest, fishing and rafting on the Animas River, Purgatory Ski Area, Trimble Hot Springs, Durango Cowboy Gathering, Mesa Verde National Park

Telluride: skiing, mountain biking, 4WD tours, film and music festivals

local historical society museums scattered about the area, many with excellent displays of Native American, mining, and railroad artifacts.

And *then* there's recreation: world-class snow skiing at Telluride, Aspen, and Crested Butte, and excellent skiing at out-of-the-way areas such as Wolf Creek Pass and Purgatory; jeep touring over high mountain passes and through ghosts of 19th-century mining towns; fly-fishing for wily native rainbow trout or trolling for landlocked salmon; white-water rafting in Class V rapids; and if that's not enough, there's hiking, snowshoeing, hot-air ballooning, camping, golfing, horseback riding.

Out here, even cynics shake their heads and mutter things about "God's Country."

And the nice thing is that much of southwestern Colorado is remote enough that you won't be fighting the crowds to see it. Oh, sure, Aspen gets packed with tourists, summer and winter alike, and when the train's running in Durango, it's tough sometimes just to find a place to park in the little town. But for the most part, southwestern Colorado—and its sprawling San Juan, Rio Grande, Gunnison, Uncompahgre, and Grand Mesa National Forests—offers the traveler an excellent opportunity to lose herself. To get away from the trappings of this fast-paced and overcrowded world. To simply enjoy being outside in one of the country's prettiest spots.

Grand Junction

Grand Junction (pop. 30,000; elev. 4,590 feet) is the largest town between Salt Lake City and Denver. Situated in the irrigated Grand Valley at the junction of the Colorado and Gunnison Rivers, Grand Junction is mainly a small industrial and agricultural community; its major crops are corn, alfalfa, and fruit, particularly apples and peaches. Other important crops include beans, small grains, pears, cherries, and apricots. The Grand Valley also supports large herds of cattle, and many sheep ranchers summer their animals in the area.

Grand Junction and the Grand Valley are surrounded by remarkable landscapes. To the northeast are the Little Bookcliffs, a miles-long row of mesa-side cliffs that drop dramatically to the valley floor. East of town, the Colorado River carves deep canyons into the rugged Colorado Plateau, and to the southeast, Grand Mesa, the world's largest flat-topped mountain, rises powerfully into the clouds. Just a half hour from Grand Junction, Grand Mesa National Forest is a treasure of alpine lakes, pine, fir, and aspen trees, and that invigorating high-country air. To the west you'll find the soft redrock canyons, stark sandstone spires, and juniper- and piñon-dotted mesa-tops of Colorado National Monument.

Which adds up to lots of wonderful country to explore. Whether by foot, Nordic skis, mountain bike, horse, or car, the Grand Junction area offers plenty of open space to wander in. As well as wonderfully friendly folks to point you in the right directions.

HISTORY

Although white settlement didn't begin in the Grand Valley and surrounding area until 1881, several Spanish and United States exploration parties had passed through in the late 18th and mid-19th centuries. The first Spanish explorers in the area, friars Francisco Antanasio Dominguez and Silvestre Velez de Escalante, traveled through in search of a route connecting the missions of New Mexico with those in California. In 1821, after Mexico won its independence from Spain, the region was claimed for the United States, and in 1853, the area was partially mapped by two U.S. expeditions—those of John C. Frémont and John Gunnison—attempting to establish a cross-country railroad route. The United States Geological Survey studied the area in detail in the early 1870s, and the resulting book of maps, the Hayden Survey, was published and sold across the country in 1876.

Settlers began to arrive in September 1881, once the Utes had been moved to the reservation, and within four months irrigation projects were under way, a store had been built, and the town of Grand Junction was incorporated. Its first winter, the new town could claim just 150 residents. But 1882 saw the arrival of the Denver and Rio Grande Railroad, as well as the town's first hotel, and soon nearly a thousand citizens were supporting a bustling business district, including a drugstore, two blacksmith shops, and five hotels and restaurants. By the end of the year, 11 more saloons went up, providing rest and recreation for cowboys who worked ranches in the area (from 15 to 75 miles away) and who would come to town to hit the saloons and red-light districts.

As Grand Junction's downtown area continued to grow, increased irrigation in the surrounding Grand Valley led to successful peach, pear, and apple orchards. Farming continued to provide stability to Grand Junction's economy into the 20th century, as improved irrigation turned the valley into one of the lushest and most productive in the state—the area was now exporting cherries, apricots, grapes, and other crops. The Grand Valley area drew the nation's attention again in 1911, when Colorado National Monument was established.

During the early and mid-1900s, oil and uranium wells were drilled throughout the northern western-slope area, from Rangely south to the Grand Junction area. Grand Junction, as the largest town between Salt Lake City and Denver, again became an important shipping center, for both product and workers, and the area saw a cycle of booms and busts. The biggest boom, fueled by the post-war demand for uranium, brought worldwide publicity to Grand Junction, though the bust of the early 1960s caused major social and economic problems.

Most recently, Grand Junction has begun to capitalize on its nearby recreation and to appeal to tourism. Still defined largely by farming, the Grand Junction area nonetheless is becoming better known for its excellent hiking, mountain biking, and other sports, as well as for the gorgeous forests and startlingly beautiful mesa lands and canyons nearby. At the same time, downtown Grand Junction has begun to honor its history and celebrate its diversity, with museums, galleries, art shows, and various festivals throughout the year.

MUSEUMS

Museum of Western Colorado

This museum complex includes the history museum downtown, the Dinosaur Journey Museum, and the Cross Orchards Historic Site.

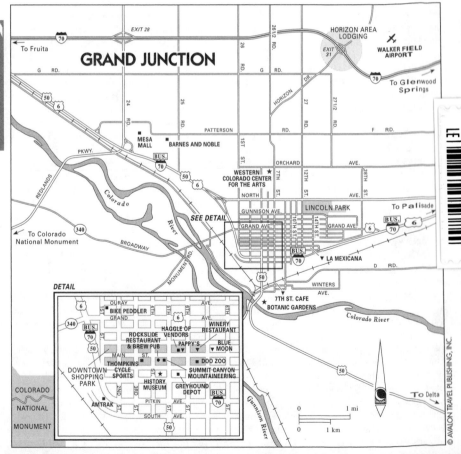

© AVALON TRAVEL PUBLISHING, INC.

The **History Museum/Sterling T. Smith Educational Tower** displays the geology, prehistory, history, and culture of western Colorado. Exhibits include a Colorado timeline (1880–1950), with tools, clothing, and artifacts from each era; Ute baskets, beadwork, and bows and arrows; Fremont culture petroglyphs, awls, fetishes; and Mimbres pottery. The Sterling T. Smith Education Tower offers a 360° view of the surrounding geography, as well as a working weather station. The museum also has a gift-and-book store, specializing in Colorado history. The museum, 462 Ute St., is open Mon.–Sat. 10 A.M.–4 P.M., Memorial Day through Labor Day; Tues.–Sat. 10 A.M.–4 P.M. the rest of the year. Admission is $5 for adults, $4 for seniors, and $3 for kids 2–17. For more information, phone 970/242-0971.

At **Dinosaur Journey Museum,** full-scale animated replicas of dinosaurs from throughout the Mesozoic period roar and growl, snort and feed in a range of incredibly lifelike displays at this museum in Fruita just west of Grand Junction. With an emphasis on education for kids and teens, this musuem features dozens of hands-on activities: buttons to push, footprints to make, clay for creating your own dinosaur. That's if you can concentrate with the huge creatures growling beside you and swaying their long necks through the air. Check out the Thalassomedon (a 45-foot-long marine reptile), or the (apparently) hungry Apatusaurus. In addition, there are replicas of more recent creatures, including a woolly mammoth and a 25-foot great white shark, plus, you can stand on an earthquake simulator and watch plate tectonics demonstrate how the earth's crust changed over the years. In a separate room, videos explain how and where the dinosaurs lived, how excavation is done, and how the models were made. There's also a gift shop with T-shirts, stuffed dinosaurs, and kids' books.

And, if that's not enough, you can also sign up to go on an actual dinosaur-quarry dig. **Dinosaur Discovery Expeditions** offers you the chance to go out and assist paleontologists on-site. Learn about excavation techniques and lab research; accommodations, transportation, and meals are included.

Dinosaur Discovery Museum is open daily 9 A.M.–5 P.M. in summer and the rest of the year Mon.–Sat. 9 A.M.–5 P.M. and Sunday noon–5 P.M. Admission is $6 for adults, $5 for seniors, and $3.50 for kids. To get there, take the Fruita exit from I-70 and follow the signs. For more information, phone 970/858-7282. For information on the expeditions, phone 888/488-DINO (488-3466).

Cross Orchards Historic Site offers thorough tours of a working apple orchard, operating since the late 1890s. Founded by Isabelle K. Cross of Massachusetts (heiress to the Red Cross Shoe Company fortune), the Cross once reigned as one of the largest and most productive orchards in the country; it covered nearly 250 acres when the average orchard was fewer than 10. Today, the orchard includes more than 20,000 apple trees on 245 acres.

An ideal school field trip, a Cross Orchards tour demonstrates planting and harvesting techniques and also takes you into the workers' bunkhouses, a dining room, and kitchen. Tour participants get to taste apples (in season) and munch on fresh-baked sugar cookies. After the tour, visitors are free to wander through several other exhibits: a barn packed with tools and equipment from an early 20th-century family farm, including wagons, plows, pitchforks, and domestic items, as well as photos and original farm records and receipts; a collection of early 20th-century road-maintenance equipment; and several cars, a partial track, and a reconstructed trestle from the Uinta narrow-guage railroad, used 1904–39 to carry Gilsonite out of the moutains to the switch-yard west of Grand Junction. A gift shop sells cards, crafts, candy, and other items. A number of annual events take place here, including a quilt show, pumpkin hunt, and "country Christmas."

Cross Orchards is open to the public Tues.–Sat. 9 A.M. to 3 P.M., mid-May to October, as well as during special events, and on Monday the rest of the year. Private tours can be arranged any time. Admission is $3 for adults, $2 for kids 2–12, and $2.50 for seniors. For more information, write Cross Orchards Historic Site, 3073 Patterson/F Rd., Grand Junction, CO 81504, or phone 970/434-9814.

The Museum of Western Colorado also administers **Dinosaur Hill** and **Riggs Hill,** sites of historic dinosaur excavations. One-mile loop trails provide access to both of these historic quarries. **Rabbit Valley Research Area and Trail through Time** is administered by the museum and the BLM. Dinosaur bones, plant fossils, and geology can be seen along this 1.5-mile self-guided trail.

For more information on the Museum of Western Colorado complex, write 462 Ute St., P.O. Box 20000-5020, Grand Junction, CO 81502, or phone 970/242-0971. The museum also maintains an exhaustive and informative website at www.wcmuseum.org.

Western Colorado Center for the Arts

This museum, 1803 N. 7th St., features a wide variety of rotating displays. Though the emphasis is on Western and Native American art, the museum also exhibits other works in various forms from around the country. On permanent display is an excellent collection of Navajo rugs. This is also a center for performing arts, with concerts held throughout the year. Hours are Tues.–Sat. 9 A.M.–4 P.M. Admission is $2 for adults; free for kids 12 and under. For more information, phone 970/243-7337.

PARKS AND RECREATION

Colorado National Monument

Sheer redrock cliffs, sandstone spires rising dramatically from valley floors, desolate mesas, and shadowed canyons dotted with juniper and piñon—Colorado National Monument sprawls just west of Grand Junction over 32 square miles of some of the Southwest's most austerely beautiful landscapes. **Rimrock Drive,** the main road through the park, rises from the lowlands of the Colorado River Valley through the canyons to the top of a broad plateau. The 23-mile road provides access to the park's visitor center, a campground, several picnic areas, more than a dozen hiking trails, and many scenic overlooks.

Be sure to stop in at the visitor center, where you'll find displays of the park's geology, flora, and fauna. You can also get information on guided na-

ture walks and campfire programs, and pick up books, maps, and other useful literature. **Saddlehorn Campground** has 81 sites available on a first-come, first-served basis; flush toilets, no showers, $7 per night. Backcountry camping is also allowed throughout the park; some restrictions apply.

Hiking trails in Colorado National Monument vary from short nature walks and quarter-mile paths leading to scenic overlooks to seven- and eight-mile backcountry routes through remote canyons. Some of the trails offer excellent cross-country skiing in the winter.

You can reach the monument from the east and west. To get to the east entrance, take Monument Road west from downtown. To get to the west entrance, take Broadway west from downtown or I-70 west to Fruita and follow the signs. Admission is $5 per vehicle for a seven-day pass; camping is $10 a night.

For further information, write Colorado National Monument, Fruita, CO 81521, or phone 970/858-3617.

City Parks

Driving through Grand Junction, you'll be surprised by the number of city parks, certainly far more than most cities this size. A couple of the nicer ones are **Lincoln Park,** on North 12th between North and Gunnison, the community's largest and best town park. Volleyball courts, swimming pools, picnic areas, a great kids' playground, huge lawns, and shade trees add to its appeal. For more information on Grand Junction parks, phone the **Parks and Recreation Department** at 970/244-3866.

Botanic Garden of Western Colorado

The new (November 1997) Grand Junction Botanic Gardens offers floraphiles a chance to view up close an array of local and tropical plants and flowers, from cacti to orchids. In addition, a huge butterfly pavilion features butterflies of North America.

The gardens, open Tues.–Sun. 10 A.M.–5 P.M., are at the corner of South 7th Street and Struthers (junction of I-70 Business Loop and Highway 50). Admission is $3 for adults, $1.50

for kids 5–12. For more information, phone 970/245-3288.

Child's Play

Grand Junction is a wonderfully "kid-oriented" town. In addition to the excellent city parks, the **Doo Zoo Children's Museum** offers a wide range of diversions for kids from about age three to eight. From play cars to a "sea" of blue plastic balls for "swimming," from a post office to a grocery store, the Doo Zoo offers enough to keep kids occupied for hours. Hands-on learning toys abound, including typewriters and computers. Parents should stay with their kids.

The Doo Zoo is right downtown at 635 Main. Admission is $4 for ages 2–12 and $1 for adults. Hours are Mon.–Sat. 10 A.M.–5 P.M. For more information, phone 970/241-5225.

Cycling

The Grand Junction area offers excellent touring and mountain biking. Rimrock Drive through Colorado National Monument is a wonderful if admittedly arduous road tour. The route rises 2,000 feet from the valley floor to the top of the

hiking trails in Colorado National Monument

plateau and back down in 23 miles; the loop from Grand Junction through the park and back to town is about 36 miles.

Kokopelli's Trail, the 128-mile first leg of the Colorado Plateau Mountain-Bike Trail System, winds from Grand Junction to Moab, Utah. The trail (named for the humpbacked, flute-playing Anasazi god of fertility) begins 15 miles west of Grand Junction at Loma (Exit 15 from I-70), parallels the interstate for about 40 miles, and then drops south at Cisco, Utah, winding down just south of Arches National Park. Difficulty ranges from moderate to strenuous. The designers of the trail system are dedicated to political awareness and environmental preservation (Kokopelli's Trail is largely old jeep trails, so little actual construction had to be done). For a map of Kokopelli's Trail or more information on the Colorado Plateau Mountain-Bike Trail Association, write P.O. Box 4602, Grand Junction, CO 81502, or phone 970/241-9561. Information is also available from the BLM, 764 Horizon Dr., Grand Junction, CO 81506, 970/244-3000, as well as from Grand Junction–area bike shops, including **Ruby Canyon Cycles,** 301 Main St., 970/241-0141; and **The Bike Shop,** 964 North Ave., 970/243-0807.

Golf

Grand Junction's public golf courses include the small, nine-hole **Lincoln Park Golf Course** in town at 12th and Gunnison, 970/242-6394, and the 18-hole **Tiara Rado Golf Course** between Grand Junction and Colorado National Monument (go west on Broadway), 970/245-8085. Grand Junction's newest golf course is the 18-hole **Redlands Mesa Golf,** with a pro shop, driving range, and restaurant.at the base of the Colorado National Monument, 970/263-9270.

Hiking

The Grand Junction area's two best hiking areas are **Colorado National Monument** and **Grand Mesa** (see Grand Mesa, below, for information on hiking in Grand Mesa National Forest). Colorado National Monument offers excellent hiking for all levels of ability and dedication. A half dozen or so short marked trails (from one-quarter mile to one mile long) will get you out of the car for a breather, while backcountry trails ranging four to 8.5 miles take up to 16 hours round-trip. The park has published a map and guide with descriptions of the different trails, including lengths in miles and approximate time allowances. You'll receive the guide when you enter the park. You can also get information on hiking in the park from the visitor center or by writing Colorado National Monument, Fruita, CO 81521, or calling 970/858-3617.

Just west of the national monument lies little-known **Rattlesnake Canyon,** a desolate and rugged area accessible only by foot or 4WD vehicle. Hardy backcountry hikers will be rewarded with some of the most austere beauty on the western slope—sandstone cliffs, piñon-dotted mesas, and several natural arches. For information on Rattlesnake Canyon, contact the regional BLM office at 764 Horizon Dr., Grand Junction, CO 81506, 970/243-3000.

Fishing

The Colorado and Gunnison Rivers probably once brimmed with healthy lunker trout, though as victims of irrigation and mining, the rivers don't offer much to modern anglers. The Grand Mesa area (see that section, below) has more than 200 lakes and offers decent fishing. For information and licenses in Grand Junction, stop in at **Gene Taylor's Sporting Goods,** 445 W. Gunnison Ave., 970/242-8165.

Rafting

Grand Junction's western-slope location makes it ideal as a base for river running, from kayaking in boiling white water to floating down broad, lazy stretches of calm river water. **Adventure Bound** is a Grand Junction-based company offering trips on the Colorado, Yampa, and Green Rivers in Colorado and Utah. Trips range in length from one to five days. Explore the canyons of Dinosaur National Monument and Utah's Green Wilderness. For a brochure with more details, including prices and reservation information,

write **Adventure Bound River Expeditions,** 2392 H Rd., Grand Junction, CO 81505, or phone 970/245-5428 or 800/423-4668. You can request brochures and read about specific trips at www.raft-colorado.com.

You can also book raft trips on the Colorado River through **Rimrock Deer Park and Outdoor Center.** Rates range from about $18 (1.5-hour trip) to $150 (two days). You can also rent canoes. Write P.O. Box 608, Fruita, CO 81521, or phone 970/858-9555 or 888/712-9555.

Horseback Riding

Grand Junction's roots are in ranching and farming, and it remains a very Western town—lots of Stetsons, string ties, and horse trailers. Several outfitters in the area rent horses and offer tours, one of the best ways to see Colorado National Monument. **Rimrock Deer Park,** whose stables are near the west entrance to the monument, offers one- and two-hour rides, as well as half-day, full-day, and overnight pack trips. In addition, rodeos are held every Tuesday evening in the summer, and Rimrock rents canoes and rafts and can provide transportation to and from put-in spots. Rates for horseback rides start at about $18 an hour. For further information, phone 970/858-9555 or 888/712-9555.

Downhill Skiing

One of Colorado's lesser-known ski resorts, **Powderhorn,** is just 35 miles from Grand Junction via I-70 and Highway 65. Powderhorn and the surrounding Grand Mesa National Forest also offer good Nordic skiing. (For information on skiing Powderhorn, see Grand Mesa, below.)

TOURS

If you've got time, you'll want to explore the Grand Junction area a bit, from the peach orchards on the east side of town to the barren backcountry to the south. Poking around by car is a great way to do it, as you'll constantly come across landscapes, farmhouses, vineyards, or tiny little towns you hadn't realized existed. Or you

© STEPHEN METZGER

Vineyards punctuate the Colorado River Valley near Grand Junction.

SOUTHWESTERN

can hook up with one of several outfits in the area that will guide you where you want to go.

Winery Tours

Though not all that new to the valley—the first arrived in the late 1970s—the wineries of the Grand River Valley have only been discovered by tourists in the past couple of years. What's more, these wines are good: several of the local wines won major awards at national competitions in recent years.

You'll find six wineries in the Palisade region alone (seven miles east of Grand Junction), including a "meadery." A wonderful way to spend an afternoon is tasting the local product and touring the operations. Because these wineries are small, you're apt to get talking to the person pouring your sample only to discover she is the winemaker/owner herself. Tours and tastings are free, and in addition to selling wine, the shops stock novelties, such as T-shirts, gift baskets, wine racks, and wine glasses. If you happen to be around in late September, check out the **Winefest,** an annual celebration of grapes, the harvest, and good wine, with special tastings, tours, entertainment, and other events in both Grand Junction and Palisade.

The Grand Junction Visitor and Convention Bureau provides a complete list of the area wineries, maps and other information, as well as exact dates of the Winefest.

ACCOMMODATIONS

The largest proportion of Grand Junction's lodging are concentrated at I-70 and Horizon (Exit 31), with the north, upper end of Horizon virtually lined with franchise inns. Downtown are a few older motels and bed-and-breakfasts in converted early 20th-century homes.

Under $50

You've got a few possibilities in this range, and if you're just passing through and aren't looking for fancy, these low-end places should serve just fine. Try the **Motel 6,** 776 Horizon, 970/243-2628, or the **Mesa Inn,** 704 Horizon, 970/245-3030 or 888/955-3080.

$50–100

Most Grand Junction lodging is in this category, with doubles at most of the upper Horizon inns going for less than $100. Among them: the **Days**

Inn, 733 Horizon, 970/245-7200; **Ramada Inn,** 752 Horizon, 970/243-5150; **Holiday Inn,** 755 Horizon, 970/243-6790; **Super 8,** 728 Horizon, 970/248-8080; **Sandman Best Western,** 708 Horizon, 970/243-4150; and **Horizon Inn Best Western,** 754 Horizon, 970/245-1410.

$100–150
If you're looking for something a bit nicer, the new **Adam's Mark Hotel,** 743 Horizon, 970/241-8888, is one of the largest (275 rooms) and best-appointed lodges in the area. For added costs, you can get suites and/or rooms with private whirlpool baths. Additionally, there are a number of bed-and-breakfasts in Grand Junction (the Grand Junction Visitor and Convention Bureau can provide a complete list). Among the best and oldest is the **Orchard House,** 3573 E. 1/2 Rd., 970/464-0529, about 10 miles east of Grand Junction on a hillside above the little town of Palisade— out and away from the hustle and bustle of town. Views from the house look out over the farms and orchards of the Grand Valley. All four rooms have private bath.

Camping and RVing
In addition to Saddlehorn Campground at Colorado National Monument (see above) and the Forest Service campgrounds on Grand Mesa (see that section, below), the Grand Junction area also offers several privately owned camping areas. The Grand Junction/Clifton **KOA** campground, 970/434-6644, is just east of town at 3238 E. Business I-70 (take Exit 37 from I-70). On the other side of town are the **Junction West RV Park,** 799 Rd. 22 (Exit 26 off I-70), 970/245-8531, and **Fruita Junction RV Park and Campground,** 970/858-3155, off I-70 in Fruita adjacent to the Colorado Welcome Center and near the west entrance to Colorado National Monument.

FOOD
Breakfast
If you're just passing through, you'll find plenty of fast-food restaurants at the major exits off I-70, particularly at the airport exit (Exit 31). **Good Pastures,** in the Days Inn at 733 Horizon Dr. (Exit 31 from I-70), 970/243-3058, is Grand Junction's version of a health-food restaurant. Beginning with fresh juices (celery, carrot, apple, etc.), Good Pastures offers several low-fat, healthful dishes, including some vegetarian specials; at breakfast, you have your choice of sausage, Canadian bacon, or "soysage" ($3.50–6). Downtown, try **Main Street Bagels,** 559 Main, 970/241-2740, serving a variety of bagels and coffees.

Other Restaurants
Fortunately, the microbrewery bandwagon didn't pass Grand Junction by. The **Rockslide Restaurant and Brewery,** 401 Main, 970/245-2111, serves excellent beer, as well as typical pub fare (burgers, fish and chips), plus dinner specials—seafood, prime rib, and pastas ($6–16).

The **7th Street Cafe,** 832 S. 7th, 970/242-7225, is Grand Junction's retro '50s diner, decorated with posters of James Dean, Marilyn, and Elvis, as well as old 45s (a 45 is a thin, round, black vinyl disk a bit larger than a CD, on each side of which is a single groove from which a tiny needle would produce music . . .). Entrées run $5–12; open for breakfast and lunch daily.

For authentic Mexican food, try **La Mexicana,** 1310 Ute, 970/245-2737. Dinners run $4–8. Closed Sun.–Monday. For excellent pizzas and sandwiches, try **Old Chicago,** 120 North Ave., 970/244-8383, which has recently opened here after having much success in other parts of the state, including Fort Collins and Colorado Springs.

If you're looking to go a bit upscale, try **The Winery Restaurant,** 642 Main, 970/242-4100, where steak, seafood, prime rib, and other specialties are served in a winery-like dining room— old wine bottles and fermentation barrels. Open for dinner daily.

Just Desserts
Pappy's Ice Cream Parlor, on the Main Street Mall at 560 Main, 970/241-5600, features ex-

cellent homemade ice cream (using Ben and Jerry's recipes), fresh-squeezed lime- and lemonade, fresh-ground coffees, and gourmet candies.

ENTERTAINMENT

Those expecting Boulder-like nightlife in Grand Junction will be disappointed. Though there are a handful of places to listen to live music, your choices are limited, and you're probably better off taking advantage of the area's daytime recreational opportunities. If nighttime does find you antsy to get out, try **Bailey's,** at the Ramada Inn, 2790 Crossroads, 970/241-8411, a nightclub/disco with DJ dancing; **Cinnamon's,** in the Holiday Inn, 755 Horizon, 970/243-6790. **Charade's,** in the Hilton, 743 Horizon, 970/241-8888, features live comedy on Tuesday night. The **Blue Moon Bar and Grille,** 120 N. 7th St., 970/242-4506, also regularly books live music.

CALENDAR

From music festivals to baseball tournaments to bike races, Grand Junction's got something going on just about every weekend. The best sources for what's happening when and where are the *Daily Sentinel* and the Grand Junction Area Chamber of Commerce.

Among the highlights: the **JUCO** (Junior College) **Baseball World Series** in late May; the **Hot-Air Balloon Rally** in early June; the **Colorado Stampede** (rodeo, music, cowboy poetry), mid-June; **Country Jam USA Music Festival** in late June or July (a week of music featuring big-name acts such as Willie Nelson); **Dinosaur Days,** late July; the **Mesa County Fair,** early August; **Palisade Peach Festival,** late August; **Renaissance Faire,** mid-September; and the **Colorado Mountain Winefest,** late September.

Throughout the summer, downtown Grand Junction features **Art on the Corner,** with a diverse group of the state's sculptors displaying their work outside on street corners. The **Grand Junction Symphony Orchestra** hosts a concert series each year, with special shows attracting big-name guest conductors and musicians. For information, phone the symphony at 970/243-6787.

SHOPPING

Try to allow yourself some time to explore downtown's Main Street Mall. Though the street has been remodeled, it's refreshingly free of Yup-scale boutiques and trendy (and pricey) shops. Instead, you'll find classic small-town clothing, band-instrument, shoe, stationery, and gift stores. There's even a nurses' uniform store, and a formal-wear rental shop. Be sure to check out **A Haggle of Vendors Emporium,** 510 Main, where every imaginable nook and cranny is packed with imports, antiques, and junk—everything from toys and fabrics to picture frames, plates, mugs, and glassware.

SERVICES

The offices of the **Grand Junction Police Department** are at 625 Ute, 970/244-3538. The **Mesa County Sheriff** is at 215 Rice, 970/244-3500. Both of Grand Junction's hospitals offer emergency and nonemergency medical care. **St. Mary's Hospital and Regional Medical Center** is at the corner of 7th and Patterson, 970/244-2273. **Grand Junction Community Hospital** is at 12th and Walnut, 970/242-0920. Grand Junction's main **post office** is at 241 N. 4th; for information on other branches or Grand Junction–area zip codes, phone 970/244-3400.

Recycling

Recycle at **United Waste and Recycle,** 2948 Business I-70, and **Western Colorado Recycling,** 2379 G Road. You can also drop off most recyclables at Grand Junction's **City Markets,** 2770 U.S. Hwy. 50, 1909 N. 1st St., 569 32nd Ave., and 200 Rood Avenue.

INFORMATION

The **Grand Junction Visitor and Convention Bureau** has a beautiful information center just off I-70 at Horizon Drive. The center is staffed with helpful volunteers and has scads of literature and other information on what to do, where to stay, and where to eat in Grand Junction. Phone the offices at 970/244-1480 or 800/962-2547. You can also get information—and order a vistor's guide—at the bureau's website at www.visitgrandjunction.com. Just west of town in Fruita is a Colorado State **Welcome Center,** where you can pick up brochures on what to do and see in the Grand Junction area, as well as in the rest of the state.

The main branch of the **Mesa County Public Library** is in Grand Junction at 530 Grand Ave., 970/243-4442. A **Barnes and Noble Booksellers** is at 2451 Patterson, 970/243-5113. You can get backcountry maps at **Summit Canyon Mountaineering,** 461 Main, 970/243-2847.

Grand Junction's *Daily Sentinel,* which comes out weekday afternoons and Saturday and Sunday mornings, has information on current events, local movie and television listings, and weather. For subscription information, phone 970/242-5050.

TRANSPORTATION

Just south of I-70 about 250 miles west of Denver, Grand Junction is easily approachable by either car or bus. The **Greyhound-Trailways** bus depot is downtown at 230 S. 5th; for information on rates and schedules, phone 970/242-6012. You can also get to Grand Junction via **Amtrak,** whose passenger station is at 2nd and South Avenue; for information, phone 970/241-2733 or 800/872-7245.

Grand Junction's **Walker Field Airport** is the largest airport in the state west of Denver and is serviced by several major airlines, with flights from cities around the country as well as connecting flights from Denver. Phone the airport at 970/244-9100.

Most of the major car-rental agencies have booths at Walker Field, including **Avis,** 970/244-9170; **Budget,** 970/244-9155; **Hertz,** 970/243-0747; and **National,** 970/243-6626. Offices of **Thrifty Rental,** 970/243-7556, are at 752 Horizon.

For taxi service in Grand Junction, phone **Sunshine Taxi** at 970/245-8294.

South and East of Grand Junction

HIGHWAY 141 SOUTH

Highway 141 winds south from Grand Junction to Dove Creek, coursing through western Colorado's remote canyon country and passing through a handful of ramshackle old mining towns. Along the way, the 150-mile stretch of highway flirts with the Utah border, twice approaching within 10 miles of the state line. Known as the **Unaweep/Tabeguache Byway,** the road slices below Grand Mesa, across the Uncompahgre Plateau, and follows the course of the Dolores River for 30 miles. Ribboning through ancient Native American hunting grounds, the route takes its name from the Utes: "Unaweep" means "Canyon with Two Mouths," and "Tabeguache" (TAB-a-wash) means "Place Where the Snow Melts First."

Unaweep Canyon is a harshly scenic draw that slices through the plateau nearly from Whitewater to Gateway. Its floor lush, green, and sometimes seemingly endless, its walls towering sharp and sheer, the canyon possesses that unmistakably familiar ability to help travelers find perspective. Out here, where the lines between nature's beauty and her cold indifference become blurred, you, and your problems, can seem awfully small.

In the late 1880s, a seven-mile wooden flume was built along the Dolores River just north of Uravan. Used to carry water from the San Miguel River to the Lone Tree Placer Site, **Hanging Flume** clings precariously to the sheer sandstone cliffs 150 feet above the water's surface. A turnout and interpretive sign provide an excellent view, as well as historical background.

Uravan was a company town founded in 1936 and named for the two elements found in the area's carnotite ore: uranium and vanadium. During the 1940s, the U.S. Army sent uranium from the tailings from the vanadium mill to Los Alamos, New Mexico, where Oppenheimer and crew used it in the Manhattan Project, the world's first atomic bomb. The mill shut down in 1984.

For a complete guide to the Unaweep-Tabeguache Byway, contact the Grand Junction Visitors and Convention Bureau. The thorough and well-written guide describes 35 points of interest along the route from Whitewater to Placerville and also provides information on the geology, history, and wildlife of the area. Write 360 Grand Ave., Grand Junction, CO 81501, or phone 970/244-1480 or 800/962-2547.

Naturita, Nucla, and Norwood

Naturita is a small town west of the junction of Highway 141 and Highway 145 with several businesses flanking the highway for a couple of blocks. The town, founded in 1882, now serves as a supply center for nearby ranchers and farmers. In addition, a handful of small motels provide base camps for the hunters who find their way out here in the summer and fall. **Children's Memorial Park** is just off the highway (at 2nd Street), next to the **Rimrock Historical Museum** (for hours and more information phone the Naturita Town Hall at 970/865-2286).

Five miles northeast of Naturita is the town of Nucla. Shortly before the turn of the 20th century, the Colorado Cooperative Community established the town as an experiment in communal living. Designed as a community where "equality and service rather than greed and competition [would be] the basis of conduct," Nucla was made up of cooperatively owned businesses. In addition, labor was evenly divided, and any product of community labor—the town's irrigation ditch, for example—became community property. Nucla was chosen for the town's name as its founders saw it as the nucleus of a socialist society that would eventually spread throughout the country. But it was not to be—the experiment was short-lived.

About 20 miles southeast of the junction of Highway 145 and Highway 141 is the little mesa-top ranching town of Norwood. Popular with outdoor enthusiasts, particularly hunters and anglers, the Norwood area is one of Colorado's little pockets of relatively undisturbed natural beauty. You can enjoy fishing and boating at nearby Miramonte Reservoir. For information on the area, phone the **Norwood Chamber of Commerce** at 970/327-4238.

GRAND MESA

Less than an hour east of Grand Junction via I-70 and Highway 65, Grand Mesa appears startling in its contrast to the Grand Valley sprawling at the base of its steep sides. Here a mountain highway winds, climbs, and switches back from the scrubby canyon country up into the firs, spruces, and aspens of Grand Mesa National Forest. The mesa is 10,000 feet above sea level (and more than 5,000 feet above Grand Junction) and covers more than 50 square miles.

With more than 200 lakes, 15 campgrounds, and miles of riding, hiking, snowmobiling, and cross-country ski trails, as well as the Powderhorn downhill ski area, Grand Mesa offers some of the best recreational opportunities in the region. In addition, the mesa affords absolutely spectacular scenery. On the drive down the back side of the mesa, several spots afford views of the San Juan Mountains shouldering massively into the sky more than a hundred miles to the south. Oftentimes in the summer, as late-afternoon storms roll in, cold rains angle across the sky, washing the needles and leaves of the trees, and the sunlight plays strange tricks with the mist and the distant clouds. Rainbows arc across the sky, and the greens shine electric.

A word of caution: even when it's warm in the valley, it can get downright cold on the mesa. I drove up one day in mid-June when it was pushing 90°F in Grand Junction, and by the time I got onto the mesa it was *snowing*. Even if it seems crazy, bring a coat or sweater.

Hiking

Grand Mesa National Forest offers hundreds of miles of trails and backcountry to explore. One of the more popular trails is **Crag Crest Trail** on the highest point of Grand Mesa. The 10-mile trail provides access to broad clearings, where you'll want to stop and take in the view, and to dense forests and beautiful mountain lakes. The Forest

Service can provide topo maps and more information on specific parts of the mesa that are best for hiking.

Fishing

Open year-round, the lakes on Grand Mesa even draw die-hard trouters for the ice fishing. Most of the lakes are quite small and get a lot of traffic; the shores of the more accessible lakes are lined with hopeful anglers, their RVs parked nearby. Even the more remote lakes are rather heavily fished.

For licenses, tackle, and information on current hot spots, stop in at the **Mesa General Store** in Mesa on Highway 65 on the north slope.

Skiing

Though primarily an intermediate area, Powderhorn offers good skiing away from the pomp and snobbery of some of the state's better-known resorts. Powderhorn skiers are also afforded some of skiing's more interesting and expansive views; because the mesa rises so dramatically from the valley below, the view becomes a mosaic of snowy mountain meadows, deep forests, and far-off canyonlands and arid desert.

Powderhorn's four lifts service 27 trails on 510 acres of trails with a 1,650-foot vertical drop. Terrain is 20 percent beginner, 50 percent intermediate, and 30 percent advanced and expert. Lessons and rental equipment are available, as is limited on-site lodging. For information, phone 970/268-5700. For lodging reservations, phone 800/241-6997. For website information, go to www.powderhorn.com.

Grand Mesa Lodging

The **Grand Mesa Lodge,** 970/856-3250, offers boating, fishing, and lakeside cabins—some with fireplaces—that sleep up to six (rates range $45–100 a night for two, with an added $7.50 for each additional person). **Mesa Lakes Resort,** 970/268-5467, has small rustic cabins (no running water), as well as larger, more modern cabins and a motel. Cabin rates run $45–150. The lodge has a small restaurant and grocery and tackle shop. Lodging is also available at **Powderhorn Ski Resort,** where summer promotional rates are attractively low (often under

$50). Phone 970/268-5799 for information or reservations.

Camping

Grand Mesa's campground's are generally open only from Memorial Day through Labor Day, thanks to the large amount of snowfall. Sometimes, there's even too much snow to open the areas until mid-June or later. **Jumbo** and **Spruce Grove** campgrounds have tent and RV sites, pit toilets, and access to hiking trails.

Information

For maps and complete information on Grand Mesa and Grand Mesa National Forest, stop by the Grand Junction District Office of the Forest Service at 764 Horizon Dr., Grand Junction, or phone 970/242-8211. Information is also available from the Grand Mesa National Forest Headquarters, 2250 U.S. Hwy. 50, Delta, CO 81416, 970/874-7691.

Cedaredge

Cedaredge (pop. 1,200; elev. 6,100 feet) is a robust and colorful small town between the lower slopes of Grand Mesa's south side and the flatlands of the Uncompahgre and Gunnison River Valleys. Backed up against the mesa, Cedaredge offers excellent views of the sprawling valleys and orchards and, on clear days, the San Juan Mountains far to the south. **Pioneer Town** is a reconstructed 19th-century Western village run by the local historical society. The village features a mining and Native American museum, plus a blacksmith shop, jail, chapel, and one-room schoolhouse. Pioneer Town is open Memorial Day through Labor Day, Mon.–Sat. 10 A.M.–4 P.M. and Sunday 1–4 P.M. Admission is $3 for adults, $2 for seniors, and $15 for kids. For more information, phone 970/856-7554.

You'll find a nice city park right downtown on Main Street/Highway 65, with picnic facilities, shade trees, and tennis courts.

HIGHWAY 133

Highway 133 winds northeast from Hotchkiss along the North Fork of the Gunnison River,

past Paonia Reservoir, over McClure Pass (elev. 8,755 feet), and then through the Crystal River Valley past Redstone and on to Carbondale. Weather permitting, this is the best and shortest route between much of southwestern Colorado and Denver, bypassing the Grand Junction-to-Glenwood Springs stretch of I-70 and cutting an hour or more off the trip. Highway 133 is also the best route connecting Telluride and the ski areas of Central Colorado, and during the winter you'll see a lot of ski-racked Subarus and Jeeps buzzing back and forth along the highway.

The first third of the way is mostly orchard and ranching country. Fertile orchards dominate the open, rolling landscapes, and grazing cattle dot the fields. Elk, commonly seen from the roadway, also graze throughout this area. At Paonia Reservoir, the road doglegs due north and lifts over McClure Pass, where you'll find trailheads of some excellent cross-country skiing trails. The highway then drops over the back side of the pass and through the beautiful White River National Forest and the Crystal River Valley, the Crystal River ribboning through the firs and gleaming argentine at roadside.

Paonia

Paonia (pop. 1,670; elev. 5,675 feet), founded in 1882, was named for the abundance of flowers in the area. The name is a bastardization of "peonie," probably resulting from misread handwriting. Agriculture, its major industry, yields excellent peaches, apples, cherries, and other fruits. Several mines can also be found nearby.

Paonia is also the rather unlikely site of the offices of one of the West's boldest, angriest, and most progressive and intelligent environmental newspapers, *High Country News*. Published out of an old one-story storefront building on Main Street, the *News*, whose motto is, "A Paper for People Who Care about the West," is supported almost solely by subscriptions and grants, including one from the Grateful Dead's Rex Foundation. This allows the paper the freedom to confront sensitive issues head-on without fear of advertisers pulling their ads. The result is a scrupulous press that does thorough investigative pieces on subjects varying from overgrazing

a Redstone fountain, frozen by near-zero Colorado winter temperatures

on New Mexico public lands to the official federal stand on grizzly bears in Yellowstone Park, and on all aspects of the West's often-destructive industries—mining, drilling, logging, and the military-industrial complex. For subscription and other information, write P.O. Box 1090, Paonia, CO 91428, or phone 970/527-4898.

If you're looking for a good place to eat in Paonia, try **La Casa,** 312 Grand Ave., 970/527-4343, where you can get Mexican and Italian food, as well as sandwiches, burgers, and salads for lunch ($5–8) and dinner ($6.50–14)—open Tues.–Saturday. Lodging is available at the **Bross Hotel Bed and Breakfast,** 312 Onarga, 970/527-6776, which offers 10 rooms (each with private bath) in a restored 1906 hotel.

For more information on Paonia, write the **Paonia Chamber of Commerce,** P.O. Box 366, Paonia, CO 81428, or phone 970/527-3885. You can also get information from the town's website at www.paonia.com, and there's a tourist information booth on Highway 65 at the turnoff to town.

Yule Marble Quarries

Some of the world's purest marble was mined at this National Historic Site. First discovered in 1870, the marble from this area has been used in government buildings around the country, including the Denver capitol. In addition, deposits here provided the largest single piece of marble ever quarried in the world: the 100-ton brick used for the Tomb of the Unknown Soldier in Arlington National Cemetery in Washington, D.C. Marble from the Yule quarries was also used in the construction of the Lincoln Memorial.

Though inactive for years, the quarries are open to the public. Wander around the old mill, view huge slabs of flawless marble once used in mill buildings, or hike along Yule Creek, where crystal-clear water polishes the marble's swirling veins and faded pastels. But be careful: some of the old pits are deep, so use caution when exploring and keep an eye on kids.

The Yule marble mill and quarries are accessible only by foot or 4WD vehicle. Turn south from Highway 133 onto County Road 3 (the turnoff is marked), and continue two miles to the town of Marble. From there it's about four miles to the quarries. You can arrange 4WD tours to the Yule quarries through **Crystal River 4x4 Tours,** 116 Main St., Redstone, 970/963-

1991. Rates are $20 per person, reservations recommended.

Redstone

Redstone, a tiny resort community on the banks of the Crystal River, dates from the turn of the 20th century, when coal baron John Cleveland Osgood (cousin of Grover Cleveland) built a village here made up of several small cottages and one magnificent "castle." Osgood, founder and director of the Colorado Fuel and Iron Company, was at one time one of the country's most successful industrialists, his peers (and houseguests) including John D. Rockefeller and Theodore Roosevelt. Osgood was reportedly worth $40 million.

The town of Redstone was built as a model industrial community. Cottages were constructed to house the families of his employees who worked in the nearby coal mines, while the large Redstone Inn was for "bachelors and guests." He built the 42-room, 16-bedroom Redstone Castle for himself, decorating it with the finest furnishings from around the world—Tiffany chandeliers, Persian rugs, and Italian oil paintings, as well as lots of goldleaf and marble. Osgood and Roosevelt are said to have sat on the front porch shooting deer that the gamekeeper released on the lawn.

Today, Redstone consists of a single narrow road paralleling the highway across the Crystal River. A handful of vacation homes and several gift shops, mostly specializing in antiques, dolls, woodcarvings, and glass, can be found there, as well as some vacation lodges, a general store, and a small park and playground.

Redstone Castle is open for tours, meetings, and weddings—rent the entire castle for $10,000 a night (sleeps 34 in 16 rooms). For information, phone 970/704-1430 or visit www .theredstonecastle.com.

The **Redstone Inn** is the lodge built to accommodate Osgood's bachelor workers and is on the National Register of Historic Places. Though not as opulent or huge as the castle, the inn is still impressive in its grandeur and elegance. If you're looking for a great place to hole up away from daily life's hustle and bustle, you'd be hard-pressed to find a better spot. Rates range from about $50 for a room with a shared bath to $220 for the larger suites. The inn also serves excellent dinners, and it is famous for its Sunday brunch ($14). Even if you're just passing through, take a few minutes to look around and maybe have a Bloody Mary in the bar, which is decorated with original Victorian furnishings. Passersthrough can get a taste of the inn's elegance by stopping for a bite at the main dining room, where you can get steaks, seafood, and lamb, or at the less formal **Patio Grill,** serving salads, sandwiches, and burgers ($6–12). For more information and reservations, phone 970/963-2526 or 800/748-2524.

Aspen

If there is an Avalon of Colorado, it is Aspen, a place where myth and reality circle round each other like freewheeling falcons under a cobalt sky. And this is the town's real charm—the way it exists as though dismembered from the rest of the world, and how in a strange way it doesn't much matter what's real and what isn't. Though you might feel more grounded after having visited, it's not as much because of the town itself but because of the perspective it provides. Like Hemingway said of journalism: Aspen is good for you, if you get out in time.

If you plan to stay, it helps to be independently wealthy. The average price of a home is over $1.5 million, while the cheapest houses (usually less than 1,000 square feet) on the market sell in the half-million-dollar range. Which helps explain why Aspen is almost synonymous with celebrity: Don Henley, Glenn Frey, Goldie Hawn, Jack Nicholson, Hunter Thompson, Oprah Winfrey, and the late John Denver are but a few who either live (or have lived) in the area or spend time here.

And it's not just housing. Walk around the downtown mall—you can almost smell the money. The boutiques and specialty shops aren't here for working people, who are, however, free to window shop and imagine a lifestyle they'll probably never experience.

What is there, then, for the untitled, the *unentitled*? Just this: some of the most magnificent scenery and greatest recreational opportunities on the planet. Though best known as a ski resort—in fact, Aspen (pop. 5,000; elev. 7,908 feet) is probably the country's quintessential ski town—the area offers untold riches for hikers, mountain bikers, anglers, and anyone else willing to explore a bit. White River National Forest literally surrounds Aspen, its woods, streams, lakes, towering peaks, and old logging roads inviting endless hours of exploration, whether you go with a group or prefer the meditative nature of solitude.

Situated in a winter-locked box canyon on the Roaring Fork River, Aspen traces its history, as do many Colorado mountain towns, to late-19th-century mining, and the town's homes and other buildings reflect that. Cozy Victorian homes—most of them tastefully remodeled and, in the summer, with lobelia, pansies, and other colorful flowers spilling out of planters and window boxes—line the town's side streets. The Hotel Jerome, at one time one of the most elegant lodges in the West and still defined by glorious opulence, stands sentrylike on Main Street, its solid, red-brick sides providing constancy to the pulsing, dynamic community that surrounds it.

During the last half century, Aspen earned a reputation as a center of sophistication and progressive cultural education. The permanent population is among the best educated in the Rockies, with 55 percent holding bachelor's degrees or better (as opposed to 20 percent nationwide), and *Mountain Sports and Living* magazine rated its school system number one among 47 ski towns. Also, a number of institutes, arts centers, and annual festivals—music, film, food and wine—bring famous writers and directors, professors and lecturers, chefs and winemakers to town every summer. In addition, the large number of well-known artists, musicians, and actors who live permanently or part-time in or near Aspen guarantee the area will remain a cultural mecca, if an overpriced one, well into the future.

HISTORY

The first mines were staked in the Roaring Fork Valley in the summer of 1879, when prospectors seeking silver arrived from Leadville by way of Independence Pass. By fall of that year, word spread that these mines, at the bases of Smuggler and Aspen Mountains, were producing respectable amounts of ore. The valley's first community, originally called Ute City, was established by Midwesterner Henry Gillespie, who stopped in Leadville en route to the valley just long enough to buy rights to the mines from the original prospectors. Gillespie didn't stay long, deciding to go to Washington, D.C., to try to raise money and establish postal service for his camp. In February 1880, B. Clark Wheeler arrived in Ute City, having skied into the valley on "Norwegian snowshoes," and, in Gillespie's absence, changed the name of the camp to Aspen.

That summer, great numbers of miners descended on the Roaring Fork Valley camps, and with them came merchants and others opening shops and services. It was reportedly a rowdy time, the lawless camp attracting men with little regard for social convention or propriety. When winter rolled around, though, and temperatures and snow fell, all but a handful hit the road for more hospitable climes. The few who stayed established the town's first newspaper, organized a Sabbath School, and sponsored regular dances and shows.

For the next three years, Aspen's ore production was kept to a minimum. The camp's remote location made hauling in equipment and domestic items difficult at best—with the nearest railroad 40 miles east, just about anything shipped into or out of the valley came via burro.

In 1883, Jerome B. Wheeler, a New York businessman vacationing in Manitou Springs, arrived in Aspen and immediately saw its investment potential. Wheeler (not related to B. Clark Wheeler) bought controlling interest in several local mines, built the town's first bank, and resurrected an abandoned smelter, which

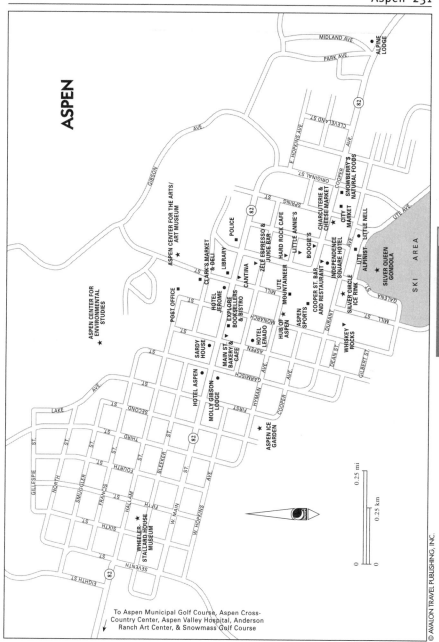

ASPEN

SOUTHWESTERN

To Aspen Municipal Golf Course, Aspen Cross-Country Center, Aspen Valley Hospital, Anderson Ranch Art Center, & Snowmass Golf Course

0.25 mi

0.25 km

© AVALON TRAVEL PUBLISHING, INC.

MIDLAND AVE.
PARK AVE.
ALPINE LODGE
GIBSON AVE.
CLEVELAND ST.
E. HOPKINS AVE.
ORIGINAL ST.
SPRING ST.
UTE AVE.
COOPER AVE.
ASPEN CENTER FOR THE ARTS/ ART MUSEUM
ASPEN CENTER FOR ENVIRONMENTAL STUDIES
POLICE
LIBRARY
CLARK'S MARKET & DELI
POST OFFICE
HOTEL JEROME
EXPLORE BOOKSELLERS & BISTRO
CANTINA
ZELE ESPRESSO & JUICE BAR
HARD ROCK CAFE
LITTLE ANNIE'S
BOOGIE'S
CHARCUTERIE & CHEESE MARKET
SNOWBERRY'S NATURAL FOODS
CITY MARKET
LITTLE NELL
ALPINIST
UTE
INDEPENDENCE SQUARE HOTEL
UTE MOUNTAINEER
COOPER ST. BAR AND RESTAURANT
HUB OF ASPEN
ASPEN SPORTS
SILVER CIRCLE ICE RINK
WHISKEY ROCKS
HOTEL LENADO
MONARCH ST.
MILL ST.
GALENA ST.
SILVER QUEEN GONDOLA
SKI AREA
SARDY HOUSE
MAIN ST. BAKERY & CAFE
HOTEL ASPEN
MOLLY GIBSON LODGE
ASPEN ICE GARDEN
ASPEN ST.
GARMISCH AVE.
HYMAN AVE.
COOPER AVE.
DEAN ST.
DURANT
GILBERT ST.
FIRST ST.
SECOND ST.
THIRD ST.
FOURTH ST.
FIFTH ST.
SIXTH ST.
SEVENTH ST.
EIGHTH ST.
GILLESPIE ST.
NORTH ST.
SMUGGLER ST.
FRANCIS ST.
HALLAM ST.
W. MAIN
W. HOPKINS
BLEEKER ST.
LAKE AVE.
WHEELER-STALLARD HOUSE MUSEUM

allowed for greatly increased ore production. Shortly after Wheeler's arrival, the little town's annual silver production was $1.25 million.

When the Denver and Rio Grande Railroad arrived in 1887, Aspen's population was approximately 15,000, making it the third-largest town in the state. Local mines, particularly the Molly Gibson, Durant, Midnight, Montezuma, and Smuggler I and II, were producing nearly 100 percent pure silver, and the value of the area's annual output had increased to $6 million. In addition, the town had earned an international reputation for free-spending wild times and wilder women. Jerome Wheeler opened the Jerome Hotel and the Wheeler Opera House in 1889 at the pinnacle of Aspen's prosperity.

Aspen's boom was destined to be silenced, however. The silver market crashed in 1893, the mines closed down, and folks packed up lock, stock, and barrel, and headed out—some hiked over Independence Pass to Leadville. For the next half decade, Aspen was little more than a handful of crumbling shacks and hardy holdouts hoping good times would return. In the early 1930s, Aspen's population dwindled to approximately 250.

Within a few years, however, the first seeds of the valley's second growth spurt were beginning to be sown. In the summer of 1936, American bobsled racer Billy Fiske and his partner Ted Ryan created the Highland-Bavarian Corporation, with plans to develop the area into the kind of ski area the two had seen in Europe. They built the valley's first inn, the Highland Bavarian Lodge, and hired Andre Roche, a Swiss mountaineer, to survey the mountains for possible ski runs. By 1939, Fiske, Ryan, and Roche had organized the town's first ski club, cut the first trail on Aspen Mountain, and hosted the Rocky Mountain Ski Racing Championships. In 1941, Aspen served as the site of the U.S. Nationals.

Throughout the 1940s, Aspen Mountain continued to host races, and its reputation as an excellent training mountain spread throughout the country. The summer of 1949 saw the founding of the Aspen Institute for Humanistic Studies, the town's first of many forays into the cultural arena. The following winter, Aspen

Mountain became the first American site to hold the World Alpine Ski Championships. The little community was now on the international map.

In 1958, the Aspen Skiing Corporation expanded, opening Buttermilk Mountain just south of Aspen. Buttermilk, with gentler slopes than Aspen Mountain, developed primarily as a teaching and beginner-to-intermediate area. Aspen Highlands opened the same winter, and Snowmass Ski Area opened 10 seasons later, in the winter of 1967–68.

MUSEUMS

Since 1949, when Aspen developer Walter Paepcke organized an international celebration in honor of Johann Wolfgang von Goethe's 200th birthday, Aspen has been a center for a wide range of cultural and educational events and permanent institutes, from music and film festivals to various seminars, workshops, and conferences. June through September, the tenor of the town is decidedly intellectual, approaching highbrow, as well-known professors, critics, writers, and artists convene in Aspen to share ideas and to explore the parameters of their disciplines and media. In addition, there are enough museums and galleries, many with a Native American and Southwestern flavor, to keep you occupied for days on end.

Wheeler-Stallard House Museum

In the restored private residence of Aspen pioneer Jerome B. Wheeler, this museum displays furniture, clothing, toys, and other period pieces collected by the Aspen Historical Society. Docent-led tours provide insights into Wheeler's life, public and private, and offer a keen sense of life in the Roaring Fork Valley before it became a winter playground for the rich and famous. You can also arrange guided walking tours of historic Aspen or pick up a map and take a self-guided tour. The Aspen Historical Society can also recommend and direct you to tours of nearby ghost towns, including Ashcroft and Independence.

The Wheeler-Stallard House Museum, 620 W. Bleeker St., is open daily 1–4 P.M. mid-June to September, and during the ski season (mid-December through mid-April). Admission is $3, and walking tours, which begin at the house, are $10. For more information, phone 970/925-3721.

Aspen Art Museum

Beside the Roaring Fork River and the Rio Grande hiking and biking trail, the Aspen Art Museum displays rotating exhibits by well-known artists from around the country, as well as the work of local artists, many of whom are highly respected and widely acclaimed. A variety of media are represented, from architecture and design art to sculpture and paintings.

With its creekside location and adjacent Rio Grande Park, the museum provides an ideal picnic spot and also offers a free wine-and-cheese reception and gallery tour each Thursday evening at 5:30. The museum, 590 N. Mill, is open Tues.–Sat. 10 A.M.–6 P.M. and Sunday noon–6 P.M. Admission is normally $3, but it's free Thursday 6–8 P.M. and all day Saturday. For more information, phone 970/925-8050.

Institutes and Galleries

In addition to these museums, the Aspen area is home to several academic and environmental institutes, arts centers open to the public, and a score or more of commercial galleries. The **Rocky Mountain Institute** is an experiment in environmentally responsible architecture and lifestyles. The 4,000-square-foot center, entirely solar heated, displays techniques in conserving energy and water. The center is in Snowmass at 1739 Snowmass Road. For information on tours, phone 970/927-3851. The **Aspen Center for Environmental Studies,** on the Roaring Fork River behind the post office, includes a 25-acre wildlife sanctuary and a bird-rehabilitation center, both open to the public. Phone 970/925-5756 for information and hours. The **Anderson Ranch Arts Center,** 5263 Owl Creek Rd. in Snowmass Village, displays works of visiting photographers, painters, woodworkers, and other artists and also offers workshops in various media. An example of the caliber of talent here was a "Winter Landscapes" workshop taught by Galen

Rowell and Robert Glenn Ketchum. For information on touring the center, or on upcoming workshops, phone 970/923-3181.

Commercial galleries in Aspen and Snowmass vary from shops specializing in prehistoric Native American art to places displaying campy art deco and art nouveau, with everything imaginable in between—large-format photography, Southwestern sculpture, 19th-century watercolors, and prints and originals by such names as Picasso, Renoir, Matisse, and Miró.

DOWNHILL SKIING

First, a clarification: there is no *one* Aspen. "Aspen" is actually four separate mountains, all of which—Aspen Mountain (also known as Ajax), Buttermilk, Aspen Highlands, and Snowmass—are owned by the Aspen Skiing Company. To further complicate things, three of the ski areas—Aspen Mountain, Aspen Highlands, and Buttermilk—lie within two miles of the *town* of Aspen. The fourth, Snowmass, is about 12 miles northwest of Aspen at Snowmass Village, not to be confused with the tiny *town* of Snowmass, about halfway back to Carbondale. Got that? Now, the ski areas, one at a time.

Aspen Mountain

First off, Aspen's terrain is designated 30 percent expert, 35 percent advanced, 35 percent intermediate, and 0 percent (!) beginner. That's not to say it should be avoided by all but the most advanced skiers, but this *is* where you'll see the polish, the finesse, the graceful speed—skiers who look like they were born on the mountain (indeed, many virtually were). Rated the fourth-best American ski resort by a 1998 *Mountain Sports and Living* magazine readers' poll, Aspen Mountain is truly one resort that every skier should hit at least once.

As with many European ski resorts, Aspen Mountain's base—the gondola, the lift ticket window, the ski school—is right in town. This is why you see skiers walking down sidewalks with skis ashoulder, and why half of those not carrying skis *are* wearing ski clothing (whether they've been skiing or not). It also creates a problem,

© STEPHEN METZGER

downtown Aspen and Aspen Mountain

though: parking. The relatively few on-street spaces in town are limited to 90 minutes and are closely monitored. Your best bet is to park in the newly built parking garage next to the Aspen Resort Chamber (two blocks north of Main Street off Mill) and then take a free bus to the lifts.

Assuming your first ascent of Aspen Mountain is via gondola (recommended), you'll probably be surprised at how far back, and up, the lift takes you. It seems never to end. In fact, Aspen Mountain's 675 skiable acres are disproportionately lanky compared to other resorts' layouts, and most of the 75 trails are long, narrow, and steep—covering a 3,267-foot vertical drop. In addition to the gondola, Aspen Mountain offers seven other lifts designed to connect the different runs on the top half and lower north side of the mountain.

Buttermilk Mountain

Designed as Aspen's teaching mountain, Buttermilk is divided into three distinct, lift-connected sections. Offering sharp contrast to Aspen Mountain's advanced- and expert-oriented terrain, Buttermilk is geared almost en-

tirely toward beginning and intermediate skiers. Six lifts service 410 acres with 45 trails rated 35 percent beginner, 39 percent intermediate, and 26 percent advanced.

Buttermilk is also much better suited to families than is Aspen Mountain, with lots of wide-open, treeless runs ideal for group cruising, or, after a decent dump, practicing those figure eights. Three-pinners not up to Aspen Mountain can tune their chops on Buttermilk's gentler slopes and take Telemark lessons through the area's ski school.

Snowmass

The Roaring Fork Valley's newest ski area, Snowmass is 12 miles "down valley" from the town of Aspen. Like Buttermilk, Snowmass best suits intermediate skiers and families—the mountain's skiable acres rate 10 percent beginner, 51 percent intermediate, and 39 percent advanced and expert. Twenty-one lifts service 3,000 acres of skiable terrain with a 4,406-foot vertical drop.

In addition, things are a little more laid-back here than they are in town, and Snowmass attracts folks not interested in the pretensions and celebrity of Aspen. In fact, each year Snowmass accounts for about half of all the skiing done at the area's four mountains.

Rated 19th among U.S. ski areas by a *Mountain Sports and Living* reader survey, Snowmass is popular for its long runs, one of which stretches more than four miles, as well as for its child-care facilities and large number of ski-in/ski-out lodges and condominiums.

Aspen Highlands

Of all the Aspen-area ski resorts, Aspen Highlands offers the most even distribution of terrain: 50 percent intermediate, 20 percent beginner, 30 percent advanced and expert, with a vertical drop of 3,635 feet.

Aspen Highlands is on Maroon Creek Road just north of the town of Aspen and the Castle Creek bridge. Situated "upvalley," Aspen Highlands generally gets plenty of snow (an average of 300 inches), and though its snowmaking capabilities are minimal, during seasons of limited snowfall its slopes often stay in better shape than those at Snowmass or Buttermilk. Aspen Highlands has four lifts and 109 trails on 700 acres of skiable terrain.

Alpine Skiing Information

For complete information on Aspen Mountain, Buttermilk, Aspen Highlands, or Snowmass, write the **Aspen Skiing Company,** P.O. Box 1248, Aspen, CO 81612, or phone 970/925-1220 or 800/825-6200. For the company's **snow report,** phone 970/925-1221. Its website is www.skiaspen.com.

CROSS-COUNTRY SKIING

Though Aspen is better known as a mecca of downhill skiing and skiers, the area also offers excellent opportunities for the Nordic skier, with miles and miles of groomed trails and vast unbroken forests and meadows where you can cut your own path. The **Aspen/Snowmass Nordic Trail System** maintains 80 km of trails between the town of Aspen and Snowmass Village. Trailheads dot the southern Roaring Fork Valley, including those at the Aspen Club, Aspen High School, the Aspen Cross-Country Center (22475

W. Hwy. 82; 970/544-9246), and the Snowmass Club Touring Center. Transportation to the trailheads is available on the Roaring Fork Transit Agency's buses. You can get detailed maps of the trail system from the visitor center in the Wheeler Opera House, 328 E. Hyman, or by writing P.O. Box 10815, Aspen, CO 81612, or calling 970/925-2145.

Twelve miles west of Aspen on Maroon Creek Road, the **Ashcroft Ski Touring Center** offers 30 km of groomed trails in the gorgeous Castle Creek Valley. After a day on the trails, return to the center's **Pine Creek Cookhouse,** where you can get a fixed-price gourmet dinner or take a sleigh ride before skiing back to your car. For complete information on ski trails, dinner, and sleigh rides, phone 970/925-1044.

Skiers looking for the ultimate cross-country experience can choose from two of the county's best backcountry trail systems. With difficult trails at high elevations, these systems are not for beginners. Skiers must be accomplished, physically fit athletes, and able to carry heavy packs.

The **10th Mountain Trail Association Hut System** offers European-style hut-to-hut skiing on 300 miles of trails stretching from Aspen to Vail and throughout much of the White River National Forest. On-trail accommodations are provided at 12 huts and lodges three to eight miles apart. The association owns eight rustic huts and maintains four privately owned lodges. Reservations are generally required months in advance. (For a complete description, see Winter Sports under Vail and Beaver Creek in the Northwestern Colorado chapter.) For information, write 1280 Ute Ave., Aspen, CO 81611, 970/925-5775. You can also get trail descriptions and other information from the website at www.huts.org.

The United States Ski Association operates the **Alfred A. Braun Hut System,** the trailhead of which you'll find on Maroon Creek Road near Ashcroft. Each of the six huts accommodates up to 18 skiers (or hikers—the center is open year-round), with a minimum of four per hut. For information, write P.O. Box 7937, Aspen, CO 81612, 970/925-6618. For reservations, phone 970/926-6775.

SOUTHWESTERN

For information on cross-country skiing in the surrounding White River National Forest, stop in at the district office at 806 W. Hallam St., Aspen, or phone 970/925-3445. You can also get information at any of the town's retail shops, including **Ute Mountaineer,** 308 S. Mill, 970/925-2849, and **The Hub of Aspen,** 315 E. Hyman, 970/925-7970. For guided tours, check out **Aspen Alpine Guides,** Box 659, Aspen, CO 81612, 970/925-6618 or 800/643-8621.

OTHER WINTER SPORTS

Snowmobiling

The **T-Lazy-7 Ranch** has become almost an institution in Aspen, with visitors returning year after year. The ranch offers snowmobile tours up into the Maroon Bells backcountry (two-hour rides are $160 for one, $240 for two), as well as rides to ghost towns and historic mining camps; four-hour rides to Independence Pass are ($200–300). You can also take a ride up the back side of Aspen Mountain to meet skiing friends for lunch at the top of the gondola. The T-Lazy-7 also offers sleigh rides and, in the summer, stage-

coach rides. For more information, phone 970/925-4614 or 888/875-6343.

You can also rent snowmobiles or join tours (three-hour or half-day) at **Western Adventures** north of Aspen at Woody Creek. For information, phone 970/923-3337.

Skating, Dogsledding, and Sleigh Rides

Aspen Ice Gardens is a 16,000-square-foot indoor rink at 233 W. Hyman, 970/925-7485. Open year-round, except for April and May, the rink offers instruction, rentals, repair, and sales. The **Silver Circle** outdoor ice rink is at 433 E. Durant, 970/925-6360.

Dogsledding in Aspen goes back to just after World War II, and **Krabloonik Kennels** carries on the tradition. Krabloonik is owned and operated by Iditarod racer Don MacEachen, who named the kennels after the first lead dog he ever raised—Krabloonik means "Big Eyebrows" and is the Eskimo term for "White Man."

Sleds pulled by 13-dog teams take visitors on full- and half-day tours through the Maroon Bells area, beginning at the ranch at 1201 Divide Rd., Snowmass Village, where MacEachen keeps

Take a carriage tour of downtown Aspen—boots by Tony Lama.

more than 300 dogs. Full-day trips include lunch on the trail, and half-day trips include lunch at the center. Prices start at about $210 for a two-hour ride for adults, $150 for kids three to eight (under three not allowed)—including lunch. For information and reservations, phone 970/923-4342 (kennel) or 970/923-3953 (restaurant). You can also get information and make reservations at www.krabloonik.com.

If you're feeling more nostalgic than Yukony, you can also tour the Aspen area by horse-drawn sleigh, with several companies offering tours (over the river and) through the woods, as well as through town. **Aspen Carriage Company,** 970/925-3394, has sleighs and carriages, with scenic and historic tours available. You'll see the rigs parked in town at the corner of Cooper and Galena.

Another longtime favorite for sleigh rides is the **T-Lazy-7 Ranch,** 970/925-7040 or 970/925-4614. Offering Maroon Creek Valley rides ranging from daytime scenic tours to evening dinner rides where you grill your own meat and enjoy live music, the T-Lazy-7 has sleighs that accommodate up to 24 people.

You can also take sleigh rides at **Ashcroft Ski Touring Center,** 970/925-1044 (lunch and dinner rides), and at **Moon Run Ranch,** 970/923-3244. The latter offers afternoon and evening rides with food and live entertainment; the rides are designed specifically for large groups and are available by reservation only.

WHEN THE SNOW MELTS

Aspen's countenance changes considerably when the lifts shut down, when running shoes and golf spikes replace ski boots as the footwear of choice and aloha shirts replace sweaters and parkas. Still, there's a common thread: a youthful vigor and an obsession with the outdoors. Running, rafting, biking, ballooning, hiking, tennis, golf, and all sorts of water sports, from fishing to windsurfing, abound. And for those who get their thrills shopping instead of rock hopping, Aspen's pricy boutiques and specialty shops offer plenty of breathtaking thrills (such as coats that cost as much as Jeep Cherokees).

Hiking

Aspen locals like to say, "You come here for the winter, but you stay for the summer," and indeed, many of Aspen's year-round citizens originally came with plans to spend a season ski bumming and then return to more serious pursuits when the resorts closed down. And the hiking in the area is without doubt one of the reasons folks stick around.

Aspen is literally surrounded by national forest land. The Aspen Ranger District of the White River National Forest alone comprises 260,000 acres and contains three wilderness areas—the Maroon Bells-Snowmass, Collegiate Peaks, and Hunter-Frying Pan regions near the Roaring Fork Valley. This means there's no shortage of excellent hiking in the area—from short nature walks to serious backcountry expeditions.

One of the area's easiest and more popular hikes, the **Rio Grande Trail,** begins where Mill Street crosses the Roaring Fork River. The two-mile trail continues northwest along Cemetery Lane and the river, offering a peaceful stroll and good views of the valley. It's also a popular mountain-bike trail.

The **Braille Trail** is a quarter-mile nature walk along the Roaring Fork River east of Aspen. Blind walkers follow a nylon rope to two dozen stations with braille as well as printed-text explanations. The trailhead and parking lot are on the south side of Highway 82 about 10 miles east of Aspen. For the rough and tumble crowd, try the five-mile **Sunnyside Trail,** which begins near the Slaughterhouse Bridge off the Rio Grande Trail. The 2,000-foot vertical rise (to almost 10,000 feet) is guaranteed to give the old ticker a workout, while affording views of spectacular scenery. And speaking of which: the 1.5-mile-long **Maroon Lake Scenic Trail** follows Maroon Creek to Maroon Lake to a view of Maroon Bells (whew!) and some scenery that will take your breath away. Take Maroon Creek Road about eight miles west of Highway 82 (summertime day-trippers will have to take the shuttle, as the road is closed except to travelers heading into the campgrounds or lodges).

Other nearby trails include the Ute Trail, American Lake Trail, and Hunter Valley Trail.

For complete information on these and other trails, see *Aspen-Snowmass Trails: A Hiking Trail Guide,* by Warren Ohlrich, available in local bookstores and outdoors shops. For information and maps of White River National Forest, stop by the district office at 806 W. Hallam, or phone 970/925-3445. You can also get maps, as well as gear and equipment, at **Ute Mountaineer,** 308 S. Mill, 970/925-2849; **Ute Alpinist,** 605 E. Durant, 970/925-2489; and **Aspen Sports,** 408 E. Cooper, 970/925-6331; and in the Snowmass Center, 970/923-3566.

Aspen Alpine Guides, 970/925-6680, offers guided day hikes and backpacking trips into the Aspen-area backcountry.

Cycling

Not surprisingly, cycling is extremely popular in the Aspen area, and mountain biking especially has caught on big in recent years. Road bikers can take any number of local passes and valley drives, although you need to exercise extreme caution: not only are many of these roads very narrow, some with steep drop-offs, but you've also got to watch out for tourists more interested in sight-seeing than bike-rider seeing.

Roadsters looking for a real workout, with an equally rewarding view, can head up Independence Pass east of Aspen. The 20-mile ride from town to the summit gains 4,000 feet in altitude, and there are excellent photo ops along the way, not only of the valley east of the pass (from the top), but of the tumbling Roaring Fork River (from just a few miles east of Aspen). Castle Creek Road to Ashcroft and Maroon Creek Road to the Maroon Lake trailhead are shorter and less demanding—each is about 10 miles and gains only 1,500 feet. The Maroon Creek Road ride can be especially nice, as it's closed during the summer except to shuttle buses and travelers heading to the campgrounds and lodges, and the lack of traffic is a refreshing respite from the hustle and bustle of town.

Mountain bikers, who have gradually begun to eclipse road bikers in the area, have far more opportunities than their skinny-tire predecessors. First of all, White River National Forest, which surrounds Aspen, is full of old logging and min-ing roads, fire trails, and other areas to explore. In addition, the ski areas themselves now solicit mountain bikers, with access roads and ski runs open for fat-tire exploration, expedition, and exhibition.

One of the more popular is the **Richmond Ridge Trail,** which is accessible either from the gondola at Aspen Mountain or via Aspen Mountain access roads (including Summer Road). Other good rides include the **Rio Grande Trail,** beginning near the post office on Puppy Smith Street, **Owl Creek Trail,** which connects Aspen and Snowmass Village on the west side of Highway 82, and the **Fisherman's Trail** tour north along the Roaring Fork from Aspen to Woody Creek.

For more information on cycling in the Aspen area, stop in at any of the excellent shops, including **Aspen Velo Bike Shop,** 465 N. Mill, 970/925-1495, or **The Hub of Aspen,** 315 E. Hyman, 970/925-7970. These shops, and dozens more in the area, also rent bicycles.

To arrange guided tours, all equipment and transportation provided, contact **Timberline Bicycle Tours,** 970/920-3217; **Aspen Velo,** 970/925-1495; or **Blazing Adventures,** 970/923-4544.

Golf

What better way to spend a warm summer afternoon in the Roaring Fork Valley than strolling about the links, taking in the great views and the crisp mountain air, and feeling the warmth of the high-altitude sun? Of course, the summer afternoon won't be all you'll be spending. Golf is a high-end sport, Aspen's a high-end resort town, and when you put the two together the results are predictable: high-end green fees.

Then again, you probably didn't come to Aspen to cut corners. You came to enjoy yourself. So swing away.

The **Aspen Municipal Golf Course** is a 7,000-yard-plus, 18-hole course across Highway 82 from the turnoff to Maroon Bells. The municipal course, known for its water hazards, offers a number of discounts (twilight play, multiday passes, etc.). Green fees are $35 for nine holes, $65 for 18. For tee times and information, phone 970/925-2145.

The **Snowmass Club Golf Course** is geared toward guests of the Snowmass Lodge but is open to the public on a space-available basis. Designed by Arnold Palmer and Ed Seay, the 18-hole course is part of the large recreation facility that also includes tennis, racquetball, and squash courts, as well as a gym and athletic club with all the luxuries you'd expect in Aspen. Green fees range from about $60 (May 1–June 14 and Sept. 16–closing) to $125, with discounts on twilight play (after 4 P.M.) and for guests staying at affiliated properties. Phone the pro shop at 970/923-3148 for tee times and information.

Tennis

Several private tennis court complexes serve the Aspen-Snowmass area, including the **Aspen Club,** 970/914-8900, and the **Snowmass Club,** 970/923-5600. In addition, the area offers a handful of public courts, though you'll still have to pay $4–5 per hour to use them. You'll find public courts on Maroon Creek Road at Iselin Park and at Aspen Highlands Ski Area, as well as at Aspen Meadows, 25 Meadows Road.

Fishing

Aspen's Roaring Fork Valley is both home to and surrounded by better trout fishing than many people realize. In addition to the two stretches of specially restricted Gold Medal streams, several other rivers and lakes in the Aspen area also offer good fishing—for rainbow, brown, cutthroat, and brook trout, as well as hybrids.

The **Roaring Fork River** flows through the town of Aspen and down the valley to its confluence with the Colorado at Glenwood Springs. The river has a fair amount of public access (respect private property) and, though it gets quite a bit of traffic, can pay off for the patient and savvy angler. The **Frying Pan River,** northeast of Aspen, runs through Ruedi Reservoir to Basalt and is famous for its BIG fish and accessible water. The stretch west of the reservoir is particularly good, with fish topping eight pounds caught regularly. Other streams worth checking out are **Maroon Creek**

and **Castle Creek. Important:** stretches of both the Roaring Fork and the Frying Pan are governed by special regulations, with specific size limits, bait restrictions, and catch-and-release rules. Pick up a copy of the regulations at local sporting-goods stores or from the **Colorado Division of Wildlife,** 6060 N. Broadway, Denver, CO 80216, 970/297-1192.

Several lakes in the area can also provide excellent fishing. In addition to **Ruedi Reservoir** east of Basalt, several smaller, tougher-to-get-to high-country lakes can be rewarding. The best sources for information on where to go when are the local shops, many of which offer guide services as well as top-quality instruction and equipment. Among the outfits with good reputations are **Taylor Creek,** 555 E. Durant, 970/920-1128 (or 970/927-4374 for the store in Basalt); and **Frying Pan Anglers,** 302 Midland (Basalt), 970/927-3441.

For Department of Wildlife fishing reports, phone 303/291-7537.

Camping

Aspen is in the heart of the White River National Forest and literally surrounded by excellent Forest Service campgrounds. And considering how packed the town and valley can get, the campgrounds tend to stay relatively uncrowded. Maybe picnic tables, sooty barbecue grills, and pit toilets are beneath the dignity of the monied noblesse, but I've driven through town on Friday afternoons when the streets were jammed with tourists and plenty of sites were available at nearby campgrounds, particularly those east of town along the upper Roaring Fork.

The following Forest Service campgrounds can be found on

rainbow trout

Highway 82 and the Roaring Fork River between Aspen and Independence Pass; all are quite nice: **Difficult,** 47 sites, five miles from Aspen; **Weller,** 11 sites, nine miles from Aspen; **Lincoln Gulch,** seven sites, 11 miles from Aspen; and **Lostman,** nine sites, 15 miles from Aspen. In addition, there are four campgrounds on Maroon Creek Road: **Silver Bar,** four sites, no trailers; **Silver Bell,** four sites, no trailers; **Silver Queen,** six sites; and **Maroon Lake,** 44 sites.

For complete information on the Forest Service campgrounds in the Aspen area, stop by the Aspen Ranger District Office, 806 W. Hallam, or phone 970/925-3445. For 24-hour recorded information, phone 970/920-1664.

If you're looking to scrub up a bit, the Aspen Recreation Department also has **public showers** for $2 per person at 110 E. Hallam St.—open Mon.–Fri. 8:30 A.M.–6 P.M.. You can also use the public showers at the James E. Moore Pool, on Maroon Creek Road. Cost there is $4.50 per person (includes use of the swimming pool)—open daily 1 P.M.–5:30 P.M.

River Running and Windsurfing

With so many rivers and streams in the area, it will come as no surprise that kayaking and rafting are very popular and that several outfitters capitalize on the quality water by offering a full range of trips. Among the popular nearby rivers are the **Roaring Fork, Colorado, Arkansas** (over Independence Pass from Aspen), and **Crystal** (west of Aspen via Highway 133).

Caution: in the spring and early summer, these rivers swell with snowmelt, and their capriciousness is the stuff of legends. Scores of people, including experienced river rats, have been killed. Check with local authorities, and don't get in the water if you don't know what you're doing.

For guided raft tours, contact **Aspen Whitewater Adventures,** 970/925-5405 or 800/873-8008, or **Blazing Adventures/Paddles,** 970/925-5651 or 800/282-7238.

Windsurfing and skiing seem to go hand in hand somehow—get a group of skiers together, and it's very likely at least a couple of them will talk about spending the "off-season" sailboarding. And though Aspen doesn't offer the thrills of the

Columbia River or the Hawaiian Islands, Aspenites do find places to catch the wind. **Ruedi Reservoir** (east of Basalt) and **Twin Lakes** (east of Aspen via Independence Pass) are among the popular spots.

Horseback Riding

A dozen or so outfitters offer rides into the Aspen mountains and Roaring Fork–area backcountry. You can either rent an animal and explore the areas on your own, or take guided tours, which vary from short, two-hour trips and dinner rides with chow on the trail to multiday pack trips into wilderness areas. Rates usually start at about $30 an hour. The best-known is probably the **T-Lazy-7 Ranch,** whose Maroon Creek Road location provides excellent access to the Maroon Bells valley; for information and reservations, phone 970/925-7040. **Capitol Peak Outfitters,** 554 Valley Rd., Carbondale, 970/963-0211, offers hourly rides from Snowmass Village and half- to seven-day pack trips into the backcountry.

Ballooning

The Roaring Fork Valley sprawls lush and rolling at the base of the towering Elk Mountains and, I imagine, is rather breathtaking from the air. A balloon ride offers the opportunity to see the landscape from an eagle's perspective without the constant in-your-face roar of an airplane engine (though the propane burners on hot-air balloons periodically roar loudly). **Unicorn Balloon Company,** 970/925-5752 or 800/468-2478, offers tours of the area's skies; $175 per person summer, $195 winter, including transportation, food, champagne, and video filming.

Recreation Information

The Aspen Visitors Center in the Wheeler Opera House at 328 E. Hyman has walls of brochures, fliers, pamphlets, and other information on the area's vast recreational opportunities. Another good source is the **Aspen Resort Chamber,** 425 Rio Grande Pl. near the downtown parking garage, 970/925-1940. Two websites, www.aspenchamber.org and www.aspenalive.com, can also provide tips, information, and rates, as well as reservation links.

Warren Ohlrich's *Aspen-Snowmass Guide to Outdoor Activities* is an excellent book of tips on everything from golf to ice climbing, running trails to snowshoeing, as well as maps and phone numbers for further information. The book is available at Aspen-area bookstores.

ACCOMMODATIONS

As you've probably heard, it's not cheap to stay in Aspen. And as in most of Colorado's resort towns, rates for accommodations fluctuate with the season. High season runs from mid-December until just after the first of the year. Rates also go up around holidays and three-day weekends. In spring and fall, when there's not a whole lot going on in town, you can get excellent rates on rooms. In fact, sometimes the lodges and inns offer promotional rates of $40–50 a night.

One of the easiest ways to book a room is through **Aspen Central Reservations,** 425 Rio Grande Place, 970/925-9000 or 888/290-1324, which handles the full range of accommodations in town.

If you're looking for cheap, basic, bargain-basement digs, you might check out lodging in Glenwood Springs, 40 miles back down the canyon (north on Highway 82), where you can usually find a room for under $50.

Note that the following accommodations categories have been collapsed to coincide with Aspen's consistently expensive lodging.

Under $100

Fah-geddit! Well, unless you happen upon some low-season promotional rate. The website, www.stayaspen.com, offers information on bargain lodging and promotions, including what the site calls a "virtual hostel." Might be worth checking out. . . .

$100–250

The **Heatherbed Lodge,** 970/925-7077 (information) or 800/356-6782 (reservations), is a funky old '50s-style ski lodge at 1679 Maroon Creek Rd., directly across the road from the park-

ing to Aspen Highlands and nestled in the pines along Maroon Creek. Heatherbed rates include breakfast and after-ski chili. Right downtown, the **Limelight Lodge,** 228 E. Cooper, 970/925-3035 or 800/433-0832, offers convenience, comfort and (for Aspen) affordable rates. Another popular inn is the **Mountain House Lodge,** 905 E. Hopkins, 970/920-2550, which features a hot tub, large lounge area, a full breakfast in the ski season, and a buffet-style continental breakfast in the summer.

Additional Roaring Fork Valley bed-and-breakfasts that have earned reputations for offering a combination of quiet charm and Aspen luxury include the **Molly Gibson Lodge,** 101 W. Main, 970/925-2580. The 50 units vary from hotel-type rooms to suites with kitchens; almost half have fireplaces. Other amenities include two jacuzzis and a heated outdoor pool. Another Aspen tradition is the **Sardy House,** 128 E. Main, 970/920-2525, a longtime favorite famous for its gourmet breakfasts, high-class decor, and overall elegance.

In Carbondale (27 miles away) is the **Ambiance Inn Bed and Breakfast,** 66 N. 2nd St. (one block off Main), 970/963-3597. Spotlighted in a feature article in the *Rocky Mountain News,* this unassuming little inn offers convenience and down-home comfort in four spacious guest rooms. Three of the four rooms have a private bath, and one has an in-room hot tub.

$250 and Up

The hotel for the ultimate Aspen experience is without doubt the **Hotel Jerome,** 330 E. Main, 970/920-1000 or 800/925-2784. Built in 1889, this gorgeous building has been completely restored and is worth a look around even if you don't plan to stay. The lobby is furnished with plush Victorian-era chairs and sofas, and the bar is a classic place where hip Aspenites rub elbows. Rates at the Hotel Jerome start at about $250 and escalate to over $2,000.

Aspen's most upscale hotel is probably the Aspen Skiing Company-owned **Little Nell,** 675 E. Durant, 970/920-4600. At the base of Aspen Mountain's gondola and offering unabashed

Aspen's Hotel Jerome

opulence and every possible amenity, the hotel has rooms, suites, and "executive apartments."

Other classic Aspen hotels include the **Hotel Lenado,** 200 S. Aspen, 970/925-6246; **Independence Square,** 404 S. Galena, 970/920-2313; and **Hotel Aspen,** 110 W. Main, 970/925-3441.

Camping and RVing

In addition to the many Forest Service campgrounds near Aspen (see Camping, above), the Roaring Fork area offers a handful of privately run, RV-oriented campgrounds. The closest, **Aspen Basalt Campground,** is 18 miles northwest, just west of Basalt; for reservations or information, phone 970/927-3532.

FOOD

There's no shortage of excellent restaurants in Aspen, and many have become institutions of their own—places to see and be seen, and to catch up on all the important local skinny. Thankfully, many of Aspen's restaurants post their menus on the door or an outside window, providing not only a sense of the type of food

and specials but of prices as well. An enjoyable way to spend part of an evening in Aspen, no matter what the season, is strolling about the downtown area "researching" the different dinner houses. In addition, *Aspen Magazine* publishes an Aspen-area *Menu Guide,* which reproduces the menus of scores of the valley's restaurants. The guides are free and available at most hotels and lodges, as well as at many gift shops.

Start Me Up

Whether you're looking for a light breakfast of muffins and espresso or something more filling, you can't go wrong at the **Main Street Bakery and Cafe,** 201 E. Main, 970/925-6446. Try the corned-beef hash, homemade granola, or a breakfast burrito ($4–8). Smaller **Zélé Espresso and Juice Bar,** 121 S. Galena, 970/925-5745, serves excellent gourmet coffees and teas, scones, muffins, and other pastries. It has an intimate, neighborhood ambience and offers three or four outside tables.

Dinner Restaurants

Mexican restaurants are always popular in ski towns—not only for their food, but for their casually festive ambience. Who can resist rehashing the day over a plate of nachos with margaritas or Dos Equis?

As perhaps America's definitive ski town, Aspen claims several restaurants serving first-rate Mexican food. Among them is the **Cantina,** 411 E. Main, 970/925-3663, offering a comfortable, laid-back atmosphere and huge windows looking out on Main Street. Burritos, fajitas, and tamale dinners and other specials run $8–20. Also good is the **Red Onion,** 420 E. Cooper, 970/925-9043, which has been in business since the late 19th century (in different incarnations). Try the burgers, steaks, ribs, or fish, or a salad or pasta special. Open for lunch and dinner daily.

I've had several excellent lunches at the high-profile, '50s-themed **Boogie's Diner,** at the corner of Cooper and Hunter, 970/925-6610. You can sit out on the second-floor patio and quaff a draft beer to wash down your delicious sesame chicken pasta salad ($8–10). Burgers, meat loaf, chicken dishes, and other entrées are $7–16.

Another distinctive and highly recommended Aspen-area restaurant is **Little Annie's Eating House,** 517 E. Hyman, 970/925-1098, where you'll find reasonably priced ($7–20) burgers, salads, ribs, and more—very popular among both tourists and locals.

Uniquely Aspen

Krabloonik, in Snowmass, 970/923-3953, is a restaurant and Yukon-style kennel; the owner keeps 300 sled dogs and regularly competes in the Iditarod. The house specialty is wild game—moose, boar, and elk. Open Wed.–Mon. for lunch (winter only) and dinner. Entrées run $25–50, while the lunch is a fixed-price menu at about $30. **Pine Creek Cookhouse,** at the Ashcroft Touring Center, 970/925-1044, serves gourmet meals to diners who (in winter) arrive after a cross-country ski trek or sleigh ride.

If you're out exploring the Roaring Fork Valley, you couldn't do much better for lunch than the **Woody Creek Tavern** (watch for the signs along Highway 82 north of the turnoff to Snowmass), 970/923-4585. The little roadhouse serves excellent burgers, Mexican food, and salads in a festive and friendly atmosphere. Open daily for lunch and dinner ($6–12; served till 10 P.M.).

Un-Uniquely Aspen

At the Aspen version of the **Hard Rock Cafe,** 210 S. Galena, 970/920-1666, burgers, sandwiches, and salads go for $7–18.

Groceries and Picnic Fixin's

The small **City Market** on East Cooper Avenue is Aspen's grocery store and a sort of social hub as well. The store has neither a salad bar nor deli (unlike most City Markets), but you can pick up sandwich makings and other picnic supplies. **Clark's Market Deli,** 300 N. Mill St., 970/925-8046, and **Charcuturie and Cheese Market,** 520 E. Durant Ave., 970/925-8010, are good places to stop in for take-out deli sandwiches, pasta salads, and soups.

Snowberry's Natural Food Store, next door to City Market at 719 E. Cooper Ave. (downstairs), carries juices, bulk grains, fresh produce, and healthful snacks and other groceries, as well as natural cosmetics, soaps, and toiletries. It also has a juice bar and salad bar.

ENTERTAINMENT

Aspen is both rowdy and sophisticated, and the entertainment options here run the gamut from smoky pool saloons to opera. If you're looking to tear things up a bit, try the **Cooper Street Bar and Restaurant,** 508 E. Cooper Ave., 970/925-7758, an often-raucous local watering hole. In addition, **Whiskey Rocks,** 315 E. Dean (in the St. Regis Hotel), 970/920-3300, books live music regularly, as does the **Wheeler Opera House**—often big-name acts passing through town on otherwise big-venue tours. Past acts at the Wheeler have included Bonnie Raitt and Lyle Lovett. Phone the ticket office at 970/920-5770.

The bar at the **Hotel Jerome,** 330 E. Main, 970/920-1000, is worth a visit, not only for its elegant Victorian decor but also to check the pulse

SOUTHWESTERN

of high-end Aspen society. The **Woody Creek Tavern,** about 10 miles north of Aspen in Woody Creek, is a great place to go for a burger and a beer. Neighbors Hunter Thompson and Don Henley stop in from time to time when in town.

CALENDAR

Detailing Aspen's myriad of cultural and recreational annual events goes far beyond the scope of this book—the town's world-famous affairs might merit a whole book of their own. To find out what's going on, phone or write the **Aspen Chamber Resort Association,** 425 Rio Grande Place, Aspen, CO 81611, 970/925-1940 or 800/262-7736. You can also phone the **Aspen Visitors Center** at 970/925-5656. Once you're here, read the *Aspen Times,* one of the country's best small-town papers, for complete listings of area happenings.

Annual Highlights

Among the highlights of Aspen's annual events: **Wintersköl,** a crazy winter festival featuring everything from a canine fashion show to a ski competition to a pancake breakfast; the *Food and Wine Magazine* **Classic at Aspen,** with chefs, winemakers, and food writers from around the world (early June); **Aspen Music Festival,** with outside concerts varying from chamber music to jazz (late June through August); **Snowmass Hot-Air Balloon Festival**

Aspen's Wheeler Opera House and visitor information center

© STEPHEN METZGER

(late June); and the **Aspen Film Festival** (late September).

SHOPPING

Confirmed shoppers will be in hog heaven in Aspen. Though nothing's cheap here—you'll find "sales" but not many bargains—there are oodles of shops to explore. Among them are jewelry stores emphasizing Southwest and Native American designs; gift shops specializing in bath oils, kitchenry, and woodcarvings; boutiques offering everything from lingerie to fur; and T-shirt and sports-apparel shops around every corner.

Part of the fun of shopping Aspen is simply wandering aimlessly from one shop to the next, wondering where folks get the money to buy that stuff (mink after-ski boots, for example). One of my favorite little shops is **Curious George Collectibles,** 410 E. Hyman Ave., which specializes in collectible Western Americana: ceremonial Native American clothing, including beaded moccasins and leggings, and frontier firearms, including 1880s' Colts and Winchesters. I stopped by one day and saw a matching pair of 18th-century dueling pistols—the same models used by Alexander Hamilton and Aaron Burr.

SERVICES

The main offices of the **Aspen Police Department** and the **Pitkin County Sheriff** are at 506 E. Main Street. Phone the police at 970/920-5400 and the sheriff at 970/920-5300. Phone the **Colorado State Patrol** at 970/945-6198 (Glenwood Springs). The full-service **Aspen Valley Hospital** is at 200 Castle Creek Rd. (Aspen), 970/925-1120.

The Aspen area's two **post offices** are in town at 235 Puppy Smith St., 970/925-7523, and in Snowmass Village at 1106 Kearns Rd., 970/923-4266.

Just Kiddin'

Aspen-area kids' programs vary from day care to weeklong race camps. Snowmass offers **Snow Cubs** for children 18 months to four years, and **Big Burn Bears** (ski instruction) for kids four through kindergarten, as well as evening child care; phone 970/923-1220. At Buttermilk, kids 3–6 can play inside or take ski lessons through **Powder Pandas,** 970/925-6336 or 970/923-3959. Aspen Highlands' **Snowbunnies** offers both day care and lessons; phone 800/525-6200.

Recycling

Pitkin County Drop-Off Sites at the county landfill, Aspen High School, Woody Creek Tavern, and Basalt Library take aluminum, glass, newspaper, plastic, and tin and steel cans. You can also recycle aluminum at the **City Market** at 711 E. Cooper Ave., 970/920-5215.

INFORMATION

A branch of the **Aspen Chamber Resort Association** is right downtown in the Wheeler Opera House, 328 E. Hyman (corner of Mill). You'll find staff to answer questions, as well as scores of brochures and other publications promoting just about everything there is to do in the area. Parking in the area can be tough, but directly in front of the building are several 15-minute spaces reserved for center visitors. Phone the visitor center at 970/925-5656. The chamber's main offices are at 425 Rio Grande Pl.; phone 970/925-1940. For **Aspen Central Reservations,** phone 800/-262-7736. Several Internet sites offer information and reservations services to the Aspen area. Try the chamber's: www.aspenchamber.org.

The **Pitkin County Public Library** is at 120 N. Mill St., 970/925-7124; hours are Mon.–Thurs. 10 A.M.–9 P.M., Fri.–Sat. 10 A.M.–6 P.M., Sunday noon–6 P.M. The **Basalt Regional Library** is at 99 Midland Ave. in Basalt, 970/927-4311.

For **road and weather information** phone 970/945-2221 (Glenwood Springs).

Bookstores

Aspen, which claims one of the most educated citizenries in the country, isn't real big on bookstores. One would expect, as in Boulder, several nooked and crannied holes-in-the-wall with easy chairs for customers, shelves spilling over into disarray, and shopkeepers more interested in reading George Eliot or Joseph Conrad than in designing window displays. But Boulder this is not.

Nonetheless, Aspen does have a couple of bookstores worth checking out. The best is **Explore Booksellers** at 211 E. Main St., 970/925-5338.

Aspen Bookstore, in the Little Nell Hotel at the base of Aspen Mountain, 665 E. Durant, 970/925-7427, also carries travel, Colorado, and self-help books, as well as magazines and a decent selection of oversized art books.

Forest Service Information

For information on White River National Forest, stop by the **Aspen District Office,** 806 W. Hallam, 970/925-3445. You can also write or visit the main offices at 9th and Grand, P.O. Box 948, Glenwood Springs, CO 81602, 970/945-2421.

TRANSPORTATION
Getting There

You can fly commercially directly to Aspen, where the little airport is lined with Lear jets and other personal aircraft. **United Express,**800/241-6522, and **America West,** 800/225-2525, offer daily connecting flights to Denver International Airport. You can also fly to DIA and take a shuttle to Aspen via **Colorado Mountain Express,** 800/525-6363.

Aspen is also easily accessible by car. The most scenic route from Denver is via I-70 to Copper Mountain, south on Highway 91 to Leadville, south on U.S. 24 from Leadville to the Highway 82 junction, then west on Highway 82 over Independence Pass. This route offers absolutely spectacular views and relatively little traffic. However, Independence Pass is closed in the winter, and if you're coming to ski, the only way to get to Aspen is via I-70 to Glenwood Springs and then Highway 82 south to Aspen (40 miles).

Amtrak offers passenger service to Glenwood Springs, where you can either rent a car or hop a Roaring Fork Transit Authority bus. Phone the

Glenwood Springs depot at 970/945-9563 or the central reservations office at 800/872-7245.

Getting Around

Roaring Fork Transit Authority offers free buses around town, and during the ski season it also runs buses from the town of Aspen to Aspen Highlands, Buttermilk, Snowmass, and the cross-country centers. Pick up shuttles at the Rubey Park Bus Station (on Durant between Galena and Mill) and at the shuttle stops throughout town. RFTA buses also serve most of the Roaring Fork Valley, with routes extending north to Glenwood Springs—fee charged for non-City Route rides. Buses depart from the Rubey Park bus station to the different ski areas. For information on schedules and fares, phone 970/925-8484.

Thrifty Car Rental, 970/243-7836, and **Eagle Rent-A-Car,** 970/925-2128, specialize in 4WD skier vehicles. For taxi service, phone **High Mountain Taxi and Limousine,** 970/925-TAXI (925-8294).

A Word about Parking

Because local authorities are encouraging public transportation and discouraging the number of cars in town, parking is a royal pain in the, well, Aspen. The best place to park is the covered Rio Grande Parking Garage at East Bleeker between Mill and Galena. Rates are about a buck an hour or $8 a day. Downtown, parking meters are distributed one to each block, and for your coin you get a receipt (proof of paying) that you put on the dash of your car. Free parking in the residential neighborhoods is restricted to two hours.

Leadville

The highest incorporated town in the United States, Leadville (pop. 3,000; elev. 10,430 feet) lies in a broad mountain valley at the base of Colorado's two tallest peaks, Mt. Elbert (elev. 14,433 feet) and Mt. Massive (elev. 14,421 feet). Once the state's second-largest community, Leadville claims a history firmly rooted in mining. Its stories were written by some of the West's most colorful characters, and its mines yielded some of the world's greatest fortunes—some wisely invested, some squandered.

Though modern Leadville is tame in comparison to the wild days of the late 19th century, when its muddy streets bustled with prospectors and prostitutes, the town still offers excellent views into the past. Tourists can visit a wide range of museums, from the new National Mining Hall of Fame and Museum to the Healy House and Dexter Cabin State Museum to the Matchless Mine (where Tabor made part of his $12 million). In fact, the town is virtually a museum in itself. Stroll the sidewalks of Leadville's main street (Harrison Avenue), which is packed with T-shirt and poster shops, as well as places to pick up everything from postcards to Native American jewelry. Wander into the old Tabor

Opera House, and hike up the little side streets, all the while taking in that thin 10,000-foot air and the indescribably beautiful scenery—there's not much better place to get a feel for what it must have been like to live in a wild Western mining town during the burlesque of Colorado's most important decade.

HISTORY

The story of Leadville is one of the most fascinating in the state, if not the country, and one of the most important in the tapestry of world mining history. It's a story of gold and silver, of rowdy miners determined to strike it rich, of lusty saloons and busy brothels, gambling halls and opera houses, and huge fortunes won and lost, and sometimes won and lost again.

Gold was first discovered in the Leadville area in the spring of 1860, and by that summer, Oro City, as the camp was called, had a population of 5,000. The gold proved particularly difficult to extract, however, and within a couple of years most of the miners had lit out for more promising lodes and the camp was all but abandoned. In 1875, "Uncle Billy" Stevens and his partner, metallurgist A. B. Wood, explored some of the deserted mines and, finding traces of silver, staked new claims. Word soon got out, and Oro City experienced a second rush, though this one on a much smaller scale. When Leadville was incorporated in 1878, postmaster H. A. W. Tabor estimated the population at about 200 people.

Tabor had been part of the Pikes Peak gold rush in 1859, having arrived in Colorado from Vermont with his wife, Augusta, and their son. A stonecutter by trade, Tabor had had little luck in the Colorado gold and silver fields and by the late 1870s had pretty much given up on ever finding the big one. In addition to acting as postmaster, Tabor worked as a storekeeper.

"At Last, Look Vat Ve Found!"

One day, two German shoemakers, George Hook and Auguste Rische, whom Tabor had grubstaked for partial interest in any ore they discovered, helped themselves to a jug of the storekeeper's booze, climbed up a hill, and started digging. What they drunkenly happened upon, almost immediately, was what would later be known as the Little Pittsburg. Almost overnight, Tabor's fortunes from the silver mine totaled $500,000; within a year he had sold his interest in it for $1 million and invested his profits in other lodes. One of them turned out to have been "salted," although digging at the site led to the discovery of the huge Chrysolite lode. More important was Tabor's investment in the famous Matchless silver mine, which would result in his becoming the district's first multimillionaire; his empire would eventually be worth $12 million. The great productivity of the Matchless also led to Leadville's being overrun, again, by prospectors, and by 1880, the town's population had surged to 25,000–60,000, the figure officially reported by the Leadville *Chronicle.*

During the early 1880s, Leadville was a rambunctious town with three breweries, brass bands playing every night along State Street, drunken women driving carriages and "smoking long black cigars," fights, vigilantes, rowdy gambling halls where the mine owners played for huge stakes,

and a general sense of silver-induced frenzy. Mines, and anything remotely resembling one, including simple holes in the ground, were sold and resold at huge profits, often over the course of a single day. One winter a grave-digger hit a silver vein while preparing to bury a body, and the cemetery was immediately staked out—the dead man was left in a snowbank, frozen stiff, until spring.

Meanwhile Tabor had become very much a public figure. He was elected lieutenant governor, built opera houses in both Leadville and Denver, and served for a brief period as a U.S. senator, filling in between Senator Henry M. Teller's appointment as Secretary of the Interior and the election of a new senator 30 days later. Tabor also divorced his wife, Augusta, and in 1883 married Elizabeth McCourt Doe, a Leadville woman with whom he had apparently been trysting for some time.

Leadville and Tabor went into the skids at the same time, and for the same reason: the devaluation of silver. In 1893, panicking investors sold interest in their mines, banks went under, and Tabor's empire crumbled. He died in 1899, the course of his life having run full circle—he was nearly broke his last years and working as a civil servant, as the postmaster in Denver. His last words to "Baby Doe," as his second wife

Horace A. Tabor

came to be known, are reputed to be "Hang on to the Matchless."

One of the strangest chapters in Leadville history was written in the early winter of 1895, when local merchants organized a "Crystal Carnival." They built, according to the WPA guide to Colorado:

> *[a] castellated structure of Norman design [that] covered five acres. [Its ice walls were eight feet thick and 50 feet high and enclosed a] ballroom, a skating rink, a restaurant, peep shows, and curio shops. Frozen into the walls were specimens of ore, produce, and meat; ice and snow statues graced the interior. The palace, visited by thousands, remained open until March 28, 1896, before it melted away.*

"Baby Doe" Tabor went on to become one of Leadville's most well-known citizens, albeit a reclusive and, some say, insane one. Though there were occasional reported sightings of her, she spent more than three decades alone in a tiny cabin beside the mine. She was found in 1935, lying on the floor, her body frozen.

Throughout the first quarter of the 20th century, Leadville continued to produce ore, though in no way approaching the amounts of its heyday. In addition to gold and silver, lead, zinc, manganese, and molybdenum were taken from the district's mines. During Prohibition, moonshiners set up shop in the old shafts, and "Leadville Moon" earned a reputation as one of the best whiskeys in the West.

MUSEUMS

Leadville probably has more museums per square foot, and certainly per capita, than any other town in Colorado. And, with the exception of the Matchless Mine, they are all within an easy walk to the center of town.

Historic Slide Show

Presented by the Leadville Chamber of Commerce, "The Earth Runs Silver—Early Leadville," is a six-projector slide show offering a dramatized glimpse of the area's history, from the gold and silver rushes of the late 19th century to modern restoration and tourism.

Showings take place daily at 10:30 A.M., 11:30 A.M., and 12:30 P.M. in the Fox Theater, 115 W. 6th. Admission is $3 for adults—discounts for seniors and kids. For more information, phone 719/486-3900.

National Mining Hall of Fame and Museum

Examining every aspect of U.S. mining, as well as bits and pieces from around the world, this fascinating museum displays a wide range of exhibits. Highlights include a state-by-state explanation of Western states' ores, production rates, and mining methods, as well as important tools and equipment. Other exhibits include dioramas showing different extraction techniques and surveying methods, a reproduction of a cableway system near Bordeaux, France, and a display of Egyptian mining techniques. The Hall of Fame, in the same building, features plaques dedicated to various pioneers of the industry.

The museum is at 120 W. 9th St., open daily 9 A.M.–5 P.M., weekdays 9 A.M.–3 P.M. Nov.–April. Admission is $4 for adults, $3 for seniors, and $2 for kids. For more information, phone 719/486-1229.

COURTESY OF COLORADO HISTORICAL SOCIETY

Augusta Tabor

the historic Baby Doe Mine, where Baby Doe Tabor was found frozen to death in 1935

Matchless Mine and Baby Doe's Cabin

Up on the hill away from the T-shirt and souvenir shops of Harrison Street, this is an excellent place to get a sense not only of the famous mine but of how Baby Doe spent the second half of her life. Guided tours take you into the mine's entrance, where original heavy equipment still sits. In addition, there's a good display of miners' tools, forged in the blacksmith shop on-site, as it was too expensive to ship them from Denver. The rickety one-room cabin, where the frozen body of Baby Doe was found in 1935, still contains her meager furnishings, and the walls display the last known photos of her.

The mine and cabin are open daily 9 A.M.–5 P.M., Memorial Day through Labor Day. Admission is $4 for adults. To get there, take 7th Street two miles east from downtown. For more information, phone 719/486-3900.

Tabor Opera House

Built in 1879 when Leadville was home to at least 25,000 people, the Tabor Opera House was at one time one of the most elegant buildings in the West. Hosting a wide range of well-known performers, from Harry Houdini and Oscar Wilde to the New York Metropolitan Opera, the Tabor Opera House originally included boutiques, a saloon, and a suite for visiting artists. Private booths were reserved for Tabor and his guests, who entered from the adjacent hotel via a second-floor walkway.

The Tabor Opera House is downtown at 308 Harrison, open daily for self-guided tours Memorial Day through Labor Day 9 A.M.–5:30 P.M.; admission is $4 for adults. For more information, phone the chamber of commerce at 719/486-3900.

Healy House and Dexter Cabin

Offering self-guided tours of an early Leadville boardinghouse and a private residence, this museum shows a side of Leadville history apart from that of the ubiquitous H. A. W. Tabor. The Healy House was built in 1878 by successful St. Louis mining engineer August Meyer and his wife, Emma. Between 1897 and 1902, the structure served as a boardinghouse, primarily for area schoolteachers.

James V. Dexter built the cabin in 1879 as a social club and poker hall. Don't be deceived by

© STEPHEN METZGER

interior of the Tabor Opera House

the cabin's Daniel Booney-like facade; inside it's lavishly furnished, reflecting Dexter's fortune and his passion for quality art and furniture.

The Healy House and Dexter Cabin, 912 Harrison St., are open 10 A.M.–4:30 P.M., daily Memorial Day through Labor Day and weekends only the rest of the year. Admission is $3.50 for adults, $3 for seniors, and $2 for kids 6–12. For information, or to book off-season tours, phone 719/486-0487.

Heritage Museum and Gallery

Offering an in-depth view of Leadville's boom days, the Heritage Museum and Gallery features mining dioramas, historical photos, Victorian furniture, a scale model of the 1896 Leadville Ice Palace, a 10th Mountain Division display, domestic items, and other late-19th-century artifacts. The art gallery diplays rotating exhibits of Colorado artists and craftspeople. The museum is at 9th and Harrison Streets and is open daily 10 A.M.–6 P.M., May through October, with limited hours of operation the rest of the year. Admission is $3.50 for adults, $3 for seniors, and $2 for kids 6–12. For more information, phone 719/486-1878.

OTHER SIGHTS

Leadville, Colorado, and Southern Railroad Company

This narrow-gauge railroad is the highest in the United States, leaving from the Leadville depot and twisting and curving and switching back to its 11,120-foot summit. Both morning and afternoon trips are available. Daily tours Memorial Day through Labor Day, weekends only through fall.

Nonreserved seating is available on a first-come, first-served basis. Fares are $24 adults, $12.50 kids 4–12. For reservations or further information, write Leadville, Colorado, and Southern Railroad Company, 326 E. 7th St., P.O. Box 916, Leadville, CO 80461, or phone 719/486-3936.

Leadville National Fish Hatchery

Established in 1889, the Leadville hatchery raises brook, rainbow, and cutthroat trout for stocking in a wide range of Rocky Mountain waters, including those in national parks and forests and Indian reservations, as well as lakes and streams under state jurisdiction. In addition to viewing hatchery operations, visitors can hike on the one-mile nature trail, where local wildflowers, trees, and other flora are identified. A picnic area is on the property.

To get to the hatchery, go south from Leadville on U.S. 24 for about two miles, then west on Highway 300 (the turnoff is well marked). For hours and information, phone 719/486-0189.

PARKS AND RECREATION

Surrounded by sprawling acres of national forest and some of the state's highest and most impressive peaks, Leadville is as rich in outdoor recre-

ation opportunities as it once was in ore. Though the historic district offers excellent insight into the town's past, the surrounding area offers chances to hike, mountain bike, ski, golf, fish, and sightsee in one of Colorado's most scenic areas.

Cycling

Tourers looking for a place to train for high-altitude competition need look no further than the roads and passes of the Leadville area. Excellent-though-grueling rides include the 60-mile Leadville-to-Aspen route, which winds over Independence Pass (elev. 12,095 feet). The route

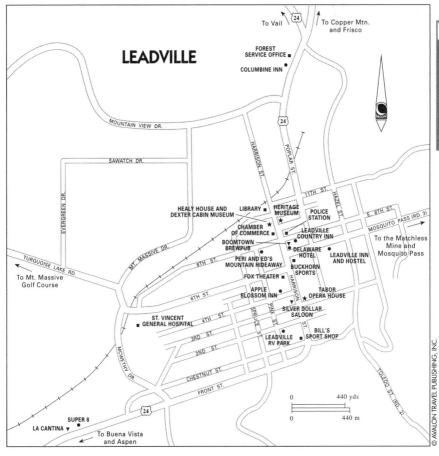

drops south and down out of Leadville, follows the upper Arkansas River, then lifts west past Twin Lakes and over the pass. You could also head north out of Leadville on Highway 91, which will take you over Fremont Pass (elev. 11,320 feet), past the mines, titanic machinery, tailings, and rusting detritus of Climax, and down into Summit County. The stretch along Ten-Mile Creek is beautiful and provides access to Summit County's other bike trails, including the path over Vail Pass (see Cycling under Vail and Beaver Creek in the Northwestern Colorado chapter). From Leadville to the junction of I-70 is about 25 miles.

Excellent trails for mountain biking are also in the region, thanks particularly to the plethora of old mining roads spider-legging over hillsides and along ridges. One good ride is up East 7th Street into the Fryer Hill and Matchless Mine area. The route, first cut in the late 1870s, eventually takes you over Mosquito Pass (elev. 13,186 feet) and then down into South Park, connecting with Highway 9 just north of Fairplay. For maps and information on mountain biking in the Leadville and Lake County area, stop by the chamber of commerce at 809 Harrison Ave., or contact the **Leadville Ranger District Office** of the Forest Service at 2015 N. Poplar St., Leadville, CO 80461, 719/486-0749.

Golf

Claiming to be North America's highest golf course, **Mount Massive Golf Club** (elev. 9,700 feet) is about four miles west of town at the foot of the appropriately named Mt. Massive (elev. 14,421 feet). Though just a nine-hole course, it offers some of the prettiest sights you'll ever see from manicured lawns. No lynx on this links, but deer, bear, elk, and cougar have all been spotted. For tee times and information, phone 719/486-2176.

Hiking

Hiking in the Lake County area varies from a short nature trail at the Leadville National Fish Hatchery to serious and physically demanding backcountry excursions, including at least three

specific marked routes to the top of **Mt. Elbert,** Colorado's highest peak (elev. 14,443 feet). Elevation gains on Mt. Elbert trails are in the 4,000–5,000-foot range, and the trails are four to six miles long. In addition, the **Colorado Trail** passes just west of Leadville.

The most popular route up Mt. Elbert, the **North Trail,** begins from Halfmoon Campground (go west on Highway 300 two miles south of Leadville, then south on Forest Service Road 110 to the campground).

For maps and more information on hiking in the area, stop by the Ranger District Office at 2015 N. Poplar St., Leadville, or phone 719/486-0749. Another excellent source of information is **Bill's Sports Shop,** 225 Harrison St., 719/486-9739 (the store also carries ski equipment and rents, repairs, and sells mountain bikes). In addition, you can get gear and information from **Buckhorn Sporting Goods,** 616 Harrison St., 719/486-3944.

Fishing

Turquoise Lake, three miles west of Leadville via Highway 300, and **Crystal Lakes,** four miles south of town on U.S. 24, are both stocked regularly. Though fished fairly heavily, the waters produce rainbow, brown, and cutthroat trout, as well as kokanee salmon, in decent numbers and occasionally of respectable size. There is also fishing at the Leadville National Fish Hatchery. Stream fishers might want to try **Halfmoon Creek,** west of Leadville off Highway 300.

For licenses and tips on local hot spots, stop in at **Buckhorn Sporting Goods,** 616 Harrison St., 719/486-3944.

Camping

Excellent Forest Service campgrounds surround Leadville, many of which are situated on or near Turquoise Lake. For a complete list, contact the Ranger District Office at 2015 N. Poplar St. in Leadville, or phone 719/486-0749 or 719/486-0752.

To get to the following Turquoise Lake campgrounds, go south from Leadville on U.S. 24 two miles, then west on County Road 37 and watch for the signs. **Baby Doe Camp-**

ground has 50 sites, all RV-suitable, on 13 acres. **Belle of Colorado Campground** is also on the lake, though its 19 sites are designated tents only. Other Turquoise Lake campgrounds include **Dexter** (26 sites), **Father Dyer** (26 sites), **May Queen** (34 sites), and **Silver Dollar** (45 sites).

Halfmoon Campground (24 sites, also maintained by the Forest Service) is on Halfmoon Creek just south of Turquoise Lake.

WINTER SPORTS

Downhill Skiing

One of Colorado's lesser-known downhill resorts, but a favorite of both locals and Denverites wanting to avoid crowds and pretensions, **Ski Cooper** is just 10 miles from Leadville. The mountain offers five lifts serving 400 acres, a 1,200-foot vertical drop (11,700-foot top), and excellent views. Terrain is rated 30 percent beginner, 40 percent intermediate, and 30 percent advanced.

Ski Cooper also offers rentals, lessons, and the "Panda Patrol" children's ski school (for ages 3–5). In addition, advanced skiers can take the "Chicago Ridge" snowcat tour to some first-rate backcountry skiing, either bowls or trees—half- and full-day tours available.

For more information on Ski Cooper, write P.O. Box 896, Leadville, CO 80461, or phone 719/486-3684. For snow conditions, phone 719/486-2277. For more information, check the resort's website: www.skicooper.com.

Cross-Country Skiing

Plenty of Nordic skiing can be found in the Leadville area, from Turquoise to Twin Lakes. **Ski Cooper** features a Nordic center with 35 km of groomed trails, as well as access to the lifts. Nordic and Telemark lessons and rentals are available. For information, phone 719/486-2277. Cross-country trails are also at the **Leadville National Fish Hatchery,** 719/486-1089.

At the Leadville/Lake County Chamber of Commerce, 809 Harrison Ave., you can pick up the *Winter Recreation Trails* guide, which lists

and describes 27 cross-country trails in the immediate area.

Other Winter Activities

Though known to relatively few, the Leadville area is truly a winter wonderland, with plenty to do outside when the mercury falls. Ice fishing is popular, particularly on Turquoise Lake, as is snowmobiling in the high valley's open meadows.

For more information on the area's winter recreation opportunities, stop by the chamber of commerce at 809 Harrison Avenue. For maps and information on skiing or snowmobiling on Forest Service land, contact the Ranger District Office, 2015 N. Poplar St., 719/486-0749.

ACCOMMODATIONS

Leadville offers a wide range of accommodations options, whether you're looking for an intimate bed-and-breakfast hideaway, a historic hotel, or a no-frills motel room, and whether you're just passing through or want digs for the season. For more information on accommodations in the area, contact the **Leadville-Twin Lakes Lodging Association,** 800/748-2057.

Under $50

The **Leadville Inn and Hostel,** 500 E. 7th St., 719/486-9334, (leadvillehostel@amigo.net), has the least expensive rooms in town. You can stay a week for as little as $100.

$50–100

Bed-and-breakfasts in Leadville include the **Leadville Country Inn,** 127 E. 8th St., 800/748-2354, an ornately restored 1880s' mansion and carriage house; **Peri and Ed's Mountain Hideaway,** 201 W. 8th St., 800/933-3715, another restored Victorian right downtown, where you'll find six rooms (some with private baths) and majestic mountain views; and **Apple Blossom Inn,** 120 W. 4th St., 800/982-9279.

You can also stay at the historic **Delaware Hotel,** 700 Harrison Ave., 719/486-1418 or 800/748-2004; rates include breakfast here. Built in 1888, the hotel was at one time one of the

© STEPHEN METZGER

downtown Leadville

classiest in town; after Leadville's fall from grace, it served as a dry goods store and has only recently been restored and reopened for lodging.

Motels in Leadville include the **Columbine Inn and Suites,** 2019 N. Poplar St., 800/954-1110, and the **Super 8,** 1128 S. Hwy. 24, 719/486-3637.

Camping and RVing

In addition to the many Forest Service campgrounds in Leadville and surrounding areas, the **Leadville RV Park,** 135 W. 2nd St., 719/486-3111, is just a block off Harrison Avenue and offers 28 full-service RV sites. **Sugar Loafin'** is another privately owned campground with RV hookups and tent sites, also offering gold panning. To get there, take U.S. 24 south to mile marker 177, and go three miles west on County Road 4. For information and reservations, phone 719/486-1031.

FOOD

Start your day with a latte and a scone at the **Cloud City Coffee House** in the historic Tabor Grand Atrium, 711 Harrison Ave., 719/486-

1317. A favorite for Mexican and New Mexican food is **La Cantina,** a mile south of town on U.S. 24, 719/486-9021. La Cantina features homemade tamales and tortillas, as well as stuffed sopaipillas and the wonderful green chili of the Southwest ($5–10). The recently opened **Boomtown Brewpub,** 115 E. 8th St., 719/486-8297, has already gained a reputation for good alehouse grub at reasonable prices ($7–14). The **Silver Dollar Saloon,** 315 Harrison Ave., 719/486-9914, decorated with historic photos and Western artifacts, is a great place for a cold one, a burger, and a sense that you never left the 19th century. (Caution: high cigarette-smoke level at the Silver Dollar.)

CALENDAR

Leadville's annual calendar isn't exactly packed back-to-back with events, but those that are scheduled tend to be big, rowdy, and well known. On weekends in late June and early July, the city hosts the **Oro City Festival,** which re-creates Leadville/Oro City's boom days. Visitors can pan for gold, sample frontier "grub," listen to plenty of good old-fashioned mountain music, and just generally cut loose in the manner of the town's founding rowdies, miners, painted ladies, and entrepreneurs. The event is sponsored by Colorado Mountain College (Timberline Campus) and takes place just south of downtown. For information, phone the college at 719/486-2015, or contact the chamber of commerce at 719/486-3900.

Another Leadville classic is **Boom Days** in early August, which includes a parade, food, music, drilling competitions, and the famous **International Pack Burro Race,** in which participants—teams of burros and humans—haul, er, ass to the top of Mosquito Pass and back to Leadville.

The **Leadville Trail 100** (mid-August) is America's highest 100-mile footrace (9,200 to 12,600 feet). Following back roads and trails deep into the woods, the course is famous among distance runners around the world as one of the most grueling.

For more information on Leadville's annual events, contact the chamber of commerce, 719/486-3900.

SERVICES

Offices of the **Leadville Police Department** are downtown across from the chamber of commerce at 800 Harrison Ave., 719/486-1365. Phone the **Lake County Sheriff** at 719/486-1249. Leadville's **St. Vincent General Hospital** has 24-hour emergency service and is at West 4th and Washington Streets, 719/486-0230. The Leadville **post office** is at 130 W. 5th St., 719/486-1667.

Recycling

You can recycle aluminum at the **Safeway** on the north end of town and at the **Coors warehouse.**

INFORMATION

Begin your visit to Leadville at the **chamber of commerce,** 809 Harrison Avenue. Pick up maps, brochures, and other information on things to do and see in the area. You can also buy tickets for the multimedia historical presentation shown next door. Write the chamber at 809 Harrison Ave., Leadville, CO 80461, or phone 719/486-3900. The chamber's website, at www.leadvilleusa.com, has lots of information on the area.

The Book Mine, 502 Harrison, 719/486-2866, sells books on local history and outdoor activities and also carries maps. The Lake County **public library** is at 1115 Harrison Ave., 719/486-0569.

South of Leadville

U.S. 24 drops almost due south out of Leadville, slicing through the beautiful Arkansas River Valley and following the tracks of the Denver and Rio Grande Western Railroad. Probably the single best place in the state to see Colorado's wealth of towering peaks, this route affords stunning—somehow humbling, even—views of the majestic Collegiate Range, a north-south formation of "14ers" paralleling the highway from the turnoff to Independence Pass to Salida.

In addition to Mt. Harvard (elev. 14,420 feet), Mt. Columbia (elev. 14,073 feet), Mt. Yale (elev. 14,196 feet), Mt. Princeton (elev. 14,197 feet), and Mt. Oxford (elev. 14,153 feet), the range includes at least seven other peaks over 14,000 feet. There are several places to pull your car off the road to take pictures or simply to enjoy the commanding views.

Just north of Salida, U.S. 24 forks: you can either veer southeast for Salida, then catch U.S. 50 east for Royal Gorge and Cañon City, or you can continue south on U.S. 285, which passes through Poncha Springs, climbs over Poncha Pass (elev. 9,010 feet), and then beelines through the San Luis Valley and Alamosa before dropping into Santa Fe, New Mexico.

TWIN LAKES AREA

About 12 miles south of Leadville is the junction with Highway 82, which connects the Arkansas River Valley with Aspen via Independence Pass

Independence Pass between Leadville and Aspen is closed in the winter.

(12,095 feet; closed in winter). South of the road are the two Twin Lakes, home to some of the largest trout in the state; patient Mackinaw anglers have taken 30-pounders. For those more interested in fight than weight, Twin Lakes are also regularly stocked with rainbow and cutthroat trout. You'll find several boat ramps, as well as lakeside picnic areas.

If you feel like holing up for a while, the lakes also offer a handful of very nice Forest Service campgrounds, and the area's moderately remote location keeps them from filling up as quickly as do many of the more easily accessible campgrounds. **Lakeview Campground** is at the east end of the lower lake, with 59 tent and RV sites (flush toilets). Other Twin Lakes campgrounds include **Parry Peak** (26 sites), **Twin Peaks** (37 sites), and **White Star** (64 sites). None of the Twin Lakes Forest Service campgrounds has showers. For information, phone the **Leadville District Office** of San Isabel National Forest at 719/486-0752 or 719/486-0749, or the Pueblo headquarters at 719/545-8737.

The **Twin Lakes Nordic Inn** ($50–100— some rooms with shared baths) offers lodging in a restored 19th-century stagecoach stop and brothel—rooms are furnished with feather beds and antiques. The inn also has a restaurant serving German and American food, and a cross-country ski center (rentals available). For reservations and information, write Twin Lakes Nordic Inn, Twin Lakes, CO 81251, or phone 719/486-1830 or 800/626-7812.

BUENA VISTA

The name of this town is no lie—this area offers some of the prettiest views in the Rockies (those who know Spanish will cringe when they hear the local pronunciation: BYOO-na VISS-ta, not BWAY-na VEES-ta).

Lying in the rich, green Upper Arkansas River Valley, at the confluence of Cottonwood Creek and the Arkansas River, Buena Vista (pop. 2,075; elev. 7,954 feet) is surrounded by massive mountains, affording views that nearly take your breath away. West of town, Mt. Yale and Mt. Princeton rise more than 6,000 feet from the valley floor to their 14,000-foot-plus peaks, providing the town with a constant reminder of nature's power and beauty. And when the sun of a late afternoon washes over the mountains' flanks, and the mist of a distant rainstorm softens their far ridge lines, well, it's almost enough to make a Believer out of you.

Silver miners founded Buena Vista in 1879, establishing it as the seat of Chaffee County the following year when they absconded with county records that had been stashed in a brewery in Granite 20 miles upriver. In 1881, an ore-sampling plant and smelter were built in Buena Vista, attracting large numbers of laborers, and through the 1880s the town was notorious throughout the West for its rowdy dance halls, gambling parlors, and brothels.

Today, Buena Vista's fortunes lie in tourism. Billing itself the "Whitewater Capital of Colorado," Buena Vista each summer attracts tens of thousands of visitors who come to sample the wide variety of runnable river water, from long stretches of calm water to nasty narrows and Class III, IV, and V rapids.

Buena Vista Heritage Museum

This four-room historical museum on the east end of Main Street (at 511) features a variety of displays spanning a range of interests. Railroad buffs will dig the miniature reconstruction of the Upper Arkansas River Valley and the working model of the three railroads that served the area in the late 19th century. One of the rooms is devoted to mining and minerals, while others display clothing and domestic utensils from the 1880s through the 1920s, as well as historical photos.

The Buena Vista Heritage Museum is open daily 9 A.M.–5 P.M., Memorial Day through Labor Day. Admission is $2 for adults and $1 for seniors. For more information, phone 719/395-8458.

City Parks

A shady lawn area on U.S. 24 behind the chamber of commerce is perfect for picnicking. You'll also find picnic tables, lawns, and shade trees at the small city park at the corner of U.S. 24 and Main Street—kids can fish in the small lake.

River Running

This is modern Buena Vista's raison d'être and pretty much defines the town during the sum-

mer. Several rafting companies offer a wide range of trips on the Arkansas River, from no-experience-required sightseeing tours to serious trips requiring not only previous experience but top physical ability and strength as well. The following Buena Vista-based outfits are well established and have good reputations: **American Adventure Expeditions,** 719/395-2409 or 800/288-0675; **Buffalo Joe River Trips,** 719/395-8757 or 800/356-7984; **Four Corners Rafting,** 719/395-4137 or 800/332-7238; **River Runners,** 710/539-2144 or 800/525-2081; and **Wilderness Aware,** 719/395-2112 or 800/462-7238.

If you'd rather watch than ride, one of the best places to view white-water rafters is an observation deck at **Five Points Arkansas Headwaters Picnic Area,** west of Salida on U.S. 50 about eight miles east of Royal Gorge.

Hiking

You could pretty much head out in any direction from Buena Vista and, being careful to avoid private property, find yourself in primo hiking country. If you feel like gaining some altitude, head west 12 miles on County Road 306 from the stoplight in downtown Buena Vista to the Denny Creek trailhead. From there, a four-mile trail leads to the top of Mt. Yale (an elevation gain of 4,300 feet).

Another approach to Mt. Yale is just a few miles north; the trail circles south from the trailhead up to a saddle, where you can either turn

the Buena Vista Heritage Museum

© STEPHEN METZGER

around or head on up to the peak. It's a four-mile hike to the saddle (elevation gain: 2,600 feet), six to the peak (gain: 4,900 feet). To get to the trailhead, go north three blocks from the light in downtown Buena Vista, and turn left on Crossman (County Road 350). Go west two miles, until you reach County Road 361, and turn right. After one mile, turn left on County Road 365, and look for the trailhead about three miles up the road on the left.

For additional information on hiking in the Buena Vista area, contact the **Salida Ranger District Office** at 325 W. Rainbow Blvd., Salida, or phone 719/539-3591.

You can also get information, as well as outdoor clothing and gear, at **The Trailhead,** 707 N. U.S. Hwy. 24, 719/395-8001.

Mountain Biking

Any area with this much excellent hiking will no doubt afford good mountain-biking opportunities as well. For maps and information on logging roads in the area, as well as single-track trails, contact the Salida Ranger District Office (see Hiking, above). For maps and information, stop by **Otero Cyclery,** 108 F St. in Salida, 719/539-6704. In addition, several of Buena Vista's rafting companies are "crossing over" and offering mountain bike tours, varying from half- and full-day outings to combination "pedal-and-paddle" trips. Both **American Adventure Expeditions,** 719/395-2409 or 800/288-0675, and **Buffalo Joe,** 719/395-8757 or 800/356-7984, can arrange guided tours that include meals, bike, and helmet rental.

Accommodations

A small resort town just a few blocks long, with a motel on nearly every one, Buena Vista often fills up in the evenings with visitors and passers-through—especially in the summer, when tourists need dry beds after spending a day on the river, and cross-country travelers need soft beds before heading back out on the trail in the morning. The following all offer doubles at the upper end of the $50–100 range.

The **Alpine Lodge,** 12845 U.S. Hwy. 24, 719/395-2415 or 888/322-4224, and the **Vista Inn,** 733 U.S. Hwy. 24, 719/395-8009, are classic motels with large comfortable rooms and proximity to town.

The **Adobe Inn Bed and Breakfast,** 303 N. U.S. Hwy. 24, 719/395-6340, is a small Southwest-style inn decorated with Mexican and Southwestern furniture and art. The inn serves a large breakfast that shows a distinct south-of-the-border influence—green chiles, sausage, eggs, Mexican hot chocolate, and the like. *¡Muy sabroso!* Just southwest of town, right on the Arkansas River, the **Blue Sky Inn Bed and Breakfast,** 719 Arizona St., 719/395-8862, is a nice, quiet home in the country. Two rooms only.

Other options include a new **Super 8** in Salida, 530 N. U.S. Hwy. 24, 719/395-2245, and **Mt. Princeton RV Park,** an RV camp a mile north of town, 719/395-6206.

Food

You'll find a handful of good restaurants in Buena Vista, ranging from Italian to Asian to Mexican, as well as down-home American. For your pre-rafting caffeine fix, check out **Bongo Billy's High Country Coffees,** 713 S. U.S. Hwy. 24, 719/395-2634, which prescribes espressos and pastries. It's also open for lunch, serving homemade soups, sandwiches, and salads. Also recommended is **Casa del Sol,** 313 N. U.S. Hwy. 24, 719/395-8810, which offers higher-end Mexican food, including Mexican-style scampi and steak ($10–18).

Entertainment

This is also a town full of river rats who need to unwind after spending their days guiding tourists downriver in rafts. And there are a couple of bars where you might stumble on some action. The **Blue Parrot** at 304 E. Main Street is usually packed with locals pounding beers; also on Main, between the highway and the Blue Parrot, the **Lariat** (whose motto is "We sell and service hangovers"), 206 E. Main, seems to cater to more serious drinkers. Live music Saturday night.

Services

The offices of the **Buena Vista Police Department** are at 101 Park Ave.; phone 719/395-2451 (in emergencies, phone 719/395-8098). The nearest hospital is the **Heart of the Rockies Regional Medical Center,** 448 E. 1st St., Salida, 719/539-6661. The Buena Vista **post office** is at 100 Park Lane, 719/395-2445.

You can recycle aluminum at the **Circle Super Food Center,** 428 U.S. Hwy. 24.

Information

The **Buena Vista Chamber of Commerce** is in the center of town on U.S. 24 and offers lots of information on things do and see in the area, as well as on places to eat and sleep. Stop in for brochures or to ask questions of the staff. Phone the offices at 719/395-6612. A good bet for books on the area, as well as the rest of Colorado, is **Creekside Books and Art,** at 300 Cedar (corner of Railroad), 719/395-6416; open Mon.–Sat. 10 A.M.–6 P.M.

Another good source for local information is the weekly *Chaffee County Times.* In addition to running local news and listing events, the paper focuses on outdoor sports—watch particularly for discussions of nearby hiking trails. The paper costs $.35 in racks throughout Chaffee County. For subscription information, phone 719/395-8621. The Buena Vista **public library** is at 131 Linderman, 719/395-8700.

SALIDA

Salida (pop. 5,200; elev. 7,036 feet) was founded in 1880 as a division point on the Denver and Rio Grande Railroad, although for years prior the area served as a stopping point for travelers passing through the mountains via the Arkansas River Valley. Throughout the late 19th century, Salida, like Buena Vista, its sister town upriver, had a reputation for rowdy, shoot-'em-up streets, and saloons and brothels famous throughout the Rockies. The railroad based its maintenance and repair operations in Salida into the second half of the 20th century.

Mount Shavano (elev. 14,229 feet), about 14 miles northwest of Salida (Sa-LIE-da), is the town's dominant landmark, named for the Ute Chief Shavano. In the spring, the mountain's melting snow is said to take the form of

the "Angel of Shavano," who appeared to the Ute chief as he prayed for his dying friend, trader Jim Beckwourth, founder of the town of Pueblo.

Today, motels and fast-food joints surround a quiet, narrow-streeted historic downtown area defined in part by antique shops, jewelers, and old taverns. Salida's definition is completed by the focus on the Arkansas River, running along the east side of town, and the many rafting and kayaking companies offering trips to tourists.

Salida Museum

Adjacent to the chamber of commerce on U.S. 50/Rainbow Boulevard (west side of town), this small historical museum displays a variety of Native American and pioneer artifacts from the Salida-Arkansas Valley area, with exhibits highlighting the region's mining and railroad histories. The museum is open daily, 10 A.M.–4 P.M. Memorial Day through Labor Day. For more information, phone the Heart of the Rockies chamber of commerce at 719/539-2068.

Parks

Salida is a true gateway to some of Colorado's best recreation areas and activities. The Arkansas River, one of the best streams for white-water rafting in the state, flows right through town, south from Leadville and then east toward Royal Gorge. To the northwest of town is the Collegiate Range and Colorado's biggest concentration of "14ers"—excellent hiking, climbing, and cross-country skiing. Also, Salida's surrounded on three sides by national forest—Pike to the north and San Isabel to the south and west. In addition, Gunnison and Rio Grande National Forests sprawl through Saguache County to the southwest of Salida, offering more camping areas and backcountry to explore.

City parks include **Riverside Park,** on the Arkansas River downtown at 1st and E Streets. The park has nice lawns and shady cottonwoods and offers good fishing and picnicking, as well as a place to watch rafts go by. **Alpine Park,** a neighborhood park at the corner of 4th and F Streets, has picnic tables, a playground, and a large lawn. There's also a small park with a playground and tennis courts adjacent to the chamber of commerce.

River Running

Like Buena Vista, Salida is a paradise for river rats, offering an exceptional base camp for a range of waters. Brown's Canyon in the Arkansas River Valley to the north is famous for its Class III and IV rapids. To the east, the Arkansas cuts through the mountains at Royal Gorge, sheer cliffs rising 1,200 feet from the riverbed. Stretching along a 148-mile section of this river lies **Arkansas Headwaters State Recreation Area,** which has established a number of campgrounds, kayak and raft put-ins, picnic facilities, and hiking trails for use by the public. You can get a guide and map to the area by writing P.O. Box 126, Salida, CO 81201, or by calling 719/539-7289. You can also get information, as well as new and rental equipment, at **Headwaters,** 228 F St., 719/539-4506.

In addition, several private companies offer a range of river trips, with one to suit just about every budget, desire, and ability. **Bill Dvorak's Kayak and Rafting Expeditions,** based in Nathrop (about 18 miles north of Salida), books half- to 17-day trips not only on the Arkansas but on rivers throughout Colorado, Idaho, New Mexico, and Utah, as well as Hawaii, New Zealand, Australia, and Mexico. Dvorak's also offers fishing, mountain biking, and pack trips. For its catalog, write 17921-B U.S. Hwy. 285, Nathrop, CO 81236, or phone 719/539-6851 or 800/824-3795. Other rafting companies based in the Salida area include **American Adventure Expeditions,** 719/539-2409; and **River Runners,** 719/539-2144 or 800/525-2081.

Hot Springs

Salida Hot Springs, Colorado's largest indoor hot-springs pool, is next to the chamber of commerce building at U.S. 50 and Rainbow Boulevard. The pools were built in 1937 by the WPA. You'll find a lap pool, wading pool, and private tubs. Salida Hot Springs is open year-round, but hours vary. For times and information, phone 719/539-6738.

Mt. Princeton Hot Springs is between Salida and Buena Vista, five miles west of Nathrop. In off-and-on operation since the late 19th century, the hot springs, lodge, and restaurant are very popular with locals and passers-through alike. In addition to three swimming pools and several private tubs, there are rock-lined pools on Chalk Creek below the lodge. For reservations or information, write 15870 County Rd. 162, Nathrop, CO 81236, or phone 719/395-2447 or 888/395-7799.

Skiing

Just west of Monarch Pass, about 15 miles west of Salida on U.S. 50, **Monarch Ski Area** offers a low-key, family-oriented alpine resort atmosphere with some of the best skiing in the Rockies (see Monarch Pass, below).

Golf

Salida Municipal Golf Course is a nine-hole course open year-round. For tee times and information, phone 719/539-6373.

Accommodations

Most lodging in Salida will run $50–100 for doubles, with the more recommended places at the higher end. The following are all good bets.

A "motel row" on U.S. 50 on the west side of town includes **Best Western Colorado Lodge,** 352 W. Rainbow Blvd., 719/539-2514; **Super 8 Motel,** 525 W. Rainbow Blvd., 719/539-6689, with an indoor pool and hot tub; and **Holiday Inn Express,** 7400 U.S. Hwy. 50, 719/539-8500.

Motels on the east side of town include **Circle R Motel,** 304 E. Rainbow Blvd., 719/539-6296; and **Days Inn,** 407 E. U.S. Hwy. 50, 719/539-6651.

In the past four or five years, Salida has seen a marked increase in the number of bed-and-breakfast inns, many of which accommodate folks in the area for the white-water rafting. Bed-and-breakfast lodging in Salida usually runs about $80–120 for two. The **River Run Inn,** 8495 County Rd. 160, 719/539-3818, is a bed-and-breakfast in a three-story brick country home built in 1892. Situated on the west bank of the Arkansas River, the cozy little lodge offers excellent mountain views and a peaceful escape from the demands of modern life—eight rooms (some with private baths, some shared).

The **Century House,** 401 E. 1st St., 719/539-7064, in downtown Salida, has four guest rooms in a restored Victorian, and the **Thomas House,** 307 E. 1st St., 719/539-7104, built in 1888 to house railroad workers, today offers five rooms to visitors. The **Tudor Rose,** 6720 Paradise Rd. (Box 89), 719/539-2002 or 800/379-0899, is just south of town and sits on 37 sprawling acres, with horse stabling and rentals available.

Heart of the Rockies RV and Tent Campground, 719/539-4051 or 800/496-2245, is on U.S. 50 (10 miles west of Salida) and has 45 RV sites, 20 tent sites, pool, playground, and excellent access to rafting, horseback riding, and sightseeing tours.

Food

A great place to head for a pre-raft-trip breakfast—whether a cup of coffee and a muffin or a full-fledged eggs-and-the-works meal—is the **First Street Cafe,** 137 E. 1st St., 719/539-4759. In the historic downtown section of Salida, the building was constructed in the late 19th century and has served as a boardinghouse, barber shop, and Ford auto garage. The café today is hipper (less smoky, for example) than most small-town joints and serves several vegetarian specials (stir-fry, etc.) in addition to traditional fare. Very reasonably priced. The First Street Cafe is also open for lunch and dinner. The **Il Vicino Wood Oven Pizza and Brewery,** 136 E. 2nd, 719/539-5219, is establishing quite a reputation. Locals recommend the pesto pizzas, calzones, and lasagna, not to mention the exceptional beers brewed on-site. Entrées run $6–10. Open daily till 11:30 P.M.

Entertainment

Check out the **Victoria Tavern,** 143 N. F St., 719/539-9003, where most nights of the week locals pound beers and listen to live music.

Calendar

The **FIBArk Boat Races** in mid-June kick off Salida's summer white-water season (FIBArk =

First in Boats on the Arkansas). In addition to a 26-mile kayak and raft race, the four-day event features footraces, novelty races (bed races, for example), a pancake breakfast, and a parade. A couple of weeks later, the town sponsors an "old-fashioned Fourth of July" with music, street dancing, a chili cook-off, and fireworks. In late summer (beginning early July), the **Aspen-Salida Music Festival** is a series of concerts featuring classical ensembles from the world-famous Aspen concert series.

For more information on these and other Salida events, contact the Heart of the Rockies Chamber of Commerce.

Services

The offices of the **Salida Police Department** and **Chaffee County Sheriff** are at 217 E. 3rd St., 719/539-2596. Phone the **State Patrol** at 719/275-0015 (Cañon City). **Heart of the Rockies Regional Medical Center** is at 448 E. 1st St., 719/539-6661. The Salida **post office** is on the corner of 3rd and D Streets.

Recycle aluminum at the **Safeway,** 232 G St., and at **Wal-Mart,** 201 E. Rainbow Boulevard.

Information

The **Heart of the Rockies Chamber of Commerce** is a good place to get information not only on Salida but on the wealth of recreational opportunities available in the Arkansas River Valley. Offices are at 406 W. Rainbow Blvd. (U.S. 50), 719/539-2068. Lodging and dining and other information about Salida is available at www.fourteenernet.com/salida.

For information on camping, hiking, and other national forest activities, contact the **Salida Ranger District Office** of the Forest Service, 230 W. 16th St., 719/539-3591.

For **road and weather information,** phone 719/539-6688 or 719/275-1637 (Cañon City).

U.S. 50 WEST

U.S. 50 continues west from Salida, connecting the Arkansas River Valley with Gunnison and Montrose. In Montrose, the highway doglegs north, joining U.S. 550 and ribboning up between the Uncompahgre Plateau and Grand Mesa through Delta to Grand Junction. The Salida-to-Gunnison section of U.S. 50 is particularly scenic, rising into Gunnison National Forest, lifting over Monarch Pass, then following Tomichi Creek. Along the way you'll find several Forest Service roads—some paved, some gravel—that lead to campgrounds and provide access to backcountry. For information on camping in Gunnison National Forest, contact the main office at 2250 U.S. Hwy. 50, Delta, CO 81416, 970/874-7691, or the Ranger District Office, 216 N. Colorado, Gunnison, CO 81230, 970/641-0471.

Poncha Springs

Five miles west of Salida, the little junction town of Poncha Springs has a couple of motels and cafés, including the **Poncha Truck Stop,** a classic little coffee shop/diner open at 6 A.M. daily. In addition to excellent breakfasts (burritos, steak and eggs, etc.), the place serves lunch and dinner (Mexican food, steak, and fried chicken), as well as the monstrous "Alaska burger." There's also a small gift shop and bookstore, as well as public showers for a small fee. Rooms are available in Poncha Springs at the **Jackson Hotel,** built in 1878 as a stage stop; the claim is that Jesse James, Billy the Kid, and Teddy Roosevelt all stayed here.

Monarch Pass

U.S. 50 crosses the Continental Divide at Monarch Pass (elev. 11,312 feet). One of the highest and most scenic highway summits in the United States, the pass affords excellent views and photo ops. To the south are the Sangre de Cristo and San Juan Mountains, both ranges continu-

ing across the border into northern New Mexico; to the north are the Ruby Mountains and the towering peaks of the Collegiate Range, several over 14,000 feet. In fact, from Monarch Pass you can see at least a dozen of Colorado's "14ers."

If the view from the roadside isn't enough, you can take the **Monarch Aerial Tram** to almost 12,000 feet. At the top is an enclosed observation tower, from which you'll have one of the best views in the Rockies. Maps and telescopes help you orient yourself and identify distant peaks. The tram is open daily 9 A.M.–4 P.M., mid-May through mid-October. For more information, phone 719/539-4789.

Monarch Ski Area, one of Colorado's classic off-the-beaten-path ski areas, is a favorite among locals, who are hip to its low-key atmosphere, relatively low prices, and uncrowded slopes. In addition, the resort's 10,800-foot base guarantees that its 350 average inches of snowfall are as fluffy as the downy flake in a Robert Frost poem—the stuff that makes converts out of pagan powder hounds.

With five lifts on 670 acres of terrrain, Monarch's 1,170-foot vertical drop offers good skiing for just about every ability level. The trails are designated 21 percent beginner, 37 percent intermediate, and 42 percent advanced. Instruction and rentals are available, and though there is no on-site lodging, you can stay down the road at the **Monarch Lodge,** 719/539-2581 or 800/332-3668, where you'll find a full-service restaurant, indoor swimming pool, jacuzzi, exercise rooms, and many more amenities.

For more information on Monarch Ski Area, phone 719/539-3573 or 888/996-7669. For snow conditions, phone 800/228-7943. The resort's website is at www.skimonarch.com.

Gunnison and Vicinity

Gunnison (pop. 5,800; elev. 7,700 feet) lies in the broad Gunnison River Valley about midway between Montrose and Salida. Home of Western State College and center for some of Colorado's finest recreation, Gunnison is a youthful and outdoor-oriented town whose roots are in ranching and mining.

Seat of Gunnison County, Gunnison has long served as a trade center for many of the smaller communities in the surrounding area. Today, the town's economy relies largely on the tourism industry and education for its stability: tourism brings in roughly $35 million annually and education $26 million; ranching brings in another $8 million.

Though Gunnison claims the sun shines almost every day, it still manages to get damn cold in the winter. The cold is due largely to its valley location: average temperatures in town are generally at least several degrees lower than in nearby towns such as Crested Butte, which lies at a higher elevation but is nestled against the mountainside. Gunnison has frequently recorded the coldest temperature in the nation.

History

The first nonnative people to explore the Gunnison area were probably those in the Escalante-Dominguez party, who in 1776 followed the Gunnison River west in their search for an overland route connecting the missions of Santa Fe, New Mexico, and Monterey, California. During the early and mid-19th century, the region was trapped and hunted by mountain men who would trade their furs at Taos and Bent's Fort.

On Sept. 6, 1853, Captain John W. Gunnison, a government surveyor, and his party camped along the Gunnison River near present-day Gunnison after having crossed the mountains in search of a transcontinental railroad route. The Gunnison party continued west into Utah, following roughly what is today the route of U.S. 50. On October 25, while looking for a place to hole up for the approaching winter, the group was attacked by Native Americans, and Gunnison and all but four of his men were killed.

In the early 1860s, prospectors began to arrive in the Gunnison area, and in 1869, the region's Utes were removed to the Los Piños Indian Agency, clearing the valley for white settlement. It wasn't until the mid-1870s, though, that farmers and ranchers moved into the region in significant numbers. In 1874, Dr. Sylvester Richardson, a Denver physician, established the town site and organized the first town company. Gunnison became the official seat of Gunnison County on May 22, 1877.

Meanwhile, local creeks, particularly Tomichi and Quartz, were beginning to produce quality gold and silver in large amounts, and thriving mining camps were springing up in the nearby mountains. Gunnison was a natural supply center. In 1880, the railroad arrived, a godsend not only to miners but to Gunnison Valley ranchers and farmers as well.

In 1909, Gunnison's Colorado State Normal School was founded; in 1915 its name was changed to Western State College.

Since the beginning of the 20th century, Gunnison has been a popular gateway to some of Colorado's best recreation areas. As early as the mid-1900s, the area's waterways—Taylor River and Tomichi and Cebolla Creeks—were known for some of the best trout fishing in the Rockies. In 1963, with the opening of Crested Butte Ski Area, Gunnison became a destination for some of the best downhill skiers in the country—today, direct flights from Dallas, Chicago, Atlanta, Houston, and Denver offer easy access to the slopes.

Pioneer Museum

Gunnison's historical museum complex includes a restored turn-of-the-20th-century schoolhouse, the town's first post office, and a railroad depot. There are also displays of railroad artifacts, Native American arrowheads, pioneer farming equipment, and lots of old photos.

To Crested Butte
135

GARLIC
▼ MIKE'S

SPENCER AVE.

0   440 yds

0   440 m

14TH ST.

DENVER   AVE.

SPRUCE ST.
PINE ST.
WISCONSIN ST.
MAIN ST.
IOWA ST.

WESTERN
STATE COLLEGE

OHIO   AVE.

8TH ST.

LIBRARY ■

TAYLOR ST.
COLORADO ST.
TELLER ST.

BOOK WORM ■

VIRGINIA   AVE.

POST OFFICE ■

VIRGINIA   AVE.

11TH ST.

CHAMBER OF
COMMERCE

HOLIDAY INN
EXPRESS

ABC MOTEL   ●   ●   ★ PIONEER
MUSEUM

To Salida

TOMICHI   AVE.

TOMICHI   AVE.   50

CATTLEMEN INN ●   ■ GENE
TAYLOR'S
SPORTING GOODS

▼
MARIO'S
PIZZERIA

▼ BLUE IGUANA

NEW YORK   AVE.

Jorgensen

Park

14TH ST.

WISCONSIN ST.

MAIN ST.

SAN JUAN   AVE.

GUNNISON

RIO   GRANDE   AVE.

■ AIRPORT TERMINAL

50

To Curecanti
National Rec. Area
and Black Canyon of the
Gunnison Nat'l Monument

GUNNISON COUNTY
AIRPORT

Tomichi Creek

© AVALON TRAVEL PUBLISHING, INC.

The Pioneer Museum is at South Adams and East U.S. 50 and is open Mon.–Sat. 9 A.M.–5 P.M., Memorial Day through Labor Day. Admission is $7, $1 for kids. For more information, phone 970/641-4530.

Western State College

Undoubtedly one of the first things you'll notice in Gunnison is the huge "W" on the side of Tenderfoot Mountain on the north side of town. Reportedly the world's largest college emblem, the "W" is made of white-washed flat rocks, carried up the mountain by students and faculty in 1923. Each line of the letter is 16 feet wide and 400 feet long; the overall dimensions are 320 by 420 feet.

For more information on the school's wide range of programs, write Western State College, Gunnison, CO 81231, or phone 970/943-0120. You can also learn more about the school at www.western.edu.

PARKS AND RECREATION

Gunnison is surrounded by some of nature's most gorgeous landscapes. Tumbling trout streams, mountain lakes, dense fir woodlands, granite peaks shouldering high above the timberline, broad valleys that come springtime are vibrant with wildflowers and shimmering waves of green—there's enough here to keep the outdoor lover grinning blissfully all year-round.

Gunnison's very pleasant **city park** is on the east side of town on U.S. 50 and has large lawns, lots of playground equipment, and public restrooms.

Fishing

This is one of Gunnison's main draws. In fact, on March 1, 1988, the state record brown trout, weighing 30.5 pounds, was taken from a pond near the East River just north of Gunnison. Though some of the best water in the area flows through private property, there is plenty of excellent easy-to-get-to public-access water in the region. In addition, the area's full of trouty backcountry streams that locals know are well worth the effort to reach.

Some of the best fishing in the area is found at **Blue Mesa Reservoir** about seven miles west of town. The 15-mile-long lake, formed when Blue Mesa Dam was built on the Gunnison River, yields lunker rainbow trout, as well as trophy-size lakes (Mackinaws) and browns. Fishing is best in early spring, shortly after the ice breaks up, and you can troll and jig from boats or work the shoreline, which varies from rocky cliffs to sandy beach. The reservoir also has a decent population of kokanee salmon—usually caught by trolling. Rent boats at either of the reservoir's two marinas. (For more information, see Curecanti National Recreation Area, below.)

Taylor Reservoir, 30 miles northeast of Gunnison at Taylor Park, is another favorite of local lake anglers, who fish for lake, brown, rainbow trout, and kokanee salmon. You can rent boats and pick up fishing supplies and groceries at Taylor Park Boathouse. To get there, take Highway 135 north from Gunnison about 10 miles and watch for the turnoff on your right.

The Gunnison area also boasts some of the best stream fishing in the state. The **Taylor River,** above Taylor Reservoir, offers good fly-fishing, while pools below the reservoir are large and deep enough for spinners and other lures. The **East River,** whose headwaters are near Schofield Pass north of Crested Butte, merges with the Taylor at Almont. The East is one of the area's best fly-fishing streams, producing good rainbow, brown, and brook trout (special restrictions apply on some stretches).

The **Gunnison River,** between Blue Mesa Reservoir and Gunnison, and north of town along Highway 135, is one of the state's best known and most productive stretches of water. Anglers have been pulling trophy brown and rainbow trout out of holes and riffles here for years, on both flies and lures.

For more information on fishing in the Gunnison area, as well as for licenses and equipment, stop in at **Gene Taylor's Sporting Goods,** 201 W. Tomichi, 970/641-1845. To arrange guided trips, contact **Three Rivers Resort and Outfitting,** P.O. Box 339, Almont, CO 81210, 970/641-1303, or check out www.3rivers resort.com.

kokanee salmon

BOB RACE

Cycling

Gunnison's proximity to Crested Butte, one of the mountain-bike capitals of the country, guarantees there will be plenty of great rides nearby. Road bikers don't have as many options, though, as there are really only two roads that go anywhere from town: U.S. 50, with major, high-speed traffic in both directions; and Highway 135 to Crested Butte, a *far* better place to take the touring bike for a spin. In fact, a bike path parallels the highway several miles north of town, and though it gets narrow after that, it would still be a rewarding ride. (For more on mountain biking in the area, see Crested Butte, below.)

SOUTHWESTERN

Golf

The **Dos Rios Golf Course** is an 18-hole course named for the *dos rios* (two rivers) at whose confluence it lies: Tomichi Creek and the Taylor River. To get there, take U.S. 50 two miles west from Gunnison and watch for the sign on your left. For information and tee times, phone 970/641-1482.

Rafting and Kayaking

With so much river water nearby, the Gunnison area is a natural for white-water sports. Kayakers, rafters, and canoers enjoy the Gunnison River from Almont to Blue Mesa Reservoir, and the Taylor River from Taylor Park Reservoir to Almont. Caution: river water in this area can get awfully fast and brawly during the snowmelt of late spring. The Taylor, particularly, can get mean and should be attempted only by experienced river rats or with guides.

Companies in the Gunnison area offering guided trips include **Three Rivers Resort and Outfitting,** 970/641-1303, and **Scenic River Tours,** 703 W. Tomichi, 970/641-3131.

Camping

At least 30 national forest and national recreation area campgrounds can be found within an hour or so of Gunnison. Gunnison National Forest alone includes a couple of dozen, both north of town in the Taylor Park region and south around Lake City. In addition, Curecanti National Recreation Area, west of Gunnison, offers a dozen or so more.

County Road 742, which parallels the Taylor River from Almont to Taylor Park, is virtually lined with Forest Service campgrounds, with at least 10 along this stretch alone. Among them: **Almont Campground,** just south of Almont off Highway 135 (10 sites); **Taylor Canyon,** about halfway to Taylor Reservoir (five sites, tents only); and **Lottis Creek,** just below the Taylor Reservoir dam (27 sites). Several other Forest Service campgrounds are at Taylor Park Reservoir. In addition, you'll find Forest Service campgrounds at the towns of Pitkin and Ohio.

Curecanti National Recreation Area campgrounds include **Cimarron,** 22 sites, dump sta-

tion; **Dry Gulch,** 10 sites, pit toilets, no showers; **Elk Creek,** 179 sites, flush toilets, dump station, boat ramp and marina, visitor center; and **Lake Fork,** 87 sites, dump station, flush toilets, boat ramp and marina, visitor center.

The Forest Service has published a detailed chart and map that lists all the campgrounds in the area and includes information on fees, number of sites, water availability, and fishing and hiking access. Write Gunnison National Forest, Taylor and Cebolla Ranger Districts, 216 N. Colorado, Gunnison, CO 81230, or phone 970/641-0471. For information on recreation area campgrounds, write Curecanti National Recreation Area, 102 Elk Creek, Gunnison, CO 81230, or phone 970/641-2337.

Sailing and Windsurfing

Though the several dams on the Gunnison River have changed forever this once wild and scenic stream, the trade-off has been an increase in the amount of available area for recreation, including sailing and windsurfing. **Curecanti National Recreation Area,** which flanks the Gunnison River west of town, includes three reservoirs. You'll find boat ramps on Blue Mesa Reservoir, while only hand-carried boats are allowed on Crystal Lake and Morrow Point Reservoir. For maps and information, stop in at any of the three visitor information centers: **Elk Creek** (16 miles west of Gunnison), **Lake Fork** (26 miles west of Gunnison), and **Cimarron** (20 miles east of Montrose).

Skiing

Gunnisonites are fortunate to live close to one of Colorado's best ski resorts, Mt. Crested Butte, just over 30 miles north of town. Offering excellent skiing for all abilities, this out-of-the-way and laid-back resort promises an honest good time, relatively uncrowded slopes, and some of the state's most breathtaking scenery. (See Crested Butte, below, for a complete description.)

TOURS
Scenic Drives

Gunnison is a wonderful starting point for several of the most scenic drives in the Rockies.

And if you've got a 4WD rig, you could spend an entire summer exploring little-used high mountain passes. Several unpaved Forest Service roads begin near Taylor Park, affording backway access to Buena Vista, Salida, and Aspen. One of the most visually arresting drives in the area is over Kebler Pass and down to Highway 133. Though unpaved, this is a well-maintained road, suitable for most vehicles (see Crested Butte, below).

Another highly recommended drive is the loop over **Cumberland Pass** via Taylor Park. Take Highway 135 north to Almont, and turn east on County Road 742. At the east end of Taylor Park Reservoir, turn south for Tincup, a mining town dating from 1880 (when it was known as Virginia City). Continue south over Cumberland Pass (elev. 12,000 feet), then down through Pitkin and Ohio, sites of late 1870s silver strikes. Continue to Parlin; then catch U.S. 50 back to Gunnison.

One of Colorado's most fascinating engineering marvels is east of Gunnison near Pitkin. **Alpine Tunnel,** a 1,771-foot bore under the Continental Divide, was completed in 1881 by the Denver, South Park, and Pacific Railroad and last used in 1910. Though the tunnel's west entrance has collapsed, you can view the remains of several old buildings, including water tanks and a boardinghouse, as well as the site of Woodstock, where the telegraph station and coal platform were. The access road is about two miles north of Pitkin (watch for the sign).

For maps and more information, contact the **Taylor River and Cebolla Ranger District of Gunnison National Forest,** 216 N. Colorado, Gunnison, CO 81230, 970/641-0471. In addition, the Gunnison Country Chamber of Commerce has published a map and guide to 20 scenic tours in the area. Write P.O. Box 36, Gunnison, CO 81230.

Historical Walking Tour

The Gunnison Country Chamber of Commerce has published a map and tour guide to historical Gunnison. Included are residences and commercial buildings dating from the 1880s, as well as several from the turn of the 20th century. The guide, which explains each structure's architectural and historical significance, is available from the chamber.

ACCOMMODATIONS

Gunnison's U.S. 50 location, its reputation for abundant nearby recreation, and the fact that it's a college town needing digs for parents and visiting professors guarantee plenty of lodging in the area, most of it reasonably priced. Motels, guest lodges, cabins, bed-and-breakfasts, in town, in a country meadow, or beside a mountain trout stream—the area should have something to suit your needs.

The Gunnison Country Chamber of Commerce has published an accommodations guide, with descriptions and photos of more than 30 places to stay in the area. You can have one sent to you by writing P.O. Box 36, Gunnison, CO 81230, or by phoning 800/274-7580. The guide is also available online at www.gunnison-co.com.

$50–100

The **ABC Motel,** 212 E. Tomichi, 970/641-2400 or 800/341-8000, is near the center of town and has among the best rates in town. The Holiday Inn has been converted to a **Holiday Inn Express,** 400 E. Tomichi, 970/641-1288. Also nice is the **Water Wheel Inn,** 2.5 miles west of town at 37478 U.S. Hwy. 50, 970/641-1650.

Two riverside Gunnison-area lodges are the **Lost Canyon Resort,** 8264 Hwy. 135, 970/641-0181, where cabins start at moderate prices, and **Three Rivers Resort and Outfitting,** in Almont, 970/641-1303, where cabins rates range from inexpensive to expensive. Three Rivers also offers RV and tent sites, guide service, a fly shop, and equipment rentals.

Harmel's Ranch Resort, P.O. Box 944, Gunnison, CO 81230, 970/641-1740, is a classic Rocky Mountain dude ranch northwest of town on the Taylor River. Harmel's has an excellent reputation, and your stay can include everything from meals to hayrides and campfire singalongs. Rates vary according to what "plan" you opt for, but range from about $70 a night per person to $180. You can also get cabins that sleep up to eight.

Camping and RVing

In addition to the dozens of national forest and national recreation area campgrounds in the area (see Camping, above), there are many private campgrounds where you can fetch up for weeks on end. **Sunnyside Campground,** 970/641-0477, is 12 miles west of Gunnison on Blue Mesa Reservoir. If you'd rather be streamside, you can get RV and tent sites, as well as cabins, at **Three Rivers Resort and Outfitting,** 970/641-1303, 10 miles north of town where the Taylor and East Rivers merge to form the headwaters of the Gunnison. A **KOA** campground is just west of town on the Gunnison River, 970/641-1358.

FOOD

For a small ranching town, Gunnison has a fairly decent number of good, reasonably priced restaurants. That might be due in part to the presence of Western State College: students get tired of dorm food and Top Ramen and love to go out to eat, especially when their folks come to town and are treating.

Garlic Mike's, 2674 N. Hwy. 135, 970/641-2493, serves traditional northern Italian food, specializing in veal, seafood, and pastas.

Mario's Pizzeria, 213 W. Tomichi, 970/641-1374, is a local favorite for thick or thin, white- or wheat-crust pizza, as well as pastas and other Italian dinners ($8–16). Free delivery. Another good bet is the **Blue Iguana,** 303 E. Tomichi, 970/641-3403, where you can get excellent Mexican food (Sonoran)—$5–9. Closed Sunday. If you're leaning more toward red meat, a big ol' steak, or a slab of prime the size of a Cadillac, it's tough to beat the **Cattlemen Inn,** 301 W. Tomichi, 970/641-1061. Entrées run $8–24.

CALENDAR

The main event on Gunnison's calendar is **Cattlemen's Days** in mid-July, which includes a rodeo, livestock shows, a parade, and street barbecues. There's also a parade, barbecues, and fireworks on the Fourth of July.

For complete information on Gunnison's annual events, write the chamber of commerce at P.O. Box 36, Gunnison, CO 81230, or phone 970/641-1501.

SERVICES

The offices of the **Gunnison Police Department** are at 201 W. Virginia, 970/641-8000. Phone the **Gunnison County Sheriff** at 970/641-1113 and the **State Patrol** at 970/641-1242. **Gunnison Valley Hospital** is at 214 E. Denver Ave., 970/641-1456. The **post office** is at 200 N. Wisconsin, 970/641-1884.

Recycling

You can recycle aluminum at the **City Market,** 401 W. Georgia, and the **Safeway,** 112 S. Spruce. Gunnison's **Citizens for Recycling** is at 702 W. Tomichi, where you can drop off aluminum, glass, and plastic; for more information, phone 970/641-2137.

INFORMATION

The **Gunnison Country Chamber of Commerce,** 500 E. Tomichi, is a good place to begin your visit. Pick up lodging and recreation guides, as well as other brochures, maps, and information. Be sure to get a copy of *Gunnison River Territory Magazine,* a free tourist-oriented publication with historical articles, profiles of locals, and pieces on exploring the Gunnison-area outdoors. Write the chamber at P.O. Box 36, Gunnison, CO 81230, or phone 970/641-1501. It also has a tourist-friendly website at www.gunnison-co.com.

For information on recreational activities in **Gunnison National Forest,** stop by the Tomichi District Office at 216 N. Colorado, 970/641-0471.

The Book Worm, 211 N. Main, 970/641-3693, specializes in books on the outdoors, recreation, and wildlife, and also sells maps. You'll find the **Ann Zegelder Library** (public) at 307 N. Wisconsin, 970/641-3485.

For **road and weather information,** phone 970/641-2896.

TRANSPORTATION

United Express, 800/241-6522, provides passenger service to Gunnison County Airport, with increased flights during the ski season.

American Airlines, 800/433-7300, has winter-only service to Gunnison. For shuttle service between Gunnison County Airport and Crested Butte, call **Alpine Express,** 800/322-4844.

Rent cars in Gunnison from **Budget,** 212 W. U.S. Hwy. 50, 970/641-4403, or **Hertz,** 708 S. 12th, 970/641-2881.

Crested Butte

A Sunday evening in June. The sun has just set over Kebler Pass, and the last light of the day is disappearing from the massive flanks of Mt. Crested Butte. I've been eating pasta and drinking red wine at Angello's and watching the Bulls beat the Lakers in the NBA play-offs. I decide to take one more stroll about town. Up Elk Avenue, past Mountain Earth Natural Foods, Coal Creek Sports, and Kochevar's, then north on 2nd and back down Maroon. And as I walk past the Union Congregational Church at the corner of 4th, I see a single image that says more about Crested Butte than any collage or long-playing study: there, in the weedy lot in front of the church, are two dozen mountain bikes—some parked, some sprawled, all muddy, dusty, and well ridden, their riders, obviously, inside. There are fewer than six cars.

Surrounded by jagged mountain peaks and the million-plus-acre Gunnison National Forest, Crested Butte (pop. 1,200; elev. 8,885 feet) is one of Colorado's true gems. A young town, Crested Butte is famous for some of the best downhill skiing in the state and is quickly gaining a reputation as its mountain bike capital. Crested Butte is actually two communities: the town of Crested Butte, which was founded in 1880, and the village of *Mt.* Crested Butte, founded nearly a century later, when Mt. Crested Butte Ski Area opened. Separated by a three-mile road and connected by a free shuttle system, Crested Butte and Mt. Crested Butte offer just about everything you could want in a vacation—history, outdoor activities, scenery, a wide range of restaurants and lodging, and friendly, down-to-earth locals.

Crested Butte's mining-era heritage is obvious from first glance: Elk Avenue, the town's main drag, is lined with Victorian homes and buildings that once served as saloons, banks, and supply shops. Today, many of them still *are* saloons, banks, and supply shops, though the supplies have changed from pickaxes and gold pans to ski poles and biking shorts. And though many of the buildings have been restored, the town has resisted gentrification, thanks in large part to the locals' respect for their history, as well as the town's off-the-beaten-path location.

History

Crested Butte dates from the early 1880s, when it was a thriving gold camp and supply headquarters for the mines in the nearby mountains, particularly in Washington Gulch, where the boom was launched when prospectors found $350,000 in gold nuggets. In the late 1880s, coal was discovered in the area, providing an economic base that would carry the community into the mid-20th century (unlike most Colorado mining camps, which were all but abandoned when ore prices fell in the 1890s).

In the early 1960s, Mt. Crested Butte Ski Area opened, changing forever the tenor of the town. At the base of the ski resort, condominiums and hotels sprang up, as did upscale restaurants and after-ski bars and pizza places. Thankfully, the town of Crested Butte was designated a National Historic District in 1974, guaranteeing the preservation of the old buildings, and an architectural review board was established to monitor renovation and new construction.

SOUTHWESTERN

In the late 1970s and early 1980s, mountain biking came to Crested Butte big-time, and the area's personality shifted again. In fact, by the late 1980s, Crested Butte, along with Durango, was one of the three or four world mountain-bike meccas. In addition to attracting more athletes to the area, both to live and visit, the sport is contributing greatly to the area's transformation to a year-round resort area. Though winter is still high season out here, summer is not far behind. And it probably won't be too much longer that local lodge owners feel compelled to lower their rates when the lifts shut down.

WINTER SPORTS

During the winter, the town of Crested Butte, the village of Mt. Crested Butte, and Crested Butte Ski Area virtually become one—indeed, they're connected every 15 minutes by free shuttle. And during the winter, just about everything revolves around winter sports: restaurants and lodges swell with vacationing skiers, students from Western State College in Gunnison cut classes and hit the slopes, and the equipment retail and rental shops do brisk business in boots and bindings, poles and parkas, sweaters and sunscreen. And for good reason: the area claims some of the finest skiing in the Rockies—cross-country and downhill—and some of the prettiest winter scenery this side of the Swiss Alps. In addition, there's a certain sense of abandon here, a nearly palpable feeling of communal *carpe diem,* the result of which is an on-the-edge inventiveness that has spawned sports unique to Crested Butte, such as dog fishing and "board joring." Dog fishing came about as a pragmatic solution to the town's notorious dog overpopulation. Though Crested Butte's dog fishermen have now mostly retired, they once trolled in the backs of pickups with fishing poles and Milk Bones, hoping to land lunker Labradors and trophy terriers (on the off-chance a poodle was hooked, it would be ceremoniously tossed back). "Board jorists" ride snowboards, water-ski-like, clinging to ropes pulled by horses galloping across meadows.

Kebler Pass Road takes you west from Crested Butte, up over Kebler Pass, and down to Highway 133—one of the best places to view fall colors.

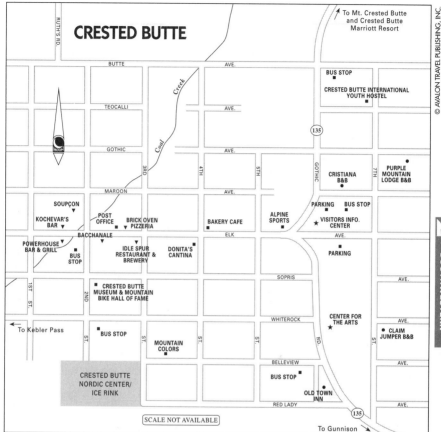

SOUTHWESTERN

Downhill Skiing

Crested Butte might not be as well known as Aspen, as big as Vail, or as easy to get to as Winter Park, but there's no denying the friggin' great snow, the runs that vary from long, gentle trails to steep-ass chutes and gnarly bump runs, and one of the friendliest, most kick-back attitudes you'll ever find at a ski resort.

With an average of 300 inches of snow falling annually on Crested Butte's 1,434 acres of skiable terrain, this mountain guarantees that if any place in the state has snow, it'll be here. In addition, there's good skiing for all ability levels, with 14 lifts providing access to 86 trails, although at Crested Butte the expert definitely has the home-court advantage: since the mid-1980s, Crested Butte has targeted extreme skiers, focusing development on black-diamond and double-black-diamond runs, and more recently opening 550 acres of backcountry chutes, bowls, and cornices. Since 1992, Crested Butte has hosted the U.S. Extreme Skiing Championships, and in 1995 it hosted the first U.S. Extreme Skiing Snowboarding Championships.

Two of Crested Butte's real prides are its ski school, which was chosen by *Rocky Mountain Sports and Fitness Magazine* as the best in the state, and its overall user-friendliness: a *Ski* magazine reader poll ranked Crested Butte 10th in the nation in customer service. Additionally, the resort's **Program for the Physically Challenged** caters to disabled skiers with disabilities, with instructors trained to teach sit and mono-skiing, three- and four-track techniques, as well as to work with blind, deaf, and developmentally disabled skiers. Skiers with disabilities can also rent adaptive equipment such as outriggers.

For more information on Mt. Crested Butte Ski Area, write Box A, 500 Gothic Rd., Mt. Crested Butte, CO 81225, phone 970/349-2333 or 800/544-8448 (reservations), or check out its website at www.crestedbutteresort.com. For ski-school information, call 970/349-2252. Phone the Program for the Physically Challenged at 970/349-2296. Call the snow-conditions line at 970/349-2323.

Cross-Country Skiing

From Telemarking in untracked backcountry bowls to speed skating on groomed track, the Crested Butte area offers plenty of high-quality Nordic skiing. Folks who want to explore the woods have the entire Gunnison National Forest at their ski tips; you can explore old logging and mining roads or take off through the trees. Experienced skiers can ascend any of several high mountain passes that are ideal for short or extended outings. For maps and information, contact the Forest Service District Office, 216 N. Colorado, Gunnison, 970/641-0471.

You can also get information, as well as equipment, at any of the area's ski shops, including **Paradise Bikes and Skis,** 224 Elk Ave., Crested Butte, 970/349-6324, and **Gene Taylor's Sporting Goods,** 19 Emmons Loop, at the base of the lifts in Mt. Crested Butte, 970/349-5386.

The **Crested Butte Nordic Center,** based at the corner of 2nd Street and Whiterock Avenue in downtown Crested Butte, has 30 km of cross-country track and skating lanes. The center offers lessons (private and group) in all types of Nordic skiing, equipment rental, and guided tours. All-day trail passes are $9 for adults, and rental equipment is $12 a day. For information or reservations, phone 970/349-1707, or go to www.visitcrestedbutte.com/nordic. **Mt. Crested Butte Ski Area** is a favorite among local

three-pinners, and its ski school offers lessons and equipment rental; phone 970/349-2252 for more information.

Other Winter Sports

Though you'll probably want to leave Crested Butte's more innovative winter sports, such as dog fishing and "board joring," to the locals, there are several more conventional winter activities available in the area. **Snowmobile** tours and rentals are offered by a couple of companies, including **Mountain Motor Sports,** 970/349-1326, which provides machine, maps, and advice.

Backcountry powder skiing is available via both helicopter and snowcat at **Irwin Lodge,** 970/349-5308. With 2,200 skiable acres and a 1,200-foot vertical drop, the lodge offers trips for both intermediate and advanced skiers (also see Accommodations, below). **Paradise Sleigh Ride Dinners** leave from the Grande Butte Hotel for Bubba's on the mountain on Tuesday, Thursday, and Saturday nights, with dinner including rib, lamb, and lobster; phone 970/349-2211 for rates and reservations. There are also two ice rinks in town.

For a complete description of the area's winter activities, contact the Crested Butte-Mt. Crested Butte Chamber of Commerce (see Information, below).

WHEN THE SNOW MELTS
Mountain Biking

Colorado mountain biking was born in Crested Butte. Following the lead of riders from Marin County, California, Crested Beauties attached motorcycle brakes and multiple gears to old "clunkers" and hit the trails. The first outings were over Pearl Pass to Aspen, but the huge number of old logging and mining roads in the area soon spawned a boom in the sport. Today, Crested Butte is one of the true mountain-bike capitals of the world.

Fat Tire Week each summer draws some of the country's best riders to a wide array of competitions, from serious dual slalom on the ski slopes to novelty events such as a limbo, a "slow race" (be the *last* one to cross the finish line, without putting your foot down), and mountain-bike polo. The week also provides an opportunity for newcomers to the sport to become better and more knowledgeable riders: clinics, workshops, and tours are offered daily. (See Calendar, below, for more information.)

The rest of the summer, too, mountain biking is big in these little communities. Tourists and locals alike explore gravel roads and single-track trails that snake through the valleys and over the ridges of the surrounding mountains. A couple of the classic rides are over **Pearl Pass** to Aspen and **Kebler Pass** to Highway 133 near Paonia. Both are steep and demanding, though physical fitness is more important than technical riding ability.

As you'd expect, there are a disproportionate number of bike shops in Crested Butte, all of which are happy to talk bikes and trails. At Mt. Crested Butte, check out **Crested Butte Sports—Ski and Bike Shop,** in the Evergreen Building at the base of Keystone lift on Emmons Loop, 970/349-7516. Rentals available.

Golf

The **Crested Butte Country Club** includes a 7,200-yard 18-hole course designed by Robert Trent Jones Junior. On 200 acres at the base of Mt. Crested Butte, this is a full-service resort complex, with tennis courts, private lake, and exercise room, as well as course-side condominiums and homes (also homesites, if you really fall in love with the place). Green fees run $65–85.

For tee times and information, phone the pro shop at 970/349-6131. For accommodations information, phone 970/349-7541.

River Running

Several rivers in the Crested Butte area offer excellent opportunities for river rats. The lower Taylor River, which flows from Taylor Park Reservoir down through Taylor Canyon to its confluence with the East River at Almont (where the Gunnison River is born), is a kayaker's delight, with rapids varying from Class II to V. The Gunnison River, slower and broader, is better suited to rafts.

A handful of outfits in the area offer guided tours of local waters, varying from short float trips to extended backcountry excursions for experienced river runners only. **Three Rivers Outfitting and Rafting,** 130 County Rd. 742 (Almont), 970/641-1303, has a full-course menu of tours. The company can also arrange horseback, mountain-biking, and snowmobile tours, as well as sleigh rides and dogsledding.

Horseback Riding

Though the area's chief recreation has taken a decidedly different tack of late, and the saddle of choice has changed from the type found on horses to the type found on mountain bikes, Crested Butte remains the quintessential Western community—ranches sprawl in the surrounding valleys, and horses stand in lots a quarter mile from downtown. And by horseback is still one of the best ways to see the high country—the Elk Mountains, the Sawatch Range, the lush river valleys.

The following are among the stables and outfitters offering horses for rent, as well as guided tours, from half-day rides to multiday pack trips: **Fantasy Ranch,** 970/349-5425; **Harmel's Ranch Resort,** 970/641-1740; and **Just Horsin' Around,** 970/349-9822.

Jeep Tours

In the heart of high-mountain mining country, with some of Colorado's most spectacular scenery beckoning, Crested Butte is an ideal base from which to explore via 4WD vehicle. In fact, some of the best tours, though they'll take you off the pavement, are perfectly suitable for conventional-traction automobiles (see Tours, below).

If you are equipped with 4WD, however, you've got substantially more options. Though it's nearly 200 miles from Crested Butte to Aspen by paved road, as the crow flies it's barely 30—just north from town, over the Elk Mountains, and across the county line. With a 4WD rig, you can at least approximate the general direction of Mr. Crow by crossing the mountains at Taylor Pass or Pearl Pass. Topo maps, with 4WD routes indicated, are available at the Gunnison Office of the Gunnison National Forest, 216 N. Colorado, 970/641-0471.

Camping

Literally surrounded by Gunnison National Forest, the Crested Butte area offers limitless camping opportunities, whether you hike in to a secluded backcountry spot or set up at one of the many nearby Forest Service campgrounds. **Lost Lake Campground** (10 sites, pit toilets, no drinking water) is about 15 miles west of Crested Butte just south of Kebler Pass Road among some of the area's finest scenery. **Cement Creek Campground** (13 sites, pit toilets) is southeast of Crested Butte via Highway 135 and Forest Service Road 740.

You'll also find Forest Service campgrounds along the Taylor River and at Taylor Park Reservoir (25–40 miles from Crested Butte), as well as National Park Service and privately owned campgrounds west of Gunnison. For more information on Crested Butte–area Forest Service Campgrounds, phone 970/641-0471.

Other Summer Activities

If the area's mountain biking, horseback riding, golf, and four-wheel-driving aren't enough for you, there's still more. You'll find excellent **fishing** in nearby lakes and streams, particularly the Taylor, East, and Gunnison Rivers, and Taylor Park and Blue Mesa Reservoirs. For licenses and information, stop in at **Gene Taylor's Sporting Goods** at the base of the lifts at Mt. Crested Butte, 970/349-5386. For information on guided fly-fishing trips in the area, try **Coal Creek Sports,** 207 Elk Ave., Crested Butte, 970/349-6166.

The area is also fraught with excellent **hiking** opportunities. Serious backpackers have the whole of Gunnison National Forest, including the beautiful Elk Mountains and the mighty Sawatch Range, while nature trailers and day hikers can wander any of the region's shorter and more accessible trails.

Several trails near Cement Creek Campground are perfect for day outings. Go south on Highway 135 for seven miles and turn east on Cement Creek Road. You'll also find excellent hiking pos-

sibilities west of Crested Butte in the Kebler Pass area; **Lost Lake Campground** is a good base for hikes through aspeny hillsides to views that'll knock your socks off. A good source for information and equipment is **The Alpineer,** 419 6th St., Crested Butte, 970/349-5210. You can also get information and maps from the Forest Service District Office in Gunnison.

ACCOMMODATIONS

Accommodations are available in both the town of Crested Butte and the village of Mt. Crested Butte. In the village, slopeside lodges and condos provide the ultimate ski-in/ski-out experience, though regular shuttle service from the smaller and more colorful inns in town makes lodging there nearly as convenient.

Keep in mind that lodging rates in the Crested Butte area, like those at most ski resorts, vary tremendously from summer to winter: rates will be highest during the peak times of the ski season (Christmas vacation, weekends, etc.) and lowest when the lifts shut down. In fact, many of the lodges offer special off-season incentives just to keep their help busy.

For complete information on lodging packages, including air and ground transportation, lift tickets, equipment, and instruction, phone **Crested Butte Reservations** at 800/215-2226. You can also get lodging information from the **Crested Butte-Mt. Crested Butte Chamber of Commerce,** P.O. Box 1288, Crested Butte, CO 81224, 800/545-4505. And you can get information from and make reservations on the chamber's website at www.crestedbuttechamber.

For condominium information or reservations, phone **Crested Butte Accommodations** at 800/821-3718. For condominiums and vacation homes, phone **Rocky Mountain Rentals** at 970/349-5354.

Mt. Crested Butte Lodging

The 27-room **Nordic Inn,** 970/349-5542, is a long-time Crested Butte favorite 300 yards from the lifts. Continental breakfast and après-ski wine and hors d'oeuvres included ($100–150 and up). The **Sheraton Resort at Crested Butte,**

970/349-8000 or 800/544-8448, is also in the village and has a large indoor pool, as well as a sauna and outdoor hot tub ($150–250).

The **Crested Butte Club Med,** 877/823-1925, is just 35 yards from the base of the lifts and features more than 260 rooms, each with whirlpool, wet bar, and other luxuries. Acquired from the Crested Butte Marriott in 2001, the club is brand new. A wide range of activities are included in lodging prices.

Under $50

You bet! In fact, not only can you get lodging at shoestring rates (under $50 a night is virtually unheard of in a ski town), but it's one of the nicest youth hostels I've seen—the new **Crested Butte International Youth Hostel,** 615 Teocalli Ave., 970/349-0588 or 888/389-0588; email hostel@crestedbutte.net. In addition to the 52 beds (in rooms sleeping four, six, or eight), the hostel offers laundry, kitchen, and shower facilities (showers are $5 for nonguests). An excellent way to visit Crested Butte on the cheap. Dorm rates are all under $30; couples rooms are available for $50–85.

In Town: $100–150

The **Purple Mountain Lodge,** 714 Gothic, 970/349-5888 or 800/286-3574, has five cozy rooms in a family home (living on the premises) and serves an excellent and large breakfast.

Just around the corner from the Purple Mountain, at 621 Maroon, the **Cristiana Guesthaus Bed and Breakfast,** 970/349-5326 or 800/824-7899, is a classic little ski lodge offering very comfortable rooms, a large downstairs lobby with fireplace, and a sauna and outdoor hot tub with a wonderful view of the mountains.

Billing itself a "unique" bed-and-breakfast, the **Claim Jumper,** 704 Whitlock, 970/349-6471, is guilty of nothing but understatement. This place is packed floor to ceiling with one of the strangest assortments of odds and ends you'll ever see. Not only is the lobby full of antiques and parlor games, but each room has a bizarre theme and the decor to match: "Ethyl's Room" has a Shell gasoline pump and a jukebox; "Soda Creek" is dedicated to Coca-Cola memorabilia; and the

best room of all, the "Sports Fan Attic," is packed with mementos and souvenirs from baseball, football, hockey, and other sports—signed game jerseys worn by Jose Canseco and John Elway, signed baseball cards, and, in a separate room, a *putting green.* Phone for reservations or a brochure describing each room in detail.

Among the best rates in the area are those at two modest motels in Crested Butte: the **Old Town Inn,** 970/349-6184, and **Forest Queen,** 970/349-5336.

FOOD

When *The Denver Post* wrote that Crested Butte "has more fine restaurants per capita than any town in America," the marketing people ate it up (sorry); you'll see the quote all over the area's promotional material. It's not hyperbole, though. There truly are an amazing number of excellent places to eat here—from burger-and-beer joints to upscale, stiff-napkin dining establishments. Some have been around forever; some are brand new; some will probably be gone by the time you read this. At any rate, *salut i force canut.*

Start Me Up

The **Bakery Cafe,** 401 Elk, 970/349-7280, opens at 7:30 A.M. daily and is a longtime favorite for breakfast, specializing in fresh baked goods (no preservatives) and gourmet coffees. The Bakery is also open for lunch and dinner, serving pastas, stuffed croissants, and homemade soups and chili.

Dinner Joints

You'll find two good Mexican restaurants in Crested Butte. **The Powerhouse Bar y Grill,** 130 Elk, 970/349-5494, serves excellent fajitas, enchiladas, and tostada salads, not to mention 65 different tequilas. Dinners run $6–16. **Donita's,** 332 Elk, 970/349-6674, a cantina-style restaurant, specializes in atmosphere and can really get to hopping (read, packed!) when the lifts shut down. Entrées are in the $8–18 range. Salsa available to go.

A wonderful after-ski (or after-any-other-activity) hangout is the **Idle Spur,** 226 Elk,

SOUTHWESTERN

970/349-5026, one of the best microbrew-pubs in the state. The huge interior, with rough-hewn beams and blazing fire, allow you to join the rowdy crowd or find a cozy corner. The menu—Mexican food, burgers, salads, and pastas—runs $7–12.

For Italian food, try the **Brick Oven Pizzeria,** 3rd and Elk, 970/349-5044, where in addition to deep-dish pizzas, you can get pastas and sub sandwiches. Pasta dishes run about $7; pizzas are $6–13. Delivery available. For more upscale, intimate Italian dining, check out **Bacchanale,** 209 Elk, 970/349-5257, where veal, chicken, and pasta dishes run $9–17.

The same *Post* article that lauded Crested Butte's many excellent restaurants singled out **Soupçon,** 127 Elk, 970/349-5448, as one of the area's best. Specializing in French country cuisine, this restaurant has a rotating menu featuring appetizers such as oysters aioli, shrimp Dijon, and duckling mousse, and entrées of seafood, veal, or beef. Ideal for an anniversary or other celebration.

Crested Butte's oldest saloon, the **Wooden Nickel,** 222 Elk, 970/349-6350, attracts a rowdy and hungry post-slope crowd (bar opens at 3 P.M.; happy hour is 4:30–5:30). Dinners include steak, soups and chili, burgers, seafood, and ribs.

ENTERTAINMENT

Crested Butte's a young town, with lots of folks doing some short-term ski and mountain bumming before facing real-world responsibilities—and of course they need places to spend the money they're saving for college. In addition, skiers and other tourists count on at least a certain degree of nightlife as part of their vacation packages. Though this is no Aspen (which is *good* news to most), the area does offer its fair share of places to let off steam.

The Rafters, at Mt. Crested Butte, conveniently located between the bus stop and the base of the Silver Queen lift, is the ski area's main bar and has a classic ski-lodge sundeck. Live music Tuesday through Sunday during the ski season, both in the afternoon for the après-skiers, then later, rockin' and rowdy—also pool and

video games, as well as sandwiches and fajitas for when the munchies kick in. You'll also find live music at the **Avalanche Bar and Grill,** 970/349-7195, and the **Artichoke Bar and Dining Room,** 970/349-6688, both right at the base of the lifts.

In town, **Kochavar's** at 127 Elk, 970/349-2299, is another local favorite, where music from live bands often spills out onto the streets. The **Wooden Nickel,** 222 Elk, has been in the hangover business (breeding and nursing) since 1929.

CALENDAR

As Crested Butte grows from a winter-only to a year-round resort, more and more events and activities are being scheduled. Throughout the winter, Mt. Crested Butte Ski Area hosts several races and other slope-side fiestas. On opening day of Mt. Crested Butte Ski Area, usually in late November, lift-ticket prices are rolled way back and the hills are alive with the euphoria induced by winter's return. For complete information on winter activities at Crested Butte Mountain Resort Ski Area, write P.O. Box A, Mt. Crested Butte, CO 81225, or phone 800/544-8448.

One of Crested Butte's popular summer events is **Fat Tire Week** in early to mid-July, when the town, already mountain-bike-crazy, becomes the hub of the country's mountain-bike activity. Attracting riders from recreational novices to hard-core racers, events include a dual-slalom race on Mt. Crested Butte's ski slopes, a bicycle rodeo, bicycle polo, clinics and workshops, tours of nearby mountain-bike trails, including Pearl Pass, the dirt road to Aspen that gave birth to Colorado mountain biking back in the mid-'70s. For information and registration forms, write Fat Tire Week, P.O. Box 782, Crested Butte, CO 81224, or phone 970/349-6817.

In addition, several other events and programs punctuate the summer in Crested Butte and Mt. Crested Butte, from softball tournaments and "fun runs" to art shows and wildflower festivals. Highlights include Fourth of July festivities, with street music, food booths, parade, and fireworks; **Aerial Weekend,** a hot-air balloon festival in late July; and the **Festival of the Arts,** a juried art show with street music, food booths, etc., in early August. For a complete calendar of special events in the Crested Butte area, write the Crested Butte-Mt. Crested Butte Chamber of Commerce, P.O. Box 1288, Crested Butte, CO 81224, or phone 970/349-6438.

TOURS

Though a trip to Crested Butte is a scenic tour unto itself, several roads in the area offer icing on the cake. Of course, you're limited in the winter, when all but the area's main routes are closed, but during the summer, assuming you don't mind getting off the pavement, you can really do some exploring. Allow a couple of hours to tour one of my favorite routes in the state, **Kebler Pass Road,** which lifts from downtown Crested Butte, winds over Kebler Pass, past Mt. Baldy, and then drops to Highway 133; there you can either turn north for Redstone and Glenwood Springs or continue west toward Paonia, Delta, and Grand Junction. A wide and well-maintained gravel road, Kebler Pass Road features enough vertical rise that you can literally watch the aspens change colors. In the spring, those at lower elevations are green and leafy, while nearer the summit they're still wintry and bare; in the fall, watch them change from green to gold to crimson.

Another interesting drive, and one that's less of a commitment, is the short jaunt to the ghost town of **Gothic,** a Victorian-era silver-mining town with superb views of the East River valley. Gothic, which was pretty much abandoned by the late 1880s, is about seven miles northeast of Crested Butte; take Forest Service Road 327 from Mt. Crested Butte.

Other scenic drives in the area include the Alpine Tunnel tour and the Gunnison, Taylor Park Reservoir, Pitkin, and back to Gunnison loop.

Walking Tour
Crested Butte was designated a National Historic District in 1974, and many of the buildings

lining Elk Avenue and some of the side streets date from the late 19th century. The Chamber of Commerce publishes a map and guide to historical Crested Butte, with more than 40 sites, many open today as restaurants, inns, and other small businesses. Full of anecdotal history, the little pamphlet is useful and intriguing whether you just want to know the history of the bar at which you plan to plant yourself or you intend to take the full tour.

SERVICES

The office of the **Crested Butte Police Department** is at 409 2nd St., 970/349-5231. Phone the **State Patrol** in Gunnison at 970/641-6382. The nearest hospital is **Gunnison Valley Hospital,** 214 E. Denver Ave., Gunnison, 970/641-1456. Limited medical facilities are available at **Crested Butte Medical Clinic,** 611 Gothic Rd., 970/349-6651. The clinic specializes in (appropriately enough) sports injuries and medicine.

The Crested Butte **post office** is at 217 Elk Ave., 970/349-5568. There's also postal service in Mt. Crested Butte at the 3 Seasons Building, 970/349-7310.

Recycling
For recycling information in Crested Butte, phone **Sunshine Garbage,** 970/349-5957. You can also drop off recyclables in Gunnison, at the **Citizens for Recycling** drop-off, 702 W. Tomichi, the **City Market,** 401 W. Georgia, and the **Safeway,** 112 S. Spruce.

Child Care
Mt. Crested Butte Ski Area's **Buttetopia Children's Program** offers a range of supervised activities for kids six months to 12 years. Programs include day care for kids six months to six years (no skiing), beginning group ski instruction for kids 3–6, private lessons for kids 2–6, and "Tag-a-Long" lessons for kids 2–12 *and* their parents—follow the class and learn how to continue instructing your child in technique and chairlift safety. For reservations or more information, phone 970/349-2259.

INFORMATION

As you approach Crested Butte by car (assuming you come in via Highway 135, the main route, and not in the back way, over one of the several unpaved mountain-pass roads), you'll meet almost head-on with a chamber of commerce **visitor information center.** This is a good place to stuff your pockets with brochures on things to do and see while you're in the area, as well as to pick up lodging and dining guides. To stock up before your visit, write **Crested Butte-Mt. Crested Butte Chamber of Commerce,** P.O. Box 1288, Crested Butte, CO 81224, or phone 800/545-4505. You can also get information at its website at www.crestedbuttechamber.com. Another excellent website is www.visitcrested butte.com.

For good selections of books on recreation and wildlife in the area, check out **The Book Store,** 327 Elk, 970/349-5304, in Crested Butte, or stop on your way into town at **The Book Worm,** 211 N. Main (Highway 135), Gunnison. The **Crested Butte Library,** 970/349-6535, is in the Old Rock Schoolhouse and is open Monday, Wednesday, and Friday 1–5 P.M. and Tuesday 6–8 P.M.

For information on **Gunnison National Forest,** stop by the ranger station at 216 N. Colorado, Gunnison, or phone 970/641-0471.

For **road and weather information,** phone 970/641-2896.

TRANSPORTATION

American Airlines and **United Express** offer regular passenger service to Gunnison, with daily nonstop flights during the ski season from Chicago, Atlanta, and Dallas/Fort Worth, as well as connecting flights from Denver. Most hotels in Crested Butte offer free airport shuttle service for guests. In addition, you can arrange ground transportation between Gunnison and Crested Butte with **Alpine Express,** 970/641-5074 or 800/822-4844.

The village of Mt. Crested Butte and the ski area are three miles from the town of Crested Butte. Free shuttle buses run between the two about every 15 minutes till midnight during ski season.

Curecanti National Recreation Area

Paralleling the Gunnison River from Gunnison to Black Canyon of the Gunnison National Monument, Curecanti National Recreation Area includes three reservoirs, 10 separate campgrounds (with more than 300 sites), 18 picnic areas, and four visitor centers, as well as marinas, boat ramps, and hiking trails. Extremely popular with anglers—who know the lakes' depths hold lunker rainbow, brown, lake, and brook trout, in addition to kokanee salmon—the area is also excellent for wildlife watching: ducks and geese and other waterfowl are common in the area, as are bald and golden eagles and great blue herons, and elk, bighorn sheep, and mule deer can be seen in the area in winter.

The three-dam system was designed to provide irrigation water and to generate hydroelectric power. Though the dams' construction met (understandably) with opposition from environmentalists and conservationists, the result has been the development of one of the state's best all-around recreation areas.

Blue Mesa, where you'll find the majority of recreational activities, is the largest of the three lakes and the system's main storage reservoir. Morrow Point and Crystal Reservoirs generate power and control water flow through Black Canyon of the Gunnison. Dozens of creeks flow into the three lakes and the stretches of Gunnison between them; the streams flowing into Blue Mesa Reservoir form long arms gouging into the surrounding mesas and plateaus and giving a fjord-like appearance to the waterway.

Camping

The four largest and most developed campgrounds at Curecanti are **Elk Creek, Lake Fork,**

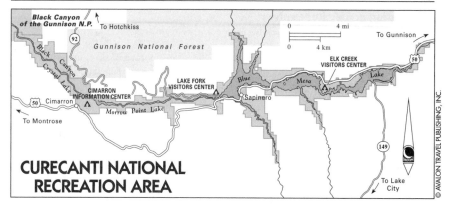

CURECANTI NATIONAL RECREATION AREA

Stevens Creek, and **Cimarron.** Other smaller campgrounds, some nestled in the lakes' narrow arms, are better suited for getting away from crowds, and several of the campgrounds offer access to hiking and self-guided interpretive trails. Group camping is available at **East Elk Creek Campground** (by reservation only). To make camping reservations, or for more information on camping at Curecanti National Recreation Area, phone 970/641-2337.

Fishing

Though rainbow trout are the most commonly caught fish in the park, the waters also hold brown, lake (Mackinaw), and brook trout, and kokanee salmon. Fishing is best in spring, shortly after ice-out, and again in the fall, when big browns head up into the tributaries to spawn. Kokanee can be legally snagged beginning in October (check regulations at nearby sporting goods stores or with the Division of Wildlife).

The area can be productive from both shore and boat, though the latter is the better way to go, especially if you're looking to hook into one of the monster lake trout, which prefer the cold, deep water (45–70 feet and deeper). Rental boats are available at Elk Creek and Lake Fork.

Water Sports

Blue Mesa Reservoir offers the broadest range of water sports and boating, with water-skiing and windsurfing popular in the summer when the water (and air) warms up. In addition, the lake is large enough—20 miles long, with three separate basins—and contains enough arms and inlets to offer sailors plenty of water to explore. Boating on Crystal and Morrow Point Lakes is restricted to hand-carried craft.

Swimming is permitted at Curecanti, but keep in mind this water's cold. Also, remember swimming is not permitted from docks, launch ramps, and unanchored boats.

Boat Tours

If you want to get out on the water but neither have your own boat nor feel like renting, you can take a tour with an interpreter/naturalist, who discusses the area's geology, history, and wildlife, as well as the role of the dams in irrigation and power generation. Tours are offered regularly throughout the summer. For information and reservations, phone the Elk Creek Marina at 970/641-0402.

Winter Sports

Winter activities in Curecanti National Recreation Area include ice fishing, snowmobiling, and cross-country skiing. Be sure to check with rangers to make sure the ice is thick enough (four inches to support an adult, seven to support a snowmobile). The area's nature trails are perfect for Nordic skiing, or you can break your own trail. You'll find a specifically designated beginning cross-country ski trail at the Elk Creek Visitor Center.

SOUTHWESTERN

Information and Visitor Centers

The **Elk Creek Visitor Center** is the best place to get oriented. In addition to viewing a slide/tape presentation on the area, you can pick up maps and other publications and ask questions of the rangers. Visitor information centers are also at Cimarron and Lake Fork.

At Cimarron, you can view a restored 19th-century Denver and Rio Grande Railroad engine and cars.

For more information on Curecanti National Recreation Area, write Superintendent, Curecanti National Recreation Area, 102 Elk Creek, Gunnison, CO 81230, or phone 970/641-2337.

Black Canyon of the Gunnison National Monument

A jagged incision—2,000 feet deep and 53 miles long—in the rocky Gunnison Uplift, Black Canyon of the Gunnison is without doubt one of the Southwest's most startling natural wonders. Named for the gorge's primarily dark gray Precambrian rocks of gneiss and schist, Black Canyon is a haven for hikers, campers, backpackers, and especially rock climbers. Black Canyon of the Gunnison National Monument was established by President Herbert Hoover on March 2, 1933, and encompasses one of the most stunning stretches of the gorge—a 12-mile length of river and sheer canyon wall. It includes two specific scenic drives (one of which, North Rim Road, is closed in winter). In addition, the monument includes two campgrounds, a handful of nature trails, view points, picnic areas, and a visitor center.

Formed more than two million years by the erosive powers of the Gunnison River, Black Canyon was known 10,000 years ago to nomadic bands of Folsom people, who hunted deer and other game along the gorge's rim. Later, in the 17th, 18th, and 19th centuries, Utes also hunted in the area, chasing deer and buffalo to the canyon's rims, where they'd trap and kill the animals at close range or force them off the cliffs so they'd fall to their deaths.

Members of the Hayden Expedition of 1873–74 were probably the first nonnatives to see the canyon. Then, toward the end of the 19th century, a survey crew for the Denver and Rio Grande Railroad proposed diverting water from the Gunnison River west to the Uncompahgre Valley for irrigation. In 1900, surveyors entered the canyon by boat, but their efforts were largely unsuccessful. A year later, two explorers lashed gear and belongings onto a rubber mattress and, after floating, swimming, and scrambling for nine days and 33 miles, emerged on the far side with the opinion that a tunnel was indeed possible. In late 1904, work was begun, and more than five years later, in September of 1909, the seven-mile Gunnison Diversion Tunnel was completed.

When visiting Black Canyon, don't miss the visitor center, just inside the National Monument boundary. Here you'll find exhibits on the area's geology, history, flora, and fauna, and you can join regularly scheduled nature walks to the very edge of the canyon's rim, where a ranger discusses the gorge's formation and natural history and will answer questions. The visitor center is open daily 8 A.M.–6 P.M. May–Oct., with reduced hours in spring and fall; closed in winter. Admission fee to the park is $7 per vehicle.

To get to Black Canyon of the Gunnison National Monument, take U.S. 50 west from Gunnison 60 miles or east from Montrose six miles and turn north on Highway 347. During the summer only, you can get to the North Rim by taking Highway 92 east from Delta or north from its junction with U.S. 50, about 30 miles west of Gunnison.

For more information, write 223 E. Main, Montrose, CO 81402, or phone 970/249-7036 (main office) or 970/249-1915 (visitor center). Visit the park's website at www.nps.gov/blca.

Camping

Both campgrounds in Black Canyon National Monument are open May through October. **South Rim Campground** (102 sites), near the visitor center off Highway 347, is the most accessible of the two. During the winter, you can't even get to **North Rim Campground** (13 sites), as the gravel road in from Highway 92 is closed.

Delta

At the junction of U.S. 50 and Highway 92, and smack dab in the middle of some of Colorado's richest ranch land, Delta (pop. 3,900; elev. 4,980 feet) is a natural hub for travelers and ranchers alike and is also the headquarters for Grand Mesa, Uncompahgre, and Gunnison National Forests. Not exactly a tourist destination in itself, Delta does offer several motels, cafés, and markets for travelers looking to rest for a while or to pull off the road for the night. It's also got a couple of nice city parks.

Billing itself "The City of Murals," Delta displays seven different murals on downtown buildings. The paintings, done by local artists, depict the history, economy, and recreational activities in the area. Examples include a pair of elk in a mountain meadow and a collection of fruit labels used by Delta County growers. Watch for the murals on Main Street (U.S. 50) as you arrive either from the north or south.

Delta County Historical Museum
A good place to get a sense of Delta's past, this museum displays an array of ranching and farming tools, including harnesses and saddles, as well as dolls and other domestic items and historical photos. Entomologists take note: the museum's butterfly collection includes extinct specimens that are the only known surviving examples.

The museum is one block east of Main Street, at the corner of 3rd and Palmer; open Tues.–Sat. 10 A.M.–4 P.M., Memorial Day through Labor Day, limited hours the rest of the year. Admission is $2. For information, or to arrange special tours, phone 970/874-8721.

Fort Uncompahgre
This is a living-history re-creation of the original fort built in 1826 by French fur trader Antoine Roubideau. Costumed docents explain, demonstrate, and allow visitors to experience firsthand the variety of activities that defined frontier life for early 19th-century Colorado pioneers.

The museum is at Confluence Park just north of Delta. Take U.S. 50 north to Gunnison River Drive and turn west. Admission is $3.50 for adults, with discounts for kids and seniors. Phone 970/874-8349.

Delta Dinosaurs
Delta County is the site of several important dinosaur-fossil discoveries. In 1971, paleontologists discovered the humerus of a brachiosaurus, and in 1979, a nine-foot scapula and a 48-inch-wide vertebra from an ultrasaurus were discovered.

Dry Mesa Quarry is a working dig open to the public, and visitors are encouraged to check it out. The quarry is a half-mile hike from the parking lot. There are picnic tables but no drinking water. Allow 90 minutes to get there on the unpaved road (suitable for passenger cars, unless it's been raining). For a map and more information, stop by the Forest Service office in Montrose, or phone 970/240-5400.

Ute Council Tree
Included in the book *Famous and Historic Trees of the United States* and recognized as a Colorado Landmark, the Ute Council Tree in north Delta is a cottonwood more than 200 years old. Between 1852 and 1887, Ute Chief Ouray and his wife, Chipeta (the only woman allowed to sit at the tree), met with white settlers in attempts to bring peace to western Colorado. The Ute Council Tree is 85 feet tall and seven feet in diameter.

To get there, watch for the small sign on U.S. 50 just north of the bridge across the river.

Ute Trail
This four-mile hiking trail, which follows one of the main routes used by Utes for centuries before settlers arrived, takes you from the south rim of the Gunnison Gorge down to the Gunnison River. This is an excellent area to view the geology of the area, as the trail switches back several times in its 1,200-foot descent, displaying sedimentary rocks, as well as metamorphic and igneous formations. In addition, bighorn sheep and river otters (both introduced by the Colorado Division of Wildlife) can be seen in the canyon.

To get to the trailhead, where you'll find picnic tables and a parking lot, take Highway 92 five miles east to Austin, and go south for three miles on County Road 2200. At County Road 2450, go east for five miles and watch for the sign to the access road (two miles of dirt; recommended for high-clearance vehicles only).

PRACTICALITIES
Accommodations

Good, clean rooms are available on the south end of town at **Sundance Best Western,** 903 Main (U.S. 50), 970/874-9781, and on the north end of town at **Comfort Inn,** 180 Gunnison River Dr., 970/874-1000. Both are at the low end of the $50–100 range. Just across the Gunnison River is the **Riverwood Inn and RV Park,** 970/874-5787.

Food

A classic Western junction town, Delta offers more than its share of cafés and fast-food restaurants. In addition, you'll find a number of specialty restaurants. **Daveto's,** 520 Main, 970/874-8277, is a favorite for Italian food, with pizzas and pastas running $6–16. The **Starvin' Arvin's** on the north end of town, 204 Ute,

970/874-7288, is popular among tourists and locals for standard, diner-type American fare—open daily for breakfast, lunch, and dinner.

Information

The **Delta Chamber of Commerce and Visitors Center,** 970/874-8616, is right downtown at 3rd and Main. An RV parking lot is directly behind the building; turn west from Main. For information on camping, fishing, hiking, etc., in any of the surrounding national forest lands, stop in at the headquarters for the Grand Mesa, Uncompahgre, and Gunnison National Forests, 2250 U.S. Hwy. 50; phone 970/874-6600.

U.S. 50/550 SOUTH

U.S. 50 drops south out of Grand Junction, shooting down between the Uncompahgre Plateau on the west and Grand Mesa on the east. The Gunnison River follows the 40-mile stretch of highway from Grand Junction to Delta, while the Uncompahgre parallels the 48-mile Delta-to-Ridgway stretch. In Montrose, U.S. 50 doglegs to the east, while U.S. 550 continues south.

Just south of Ridgway, the highway begins to lift into the mountains, and then, suddenly, at Ouray, you're facing an apparently unpassable wall of mountain granite. Don't worry: the road continues. In fact, at Ouray, U.S. 550 begins a dramatic series of switchbacks over Red Mountain Pass (elev. 11,008 feet), and then drops again into Silverton before winding back over Molas Divide (elev. 10,910 feet) and through some of the state's most gorgeous scenery. Fifty miles south of Silverton, U.S. 550 slips into Durango.

This is one of the western slope's most well-traveled roadways. Not only do many motorists take advantage of the quick northern section, which provides the best access between Grand Junction and Telluride, but many drive the southern route for its scenery alone. The Ouray-to-Silverton section, known as the Million Dollar Highway, offers unparalleled views of the Colorado Rockies at their most dramatic.

SOUTHWESTERN

Montrose

The seat of Montrose County, Montrose (pop. 8,884; elev. 5,794 feet) is a small crossroads town in the center of the fertile Uncompahgre Valley on the Rocky Mountain's stark western slope. Used during the late 19th century as a supply point for miners working the Uncompahgre River, which flows through the valley, and for those probing the 14,000-foot San Juan Mountains to the south, Montrose today serves as a hub for ranchers, hunters, and others exploring the vast recreational opportunities afforded by the southwestern Rockies, particularly Black Canyon of the Gunnison National Monument, and the Native American ruins of the Four Corners area.

Just over a mile above sea level, Montrose is blessed with a fairly moderate year-round climate, the town's lowest average temperatures scarcely dropping into the high 30s (in January) and its highs maxing out at about 90° (in July).

Average maximum temperature is 63°, and local boosters like to brag about Montrose's 250 or so annual days of sunshine.

History

Like most of the country's most desirable areas, the Uncompahgre Valley was once Native American land. Southern Utes had farmed and hunted in the region for centuries before Europeans arrived, Chief Ouray and his wife, Chipeta, overseeing local Utes in the fertile river valley in the mid- to late 19th century—until the tribe was "removed" in 1881 by the United States government.

Oliver D. "Pappy" Loutsenhizer was one of the first white settlers in the valley, arriving first in the fall of 1873 with a group of gold-seeking adventurers led by Alferd Packer. Though Loutsenhizer and part of the group eventually turned back (at the urging of Ouray), Packer continued, even as winter temperatures and snow began to fall. Ultimately, Packer was convicted of cannibalizing five members of his splinter group after they became snowbound near Lake City (see Lake City, under North of Pagosa Springs below).

Loutsenhizer returned to the valley several years later and, in 1881, with his friend Joseph Selig, laid out what was to become the town of Montrose—first dubbed "Pomona," after the Roman goddess of fruit, but later renamed after the Duchess of Montrose, a character in a Walter Scott novel. Shortly after its founding, Montrose saw two big changes that would have great effects on its face and character. The first was the railroad, which pushed through in 1882, providing opportunities for local farmers to ship their crops, especially cotton and sugar beets, to destinations throughout the United States. The second was the Gunnison Diversion Tunnel. Begun in 1904 and completed in 1909, the seven-mile passage provided irrigation water from the Gunnison River northeast of town to Uncompahgre Valley farmers whose increasing croplands were requiring more and more water. One of the Bureau of Reclamation's first projects, the tunnel had a much-celebrated inauguration, with the dedication conducted by President Taft.

Ute Indian Museum and Ouray Memorial Park

Dedicated in 1956 by the Colorado Historical Society, this small museum sits on land once farmed by the Southern Ute chief Ouray and displays artifacts from the Ute culture as well as dioramas and exhibits describing European exploration of the area, including the Dominguez-Escalante expedition of 1776. In addition to the collections of ceremonial artifacts, some of which once belonged to Ouray himself, the museum and park include a monument to the chief and the grave of his wife, Chipeta, as well as picnic facilities for passers-through.

The museum is two miles south of the town center on U.S. 550 and is open daily June–Oct., Mon.–Sat. 9 A.M.–4:30 P.M., and the rest of the year Mon.–Sat. 9 A.M.–4 P.M. The museum is also open for school groups and prearranged tours. Admission is $3 for adults, $2.50 for seniors, and $1.50 for kids. For more information, phone 970/249-3098, or write P.O. Box 1736, Montrose, CO 81402.

Montrose County Historical Museum

Providing a general history of the Uncompahgre Valley and the western slope—from Ute occupation through 20th-century irrigation and development—this museum highlights the late 19th-century pioneer and settler. Especially impressive are the museum's excellent displays of historical photos, particularly of Chief Ouray and his wife, Chipeta, and of the early days of the railroad—as well as the collections of artifacts, including Ute arrowheads and domestic items, from toys to medical equipment to musical instruments. Also of interest are replicas of nearby petroglyphs and a full-size homesteader's cabin with original furnishings. The museum's library includes Montrose newspapers 1896–1940, photos, and several historical publications.

The Montrose County Historical Museum is open Memorial Day through September Mon.–Sat. 9 A.M.–5 P.M. The museum is on West

COLORADO HISTORICAL SOCIETY

Colorado State Prison was Alferd Packer's home for several years after his conviction on charges of culinary impropriety.

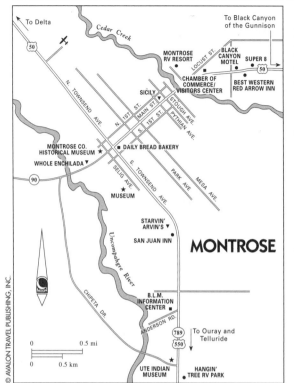

Several Montrose companies offer trips, including **Gunnison River Expeditions,** 970/249-4441. For fishing tackle and information, stop by **Cimarron Creek,** 317 E. Main St., 970/249-0408.

ACCOMMODATIONS
$50–100
Montrose's "Motel Row" is on the east end of town on Main Street/U.S. 50 East, where you'll find a dozen or so places to bed down. There are newer hotel-type lodges, as well as mom-and-pop places. The **Best Western Red Arrow Inn,** 1702 E. Main, 970/249-9641 or 800/468-9323, is one of the more fully appointed lodges in town (exercise room, fax and copy services, convention facilities, etc.) and has 60 rooms. Also on U.S. 50 East, the **Black Canyon Motel,** 1605 E. Main, 970/249-3495 or 800/453-4911, and the **Super 8,** 1705

SOUTHWESTERN

Main Street; admission is $2.50 for adults, with discounts for kids and seniors. For more information, phone 970/249-2085.

PARKS AND RECREATION
Golf
Montrose's 18-hole golf course (1350 Birch St., by way of Hillcrest Drive) is open to the public 7 A.M.–7 P.M. For information and tee times, phone 970/249-8551.

On the Water
Rafting, float trips, and fishing are extremely popular on Montrose-area rivers, including the nearby Gunnison and Uncompahgre. Most outfits also book trips to other Colorado waters. Go for a half day, or take a three- or four-day excursion. Prices start around $60.

E. Main, 970/249-9294, also have good, clean rooms; RV and truck parking available.

The **San Juan Inn,** 1480 U.S. Hwy. 550 S, 970/249-6644, is one of the first you'll come to as you approach from the south. The indoor pool and jacuzzi are especially nice after a day on the road.

Camping and RVing
Though it gets a bit cold on the Rockies' western slope for winter camping, from late spring to early fall the weather's much more accommodating, and the Montrose area offers a number of campgrounds, both private and government-run. The **Hangin' Tree RV Park,** 17250 U.S. Hwy. 50, 970/249-9966, has laundry facilities, showers, and a convenience store, and sites with full hookups; open year-round. The **Montrose RV Resort,** 200 N. Cedar, 970/249-9177, is

open Memorial Day through Labor Day and has both tent and RV sites, showers, a laundry, pool, and small store.

In addition to the campgrounds at Black Canyon of the Gunnison and Curecanti National Recreation Area (see above), you'll find a number of Forest Service campgrounds near Cimarron, in the Uncompahgre National Forest about a half hour east of Montrose: **Big Cimarron Campground** offers free camping at 16 sites along the Big Cimarron River—no drinking water available; **Beaver Lake Campground** has 16 sites on Beaver Creek; the 60 units at **Silver Jack Campground** on Silver Jack Lake provide access to good boating and fishing on the reservoir, as well as to hiking into the Big Blue Wilderness Area. To get to all three campgrounds, take U.S. 50 about 24 miles east of Montrose and then Owl Creek/Cimarron Road (dirt) 20 miles south.

FOOD

Montrose offers a decent number of nonfranchise, non-fast-food restaurants. **The Whole Enchilada,** 44 S. Grand, 970/249-1881, serves a variety of Mexican and Southwestern dishes, including fajitas, chimichangas, and blue-corn enchiladas. Most dinners are under $10. Open daily for lunch and dinner. For Italian food, try **Sicily's,** 1135 E. Main, 970/240-9199, specializing in homemade pizza and pastas and, weather permitting, serving on a cozy outdoor patio. Open for lunch and dinner Mon.–Sat., with a brunch on Sunday.

For an early-morning caffeine and sugar fix, stop in at **Daily Bread,** 346 Main, 970/249-8444, for fresh-baked breads and pastries and coffee to get your motor runnin'.

Starvin' Arvin's, 970/249-7787, is on U.S. 50 on the south side of town, right next door to the San Juan Inn. This moderately priced family-style restaurant serves breakfasts, lunches, and dinners daily 6 A.M.–10 P.M.

CALENDAR

Montrose is busy with events throughout the year. A few highlights are the **Fourth of July** parade and fireworks display, the **Montrose County Fair** (August), and a number of **Christmas shows and pageants** (December). For a complete listing of annual events, write the Montrose Chamber of Commerce (1519 E. Main St., Montrose, CO 81401).

TOURS

The Montrose Chamber of Commerce has delineated several specific scenic day trips from town and has published maps with mileages, average driving times, and other tips. Visit Ridgway State Recreation Area, Black Canyon National Monument, Curecanti National Recreation Area, or Grand Mesa National Forest—all of which are also discussed in this book. For maps and information, contact the chamber at 1519 E. Main, Montrose, CO 81401, or phone 970/249-5000 or 800/923-5515.

SERVICES

Phone the **Montrose Police Department** at 970/249-6609 and the **Montrose County Sheriff** at 970/249-6606. The offices of the **State Patrol** are at 2420 N. Townsend, 970/249-4392. **Montrose Memorial Hospital** is at 800 S. 3rd St., 970/249-2211. Montrose's main **post office** is at 321 S. 1st Street.

Recycling

Drop off most recyclables at **Montrose Recycle Center,** 1215 N. Townsend. The **City Market,** 128 S. Townsend, and **Safeway,** 1329 S. Townsend, will take aluminum.

INFORMATION

You can obtain further information about the Montrose area by stopping by or writing the **visitor information center,** 433 S. 1st, Montrose, CO 81401, or by phoning 800/873-0244. The visitor center is open Mon.–Sat.; if you're passing through on a Sunday, visitor information is available at the Ute Indian Museum (see above). Be sure to ask for the *Montrose Visitors Guide,* which includes a full listing of lodging and restaurants, as well as information sources for various recreational pursuits (hunting to scuba diving). For Internet information, or to request a hard-copy visitor's guide, visit www.visitmontrose.net.

Montrose's daily newspaper is the independently owned *Montrose Daily Press* (not published weekends or holidays), available for $.25 in racks around town. For subscription information, write 535 1st St., Montrose, CO 81401, or phone 970/249-3444.

For **road conditions and weather information,** phone 970/249-9363 or 800/821-4765.

TRANSPORTATION

United Express 800/241-6522, offers passenger service to **Montrose Airport,** 970/249-3203, on the north end of town, where you can also rent cars. Air service is also provided by **America West/Mesa,** 800/235-9292. Phone **Budget** at 970/249-6083, **Hertz** at 970/249-9447, or **Dollar,** 970/249-3770.

The Montrose **bus depot** is at 132 N. 1st, 970/249-6673. For taxi service, phone **Western Express Taxi,** 970/249-8880.

Ridgway

At the junction of U.S. 550 and Highway 62, Ridgway (pop. 400; elev. 6,900 feet) marks the point where scenery for southbound travelers begins to get absolutely breathtaking. Telluride-bound travelers will turn west at Ridgway, ascending the 8,970-foot Dallas Divide Pass before dropping back to Highway 145 and looping back into the little box canyon from the west. As you rise out of Ridgway toward the pass, look back over your shoulder to your left at the towering Mt. Sneffels Range, the highest point of which is 14,150-foot Mt. Sneffels.

If you're continuing south from Ridgway, you'll follow the course of the Uncompahgre River for 10 miles before reaching Ouray, a tiny Swiss-like village at the foot of Red Mountain Pass. From Ouray, you'll begin a switchback assault on the pass, climbing almost 3,500 feet in about a half dozen miles.

Ridgway dates from 1891, when it was a link on the Rio Grande Southern Railroad's route to Durango (175 miles to the south). Throughout the 20th century, Ridgway served as a supply center for miners working claims scattered in the San Juan Mountains. In addition, the little town is a natural hub for cattle ranchers in the surrounding valley.

Rail service to Ridgway was halted in 1951, when shipping rates became prohibitively expensive, though the little town still sees plenty

of travelers, in large part because of its "gateway" location. In the early 1970s, the movie *True Grit* was filmed in Ridgway.

Ridgway State Park

One of the state's newer parks (1989), this very nice recreation area two miles north of Ridgway surrounds a 1,000-acre reservoir on the Uncompahgre River. Three separate campgrounds offer nearly 300 campsites (some wheelchair-accessible), a boat-launching ramp, picnic facilities, and a visitor center, where you can get information on hiking, fishing, and nature programs.

For information or to reserve campsites, phone 970/626-5822.

Accommodations

Looking as if it belongs in Santa Fe instead of a Colorado mountain town, the gorgeous adobe **Chipeta Sun Lodge and Spa,** 304 S. Lena, 970/626-3737, offers great views of the Uncompahgre Valley and surrounding mountains. There are twelve rooms, and highlights are the solarium and the third-floor spa. A variety of packages are available, with rates running about $90–225. For more information and photos, check out www.chipeta.com. You can also get rooms at the **Super 8 Lodge,** 373 Palomino Trail (junction of U.S. 550 and Highway 62), 970/626-5444—$50–100.

Food

At the **Ridgway Mountain Market,** on Highway 62, 970/626-5811, you can build your own sandwich (and pay by the pound), or choose from other deli items, including "everything from wieners to caviar." It's also a great place to stock up before heading out into the backcountry. At the **True Grit Cafe,** 123 N. Lena, 970/626-5739, you can chow down on hearty burgers and sandwiches while checking out a variety of memorabilia from the John Wayne film for which the café was named.

Information

For more information on Ridgway, write the **Ouray County Chamber of Commerce,** P.O. Box 145, Ouray, CO 81427, 970/325-4747 or 800/228-1876. Be sure to ask for a copy of the *Ouray County Vacation Guide,* a very thorough guide (60 pages) to communities in the area, including lodging, dining, and recreation opportunities. The **Ridgway Visitor Center** is at 102 Village Square W (junction of 550 and Highway 62), 970/626-5868.

Ouray

Nestled in a natural amphitheater in a narrow box canyon and surrounded by peaks that tower 5,000 feet above the valley floor, Ouray (pop. 700; elev. 7,800 feet) is known as the "Little Switzerland of America." Approached from either the north or the south, Ouray will certainly arrest the eye. As you enter the valley from the north, the high walls seem to close in on you, and as you pass through the quiet little town—its streets lined with Victorian-era homes and lavish old hotels—you can't help but be struck by the seemingly unpassable pass ahead. All around you the mountains rise: to the west, White House Mountain (elev. 13,493 feet); to the south, Hayden Mountain (elev. 13,100 feet); and to the northwest, Cascade Mountain (elev. 12,100 feet). Ouray (you-RAY) seems trivialized by nature.

If you arrive from the south, you'll be switchbacking down Red Mountain Pass and looking at the town from almost straight above. This is when it really seems like a Little Switzerland, the colorful buildings and green meadows at the base of these towering peaks looking like something right off a calendar or the cover of a travel magazine. The view is breathtaking.

Don't let it take so much of your breath that you forget to keep your eyes on the road; this is a steep sucker, with dramatic horseshoe turns. Look away from the road for too long and you could end up taking the shortcut to town. Instead, take advantage of the turnouts provided for sightseeing and picture-taking.

The town takes its name from the Southern Ute Chief Ouray, whose people had been coming to the valley for centuries before the white men came to mine and ranch. The hot mineral waters that bubble from the ground in several different places were said to have healing powers. Today those same waters soothe the aches of road-weary motorists, as well as hikers, cross-country skiers, horseback riders, and others who enjoy relaxing in the hot mineral waters after a day of recreation. You'll find hot springs at several local lodges and at the municipal pool and park at the north end of town.

History

Ouray dates from 1875, when prospectors entered the valley and discovered a number of rich silver lodes in the nearby mountains. The town was incorporated in the fall of the next year and named for Chief Ouray, universally praised for his intellect and attempts to bring whites and Native Americans together in harmony. Soon, the Uncompahgre area's first newspaper, the *Ouray Times,* was founded after a wagon train hauled type and presses from Cañon City.

Ouray boomed in the early 1880s but then went temporarily belly up when the silver market crashed in 1893. In 1896, however, carpenter Thomas F. Walsh discovered gold in the Camp Bird silver mine, bought rights to the mine for $20,000, and quickly became one of Colorado's laborer-turned-millionaires. Until 1902, the mine yielded ore worth between $3 and $4 million a year, sometimes matching Walsh's initial investment in a single week. By 1910, the mine had produced $26 million in gold.

Many of the Ouray-area mines are still worked, although as costs of extraction have increased disproportionately to the price of gold, the industry has become less and less important. Instead, Ouray and Ouray County rely on tourism and ranching to keep local economies vital.

SIGHTS

Bachelor-Syracuse Mine

Named for three bachelors and a group of miners from Syracuse, New York, this mine produced $90 million in gold and $8 million in silver, as well as respectable amounts of lead, zinc, and copper. Tours of the mine, which take you 3,350 feet into the side of Gold Hill, offer an excellent sense of Ouray's early (and dangerous!) mining days. Be sure to bring a sweater, as the temperatures inside stay right about 50° Fahrenheit.

The Bachelor-Syracuse Mine is open to the public late May through mid-September. Tours are on the hour 9 A.M.–6 P.M. mid-May through September, with reduced hours of operation the rest of the year. Rates are $12.95 for adults, $10.95 for seniors, and $6.95 for kids. For an

COURTESY OF THE NATIONAL ARCHIVES

Ouray (the arrow), the Southern Ute Chief for whom the town is named

added fee, you can pan for gold and keep what you find. For information or reservations, write Bachelor-Syracuse Mine Tour, County Rd. 14, Drawer 380W, Ouray, CO 81427, or phone 970/325-4500.

Ouray County Historical Museum

With an emphasis on the area's mining and railroading history, this museum, housed in an old hospital dating from 1887, also features exhibits highlighting contributions of the Southern Utes, ranchers, educators, doctors, and other settlers. The museum is at the corner of 5th Street and 6th Avenue. Open daily May–Sept., 10 A.M.–5 P.M., weekends only the rest of the year. Admission is $4, $1 for kids. For more information, phone 970/325-4576.

Walking Tour

Ouray is small enough (downtown is about six by four blocks) that you can easily tour the town by foot in an afternoon—it is hilly, though. The Ouray County Chamber of Commerce has designated a specific walking tour of the National Historic District, with more than two dozen buildings of historical significance. Among them: **St. Elmo Hotel,** 426 Main, built in 1898, since restored, and today operating as a restaurant and inn; the **Western Hotel** (est. 1891), 220 7th Ave., Ouray's original deluxe lodge; and **Wright's Opera House** (est. 1888), fascinating for its Romanesque and Greek Revival architecture. Pick up a map and detailed guide at the visitor center next to Ouray Hot Springs Pool, or write the chamber of commerce, P.O. Box 145, Ouray, CO 81427.

Million Dollar Highway

In the early 1880s, Otto Mears built a toll road over Red Mountain Pass to make it easier to get Ouray ore out of the valley; the road greatly increased the efficiency of mining in the Ouray-Silverton-Telluride District. Today, U.S. 550 from Ouray to Silverton follows the old route much of the way and is known as the Million Dollar Highway. Why? No one seems to be able to say for sure, though there are at least three explanations you'll get, depending on which "expert" you talk to: the road was paved with gold-bearing gravel, the value of which was not discovered until the project was completed; the road was so steep and so precarious that an early traveler was heard to claim, "You couldn't pay me a million dollars to go back over that pass"; or, the road cost about $1 million to pave in the mid-20th century.

PARKS AND RECREATION

Ouray Hot Springs Pool and Park

Ideal for soaking away a day's hiking or skiing aches, or cooling off after a long day's driving, this municipal facility features hot springs, soaking pools, and cool-water lap and goof-around pools. And the location couldn't be better: kick back in the 104°F water and dig the towering peaks that rise 5,000 feet from the valley floor and box Ouray into the canyon.

If you don't feel like getting wet, there's a spacious grassy lawn, perfect for tossing the Frisbee about, as well as picnic facilities and a playground. The hot springs and park are right on U.S. 550 at the north end of town. The pools are open daily 10 A.M.–10 P.M. in the summer, noon–9 P.M. in the winter. For more information, phone 970/325-4638.

Box Canyon Falls and Park

With the waters of Clear Creek crashing nearly 300 feet into the narrow granite-walled Box Canyon, this city-owned park offers spectacular views and hiking trails. In addition, a steel suspension footbridge across the canyon affords a stunning view of the falls and creek. There are also restrooms and picnic facilities.

The falls and park are just south of town off U.S. 550 (watch for the signs). Hours are 8 A.M.–dusk, mid-May through mid-October. Admission is $1.25 for adults and $.75 for kids. For more information, phone 970/325-4464.

Jeep Touring

This is one of the primary reasons folks come to Ouray. Scores of rocky back roads wind into remote canyons, past abandoned mines, through ghosts of old mining camps, and along cliffsides with sheer dropoffs to valley floors thousands of feet below. Trips vary from the fairly easy tour to

Yankee Boy Basin to the more difficult (and dangerous) drive over Imogene Pass to Telluride. The Yankee Boy Basin tour begins on Camp Bird Road just south of Ouray, follows Canyon Creek to the Camp Bird Mine (five miles from Ouray), and then veers west toward a series of wildflower-laden valleys at the base of Dallas and Gilpin Peaks and Mt. Emma. The Imogene Pass road begins at the Camp Bird Mine and winds over the 13,509-foot summit, affording views of some of the best scenery in one of most scenic areas of the state.

If you're looking to explore on your own, pick up Forest Service maps at the Ouray Ranger District Office, 2505 S. Townsend, Montrose, 970/249-3711. You'll also find a 4WD map and descriptions of routes in Ouray County's *Vacation Guide*.

San Juan Scenic Jeep Tours, in operation since 1946, offers half- and full-day tours throughout the area. Go on a predesigned tour, or make your own itinerary. Prices start at about $25 for adults for half-day trips. You can also rent vehicles. For reservations or information, write P.O. Box 143, Ouray, CO 81427, or phone 970/325-4444 or 970/325-4154.

Several other companies in Ouray also offer Jeep rentals and 4WD tours. Among them are Switzerland of America, P.O. Box 184, Ouray, CO 81427, 970/325-4484, and Colorado West, 332 5th Ave., 970/325-4014. You can also rent Jeeps at the KOA campground north of town.

Hiking

The woods, peaks, and steep canyons of the Ouray area are ideal for exploring by foot, and hikers will find a wide variety of trails. The following are but a sampling of the hikes in the area. The *Ouray County Vacation Guide* describes a dozen or so more, providing lengths and degrees of difficulty. Lower Cascade Falls Trail is a short (half-mile) but fairly rugged trail that begins at the top of 8th Avenue and takes you down into the canyon to the bottom of Cascade Falls—expect to do some scrambling over boulders, and be careful of slick spots caused by melting snow. For something a little longer, although not as demanding, try the five-mile Portland Trail, which begins on the east side of town at Amphitheater Campground in Portland Basin. **Upper Cascade Trail** also begins at Amphitheater Campground and though half as long gains more than twice the altitude (1,500 as opposed to 700 feet). The trail offers great views of the valley, as well as of waterfalls on Cascade Creek.

For more information on hiking in the area, stop by the Ouray Visitors Center next to Ouray Hot Springs Pool, or contact **Uncompahgre National Forest,** either at its headquarters at 2250 U.S. Hwy. 50, Delta, 970/874-7691, or at the **Ouray Ranger District Office,** 2505 S. Townsend, Montrose, 970/249-3711. You can also get information, as well as maps and gear, at **Cabin Fever,** 624 Main.

Fishing

Ridgway Reservoir at the **Ridgway State Recreation Area,** about 12 miles north of town on U.S. 550, is regularly stocked with rainbow and brown trout. Fish the 1,000-acre lake either from shore or from a boat; launch your own boat from the six-lane ramp near the main entrance, or rent a boat from **San Juan Skyway Marina** on the lake, 970/626-5480. You can also fish for trout at the tiny but scenic **Molas Lake** on the Silverton side of Molas Pass, where you'll also find camping and picnicking facilities (fee charged, except for in a very small public area). The **Uncompahgre River** between Ouray and the reservoir is also stocked, though much of the river passes through private property.

Cross-Country Skiing

The nonprofit Ouray County Nordic Council operates **Red Mountain/Ironton Park Cross-Country Trails,** with several designated routes and loops that wind among eight historic landmarks and sites. There are both beginner and intermediate trails. For information, write P.O. Box 468, Ouray, CO 81427.

Other Activities

Though one could devote most of a summer to hiking or Jeep touring in the Ouray area, there are other things to do. One of the best ways to get into the heart of the backcountry is by horse-

back. **San Juan Mountain Outfitters/San Juan Dude and Guest Ranch,** whose stables are along the Uncompahgre River two miles north of town, offers half- and full-day trips, as well as overnight camp-out rides and full-service hunting pack trips. Reservations required. Write 2882 County Rd. 23, Ridgway, CO 81432, or phone 970/626-5630 or 800/331-3015.

Ouray Livery Barn on Main Street in Ouray, 970/325-4606, has one- and two-hour and half-day rides along some of the nearby area's hiking trails, including Oak Creek and Portland Trail.

San Juan Balloon Adventures offers half- and one-hour balloon tours of the Uncompahgre River Valley, as well as a "Balloon-N-Brunch" flight; soar out to a secluded picnic brunch, sip champagne with your meal, and climb back aboard for the trip home. Reservations required at least 12 hours in advance. Write P.O. Box 66, Ridgway, CO 81432, or phone 970/626-5495.

ACCOMMODATIONS

Ouray is a wonderful little hideaway town, a perfect place to hole up after a particularly demanding job project or semester of graduate school. Personally, I've always wanted to rent a little room in town, set up my word processor, and write all those scripts I've been telling myself Hollywood is aching to produce.

Ouray offers a variety of accommodation options, with one common denominator: they all tend to fill up. Don't expect to be choosy if you're looking Friday afternoon for digs for Friday night. In fact, you might not be able to find anything at all, at least in the summer, when southwestern Colorado swells with sightseers and vacationers. Call ahead for a room.

The small **Antlers at Ouray,** right downtown at 407 Main St., 970/325-4589, has no-frills doubles ($100–150), and the **Best Western Twin Peaks Motel,** 125 3rd Ave., 970/325-4427, has a natural hot-springs whirlpool ($50–100). Both the Antlers and the Twin Peaks are closed in the winter. You'll also find natural outdoor hot tubs at **Box Canyon Lodge and Hot Springs,** 45 3rd Ave., 970/325-4981 ($50–100).

In the center of town at 426 Main St., the **St. Elmo Hotel,** 970/325-4951, was built before the turn of the 20th century and has recently been remodeled. It's now an 11-room bed-and-breakfast inn furnished with Victorian-era antiques. Doubles run $100–150.

For top-of-the-line bed-and-breakfast accommodations, try the **Damn Yankee Country Inn,** 100 6th Ave., 970/3254219 or 800/845-7512, offering elegance and stunning views, as well as discounted lift tickets at Telluride Ski Area—$100–150.

For more information on lodging in Ouray, write the Ouray Chamber Resort Association, P.O. Box 145, Ouray, CO 81427, or phone 970/325-4746, website: www.ouraycolorado.com.

Camping and RVing

Ouray Rotary Park on U.S. 550 at the north end of town offers free overnight camping and picnicking. **Amphitheater Campground,** 970/249-3711, immediately south of town (east side), is operated by Uncompahgre National Forest and has 30 sites, pit toilets, and no showers.

A **KOA** campground, 970/325-4736, is four miles north of Ouray—110 tent and RV sites, plus a few cabins. You can also camp at **Timber Ridge Motel and Campground,** just north of town on U.S. 550, 970/325-4523. Motel rooms have fireplaces and steam rooms.

FOOD

Ouray has a respectable number of good restaurants, some of which draw folks from throughout the Uncompahgre Valley area. Keep in mind that Ouray is largely a summer-oriented town, and that many of the businesses, including restaurants, shut down from November or so through April or May.

The **Grounds Keeper Coffee House** at 6th and Main, 970/325-0550, has wonderful health-oriented breakfasts and lunches, including homemade cobblers, soups, and salads, for $3–6. A longtime favorite is the **Bon Ton Restaurant,** next door to the St. Elmo Hotel at 426 Main, 970/325-4951. The Bon Ton spe-

cializes in Italian food, as well as steaks, seafood, and chicken, with dinners ranging from $12 to $24. Sunday brunch is served 10 A.M.–1 P.M. For something a bit more casual, try **Cecelia's Family Restaurant,** 630 Main St., 970/325-4223, where you can get burgers, fried chicken, grilled-cheese sandwiches, and soups and salads. Dinner entrées run $6–15. Open for breakfast, lunch, and dinner daily June through mid-October. The **Outlaw Steakhouse,** 610 Main, 970/325-9996, is a classic Western steakhouse that was spotlighted by *National Geographic Traveler* in 1990. You can also get seafood and chicken dinners. Dinners are $10–22. Open daily for dinner May through mid-October, with limited hours of operation the rest of the year.

ENTERTAINMENT AND EVENTS

As the commercial, recreational, and cultural center of Ouray County, Ouray offers lots of goings-on throughout the year, from arts-and-crafts shows to music festivals to the **Jeepers Jamboree.** Highlights include the **Music in Ouray** classical concert series (mid-June); the **Imogene Pass Run** footrace up Imogene Pass, which connects Ouray and Telluride (early September); and the **Octoberfest** (early October). Write the Ouray County Chamber of Commerce (see Information, below) for a complete calendar of annual and special events.

Suzanne's Broadway to Branson is a multigenre musical variety show (country, big band, gospel, Broadway, etc.) offering evening shows throughout the week and Sunday afternoon at 630 Main (above Cecilia's Family restaurant). Phone 970/325-0357 for show times, reservations, and rates (which run about $12 for adults, with discounts for seniors, kids, and at Sunday matinees).

INFORMATION

If you're passing through, be sure to stop at the **tourist information center** on the north end of town next to Ouray Hot Springs and Pool. If you're planning to visit, write **Ouray**

Chamber Resort Association, P.O. Box 145, Ouray, CO 81427, or phone 970/325-4746, website: www.ouraycolorado.com. Be sure to request a copy of the *Ouray Visitor's Guide,* which is full of maps, suggestions for hiking and jeep-touring trails, and listings of accommodations, restaurants, and other businesses. For information on Uncompahgre National Forest, phone the main office in Delta at 970/874-7691, or stop by the **Ouray Ranger**

District Office, 2505 S. Townsend, Montrose, 970/249-3711.

You can also get maps (topo, 4WD, hiking, etc.), as well as books on local and regional history at **Cabin Fever,** 624 Main Street.

The *Ouray County Plain Dealer* newspaper is published weekly and is available in racks and shops throughout the area. For subscription information, write P.O. Box 607, Ouray, CO 81427-0607, 970/325-4412.

Silverton

Silverton (pop. 790; elev. 9,300 feet) is the seat of San Juan County and the center of the Las Animas Mining District. Situated in a tiny pocket between Molas and Red Mountain Passes, and literally ringed with towering mountain peaks, Silverton began as an isolated mining camp, became a railroad supply center, and between 1880 and 1910 had a reputation as one rip-roarin' town, where whoring, drinking, and gunfighting went on around the clock.

Known as the "mining town that never quit," Silverton finally shut down its last mine in August 1991, after a century and a quarter of silver, gold, lead, zinc, and copper production. Eureka, Howardsville, Red Mountain, and other once-thriving mountain communities are accessible by back roads; get information and maps from the Silverton Visitors Center on the west end of town.

Silverton is also known today as the northern terminus of the Durango and Silverton Narrow Gauge Railroad, and for the dozens of gift shops, as well as restaurants and hotels, that occupy 100-year-old buildings. In the summer, passengers take the winding railroad up from Durango, spend a few hours wandering through the shops of Silverton (or spend the night), and then get back on the train for the trip back to Durango (you can also begin the trip in Silverton; see Sights, below). The Silverton Gunfighters Association entertains tourists every evening at 5 with gunfights in the street.

History

A mining camp dating from 1871, when the first lodes were discovered here, Silverton was originally known as Baker's Park, after Captain Charles Baker, who had explored the area in the early 1860s. According to local legend, the town's name was changed in 1874 when a local mine operator announced, "We may not have gold here, but we have silver by the ton."

The camp prospered in the late 1870s and early '80s. Several large hotels and other buildings were constructed, among them the Grand Imperial Hotel and the gold-domed courthouse. In 1882, the Denver and Rio Grande Railroad arrived in town, greatly improving accessibility to the little community. During this time, Silverton's Blair Street, one block east of Greene, was a hotbed of brothels, saloons, and gambling houses. Madams such as Mamie Murphy, Kate Starr, and Jew Fanny operated 24-hour-a-day "pleasure palaces" that drew huge numbers of miners and other callers from throughout western Colorado. Things got so wild, in fact, that Silverton eventually recruited Bat Masterson from Dodge City to "clean up the town."

Silverton fared better during the silver crash of 1893 than did many of Colorado's ore-dependent towns, its mines continuing to produce an average of $2 million a year. In fact, Silverton prospered well into the next century; the population in 1910 was 2,153, more than twice what it is today. By 1918, more than $65 million in silver had been taken from Silverton-area mines.

SIGHTS

Durango and Silverton Narrow Gauge Railroad

One sightseeing highlight of a visit to Silverton is a ride aboard this famous narrow-gauge railway. Though the vast majority of tourists catch the train at its southern terminus, Durango, you can also begin in Silverton. Options include one-day, round-trip tours; round-trip tours with an overnight layover in Durango; one-way trips; and combination bus-train round-trip tours. Reservations highly recommended. Round-trip fares are about $55 for adults. Phone the Durango depot at 970/247-2733, or write Durango and Silverton Narrow Gauge Railroad Company, 479 Main Ave., Durango, CO 81301. (Also see Sights under Durango, below.)

San Juan County Museum

In the old San Juan County jail, this small museum, operated by the San Juan County Historical Society, is geared mostly toward the area's railroad and mining history. The first floor of the building, constructed in 1902, served as the sheriff's living quarters, while the jail cells, which have not been removed, are on the second floor.

The San Juan County Museum, on Greene Street between 15th and 16th, is open daily 9 A.M.–5 P.M., Memorial Day through Labor Day, and thereafter daily 10 A.M.–3 P.M. through mid-October. Admission is $2.50 for adults. For information, phone 970/387-5838.

COURTESY OF COLORADO HISTORICAL MUSEUM

downtown Silverton in the late 19th century

Historical Walking Tour

Whether you realize it or not, if you're walking around Silverton, you're taking a historical walking tour. You can't help it: Silverton *is* history. The two main north-south streets—Greene and Blair—offer a tour of the town's past, from its most elegant to its most indecorous; while most of the "respectable" businesses were on Greene, Blair was known for its brothels and wild saloons.

The Silverton Chamber of Commerce and the San Juan County Historical Society have printed a map and thorough description of historic Silverton. Included are more than 50 structures within a few short blocks of each other. Among the buildings on the tour are the **Grand Imperial Hotel,** 1221 Greene, which was built in 1883; the **Exchange Livery,** 1244 Greene, built in 1906 (buggies and wagons were stored downstairs, horses upstairs); and **Natalia's,** 1161 Blair, and the **Shady Lady,** 1154 Blair, both of which were popular brothels around the turn of the 20th century.

The map and guide are published in the back pages of the *Silverton-San Juan Vacation Guide,* available at the chamber of commerce visitor center at the town's entrance.

Christ of the Mines Shrine

Dedicated to Silverton's miners, past and present, this statue of a 12-ton Rio-like Jesus stands arms spread in a stone alcove on the hillside above Silverton. Erected in 1959, the statue, made of Italian marble, is thought to have been the source of several local "miracles," including the fact that no workers were present when a local mine exploded one Sunday night. To get there, take 10th Street west from downtown Silverton.

RECREATION

Hiking

Silverton is surrounded by the San Juan National Forest and is just northwest of 405,000-acre Weminuche Wilderness, the state's largest and most visited wilderness area. This is steep and high country, though, with the Continental Divide passing just a few miles east of town, and hikers should know what they're doing.

For topo maps of the area, and for suggestions on hiking, contact the **Animas Ranger District Office** of the Forest Service, 701 Camino Del Rio, Durango, CO 81301, 970/247-4874. The Silverton Visitors Center also has information and maps, as does **Outdoor World,** 1234 Greene, Silverton, 970/387-5628.

Though you can get into the backcountry by walking from downtown Silverton, you can also take the Durango-Silverton Railroad. Certain runs stop for backpackers (to let you on or off). For information, phone 970/387-5416 (Silverton) or 970/247-2733 (Durango).

Jeep Tours
Like Ouray, Silverton is a four-wheel-driver's paradise, and the old cliff-hanging mining roads are litmus tests for driving skills. One popular trail is the **Alpine Loop,** which connects Silverton, Lake City, and Ouray and crosses **Engineer Pass** (elev. 12,800 feet) and **Cinnamon Pass** (elev. 12,620 feet). The 65-mile route is designated a **Backcountry Scenic Byway,** and is not one of the more treacherous in the area.

Several companies in town offer 4WD rentals, including **Triangle Jeep Rental,** 864 Greene St., 970/387-9990; **Silver Summit Jeep Rentals,** 640 Mineral St., 970/387-0240; and **Red Mountain Jeep Rentals,** 664 Greene St., 888/970-5512.

Pick up 4WD and topo maps at **Outdoor World,** 1234 Greene, 970/387-5628.

ACCOMMODATIONS

For such a tourist-oriented town, Silverton has a number of good places to stay at decent rates, from hotels in century-old buildings to modern motels. There's not a whole lot in terms of numbers, though, and you'd be wise to make reservations ahead of time. Remember, too, that things slow down in Silverton considerably during the winter, and some of the lodges are available mid-May through September only.

Hotels and Motels
The **Alma House,** 220 E. 10th., 970/387-5336, is a small (11-room) very nice inn two blocks from the train depot and one block from Greene. Built in 1902 and empty for years, the old stone hotel has now been restored. Full breakfast included. Rooms run $100–150, with a couple at $75. The red sandstone **Wyman Hotel and Inn,** 1371 Greene in the upper-downtown area, 970/387-5372, was built in 1902 and offers 19 large rooms, with rates also including full breakfast—18 rooms running $95–190.

You can also get rooms in the **Alpine House,** 1234 Greene, 970/387-5628 ($50–100), some of which have full kitchens. At the **Teller House Hotel,** 1250 Greene, 970/387-5423, which was built in 1886, rooms run $50–100, some with shared bath.

The lowest rates in town are undoubtedly at the **Silverton Hostel,** 1025 Blair St., 970/387-0115. All seven of the private rooms go for under $50, and you can get dorm lodging for about $12 a night ($75 a week, $260 a month).

Camping and RVing
Molas Lake Park, 970/387-5410, five miles south of Silverton on U.S. 550, is a privately run campground with 60 sites on a 40-acre trout-stocked lake. The area gets a certifiable A+ for scenery. **Silverton Lakes Campground,** 970/387-5721, has tent and RV sites right next to town at the junction with Highway 110. **South Mineral** Forest Service campground just north of town has 23 sites and flush toilets (no showers). Take U.S. 550 four miles north, then Forest Service Road 585 five miles west. Phone the Durango District Office of San Juan National Forest at 970/247-4874 for reservations or more information.

FOOD

An excellent place to get started in the morning is at the **Avalanche Coffee House,** 1067 Blair, 970/387-5282, specializing in pastries by the Silverton Baking Company and espresso coffees.

If you're looking for a premade lunch to take into the backcountry, try **Mad Mama's Pies,** a bakery and deli at 1157 Greene St., 970/387-5877.

For Mexican food, try **Romero's Restaurant y Cantina,** 1151 Greene, 970/387-5561. Open for three decades and specializing in margaritas, Romero's also serves *menudo* (a sure sign the place is authentic!). Dinners are in the $7–10 range.

Another highly recommended Silverton restaurant is **Handlebars,** 117 E. 13th St., where lunch salads (spinach, pasta, and veggie) run about $7 and soups, burgers (beef and buffalo), and sandwiches are $6–9. Dinners, which include beef and chicken plates, range $8–20.

ENTERTAINMENT AND EVENTS

Although Silverton is absolutely beautiful during the snowy months, its location and elevation make it less a winter than summer destination. Among the highlights of the summer season are the **Jubilee Folk Festival,** late June; **Fourth of July,** with a parade and fireworks; **Kendall Mountain Run,** a 13-mile footrace up Kendall Mountain (4,000-feet altitude gain) in mid-July; and the **Hardrockers Holiday Mining Celebration,** with tugs-o'-war, drilling competitions, wheelbarrow races, etc., in mid-August; and the **Great Rocky Mountain Brass Band Festival,** mid-August. In addition, the **Silverton Theatre Group,** which began producing plays in 1988, has a half dozen or so offerings each season, varying from standards by Neil Simon and George Bernard Shaw to lesser-known and sometimes locally penned works. Performances are in the Miners Union Theatre, at the corner of 11th and Greene; $10–15 for adults, $6–10 for kids. For information and reservations, phone 970/387-5337 or 800/752-4494.

For more information on these and other Silverton events, contact the Silverton Chamber of Commerce at 970/387-5654.

SHOPPING

Though Silverton was at one time defined by miners, saloons, gambling halls, and brothels, today the little town is defined by tourists, restaurants, gift shops, and more gift shops.

Like several other Colorado mining-camps-turned-tourist-towns (Cripple Creek, Georgetown), Silverton relies heavily on the out-of-town dollar to keep the head of its struggling economy above water, and its main drag (Greene Street) is virtually lined with gift and souvenir shops. So, if you're looking for something to bring home, look no further. And even if you're not, allow yourself a couple of hours to wander up and down Greene Street and down the side streets. Poke your head into the little specialty shops; you'll find the owners very friendly and laid-back (no high-pressure selling in this low-key little town).

In addition to the shops you'd find in most tourist-oriented towns (Christmas, jewelry, minerals, T-shirts, Native American art), Silverton also has a handful of stores specializing in the area's history.

INFORMATION

You'll want to stop in at the two chamber of commerce visitor centers in Silverton. The main one, at the town's entrance, is stocked with literature on Silverton and the surrounding area, and there are staff members to answer questions—open year-round. The second one, the Blair Street Information Booth, on Blair between 12th and 13th, has brochures and information on local businesses, including the menus of many of Silverton's restaurants. There are also picnic tables and public restrooms—open summer only.

You can get information before your visit by writing the **Silverton Chamber of Commerce,** 414 Greene St., P.O. Box 565, Silverton, CO 81433, or by calling 800/752-4494 or 970/387-5654. Be sure to get copies of the *Silverton-San Juan Vacation Guide* (published by *The Silverton Standard* and *The Miner*), which includes coupons good at local gift shops, as well as stories on Silverton's history and suggestions for things to do in the area.

For Internet information, visit www.silverton.org, where you'll find an extremely user-friendly site covering Silverton and the surrounding area in great detail.

Telluride and Vicinity

A mining town that has turned world-class resort village, Telluride (pop. 1,400; elev. 8,745 feet) is full of juxtapositions and ironies: gingerbread Victorian homes stand in the shadows of ultra-modern condominium complexes; grizzled life-time locals share bar space with Austrian ski racers named Wolfgang, while young WASPy passers-through with wannabe dreadlocks hang out on benches on the sidewalk; chic boutiques, new-age bistros, and Southwestern art galleries line the streets; and, in perhaps the most potentially explosive stand-off of all, developers, no- and slow-growthers debate the town's future according to their own visions.

> *On a dark, cold December night with a light snow falling softly on deserted side streets and fire-light flickering in windows of century-old Victorians, the place becomes truly magical.*

Situated at the end of a box canyon deep in the San Juan Mountains, Telluride almost overnight has mushroomed from a sleepy little community with summer music and film festivals and some of the best uncrowded skiing in the country to a hot spot attracting the likes of Tom Cruise and Donald Trump. Which, of course, is why there are such strong feelings among the community. Locals have seen real estate prices skyrocket in recent years (a *modest* restored Victorian in town can fetch anywhere from $500,000 to $1.5 million), and people fear the little town will become another Aspen.

In addition to their ambivalence about the gentrification and possible overdevelopment of the town of Telluride, locals are split over the development of Telluride Village, the new megabucks resort at the base of the ski area. Though the deluxe hotels and other lodging promise to pump big money into the economy, and to provide more jobs for Telluridians trying to eke out a living in the canyon, the new housing is clearly aimed at outside budgets. As Telluride Village began to take shape in the late 1980s, and the cost of living in town zoomed skyward, many local workers were forced to move "down valley," where housing was still affordable.

Apparently things have slowed down a bit, though, and real estate, for example, has reached a plateau. In addition, several nearby housing developments, including Lawson Hill (two miles from Telluride; three-bedroom duplex: $155,000), have put home ownership within the reach of locals. Plus, some of the housing is "deed restricted," meaning new homes are designated for purchase by locals only, and they must meet several criteria, including living and working within the local school district, to qualify.

Still, developable land is scarce and demand for it high, so you can expect housing to continue to command top dollar. And though Telluride's future hangs uncertain, it's still one of the prettiest and classiest places in Colorado. And on a dark, cold December night with a light snow falling softly on deserted side streets and firelight flickering in windows of century-old Victorians, the place becomes truly magical. If you plan to hit the slopes in the morning, it's easy to think you've found paradise.

HISTORY

Telluride's history dates from 1875, when it served as a supply center for several mines—including the Sheridan, Ajax, and Smuggler—that had been staked in the high mountains just east of the little box canyon. Originally known as Columbia, Telluride took its name from tellurium, a sulphurous compound prevalent in the district and often found in the gold itself. (There's little evidence to support the claim of barstool historians that the name comes from "To Hell You Ride," a saying that apparently once quite accurately described the nature of the trip to the rugged and rowdy little town.)

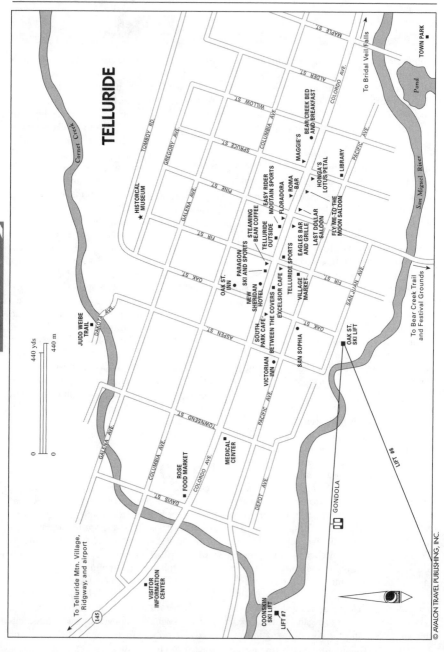

SOUTHWESTERN

TELLURIDE

0   440 yds
0   440 m

To Telluride Mtn. Village, Ridgway, and airport

VISITOR INFORMATION CENTER

COONSKIN SKI LIFT
LIFT #7

GONDOLA

LIFT #8

To Bear Creek Trail and Festival Grounds

OAK ST. SKI LIFT

Cornet Creek

Corbet Creek

JUDD WEIBE TRAIL

HISTORICAL MUSEUM

ROSE FOOD MARKET

MEDICAL CENTER

VICTORIAN INN

SAN SOPHIA

SOUTH PARK CAFÉ

BETWEEN THE COVERS

EXCELSIOR CAFÉ

NEW SHERIDAN HOTEL

OAK ST. INN

PARAGON SKI AND SPORTS

STEAMING BEAN COFFEE

TELLURIDE OUTSIDE

TELLURIDE SPORTS

VILLAGE MARKET

EAGLES BAR AND GRILLE

EASY RIDER MOUTAIN SPORTS

FLORADORA

ROMA BAR

LAST DOLLAR SALOON

HONGA'S LOTUS PETAL

FLY ME TO THE MOON SALOON

LIBRARY

MAGGIE'S

BEAR CREEK BED AND BREAKFAST

To Bridal Veil Falls

TOWN PARK

Pond

San Miguel River

TOMBOY RD.

GREGORY AVE.

COLUMBIA AVE.

PACIFIC AVE.

COLORDO AVE.

MAPLE ST.

ALDER ST.

WILLOW ST.

SPRUCE ST.

PINE ST.

FIR ST.

OAK ST.

ASPEN ST.

TOWNSEND ST.

DAVIS ST.

DAKOTA AVE.

GALENA AVE.

COLUMBIA AVE.

GALENA AVE.

COLORDO AVE.

DEPOT AVE.

PACIFIC AVE.

SAN JUAN AVE.

OAK ST.

FIR ST.

145

The Rio Grande Southern Railroad arrived in Telluride in 1890, making the camp far more accessible. Almost overnight, the tents and shacks that had lined Colorado Avenue were replaced by homes, shops, brothels, and hotels. By some estimates, more than 5,000 people were living in Telluride in the early 1890s.

The New Sheridan Hotel was constructed between 1890 and 1895. Typifying the lavishness of Colorado's mining industry-financed hotels, the New Sheridan offered luxurious accommodations for passers-through, as well as a dining room said to rival that at Denver's Brown Palace. Sarah Bernhardt and Lillian Gish were among the hotel's early guests.

Telluride's boom was short-lived, however. After the silver market crashed in 1893, many of the town's mines shut down, and homes and businesses were abandoned. By the last years of the 19th century, overall productivity had greatly decreased and the remaining miners were disgruntled; the euphoria of the early part of the decade had vanished. In 1901, mine owners presented workers new contracts, and guess what? They stipulated more money to owners and management and less to labor. The

union struck, though nonunion miners were brought in, resulting in intense standoffs and violence, with the National Guard being called in during the winter of 1904 to impose peace on the town.

Though a handful of mines remained open through the first part of the 20th century, the Bank of Telluride closed, and all but a few people left town. The population in 1930 was 512. Still, Telluride's contribution to Colorado mining history had been impressive. By 1909, the district had produced more than $60 million in gold, silver, copper, lead, and zinc.

Telluride lay remote and mostly idle for most of the midcentury, though its second boom was on the horizon. As early as 1938, the town was realizing its potential as a winter resort area, although poor snowfalls and World War II combined to discourage the idea's first backers. However, in 1945, after the war, Telluride's first rope tow was built. The lift ran for two seasons, lay inoperative for more than a decade, and then was rebuilt in 1958 using an old car engine for power. That winter, season passes sold for $5.

It was still another decade before Telluride would make the transition from a tiny ski area

downtown Telluride shortly after a light January snowfall

© STEPHEN METZGER

used almost exclusively by locals to one ultimately attracting some of the best and most sophisticated skiers from around the world. In 1968, in a move that could eventually be seen as disconcertingly prophetic, businessman Joe Zoline arrived in Telluride from Beverly Hills with plans to develop a "winter recreation area second to none." Work began almost immediately, and Telluride Ski Area was dedicated in April 1971.

For the next 15 years or so, although the town was again hitting pay dirt, it enjoyed a relatively downscale and unpretentious elegance, guaranteed by its remote location. Though it had a reputation for some of the best skiing—as well as some of the best music and film festivals—in the state, you had to really *want* to go there: while Denver skiers could get to Winter Park in 1.5 hours, Telluride was a six- or seven-hour drive, more if the weather was at all threatening.

Then in the late 1980s, Telluride Regional Airport was built, and it became as easy to get to Telluride as to get to Vail or Aspen. Regular flights were offered from Los Angeles, Phoenix, and Albuquerque, and express jets were flying into Telluride daily from Denver. The face and tenor of the town changed dramatically and permanently. By 1990, local waiters and ski-lift operators were no longer renting cheap rooms in town; there weren't any. By now, property values had skyrocketed, and working people for the most part couldn't afford to live in town. Huge resort complexes—hotels and conference centers—were springing up at Telluride Mountain Village. Movie stars and rock musicians were being seen in shops buying sealskin after-ski boots; realtors found themselves dealing with a whole new breed of buyer, folks who flew into town in their own jets.

Still, at least as of last inspection, Telluride has managed to survive the onslaught of outside money. As long as local music promoters continue to book (and sell tickets to) acts such as James Taylor, Emmy Lou Harris, and John Prine, and as long as the mountain continues to attract skiers to whom nothing matters but deep snow and steep slopes, the town should retain most

of its integrity and charm, and should remain one of Colorado's true treasures.

Historical Walking Tours

The Town of Telluride has published a map and guide to historical Telluride. With more than a dozen sites, the tour includes the **San Miguel County Courthouse** (in use since 1887), the **town hall** (built in 1883), the **New Sheridan Hotel** (early 1890s), as well as several private residences dating from before the turn of the last century. The map and guide are printed in the vacation guide in *Telluride Magazine* and are available at the Telluride Visitor Center and most real estate offices. **Historic Tours of Telluride** offers guided tours of town, including both famous and lesser-known Telluride landmarks. Catch them at 10 A.M. daily from Elk's Park June to September. Cost is $8 per person. Phone 970/728-6639 for reservations and information.

PARKS AND RECREATION

This is why folks both live and visit here. Situated in one of the prettiest pockets of Colorado's

Olympic gold medalist Phil Mahre crosses the finish line just ahead of his dual-slalom competitor.

gorgeous San Juan Mountains, Telluride offers a range of activities guaranteed to satisfy even the most demanding outdoor enthusiast. Though best known for its downhill skiing, Telluride is also an excellent base for myriad other recreational pursuits, from hiking, horseback riding, and mountain biking to jeep touring, fishing, and white-water rafting. In addition, it's a great place just to experience *being* outdoors. In the fall, when the aspen leaves turn to gold and crimson, there may not be a lovelier place on earth.

Downhill Skiing and Snowboarding

Known until recently as a mountain geared mostly toward advanced and expert skiers, Telluride has spent several summers cutting more trails and opening things up for intermediate and beginning skiers. The mountain straddles a high ridge, which provides two separate base areas. Two lifts are based in town and take skiers up the steep face that looks down on Telluride's streets; the main base area is accessible by driving around the ridge to Telluride Mountain Village, where you'll find the ski school, administrative offices, and other base facilities. A free skier shuttle runs regularly between the two areas.

Generally, the advanced and expert skiing is on the town-of-Telluride side. Several of these runs—Spiral Stairs, for example—offer some of the steepest, nastiest lift-serviced skiing in the country. In addition, you'll find excellent bump skiing over here, as well as the best powder—the northern exposure means snow staying in better shape longer. Meanwhile, the Telluride Mountain Village side caters more to intermediate and beginning skiers, with lots of long, sweeping runs, perfect for GS-style cruising, in packs or all by your lonesome.

With 12 lifts servicing 1,055 acres, Telluride has one of the longest vertical drops in the state: 3,522 feet. In addition, *Mountain Sports and Living* magazine reader polls ranked Telluride's lift lines the state's shortest and the bumps the West's best. The terrain is officially designated 21 percent beginner, 47 percent intermediate, and 32 percent advanced and expert. **Free tours** of the mountain are offered daily at 10 A.M. Look for

the guides in the turquoise ski parkas. The Telluride Ski School includes instruction in Telemarking and snowboarding.

For more information on Telluride Ski Area (reservations, ski school, lift tickets, etc.), write P.O. Box 1115, Telluride, CO 81435, or phone 970/728-6900 or 888/355-8743. For **snow conditions,** phone 970/728-7425. The resort's website is www.telski.com.

Cross-Country Skiing

Nordic skiing in all its forms is very popular in Telluride. Telemarkers, skaters, and tourers can all find plenty of action. If you just want to get some fresh air and check out the valley a little bit, try the **Town Park and River Trail,** which is maintained by the city and runs east from the town park along the San Juan River. **Telluride Resort Nordic Center** is a full-service center at Telluride Mountain Village. Sunshine Express lift at the ski area provides access to more than 30 km of excellent trails of varying ability levels. You can also arrange guided backcountry tours. Phone 970/728-4424.

For the more ambitious, **San Juan Hut Systems** offers a series of backcountry cabins linked by cross-country ski trails. The huts are five to six miles apart, and the scenic trails are skiable even for beginning Nordic skiers. For information or reservations, write Box 773, Telluride, CO 81435, or phone 970/626-3033; you can also visit the website at www.telluride2.com/colorado/San-Juan-Hut-System.

WHEN THE SNOW MELTS
City Parks

On the east side of town, along the San Juan River, **Telluride Town Park** is perfectly befitting the little community's character and charm. In addition to two dozen campsites (no hookups, small fee), the park has picnic facilities, volleyball, basketball, and tennis courts, playground equipment, a skateboard park, and a small lake where kids can catch trout recently arrived from the hatchery. For information phone 970/728-3071. An alternative picnic area is the very nice little **San Miguel County Park** on the San Miguel

River in Placerville, about 15 miles northwest of Telluride (no overnight camping).

Cycling

The old mining roads twisting and slicing throughout the San Juan Mountains make Telluride a natural for mountain biking, and the sport has really taken off in recent years. For the ultimate southern Colorado mountain-bike experience, check out **San Juan Hut Systems'** Telluride-to-Moab trip. This 215-mile weeklong tour features stops at six cabins along the way, and all you have to do is ride (you can go with or without a guide). The huts are 35 miles apart and each has 12 padded bunks (with blankets), a propane stove, kitchen utensils, a wood-burning stove, and firewood. You can also arrange day trips through San Juan Hut Systems. Guided tours start at about $40 a day. For information or reservations, write P.O. Box 733, Telluride, CO 81435, or phone 970/626-3033. The organization's website is www.telluride2.com /colorado/San-Juan-Hut-System. In town, stop by 224 E. Colorado.

For accessories, tips on biking in the Telluride area, or to rent bikes, stop in at **Paragon Ski and Sports,** 213 W. Colorado, 970/728-4525, or **Telluride Sports,** 150 W. Colorado, 970/728-4477.

Guided bicycle tours are available through Paragon Sports and **Telluride Outside,** 800/831-6230. Get topo maps of Uncompahgre National Forest from the **Norwood Ranger District Office,** 1760 Grand, Norwood, CO 81423, 970/327-4261.

Golf

The 18-hole, 7,009-foot **Telluride Golf Course** is at Telluride Mountain Village, five miles south of town. For information and tee times, phone 970/728-6366.

Hiking

Hiking is one of the best ways to get out and enjoy southwestern Colorado, and the Telluride area offers a wide array of trails, from short walks to backcountry excursions. The town's de rigueur outing is to **Bridal Veil Falls.** This relatively easy two-mile round-trip walk on a dirt road takes about two hours and leads to the largest waterfall in the state; the water cascades off a 425-foot cliff. Begin at Pandora Mill on the east end of town. Total elevation gain is about 1,000 feet. The two-mile **Judd Weibe Trail** begins at the north end of Aspen Street, where it crosses Cornet Creek. Allow up to three hours, but expect excellent views. Along the way, you'll also pass the remnants of Telluride's old "pesthouse," where horse-drawn wagons once carried Telluride's contagious to quarantine. Another hike known for its stunning scenery begins in town at Pine Street and climbs two miles and 1,300 feet in elevation through **Bear Creek Canyon** to a multi-tiered waterfall.

For complete information on hiking in the area, pick up a copy of Susan Kees's *Telluride Hiking Guide* (Pruett Publishing Co., Boulder), available in bookstores and some outdoors shops in the area. Get topo maps from the Forest Service District Office in Norwood, 970/327-4261.

Fishing

With lots of good fishing in southwestern Colorado, particularly in the San Juan Mountains, Telluride's as good a place as any to base yourself. Though you won't find the lunker Mackinaw that you might at Blue Mesa or Shadow Mountain Reservoir, there's plenty of good stream fishing, especially for those who'd rather entice a native fish to rise to a hand-tied fly than hook a larger hatchery fish on bait or hardware.

The west fork of the **Dolores River,** which parallels Highway 145 south of town, has rainbows, browns, and cutthroats. Fish for rainbows in the faster water and rapids below pools; fish for browns in deeper, slower water. Closer to town, the **San Miguel River** is regularly stocked with pan-size rainbows, as is the little lake at **Town Park,** an excellent spot to give younger kids their first lessons in the sport (fishing here is for kids 12 and younger only).

Popular lakes in the area include **Alta Lake, Priest Lake,** and **Trout Lake,** all accessible via Highway 145 south of town; **Woods Lake** is west on Highway 145 toward Placerville.

For information, licenses, equipment, and guided fly-fishing trips, stop in at **Telluride Sports/Telluride Flyfishers,** 150 W. Colorado Ave., 970/728-4477, or **Telluride Outside,** 121 W. Colorado, 970/728-3895, the latter also offering a fly-fishing school.

Rafting

Though most Telluride-area streams are too small for rafting, you can book a range of trips on other southwestern Colorado rivers—the Gunnison, Dolores, Animas—through **Telluride Sports,** 970/728-4477, or **Telluride Outside,** 970/728-3895.

Four-Wheel-Drive Tours

Four-wheel-drive rigs and southwestern Colorado go together like motor scooters and Bangkok. Not only are they ideal for simply getting around in the winter, but in the summer they're the only (well, okay, quickest and easiest . . .) way to some of the region's more secluded and scenic spots.

The mountains around Telluride are interlaced with old mining roads perfect for four-wheeling. And since the roads have already been cut, your contribution to environmental damage is limited. (Do stay on those roads, though: as tempting as it might be to take a short cut across a high-mountain meadow, keep in mind how vulnerable and fragile these ecosystems are.)

Imogene Pass (elev. 13,509 feet) is the cliff-hanging historical route connecting Telluride and Ouray (about 18 miles). You'll pass both the abandoned Tomboy Mine and the remains of Fort Peabody, which was a guard station during the labor-management conflicts at the turn of the 20th century. For neither the timid nor the amateur back-roadster, the pass is as difficult as it is scenic. Experienced drivers: take Oak Street north, and turn east onto the Forest Service-maintained pass road.

A much easier and less dangerous 4WD route is **Ophir Pass** (elev. 11,740 feet), an 1881 toll road that connected Telluride and Silverton. Today, it's one of the most popular backcountry scenic routes in the area. Note: this is a one-way road, with traffic moving east to west. Start in Silverton, and go north on U.S. 550 about five miles; the road is unmarked, but directly across from it is a sign for Red Mountain Summit (five miles). From Silverton to Ophir is about 15 miles.

For information, tours, and 4WD rentals, contact **Telluride Outside,** 970/728-4477 or 800/831-6230, or **Dave's Mountain Tours,** 970/728-7737.

Gondola Rides

In summer, Telluride Ski Area offers free gondola rides. This is an excellent opportunity—especially for nonskiers, who don't ordinarily get to these peak-tops—to view the grandeur of the southern Rocky Mountains. For information, phone 970/728-6900.

ACCOMMODATIONS

Because of Telluride's remote location, and the fact that it's grown increasingly popular in recent years, especially in winter, lodge owners can pretty much get whatever they want for a room. Though not yet on a par with Aspen, rooms in Telluride are expensive (winter high season is from mid-December till just after the first of the year; summer rates go up during festivals and special events). If you can, plan to come when things are slower. During January, for example, rooms are the least expensive (of the ski season), and the skiing's at its best.

For a complete listing of accommodations available in Telluride, or to make reservations, contact **Telluride Central Reservations** at 888/605-2578.

$50–100

Surprisingly, lodging is still available in this price range, though you don't have a whole lot from which to choose. The **Oak Street Inn,** 970/728-3383, one block off the main drag, offers small rooms with baths down the hall ($58), as well a limited number of rooms with private baths for a few bucks more. Don't expect anything fancy and you won't be disappointed.

$100–150

For a real taste of Telluride, try the recently remodeled (1995) **New Sheridan Hotel,** 231 W. Colorado Ave., 970/728-4351 or 800/200-1891, which has a wide range of rates, including rooms in this price category (suites go for $400 a night). The **Victorian Inn,** 401 W. Pacific Ave., 970/728-6601 or 800/537-2614, though built in 1976, blends in gracefully with the surrounding 19th-century structures and is within a short walk of the Coonskin and Oak Street lifts. The **Bear Creek Bed and Breakfast,** 221 E. Colorado Ave., P.O. Box 2369, Telluride, CO 81435, 970/728-6681 or 800/338-7064, also has rooms in this range, though the inn's rates vary tremendously depending on season and size of room ($80–250).

$150–250

Another distinctly Telluride inn is the **San Sophia Inn,** 970/728-3001 or 800/537-4781. This elegant bed-and-breakfast is right downtown near the base of the lifts, and ski packages are available. **Telluride Mountain Village** is a short drive from town (another series of base lifts for the ski area), where you'll find plenty

of lodging in condominium complexes and upscale hotels. Though they don't offer the charm of staying in one of Telluride's historical hotels or refurbished old homes, they do offer convenience and just about every amenity you can imagine, including ski and golf packages. One of the fanciest hotels is **Wyndham Peaks Resort,** 970/728-6800, a 181-unit, $60 million number with a huge athletic club, as well as conference and banquet facilities.

FOOD

Gone Skiing?

Telluride is first and foremost a ski town, and if there's been a good dump during the night, it's not unusual for a restaurant to shut its doors for the day. Don't be surprised when looking for breakfast to find signs on doors that read, "Powder day. Closed. See you this afternoon."

Start Me Up

The **Steaming Bean Coffee Co.,** right downtown at 201 W. Colorado, 970/728-0793, serves espressos, cappuccinos, and other cof-

© STEPHEN METZGER

The New Sheridan Hotel in downtown Telluride dates from the early 1890s.

fees guaranteed to put a bite in your morning, as well as pastries and other goodies. Another local favorite is **Maggie's Bakery,** 217 E. Colorado, 970/728-3334, where you can get espressos, regular coffees, pastries, and complete breakfasts. A casual café attracting everyone from white rastas on the road to longtime Telluridians, Maggie's also serves lunch, with an emphasis on health and vegetarian dishes.

Other Telluride Restaurants

The **Roma Bar and Cafe,** 133 E. Colorado, 970/728-3669, serves excellent Italian food in an anything-but-pretentious atmosphere (listen to the pool balls smacking each other in the next room). Entrées are in the $9–13 range, and you can also order off the appetizer-pizza menu (pizzas start at about $10). For burgers, pastas, pizzas, and other lunch specials ($6–14), try **Eagles Bar and Grille,** 100 W. Colorado, 970/728-0866, which also serves upscale dinners, including steak and seafood ($12–38). **Floradora,** 103 W. Colorado, 970/728-3888, supposedly named after a couple of Telluride pioneers (Flora and Dora, who worked the Red Light District), serves excellent lunches and dinners at reasonable prices. From burgers to steaks to chicken and Mexican dishes, with daily specials and soup *du jour.* Great bar for munching nachos and catching a game on television.

Another good bet is the **South Park Cafe,** 300 W. Colorado, 970/728-5335, serving salads, sandwiches, burgers, and pasta dinners ($5–14). For Asian food, try **Honga's Lotus Petal,** 970/728-5134.

Grocery Stores

Rose Victorian Food Market and Deli, 700 W. Colorado, 970/728-3124, and **Village Market,** 157 S. Fir, 970/728-4566, both carry meats, produce, and other grocery products, with emphasis on natural and health foods.

ENTERTAINMENT

And a Good Saloon in Every Single Town

Sometimes you're in the mood for something smoky, poolly, loud, and local. The **Last Dollar Saloon,** 100 E. Colorado, is it. Put your quarter down on the table, order a draft, and soak in the local flavor. During the summer the talk is of softball—aging adolescents' tales of catches almost made and hard grounders almost run out—and during the winter it's of skiing—how much snow'll fall tonight, the awesome bumps under Number 9, the new Rossi slalom ski. Just know that you'll have to wash the Marlboro out of your sweater (and hair) in the morning.

For live rock and rhythm and blues, check out **Fly Me to the Moon Saloon,** 132 E. Colorado, 970/728-6666. You can also sometimes hear live tunes at the bar at **One World Cafe,** 970/728-5530.

CALENDAR

In addition to Telluride's better-known events—the bluegrass, jazz, and film festivals—the community offers dozens of other intriguing workshops, conferences, bike and foot races, and other festivals. In early June, you can attend the simultaneous **Wine Festival** and **Balloon Rally.** Taste fine wines or sip champagne as the skies fill with colorful hot-air balloons. The world-famous **Telluride Bluegrass and Country Music Festival** is the highlight of the summer. Hotels and campgrounds fill up, and music fills the valley from the stages at Town Park. Wednesday through Friday, lesser-known acts take the stage, while Friday night through Sunday afternoon, players such as Bill Monroe, James Taylor, John Prine, the Nitty Gritty Dirt Band, Bela Fleck, and Wolfstone entertain the crowds. **Fourth of July** has always been a time of festivities and fireworks in Telluride, with much of the action in Town Park.

The **Telluride Jazz Festival** in early August began in the late 1970s and has featured mainstream and experimental artists from around the world, including Herbie Hancock, Branford and Wynton Marsalis, Etta James, and the Neville Brothers. **Wild Mushrooms Telluride** is a three-day celebration of the edible fungus. Included in the late August festival are lectures, workshops, identification hikes, and cooking and tasting events.

Over Labor Day weekend, the **Telluride Film Festival** attracts big- and not-so-big-name directors, writers, and other scholars to retrospectives and national and world premieres. Seminars, featuring directors and actors, take place in Town Park and are free. **Talking Gourds** in September is an annual gathering of poets, storytellers, and performance artists for workshops, readings, and shows. Finally, the weeklong **Telluride Airmen's Rendezvous** in June is the longest-running and largest hang-gliding affair in the world. Top flyers sponsor lectures and workshops and compete in the World Hang Gliding Championships.

For festival tickets and information, phone 800/525-3455.

SHOPPING

Although no Aspen, Telluride does claim a number of moderately fancy specialty shops, galleries, and boutiques where without a movie-star income you're not going to be able to do much more than look and hope. In addition, some of the ski shops display duds that are far more flash than function. Still, isn't that partly what vacation shopping's all about?

Whether you're looking to buy or simply to ogle, Telluride's galleries are a kick to poke around in. With primarily Native American- and Southwestern-flavored artwork, the shops sell pottery, jewelry, rugs, paintings, prints, and sculpture.

SERVICES

The offices of the **Telluride Police Department** are in the town hall building at 113 W. Columbia, 970/728-3071. The **Telluride Medical Center** is at 500 W. Pacific, 970/728-3848. The **post office** is at 101 E. Colorado.

Recycling

Drop off most recyclables at the transfer station for **United Waste and Recycle,** 330 Colorado Avenue.

INFORMATION

Telluride Visitor Services operates a 24-hour automated **visitor information center** at 666 W. Colorado (on the west side of town, on your right as you approach). This is an excellent place to pick up brochures and other information on accommodations and things to do in the area. Before your visit, write P.O. Box 653, Telluride, CO 81435, phone 888/605-2578, or go online to www.telluridemm.com.

Telluride has two excellent newspapers, the daily *Telluride Times-Journal* and the weekly *Daily Planet.* Check both ($.25 each) for word on local events as well as on matters of interest to the community and visitors alike. Peter Shelton, of nearby Ridgway, named America's Ski Writer of the Year three times, has a regular column in the *Times-Journal.*

Telluride Magazine, published twice a year (summer and winter editions), is rife with information on things to do, and where to eat, stay, and play; it also profiles local celebrities, developers, and developments. Though this is a very commercial and slick publication, heavy on promotional fluff, reading between the lines will teach you a lot about Telluride. It's available at the Telluride Visitor Center and at most real estate offices in town.

Between the Covers Books and Music, 224 W. Colorado, 970/728-4504, carries an excellent selection of travel- and Colorado-related publications, with a lot of books of local interest. The **Wilkinson Public Library,** 970/728-4519 or 970/728-6613, is at 134 S. Spruce—closed Sunday and Monday.

For **road and weather conditions,** phone 970/728-3330.

TRANSPORTATION

Considering its remote, box-canyon location, Telluride's remarkably easy to get into and out of, thanks (or curses, depending on your perspective) largely to the jet airport in town. **United Express,** 800/241-6522, **Continental Connection,** 800/525-0280, and **America West Express,** 800/235-9292, offer passenger service to **Telluride Regional Airport** 970/728-5313. And once in town, you'll have no trouble at all getting around. You can walk in five minutes from one end of Telluride to the other, and free shuttles run regularly to Telluride Village and the base of the lifts (or you can ski directly from town, with two of the resort's lifts beginning two blocks from the main drag).

HIGHWAY 145 SOUTH TO CORTEZ

One of the most scenic legs of the **San Juan Scenic Byway,** this 80-mile stretch of state highway cuts across San Juan National Forest and drops out of the San Juan Mountains toward the Four Corners area and the Ute Mountain Indian Reservation. About 10 miles out of Telluride, you'll pass through the tiny town of **Ophir,** a silver camp named for the location of the mines of mythical King Solomon. During the 1870s, the little community boasted 500 people. Today,

it's the starting point for the Ophir Pass road to Silverton.

Lizard Head Pass (elev. 10,222 feet), just a few miles south of Ophir, is named for the 400-foot-high monolith northwest of the highway. Apparently, the needle more closely resembled the head of a lizard before a slab of rock broke off.

Along this route, you'll drive along the east fork of the Dolores River, and pass by several high mountain lakes. The highway also parallels the west fork of the Dolores, a few miles to the west. About five miles north of Rico, you can catch a Forest Service-maintained dirt road that will take you over to and down the west fork before rejoining Highway 145 near the confluence of the two forks, just west of Stoner. From here south, the Dolores runs alongside the highway for 15 miles, past the town of the same name, before feeding into McPhee Reservoir. Among several campgrounds lining the river is **Priest Gulch Campground and RV Park,** 26750 Hwy. 145, 970/562-3810, where you can also pick up fishing tackle and licenses.

Cortez and Vicinity

Seat of Montezuma County, Cortez (pop. 9,000; elev. 6,200 feet) is the closest large town to Mesa Verde National Park. Situated in the heart of the Four Corners area, the community is surrounded by scrubby mesas and canyonlands once home to tens of thousands of Anasazis. Between about A.D. 550 and 1300, the Anasazi farmed this area, living in elaborate "cities" of stone pueblos, some clinging to cliffsides, some freestanding. The most well known, of course, are the cliff dwellings at Mesa Verde, but this entire area is full of ruins, and the region is remote enough that some of them will probably remain undiscovered forever. In addition, the area is so thick with ruins that even many of those that have been discovered—the smaller ones, that is—are considered no big deal. In fact, in the summer of 1995, a private developer offered to sell 35 acres of land just a couple miles north of Cortez, with at least one ruin guaranteed to exist on each parcel.

Cortez was first settled by nonnatives in 1885,

when a group of farmers arrived in the area with plans to irrigate crops with water from the Dolores River. Within a year, the Mitchell Springs Project was pumping water from the river into nearby fields, and in 1887 the town of Cortez was officially founded. The town served throughout the 20th century as a trading and supply center for local farmers and sheep and cattle ranchers—Ute, Navajo, Hispanic, and white. Recently, tourism has become of more importance, as Cortez capitalizes not only on its proximity to Four Corners–area ruins but to prime recreation areas as well.

SIGHTS
Anasazi Heritage Center
Ten miles north of Cortez and three miles west of Dolores, this BLM-operated research and display center includes laboratories, collection areas, a library, theater, museum, and gift shop,

as well as a reproduction of an Anasazi dwelling. The center houses nearly two million artifacts and documents—some of which were recovered from the 12th-century Anasazi site where the center was built—from yucca sandals to blankets and embroidery, and the museum is highlighted by several hands-on displays: grind corn like the Anasazi did or examine other seeds, pieces of bone, flint, or pottery shards under a microscope. In addition, the museum explains dig strategies and lab analyses, portrays the prehistoric Southwest on an Anasazi timeline, and includes a photograpic and textual explanation of the Dolores Valley Water Project and McPhee Dam. There's also an excellent gift-and-book store.

The Anasazi Heritage Center is at 27501 Hwy. 184, just west of downtown Dolores. Open March–Oct., daily 9 A.M.–5 P.M.; the rest of the year, daily 9 A.M.–4 P.M. For more information, phone 970/882-4811. Admission is $3; kids 17 and under admitted free.

Canyons of the Ancients National Monument

Established in June 2000 (under President Clinton's Antiquities Act proclamation), this 163,000-acre monument contains a wide range of historic and prehistoric structures and geologic formations—many of them of significant scientific importance. Included within the boundaries of the BLM-administered monument is the 370-acre Hovenweep National Monument, which is still administered by the National Park Service (see Four Corners Area, below). The new monument is open to visitors, and plans are to develop some of the sites for camping.

Among the points of interest in Canyons of the Ancients is **Lowry Pueblo National Historic Landmark.** Occupied by 100 Anasazis between A.D. 800 and 1000, Lowry was restored in the mid-1960s and includes eight kivas, a great kiva, and 40 rooms. The ruins are nine miles west of Pleasant View off U.S. 666 (turn west on County Road CC). There are picnic tables, drinking water, and toilets, and the ruins are wheelchair-accessible. Pick up a brochure detailing the self-guiding tour.

Further information is available at the Anasazi Heritage Center, 970/882-4811, or at the BLM San Juan field office in Durango, 970/247-4874. Detailed information is also available from the monument's website at www.co.blm.gov /caninfo.

The Cortez Center/University of Colorado Museum

This small museum in downtown Cortez emphasizes pre- and post-Columbian Native American cultures of the Southwest. Included are explanations of cliff-dwelliing construction, examples of Anasazi pottery and basketry, and Ute and Navajo pottery and embroidery. Artifacts have been collected from throughout the Four Corners area. In addition, there are traveling exhibits; summer of 1995 boasted an extremely moving collection of Edward Curtis photographs of Native Americans taken during the 1920s (on loan from the CU museum in Boulder). There's also a small gift shop.

Summer evenings at 7:30, Native American dances are held on the grounds next door to the museum. Sometimes Native American storytellers recount ancient tales. Admission to the museum, dances, and storytelling is free, donations accepted. The museum is at 25 N. Market (a half block north of Main/U.S. 160). Call 719/565-1151 for more information.

A word of caution about scheduling and dependability: Native American dances are absolutely riveting, linked as they are to ancient mythologies and stories and ways of viewing life on Earth. However, because of various conflicts, scheduled Native American dances don't always occur, well, on schedule. In fact, sometimes scheduled Native American dances don't occur at all. I would definitely *not* plan my vacation around a scheduled performance, nor go too awfully far out of my way to attend one without confirmation first. Call ahead, and then keep in mind that if they say the pageant will happen, it *probably* will. Probably.

Crow Canyon Archaeological Center

If you've ever wanted to take part in a dig, actually to visit and work at a legitimate archaeological site, here's your chance. Crow Canyon Archaeological Center is a serious research center, with library, laboratories, and computer tie-ins to other centers, all with an emphasis on the prehistoric cultures of the Southwest. In addition, the center offers an innovative program by which visitors can join in the research. A variety of programs are offered, from daylong to weeklong, as well as workshops designed especially for teachers. Cost for the daylong programs—offered twice or thrice midweek, June through mid-October—start at about $30 a day for adults ($20 for ages 12–18, $15 for under 12), which includes lunch. Reservations are required at least a day in advance. To get to Crow Canyon, take U.S. 666 four miles north from Cortez, turn left on Road L, and follow the signs. Note: the road is not paved the last couple of miles. For reservations, or more information on the programs available, call 970/565-8975 or 800/422-8975.

Dove Creek

Still farther north on U.S. 666 is Dove Creek, seat of Dolores County, where many Dust Bowl farmers ended up after fleeing Oklahoma in the 1930s. Zane Grey lived here for a brief period, and his *Riders of the Purple Sage* is supposedly set here.

In the summer of 1990, two University of Colorado hikers who were tracking bighorn sheep in the Dove Creek area stumbled on the virtually untouched ruins of a 1,100-year-old Anasazi village. Mountain Sheep Village, as the site was named, is significant to archaeologists for several reasons, not the least of which is that it is one of the northernmost Anasazi sites ever discovered. The village, which dates from around A.D. 800 and is off limits to the public, probably consisted of about 200 rooms on six acres and housed between 150 and 200 people.

Ute Mountain Casino

Feelin' lucky? Want to see what the one-armed bandits have in store? Think you can draw to beat the dealer's 19? Ute Mountain Casinos offers limited-stakes gambling ($5 max), with blackjack tables, video poker, keno, and more than 300 slot machines. The casino is open daily 8 A.M.–4 A.M. To get there, take U.S. 160 south from Cortez for 11 miles. You can't miss it.

PARKS AND RECREATION
Cortez City Park

Next to the Cortez Visitor and Colorado Welcome Centers, this grassy hillside park has very good picnic facilities—plenty of shade—as well as a kids' playground, basketball hoops, and a public swimming pool. Directly adjacent to the park (behind and to the north), **Centennial Park** sprawls for several city blocks, offering more picnic tables, large lawns, and a lake/pond where you can feed the resident ducks and geese.

McPhee Reservoir

In 1987, when McPhee Dam was completed and McPhee Reservoir filled in, the world lost some of its most gorgeous river and canyon country, as well as some of its most valuable archaeological treasures. Hundreds of ancient Anasazi ruins, and probably hundreds of thousands of artifacts, now lie deep beneath the surface of the lake, one of the largest in Colorado. Perhaps, though, that is a better place for them. Leaving them undisturbed at the bottom of a reservoir is certainly better than destroying them to build roadways, and maybe more ethical than transplanting them to museum storage rooms. At any rate, as you look out across the water, think about the people who lived in the river valley 1,100–1,300 years ago, farming beans, corn, and squash, and building intricate stone pueblos. Think about nature's *true* course.

McPhee Reservoir is about 12 miles north of Cortez via U.S. 160, Highway 145, and a short access road—also via Highway 184. The lake offers boating, water-skiing, camping, and fishing (for rainbow trout as well as warm-water fish such as bass and bluegill). Two Forest Service campgrounds, **McPhee** and **House Creek,** offer a combined 133 sites (no showers at either). For information, phone 970/882-7296; for reservations, phone 800/283-CAMP (283-2267).

River Running

The Dolores River is one of western Colorado's premier streams, though McPhee Dam has affected it in still-untold ways. Stretches can still be run, however, with any of several Four Corners–area outfitters, among them: **Durango Rivertrippers,** 720 Main, Durango, 970/259-0289; **Peregrine Outfitters,** also in Durango, 970/385-7600; and **Wilderness Aware,** in Buena Vista, 719/395-2112.

Fishing

The Dolores is also one of the Southwest's premier trout streams, and Cortez is a good point at which to begin an exploration of the river's upper stretches or the 11-mile stretch below McPhee Reservoir. The reservoir itself offers good fishing for trout, as well as warm-water fish. For licenses, supplies, and information, stop by **The Tackle Shack,** 11290 Hwy. 145, 970/565-6090.

PRACTICALITIES

Accommodations

A junction town and base for folks exploring Mesa Verde National Park, Cortez offers plenty of relatively inexpensive lodging, with numerous motels along the main routes through town (Main Street and Broadway).

Under $50

Among the least expensive digs in town are **Tomahawk Lodge,** 728 S. Broadway, 970/565-8521, and **TraveLodge,** 440 S. Broadway, 970/565-7778. Nothing fancy, but clean and comfortable.

$50–100

The **Anasazi Motor Inn,** 640 S. Broadway, 970/565-3773 or 800/972-6232, is one of the nicer lodges in Cortez. Also nice are the **Best Western Sands,** 1120 E. Main, 970/565-3761, and **Best Western Turquoise Inn and Suites,** 535 E. Main, 970/565-3778. A *huge* **Comfort Inn** is at 2321 E. Main, 970/565-3400, next to a **Holiday Inn Express,** 2121 Main, 970/565-3764.

The **Grizzly Roadhouse Bed and Breakfast,** 3450 U.S. Hwy. 160 S, 970/565-7738 or 800/330-7286, accommodates up to eight guests;

accommodations include rooms in the main house or a two-bedroom, two-bath guest cottage with full kitchen. **A Bed and Breakfast on Maple Street,** 102 S. Maple, 970/565-3906 or 800/665-3906, offers a range of rooms and packages, including horseback riding, tickets to Ute Mountain Tribal Park, massage, sack lunches, and dinner at local restaurants. Rates go up to $300 but include two nights' lodging for two people, with dinner and other bonuses.

You'll also find several RV campgrounds in the Cortez area, including the **Cortez–Mesa Verde KOA,** east of downtown on U.S. 160, 970/565-9301, and the **Lazy-G Campground and Motel,** at the U.S. 160–Highway 145 junction, 970/565-8577 or 800/628-2183.

Food

Cortez offers lots of fast-food restaurants and trucker-style cafés. In addition, several longtime favorites have been feeding locals and passers-through for years. The **Main Street Brewery,** 21 E. Main, 970/564-9112, is Cortez's answer to the brewpub craze, offering good brewed-on-the-premises beers and pub fare to go with. Entrées run $6–14. Open for dinner daily and for lunch Mon.–Saturday. **Francisca's,** 125 E. Main, 970/565-4093, is a favorite for Mexican food, serving burritos, chimichangas, and other favorites—$5–10. Closed Sunday. For Italian, try **Nero's Restaurant,** 303 W. Main, 970/565-7366, where dinner entrées run $10–15, with excellent pasta dinners in the $8–10 range. The **M and M Truckstop and Family Restaurant,** 7006 U.S. Hwy. 160, 970/565-6511, is a classic roadhouse, specializing in green chili, Navajo tacos (like a tostada, but on fry bread instead of a tortilla), and Mexican food—open 24 hours a day.

If you've been out in the backcountry living off freeze-dried campfood and just feel like binging, try the **Warsaw Inn Restaurant,** U.S. 160 East at the junction with Highway 145, 970/565-8585, where a full-service, all-you-can-eat smorgasbord awaits empty tummies.

Shopping

In the heart of Native American country, Cortez has more than a sampling of Native American gift shops and "trading posts." If you're looking for authentic art—jewelry, sculpture, kachina dolls, etc.—expect to pay for it. The work has gotten very popular in recent years, and gone are the days when you could get a Navajo rug for $50. You'll also find that the prices don't vary a whole lot from one store to the next, though you still should shop and compare. Also, don't fall for the ubiquitous "50 percent off sale." Seems jewelry is *always* 50 percent off.

One store worth checking out is **Mesa Verde Pottery and Gallery Southwest,** 27601 U.S. Hwy. 160 E, 970/565-4492. Even if you're not interested in buying, poke your head in and take a look around—in addition to quality art, you'll also find inexpensive souvenirs.

Services

The offices of the **Cortez Police Department,** 970/565-8441, and the **Montezuma County** **Sheriff,** 970/565-8444 (or 970/565-8441 in emergencies), are at 601 N. Mildred. **Southwest Memorial Hospital** is at 1311 N. Mildred, 970/565-6666. The Cortez **post office** is at 35 S. Beech, 970/565-3181.

Information

The **Cortez Visitor Center** and a **Colorado Welcome Center** are housed in an adobe-style building at City Park on Main Street. Stop in for information on lodging, dining, recreation, and sightseeing in Cortez, the Four Corners area, and the rest of Colorado. For information before your visit, write **Cortez Area Chamber of Commerce,** P.O. Box 968, Cortez, CO 81321, or phone 970/565-3414 or 800/346-6526. Information is also available online at www.southwestdirectory.com/Cortez.

For **road and weather information,** phone 970/565-4511.

Four Corners Area

Four Corners is the only place in the United States where the borders of four different states meet. Colorado, New Mexico, Arizona, and Utah all touch here, and the spot is commemorated by an inlaid slab of concrete and a small visitor center.

This is the heart of Native American country. The Navajo, Ute, and Hopi tribes all lay claim to land nearby—the Navajo and Ute reservations abut here, and the Navajos, particularly, count the country around the Four Corners area among its most sacred. As you drive through, you can see why: it's a haunting and strangely beautiful land, miles and miles of barren plains marked by sudden mesas, red rock, and bizarre sandstone cliffs crumbling and melting away like Dali landscapes. The hills, dotted with juniper and piñon, roll away like the soft waves of an ocean current to meet the deep sky on a far horizon.

FOUR CORNERS MONUMENT

A stone slab marks the spot where all four states' borders meet, and tourists gather for the requisite photo opportunity (pose on all fours—a foot in Arizona, a foot in Utah, a hand in Colorado, and a hand in New Mexico, and bring a slide of *that* back to show your friends . . .). Native Americans, all of whom are licensed, have booths set up near the parking lot and sell jewelry, pottery, sand paintings, and snacks and refreshments. Maps, brochures, and drinking water are available at the small visitor center, and there are portable toilets in the parking lot. To get to the monument from Cortez, continue south on U.S. 160 for about 38 miles and watch for the signs. The monument is open daily 7 A.M.–7 P.M. Memorial Day through Labor Day, and 8 A.M.–5 P.M. the rest of the year. Entrance fee is $1.50 per vehicle.

HOVENWEEP NATIONAL MONUMENT

Straddling the Colorado-Utah state line, Hovenweep National Monument consists of six individual ruins, although only one of them, Square Tower, is easily and commonly visited. Built by the Anasazi between A.D. 1000 and 1200, the pueblos, like those at Mesa Verde and Chaco Canyon, were abandoned by 1300. The buildings are characterized by tall square, circular, oval, and D-shaped towers, some of them appearing almost medieval.

The ruins at Hovenweep (a Ute word meaning "Deserted Valley") were first photographed in 1874 by William Henry Jackson. The site was explored in 1917–18 by the Smithsonian Institution, which lobbied for its designation as a national monument; it was given that status in 1923.

The headquarters of Hovenweep are at Square Tower Pueblos, across the border in Utah, though you can approach the monument from the Colorado side; neither road in is paved, and though they're well maintained they can get pretty nasty during summer's regular afternoon storms. At headquarters, you can get maps and advice for exploring the other ruins: Holly, Cutthroat Castle, Cajon, Horseshoe, and Hackberry (none of which you can drive to). To get to Hovenweep National Monument from Cortez, go south for three miles on U.S. 160, and turn west on McElmo Canyon Road. From there, it's 39 miles to the monument (you'll turn north again just over the Utah state line). You can also get there from Pleasant View and Lowry Ruins (see Sights under Cortez and Vicinity, above). From Pleasant View (20 miles north of Cortez on U.S. 666), go west 27 miles. The turnoff is well marked. Admission is free.

Hovenweep Campground, operated year-round by the National Park Service, has 31 sites and is open on a first-come, first-served basis ($4). For more information on the campground or the monument, write Mesa Verde National Park, CO 81330, or phone 970/529-4465.

UTE MOUNTAIN TRIBAL PARK

Encompassing 125,000 acres of the Ute Mountain Indian Reservation south of Cortez, this is a sanctuary set aside to preserve the Anasazi ruins of the region. Native Americans lead day-hikers and backcountry overnighters to ruins and remains of the ancient culture: cliff dwellings, free-standing pueblos, and petroglyphs.

Be forewarned, though: this may be the most natural and authentic way to see the ruins (no German tour buses), but it's not for lightweights. You'll travel by your own rig over 40 miles of dirt road, hike narrow trails into remote parts of the park, and scramble up primitive ladders to secluded kivas.

Tours usually begin around 8 A.M. June–Oct. and meet at the **Ute Mountain Pottery Plant** 15 miles south of Cortez on U.S. 666. Be sure to call ahead. Tours are often delayed. For reservations and information, write Ute Mountain Tribal Park, Towaoc, CO 81334, or phone 970/565-3751, ext. 282, or 970/565-8548.

MESA VERDE NATIONAL PARK

Mesa Verde ("Green Table") is an 80-square-mile plateau rising 1,600 feet from the surrounding desert and river valley. As early as A.D. 550, Anasazi were living on the plateau, mainly in the shelter of the many narrow canyons that cleave its top. By 1200, their crude shelters had developed into lavish communities, and multi-story pueblos were being built into the cliffsides. By the middle of the 13th century, as many as 5,000 people were living in pueblos scattered about the mesa, and the site was a bustling trade center for other pueblos and communities throughout the Four Corners area. Today, the ruins at Mesa Verde National Park are some of the world's largest and best-preserved testaments to ancient civilization.

The first whites to see the cliff dwellings at Mesa Verde were probably members of an 1874 U.S. Geological and Geographic Survey party. Among them was photographer William Henry Jackson, who took the first photos of the ruins.

The mesa's main ruins were discovered quite by accident, however. On December 18, 1888, Mancos Valley ranchers Richard Wetherill and Charlie Mason were riding across the mesa in search of stray cattle. As they peered over a canyon rim, they were shocked to see the ruins of Cliff Palace—several stories high with 200 rooms and 23 kivas. They scrambled down into the canyon and explored the ruin, taking with them

partial view of Cliff Palace at Mesa Verde National Park

bits of pottery and other artifacts, then returned to the top of the mesa, where they split up to look for more ruins. Wetherill soon discovered Spruce Tree House near where the museum now stands. The next day they stumbled upon Square Tower House.

Wetherill eventually became so fascinated with the Mesa Verde ruins he devoted his life to them. He and his family collected thousands of artifacts, most of which they sold to the Colorado State Historical Society and the C. D. Hazard and Jay Smith Exploring Company, which displayed them at the 1893 World's Fair in Chicago.

By the turn of the 20th century, Mesa Verde was being deluged with treasure hunters, and the ruins were in danger of being destroyed. In June 1906, Theodore Roosevelt signed a bill creating Mesa Verde National Park.

The Anasazi, or Ancient Pueblo People

Current courtesies acknowledge that the word "Anasazi," Navajo for "Enemies of Our Ancestors" or "Ancient Foreigners," could be interpreted as disparaging or demeaning to these people's descendants, who still populate large areas of the Southwest. The more sensitive term, then, is "Ancient Pueblo Peoples." While sympathizing entirely—and respecting the immense power of the Word—I'll continue to use "Anasazi" in this book, hoping it's understood that I intend that no offense be taken.

Two thousand years ago, Native Americans were farming along the banks of the Rio Grande south of present-day Albuquerque. Using techniques that had spread north from Mexico and Central America, the Rio Grande tribes farmed corn, beans, and squash, made baskets, and lived in primitive shelters along the river's shores. So fertile was this land and so successful were these early farmers that scientists believe the area actually experienced overcrowding.

Eventually, some of the people left the river area. By A.D. 550, splinter groups had begun to build pit houses and establish small communities on both sides of the Rio Grande, and others had begun to move north toward the Four Corners area.

Although anthropologists refer also to the early Rio Grande civilizations as Anasazi (Basketmaker period, A.D. 1–750), the term is most often used to describe the people who thrived in the Four Corners area about A.D. 800–1300. The Anasazi were a peaceful people—farmers and potters—and highly religious. Their huge adobe and stone pueblos are thought today to have been culture and trade centers, and evidence suggests they traded with other tribes as far west as the Pacific Ocean and as far south as what is now southern Mexico. Their pueblos, three- and four-story apartment-style buildings—both built into cliffs and freestanding—often contained up to 400 rooms, some of which were living quarters, some of which were used to store grain. Also characteristic of the pueblos were kivas, ceremonial meeting places, built partially underground and round—perhaps symbolic of the womb of Mother Earth. The largest of these Anasazi "cities" exist in ruins at Chaco Canyon National Historic Park about midway between Gallup and Farmington, New Mexico, and at Mesa Verde National Park.

The first evidence of occupation of the Mesa Verde plateau is from the Modified Basketmaker Period (A.D. 550–750). Ruins of their pit houses, as well as their baskets and primitive pottery, have been found in the area. During the Developmental Pueblo Period (A.D. 750–1100) the Anasazi began to reach their full stride. Pit houses were replaced by larger, family-based dwellings, the classic black-on-white Anasazi pottery was being produced, and there is speculation that water-management systems were being developed. It wasn't until the middle of the Great Pueblo Period (A.D. 1100–1300), though, that they began moving into the alcoves formed by the overhanging cliffs. After living on mesas and in river valleys for 1200 years, they suddenly began work on the cliff dwellings. For years the commonly held anthropological theory was that the dwellings had been built for protection from enemies. Recent research questions that, however. The Athapascan peoples (Navajos and Apaches) weren't to arrive in the area until later, and the Utes probably after them. The Anasazi don't seem to have *had* any enemies. It could be, too, that they moved into the alcoves to more easily control the temperature of their dwellings. For whatever reason, the cliff dwellings at Mesa Verde were built and by the middle of the 13th century they were home to 5,000 people.

And then they left. Perhaps within the span of a single generation, the pueblos were abandoned.

And just as anthropologists debate the reasons for the dwellings' construction, so do they debate the reasons for their abandonment. One theory holds, however, that the Native Americans simply overfarmed their land and had to seek arable land elsewhere. Other contributing factors may have included a very long drought, as well as, according to former Park Superintendent Robert Heyder, a "mini-ice age." These factors and perhaps others, including the possible arrival of other native peoples, combined with dwindling resources in the late 1200s and possibly the problems that typically attend a city bursting at the seams—overcrowding, disease, unrest, internecine hostilities—most likely led to Mesa Verde's downfall. And yet another theory holds that it wasn't a "downfall" at all. In fact, some modern Pueblos claim that Mesa Verde was just a "stepping stone" for the Anasazi and that they weren't moving away from problems so much as moving on to new homes, perhaps inspired by their trade with other Anasazi in Arizona and New Mexico. At any rate, by 1300, they were gone.

But where'd they go?

As the Anasazi abandoned their large communities, they dispersed, living in small groups and ending up in different parts of the Southwest. Most likely the pueblo people living in northern New Mexico and Arizona—the Hopi, Zuni, Taos, Acoma, and others—are descendants of the people who once lived at Mesa Verde.

An Endangered Species?

Sadly, many of the Mesa Verde dwellings have fallen victim to the ravages of 700 years of weather, seeping groundwater, nesting animals, and nearly a century of tourism. Walls have crumbled. Adobe bricks lay scattered. And funding to preserve the ancient archaeological sites has been inadequate. So severe is the problem that the National Trust for Historic Places has listed Mesa Verde as one of the 11 most endangered sites in the country.

Meanwhile, preservationists lobby for more funding, and sites once open to the public are roped off.

Visiting the Park

A visit to Mesa Verde is a highlight of any trip to the Southwest or to Colorado. Ideally, you'd spend several days here, exploring the ruins and the museum, and hiking about the mesa to get a sense of how its early inhabitants lived. But even if you've got half a day, you can still enjoy and benefit from the park. A couple of the ruins are very easy to get to, and even if you're not up for the short hikes to them, there are viewing platforms (wheelchair-accessible) from which you can see the impressive ruins less than 100 yards away. In addition, a short visit to the museum and visitor center offers a fascinating lesson in the archaeology of the area and especially of the culture of the Mesa Verde Anasazi. On display are pottery, baskets, cradle boards, fetishes, and countless other artifacts, as well as exquisitely detailed dioramas suggesting how things at the cliff dwellings must have looked when they were thriving—when hunters were returning with game, farmers were harvesting crops, potters were making jars, and children were playing by the water. Other displays explain in great detail the construction and restoration of the pueblos, as well as the various stages of Anasazi culture.

Ruins Road takes motorists along Chapin Mesa to several of the major sites on two six-mile loops. Along the way are viewing platforms or trailheads to more than 40 different pueblo ruins. A separate road leads to Weatherill Mesa, where you'll find other sites.

One of the largest, best-preserved, and most accessible cliff dwellings is **Spruce Tree House,** just behind the museum at park headquarters. A short walk on a paved pathway will take you down to the canyon floor and the base of the pueblo. The best-known ruin is **Cliff Palace,** on the east wall of Cliff Canyon. A little tougher, the

hike to Cliff Palace requires some scrambling over and between huge boulders. Self-guided Spruce Tree House tours are offered in the summer, and in the winter you can join ranger-led tours. Cliff Palace is open only to guided tours. Another popular ruin is **Balcony House,** which is open during the summer for ranger-guided tours. The tours to Balcony House and Cliff Palace cost $1 per person; buy tickets and make reservations at the Far View Visitor Center.

As you enter the park, you'll get a detailed map of the mesa, with ruins, turnouts, and other points of interest identified. Just beyond the park entrance is a special parking area for trailers—this will save you from hauling your rig up onto the mesa and trying to find a parking place—trailers are not allowed past Morefield Campground (see below), six miles past the park entrance. In addition to the campground, **Morefield Village** has a small store, gas station, and ranger station. At **Far View Terrace,**

SOUTHWESTERN

© STEPHEN METZGER

exploring Balcony House

another 10 miles in, there's a lodge (see below), gift shop, cafeteria, and gas station.

Mesa Verde National Park is open year-round, although lodging and gasoline are available in summer only. In addition, some of the ruins are closed in the winter, when snow and wet weather make the trails dangerous. Admission is $10 per vehicle; the pass is good for seven days.

Accommodations

To really appreciate Mesa Verde National Park, you need to spend a night here. You need to remain after the tour buses depart and the museum doors close. You need to watch the sun go down, and to listen to wind whispering through the piñons and canyons and ruins; you need to sense the magic and the spirit of the mesa, intensified by the eerie quiet of the night.

Morefield Campground is a huge area inside the park with 477 sites on 92 acres. The campground is open mid-April through mid-October and has showers, laundry, a grocery store and gift shop, and evening ranger-led campfire talks. For information or reservations, phone 970/533-7731.

The **Far View Lodge** is a scattering of single-story multiunit structures nestled in the juniper and piñons of the mesa. With private viewing porches offering stunning panoramas across the mesa and the Southwest (clear to New Mexico's Shiprock), the Far View offers one of the state's unique lodging experiences. Doubles run about $100. The upscale dining room at the lodge serves chicken, seafood, veal, venison, and Mexican specialties (accompanied by Anasazi salad) for $12–20. For information or reservations, phone 970/529-4421.

Information

For more information on the ruins, the museum, and special group programs, write Mesa Verde National Park, CO 81330, or phone 970/529-4465.

MANCOS

Mancos (pop. 870; elev. 6,993 feet) is a small ranching and shipping town about eight miles east of Mesa Verde and 30 miles west of Durango. Situated in a lush valley on the Mancos River, this is a laid-back and quiet little town in some of the prettiest country in Colorado. You'll find a very nice visitor center just off the highway at Railroad Avenue. In addition to literature on where to stay and what to do nearby, the center has a small museum, mostly displaying pioneer history. **Free camping** for tenters and RVers is available at **Boyle Park/Mancos Wayside Park** (two-week limit), where there's also a shady playground for kids.

Echo Basin Dude Ranch and RV Park

Perched on a hillside overlooking the Mancos River Valley, this lodge and recreational paradise offers just about everything you could imagine in an absolutely beautiful setting. Stay in a log cabin, haul your RV in, or set up your tent beside one of the property's two lakes. Fish, ride horses, play tennis, croquet, and basketball; in the winter, go cross-country skiing, snowmobiling, sledding, or ice fishing.

Cabin rates start at about $100 for two people, with weekly rates at $550. For information or reservations phone 970/533-7000 or 800/426-1890, or visit www.echobasin.com.

Information

There's a very nice visitor information center in Mancos at the corner of North Main and Railroad (frontage road through town). Pick up brochures on lodging, dining, and activities in the area, and talk to staff about the area's highlights. In addition, there's a small museum in back, with historical photos, pioneer clothing, branding irons, etc. Write for Mancos information at P.O. Box 494, Mancos, CO 81328, or phone 970/533-7434.

Durango

The largest town in the Four Corners area of Colorado, Durango (pop. 13,560; elev. 6,512 feet) offers excellent access to the area's many attractions—historical, cultural, and recreational. Situated between the southern border of the two-million-acre San Juan National Forest and the northern reaches of the Southwest's stark canyon country, the little community reflects all the vitality, contrast, and diversity of the surrounding geography.

Durango is a youthful and outdoor-oriented town, graced with a wonderful climate and crisp mountain sunshine. During the summer, the otherwise slow-paced town swells with tourists, many of whom come to ride the famous Durango and Silverton Narrow Gauge Railroad and to visit the Anasazi cliff dwellings at nearby Mesa Verde National Park. On those afternoons, motor homes line the streets; droves of shoppers pack into the gift shops, boutiques, and Native American galleries; and locals and passers-through cram the town's many restaurants and taverns, all enjoying a good time in this fun-loving little community.

History

In the mid-1870s, Animas City, two miles north of present-day Durango, was a thriving town with 2,000 people and its own newspaper. When the Denver and Rio Grande Railroad pushed through, in 1880, it bypassed Animas City and built its own town. Almost immediately, most Animas City residents transplanted themselves south to the new community, Durango, named by a railroad stockholder who had recently returned from Mexico. By late 1880, Durango was home to about 2,500 people, and 500 buildings had been erected.

With a reputation for being a rowdy, shoot-'em-up town in its early days, Durango and the surrounding area were frequented by ranchers and rustlers, miners and claim jumpers, as well as railroad workers and vigilantes attempting to maintain some semblance of order. Between 1880 and the turn of the 20th century, Durango served as a supply center for the mines in the region and also as an ore-processing center.

By the early 20th century, though, as the mining industry throughout the state began to see the full and long-term effects of the silver crash of 1893, Durango followed suit. Its boom days over, Durango became a quiet little shipping center for farmers and ranchers in the Animas River Valley and in the mesa country to the west.

Then things began to pick up again. As more and more people became interested in the cliff dwellings at Mesa Verde National Park and other Four Corners–area sites, and as roads made getting to them easier, Durango became a natural base camp for tourists. In addition, more and more travelers began to take advantage of southwestern Colorado's myriad recreation activities, from fishing to snow skiing. Finally, in the early 1980s, the Durango and Silverton Narrow Gauge Railroad began to attract railroad buffs and other tourists from around the country.

So today Durango is experiencing another boom. During the summer, the little town's streets are overrun with motor homes, its sidewalks bustling with shoppers looking for Native American jewelry and railroad memorabilia, and outdoor enthusiasts waiting for their shuttles to the river.

SIGHTS

Durango and Silverton Narrow Gauge Railroad

In continuous operation since 1882, the 45-mile railway was for many years the main connection between Durango and Silverton, supplying miners and transporting ore down out of the high country. Today, coal-burning trains take 200,000 sightseers per season (May–Oct.) through the lush Animas River Valley and the gorgeous San Juan National Forest to Silverton. The round-trip takes eight hours (three each way, plus a two-hour layover), although you can also arrange

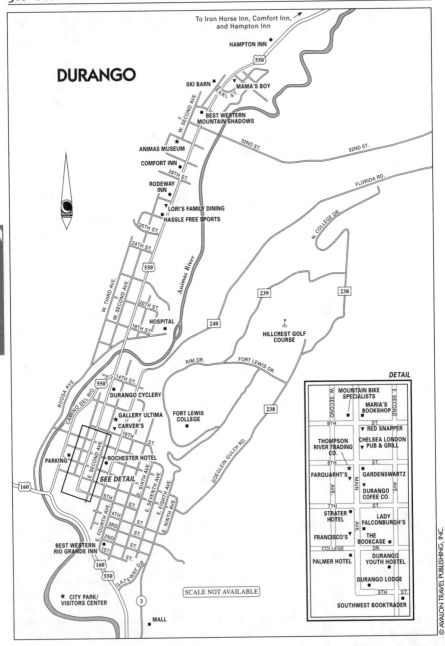

DURANGO

To Iron Horse Inn, Comfort Inn, and Hampton Inn

HAMPTON INN

550

SKI BARN ■ ▾ MAMA'S BOY

■ BEST WESTERN
MOUNTAIN SHADOWS

★ ANIMAS MUSEUM

COMFORT INN ●

RODEWAY
INN ●

▾ LORI'S FAMILY DINING
■ HASSLE FREE SPORTS

HOSPITAL ■

32ND ST.
32ND ST.

FLORIDA RD.

239   238

240

HILLCREST GOLF
COURSE

RIM DR.   FORT LEWIS DR.

238

■ DURANGO CYCLERY

■ GALLERY ULTIMA
▾ CARVER'S

FORT LEWIS
COLLEGE

PARKING ■

● ROCHESTER HOTEL

SEE DETAIL

BEST WESTERN
RIO GRANDE INN

160
550

★ CITY PARK/
VISITORS CENTER

3

■ MALL

SCALE NOT AVAILABLE

DETAIL

■ MOUNTAIN BIKE
SPECIALISTS

● MARIA'S
BOOKSHOP

▾ RED SNAPPER

THOMPSON
RIVER TRADING
CO.   ■

CHELSEA LONDON
PUB & GRILL ▾

■ FARQUARHT'S   ★   ● GARDENSWARTZ

▾ DURANGO
COFEE CO.

STRATER ●
HOTEL

LADY
FALCONBURGH'S

FRANCISCO'S ▾

■ THE
BOOKCASE ■

PALMER HOTEL ●

● DURANGO
YOUTH HOSTEL

■ DURANGO LODGE

SOUTHWEST BOOKTRADER

overnight lodging in Silverton or go one direction by bus (six hours is a *long* time to be on a loud, slow-moving, ash-spewing train no matter how gorgeous the scenery or authentic the experience).

Trains depart four times daily (between 7:30 and 9:45 A.M., returning between 4:45 and 7 P.M.) from the depot at 479 Main Ave. in downtown Durango. High-season fare is about $50 for adults, $30 for kids 5–11; no charge for a child under five sitting on an adult's lap.

This is Durango's primary summer draw, and reservations are highly recommended (the main office suggests booking your trip at least 30 days in advance). However, if you're lucky, you can sometimes get last-minute tickets. For reservations and information write Durango and Silverton Narrow Gauge Railroad Company, 479 Main Ave., Durango, CO 81310, or phone 970/247-2733. You can also get extensive schedule and rate information at www.durango.org/vp/train.

Animas Museum

This small museum at Durango's north end displays a wide array of historical artifacts from the area, from Anasazi pottery to early ranching gear to domestic items, as well as historical photos. The museum also has a small gift store.

The Animas Museum, 31st Streeet at West 2nd Avenue, is open May–Oct., Mon.–Sat. 10 A.M.–6 P.M. Admission is $2 for adults. For more information, phone 970/259-2402.

Southern Ute Indian Cultural Center

On the Southern Ute Reservation in Ignacio, about 25 miles southeast of Durango, this museum emphasizes the history and culture of the Utes and also displays a variety of Anasazi artifacts, including pottery from nearby ruins. Among the highlights of the museum's exhibits are elaborate 19th-century Ute bead leatherwork. An adjoining gift shop sells authentic arts and crafts. The museum is open Mon.–Sat. 9 A.M.–6 P.M. and Sunday 10 A.M.–3 P.M. For more information, phone 970/ 563-9583.

PARKS AND RECREATION

City Park

You'll find a very nice city park on the Animas River, where you can picnic and let the kids play on the swings and slides while river rafters go by just yards away on the other side of the cottonwoods. Go west from U.S. 550 at the Holiday Inn, and turn right when you get across the river. Kayakers can also put in here. There's also a very nice city park beside the visitor information center on the east side of town (U.S. 160 coming in from Pagosa Springs), with more lawns, playground equipment, and picnic tables.

Vallecito Reservoir

About 20 miles northeast of Durango, this reservoir, originally built to store irrigation water, offers a wide range of recreational pursuits. A favorite among local lake anglers, the reservoir has more than 22 miles of accessible shoreline and five marinas, where you can rent fishing boats, sailboats, and canoes. The waters hold brown, rainbow, and cutthroat trout, plus kokanee salmon, northern pike, and walleye.

Vallecito Reservoir also offers excellent hiking, with trailheads leading into the Weminuche Wilderness Area. In addition, there are several Forest Service and private campgrounds. **The Wit's End Guest Ranch and Resort** at the lake

A Durango and Silverton Narrow Gauge Railroad train heads out of town.

offers lodging in "luxury log cabins" and a main lodge built in 1870. Here also are a dining room and tavern, with mirrors from the 1853 World Exposition. Summer guests can fish, hike, swim, and go horseback riding; winter guests can go snowmobiling, cross-country skiing, ice fishing, and showshoeing. Rates start at about $2,500 a week per person, plus a 15 percent service charge. For reservations or information, write The Wit's End, 254 County Rd. 500, Vallecito Lake, CO 81122, or phone 970/884-4113 or 800/236-9483.

For more information on Vallecito Reservoir, phone the **Vallecito Lake Chamber of Commerce** at 970/884-9782, or write P.O. Box 804, Bayfield, CO 81122.

Hot Springs

Looking for a place to soak away the aches after a day of skiing, mountain biking, or scrambling around the ruins at Mesa Verde? Try **Trimble Hot Springs,** where you can relax in a private tub, swim laps in the Olympic-size swimming pool, or, if you're really hurtin', treat yourself to a massage. There's also a picnic area.

Trimble Hot Springs is six miles north of Durango on U.S. 550. For information, phone 970/247-0111.

River Running

Next to the narrow-gauge railroad, this is probably Durango's main tourist attraction, with numerous companies offering trips on the Animas and other nearby rivers. Booking a trip is easy. You'll find temporary booths set up along Main Avenue near the train depot, as well as flyers and posters tacked to telephone poles and taped to windows. You can also book river trips through most of the local sporting-goods stores.

The following companies have excellent reputations and offer a wide range of trips— half-day and full-day, in canoes, kayaks, and rafts, on the Animas, Piedras, and Dolores Rivers: **Durango Rivertrippers,** 970/259-0289 or 800/292-2885; **Flexible Flyers Rafting,** 970/247-4628; **Mountain Waters Rafting,** 970/259-4191; **Peregrine River Outfitters,** 970/385-7600 or 800/598-7600.; and

Rivers West Adventures, 970/259-5077 or 800/622-0852.

Cycling

Both touring and mountain biking are very big in Durango, as you'll quickly notice: Lycra-thighed riders pump lightweight racing bikes along roadsides, and it seems every porch has a muddy mountain bike locked to its railing. In fact, as one of Colorado's mountain-biking meccas, Durango is second only to Crested Butte. In addition, Durango is home to Ned Overend, one of the country's premier riders/racers.

Among the trails locals recommend are the **Colorado Trail, Hermosa Creek Trail,** and **La Plata Canyon Road.** The truly adventurous can drive 28 miles north to **Purgatory Ski Area,** 970/247-9000, haul their bikes to the top of the mountain via chairlift, and ride down on the ski trails.

For maps and information on mountain biking in the surrounding San Juan National Forest, stop by the **Animas Ranger District Office,** 701 Camino Del Rio #310, or phone 970/247-4874. You can also get maps, information, and expert advice from most Durango-area cycling shops, including the **Mountain Bike Specialists,** 949 Main Ave., 970/247-4066, and **Hassle Free Sports,** 2615 Main Ave., 970/259-3874— Hassle Free and Mountain Bike Specialist both rent bikes.

To arrange tours, contact Mountain Bike Specialists.

Hiking

From Durango you can head out into the woods for a full gamut of hiking experiences. Wander along the river for a couple of miles, taking in the scenery and the mountain air; hike up into the La Plata Mountains and the San Juan National Forest; or tackle part of the 469-mile Colorado Trail, whose southwestern trailhead is just outside town. A good midrange hike is the six-mile **Red Creek Trail,** which winds through aspens to the top of Missionary Ridge and affords excellent views of the valley below. To get to the trailhead, go northeast on East 3rd Avenue for 10 miles, turn left at the sign for Colvig Silver Camps, and continue for two more miles. You'll also find excellent hiking trails at Vallecito Reservoir, including several into the Weminuche Wilderness Area.

For more information on hiking and backpacking in the Durango area, stop by **Backcountry Experience**, 780 Main, 970/247-5830, where you'll find an excellent selection of maps and books, as well as equipment and clothing (rentals available). You can also get maps and information from the **Animas Ranger District Office** of San Juan National Forest, 701 Camino Del Rio #310, 970/247-4874.

Fishing

One of the most popular Durango-area fishing spots is **Vallecito Reservoir**, 18 miles northeast of town. Fish along the 22 accessible miles of shoreline or take a boat out into deeper waters and troll for lunker rainbow, brown, cutthroat trout, northern pike, walleye, and kokanee salmon. Boat rentals are available at the lake.

Stream anglers can work the Animas River. Though you can catch trout within the city limits, you're better off heading north or south where there's less traffic. Locals recommend the **Devils Falls** area near the Takoma Power Plant, about 20 miles north of town via U.S. 550.

For tours, gear, licenses, and information, stop by **Duranglers**, 923 Main, 970/385-4081 or 888/347-4346. You can also book guided tours through **Anasazi Angler**, 970/385-HOOK (385-4665).

Camping

With San Juan National Forest sprawling to the north, Durango offers plenty of camping possibilities. The largest concentration of campgrounds is in the Vallecito Reservoir area, about 20 miles northeast of town. You'll find more than a half dozen different areas with more than 200 sites. The largest is **Vallecito Campground**, with 88 sites (pit toilets, no showers). The smaller and more private **Pine Point Campground**, also at Vallecito Reservoir, has 30 sites (pit toilets, no showers). For information on these and other Vallecito Reservoir campgrounds, phone the **Pine Ranger District Office** in Bayfield at 970/884-2512. For

campsite reservations, phone 800/283-CAMP (283-2267).

You'll also find several Forest Service campgrounds at the Haviland Lake area about 20 miles north of Durango on U.S. 550. **Haviland Lake Campground** has 45 sites on 20 acres (pit toilets, no showers). In addition, there are several Forest Service campgrounds just off U.S. 160 between Durango and Mancos, including **Target Tree**, where you'll find more than 40 nicely secluded sites. Phone the **Animas Ranger District Office** at 970/247-4874 for more information.

Golf

Durango's public course is the 18-hole **Hillcrest Golf Course** on the Fort Lewis College Mesa overlooking town. Phone 970/247-1499 for information and tee times. The public can also play the private **Sheraton Tamarron Resort Golf Course**, though Tamarron guests are given priority. Phone 970/259-2000, ext. 2000.

Downhill Skiing and Snowboarding

Though not the best-known resort in the Rockies, **Purgatory Ski Area**, 25 miles north of Durango on U.S. 550, has its devoted fans—folks who care more about amount and quality of snow than about flash and fashion. With 11 lifts on 1,200 acres and a vertical drop of 2,200 feet, Purgatory offers good skiing for all ability levels; its terrain is ideally diversified, rated 23 percent beginner, 51 percent intermediate, and 26 percent advanced.

Though Purgatory is primarily a day-use area, in recent years the resort has developed its base facilities. These include a shopping area, several restaurants, and on-site accommodations. Shuttles run regularly between Durango and the lifts; phone 970/259-5438 for rates and schedule. If you're driving, note that the last few miles can get a bit icy during and after storms. Call ahead for road conditions. Ski rentals and instruction are available. You can also rent equipment at many of the sporting-goods shops in town, including **The Ski Barn**, 3533 Main, 970/247-1923, where you'll find a wide range of gear and accessories.

For more information on Purgatory Ski Area,

phone 970/247-9000 or 800/525-0892. Its website is www.ski.purg.com.

Cross-Country Skiing

The lush valleys and deep forests of San Juan National Forest north of Durango offer some of the best Nordic skiing in Colorado. Check out the trails in the **Haviland Lake** area (beginning at Haviland Campground, about 18 miles north of Durango) and at **Molas Pass,** about 35 miles north of town. Both afford perfect opportunities for heading off into the quiet white backcountry—the views in the Molas Pass area are particularly exquisite. There are plenty of places to pull off the road and park.

For groomed trails, check out **Purgatory Ski Touring Center,** at the Purgatory Ski Area 30 miles north of Durango on U.S. 550. The center offers 15 km of trails, and rentals and instruction (in Telemarking and touring). For more information on the Purgatory Ski Touring Center, phone 970/247-9000.

For more information on cross-country skiing in the area, and for rentals, contact **Hassle Free Sports,** 2615 Main Ave., Durango, 970/259-3874. You can also get information from the Animas Ranger District Office of the Forest Service, 701 Camino Del Rio #310, Durango, CO 81301, 970/247-4874.

TOUR

San Juan Skyway

Durango is an ideal starting point for the 236-mile San Juan Skyway, mile by mile one of the most scenic drives in the country. From Durango, the route heads due north on U.S. 550, winds over Molas Pass (elev. 10,910 feet), drops into Silverton, rises on the Million Dollar Highway again over Red Mountain Pass (elev. 11,008 feet), then falls dramatically down a series of switchbacks into Ouray. From Ouray, continue north to Ridgway, where you turn west on Highway 62, which lifts gently over Dallas Divide (elev. 8,970 feet) and provides excellent views of the Mt. Sneffels Range. On the back side of Dallas Divide, Highway 62 tees into Highway 145; here, turn southeast

for Telluride. From Telluride, continue south over Lizard Head Pass (elev. 10,222 feet), and then head toward the Four Corners area and Cortez. In Cortez, catch U.S. 160 east back to Durango.

Note: the entire loop can be driven in a day—a long day—when the weather's good. However, there are enough interesting diversions along the way that you could easily take three or more days. (All the points of interest on the San Juan Skyway are covered in detail elsewhere in this book.)

ACCOMMODATIONS

Durango's got tons of places in which to hole up, from private RV parks and budget motels to condos, bed-and-breakfasts, guest ranches and private cabins, as well as a number of restored historic hotels. In fact, if you drive in from the north on U.S. 550, you'll probably think Durango is nothing *but* lodging, as it seems two of every three buildings along this route are motels. Be forewarned, though: Durango fills up during the high season (July and August), and if you show up without reservations you may find yourself scrambling to get a room. In addition, though many of the motels advertise budget rates, you might be surprised at what they are. In Durango in summer, "budget" generally means starting at around $50 for a double.

You've even got a range of choices (read *prices*) should you want to set up camp as close as possible to the train depot. Four accommodation options are within one block: the Durango Youth Hostel, the Durango Lodge, the Rio Grande Inn Best Western, and the General Palmer Hotel.

For more information on lodging in Durango, or for assistance booking a room, phone **Durango Area Chamber Resort Association** at 800/525-8855.

Under $50

The least expensive rooms in town are probably at the **Durango Youth Hostel,** 543 E. 2nd Ave., right across from the train depot, 970/247-9905. For $20, you can get a bunk in a shared room.

Downtown: $50–100

Several motels and lodges in this price range are within easy walking distance of the train depot, including the **Durango Lodge,** 150 E. 5th St., 970/247-0955, and the **Best Western Rio Grande Inn,** 400 E. 2nd Ave., 970/385-4980 (though rates at the latter begin to sneak over $100.)

Motel Row and Farther North: $50–100

U.S. 550 on the north end of town is virtually lined with motels, and rates don't vary a whole lot—all $50–100. Among the best bets on the strip are the **Alpine Motel,** 3515 N. Main, 970/247-4042; the **Rodeway Inn,** 2701 N. Main, 970/259-2540; the **Best Western Mountain Shadows,** 3255 N. Main, 970/247-5200; and the **Comfort Inn,** 2930 N. Main, 970/259-5373.

A couple of miles north of the last streetlight in town lie a handful of motels that still offer convenience (they're on the trolley route) yet a bit more peace and quiet than those right downtown. Good rooms at the following are around $100.

I've stayed several times at the **Iron Horse Inn,** 5800 N. Main, 970/259-1010, a sprawling complex with everything from small motel rooms to rooms with lofts and kitchenettes. Be sure to ask for a room overlooking the railroad tracks, for a view of the valley and waving train passengers. The Iron Horse also offers horseback riding. Nearby are the **Comfort Inn,** 970/259-1430, and the **Hampton Inn,** 970/247-2600.

$100–150

Adjacent to the train depot, the medium-size (39-room) **General Palmer Hotel,** 567 N. Main, 970/247-4747, offers decor and architecture that will take you back to the 19th century—the hotel was built in 1890. Continental breakfast is included. Nearby is the **Jarvis Suite Hotel,** 125 W. 10th St., 970/259-6190 or 800/824-1024, which was built in the early 1890s and housed a variety of businesses, including a cobbler, a printer, and a tailor. From 1910 to 1915, Durango's first theater operated on the ground floor. The building was remodeled in 1984 and today features 22 suites, each with a fully equipped kitchen. Ski packages available.

$150–250

One of the newest additions to Durango's list of renovated historic hotels is the **Rochester Hotel,** 726 E. 2nd Ave., 970/385-1920 or 800/664-1920. The hotel was originally built in 1891 and today offers 14 rooms, each decorated around a movie filmed in the Durango area (including *City Slickers, National Lampoon's Vacation, Around the World in 80 Days,* and *Support Your Local Gunfighter*). Home-cooked breakfasts included.

The elegant **Strater Hotel,** 800/247-4431 or 970/247-4431, also offers history, charm, and convenience. A real bonus here: the **Diamond Belle Saloon** adjoining the lobby, where the bartender and waitresses dress in Gay Nineties garb, garters and all, and you can drink a draft while imagining you're a miner or railroad worker from Durango's early days.

Camping and RVing

At the southern border of San Juan National Forest, Durango offers lots of good Forest Service camping. In addition, there are dozens of private campgrounds in the area, many of which flank the highway between Cortez and Durango. The **Durango East KOA,** 970/247-0783, is just east of town on U.S. 160 heading toward Pagosa Springs. North of town (15 miles) is **Ponderosa North KOA,** 970/247-4499.

FOOD

Start Me Up

My favorite place to begin a Durango morning is the **Durango Coffee Company,** 730 Main, 970/259-2059, where you can get excellent lattes and other espresso drinks, as well as muffins, pastries, and desserts, while you peruse the morning paper or plan your day. The little shop stocks an interesting selection of kitchen accessories, from garlic presses to cookbooks to espresso makers, and it also carries homebrew equipment and ingredients. Another excellent bakery/coffee shop is **Carv-**

er's **Bakery and Brew Pub,** 1022 Main, 970/259-2545.

North of downtown, where you'll find the majority of the motels, **Lori's Family Dining,** 2653 Main, 970/247-1224, has earned a solid reputation for its breakfast specials and friendly atmosphere. Lori's is also open for lunch and dinner; the salad bar is a favorite.

Other Durango Restaurants

At **Mama's Boy,** 36th and Main, 970/247-0060, the lasagna was one of the best I've ever had in a restaurant. Other tempting entrées include pastas, veal, beef, and seafood; prices top out at about $16. There's also a Mama's Boy north of town on U.S. 550 in Hermosa, 970/247-9053.

Specializing in healthful meals, including bread (and beer) baked (and brewed) on-site, is **Carver's Bakery and Brew Pub,** 1022 Main, 970/259-2545, offering veggie specials (salads, stews, and stir-fry), with delicious black-bean dishes, as well as beef and chicken plates. Dinners run $5–9. Local musicians play informal live music.

If your tastes, or mood, run more toward pizza, try **Farquahrts Pizza Mia,** 725 Main, 970/247-5442, a local favorite for a variety of pizzas and Italian dishes, as well as Mexican food. A classic, saloon-style restaurant, the place is loud, smoky, and full of local color. Dinners run $8–12, and the restaurant regularly features live music (blues and rock 'n' roll), with open-stage jams every Sunday night. For Mexican food served in a large, cantina-style restaurant, try **Francisco's,** 619 Main, 970/247-4098, a Durango tradition since the late 1960s. In addition to Mexican food, Francisco's also serves steaks, seafood, and pastas. Dinners run $8–18. Another longtime favorite is the **Red Snapper,** 144 E. 9th St., 970/259-3417, where in addition to seafood, you can get steaks, beef, and pastas, as well as salad from an excellent salad bar; entrées average about $16–18.

The **Chelsea London Pub and Grill,** 862 Main, 970/247-2432, offers good Mexican food, burgers, sandwiches, and steaks ($8–15). It's a large place, with a high ceiling and great ambi-

ence. Open daily till midnight, with live music every night except Sunday.

The Waiting is the Best Part

Downstairs in the Century Mall, 640 N. Main, **Lady Falconburgh's Barley Exchange,** 970/382-9664, stocks more than 125 microbrews and import beers, from all corners of the earth . . . well, at least most corners of the United States and Europe. With a large rectangular bar in the center of the restaurant and tables situated around it, and high ceilings and skylights, the place has a wonderfully casual feel about it, with picnic tables as well as smaller tables tucked into corners. Wash down your beer with appetizers (fries, pretzels, etc.), or have dinner; salads, burgers, and pita sandwiches run $6–12.

ENTERTAINMENT

Durango's a hopping little town, especially during the summer when its motels swell with railroaders and river rats, and locals look for places to unwind after a day on their mountain bikes. A continually popular tourist attraction, the **Bar-D Wranglers** offer a combo plate of live country-and-western music and chuck-wagon suppers Memorial Day through Labor Day. A Durango institution since the mid-70s, the Wranglers serve a dinner of barbecued beef, baked potatoes, beans, and biscuits nightly at 7:30, "rain or shine." Get there early and explore the Wranglers' "spread"—blacksmith shop, record store (buy Wranglers' records, tapes, and CDs), and other gift shops. Tickets are $16 for adults, $8 for kids eight and younger (dinner and show). Reservations required. Phone 970/247-5753. To get there, go north about seven miles from downtown to Trimble Lane/County Road 252, where you'll turn right. Cross the railroad tracks and the Animas River, and then continue north on County Road 250.

The Strater Hotel presents the annual summer **Diamond Circle Melodrama,** described by *Time* magazine as one of the top three in the country. The season usually runs from early June through September. Ticket prices run about $17 for adults and $13 for kids 11 and younger.

If you're looking for live music in Durango, you don't have to look far; several local watering holes offer a variety of music. The **Chelsea London Pub and Grill,** 862 Main, 970/247-2432, features a variety of tasteful music—not so loud that you can't enjoy conversation—Mon.–Sat. nights. **Carver's,** 1022 Main, 970/259-2545, hosts very informal concerts beginning in the early evenings.

Watch the Durango *Herald* for current listings of who's playing where and what else is going on around town.

SHOPPING

Be sure to allow yourself at least a couple of hours to wander around the shops of Durango's downtown area, where you'll find a variety of galleries and gift shops, many of which specialize in Native American jewelry, pottery, sculpture, and prints. Among the galleries worth checking out are **Toh-Atin,** 145 W. 9th St., 970/247-8277, where you'll find an excellent selection of Navajo rugs, and **Gallery Ultima,** 1018 Main, 970/247-1812, specializing in contemporary Southwestern art. The **Thompson River Trade Company,** 140 W. 8th St., 970/247-5681, specializes in pre-1940 Native American baskets, weavings, pottery, and other artifacts.

You'll find several sporting-goods stores—whose emphases are on adventure and backcountry outings—as well as a couple of dozen factory outlet stores, including London Fog and Benetton. In addition, there are several boutiques, emphasizing upscale Southwestern styles, and souvenir shops, including several at the train depot, as well as the requisite T-shirt emporiums.

East of town on U.S. 160, the Durango Mall has a JCPenney, Sears, and other standard mall shops.

CALENDAR

Durango's calendar is practically fully booked, especially during the summer when the town's

packed with tourists. Your best sources for details on upcoming events are *Durango Magazine* and *Southwest Summer,* both of which are promotional publications with complete listings. Pick up copies at the Resort Chamber office. In addition, watch the Durango *Herald* and its regular supplements.

Among the highlights of Durango's annual events: the **Iron Horse Bicycle Classic,** which attracts 1,500 riders in a Memorial Day weekend race against a Durango and Silverton Narrow Gauge locomotive to Silverton (47 miles); **Whitewater Races,** a series of races and seminars on the Animas River, attracting some of the country's best-known river runners (early June); **Fiesta Days,** three days celebrating Durango's heritage, with a parade, music, and rodeo (late June); the **Durango Cowboy Gathering,** a three-day festival with musicians, storytellers, and cowboy poets (early October); and **Colorfest,** a multievent "celebration of color, culture, and adventure" (Sept.–Oct.).

Since 1976, a highlight of Durango's winter has been the annual **Snowdown** in late January. This five-day celebration includes more than 60 different events, from snowsculpting to ski golf and softball, with lots of live music and good eats for competitors and spectators alike. For information on these and other events, contact the **Durango Chamber Resort Association** at 970/247-0312 or 800/525-8855.

SERVICES

The offices of the **Durango Police Department** are at 990 E. 2nd Ave., 970/247-3232. The **La Plata County Sheriff** is at 742 Turner, 970/247-1155. Phone the **State Patrol** at 970/247-4722. Durango's **Mercy Medical Center** is at 375 E. Park Ave., 970/247-4311. The main **post office** is at 222 W. 8th, 970/247-3434.

Recycling

The City of Durango has its own recycling program, with several drop-off sites where you can leave aluminum, glass, newspaper, and tin cans. The most convenient are at the **City Markets,** 3130 N. Main and 6 Town Plaza (near the train depot). For information on recycling in Durango, or for a listing of other drop-off sites, phone 970/247-5622.

INFORMATION

The office of the **Durango Chamber Resort Association** is an excellent source for brochures, dining and lodging guides, and complete lists of Durango-area services. Stop by 111 S. Camino Del Rio. In the same building is a national forest visitor center, where you can get information on hiking, mountain biking, and backcountry skiing in the area. Before your visit, check out the association's website at www.durango.org, or write P.O. Box 2587, Durango, CO 81302; you can also phone 970/247-0312 or 800/525-8855. The Durango **public library** is at 1188 E. 2nd Ave., 970/247-2492.

The independently published *Durango Herald* is published daily and is available in racks around town for $.35.

You can get information on lodging, dining, and outdoor activities through the Durango Chamber Resort Association's email address: **durango@frontier.net.**

Bookstores

Durango has three exceptional bookstores always well stocked with books on the Southwest. **The Bookcase,** 601 E. 2nd Ave., 970/247-3776, features collectors' and first editions, including some rare enough to be locked away in glass cases. The shop also carries used paperbacks and new books on Colorado and the Southwest, particularly the Four Corners area. **The Southwest Book Trader,** 175 E. 5th., 970/247-8479, has an excellent selection of books on Colorado and the Southwest, though you might have to dig around, as the little shop is wonderfully cluttered, with books piled on the floor, in every corner, and spilling out into aisles. **Maria's Bookshop,** 960 Main, 970/247-1438, specializes in books on the Southwest and Native Americana and also sells Navajo rugs and topographical maps of the area. There's also a **Waldenbooks** next to the train depot.

TRANSPORTATION

The **Durango–La Plata County Airport,** 14 miles east of Durango off Highway 172, provides passenger service by **America West, United Express, Continental Express,** and **Mesa Airlines.** Durango's **Greyhound-Trailways bus depot** is at 275 E. 8th Ave., 970/247-2755.

The **Durango Lift** is the town's public transportation system. Buses run regularly through town year-round, and to Purgatory Ski Area during the ski season. For routes and information, phone 970/247-5438. For 24-hour taxi service in Durango, phone **Durango Transportation** at 970/259-4818.

Pagosa Springs

Pagosa Springs is a combination Old West town and soon-to-be booming resort town. You'll probably be surprised at the huge number of real estate and land-sale offices, particularly on the west side of town. The **Fairfield Pagosa Resort,** also on the west side, is a deluxe spread, with gorgeous executive-style homes right on the golf course.

Named for the nearby hot mineral springs (Pagosa is Ute for "Healing Waters"), which average 153°F, Pagosa Springs was the focus of a centuries-long dispute between Navajos and Utes. According to the WPA guide to Colorado, in 1866 the two tribes agreed to a final one-on-one duel over the springs' rightful ownership. The Utes chose as their representative Albert Henry Pfieffer, a Scotsman who had worked alongside Kit Carson and who had served as a U.S. Indian agent in New Mexico, where Pfieffer's Spanish wife had been killed by natives. Pfieffer chose Bowie knives for the duel. Apparently, the two men rushed at each other, and Pfieffer flung his knife at his Navajo rival, killing him, and the Utes took undisputed possession of the springs.

Of course, Native American possession of anything of value was not part of the Great European Plan, and Pagosa Springs was no exception. By 1880, a one-square-mile area surrounding the springs had been claimed by the U.S. government, and a townsite was plotted that year.

Throughout the early 20th century, local boosters tried to promote Pagosa Springs as a resort spa, although they were largely unsuccessful. Only lately has the area begun to see growth and development to any significant degree.

SIGHTS
Chimney Rock Anasazi Ruins
An "outlier" community of the Chaco Canyon pueblos and cultural center, the Chimney Rock site is a fascinating thread in the Anasazi tapestry of the Southwest—a tapestry that includes not only Chaco, but Aztec, Bandelier (all three in

New Mexico), Mesa Verde, and literally thousands of other ruins.

Chimney Rock was named for the twin spires that stand guard over the ruins, which during the 11th century were home to as many as 2,000 people. Recent archaeological research suggests the Chimney Rock site was very likely of great religious significance, and one theory is that the inhabitants of this remote outpost were priests sent north from Chaco. Other anthropologists suggest the community was a trading and shipping center, and timbers from the northern forests may have been harvested here and shipped south for pueblo construction in the barren area around Chaco.

Encompassing six square miles, the Chimney Rock site includes dozens of structures, many of which have been partially restored. Homes, ceremonial kivas, and storage rooms are scattered about the pueblo. Walking among these isolated ruins is a powerful spiritual experience that may help you ask questions to better understand your earth, your self, your ancestors, and your gods.

Touring Chimney Rock is possible only with Forest Service guides, May 15–Sept. 30, at 9:30 and 10:30 A.M. and at 1 and 2 P.M. (occasionally at noon). Groups of 30 leave from the Chimney Rock entrance 17 miles west of Pagosa Springs via U.S. 160 and and three miles south on Highway 151. The two-hour tours are $5 for adults, $2 for kids 5–11; reservations for groups of 10 or more are required. Full-moon tours are also offered at $7.50 (children discouraged). For information or reservations, contact the **Chimney Rock Visitor Center** at 970/883-5359. You can also get information from the **Pagosa Springs Ranger District** of San Juan National Forest, P.O. Box 310, Pagosa Springs, CO 81147, 970/264-2268, or the **Pagosa Springs Chamber of Commerce,** 970/246-2360.

San Juan Historical Museum
This small museum features most of the requisite historical-society-type displays, focusing on the Pagosa Springs area's Anglo settlement. Lots of

ranching and farming artifacts are featured, as are early domestic items: a horsehide coat, a turn-of-the-20th-century loom, and early dentists' equipment. Admission is $3 for adults and $1 for kids.

The museum, on the east side of town at Pagosa and 1st, is open Mon.–Fri. 9 A.M.–4 P.M., Memorial Day through Labor Day. For more information, phone 970/264-4424.

PARKS AND RECREATION

City Park

You'll find a very nice city park along the San Juan River next to Pagosa Springs visitor center. In addition to the recently built (1995) riverwalk, there's a lawn, playground equipment, picnic tables, and restrooms. On the other side of the parking lot is the Pagosa Springs Visitor Center.

Hot Springs

Down on the river near the Pagosa Springs visitor center, the mineral-water tubs at **Spa Hot Mineral Baths,** 970/264-5910, and at the **Springs,** 970/264-0934, are open to the public. Water temperature in the hot pools runs about 108°F. Both places also have warm, 85°F pools.

Golf

The **Fairfield Pagosa Resort** has both a nine- and an 18-hole course. The wide-open terrain offers excellent views of the mountains to the north and east, and of rolling hills and canyons to the south and west. For information, phone 970/731-4141 or 800/523-7704.

Fishing

Good fishing opportunities abound in the Pagosa Springs area, whether you like to stalk native rainbows with #18 flies or prefer to sit in a lawn chair and tip brews with a bell on your rod. Stream anglers can pull decent rainbows out of both the east and west forks of the **San Juan River;** the confluence of the two forks is 10 miles north of Pagosa Springs. From town, the San Juan flows southwest, eventually dumping into **Navajo Reservoir,** which straddles the Colorado–New Mexico state line. Another popular trout stream is the

Piedra River, which drops out of the Weminuche Wilderness Area about 20 miles west of Pagosa Springs.

Lake anglers often do well at **Capote Lake,** 16 miles west of Pagosa Springs at the junction of U.S. 160 and Highway 151 (boat rentals available), and at **Echo Lake,** five miles south of town via U.S. 84. For more information on fishing in the area, stop by **Duranglers Flies and Supplies,** 801-B Main Ave., Durango, 970/385-4081.

Cycling

Biking's a natural here, and though some hardy road warriors attack these high passes, off-road cycling is much more popular. A moderate ride that will introduce you to the area is the 16-mile Willow Draw Loop. Go east on U.S. 160 to U.S. 84, and turn south. At Mill Creek Road/County Road 302, turn left, and continue for four miles. The double-track dirt road will be on your left after you pass the third cattle guard. Other rides include several in the Turkey Springs and Chris Mountain areas. For maps and information, stop by any of Pagosa Springs's bike and sporting-goods stores, including **Juan's Mountain Sports,** 155 Hot Springs Blvd., 970/264-4730, and **Pedal the Peaks,** in the River Center, 970/264-4110.

Jeep Tours

Pagosa Springs is a popular jumping-off point for folks 4WD-ing up into the high country. A favorite trip is out East Fork Road to Elwood Pass and the Summitville Historic Mining District, a gold-mining camp dating from the early 1870s. **Pedal the Peaks** offers Jeep tours to Summitville, and, if you're so inclined, staffers will haul your mountain bike up for you so you can ride back down. Phone 970/264-4110.

Camping

Pagosa Springs is literally surrounded by San Juan National Forest, so the camping opportunities in the area are virtually limitless. In addition to the primitive camping allowed by the Forest Service, you can head out in just about any direction and arrive at a designated Forest Service campground. To the northeast lie **Wolf Creek** and **West Fork** campgrounds

(75 sites total); take U.S. 160 13 miles to Forest Service Road 684. To the south is **Blanco Campground** (18 sites on eight acres, no water); take U.S. 84 13 miles to Forest Service Road 656. To the west is **Cimarrona Campground** (21 sites on six acres); take U.S. 160 two miles to Forest Service Road 631, and then follow 631 for 22 miles to Forest Service Road 640.

For more information on these and other Pagosa Springs–area Forest Service campgrounds, contact the **Pagosa Springs Ranger District** office, P.O. Box 310, Pagosa Springs, CO 81147, or phone 970/264-2268.

Skiing
Wolf Creek Pass Ski Area is one of Colorado's little-known gems. Averaging well over 450 annual inches (!) of the Rockies' finest powder, Wolf Creek is a favorite of some of the sport's most discriminating connoisseurs.

Wolf Creek's six lifts service 1,600 acres and a 1,604-foot vertical drop, and the area's terrain is about as well divided as you could hope for—20 percent beginner, 35 percent intermediate, 25 percent advanced, and 20 percent expert. The 10,300-foot base guarantees that all that snow will be nothing but the lightest, fluffiest, most skiable *powder* imaginable.

There are no overnight facilities at Wolf Creek, though there is a restaurant, cafeteria, and the proverbial bar for that post-ski nip. For more information, phone 970/264-5639, or visit the website: www.wolfcreekski.com.

Cross-Country Skiing
Pagosa Pines Touring Center is west of town at the Fairfield Pagosa Resort. With 12 km of groomed trails winding about the resort's two golf courses, the area offers instruction and rental equipment. For information on rates and hours of operation, phone 970/731-4141.

The Wolf Creek Pass area is very popular among Nordic skiers who prefer to cut their own trails through the fluff; the views from up here are exceptional. For maps and information on cross-country skiing in the San Juan National Forest, phone the **Pagosa Ranger District Office** at

970/264-2268. You can also get information and maps, as well as rental equipment, from **The Ski and Bow Rack,** at the east end of Pagosa Springs, 970/264-2370.

PRACTICALITIES
Accommodations
If you plan to stay here, you might as well take advantage of the hot springs, which you can do at the following for $50–100. The **Spa Motel,** 970/264-5910, the **Best Western Oak Ridge Mineral Spring Inn,** 970/264-4173, and the **Springs Motel,** 970/264-4168, all offer free mineral-water hot tubbing for guests. All three are on Hot Springs Boulevard downtown near the river and visitor center.

A **Holiday Inn Express,** 2 Solomon Dr. (off U.S. 160), 970/731-5101, is on the east side of town and also has good, clean rooms ($70–120).

Food
A Pagosa Springs tradition, the **Elkhorn Cafe,** 438 Main, 970/264-2146, has a reputation for some of the best Mexican food in the area, as well as hearty American fare—in the center of the downtown area. For beef, try the **Branding Iron Barbecue,** three miles east of town on U.S. 160, 970/264-4268, which specializes in ribs, links, and chicken. Dinners, which include all the fixin's (choose from corn on the cob, cole slaw, and beans) run $7–14. Lunch specials are $5–7. For Chinese food, try **Hunan Restaurant,** 180 E. Pagosa, 970/264-5922, where lunch entrées run $6–10 and dinners $6–12. An excellent deal is the Sunday all-you-can-eat buffet for about $7.

For pizzas, pastas, salads, and other brew-pub fare, try the **Paradise Brew Pub and Grill,** 164 N. Pagosa, 970/731-9101.

Information
Pagosa Springs's new **visitor center** building is in the center of town on the river (watch for the signs). You'll find lots of brochures and maps, particularly on recreation in southern Colorado, as well as information on lodging and real estate. To have information on the area sent to you, write the chamber at P.O. Box 787, Pagosa

Springs, CO 81147, or phone 970/264-2360 or 800/252-2204. Better yet, check out its website at www.pagosaspringschamber.com.

Moonlight Books, right downtown, 970/264-5666, stocks a good selection of books of local and regional interest.

North of Pagosa Springs

U.S. 160 rises northeast out of Pagosa Springs into San Juan National Forest, crosses the Continental Divide into Rio Grande National Forest at Wolf Creek Pass (elev. 10,850 feet) and then drops west of Del Norte Peak (elev. 12,400 feet) on its way toward the San Luis Valley. Without doubt one of the prettiest 45-mile stretches of highway in the country, the route offers views guaranteed to take your breath away. Along the way are a dozen or so Forest Service campgrounds, as well as trailheads into the backcountry. The first time I drove along here I was returning to California after spending a summer in New Mexico. The lush green forests, the massive peaks, the sprawling lonesomeness of the countryside had me convinced I'd found paradise on earth. I'm not sure I hadn't.

Near the eastern base of the pass lies the little town of **South Fork,** a jumping-off spot for hikers, campers, fishers, and skiers. The **Wolf Creek Ski Lodge** in South Fork, 970/873-5547, has nice clean rooms and a restaurant. The **Hungry Logger Restaurant,** 970/873-5504, is a popular refueling stop for locals and passers-through alike. Open daily. Six miles west of South Fork is **Moon Valley Campground,** 970/873-5216, with RV sites, as well as guided fishing trips, horseback rides, evening campfires, and a "Sunday devotional."

DEL NORTE

Situated on the far west side of the San Luis Valley, Del Norte (pop. 1,700; elev. 7,874 feet) is the seat of Rio Grande County. Founded in 1860, it was a supply center in its early days for miners working the San Juan district to the west. Apparently those early days were rowdy ones, and a vigilante group was organized to try to bring peace to the community. A ragtag group, the vigilantes succeeded in doing more harm than

good, one night shooting up much of the town, including each other—vigilante activity decreased substantially thereafter.

Rio Grande County Museum

Devoted to the multicultural heritage of the area, this small museum features exhibits highlighting the contributions of prehistoric peoples, early Spanish explorers, and Anglo trappers, miners, and farmers. The museum, at 580 Oak St., is open daily 10 A.M.–5 P.M. June–Aug., and 11 A.M.–4 P.M. September to mid-December and Feb.–May. Admission $1, or $2.50 per family. For more information, phone 719/697-2847.

HIGHWAY 149 NORTH

Highway 149 tees into U.S. 160 about 15 miles west of Del Norte, winds north through Creede, crosses the Continental Divide at Spring Creek Pass (elev. 10,901 feet), rises again over Slumgullion Pass (elev. 11,361 feet), drops into Lake City, and then connects with U.S. 50 about 10 miles west of Gunnison. Hardly one of the better-traveled routes in Colorado, it nonetheless offers the adventurous traveler a unique perspective on the state, including glimpses of one of the strangest chapters in Western history. Also, the route provides a gateway to some of Colorado's most scenic recreation areas. Side trips to excellent fishing, skiing, and 4WD areas begin along here.

In addition, the scenery is downright gorgeous. In fact, the 75-mile stretch from South Fork to Lake City has been designated the "Silver Thread Scenic Byway" by the Forest Service. From the upper Rio Grande that parallels the roadside to waterfalls in distant canyons, from high mountain lakes to ghost towns, the scenery here is ever changing and uniquely Colorado.

CREEDE

Seat of Mineral County, Creede (pop. 610; elev. 8,852 feet) dates from 1890, when Nicholas C. Creede discovered silver and staked out the Holy Moses mine. In 1893, the population of Creede was 8,000, and the community had earned a reputation as one of Colorado's rowdiest mining camps. Gunfights were commonplace, and saloons, gambling houses, and brothels operated 'round the clock. One of Creede's early entrepreneurs was Bob Ford, who killed Jesse James (shot him in the back); Ford was murdered in Creede in 1892.

Creede's first newspaper, *The Candle,* was published by Cy Warman, whose versified description of the town became as well known in the mining camps and as oft recited as the poetry of Robert Service:

> *. . . the cliffs are solid silver,*
> *With wond'rous wealth untold,*
> *And the beds of running rivers*
> *Are lined with the purest gold*
> *While the world is filled with sorrow,*
> *And hearts must break and bleed—*
> *It's day all day in daytime,*
> *And there is no night in Creede.*

Creede has faced more than its share of setbacks over the years. In addition to being pummeled by the crash of the silver market in 1893, Creede has four times been destroyed or nearly destroyed by fire, most recently in 1936. The small number of folks who make their home here today, though, are a hardy lot, with much in common with the miners who first settled the town. They appreciate the rugged scenery and the independence guaranteed by their remote location.

Visitors to Creede will find shops and restaurants along the several-block main drag, Creede Avenue, which dates from the town's glory days. Creede's tourism, though, is oriented almost entirely toward summer, when folks flock to town to see the famous Creede Repertory Theater, and many of the town's businesses shut down for the winter.

Creede Repertory Theater

Featuring talented and well-known actors each summer in one of the Rocky Mountains' prettiest pockets, this little theater group presents highly polished productions that have been favorably reviewed by newspapers throughout the country. Established in 1966, the nonprofit company has been steadily growing in quality and reputation, and many playgoers are longtime "regulars." Plays, a different one each night of the week, are performed downtown in the Creede Opera House. They vary from modern classics (Synge's *Playboy of the Western World*) to adaptations for kids. Tickets run $10–17 for adults. Reservations highly recommended.

For tickets and information, write Creede Repertory Theater, P.O. Box 269, Creede, CO 81130, or phone 719/658-2540.

Creede Underground Mining Museum

Operated in 23,000 square feet of tunnels, rooms, and bays, this museum displays artifacts and historical photos from the mining camp's heyday. On exhibit are the town's first fire truck (hand-pulled), a horse-drawn hearse, and mining tools and equipment. The museum, at 6th and San Luis, is open daily, 10 A.M.–4 P.M. Memorial Day through Labor Day and 10 A.M.–3 P.M. the rest of the year, with tour times varying according to season. Admission is $5 for adults, $4 for seniors, and $3 for kids 6–16. For information, write P.O. Box 608, Creede, CO 81130, or phone 719/658-2303 or 800/327-2102 (chamber of commerce).

Accommodations and Food

Lodging is available in Creede at the rustic **Creede Hotel** (built in 1890), 719/658-2608, as are breakfast, lunch, and dinner (rotating dinner menu). Doubles are available for $50–100, which includes a full breakfast. About 20 miles south of Creede on Highway 149 is the **Bristol Inn,** 719/658-2455, which locals recommend for dinner ($8–14)—open Wed.–Saturday.

Information

For more information on the Creede area, write the **Creede–Mineral County Chamber of Commerce,** P.O. Box 580, Creede, CO 81130, or phone 719/658-2374 or 800/327-2102. For information on Rio Grande National Forest, phone the **Creede Ranger District Office** at 719/658-2556.

LAKE CITY

Sandwiched between Uncompahgre and Rio Grande National Forests, Lake City (pop. 250; elev. 8,671 feet) is an 1870s-era mining town with a unique history. First of all, the community seems to have been fortunate enough to avoid the traditional trappings of the other mountain mining camps—brothels, gunfights, gambling, and other assorted manifestations of lawlessness. In fact, by 1877, the town was defined largely by its healthy religious community, with its flocks divided into four churches—Presbyterian, Baptist, Episcopalian, and Catholic. Susan B. Anthony passed through the area on September 20, 1887, speaking for two hours on the suffrage movement.

History remembers lurid excess more than righteousness, though, malevolence more than virtue. And Lake City remembers Alferd Packer, cannibal.

Though Packer's tale has been mythologized over the last century, and historians will probably never fully untangle fact from fiction, a basic story has emerged. Packer had been part of a party of prospectors that stopped at a Ute camp near present-day Delta as the winter of 1874 set in. Chief Ouray, sensing the risk of heading into the mountains, encouraged them to turn back. But men are often blinded by the glare of gold and silver, and Packer and five others didn't listen to the chief. Instead they continued into the mountains. Come spring, Packer alone came down out of the mountains; he claimed he had gone lame and his fellows had deserted him. He had, he said, survived on roots and small game. When offered food, he turned it down; he wanted whiskey instead. He also claimed he was broke, but days later appeared drunk at a gambling hall; some say he was taking money out of several different wallets.

Shortly after a Ute stumbled upon strips of human flesh about five miles from Lake City, a photographer from *Harper's Weekly* discovered in the same area the remains of five men. Their skulls had been crushed and strips of flesh had been torn from their bodies.

Packer maintained his innocence, claiming the men had gone insane and that he had killed one of them, but in self-defense. He was arrested, but escaped shortly thereafter and evaded the law for nine years—until 1883, when he was captured in Wyoming. On April 13, Packer was tried in Lake City and sentenced to hang. However, he got off on a technicality and was instead convicted of manslaughter. He was paroled in 1906 and died of natural causes a year later.

The site where the bodies were found, on the northeast side of Lake San Cristobal, is now known as Cannibal Plateau. Colorado remembers Packer himself in strange ways: Lake City hosts an annual Alferd Packer Jeep Tour and Barbecue, and the cafeteria in the student union at the University of Colorado (Boulder) is the Alferd Packer Memorial Grill.

Lake City, meanwhile, has seen a recent rise in tourism. Though too remote to attract many winter visitors, summer sees the little town swell with passers-through, many of whom take advantage of the great recreational opportunities the area affords.

Summer Activities

Fishing is one of the Lake City area's primary draws, with nearby **Lake San Cristobal,** the state's second-largest natural body of water, known for its rainbow and brown trout. Try a Mepps, Kastmaster, or a red-and-white spoon for rainbows; browns, typically voracious and greedy, can often be taken with Rapalas and other lures that look like small bait fish. Of course, some diehards never give up their salmon eggs. Just below the lake, the **Lake Fork** of the Gunnison River offers good dry-fly fishing, with some decent holes right in town. Both the lake and the river are stocked regularly. For gear, tips, and guided trips (about $100 per person), stop by **Dan's Fly Shop** downtown, 970/944-2281. This little shop has everything you'd ever need for a day—or a summer—on the water, from hats and nets to high-quality reels and rods. For a catalog, write P.O. Box 220, Lake City, CO 81235.

Another popular diversion in the area is four-wheeling, with one of the state's best loops beginning just outside town. The 49-mile **Engineer Pass/Cinnamon Pass Loop** takes you west from Lake City through Henson Creek Canyon and over Engineer Pass (elev. 12,810 feet). Once over the pass, you can either continue to Silverton or Ouray or circle back to Lake City via Cinnamon Pass (elev. 12,620 feet). Between Lake City and Engineer Pass, you'll travel through several ghost towns, including **Capital City, Engineer City,** and **Rose's Cabin.**

The Lake City area also offers excellent hiking and climbing opportunities. **Uncompahgre Peak** is the state's sixth-highest mountain and one of the least technical "14ers." The day-long round-trip hike gains 5,000 feet in elevation. In addition, the surrounding San Juan National Forest offers unlimited backcountry hikes.

Forest Service camping is available at **Slumgullion Pass Campground,** about nine miles south on Highway 149 (21 sites on seven acres, no showers). **River Fork Camper Park,** 970/944-2389, offers RV and tent camping along the Lake Fork of the Gunnison River. It's right in town.

Winter Activities

Though winter doesn't see the tourists in the Lake City area that summer does, some still like to get out and explore the area. Cross-country skiers can head out in virtually any direction and find the soft peace and winter quiet that a snowfall in the Rockies ensures. Those who prefer thrills and speed over peace and quiet take to the old 4WD roads on snowmobiles.

Accommodations and Food

Lake City offers a number of motels and cabins, and a couple of bed-and-breakfasts. The **Wagon Wheel Resort,** right downtown on Highway 149, 970/944-2264, has cabins with kitchenettes ($50–100), while the **Silver Spur Motel,** at the corner of 3rd and Gunnison, 970/944-2231 or 800/499-9701, offers no-frills digs with a convenient downtown location (under $50).

For good home-style cooking, try the **Mountain Harvest Restaurant,** on the east end of town at Highway 149 and Ocean Wave, 970/944-2332; open for lunch and dinner daily with chicken, pastas, steaks, and Mexican entrées ($8–14).

Information

For more information on Lake City, write the **Lake City Chamber of Commerce,** P.O. Box 430, Lake City, CO 81235, or phone 970/944-2527 or 800/569-1874.

For tips and information on recreation, stop by **The Sportsman,** in town on Highway 149 South, 719/944-2526. For maps and outdoor information, check out **Back Country Navigator,** in the Alpine Gateway Shops (east end of town), 970/944-MAPS (944-6277) or 888/700-4174. You can get information on camping in San Juan National Forest from the **Creede Ranger District Office,** 719/658-2556.

SOUTHWESTERN

Summit County

Introduction

This is one of Colorado's best and most popular year-round playgrounds. Just 70 miles west of Denver via I-70, Summit County—80 percent of which is within the borders of Arapaho National Forest—offers more recreational opportunities per square foot than any other area in the state, perhaps the country. Skiing, cycling, hiking, off-road touring, and water sports from fishing to windsurfing draw three million visitors a year.

Situated just west of the Continental Divide in the high mountains of the Gore and Tenmile Ranges, Summit County is an outdoor lover's Garden of Eden, with the Snake and Blue Rivers, as well as Tenmile Creek, all tumbling through steep canyons and lush mountain valleys; Dillon Reservoir sprawls as the county's centerpiece. With many of the surrounding peaks topping 13,000 feet, and the towns themselves nestled in 9,000-foot-high valleys, this is about as close to the Rockies' soul as one can get.

During the winter, Summit County, whose full-time population is about 8,000, swells with winter sports enthusiasts from around the world. Skiers flock to the slopes of four of the state's best ski areas: Arapahoe Basin, Breckenridge, Copper Mountain, and Keystone. The funky little streets of Frisco and Breckenridge—mining towns rich in history—are full of shoppers and après-skiers, bundled up against the cold, their ski boots crunching the dry snow. More skiers visit Summit County per year than Aspen and Vail combined.

When the snow disappears from the mountainsides and the ski lifts shut down, Summit County turns its attention to warm-weather recreation. Sails appear on Dillon Reservoir. Bicycles come out of storage, then are tuned and readied for the nearly 50 miles of paved bike paths and hundreds of miles of backcountry trails. Golf clubs are dusted off, tennis nets unfurled and strung across courts, softball gloves oiled for another season.

All of which means you won't have any trouble occupying yourself during your visit to Summit County. And on the off chance that occupying yourself isn't what you had in mind, this is one of the best places in Colorado to simply relax. The mountain sunshine, the scent of pines,

sailing on a summer afternoon on Lake Dillon

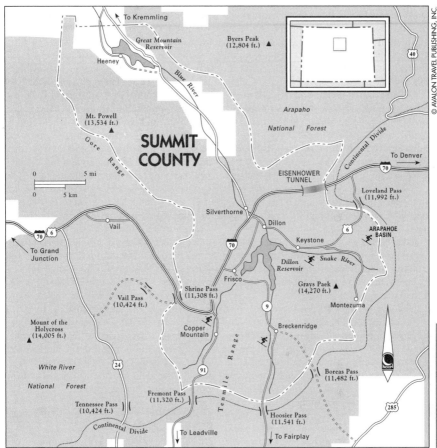

To Kremmling

Great Mountain
Reservoir

Byers Peak
(12,804 ft.) ▲

Heeney

Blue River

Arapaho

Mt. Powell
(13,534 ft.)
▲

National Forest

**SUMMIT
COUNTY**

Gore Range

Continental Divide

To Denver

EISENHOWER
TUNNEL

0   5 mi

0   5 km

Loveland Pass
(11,992 ft.)

Silverthorne

ARAPAHOE
BASIN

Vail

Dillon

Keystone

To Grand
Junction

Snake River

Dillon
Reservoir

Frisco

Grays Peak ▲
(14,270 ft.)

Shrine Pass
(11,308 ft.)

Vail Pass
(10,424 ft.)

Montezuma

Mount of the
Holycross
(14,005 ft.)
▲

Copper
Mountain

Breckenridge

White River

Tenmile Range

Boreas Pass
(11,482 ft.)

National Forest

Fremont Pass
(11,320 ft.)

Tennessee Pass
(10,424 ft.)

Continental Divide

Hoosier Pass
(11,541 ft.)

To Leadville

To Fairplay

SUMMIT COUNTY

the sound of water gently lapping against the shore—Summit County is the best prescription you'll find for urban anxiety, whether you're just passing through or you're here for the long haul.

HISTORY

Summit County's history dates from summer 1859, when prospectors discovered gold on the Blue River and built a blockhouse near what is now **Breckenridge** as protection from the Utes, who had long claimed this land for their own. Word of the strike soon got out, and when the

snows melted the following year, hordes of miners descended on the valley from Denver. Before long, a substantial mining camp had sprung up, with several other smaller ones in the surrounding area. Because the camps were so isolated, the miners sought to be assigned their own post office, and in a political move named their community for Vice President John C. Breckinridge. The town was then granted mail service. When the Civil War broke out and Breckinridge sided with the South, angry citizens changed the spelling of the town's name to Breckenridge.

Silverthorne was founded in 1881, when Judge Marshal Silverthorne bought 160 acres of land from the U.S. government. Within a couple of years, the savvy Silverthorne, who ran the Silverthorne Hotel in Breckenridge, had discovered an efficient way to extract gold from the Blue River. He eventually got a patent for the Silverthorne Placer.

Dillon was founded around the same time as Silverthorne, although the present-day town is actually Dillon number three. The town was originally built east of the Snake River; when the railroad arrived, it was moved across the Blue River to be closer to the depot. The new little town did quite well, supporting two newspapers, four saloons, and a couple of general stores. In the early 20th century, local skiers built a ski run above the town, which in 1919 was the site of a world-record-setting ski jump: 213 feet.

In the late 1950s, though, in response to Denver's water shortage, the Blue River was dammed to form Dillon Reservoir. Old Dillon and the ski hill were submerged deep beneath the lake. Dillon was moved to its present site in 1961.

Though miners had used snow skis to get around as early as the 1880s, and turn-of-the-20th-century Summit County residents had begun to use skis for recreation, it wasn't until the late 1940s that skiing really began to take off in the area. That was the year Arapahoe Basin opened, and a number of lodges and inns were built in the Dillon-Keystone area, turning the county into a prototypical ski resort. By the mid-1960s, the nation had caught "ski fever," and Summit County was in the perfect position to take advantage of it. By the winter of 1972–73, all four of Summit County's ski areas were open for business and attracting skiers from all over the world. That winter also saw the completion of the first bore of Eisenhower Tunnel through Loveland Pass, making for a safer and faster drive from Denver. (See the Eisenhower Memorial Tunnel special topic.)

The 1970s and '80s witnessed huge improvements at the ski areas, not only in additional acres and increased numbers of lifts, but in technology (better, faster, and safer lifts), instructional methods, shuttle services, lodging facilities, and on-mountain amenities. Also during the '70s and '80s, Summit County began to develop into a four-season resort area, with summer visitors flocking to the area to golf, mountain bike, white-water raft, and hike the back trails of Arapaho National Forest.

And as more came to play, more came and stayed. In the mid-1990s, Summit County began to show the unpleasant signs of growth. New housing developments crept toward Lake Dillon, and forested hillsides were laid bare to make way for shopping centers and condominium complexes. Traffic snarled at intersections, and folks began to resent newcomers, whom they blamed for the problems. So Summit County, like many of Colorado's wonderfully desirable destinations, will have some choices to make; if it is to remain the Eden it is, planning will have to be intelligent, sensitive, and far-sighted.

Meanwhile, Summit County today offers many chances to view its history, offering sometimes startling comparisons between past and present. The Summit County Historical Society sponsors walking tours of Breckenridge Historical District, as well as tours to mining towns; Frisco Historic Park displays buildings from that town's heyday. And if that's not enough, just take a gander at the tailings along the Blue River between Frisco and Breckenridge. Unfortunately, mining leaves ugly scars, and the county hasn't wholly escaped the fate that has befallen so many other Colorado mining regions.

SUMMIT COUNTY HIGHLIGHTS

Skiing: Arapahoe Basin, Keystone, Copper Mountain, Breckenridge

Fishing: Dillon Reservoir, Green Mountain Reservoir, Blue River, Tenmile Creek

White-water rafting: Blue River, plus access to nearby Arkansas and Colorado Rivers

Bicycling: Blue River Bikeway, Tenmile Canyon National Recreation Trail, Vail Pass Bikeway

More: summer chairlift rides at Breckenridge and Copper Mountain, sleigh rides, snow tubing, museums, golf, hiking, horseback riding, jeep tours, historical tours, ballooning in Dillon, shopping, Breckenridge's Ullr Fest, Copper Mountain's CopperFest

SILVERTHORNE

Silverthorne lies at the junction of I-70, U.S. 6, and Highway 9, and though it dates from the 1860s, the town has the feel of the popular tourist stop that it is. Silverthorne sees millions of travelers annually, many of whom stop to take advantage of the chain motels and hotels, fast-food outlets, gas stations, recreation-equipment-rental outfits, and the huge Silverthorne Factory Stores mall. Get a sense of less-traveled Silverthorne, and take a drive north on Highway 9; this is the gateway to the Blue River Valley and Eagles Nest Wilderness Area. Hidden in the pines directly west of the central shopping areas, on the hillside overlooking I-70 and the lake, are a number of condominium complexes and deluxe vacation homes.

DILLON

On the shore of Summit County's centerpiece, Dillon Reservoir, Dillon is a blend of backwoods cabins, modern vacation homes, and deluxe hotels and condo complexes. Its streets winding through the pines and down by the lake, Dillon is without a real "downtown," though the Dillon Mall is home to several restaurants, business offices, ski shops, and other retailers.

Dillon has been a popular resort community since the 1940s, when Arapahoe Basin skiers built log cabins in the area and the first restaurants and lodges opened. Today, the community offers some of the most upscale lodging in the county. During the summer, Dillon is very popular with sailors, anglers, and other water-sports enthusiasts, who can lodge within yards of the lakeshore.

KEYSTONE

Like Copper, Keystone is a self-contained vacation resort area devoted largely to skiing. Found in the lush Snake River Valley above Dillon Reservoir, Keystone is surrounded by massive mountains rising to over 13,000 feet. Keystone first opened for skiing in the winter of 1969–70.

Tucked away among thick pine forests, Keystone comprises condominium complexes, the Keystone Conference Center, and a small village with ski stores, gift shops, and restaurants. To keep the cash flow at least moderate between ski seasons, Keystone offers a wide range of summer activities, including gondola rides, horseback riding, and golf. The resort also hosts the annual Keystone Music Festival with classical and pop concerts by the National Repertory Theater and the Summit Brass.

MONTEZUMA

The second-highest occupied community in the United States (elev. 10,268 feet), Montezuma is a tiny town isolated just off the Continental Divide five miles east of Keystone; the main street through town is still unpaved. Dating from the late 1800s, Montezuma has yet to be taken over by T-shirt and souvenir shops, unlike other 19th-century silver-mining towns such as Cripple Creek and Central City, although you will find a small grocery-and-supplies store in town. A small handful of hardy Summit Countians call Montezuma home. To get there take Montezuma Road off U.S. 6 just east of Keystone.

HEENEY

Heeney is the northernmost community in Summit County. Established on Green Mountain

Keystone is a very kid-friendly ski resort.

© STEPHEN METZGER

Reservoir off Highway 9, the town is small enough and far enough away from the ski resorts that it doesn't take itself too seriously. To wit: each June, the town sponsors the Heeney Tick Festival, which, according to one story, began when a popular Heeneyite recovered from a tick-bite related sick spell. The highlight of the festival, which also features a dance and kids' programs, is the parade down Main Street, with "tick-sized floats."

FRISCO

At the junction of I-70 and Highway 9 in the center of Summit County, Frisco (pop. 1,320; elev. 9,000 feet) offers excellent access to the county's skiing and other recreational sports. A late 19th-century mining town, Frisco today is an unpretentious little community defined by friendly people who seem somehow less caught up in the glamour of the ski industry, though the town's economy is still largely dependent on winter tourists.

The town's quiet main drag has a handful of restaurants, older motels, and sports and gift stores. The back streets south of Main are lined with old homes and cabins, some converted to bed-and-breakfasts; larger vacation-type homes and complexes are scattered in the woods just north of Main. Not far from the downtown area, Frisco loses some of its intimacy and charm, the highway both north and south lined with fast-food restaurants, gas stations, and malls (with a Wal-Mart, a Safeway, and other modern conveniences).

BRECKENRIDGE

Breckenridge, the county seat (pop. 1,200; elev. 9,500 feet), is both the oldest and the largest community in Summit County. In the Blue River Valley at the base of the massive Tenmile Range, Breckenridge is a ski town in the truest sense of the term, with the three-mountain Breckenridge Ski Resort dropping nearly to the little town's ski-shop-lined Main Street.

Dating from the mid-19th century, when it was a roaring mining camp, Breckenridge is a National Historic District, and many of its Victorians have been gorgeously restored, today housing bed-and-breakfasts, restaurants, and retail shops. In contrast, several deluxe hotels, convention centers, and condominium complexes are scattered on the hills between Main Street and the ski area.

One of the oldest continually occupied mining towns in the state, Breckenridge still has a bit of a frontier feel to it. It's a young and vital town that can still get awfully rowdy on Saturday night when the bars are packed with ski resort employees, grunged-out snowboarders, and miners down out of the mountains spending their paychecks.

During the summer, downtown Breckenridge becomes a shopping mecca, its sidewalks packed with visitors exploring the scores of gift and souvenir stores, boutiques, and T-shirt shops. Many of the restaurants feature patio seating, and you can sit and enjoy a salad and a lemonade, or a burger and a beer, in the crisp thin-air sunshine.

COPPER MOUNTAIN

Copper Mountain is a self-contained resort community, with several high-rise condominium complexes and lodges, as well as a central plaza area where you'll find a conference center, ski shops, boutiques, and restaurants. Many Copper employees live in on-site resort-owned housing.

Copper Mountain first opened in the winter of 1972–73 and revolves primarily around snow skiing. During the winter, the place bustles with skiers in for the day from Denver as well as Texans, New Yorkers, and Europeans here to hit the slopes for a week or more. In the summer, things die down considerably, though the resort also offers a variety of recreation, including golf at Copper Creek Golf Club, and tennis, fishing, and whitewater rafting.

MUSEUMS

Summit County is much richer in history than it is in museums, although the Summit Historical Society has recently increased efforts to

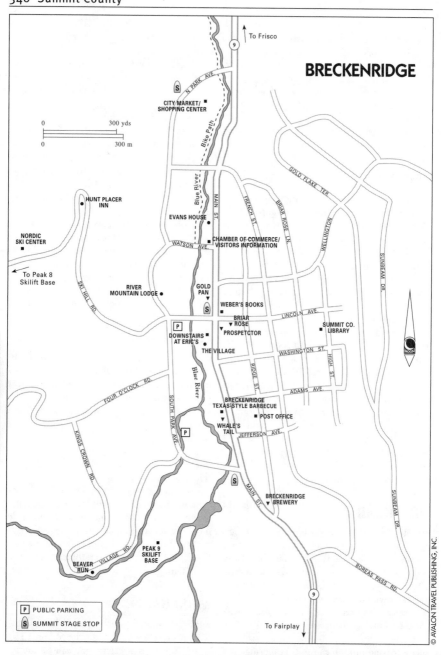

BRECKENRIDGE

To Frisco

City Market/ Shopping Center

Hunt Placer Inn

Nordic Ski Center

To Peak 8 Skilift Base

Evans House

Chamber of Commerce/ Visitors Information

River Mountain Lodge

Gold Pan

Weber's Books

Briar Rose

Prospector

Downstairs at Eric's

The Village

Summit Co. Library

Breckenridge Texas-Style Barbecue

Post Office

Whale's Tail

Breckenridge Brewery

Beaver Run

Peak 9 Skilift Base

To Fairplay

0   300 yds
0   300 m

N PARK AVE.
Bike Path
Blue River
MAIN ST.
WATSON AVE.
FRENCH ST.
BRIAR ROSE LN.
GOLD FLAKE TER.
WELLINGTON
SUNBEAM DR.
LINCOLN AVE.
WASHINGTON ST.
RIDGE ST.
ADAMS AVE.
HIGH ST.
SKI HILL RD.
FOUR O'CLOCK RD.
SOUTH PARK AVE.
Blue River
JEFFERSON AVE.
KINGS CROWN RD.
VILLAGE RD.
MAIN ST.
BOREAS PASS RD.
SUNBEAM DR.

P PUBLIC PARKING
S SUMMIT STAGE STOP

SUMMIT COUNTY

© AVALON TRAVEL PUBLISHING, INC.

bring history to the public. The **Dillon Schoolhouse Museum,** a 19th-century one-room schoolhouse, displays early educational supplies, desks, readers, and musical instruments. The museum is at 403 La Bonte St., Dillon, and is open late May to early September, Tues.–Sat., with tours at 1:30 and 3 P.M.

Also administered by the Summit Historical Society is the **Montezuma Schoolhouse Museum,** isolated in the deep woods east of Keystone at the old Montezuma mining camp. A visit here is an excellent way to learn about mining and the early settling of Summit County. The Montezuma Schoolhouse Museum is open Saturday only, early July through mid-August. To get there, take U.S. 6 past Keystone to Montezuma Road, and continue

about five miles to the town of Montezuma. Admission to both museums is by donation. For more information on either, phone 970/453-9022.

Frisco Historic Park, a collection of seven buildings from late-19th-century Frisco, will give you a good idea of what the town was like as a logging and mining center. Included are a one-room schoolhouse, a jail, a ranch house, and a chapel. The museum also displays historical photos, clothing, and other artifacts from the period.

Frisco Historic Park, at the corner of Main and 2nd (120 Main), is open Tues.–Sat. 11 A.M.–4 P.M. (through Sunday, Memorial Day through Labor Day). Admission is free. For more information, phone 970/668-3428.

Parks and Recreation

Okay, museums are all fine and well, but you can't fool me. You didn't come to Summit County to brush up on your history. You came to play. Though one of the side benefits of this playground is its marvelous sense of history, its main draw is recreation. And though Summit County's begun to sell itself lately as a year-round resort, the area's really about skiing. When the first downy flakes of the white stuff begin to swirl from a dark autumn sky, Summit County turns its attention to the slopes.

For complete information on the wide range of recreational possibilities in Summit County, contact the Forest Service office at 135 Hwy. 9 in Silverthorne, 970/468-5400, and ask for its *Recreation Opportunity Guide.*

SKIING AND SNOWBOARDING

Four of Colorado's best ski areas are concentrated within the borders of relatively tiny Summit County. No matter what your level—whether you're a first-time beginner or a retiring weideler, bump basher, powderhound, or chute shredder—you're bound to find something in Summit County to your liking. With a total of nearly 60 lifts servicing almost 300 marked trails on 4,000 acres of skiable

terrain, Arapahoe Basin, Breckenridge, Copper Mountain, and Keystone combine to offer some of the finest skiing in the country.

Avoiding the Crowds

And, unfortunately, sometimes it seems as though *everyone* is here. Not only are these some of the best ski areas in the state, but they're also about the most accessible—just 70 miles from Denver, with shuttles running back and forth about every 10 minutes. So the slopes can get crowded.

And so can the roads.

Not only does I-70 bottleneck between the resorts and Denver on Friday and Sunday afternoons, but some of the smaller access roads can also grind to standstills. Hints to avoid crowds: unfortunately, no profound secrets here. In fact, most folks know exactly how to avoid crowded slopes—it's just that their jobs won't let them. If yours does, try this: don't ski weekends, especially long ones; don't ski during Christmas vacation (approximately Dec. 26–Jan. 2 or 3). If you have no choice but to ski during those crowded times, get up early, get to the parking lot early, buy your ticket early, start skiing early, break for lunch early, quit early. Then get to bed early and do it again.

SUMMIT COUNTY

EISENHOWER MEMORIAL TUNNEL

First open to traffic in the spring of 1973 and completed in 1979, when the second bore was punched through, Eisenhower Memorial Tunnel cost just under $300 million and tremendously increased the accessibility of Colorado's ski resorts. The new route cut as much as an hour off the drive from Denver to the lifts at Vail, Copper Mountain, Breckenridge, and the others. In fact, the new tunnel so dramatically opened up the mountain resorts to motorists (in its first year 4.6 million cars passed through) that within 10 years of its completion it was already being viewed as inadequate, and the highway department was bemoaning that the tunnel's four lanes weren't six. By 2001, an average of about 30,000 cars were passing through each day, with nearly 10,300,000 total in 2001—far more than it was designed to accommodate.

In addition to the snags on the back sides of the two major summer holidays (Memorial and Labor Days), Eisenhower and I-70 also get snarled on winter weekends, especially the three- and four-day presidents' celebrations in February.

For road conditions in the Eisenhower Tunnel area, phone the statewide road conditions hotline at 303/639-1111 or 970/668-1090.

Also, don't forget about late-season skiing. Arapahoe Basin regularly stays open until June, and then it might close only close because of lack of customers. Just because your friends are calling you to play tennis or to chase trout, don't think the ski season's over. Indeed, you could very easily head up to the Basin one fine spring day and look around you and find that you *are* the lift line, that you're the only one on the entire lift, or that you've got a whole 1.5-mile run all to your lonesome. Ain't nobody but you and the mountain, one of the greatest feelings in the world.

Lift Tickets

As lift-ticket prices reach the $60-a-day mark, a day's skiing takes a bigger and bigger chunk of your life's savings. And unless you're Bill Gates, you'll probably want to keep an eye out for ways to trim the cost. You won't be able to save a whole lot, but if you play your cards right, you will find breaks here and there. First of all, most of the resorts offer multiday discounts, and you can buy tickets good at all four resorts. Second, many of the retailers in the area—from grocery stores to ski-rental outlets—offer discounts. Watch the local papers, coupon booklets, and advertising. Three bucks saved on a lift ticket will almost buy you a beer at the end of the day.

Another lift-ticket tip: in the winter of 1998–99, several Summit County-area ski resorts, in response to a declining skier base, actually *lowered* their lift-ticket prices . . . sort of. Resorts began offering extremely discounted season passes. For example, for about $750, you can get an unlimited four-person (users need not be related) pass good at Breckenridge and Keystone (available through Vail Resorts), while Copper Mountain and Winter Park are offering similar deals. Do the math: with daily passes at $50, all four participating members begin saving money sometime in midafternoon on the fourth day.

Arapahoe Basin

A look at A-Basin's terrain statistics—40 percent advanced and expert, 45 percent intermediate, 15 percent beginner—tells you A-Basin is one demanding ski area. Steep, challenging, unforgiving—where some of the toughest skiers in the area fine-tune their chops. Skiers who don't care that this is the smallest ski area in Summit County know it's the best, and a lot of them wouldn't ski anywhere else. Not only that, it's also the one with the longest season. Its high base ensures a late snowpack, and the resort regularly stays open until June. In fact, in 1995 A-Basin was not only open for skiing on July Fourth, but it got seven new inches of snow that day.

Arapahoe Basin first opened shortly after World War II, when members of the U.S. Army's 10th Mountain Division improvised a cable ski lift using old mining equipment. The resort stayed small and low-key, even as many of the state's other ski areas were being developed into major destination resorts. In the late 1970s, A-Basin was bought by Keystone, whose owners invested money in upgrading the Basin; still, it remains refreshingly unglitzy. This is in part because it's the least accessible of the four Summit County ski areas. Sitting high on the west side of Loveland Pass, Denver skiers must get there either by driving through Eisenhower Tunnel to Dillon and then turning around and going east again via U.S. 6, or they must drive over the top of the pass, a harrowing if awesomely scenic road, and drop to the base of the lifts.

Today, A-Basin has five lifts servicing 30 trails on 490 mostly above-timberline acres. Its 360-inch average snowfall, coupled with its 10,780-foot *base,* ensures a season through June, oftentimes longer. Those whose goal is to sample the range of American skiing owe it to themselves to try the Basin, where you're as close to the top of the world as any chairlift will take you.

For more information on Arapahoe Basin, phone the resort at 970/468-0718 or 888/ARA-PAHO (272-7246). Its website is www.arapahoebasin.com.

Keystone

Keystone has long had a reputation as an area ideally suited to beginners and intermediate skiers and boarders, and folks at those levels will still find plenty of terrain to their liking. However, as the resort has expanded, it has increased significantly the amount of advanced and expert skiing and boarding. The area is now roughly 12 percent beginner, 30 percent intermediate, 5 percent advanced, and 55 percent expert, due in large part to the separate North Peak/Outback part of the mountain, which alone is 71 percent expert. Excluding the North Peak area (see below), Keystone's terrain is 20 percent beginner, 65 percent intermediate, and 15 percent advanced. Combined, the two areas' 22 lifts service a 2,900-foot

vertical drop (snowmaking on 849 acres). The longest run is longer than three miles.

Keystone is the epitome of a user-friendly resort. Among its attractions: well-groomed slopes ideal for effortless cruising, high-tech lifts and equipment, exceptional instructional programs, convenient accommodations and facilities, and night skiing—lifts run for 13 hours.

To get there, take U.S. 6 east from Dillon about eight miles and watch for the signs.

For more information on skiing Keystone, contact the resort at P.O. Box 38, Keystone, CO 80435, 800/258-9553. For snow conditions, phone 970/468-4111. Look at the website at www.keystoneresort.com.

Copper Mountain

Copper Mountain first opened in the winter of 1972–73 as a completely self-contained resort community. Once the second-largest ski resort in Summit County, Copper Mountain leases from the Forest Service three separate mountains, which naturally divide the resort's terrain fairly evenly among ski abilities (21 percent beginner, 25 percent intermediate, 36 percent advanced, 18 percent expert). Expansion in the late summer of 1999 added more than 300 more acres of skiable terrain, bringing the total

Skiers pause to take in the view at Keystone.

© STEPHEN METZGER

SUMMIT COUNTY

catching air at Copper Mountain

to 2,400 acres (and making it Summit County's largest ski area). Additional developments included two new high-speed chairlifts (for a total of 21 lifts), increased snowmaking capabilities, and a new 40,000-square-foot base lodge.

Because of the wide range of excellent skiing, as well as the resort's wonderful accessibility (it's just yards from I-70 on the east side of Vail Pass), it's a favorite of Denver day-trippers. Its range of fine skiing also attracts families and other groups within which ability levels vary. Groups can ski together awhile, then head off for terrain suited to their individual abilities, then meet again for lunch or to show off for each other before retiring at day's end.

Another one of Copper's advantages is its self-containment. There's plenty of on-site lodging, shopping, and dining, and it's a great place to hole up for a week doing nothing but skiing—you can be out your door and on the slopes in minutes.

For more information on skiing or accommodations at Copper Mountain, write Copper Mountain Resort Association, P.O. Box 3001, Copper Mountain, CO 80433, 970/968-2882 or 800/458-8386. For snow conditions, phone 800/789-7609 or 970/968-2100. The website is www.ski-copper.com.

Breckenridge

With more than 2,000 skiable acres, Breckenridge is Summit County's second-largest ski area. Twenty-five lifts service 139 designated trails, the longest of which is 3.5 miles long. Like Copper Mountain, Breckenridge offers good skiing for all ability levels, though recent expansion has made the area increasingly attractive to advanced skiers (the actual breakdown is 15 percent beginner, 28 percent intermediate, 22 percent advanced, and 35 percent expert). Also like Copper, Breckenridge sprawls over three separate mountains—Peaks 8, 9, and 10. Beginning and low-intermediate skiers have the lower parts of Peaks 8 and 9 to roam, while advanced skiers claim the back sides of peaks 8 and 10, which are also good places to avoid crowds. The two base areas provide access to all three mountains.

One of Breckenridge's real pluses is its open-mindedness and the resulting on-mountain eclecticness. One of the first ski areas in the state to okay snowboarding and then actively to court the wild snow surfers, Breckenridge has hosted the World Snowboard Championships. The resort is also popular with Telemarkers.

Something else distinguishing Breckenridge from Copper, Keystone, and A-Basin is both a town and the ski resort—in fact, the town and the ski area are virtually one and the same. Much like Telluride and Aspen, Breckenridge is a ski town in the truest and most aesthetically pleasing sense. Though Breckenridge claims its share of condos and fancy modern motels, the town is much more defined by its Victorian-lined main streets, its tiny shops, and its laid-back locals—young, unpretentious, and completely ski-oriented. After a good dump, the little town's streets are all but deserted, as just about everyone's "gone skiin'."

For more information on skiing and accommodations in Breckenridge, write P.O. Box 1058, Breckenridge, CO 80424, or phone 970/453-5000 or 800/789-7669. For snow conditions, phone 800/789-7669. You can also get snow conditions from the website: www.breckenridge.com.

Cross-Country Skiing

Take a look at the racks atop cars coming into Summit County from Denver, as well as those on local rigs, and you'll see that cross-country skiing is, if not as popular as downhill, certainly the passion of *many* people. In fact, Summit County skinny skiers have even more to choose from than Alpiners do: everything from quiet, ungroomed lakeside trails to groomed skating tracks to the lift-serviced runs of the resorts themselves, where three-pinners practice Tele turns on the same slopes as downhillers.

Frisco Nordic Center, 1121 N. Summit Blvd., Frisco, 970/668-0866, offers nearly 40 km of trails (one-way loops) in the woods near Dillon Reservoir. Lessons and rentals are available. **Copper Mountain Nordic Center,** P.O. Box 3001, Copper Mountain, CO 80443, 970/968-2882, ext. 6342, has 25 km of groomed track and skate lanes. A favorite among intermediate and advanced Nordic skiers, this center also provides access to Copper Mountain's lifts, as well as a variety of special programs, including races, moonlight tours, and Telemark, waxing, and snow-safety workshops. **Breckenridge Nordic**

Ski Center, P.O. Box 1200, Breckenridge, CO 80424, 970/453-6855, has 30 km, rentals, and lessons (a mile west of town on Ski Hill Road). Cruise the Keystone area at **Keystone Cross-Country Center,** P.O. Box 38, Keystone, CO 80435, 970/468-4275, where 30 km of trails meander along the backcountry lodges, creek, and valley.

In addition, the county has many easily accessible trails ideally suited to cross-country skiers, including some of the bike paths and areas around Dillon Reservoir. Parts of the 15-mile bike path paralleling Highway 9 between Frisco and Breckenridge are perfect for easy-access sliding, as are some of the Forest Service campgrounds on the lake (roads and weather permitting).

For further information on Nordic skiing, contact the Dillon District Office of **Arapaho National Forest,** 135 Hwy. 9, Silverthorne, CO 80498, 970/468-5400. You can also get information from the retail ski shops in the area, including **Christy Sports,** 645 S. Park, Breckenridge, 970/453-0987, and **Breckenridge Ski Shop,** 211 N. Main, 970/453-7039. In Silverthorne, stop in at **Wilderness Sports,** 171 Blue River Pkwy., 970/468-8519, and in Frisco, try **Antler's Ski and Sport Shop,** 900 N. Summit, 970/668-0248.

OTHER WINTER ACTIVITIES

Snowmobiling

Though controversial by definition (the machines are loud, exhausty, and fossil-fuel gobbling), this sport has its fans, with several outfits in the county providing a range of services and activities. **Tiger Run Resort,** P.O. Box 1418, Breckenridge, CO 80424, 970/453-2231, has 150 snowmobiles for rent (as well as boots and snowsuits). Tiger Run is four miles north of Breckenridge on Highway 9. **White Mountain Snowmobile Tours,** 970/668-5323 or 800/247-7238, offers hourly and half-day tours, with discounts available to groups.

Ice Skating

Summit County probably has more ice-skating rinks than any similar-size area west of New York and south of the Canadian border. One of the most popular is **Keystone Lake** in Keystone Village, open daily 10 A.M.–10 P.M. Rental skates available. Phone Keystone Resort at 970/468-2316 for more information.

Ice skating is also available on Maggie Pond in Breckenridge (next to the Bell Tower Mall) and on West Lake at Copper Mountain.

Over the River and through the Woods

A number of Summit County outfits offer day and evening sleigh rides, from short jaunts to dinner rides that might include buffalo soup or baked salmon. Sleighs depart from the alpine and cross-country ski areas, as well as from private enterprises. For a listing of companies with descriptions of services, contact **Summit Activity Center,** 970/547-1594, or www.summitactivities.com.

WHEN THE SNOW MELTS

Though Summit boosters have been very successful changing the area's image from that of a cluster of ski towns to a year-round resort, Summit County remains predominantly winter-oriented. So far. But each summer, more and more tourists are drawn to the area for its myriad recreational opportunities—from cycling to windsurfing, fishing to horseback riding to just plain sightseeing.

Cycling

Anyone skeptical that Summit County is one of the premier biking areas in the country need only take a look around. Miles and miles of bicycle paths connect the various communities; not only are they ideal for exploring, but they make commuting easy for locals. Come spring, don't be surprised to see a mountain biker on Main Street in Breckenridge with a pair of skis under his arm or bungie-corded to his top bar. In fact, many of the ski shops serve double duty by turning to cycling—sales, rentals—in the spring, summer, and fall.

Among the excellent paved bike paths in the area are the **Blue River Bikeway,** which connects Breckenridge and Frisco and winds in and out of meadows and forests of sweet-smelling pines; **Tenmile Canyon National Recreation Trail** between Copper Mountain and Frisco; and **Vail Pass Bikeway,** a 20-mile route over the 10,600-foot pass that drops into Vail Village—excellent scenery en route.

For more serious touring, you can head off in just about any direction, though traffic will of course be heavier on some routes. Highway 9 north along the Blue River is a moderate ride, with rises but no significant hills. At the other end of the range, U.S. 6 east passes A-Basin and climbs over the grueling **Loveland Pass** (11,990 feet). Even Ah-nold might huff and puff a bit.

The county is also rife with mountain-bike trails, with several designated paths over nearby mountain passes, including **Boreas, Georgia,** and **Webster** Passes. Your best source for information on biking in the area is *Summit County Mountain Bike Trail Guide,* which details some 30 bike-path and off-road trails in the area, providing lengths and degrees of difficulty for each. The free guide is available at all area visitor information centers and at many local bike shops. You can also get information from the Dillon District Office of **Arapaho National Forest,** 135 Hwy. 9, Silverthorne, 970/468-5400. The Forest Service, in conjunction with the county, has published an excellent map showing the various trails in the area, which provides mileage, difficulty ratings, safety and camping information, and recommended tours. The maps are available free at the Forest Service office and at most bike shops in the area.

Golf

Golf is another exceptionally popular summer activity in Summit County, and some of the ski resorts, specifically Keystone and Copper Mountain, promote golf-and-lodging packages with the same enthusiasm with which they promote skiing plans during the winter. The public **Breckenridge Golf Course** is owned and operated by the town of Breckenridge. Designed by Jack Nicklaus, the 18-hole course, at 200 Clubhouse Drive, offers a wonderful natural setting in the

Blue River Valley just north of town. Phone 970/453-5544 for tee times and information. **Copper Creek Golf Club** at Copper Mountain, another lush 18-hole course with excellent views, claims to be the highest-elevation PGA course in the country. Phone 970/968-2339.

Keystone Ranch Golf Course at Keystone Resort is an 18-hole course designed by Robert Trent Jones Jr., and is reserved for Keystone guests, except on a space-available basis. Phone the golf course at 970/468-4250 or Keystone Resort at 970/468-2316. The nine-hole **Eagles Nest Golf Course** is in north Silverthorne off Highway 9, 970/468-0681.

Hiking

Summit County abounds in hiking trails, from half-mile walks to scenic overlooks to 10-mile (and longer), full-day wilderness excursions. The Forest Service, in conjunction with several local businesses, publishes an excellent *Summer Trailhead Guide,* which discusses a dozen trails of varying lengths and difficulty levels. The guide also includes recommendations for specific topo maps and provides a day-pack checklist and suggestions for environmental responsibility.

Here is a small sampling of Forest Service-suggested hikes: **Tenderfoot Mountain** is an easy 1.25-mile hike offering views of Dillon Reservoir and the Gore and Tenmile mountain ranges. Turn north from the stoplight on U.S. 6 in Dillon, and turn immediately right onto the frontage road, which you'll follow to the trailhead. **Gold Hill Trail** is a popular three-mile hike beginning five miles south of Frisco on Highway 9. Ranked "more difficult," Gold Hill is part of the Colorado Trail and joins **Peaks Trail** three miles south of Frisco. **Wheeler National Recreation Trail** is an 11-mile hike, also ranked "more difficult," linking Breckenridge and Copper Mountain. The trail crosses the Tenmile Range through Breckenridge ski area, and offers views of the Tenmile, Gore, Sawatch, and Flat Top Ranges. Lots of excellent hiking trails are also in the **Eagles Nest Wilderness Area** north of Silverthorne. The Forest Service can provide complete information.

Fishing

There's a lot of water in Summit County, most obviously the sprawling arms and main body of Dillon Reservoir. In addition, there are many streams and rivers, with lots of accessible shoreline. Also, Green Mountain Reservoir north of Dillon midway to Kremmling offers lots of fishing opportunities for both the shore and boat angler. Among the fish you'll find in the county's various waters are brook, brown, rainbow, and lake trout, and kokanee salmon.

Summit County waters are so accessible that they see an awful lot of traffic, and you've got to be pretty persistent and trout-savvy to hook into big fish. Remember, too, some of the streams have special restrictions; make sure you read and understand all regulations before making that first cast.

Dillon Reservoir offers decent fishing year-round (ice fishing in the winter) for trout and kokanee salmon. Boats are ideal, though fishing from the shore can be successful. **Green Mountain Reservoir** is also open year-round, with the narrower Blue River Channel stretches, and the area between the town of Heeney and the dam, offering the best bets.

The **Blue River** north of Silverthorne is a Gold Medal Water-designated trout stream with some excellent catch-and-release-only sections (fly-fishing only). **Tenmile Creek** between Frisco and Copper Mountain can also be good.

An excellent source of information is *Fish the Summit,* a map and guide that discusses the Summit's various streams and lakes in detail, offering a season-by-season series of tips on lures, bait, and hot spots. The guide also identifies the individual species of fish (with both drawings and text), discusses stream restrictions, and provides a list of fishing-license agents. The map and guide is available at most tourist and chamber of commerce offices.

A number of shops and outfitters in the county provide guided fishing trips, licenses, equipment, and tips. **Cutthroat Anglers,** 400 Blue River Pkwy., Silverthorne, 970/262-2878, website: www.fishcolorado.com, specializes in fly fishing and offers guided trips, gear, and instructions. You can also get gear and information at **Antler's,** 900 N. Summit Rd., Frisco, 970/668-0248.

White-Water Rafting

Though there's not a whole lot of raftable white water in Summit County, there's plenty nearby, and a number of companies offer half- and full-day trips on the county's Blue River, as well as on the Arkansas and Colorado. Contact **Performance Tours Rafting,** 110 Ski Hill Rd., Breckenridge, 970/453-0661; **Breckenridge Whitewater Rafting,** P.O. Box 3732, Dillon, CO 80435, 970/668-1665; **Tiger Run Resort,** 128 S. Main St., Breckenridge, 970/453-2231; or **Adventure Specialists,** 970/668-1689.

Boating, Sailing, and Windsurfing

Dillon Reservoir and Green Mountain Reservoir are exceptionally popular for most water sports (though the water's *awfully* cold for swimming). There are several public boat launches around Dillon Reservoir, and the shore is generally gently sloped for easy put-ins. In addition, a handful of marinas rent sailboats, paddleboats, and fishing boats. In Dillon, check out **Dillon Yacht Basin,** on East Lodgepole, 970/468-2396. In Frisco, you can rent canoes and motorboats at **Osprey Adventures,** 900 Main St., 970/668-5573 or 888/780-4970, which also offers guided canoe tours.

Ballooning

To see Summit County from the basket of a hot-air balloon, contact **Colorado Balloon Rides,** 970/468-9280, which advertises the highest-altitude balloon rides in North America.

Horseback Rides

This is superb country to explore by horseback, and a number of pack companies in the area offer a range of trips. Rates usually start at about $20 an hour. **Alpine Adventures,** P.O. Box 2620-B, Breckenridge, CO 80424, 970/468-9297, offers short trail rides as well as overnight pack trips to the Montezuma Mining District and into Arapaho National Forest; meals and a sleeping bag provided. **Eagles Nest Equestrian Center,** P.O. Box 495, Silverthorne, CO 80498, 970/468-

0677, also offers a full range of trips, specializing in extended backcountry tours and fall hunts. You can also arrange rides, from one hour to a full day, through **Keystone Stables,** 970/468-4156, and **Breckenridge Stables,** P.O. Box 1816, Breckenridge, CO 80424, 970/453-4438, both of which welcome large groups and offer rides that include meals.

Chairlift Rides

Breckenridge and Copper Mountain both offer off-season chairlift rides for sightseers, while you can ride Keystone's gondola. At the top, grab something to eat while you take in the panoramas, and then either ride or hike back down. Lifts are usually open from late spring through September. For more information, phone **Breckenridge Ski Area,** 970/453-2368; **Copper Mountain Resort,** 970/968-2318; or **Keystone Resort,** 970/468-2316.

Jeep Tours

The old mining roads and high mountain passes in Summit County make the area a natural for exploring with an off-road vehicle. From ghosts of old mining towns to high lakes, some of Summit's most interesting areas are accessible only by 4WD. For maps and information, stop by the Forest Service, 135 Hwy. 9 in Silverthorne. **Tiger Run Resort,** 970/453-2231, and **Tenderfoot Tours,** 970/468-5000, can arrange Jeep tours of the backcountry.

Historical Tours

The Summit County Historical Society has designed a number of guided and self-guided tours of the area, including Breckenridge and local ghost and mining towns. Guided tours of the Breckenridge Historic District are offered Wed.–Sat. mornings (summers only)—a ghost is said to haunt the bathroom of the Brown Hotel. The society also sponsors tours to Washington Gold Mine and the Edwin Carter Museum. A separate tour to the Lomax Placer Gulch includes mining demonstrations, gold panning, and a slide show. For starting times and more information on the tours, stop by the Breckenridge Actvities Center, 201 S. Main St., or phone 970/453-9022.

Take Me Out to the Ball Game

One of the most relaxing ways to spend a summer evening or Saturday afternoon is by watching a local slow-pitch softball game. Spirits are high as teams representing local pizza parlors, construction companies, and ski shops vie for Summit County trophies. Watch excellent athletes (many of the best skiers in the area) drive ground balls up the middle or line deep ropes into the gaps. The Breckenridge fields are just north of town off North Park Avenue, behind City Market.

Indoor Recreation

In addition to the health clubs at many of the larger hotels and condo complexes, the **Silverthorne Recreation Center** is a public facility with racketball courts, cardiovascular machines, free weights, indoor basketball, and swimming pools with a water slide, as well as classes in yoga, tumbling, martial arts, etc. Drop-in fee is $8.50 a day. The rec center is at the corner of Rainbow and 4th in Silverthorne, behind the factory stores. Phone 970/468-0711.

Practicalities

You'll find a huge range of accommodations in Summit County, from small mom-and-pop motels to luxurious condominium complexes and convention centers—each year fewer and fewer of the former and more and more of the latter. You can also rent individual homes, some sprawling and estatelike, others smaller and more budget-oriented. Generally, if you're looking for cheap digs, you'll be least disappointed in Frisco and Silverthorne, both virtually lakeside to Dillon Reservoir, whereas if you're more interested in being pampered, you might want to check out the condos and hotels in Breckenridge, Dillon, Keystone, or Copper Mountain. Between the two extremes are a handful of highway-side franchise inns both in Frisco and Dillon. Most of the lodges offer free shuttle service to the ski areas, as well as package deals that include lift tickets, equipment rentals, and transportation.

When it comes to lodging (and what you'll pay), though, the main consideration, as in most resort towns, is season: most places adjust their rates to the ol' law of supply and demand—when the snow comes down, prices go up. High-season prices generally revolve around the ski resorts and holidays. Rates will be highest between Christmas and the end of New Year's weekend. They'll also be high in February, around the time of Washington's and Lincoln's birthdays (often shoved together and celebrated jointly in ski country to allow schoolkids a whole week off). Pre-

dictably, rates will be lower once the snow melts, especially in late spring before the weather warms up enough to allow for swimming, sailing, and shirt-sleeved bike riding and hiking, and in the fall, when it cools off again and before the clearcuts on the mountainsides are snow covered and the engines of the chairlifts get fired up.

The other thing to keep in mind is that even though rates go up significantly when the skiing gets good, people still clamor to pay them. Don't even think of trying without reservations to find a room in this part of the country when the skiing's good. Book a room at least a month before you plan to come. Or better yet, two months. Or six. A year if you can. The only way you might find a room at the last minute during high season is by calling to see if there have been any cancellations.

Summit County Lodging Information

For complete information on accommodations in Summit County, write the **Summit County Chamber of Commerce,** P.O. Box 214, Frisco, CO 80443, or phone 800/530-3099. You can also get lodging information from the following ski resorts: **Breckenridge,** 800/221-1091; **Copper Mountain,** 800/458-8386; and **Keystone,** 800/468-5004. You can also book vacation rentals, summer or winter, through **Summit County Central Reservations,** P.O. Box 446, Dillon, CO 80435, 800/365-6365.

MOTELS AND HOTELS

Most of the smaller motels and hotels are in Frisco and Dillon, each within a short drive of all of the Summit County ski areas, as well as Vail and Beaver Creek. They're also right in the heart of most of the summer resort activity—sailing, cycling, hiking, rafting, and golfing.

$50–100

A handful of motels in downtown Frisco offer reasonably priced but dependable lodging. The **Sky-Vue Motel,** 305 S. 2nd, 970/668-3311, and the **Snowshoe Motel,** 521 Main, 970/668-3444, both have long-standing reputations; guests return year after year. Newer lodges in Frisco, with doubles starting in this price range, include the **Alpine Inn,** 105 Lusher Ct. (behind the Safeway), 970/668-3122, and the **Summit Inn,** 1205 N. Summit Blvd., 970/668-3220.

$100–150

Also in Frisco, the **Holiday Inn,** 970/668-5000 or 800/782-7669, offers six stories of rooms and a heated pool and spa. Nice, too, is the **Best Western Lake Dillon Lodge,** 1202 N. Summit Blvd., Frisco, 970/668-5094. Over in Dillon, try the **Best Western Ptarmigan Lodge,** 970/468-2341 or 800/727-0607, or the **Super 8 Motel,** 808 Little Beaver Trail, 970/468-8888 or 800/843-1991.

CONDOMINIUMS AND MORE EXPENSIVE HOTELS

Breckenridge

The Village at Breckenridge Resort is a sprawling complex (actually encompassing three separate lodges) with more than 400 rooms, varying from studios to penthouse suites. Though prices vary as well, this is generally for the expense-account crowd, those who've saved for the Big Splurge, and the fortunate (?) few who never have to ask, "How much?" Amenities include the standard exercise room, spa, and pool, as well as kitchens. Phone 970/453-2000 or 800/321-8552. Larger rooms that sleep more will decrease the cost per person, with doubles starting in the $150 range.

Among other Breckenridge deluxe accommodations are **Beaver Run Resort,** 970/453-6000 or 800/525-2253 ($100–300); and **River Mountain Lodge,** 970/453-4711 ($100–300).

Copper Mountain

The base of Copper Mountain is dotted with condominiums and lodges, many of which offer to-your-doorstep skiing, and all of which are steps away from a shuttle-bus stop. Copper's **Club Med** (the first in the United States), 970/968-2121, is near the central plaza right at the base of the lifts. For rates and a full listing of accommodations and ski and summer-vacation packages, write **Copper Mountain Resort Lodging Services,** P.O. Box 3001, Copper Mountain, CO 80443; or phone 800/458-8386, ext. 1; locally, phone 970/968-2882. Winter rates ($150–300) include skiing. Summer rates ($100–250) include chairlift rides, fly-fishing, and other bonuses.

Dillon

Dillon offers about two dozen hotels and condominium complexes, many of which are right on or overlook the lake. Among them: **Summit Yacht Club,** 970/468-2703; **Lake Dillon Condotel,** 970/468-2409 or 800/323-7892; and **The Spinnaker at Lake Dillon,** 970/468-8001. All are in the $100–150 (and up) range. For more information on lodging in Dillon, write Town of Dillon, P.O. Box 8, Dillon, CO 80435, or phone 970/468-2403 or 970/629-6342 from Denver.

Keystone

Like Copper Mountain, Keystone is a small village of condominium complexes, restaurants, ski shops, and boutiques built to accommodate the ski crowd but which in recent years has begun (successfully) to woo summer vacationers as well. Three basic options here: the lodge at the resort, the Ski Tip Lodge (see below), or one of the many condo complexes (about 800 suites total). Either way you can book rooms by the night or buy full-bore ski-golf-ride-sail-fish-bike-eat-drink-and-be-merry packages. Five-night ski packages at the **Keystone Lodge** or a nearby condo begin at around $300 per person, and include four days' skiing at Keystone and/or Arapahoe Basin. For more information, write **Keystone Resort,** P.O. Box 38, Keystone, CO 80435, or phone 800/541-0346 (the lodge) or 800/222-0188 (condos); from Denver phone 970/534-4806 (the lodge) or 970/534-7712 (condos).

BED-AND-BREAKFASTS

Gaining in popularity recently, bed-and-breakfasts offer a wider range of prices (and comfort levels) than one might imagine. The **Summit County Bed and Breakfast Association** (www.summitcountybnbs.com) includes more than 20 members in the area. For a complete listing, write the Summit County Chamber of Commerce, P.O. Box 214, Frisco, CO 80443.

In Frisco, the **Galena Street Mountain Inn,** 106 Galena St., 970/668-3224 or 800/248-9138, has a solid reputation for catering to skiers and summer visitors alike, with many visitors returning year after year. Fifteen very nice rooms in the $100–150 range.

In Breckenridge, the **Evans House,** 102 S. French St., 970/453-5509, offers seven guest rooms in a restored Victorian home dating from 1886 and listed on the National Register of Historic Places. Rooms are $100–150 in winter, less in summer. Also in Breckenridge, the **Hunt Placer Inn,** a newer, European chalet-style inn at 275 Ski Hill Rd., 970/453-7573 or 800/472-1430, has eight elegantly decorated rooms and is a three-block walk from downtown and two from the lifts. Doubles run $125–250.

If you're looking to get away from the hustle and bustle of the busy streets and ski areas, a lodge or bed-and-breakfast in the trees might be the ticket to the perfect escape.

Dillon's **Western Skies Bed and Breakfast,** 5040 Montezuma Rd., 970/468-9445, offers both individual cabins and rooms in the main lodge. Along the Snake River on 22 acres of pines, the lodge is still just a few minutes from the lifts at Keystone. Rooms and cabins are $100–150.

VACATION HOMES

Generally at the high end of vacation accommodations options, individual homes offer privacy and oftentimes the size needed to accommodate large groups, and they sometimes offer better long-term rates. To rent from owners, look in the "Vacation Homes" section of *The Denver Post* classified ads. In addition, you can arrange lodging at individual homes in Summit County through **Vacation Rentals Property Management,** Box 3549, Dillon, CO 80435, 970/262-1269 or 800/944-5994. Check out its website at www.vrpm.com.

CAMPING AND RVING

Summit County is entirely contained within the borders of Arapaho National Forest, so summer visitors will find a variety of Forest Service-maintained campgrounds within short drives of Breckenridge, Copper Mountain, Dillon, and Keystone, including several at Dillon Reservoir. Be forewarned, though: those on the lake (Heaton Bay, Peak One, Pine Grove, and Prospector campgrounds—more than 300 sites total), though very nice, fill up quickly when the weather's warm. Don't expect to get a site without reservations. Some areas are designated hike-in and bike-in only.

Several campgrounds in the north arm of Summit County offer less developed but also somewhat less crowded facilities. Take Highway 9 north from Silverthorne. The road winds through the beautiful Blue River Valley past Green Mountain Reservoir to Kremmling, with several campgrounds on the way. **Blue River Campground** is about five miles north of Silverthorne on Highway 9 (well water and pit toilets only).

Cow Creek Campground offers free camping on the east shore of Green Mountain Reservoir just off Highway 9. Another fairly primitive area (pit toilets), this campground has zippo in terms of shade, but the lack of trees makes for good winds, and the spot is very popular with sailboarders. Not much shade at **Prairie Point Campground,** either, at the south end of Green Mountain Reservoir, though the views, particularly of the massive Gore Range, make for a fair trade.

For information on camping in the area, or to make reservations, stop in at the Forest Service District Office at 191 Blue River Pkwy., Silverthorne, 970/468-5400.

Tiger Run RV Resort, 970/453-9690, on the Blue River between Frisco and Breckenridge, is the only RV park in the county, and, in true Summit County style, it's actually a full-fledged resort, with tennis courts, pool, hot tub, etc. Write P.O. Box 815, Breckenridge, CO 80424.

FOOD

I've been coming to Summit County regularly for more than 25 years, and each time I return I am amazed at the huge number of new restaurants, as well as at the number that have managed to hang on. Following are a small sampling of some of my favorites, as well as places readers and locals have recommended over the years.

Frisco

One of my favorite places to start the day, over espressos and pastries, is **Rocky Mountain Coffee Roasters,** 285 Main St., 970/668-3470, where you can read the newspaper, chat with locals, and watch downtown Frisco come to life. For lunch and dinner, try **El Rio Cantina,** 450 W. Main, 970/668-5043, which offers excellent Mexican food with a health twist—my burrito had black beans and corn—and good prices to boot. Entrées are in the $6–12 range.

The **Moose Jaw,** downtown at 208 Main, 970/668-3931, is a classic little diner and bar for the pool/softball/country-music/just-finished-framing-a-house-up-in-Breck crowd. Originally built in the 1950s as a bunkhouse for Dillon Dam workers, the structure was cut in half in 1961 and moved to its present site, where it initially served as a grocery store. Today, a burger with a basket of fries will run you $5–8, or you can get a fish sandwich or a bowl of chili and fries for about the same price.

Two of Frisco's higher-end restaurants are **Ristorante Ti Amo,** 730 N. Summit Blvd, 970/668-1993, which specializes in Tuscan and Florentine food, including calamari, sauteed artichokes, and polentas and pastas (open daily for dinner); and the **Blue Spruce Inn,** 120 W. Main, 970/668-5900, which serves beef, veal, and seafood dishes ranging from $14 to $25 (steak and lobster).

For good and reasonably priced Chinese restaurants, try **Szechuan Taste,** 301 Main St., 970/668-5685. Specials (duck and seafood) run $11–15, but you can also get good-sized vegetable, beef, and noodle dishes for $7–12.

Dillon and Silverthorne

A veritable Summit County institution, established in the early 1940s when skiers would stop en route to a day at Arapahoe Basin, the **Arapahoe Cafe and Pub,** in Dillon at the corner of Lake Dillon and La Bonte (626 Lake Dillon Dr.), 970/468-0873, serves a breakfast guaranteed to kick your morning in the backside. Egg dishes and other standards run $5–9. The Arapahoe is also open for lunch and dinner, serving burgers, soups, salads, and other hearty fare.

For Italian food, it's hard to beat **Ristorante Al Lago,** 240 Lake Dillon, 970/468-6111, where veal, chicken, seafood, and pasta dinners run $12–22. Another Dillon favorite is **Pug Ryan's Steakhouse,** 104 Village Place, 970/453-2145, where steaks, prime rib, chicken, and fish dinners run $12–25.

Opened in February of 1997, the **Dillon Dam Brewery,** 100 Little Dam Rd., 970/262-7777, is one of the best brewpubs in the state. Not only is the beer outstanding, but its food is very good and reasonably priced. Salads, burgers, pastas, and sandwiches, as well as steak and seafood and other specials, are $6–18.

Breckenridge

The Stage Door Cafe, 203 S. Main, 970/453-6964, is a great little place to stop in for a muffin and latte. Open at 7 A.M. daily; some outdoor seating is available in the summer.

Another good breakfast call is the **Prospector,** 130 S. Main, 970/453-6858, where big American breakfasts run $5–8. The Prospector also serves excellent lunches; a burger, omelette, or bowl of hot soup will run $5–8. Also serving breakfast (including breakfast burritos and *huevos* rancheros) is the **Gold Pan Restaurant and Bar,** 103 N. Main St., 970/453-5499, a true Summit County classic. In a building dating from the 1880s that has housed over the years a dry goods store, a bowling alley, and a gas station, the Gold Pan claims to hold the longest continually operating liquor license west of the Mississippi. The Gold Pan Bar is a longtime favorite of locals of all stripes, from Glen Plake wannabes to miners who look as if they haven't seen daylight in years. The restaurant tends to cater to a slightly more civil crowd, après-skiers who munch on Mexican food (try the nachos) or the famous Gold Pan burgers. Dinners run $5–12.

Breckenridge Brewery and Pub, at the south end of town at 600 Main St., 970/453-1550, offers a half dozen or so different house beers (ranging from the Avalanche Ale—"it can overtake you before you know it"—to an oatmeal stout). The pub also serves a variety of traditional pub grub—shepherd's pie, fish and chips, burgers, sandwiches, and salads. Lunches run about $7–14. Open for lunch and dinner daily (bar until 2 A.M.). Home-brewed ginger ale and root beer are also available. Also good is **Breckenridge Texas-Style Barbecue,** 301 S. Main, 970/453-7313, where you can get links, briskets, chicken, etc., and sample from the 20 microbrews on tap. Entrées are in the $6–12 range. Watch for the all-you-can-eat-ribs specials.

Among the better upscale Breckenridge restaurants are the **Briar Rose,** 109 E. Lincoln, 970/453-9948, specializing in exotic game dishes (elk, venison), beef, and seafood (closed Monday); and the **Whale's Tail,** 323 S. Main, 970/453-2221, serving seafood.

ENTERTAINMENT

When ski season's in full swing and Summit County's swollen with skiers of every hue—honeymooners from Houston, families from Fargo, and countless college students here between (or instead of) semesters—there's a lot going on, and you'd be hard-pressed not to find something to do when you pull your ski boots off. Most of the ski-area bars feature live music,

and there's a huge range of clubs and nighteries around the county. Summer's a bit slower, though, and spring and fall slower still.

For current information on what's happening where, check out the local papers. The *Summit County Journal* and the *Summit Daily News* provide up-to-date information on everything from reggae concerts to dinner theater, gallery openings to pool tournaments. Both papers are available in racks around town.

Though you'll find live music and other entertainment throughout the county, the largest cluster is in Breckenridge, and come nightfall, locals as well as visiting skiers often head into "Breck," where a dozen or so clubs are within walking distance of each other. **Downstairs at Eric's,** in the Georgian Square (111 S. Main), 970/543-0999, regularly features live music and dancing for the younger crowd. **The Gold Pan,** 105 N. Main St., 970/453-5499, books live music "when we feel like it," generally soft rock in the Kenny Rankin–James Taylor–Jackson Browne mode.

In Keystone, several clubs offer live and dance music, including the **Snake River Saloon,** 23074 U.S. Hwy. 6 in Keystone, 970/468-2788 (ski movies in the winter), and in Keystone Village, the **Last Chance Saloon,** 970/468-9501.

The **ski areas** themselves often host live music on winter afternoons, particularly Friday and Saturday—in the bars, or, come springtime, outside on their patios.

Theater

Breckenridge's **Backstage Theater** is a local favorite and has been putting up a range of productions for nearly 30 years. Seasons are July through August and mid-December through April. For information and reservations, phone 970/463-0199.

CALENDAR

Summit County's annual events vary from ice sculpture and snowboard competition to sailing regattas, horse and bike races, and a wide range of concerts. The winter biggie is Breckenridge's **Ullr Fest** in mid-January, honoring the Norse god

Ullr, Thor's son. According to a slightly revisionist version of the legend, the mighty Thor and his gorgeous wife, Sif, had no time for Ullr, and so out of boredom, the kid hit the road. And where do you think he ended up? Why, Breckenridge, of course, where he fell in love with the beautiful Blue River Valley.

The weeklong party commences with the International Snow Sculpting Competition (in town on Main Street), and includes a variety of skiing competitions (aerials, moguls, ballet), a parade, and the "Mr. and Mrs. Ullr Beauty Pageant and Dance." In March, Breckenridge hosts the increasingly popular **Snowboard Race Series.** Also in Breckenridge is the **Alamo Freestyle Classic,** in mid-January, where you can watch the country's best freestylers compete in ballet, moguls, and aerials.

At the other end of the scale is the **Bach, Beethoven, and Breckenridge** concert series in July. Not limited to the two Big Bs of classical music, performances also include the works of other major and minor composers, from Copland to Wagner. The monthlong season also features workshops—on music theory, education, and individual instruments. For more information, write P.O. Box 1254, Breckenridge, CO 80424, or phone 970/453-9142.

A variety of festivities and events punctuate the Fourth of July weekend throughout Summit County, including fireworks, food booths, and concerts. The route of mid-July's **Montezuma's Revenge Mountain Bike Race** crosses the Continental Divide seven times in the course of 200 miles. Over Labor Day weekend, Copper Mountain hosts the **Copper-Fest,** which focuses on the art and culture of the Western and Southwestern United States. Lots of Native American art and jewelry, as well as music and food. Phone 800/458-8386 for more information. Also in September is Breckenridge's **Fall Classic Mountain Bike Race,** which attracts the best riders in the country.

For complete listings of the county's myriad events, contact the Summit County Chamber of Commerce. Also, watch the *Summit Daily News* and the *Summit County Journal,* available in racks all over town.

SHOPPING

A favorite recreational activity among visitors to Summit County, shopping knows no bounds here in what would seem to be an unlikely place to find everything from Native American pottery to bargains on lingerie, from Christmas ornaments to T-shirts. (Breckenridge must have the highest number of T-shirt shops per capita in the country.)

Silverthorne Factory Outlets

A seemingly unlikely spot for a factory outlet mall, the Silverthorne site is nonetheless extremely popular. For those who'd rather shop than ski or mountain bike, there are Van Heusen, Bass shoes, Evan-Picone, American Tourister, Liz Claiborne, London Fog, and Nike outlets—more than 80 stores in all. Take the Silverthorne exit from I-70 and follow the signs; keep a leash on your credit card.

SERVICES

The **Breckenridge Police Department** is at 150 Ski Hill Rd., 970/453-2941. Reach the **Dillon Police** at 970/468-6078. The offices of the **Summit County Sheriff** are in Breckenridge at 501 N. Park, 970/453-2232.

Provenant Medical Center in Frisco is open weekdays 9 A.M.–5 P.M. (plus 24-hour emergency care). The clinic is at the corner of Highway 9 and School Road, 970/668-3300 or 800/843-0953. The **Breckenridge Medical Center** is at 535 S. Park St., 970/453-9000.

Post offices are found at the following addresses: Breckenridge, 300 S. Ridge, 970/453-2310; Dillon, 224 Dillon Mall, 970/468-2501; Frisco, 400 Granite, 970/668-5505; and Silverthorne, 390 N. Brian Ave., 970/468-8112.

Recycling

The **Summit Recycling Project** has two drop-off spots, both of which will take most recyclables: 301 8th Ave., Frisco, and on Summit Lane, Breckenridge.

Child Care

Breckenridge, Copper Mountain, and Keystone

ski areas all have children's centers, providing day care for kids two months to five years old, with snow and ski programs for kids three and older. Reservations are required at all three. Phone Copper Mountain's **Belly Button Bakery** at 800/458-8386, ext. 5; **Breckenridge Children's Center** at 970/453-2368; and **Keystone's Children's Center** at 970/468-4182.

INFORMATION

One of the best places to begin your visit to the area is the **Summit County Chamber of Commerce** in Frisco at the east end of Main Street between Dillon Reservoir and Highway 9. Pick up maps, brochures, and tips on everything from lodging to cycling, fishing, rafting, and after-hours entertainment. Write the chamber at P.O. Box 2010, Frisco, CO 80443, or phone 970/668-2051 or 800/530-3099. Its website is www.summitchamber.org.

The chamber also operates a tourist information center just off U.S. 6 between Silverthorne and Dillon with lots of information on places to stay and eat, and things to do and buy, 970/262-0817. Watch for the road signs. The Breckenridge Resort Chamber operates the **Breckenridge Information Center** out of its offices at 309 N. Main.

The toll-free number for **Summit County Central Reservations** is 800/365-6365 (www.skierlodging.com). You can make lodging reservations by calling the following numbers: 800/221-1091 (Breckenridge); 800/458-8386 (Copper Mountain); and 800/222-0188 (Keystone/Arapahoe Basin).

You can also get more information from the **Breckenridge Resort Chamber,** P.O. Box 1909, Breckenridge, CO 80424, 970/453-6018, and the **Town of Dillon,** P.O. Box 8, Dillon, CO 80435, 970/468-2403.

Libraries and Bookstores
The main branch of the Summit County **public library** is in Frisco at 43 Mt. Royal Dr., 970/668-5555. The north branch is at the town hall in Silverthorne, 970/468-5887, and the south

branch is in Breckenridge at 103 S. Harris, 970/453-6098.

Write the **Summit County Historical Society** at P.O. Box 747, Dillon, CO 80435, 970/468-6079. Offices are at 104 N. Harris, Breckenridge, 970/453-9022, and 403 La Bonte, Dillon.

Bookstores stocking books and other publications on local history, recreation, and goings-on include the **Daily Planet,** 308 Main, Frisco, 970/668-5015, and **Weber's Books,** in the Lincoln West Mall, Breckenridge, 970/453-4723.

Forest Service Information
For maps and information on camping, hiking, mountain biking, Jeep touring, and backcountry skiing in Summit County, contact the Silverthorne District Office of **Arapaho National Forest,** 191 Blue River Pkwy., 970/468-5400.

Ski Reports and Weather Conditions
Remember when calling ski resorts for their snow conditions that they're in business to make money, and their reports are often optimistic and overly enthusiastic. Sometimes you're better off stopping by a local ski shop.

For information from the resorts, phone 970/453-5000 (Breckenridge), 970/968-2882 (Copper Mountain), 970/468-2316 (Keystone), or 970/272-7246 (Arapahoe Basin). For the latest in **road and weather conditions** in Summit County, phone 970/453-1090.

Newspapers
In addition to the several locally published commercial guides to Summit County, check out the *Summit County Journal* and the *Summit Daily News,* available in racks throughout the area. Both list upcoming events and run stories spotlighting local celebrities, as well as pieces on local political maneuvering.

Further Reading
Janet Marie Clawson's *Echoes of the Past: Copper Mountain Colorado* (published by Copper Mountain Resort, 1986) is a thoroughly researched narrative history of the old mining-camp-turned-

resort, and except for the last few pages is mostly free of PR-type promotion for the ski area.

An excellent account of the history of Frisco and the area is *Frisco! A Colorful Colorado Community* (it's livelier than the title would suggest!), by local writer Mary Ellen Gilliland and published by the Frisco Historical Society. After a brief discussion of the area's natives (the Utes), Gilliland chronicles the town's development and discusses its major players.

TRANSPORTATION

Summit County's very easy to get to and around in. Only 70 miles from Denver via the I-70 autostrada, the area is serviced by a number of independent shuttle services, and many of the hotels offer free transportation from Denver's International Airport (serviced by most major domestic airlines). You can also fly into DIA and rent a car for the short drive over Loveland Pass.

Buses and Shuttles

The **Resort Express,** a Summit County/Denver International Airport shuttle, offers shuttles hourly during the ski season and every 1.5 hours the rest of the year. Cost is about $80 (round-trip), and reservations are required. Phone 970/468-7600 or 800/334-7433, or write P.O. Box 1429, Silverthorne, CO 80498. The main office is at 273 Warren Ave. in Silverthorne.

In addition, free shuttle service is offered within the county by the **Summit Stage.** Bus routes link Breckenridge, Frisco, Copper Mountain, Dillon, Silverthorne, and Keystone (no service to Arapahoe Basin). For route schedules and more information, phone 970/453-1241 or 970/453-1339. The **Breckenridge Free Shuttle and Town Trolley** provides service through town and up to the ski resort (both base areas). For schedule information, phone 970/453-2368. The **Frisco Flyer** has routes throughout Frisco, from the Safeway at I-70 and Highway 9 up into town on Main and back through into the condos and vacation homes. Phone 970/668-5276 for a map and schedule. Keystone offers regular shuttle service between Keystone Ski Area and Arapahoe Basin.

Greyhound, 970/668-5703, www.greyhound.com, offers passenger service to Summit County (Silverthorne).

The Denver Area

Denver

The only Word I had was "Wow!"
. . . Here I was in Denver . . . I stumbled
along with the most wicked grin of joy in
the world, among the bums and beat cow-
boys of Larimer Street.

Jack Kerouac, **On the Road**

Situated at the far western edge of North America's Great Plains, and sprawling north, south, east, and west almost into the foothills of the massive blue Rocky Mountains, Denver (elev. 5,280 feet) holds about half a million people within its city limits and about two million in the metro area. It's the American Rockies' largest and busiest city; Colorado's commercial, governmental, and transportation center; and a major tourist destination, offering abundant attractions within the city limits as well as easy access to some of the state's premier playgrounds and historical sites.

It's also a city on the move. In the mid-1990s alone, Denver built a new international airport, a beautiful downtown baseball stadium (home to the Colorado Rockies, a National League baseball expansion team), and an indoor sports pavilion (home to the Colorado Avalanche pro hockey team and the Denver Nuggets NBA basketball team). And downtown's elegant, ultramodern office towers, soaring steep and glassy off the plain, form a hive of business activity that buzzes with legions of gray-suited and power-tied young urban professionals. (Thirty-five percent of Denver's residents are between the ages of 18 and 35, and the city claims the country's fourth-highest number of college graduates—behind only Washington, D.C., San Francisco, and Boston).

All of which runs contrary to the image many people have of Denver as a glorified cow town, or simply a cold, wintry stepping-stone to the world-class ski resorts fewer than 100 miles west. Denverites, perhaps unduly self-conscious of their image, will go out of their way to dispel these myths and teach outsiders the truth—which is that the city isn't a cow town at all (save for a couple of weeks each January, when the country's biggest rodeo comes to town), and it's hardly as cold and wintry as many people think.

© STEPHEN METZGER

State Capitol in Denver

THE DENVER AREA

To Sterling

Prospect Valley

Keenesburg

Fort Lupton

Dacono

Brighton

Lafayette

Broomfield

Niwot

Boulder

Pinecliffe

Eldora

Central City

Idaho Springs

Empire

Georgetown

Silver Plume

To Vail and Grand Junction

Tabernash

Granby

Lake Granby

Rocky Mountain National Park

Arapaho National Rec. Area

Mt. Evans (14,264 ft.)

Evergreen

Conifer

Bailey

Grant

Jefferson

To Fairplay

Golden

Westminster

Arvada

Thornton

DENVER

Aurora

Englewood

Littleton

Roxborough State Park

Sedalia

To Colorado Springs

Parker

Franktown

Kiowa

Bennett

Manila

DENVER INTERNATIONAL AIRPORT

Barr Lake

Barr Lake State Park

Rocky Mountain Arsenal N.W.R.

Cherry Creek Lake

(TOLLWAY)

To Fort Collins and Cheyenne

To Limon

20 mi

20 km

© AVALON TRAVEL PUBLISHING, INC.

DENVER AREA HIGHLIGHTS

Denver: state capitol, historic and art museums, botanical gardens, Denver Zoo, recreation areas, hiking, biking, and skiing along the Colorado Urban Trail System, dining, nightlife, Tattered Cover bookstore, 16th Street Mall, Capitol Hill People's Fair, LoDo (transformed and rejuvenated) lower-downtown area, Coors Stadium and Colorado Rockies baseball games

Boulder: climbing, cycling, and virtually all forms of recreation, people-watching, shopping, nightlife, bookstores and cafés, Colorado Music Festival, Kinetic Sculpture Challenge, Colorado Indian Market

Golden: Coors Brewery, Colorado School of Mines, hiking and biking in Golden Gate Canyon State Park, museums, International Heritage Festival of Folk Arts

Georgetown/Idaho Springs: museums, historic districts, the Georgetown Loop Railroad, skiing, hiking, and camping in Arapaho National Forest, Indian Springs Resort

Central City/Black Hawk: museums, mine tours, shopping, gambling, festivals, Central City Opera

According to city statistics, the sun shines on Denver an average of 300 days a year (the U.S. Weather Bureau claims Denver gets "more hours of annual sun than San Diego or Miami Beach") and the city receives less than 15 inches of precipitation annually. Of course, cold winter winds sometimes sweep across the plains, whipping icy particles of snow against unprotected cheeks (as anyone who's watched a Broncos' home game knows). Anyone visiting town between October and April would be well advised to bring a hat, scarf, gloves, thermal underwear, and a down jacket (Denver's annual average minimum temperature is 37.2°F). But even when it's cold, it's dry (and often sunny), and dry, cold air is a *lot* easier to take than cold, moisture-laden air.

A lot's changed in Denver since Jack Kerouac and Neal Cassady and the gang were raising hell on Larimer Street and trying their damnedest to live life on the stark edges of experience. Most of the old pool halls and flophouses are long gone, much to the chagrin of purists who deplore the city's gentrification. But it's still a wonderful place, very much tied to the psyche of the American West. Modern travelers looking for the heart of America must not overlook Denver—a city sprawling at the confluence of two of the country's greatest geological features and offering a history rich with the deepest textures of the American experience.

HISTORY

Though Denver is Colorado's capital and largest city, its history is more recent than many of the other cities and towns in the state. And it's much younger, historically, than other parts of the West—particularly the coast and New Mexico, which Spaniards explored and began to colonize as early as the late 16th century. The first outpost in the Denver area was built in 1832 by fur trader Louis Vasquez, though there were no permanent settlers in the region until 1858. That year William Green Russell discovered small amounts of gold along the South Platte River. When word of his strike spread southeast to Pikes Peak, which wasn't living up to its promises, a handful of hopefuls packed up in search of better prospects. Along what is now West Evans Avenue, the new arrivals built several cabins, which they named Montana City. The gold there soon played out, however, and the group, led by Charles Nichols, moved downstream to the confluence of the Platte and Cherry Creek, where in the fall of 1858 they drew up plans for their new town, St. Charles City.

Meanwhile, word of gold in the Cherry Creek-South Platte area reached the East Coast, and optimistic miners soon rushed west to try to make their fortunes. Also, members of William Russell's party, who had moved back into the mountains, learned that their original find may have been more significant than they first thought; they returned to the Cherry Creek area and built a small settlement, which they named Auraria, across the stream from St. Charles City. Shortly afterward, General William Larimer arrived from Kansas and established next door to St. Charles City the area's third townsite, which he named Denver City, after General James W. Denver, a former governor of Kansas Territory (of which Colorado was still part). Almost immediately, though, Larimer's party "incorporated" Nichols's camp (some say by force), and once again there were just the two towns, Denver City and Auraria.

Denver's Silver Lining

For the next several years, the two towns grew in size, with saloons, hotels, schools, and churches springing up along the creek. The first edition of the *Rocky Mountain News* was published from its "office" on midstream pilings between the camps on April 23, 1859. Meanwhile, more gold strikes occurred in the area—some highly exaggerated—many of which played out almost as soon as word of their existence reached the public. Still, prospectors continued to flock to the area, and on April 3, 1860, Denver and Auraria were consolidated; in January 1861, when the new town held its first election, the population was approximately 6,000.

Over the next 20 years, gold fell off in Denver, and with it so did the infant city's economy. Prices fell, and discouraged miners left for greener pastures. In the early 1880s, however, focus on Colorado's ore changed from gold to silver. Prospectors in the mountains west of Denver discovered immensely lucrative lodes, particularly at Cripple Creek, Leadville, Aspen, and Georgetown. Almost overnight, Denver's future again looked bright. Between 1880 and 1890, Denver's population tripled; banks, machine shops, smelters, and other businesses sprouted up downtown; and boutiques and other retail shops opened on Lawrence Street. By the end of the decade, Denver was producing more mining machinery than any other city in the world. In addition, Denver was becoming somewhat of a social hub, as miners who had made their fortunes in the nearby mountains

moved to the city and built elaborate houses and threw lavish parties. Among the silver barons who brought their prosperity and high living to Denver was Horace Tabor, who opened the Tabor Opera House (on 16th Street where the Tabor Center now stands) in 1881 and soon afterward built a magnificent mansion whose grounds covered an entire city block on Capitol Hill (see History under Leadville in the Southwestern Colorado chapter).

The 1890s saw a depression in Denver's economy, brought on by a sudden drop in silver prices, although by the turn of the century the city was already well on the road to recovery. Throughout the early 1900s, Denver continued to grow, with great improvements in roadways, schools, and parks, although the massive Rocky Mountains pretty much kept the city isolated from the rapidly developing cities on the West Coast, Los Angeles and San Francisco in particular. In 1928, however, Moffat Tunnel was blasted through the Rockies, providing a direct railway to the coast, and Denver was finally a part of the burgeoning national village.

Modern Times

Still, though, Denver retained its image as a Wild West frontier town. Its location in America's heartland, as well as the fact that it had become a veritable hub for an expanding national highway and railway system, ensured lots of short- and long-term visitors—from the upper crust to the down and out. In fact, until the city's "urbanization" in the late 1970s and early '80s, Denver still boasted (or bemoaned, depending on your perspective) many of the things that attracted the Kerouac gang in the '50s: pool halls, saloons, flophouses, and more than its share of folks who had slipped through the cracks in the American Dream.

In the early 1980s, natural resources again changed the face of Denver—this time in the form of oil and coal, which brought new revenues to the city. Although preservationists argued for the restoration of Denver's historic buildings, many—including the Tabor Opera House, of course—were razed and replaced with shopping centers, office buildings, and hotels. Though costing Denver much of its unique architectural heritage, this resulted in a very attractive and contemporary city, thoroughly modern in every sense of the word.

National League Baseball and an International Airport

Still more and bigger changes were in store, beginning in 1992, when the people of the state voted to build Coors Field on the west side of the downtown area near the train station. Though the stadium wasn't ready for play until the 1995 season, as soon as it was under way, the area, which came to be known as LoDo (for Lower Downtown District), began a true transformation: long-empty machine shops and warehouses were converted to brewpubs, antiques stores, coffee shops, and art galleries; live music filled the streets on summer evenings; and, of course, rents skyrocketed. Today, no visit to Denver is complete without a trip to LoDo. Sip a latte at a sidewalk table beside local businessfolk poring over blueprints for more restoration. Sample a local ale or stout from one of the microbreweries. And, if they're in town, go see the Colorado Rockies play, and marvel at one of the nation's finest baseball stadiums.

Like Colorado baseball, a new Denver airport had been a long time coming. The city's old airport, Stapleton, had long since outlived its design and small size, and passengers frequently complained of delays, traffic jams (both auto and airplane), and of generally outdated facilities. Denver International Airport (DIA), which opened for business in early 1995, was the solution. Though not without problems itself—not least among them the technical problems that delayed its opening, sparking a legal nightmare—DIA is an efficient and attractive airport that makes getting in and out of town and the mountains a whole lot easier.

MUSEUMS

A children's museum and museums of history, art, natural history, transportation, and fire fighting—many of which are right downtown—will keep museophiles entertained for days. Spend a morning learning about the history of the state; break for lunch; then take in prehistoric, Native American, modern, and postmodern art in the afternoon. Or head out to the Transportation Museum, and (appropriately enough) take a trolley along the Platte River to Denver's Children's Museum.

Colorado History Museum

Without doubt one of the best places to begin your exploration of Denver, particularly if your knowledge of the state's and city's history is at all sketchy, this beautifully designed and impressively laid-out museum provides the opportunity to wander among a huge assortment of exhibits. Start at the Colorado time line, a multidimensional and multimedia display that explains the history of the state from just before the Louisiana Purchase of 1803. You'll also want to check out the re-created machine shop, the displays of the various mining techniques used in Colorado's past, and the beautiful textile exhibit with Native American rugs, mostly from the Rio Grande Valley, from the mid-19th through the late 20th century. The museum also features lots of Plains and Ute Native American clothing (take a look at the beaded leggings), a Conestoga-style wagon built in 1824, and a 100-Mile Fritchle Electric Car (which could go 100 miles between battery chargings) built in 1910—displayed with the car are the original owner's manual, the purchase deed, and various advertisements for the early autos, manufactured in Denver between 1904 and 1917. The museum is downtown at the corner of 13th and Broadway and is open Mon.–Sat. 10 A.M.–4:30 P.M. and Sunday noon–4:30 P.M. Admission is $4.50 for adults, $4 for seniors, and $2.50 for kids 6–16. For more information, phone 303/866-3682.

Denver Museum of Nature and Science

Ideally, you'd allow yourself at least an entire day to wander around this place and see everything, and one could easily spend more than that here. The seventh-largest museum in the United States, this is a beautifully and intelligently designed multistory complex of exhibits that will delight visitors of all ages. A sampling: dinosaur fossils and skeletons (including the stegosaurus, Colorado's state fossil), skeletons from La Brea Tar Pits (a saber-toothed tiger, dire wolf, and ground sloth); a display of the world's minerals; a small Egyptology exhibit, with a mummy, a casket, and an illustrated explanation of the mummification process; a "Development of Man" display, beginning with a facsimile of the remains of "Lucy," who, named for the Beatles' song *Lucy in the Sky with Diamonds,* is probably 3.2 million years old; and exhibits of whales of the world, fishes of Colorado, and, well, you get the picture.

Don't miss the museum's **IMAX Theater,** the world's largest motion picture system. Films are projected onto a four-story-tall screen, and the wide-angle photography is absolutely stunning. Shows are also regularly offered at the museum's **Charles C. Gates Planetarium,** which is closed until 2003 for renovation. Admission to either the museum or theater is $8; combined ticket is $12 (with discounts for kids, students, and seniors). An excellent gift shop is in the museum's lobby. The museum is at 2001 Colorado Blvd.; phone 303/322-7009 or 800/925-2250 for more information.

Children's Museum of Denver

With regularly changing exhibits, as well as permanent displays, this museum offers dozens of hands-on experiences, including "classes" on such things as recycling and candy-making, and "Kidslope," an

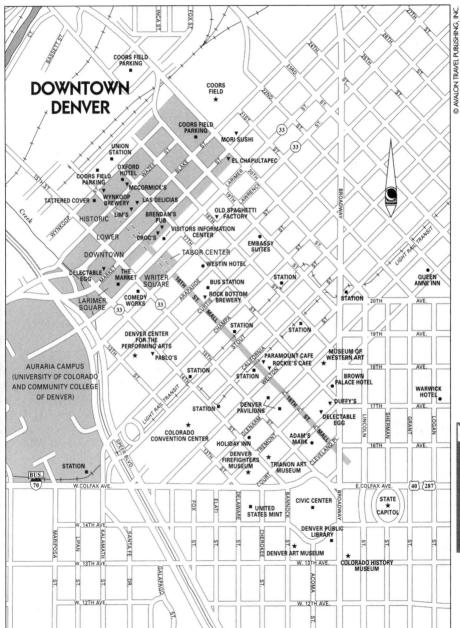

DOWNTOWN DENVER

COORS FIELD PARKING

COORS FIELD ★

COORS FIELD PARKING

UNION STATION

MORI SUSHI ▼

EL CHAPULTAPEC ▼

OXFORD HOTEL ●

COORS FIELD PARKING ■

McCORMICK'S ●

TATTERED COVER ■

WYNKOOP BREWERY ●

LAS DELICIAS ●

LIM'S ●

BRENDAN'S PUB ●

OLD SPAGHETTI FACTORY ▼

HISTORIC

VISITORS INFORMATION CENTER ●

LOWER

CROC'S ●

EMBASSY SUITES ▲

DOWNTOWN

TABOR CENTER

DELECTABLE EGG ▼

THE MARKET ■

WESTIN HOTEL ●

STATION ■

WRITER SQUARE

BUS STATION ■

LARIMER SQUARE

COMEDY WORKS

ROCK BOTTOM BREWERY ●

STATION ■

STATION ■

20TH AVE.

QUEEN ANNE INN ●

DENVER CENTER FOR THE PERFORMING ARTS ★

STATION ■

STATION ■

19TH AVE.

PABLO'S ●

PARAMOUNT CAFE ●
ROCKIE'S CAFE ●

MUSEUM OF WESTERN ART ★

18TH AVE.

AURARIA CAMPUS (UNIVERSITY OF COLORADO AND COMMUNITY COLLEGE OF DENVER)

STATION ■

STATION ■

BROWN PALACE HOTEL ●

WARWICK HOTEL ●

DUFFY'S ●

17TH AVE.

STATION ■

DENVER PAVILIONS ●

DELECTABLE EGG ▼

COLORADO CONVENTION CENTER ★

ADAM'S MARK ●

16TH AVE.

HOLIDAY INN ●

DENVER FIREFIGHTERS MUSEUM ★

TRIANON ART MUSEUM ★

STATION ■

BUS. 70

W. COLFAX AVE.

E. COLFAX AVE.

40 287

CIVIC CENTER

STATE CAPITOL ★

W. 14TH AVE.

UNITED STATES MINT ■

DENVER PUBLIC LIBRARY

W. 13TH AVE.

DENVER ART MUSEUM ★

W. 13TH AVE.

COLORADO HISTORY MUSEUM ★

W. 12TH AVE.

W. 12TH AVE.

THE DENVER AREA

artificial ski hill where kids can practice their technique and take lessons from professional ski instructors. And if that's not enough to wear them out, there's a park outside with all kinds of equipment to climb around on *and* a trolley that'll take the clan two miles along the South Platte to the Transportation Museum (the trolley costs $2 for adults and $1 for seniors and kids and takes about 25 minutes). Special days at the museum include Cinco de Mayo (May 5, Mexican Independence Day), Disney Days (late June), Young People's Mini Prix (mid-August), Big Shoes to Fill Career Day (late September), and Trick or Treat Street (you guessed it, late October).

The Children's Museum is just off I-25 (take Exit 211) across from Mile-High Stadium at 2121 Crescent Drive. Admission is $6.50, $3.50 seniors and kids. The museum is open weekdays 9 A.M.–4 P.M. and weekends 10 A.M.–5 P.M. Closed Monday the rest of the year. For more information, phone 303/433-7444.

Denver Firefighters Museum

An unassuming little building at 1326 Tremont houses Denver's original firehouse, dating from the mid-19th century. View old uniforms, fire carts and trucks, nets (used in drills only, never in real fires), switchboards, and bells. Learn about how dalmatians came to be used—to keep the horses clipping along en route to the fire, the dogs nipped at their hooves; then once they got there, the dogs led them away from the fire and kept them waiting until it was time to return to the stables in the back of the firehouse. Kids can try on the old firefighting uniforms at the end of the tour.

Today, the museum is on the first floor, where the carts (and later, trucks) were kept, and a restaurant (see Food, below) is on the second, formerly the men's living quarters. The Denver Firefighters Museum is open Mon.–Fri. 10 A.M.–4 P.M. Admission is $3, $2 for kids and seniors. Phone 303/892-1436 for more information.

Molly Brown House and Museum

As you'd expect, attendance at the Molly Brown House has increased dramatically since the release of *Titanic,* the unsinkable film that put Molly Brown back in the public eye. (Some still

© STEPHEN METZGER

The number of visitors to the Molly Brown House and Museum increased dramatically after the release of the movie *Titanic*.

recall Debbie Reynolds as the title character in the 1960s' MGM movie *The Unsinkable Molly Brown*.)

Part redheaded Irish-Catholic pioneer, part early women's-rights activist, rabble-rouser, and all-around bon vivant, Molly Brown (née Margaret Tobin) was born in 1867 in Hannibal, Missouri. She moved to Leadville at age 18 and married J. J. Brown there on September 1, 1886. After their two children were born (Larry in 1887 and Helen in 1889), the family moved to Denver, where in 1909, as a result of the conflict between Molly's love of traveling and J. J.'s commitment to Colorado business, the couple legally separated.

In 1912, the world learned of Molly. Traveling on the "maiden" voyage of the *Titanic,* Molly, with her knowledge of seven languages, helped save many of the immigrants and later went on to help the survivors chart new courses for their lives—by organizing them and donating money to them.

The Molly Brown House and Museum is an ornate Victorian mansion built in 1889 and bought by the Browns in 1894. It has been completely restored (having been used for many purposes over the years, including a men's boardinghouse), and the furniture is either original (such as the horsehair sofa) or replicated (such as the piano). Particularly impressive is the gilt-relief wallpaper throughout the house, lending the walls a look that's part European parlor, part Las Vegas brothel.

The Molly Brown House can be found at 1340 Pennsylvania (between 13th and 14th Streets). Note: no off-street parking is available, and you're probably better off walking from downtown than driving the few blocks and trying to park. Tours (by docents dressed in Victorian garb) are offered year-round; admission is $6 for adults, $4 for seniors over 64, and $2 for ages 6–12. Museum/tour hours are June–Aug., Mon.–Sat. 10 A.M.–3:30 P.M. and Sunday noon–3:30 P.M.; Sept.–May, Tues.–Sat. 10 A.M.–3:30 P.M. and noon–3:30 P.M. For more information or to buy tickets in advance (a good idea, especially in summer), phone 303/832-4092.

Black American West Museum and Heritage Center
Though overlooked in the whitewashed histories of the country, blacks played an important role opening up the West. In fact, according to documentation at this unique museum, roughly a third of the West's cowboys were black, as were many pioneer doctors, politicians, and teachers. Fortunately, historians are beginning to realize their vast contributions to American history, and textbooks are slowly beginning to reflect the truth. Maybe someday, museums like this one won't seem such anomalies, and the history of black America will be fully integrated into our museums, books, and consciousnesses.

The museum is at 3091 California Street, right on the city's light-rail system. Hours are Mon.–Fri. 10 A.M.–5 P.M. and weekends noon–5 P.M. May–Sept. and the rest of the year Wed.–Fri 10 A.M.–2 P.M. and weekends noon–5 P.M. Admission is $6 for adults, $5.50 for seniors, $4 for kids. Phone 303/292-2566.

Museo de las Americas
This museum, which opened on Santa Fe Avenue after moving from several different directors' homes, aims to reach out to the Hispanic community in the Denver area by focusing on the art, culture, and history of Latino Americans. In addition to the regular displays, the museum offers a range of educational programs and works with local schools. The museum is at 861 Santa Fe and is open Tues.–Sat. 10 A.M.–5 P.M. Admission is $3 for adults, $2 for seniors, and $1 for students; phone 303/571-4401 for more information.

Forney Museum of Transportation
This museum features a gigantic array of vintage automobiles, railroad cars, sleighs, carriages, and just about anything else that once carried human beings (or cargo) from one place to another. Among the cars are an 1898 Renault Opera Coupe, a 1915 Hudson, 1919 Fiat limousine, and 1924 Moon sedan (built between 1906 and 1929), and scores more—from 1930s roadsters to a 1970 limited-edition Ford Mustang. An eccentric and eclectic museum,

the Forney offers a chance to wander around—even to get lost—in the maze of half-completed exhibits, storerooms, and the weedy, overgrown yard full of rusted train engines, passenger cars, and careening sailing ships, their paint faded and chipped; one room, and I'm not sure how it fits into the general theme, is full of mounted game fish in glass cases, all of apparently near-record size. A small gift shop sells posters, postcards, model airplanes, and other souvenirs. The Forney Transportation Museum is at 4303 Brighton and is open Mon.–Sat. 9 A.M.–5 P.M. Admission is $6, $4 for ages 12–18, and $3 for kids 6–11. Phone 303/433-3643 for more information.

Mizel Museum of Judaica

This museum features permanent and changing exhibits demonstrating Jewish heritage and cultural contributions throughout the world. Included in the free admission are films, tours, and lectures. The museum is at 560 S. Monaco Parkway. Hours are Mon.–Fri. 10 A.M.–4 P.M., Saturday 11 A.M.–1 P.M., and Sunday noon–4 P.M. Phone 303/333-4156.

Denver Art Museum

This modern six-story downtown facility offers visitors a mind-boggling array of art and information about the countries and societies where the works originated. One of the true beauties of this museum is that the exhibits are arranged to demonstrate the distinct links between the various cultures and societies. Just a preview of what you'll find: African masks, sculpture, and beaded belts and necklaces, along with Northwest Native American totems, gigantic carved masks, and rattles, and South Pacific ceremonial staffs, masks, and clothing (pieces from prehistoric to mid-20th century); Spanish colonial paintings and sculpture, including a beautiful collection of Santos (carved cottonwood or pine figures, usually of Christ on the cross or the Madonna), a recreated 17th-century New Mexican church; European and Mediterranean art, Egyptian caskets, Greek statues, and Roman urns; modern pieces by Picasso, Juan Gris, Georges Braque, Matisse, and

Breton; and art from the United States and the American West, with pieces by Frederic Remington, Winslow Homer, Thomas Hart Benton, and E. Irving Crouse and Joseph Sharp, two of the founders of the early 20th-century Taos artists' colony.

The Denver Art Museum is at 14th and Bannock (near Broadway); open Tues.–Sat. 10 A.M.–5 P.M. and Sunday noon–5 P.M. (also Wednesday evenings till 9 P.M.). Admission is $4.50 for adults, $2.50 for seniors and students (higher during some exhibits)—free admission to Colorado residents on Saturday. The museum also has a classy gift shop with an especially fine selection of books. For more information, phone 720/865-5000.

Trianon Museum and Art Gallery

Half a block from the Denver Firefighters Museum is this classic example of the adage, "Don't judge a book by its cover." From the outside this little place looks all but abandoned, save for the small awning out front. But step inside, and you're in a world of stunningly beautiful antique vases, furniture, silver, china, Oriental screens, and much more, all arranged—some might say cluttered—into two small rooms. Betty Metzger (no direct relation) gives tours as minutely detailed as the pieces she shows. Among the works are Louis XVI service plates, a silver tray once owned by Czar Peter the Great, and a 60-key Steinway piano from the early 18th century. In addition, there's an antique gun collection dating from the 16th century, as well as a late 19th-century Gatling gun and a 12-pound mountain howitzer. Visit the Trianon at the corner of 14th Street and Tremont; it's open Mon.–Sat. 10 A.M. to 4 P.M. Admission is $1. Some art, antiques, and prints for sale. For more information, phone 303/623-0739.

OTHER SIGHTS
State Capitol

On July 5, 1886, almost 10 years after Colorado achieved statehood, and after the territorial government had been moved first from

Colorado City and then from Golden City, excavation began on the state capitol building. Built on 10 acres of land donated by Henry C. Brown—who retained much of the surrounding property and grew rich by developing it for settlers and merchants who wanted to be near the state's new headquarters—the capitol took 22 years to complete, though 160 rooms were in use for the last 12 years of construction. In an attempt to represent Colorado in the building, designers worked primarily with materials from the state: the outer walls are of granite from the Gunnison area; the marble floors are from Marble; and the interior walls are wainscoted with rose onyx from Buelah (whose resources were exhausted by the shipments to Denver).

Particularly impressive are the building's gold-plated outer dome, the gorgeous stained-glass and hand-carved white oak throughout the building, and the monstrous chandeliers—the one in the original Supreme Court chambers weighs a ton and was originally lighted with gas, as the engineers didn't trust the newly discovered electricity.

The Colorado State Capitol is at Colfax and Broadway. Free 30-minute tours, which end at the rotunda and provide wonderful views of both downtown and the distant mountains, are offered weekdays 9:30 A.M.–3 P.M. (on the half hour). For more information, phone 303/866-2604.

United States Mint

Free guided tours of this penny-printing press explain the history of the mint (next to Fort Knox, the second-largest gold depository in the United States) and the process of making coins. During the height of the tourist season in summer, you'll want to get here early to beat the crowds; otherwise, expect to stand in line for up to a half hour (sometimes more). Avoid the crowd (and the tour) by going to the gift store entrance around back—pick up freshly minted commemorative coins for your collection. The mint is open for free tours Mon.–Fri. 8 A.M.–2:45 P.M. It's directly behind the city and county building at West Colfax and Cherokee, 303/405-4765.

PARKS AND RECREATION

With Denver's youthful and outdoor-oriented population, an abundance of parks should come as no surprise. More than 200 parks dot the metro area, and Denverites take full advantage of them—for cycling, picnicking, swimming, tennis, or just sprawling on a lawn and napping. For a complete listing of city parks, call the Denver Parks and Recreation Department at 303/575-3043.

City Park

When this park was first established in 1881, it was a good horse-and-buggy day trip from Denver out to the lawns and lakes. Since then, the city has grown up around it, and though still a bit of a drive from downtown, this is a city park in the truest sense of the word. In addition to the spacious lawns perfect for picnicking, the small lakes where you can rent rowboats, and the rose gardens (the place makes you feel as if you're living in a Matisse painting), the park also contains the **Denver Zoo,** the **Denver Museum of Science and Nature,** and a golf course (see below). You could spend an entire day here, maybe even a weekend, and still not see everything. To get to the park from downtown, take Colorado Boulevard to 17th Street.

Denver Zoo

Now I'll admit to being somewhat of a cynic when it comes to zoos—the sight of sickly looking animals baking under a too-hot sun in too-small cages doesn't do a whole lot for me. But some zoos seem to respect the animals more than others, and as zoos go, Denver's is all right. In fact, it's a participant in the North American Species Survival Program, which attempts to keep the bloodlines of different species thriving and to educate the public about the plight of animals other than the human type. The Denver Zoo draws special attention to endangered species (officially recognized and otherwise), and among the gift shop's more popular T-shirts are the ones with the logo "Extinction is Forever."

© STEPHEN METZGER

Denver's Botanic Gardens

If you're not up for wandering footloose around the 76-acre compound, viewing the lions, and tigers, and bears (oh, my!), hop on the "Zooliner," a nonstop train through the zoo complete with a "safari lecture." Interested in pinnipeds? Stop by the seal and sea lion exhibit, where regular feedings and shows are scheduled.

Snack huts are scattered around the complex, though the many lawns make ideal picnic areas, as do the lawns at the City Park, just outside the gate. (By the way, full literary pun awards go to the snack shack "Ice Cream Station Zebra.")

The Denver Zoo is at East 23rd and Steel Streets (on weekends, a shuttle runs between the zoo and the Museum of Science and Nature, and concerts are scheduled throughout the summer). Admission is $9 for adults, $7 for seniors, and $5 for kids 4–12. For more information, phone 303/376-4800.

Denver Botanic Gardens

If you've been pounding the pavement of downtown Denver, taking in the sights and sounds of the city, chances are you're starting to feel the effects: the noise and crowds have gone from at-tractive novelties to overbearing encroachments on your senses. If this is the case, one of the best places in town to restore your sanity is the Botanic Gardens, where you'll find acres of gardens, from gorgeous spreads of wildflowers and native grasses to plots of domesticated perennials, vegetables, and a water garden with a dozen or more different types of water lilies. With paved sidewalks winding among the various gardens, benches, and gazebos, and arboretums for shade, the Botanic Gardens—still in the heart of the city—is one of the best places to come for a change of pace. (In addition, people planning to do a little landscaping of their own might want to wander around simply gathering ideas and inspiration; pamphlets and fliers explaining the different plants are available in racks throughout.) Also here is a gift shop and huge library. In the summer, the gardens feature a series of evening concerts.

Denver's Botanic Gardens, 1005 York, are open daily 9 A.M.–5 P.M. Admission is $5.50 for adults May–Sept., with discounts the rest of the year and for kids and seniors. To get there from downtown, take 14th Street to York. For general information, phone 303/331-4000.

THE DENVER AREA

Colorado's Ocean Journey

Denver's new aquarium, Ocean Journey, opened in summer 1999 at a cost of $93 million. It includes a large array of visual and interactive exhibits and features five re-created aquatic environments: Colorado River Journey, Sea of Cortez, Indonesian River Journey, Depths of the Pacific, and Ocean Discovery Plaza. You'll see more than 15,000 live specimens, including sharks, starfish, sea otters, turtles, trout, and tuna.

The aquarium is minutes from downtown Denver, on the Platte River just north of the Children's Museum. Open daily 9 A.M.–6 P.M. Memorial Day through Labor Day, 10 A.M.–6 P.M. the rest of the year. Admissions is $15 for adults, $13 for seniors and kids 13–17, and $7 for kids 4–12. To get there, take Speer Boulevard west from downtown; from I-70, take the Speer exit. For more information, phone 303/561-4450.

Bear Creek Lake State Park

Operated by the City of Lakewood Parks and Recreation Department, this small park (just short of 3,000 acres) also contains the two smaller Soda Lakes and offers many different recreation opportunities—from windsurfing and fishing to picnicking, overnight camping, horseback riding, and bird-watching (waterfowl and birds of prey). You can rent sailboards, paddleboats, canoes, and sailboats. The best way to get there is to take Kipling Avenue to Morrison Road and go west. Entrance fee is $4 per vehicle. Open 6 A.M.–10 P.M. Memorial Day through Labor Day. For more information, phone 303/697-6159.

Cherry Creek Lake State Recreation Area

Offering easy-access relief from the strip malls, townhouses, and high-rise office buildings of surrounding Aurora, this multipurpose recreation area is popular among Denverites looking to cool off on hot summer days. Lately, the lake has become especially popular with jet-skiers, who jam around the lake, much to the chagrin of some of the other folks—waterskiers, windsurfers, fishermen, picnickers, cyclists, and campers. In

the winter, the lake opens for ice fishing, skating, and boating, as well as cross-country skiing and snowmobiling (it has more than 1.5 million visitors a year).

Built between 1946 and 1950 as a flood-control project, Cherry Creek Dam is nearly 1,500 feet long and 150 feet high; the lake is 3.5 miles long. Public recreation facilities include bicycle and jet-ski rental, campgrounds and picnic areas, a golf course, riding stables, nature trails, and fishing areas, with some especially designated for use by people with disabilities.

For general information on Cherry Creek Lake State Recreation Area, phone 303/690-1166, or write 4201 S. Parker Rd., Aurora, CO 80014. For information on horseback riding, phone 303/690-8235; for information on nature walks, picnicking (to reserve sites), and special events, phone 303/690-1166.

To get to the lake from downtown, take Leetsdale to Parker Road; from I-225, take the Parker Road exit. The gates are well marked. Admission is $4 per vehicle.

Chatfield Lake State Recreation Area

Quite a bit nicer than Cherry Creek Lake (you can't see high-rises from the shores), Chatfield isn't quite as accessible from downtown. But it's worth the drive, especially for nature lovers. In addition to a blue heron reserve at the lake, the area has a nicely presented visitor center with the skull of a mammoth found during dam excavation, a U.S. Army Corps of Engineers exhibit of rivers, flooding, and damming, and includes excellent historical photos of 19th-century floods. The lake has several marinas and campgrounds (more than 150 sites, with water and flush toilets), and riding stables, bike trails, and hiking paths. In the winter, Denverites go with the floe (sorry . . .) and head to Chatfield for ice fishing and cross-country skiing.

The Army Corps of Engineers offers free 1.5-hour tours of Chatfield Dam on Saturday morning from late May through August. Call 303/979-4120 for information about tours, or 303/791-7275 for information about the recreation area. To make camping reservations, phone 303/470-1144.

To get there, take I-70 south to Highway 470 to Wadsworth, and follow the signs. Admission is $4 per vehicle. You can also get there by taking Wadsworth south from central Denver.

SPORTS AND OUTDOOR ACTIVITIES

Skiing

Skiing is the sport most people associate with Denver. And with good reason—the city's the gateway to a concentration of ski resorts offering some of the finest runs, conditions, and facilities the sport has to offer. Not only are there huge destination resort complexes—Vail, Aspen, Breckenridge, and others—within easy drives of Denver International Airport, but several other smaller resorts—Arapahoe Basin, for example—offer world-class skiing in less crowded (as well as less pretentious) areas, also within easy reach of the metropolitan area.

From Denver, it's very easy to get to the slopes. Whether your destination is Winter Park, Copper Mountain, or Vail, you can drive your own car, rent one, or take a shuttle, and be buckling your boots in under two hours (weather permitting). For more information on the ski areas, as well as on transportation to them, refer to the specific destination chapters. **Colorado Mountain Express,** 800/525-6363, offers ground transportation from Denver International Airport to Winter Park, Vail, and the Summit County ski areas.

For an only-in-Denver ski experience, take a ride on the **Ski Train.** Departing from Union Station on weekends at 7:15 A.M., Dec.–April, the train takes you out of the city, northwest into the mountains, through Moffat Tunnel (completed in 1928), and eventually deposits you at the base of **Winter Park Ski Resort.** The train leaves the ski area in late afternoon, and will have you back at Union Station (conveniently located across the street from the Wynkoop Brewery) by early evening (it's a two-hour trip). Coach tickets are $45 round-trip; first-class tickets are $70.

For more information on the Ski Train, write 555 17th St. #2400, Denver, CO 80202, or phone 303/296-I-SKI (296-4754). You can also get up-to-date information from its website at www.skitrain.com.

Cycling

Bicycling is so popular in Denver that speed limits are enforced in the city parks. In addition, the city offers a huge network of bike paths that can take the adventurous cyclist into most areas of the metro Denver area. From downtown, a bike path follows Speer out to Cherry Creek Shopping Center. The outlying areas offer limitless cycling, and some Colorado bikers "collect" passes: Berthoud (elev. 11,315 feet), Loveland (elev. 11,992 feet), Independence (elev. 12,095 feet), and others.

The **Denver Bicycle Touring Club** offers regular rides at all levels of interest and ability, and also publishes maps and a newsletter (with complete listings of events and rides). For information, write P.O. Box 8973, Denver, CO 80201. To obtain current ride schedules, meeting places, the names and numbers of ride leaders, or to join the club, log onto www.dbtc.org.

Golf

There are so many public golf courses in the Denver metro area that you could almost play a different course every day for a month without walking (or driving) the same fairway. Varying from plain and pleby to elaborate and aristocratic, Denver's courses offer something for just about every level of skill and dedication. Several websites support Colorado golf and provide information on courses. Try www.rockiesgolf.com.

One of the Denver area's most popular courses is **Arrowhead Golf Club,** 10850 W. Sundown, Littletown (in Roxborough State Park, 45 minutes southwest of Denver—south of Chatfield Dam). Designed by Robert Trent Jones Jr., Arrowhead is famous for its views, setting, and the challenge it provides golfers of all abilities. Green fee is $85, which includes cart rental. For information and tee times, phone 303/973-9614.

City Park Golf Course, East 25th Avenue and York, is an ideal family course, especially for the family whose members don't all share the same enthusiasm for the sport—also at the park are tennis courts, the Denver Zoo, the Museum of Science and Nature, and 134 acres of sprawling lawns. For more information, phone 303/295-4420.

Other popular Denver-area courses include: **Meridian Golf Club,** 9742 S. Meridian, Englewood, 303/799-4043 (green fee, $50); and **Riverdale,** 13300 Riverdale, Brighton, 303/659-4700 ($27).

Denver's **Golf Line,** 303/964-2563, provides information on the dozens of courses in the greater Denver area. For details on the courses owned and operated by the Denver Parks and Recreation Department, phone 303/575-3155.

Colorado Urban Trail System

The Colorado State Trails Program, a division of the state Parks and Outdoor Recreation Department, organizes a series of nearly 100 hiking, cycling, horseback riding, and cross-country ski trails throughout the Denver metro area, from Golden to Aurora to Roxborough State Park. You can get maps, which designate degrees of difficulty and list facilities (restrooms, picnic tables, shelters, etc.), by writing the Colorado Division of Parks and Outdoor Recreation, 1313 Sherman St. #618, Denver, CO 80203, or by phoning 303/866-3437.

Amusement Centers and Parks

Six Flags Elitch Gardens is sort of a Rocky Mountain version of Coney Island, with more than 40 rides, including white-water rafting and a huge roller coaster, plus miniature golf, musical revues, and islands of flowers, as well as fast food at every turn. Dating from the early part of the 20th century, Elitch's was home for years to one of the country's original summer stock theaters. In the spring of 1995, Elitch's moved (and expanded) from its location west of town to a more central downtown site near Coors Stadium. The park is open daily June through Labor Day (and weekends in May). Unlimited ride admission is about $30 for adults and $15 for kids. Parking is $4. Phone 303/595-4386. To get there, take Speer west from downtown and watch for the roller coaster.

If you drove into Denver from the west, chances are you noticed **Lakeside Amusement Park** just before you got into town. Like Elitch's, Lakeside is a classic amusement park, evoking a simpler and more innocent America. Get your thrills on the roller coaster, speedboat rides on the lake, or any number of other rides; there are also rides for the less adventurous and for those whose stomachs insist they stay in tamer territory (see you there. . .). Admission is $1.50, with rides at extra cost, or $11.25 ($14.75 weekends) for unlimited ride access. You'll find it at I-70 and Sheridan, 303/477-1621.

Take Me Out to the Ball Game

On July 5, 1991, less than a year after Colorado voters approved the construction of a new baseball stadium, Denver was awarded a National League Baseball team. The Colorado Rockies began playing on April 9, 1993, in Mile High Stadium, home of the Denver Broncos, and in spring of 1995 moved to the gorgeous new Coors Field in lower downtown Denver. This stadium has been instrumental in transforming that area from a warehouse district to an upscale one of antique stores, brewpubs, nightclubs, and coffee shops.

In 1998, Coors Field was host to the Major League Baseball all-star game, and for a week in early July, the stadium, and much of downtown Denver, was a circus of media and baseball fans. Various promotions at the ballpark, from celebrity home-run derbies (Kevin Costner hit one out) to Beanie-Baby giveaways, kept things popping at the field and the surrounding neighborhood, and most sports fans' eyes were on the field by game time.

More recently, Barry Bonds visited the stadium. In his record-breaking 2001 season, Bonds hit home run numbers 61, 62, and 63 at Coors Field—all on the same day (September 9).

Admission to Colorado Rockies' games ranges $4–37, and the season runs from early April through late September. For tickets or more information, phone 800/388-ROCK (388-7625). You can also usually get tickets before games at the on-site box office (Blake and 20th), and you can arrange ticket/hotel/rental-car packages through the Denver Metro Convention and Visitors Bureau, 303/892-1112. You can also get tickets at the Rockies' website at rockies.mlb.com (which, if you're a baseball fan at all, is a wonderful site simply to explore!).

TOURS

Best Mountain Tours by The Mountain Men, 303/750-5200, offers half- and full-day historic and scenic tours, as well as ski charters. Write to 3003 S. Macon Circle, Aurora, CO 80014. **Gray Line of Denver,** 303/289-2841 or 800/348-6847, offers sightseeing tours of the city and the area, and it can arrange tours of other areas outside the city. **British Double Decker,** 303/892-1800 (www.doubledeckerbus.com), has a fleet of 10 buses available for sporting events, conventions, etc.

For what ales you, try **Actually Quite Nice,** a company offering tours of Colorado's brewpubs. Rates range from about $50 (4.5 hours, lunch included) to $75 (seven hours, dinner), and private tours can be arranged. Tours include "not too serious" educational talks. Phone 303/431-1440 or 800/951-PUBS (951-7827) for reservations or more information.

ACCOMMODATIONS

Although you can find motels throughout the Denver metropolitan area, particularly at major artery junctions and interstate offramps, the city's accommodations are primarily concentrated in the downtown area and in the southeastern region. If you can afford to, the best area to stay is downtown, where a good number of Denver's main attractions lie within walking distance—the 16th Street Mall, the capitol building, several excellent museums and historical landmarks, and some of the city's best restaurants are concentrated within an area not much bigger than a couple of square miles. And the best way to see them is by stepping outside your hotel and hoofing it (or taking the very-easy-to-use public transportation).

Downtown: $150–250

Naturally, you'll pay a bit more to stay downtown than you would at one of Denver's cookie-

downtown Denver from the Capitol Building

© STEPHEN METZGER

cutter franchise inns along the interstate, and it's your call, obviously, as to whether the convenience and personality of downtown accommodations are worth the investment. The following hotels all offer a wide range of rates, some with suites up to $1,200.

Denver's oldest and most elegant downtown hotel is the **Brown Palace,** 321 17th St. between Tremont and Broadway, 303/297-3111 or 800/321-2599, or 800/228-2917 in Denver. Completed in 1892 and designed in Italian Renaissance style, this four-star grande dame of Denver's hotels is worth a visit just to have a look around—even if you're staying somewhere a bit less ostentatious. Management has actually printed up a descriptive walking-tour guide (available at the registration desk) providing information on design, construction materials, former guests, and furnishings.

Another of downtown's nicer and more elegant hotels is the **Oxford Hotel,** 303/628-5400 or 800/228-5838. This European-style hotel at the corner of 17th Street and Wazee offers luxurious, if small, rooms, and all the pampering you can take—including a health club, free limousine service downtown, and hosts who take the time to know their guests almost as family. Plus, it's the closest hotel to Coors Field and LoDo.

The **Westin Hotel Tabor Center,** 1776 Grant, 303/572-9100 or 800/228-3000, is conveniently located right downtown on the 16th Street

Mall. It boasts an elegant lobby, large rooms, and a rooftop pool and hot tub. Also nice and very convenient is the newly expanded **Adam's Mark** (née Radisson), 1550 Court, 303/893-3333, which offers first-class digs and easy access to downtown.

The **Warwick Hotel,** at the corner of 17th and Grant, 303/861-2000 or 800/525-2888, is a classically high-styled high-rise offering free downtown transportation, athletic facilities, and a rooftop pool looking out over the modern, glassy city skyline.

Downtown on Curtis between 18th and 19th is the **Embassy Suites Hotel,** 1881 Curtis, 303/297-8888, where large rooms afford privacy and easy access to LoDo and Coors Stadium.

The **Comfort Inn,** 401 17th St., 303/296-0400, has high-rise rooms overlooking the city—the corner rooms are especially impressive, with wraparound floor-to-ceiling windows for excellent views of the downtown area. The upscale **Holiday Inn** is downtown at 1450 Glenarm, 303/573-1450 or 800/423-5128. The Comfort Inn and Holiday Inn both offer rooms a tad less expensive than the other hotels—you might be able to find a double for under $150.

The South End: $100–150

Stay at the towering and elegant **Loews Giorgio Hotel,** 4150 E. Mississippi, 303/782-9300, and you'll feel like you're in Milan and that La Scala or DaVinci's *Last Supper* is just a short cab ride

The Brown Palace is still one of the state's grandest hotels.

COURTESY OF COLORADO HISTORICAL SOCIETY

away. Indeed, this Italian-style hotel is one of Denver's real luxuries, and though a bit south of downtown still affords easy access to most of the city's attractions. An added bonus is that you don't have to pay for parking here, unless you opt for valet (most places downtown require pay parking, which can add a sizable sum to your bill). To get there, take the Colorado Boulevard exit from I-25, go east on Mississippi, and turn left.

The South End: $50–100

Other, more moderate lodgings at the south end of town (still at the junction of Colorado and I-25—Exit 204) include the **Landmark Best Western,** 303/388-5561, and the **La Quinta Inn,** 303/758-8886. Both offer easy access to the Cherry Creek Mall.

Bed-and-Breakfasts: $100–150

The **Queen Anne Inn,** 303/296-6666, is just east of downtown at 2147 Tremont. Constructed in 1879, the building is on the National Register of Historic Places, was beautifully restored and decorated, has been touted in dozens of national publications, and was named Denver's best bed-and-breakfast by the local weekly, *Westword.* Its residential neighborhood is within easy walking distance of most downtown attractions and restaurants. The most expensive of the fourteen rooms is $175 for two. To get to the Queen Anne from I-25, take the Colfax exit, and follow Colfax past the capitol to Logan; go left on Logan until it tees into a small park (you'll be looking straight across at the Queen Anne); go left, and then veer right onto Tremont.

The **Capitol Hill Mansion Bed and Breakfast,** 1207 Pennsylvania, 303/839-5221, occupies a grand stone home built in 1891 just before the silver crash. On the National Register of Historic Places, it features oak paneling, hand-painted murals, and other examples of late-19th-century opulence. It's just a couple of blocks from the state capitol and within walking distance to most of Denver's downtown attractions. All eight rooms, the most expensive of which is $175, have private baths. You can also

THE DENVER AREA

rent an entire floor (three rooms, eight guests max) for about $400 winter, $450 summer.

Hostels: Under $50

Generally the least expensive way to travel, and one of the best ways to meet fellow travelers, hosteling can be a real adventure, though it's not for everyone. The typical dorm-style accommodations, the chore(s) you'll be asked to do to offset the exceptionally low rates, and the socializing demanded by the lack of privacy can either suit your needs and moods or not. If this is the kind of digs you prefer, or one that your budget insists upon, the city offers the **Hostel of the Rocky Mountains,** 1530 Downing St., 303/861-7777, and the **Denver International Youth Hostel,** 630 16th Ave., 303/832-9996. For more information on hosteling in the Rocky Mountain area, write **American Youth Hostels,** Rocky Mountain Division, P.O. Box 2730, Boulder, CO 80306, website: www.bcn.boulder.co.us.

Camping and RVing

Of course the mountains west of Denver are full of campgrounds, both privately owned and government run, and hundreds of thousands of acres of national forest and wilderness areas lie within a short drive of the city (see specific destination chapters). If you're heading into Denver and just need a place to pull off the road, you've got several options, including **Chief Hosa Campground,** 303/526-0364, west of town just off I-70 at Exit 253, and **Denver-North Campground,** 303/452-4120, north of town at Exit 229 (Broomfield) off I-25.

FOOD

Start Me Up

One of the best places to face the morning in Denver is at **The Market,** in LoDo on Larimer Square at 1445 Larimer, 303/534-5140. Grab a newspaper and get in line at the espresso bar for a latte, cappuccino, or house coffee and a croissant or fresh-baked muffin. Open at 6:45 weekday mornings (8:30 on Saturday) and till midnight on Friday and Saturday. The Market also sells gourmet groceries, deli sandwiches, and

desserts (try a cream puff or truffle). Seating is available both inside and on the sidewalk outside, weather permitting. At the Tabor Center, try **Peaberry's Coffee,** part of a local chain that offers a multitude of other nearby locations. Many other coffee shops are scattered around the downtown area. For theatergoers, **Pablo's,** 1060 14th St., 303/571-5662, is a great place to stop before or after a show, for coffee, quiche, and *empanada.* Open at 6:30 A.M. on weekdays and 9:30 A.M. on weekends and until 11 P.M. Sun.–Tues. and till midnight Thurs.–Saturday.

If you're in the mood for something heartier, you might try the **Delectable Egg,** 1642 Market (between 16th and 17th streets in LoDo), 303/572-8146. Open at 6:30 weekday mornings and 7 A.M. on Saturday, the Egg serves daily specials for around $5 in a large, airy, woody, and ceiling-fanned dining room. There's also a Delectable Egg at the other end of the 16th Street Mall at 1625 Court Pl., 303/892-5720. Both also serve very good lunches, including croissant and pita sandwiches, salads, and frittatas; lunch will run you $5–8.

Dozens, 236 W. 13th, 303/572-0066, is a veritable downtown institution. Housed in a restored Victorian, the restaurant is walking distance from downtown businesses and many of the local tourist attractions. That fact, along with its reputation for excellent food at reasonable prices, ensures its popularity with locals and out-of-towners alike. Open daily 6:30 A.M.–2 P.M. Another downtown tradition is **Duffy's Shamrock Restaurant and Bar,** 1635 Court Pl., 303/534-4935, where you can get reasonably priced steak and eggs, omelettes, and waffles, as well as Bloody Marys to wash it all down with (full bar service begins at 7 A.M.). Duffy's also serves lunch (burgers, prime rib, salads: $4–7) and dinner (burgers, steaks, seafood, spaghetti: $4–12). Hours are Mon.–Sat. 7–2 A.M. and Sunday 11 A.M.–midnight.

Mexican

One local favorite—regularly recognized by *Westword's* "Best of Denver"—is the **Blue Bonnet Café,** at 457 S. Broadway, 303/778-0147. Be prepared to wait, though: the Blue Bonnet's no secret. But even the wait is part of the picture—try one of the half dozen or so types of margaritas, by the glass or by the pitcher, on which the Blue Bonnet prides itself. Dinner combos run $6–8, specials $6–10; à la carte tacos, burritos, enchiladas, and tamales are $2–4.

Right up there with the Blue Bonnet, and even more authentic, is **Las Delicias,** 303/839-5675, at the corner of East 19th and Pennsylvania. With the television in the lobby tuned to a Spanish-language station and the waitresses, busboys, and cooks rarely breaking into English, this is the *cosa real* (real thing). And the prices are unbeatable: dinners run $3–8, with most right around $4. All of Las Delicias's food is available for carryout (including the green chile stew, at $2.90 a pint). In addition to the restaurant on 19th, **Las Delicias II** is at 50 E. Del Norte, 303/430-0422, and **Las Delicias III** has opened up in LoDo at 1530 Blake, 303/629-5051. Hours at Las Delicias are Mon.-Sat. 8 A.M.–9 P.M. and Sunday 9 A.M.–9 P.M.

Croc's Cafe, in LoDo at 1630 Market, 303/436-1144, caters to a younger crowd and is an excellent place to sip a margarita or microbrew before a Rockies' game. Mexican-style pastas, seafood, chili, and burrito dinners run $6–12.

Brewpubs

The flagship of Colorado's microbrewery fleet, **Wynkoop Brewing Company,** 303/297-2700, is at the corner of 18th and Wynkoop, just a couple of blocks from Coors Stadium. Whether you stop in to taste the half dozen or so beers, or you're more interested in pub chow, this place is a must. The brews vary from week to week, and, particularly, from season to season, but they usually vary from a light ale to a dark stout or porter. Lunch specials include salads, soups (including the Gorgonzola Ale, made with cheese and beer, natch!), sandwiches, the Ploughman's Platter (buffalo and veal bratwurst, cheeses, eggs, onions, beer mustard, and fresh fruit chutney), as well as shepherd's pie, bangers and mashers, bockwurst, and Italian sausage—all lunches range $5–7. For dinner, try grilled game hen, curried coconut chicken, trout or shark—running from about $8 to $12. What-

ever your preference, whether it's bangers or bratwurst, be sure to wash it down with a Wynkoop's beer (assuming you're of age). It'd be sacrilege to drink anything else—I actually witnessed an otherwise intelligent-appearing gentleman order a Miller Lite, *and drink it.* Wynkoop's also has 40 deluxe pool tables upstairs and a cabaret theater downstairs, as well as meeting and banquet rooms rooms adjoining the main bar and restaurant.

The Rock Bottom Brewery, 1001 16th St. (16th Street Mall at Curtis), 303/534-7616, is another brewpub, especially popular with the downtown business set. We stopped by on a Friday for a late lunch to find it packed with suited businesspeople who, judging by the amount of beer being quaffed, were apparently planning to take the afternoon off. Food is excellent here, too. Try the brew burger, the Taos chicken sandwich, pesto Genovese, or buffalo fajitas. Lunch entrées run $6–9, and dinner $6–14. Open daily 11 A.M.–11 P.M.—till midnight Friday and Saturday (the bar is open till 2 A.M. daily).

Asian Food

Denver has scores of excellent Asian restaurants, offering everything from authentic cuisine direct from Saigon to excellent Mandarin, Hunan, and Mongolian dishes. And many of these restaurants are perfect for the budget traveler, because you often get a *lot* of food for your buck. Voted best Chinese restaurant by *Westword* (2001), **Little Ollie's,** 2364 E. 3rd Ave., 303/316-8888, is a great place for classic Chinese dishes, plus many you've probably never tried. Ollie's Shrimp and Crispy Sea Bass are sure to entice the seafood lover, and the basil chicken is excellent. Dinners run $8–20. Open daily 3–10 P.M.

Another favorite Chinese restaurant is **Imperial,** 431 S. Broadway, 303/698-2800. Locals swear by sushi at the **Mori Sushi Bar and Tokyo Cuisine,** 2019 Market, 303/298-1864, and at **Sushi Heights,** 2301 E. Colfax, 303/355-2777.

For Thai food, try **Wild Ginger,** 309 W. Littleton (in Littleton), 303/794-1115. A perennial favorite for Vietnamese food is **New Saigon,** 630 S. Federal, 303/936-4954.

THE DENVER AREA

Other Downtown Restaurants

One of the best places downtown to see and be seen, and to get decent grub at reasonable prices, is the **Paramount Café,** 511 16th St., 303/893-2000. This little bar and café, with plenty of outside tables for watching 16th Street strollers, serves fajitas, Cajun chicken, meatloaf or albacore sandwiches, Tex-Mex specialties ($6–10), and a variety of appetizers, from wontons to potato skins ($4–6). Daily specials are $6–8.

A favorite for fish and other seafood is **McCormick's,** 303/825-1107, a classic fish house and oyster bar on the corner of 17th and Wazee (right next door to the Oxford Hotel). A long-standing west-Denver tradition, McCormick's is these days enjoying its location near Coors Field: before and after ballgames the place is packed with Rockies' fans powering microbrews and scarfing everything from burgers and fries to fresh swordfish, salmon, and crab, as well as bouillabaisse and Bluepoint oysters. Entrées run $8–20. Open daily 4:30–11 P.M.

High-End Denver Classics

Claiming to be Denver's oldest restaurant, and having served countless luminaries through the years—many of whose photos adorn the walls—**The Buckhorn Exchange,** 10th Avenue and Osage, 303/534-9505, is another Denver tradition. Specialties include buffalo, elk, alligator, rattlesnake, and Rocky Mountain oysters. A word of caution: if the sight of animal trophies makes you at all uncomfortable, you won't enjoy the Buckhorn. Heads of elk, reindeer, bison, deer, and antelope, and mounted ducks, foxes, and other critters, fill every square inch of wall space and stare down at the tables; we happened to be sitting directly below a coyote with a pheasant in its mouth—Betsy ordered the salmon. Dinner for two will run you a minimum of $60, easily more if you have drinks and/or appetizers. Dinner is served Mon.–Thurs. 5:30–9 P.M., Friday and Saturday 5–9:30 P.M., and Sunday 5–9 P.M. Live folk music Friday and Saturday nights.

For the best buffalo in town, the choice is made obvious by the name: **The Denver Buffalo Company,** 1109 Lincoln, 303/832-0880, which specializes in high-end cuts such as tenderloin and prime rib. The restaurant also offers game meats such as wild boar. Dinners run $19–39. Hours are Mon.–Thurs. 11 A.M.–9 P.M. and Friday and Saturday 11 A.M.–10 P.M. Entertainment is also offered 52 weekends a year, but is not recommended for children; call ahead to see what's on tap. Be sure to make reservations well in advance.

Another Denver-area tradition is **The Fort,** 19192 Hwy. 8, in Morrison, 303/697-4771, which was built in 1962 as a full-size replica of Bent's fort. The restaurant specializes in "Old West" favorites, such as Rocky Mountain oysters, buffalo heart and tongue, rattlesnake, and elk, and has been written up in *Esquire, Bon Appétit, Gourmet,* and *The New York Times.* Entrées run $14–28. The Fort is 22 miles from Denver. Take I-70 west to Hampden (U.S. 285), and go south to the junction with Highway 8. Open Mon.–Fri. 5:30–9:30 P.M., Saturday 5–9:30 P.M., and Sunday 5–8:30 P.M. Reservations are a must.

For the definition of luxurious dining, try the **Palace Arms,** inside the beautiful Brown Palace Hotel, 303/297-3111. Awarded four stars by the Mobil Travel Guide, the Palace Arms is guaranteed to please. The interior is decorated with antiques dating from 1670 and 22 replicas of American flags—from the Revolutionary War and different periods of westward expansion. Try the roasted rack of Colorado lamb or the pan-roasted loin of veal. Jackets are required for men, ties optional. Open Mon.–Fri. for lunch 11:30 A.M.–2 P.M. ($12.50-18) and daily for dinner, 6–10 P.M. ($30–70). Reservations required.

Farmers Market

Each Saturday morning from late June through late October, farmers back their pickups against the curb at 17th and Market Streets and sell fresh produce. There's usually live music and an array of T-shirt booths as well. Open from 7 A.M. to 1 P.M.

ENTERTAINMENT

Again, with the transformation of lower downtown from a run-down warehouse district to LoDo, where clubs and pubs are two, three, and four to a block, entertainment in Denver has taken a giant leap forward. In fact, it can be downright entertaining just wandering through the area, especially before and after Rockies' games, when the streets fill with folks sharing their love of the city and their team with a vibrant energy that's unusually infectious. There's also lots of music, comedy, and dance. The best way to find out what's going on where is to check the *Weekend* magazine supplement to *The Denver Post* and *Westword,* the free weekly distributed in racks and in cafés and restaurants around town.

According to the 2001 "Best of Denver" survey in *Westword,* Denver's best rock club is the **15th Street Tavern,** 623 15th St., 303/572-0822, where it gets loud and sweaty with rowdy-indie rock, punk, even occasionally some old-fashioned R&B.

If you feel like kickin' up your heels and doin' some two-steppin', check out the **Grizzly Rose Saloon and Dance Emporium,** 5450 N. Valley Hwy., 303/295-1330, regularly named best country-and-western club by *Westword.* Big-name performers—from Willie Nelson to Stephen Stills—stop in here and there's always something country going on.

The **Comedy Works,** 303/595-3637, also right downtown at 1226 15th St., in Larimer Square, features local and comedy-circuit comedians most nights of the week. Two shows Friday and Saturday nights. A recorded message will give you showtimes and prices.

Concert Venues

Among Denver's places to see acts big enough to draw huge crowds is **Red Rocks,** 303/295-4444, a gorgeous natural amphitheater in the hills on the city's west side. Past acts include Rickie Lee Jones, Lyle Lovett, and Jimmy Cliff. **Fiddler's Green,** 303/220-7000, also features outdoor concerts varying from pop (James Taylor) to rock (the Foo Fighters), as well as jazz

and classical music (local and national orchestras and symphonies).

Six Flags Elitch Gardens , 303/595-4386, also known for its roller coaster and other rides, as well as its perennial county-fair atmosphere, books live music throughout the summer. Often country-flavored, acts have included Emmylou Harris, Riders in the Sky, and Air Supply.

Denver Performing Arts Complex

This center, downtown at 14th and Curtis, is home to many of Denver's entertainment and cultural events, shows, and troupes, including the Denver Symphony Orchestra, the Colorado Ballet, and the Denver Theater Company, which produces 12 plays each season on the center's four stages. Performances at the center range from well-known traveling acts such as Eartha Kitt and Jackie Mason to productions of Shakespeare and Rodgers and Hammerstein. Check the website at www.denvercenter.org for information and schedules, or phone 303/893-4100 or 800/641-1222.

CALENDAR

Denver's a big city, the biggest for more than 600 miles in any direction, and there's something going on almost every day, evening, and weekend—from arts-and-crafts fairs to auto races, from music festivals (*lots* of music in this town) to golf tournaments. The new year kicks off in mid-January with the two-week **National Western Stock Show and Rodeo,** the largest such show on the planet. In addition to pro and amateur rodeos and livestock competitions, you can watch the city transmogrify into a shit-kickin' cow town with Ralph Lauren and Obsession stepping aside for Wrangler and *eau de chevaux.* If you plan to be in Denver during the festivities, whether you're ridin' and ropin' or just watching from the rails, be sure to make hotel reservations well in advance. For schedule and ticket information, phone 303/297-1166.

Denver's annual two-day **Cinco de Mayo** party takes place on the 16th Street Mall and features music, dancing, arts and crafts, and

WHERE TO FIND LIVE MUSIC

On the music front, the overhaul in Denver over the last dozen years has been rewarding. The music scene improvement is right up there with adding major league baseball and proving that Denver's suburbs can sprawl their way across perfectly good prairie as fast as any good metropolis on earth. So there.

No, really. Something's changed. This is a good thing. First, all bands stop here now. They used to skip Denver at 35,000 feet. Now, they stop. And perform. Second, there is a nifty array of venues for the up-and-coming, the won't-go-away, and the came-and-wents (or at least, until they came back).

Herewith a quick guide to the live music scene and improved, tune-filled landscape. One note: any night that ends at the Lion's Lair is a good one.

Bluebird Theater, 3317 E. Colfax Ave., 303/322-2308: A converted movie theater with friendly bar and service where the back rows used to be. Cool blue marquee (best marquee going), hip touring and local acts (anything goes) with a not-quite-ready-for-prime-time feel. Not much else happens on this end of Colfax, but it's worth tracking down. Across the street, you'll find fine beer along with tasty pizza and sandwiches at the Goose Town Tavern.

The Church, 1160 Lincoln St., 303/832-3528: Yes, a church. An old, cool church with multiple layers and scenes that keep unfolding as you explore. Some live music, some hip DJ action. Three dance floors, usually at least one propelled by a good, live cover band. House, progressive house, and electronica fill the DJ rooms. Usually a tad pricey, but the people-watching almost matches the deep thudding pulse. (Usually no cover before 10 P.M.) The in-

side includes multiple bars and food options (it's not that big, really) all in shades of dim light. Not the place for a quiet rendezvous, and locals can count on running into anybody and everybody. It's busy. And, really, a must-see—and feel.

Cricket on the Hill, 1209 E. 13th Ave., 303/830-9020: Simple, basic, straightforward, usually lots of fun. It's been rocking here for a very long time. Bands Thursday, Friday, and Saturday. The band setup spills right on top of the tables. It looks small from the outside and it is. Pretension factor? Zippola. Great spot if simple is your shtick.

15th Street Tavern, 623 15th St., 303/572-0822: Unpredictable quality, but dependable venue for mostly local acts. A good choice for those stuck downtown on a budget.

Fox Theatre, 1135 13th St. (in Boulder), 303/443-3399: A setup similar to the Bluebird's with more bars (three) and a good pit area for jamming (say, to Cracker) and lots of tables for the sedate stuff (say, Kim Richey). A good, hassle-free environment.

Gothic Theatre, 3263 S. Broadway (in Englewood), 303/380-2333: Not too far from downtown Denver (15 minutes on Broadway, straight south) is another movie theater conversion project with a more intimate feel, neat balcony, and high-up stage with a great view for all. This place forces folks to have a good time. It's not afraid to book the occasional offbeat artsy act or world-beat show. Gritty and real. Downside? There's nothing else nearby.

Herman's Hideaway, 1578 S. Broadway, 303/777-5840. Well, you could cab it up a couple of miles from the Gothic heading north—or vice

food—in a salute to Denver's Chicano heritage and to Mexican independence. For more information, phone 303/534-6161.

Also in May, things get crazy for a couple of days at the Civic Center Park during the annual **Capitol Hill People's Fair.** Join the more than 100,000 revelers, politicos, and New-Agers, and check out everything from the latest in low-impact high technology to noncompetitive games, from herbal teas to current political agendas. Virtually nonstop live music.

Phone 303/388-2716. (See accompanying special topic.)

Another folky favorite is the **Colorado Renaissance Festival,** in Larkspur, south of Denver, on weekends in June and early July. Paint your face, don a beret and plume, or squeeze into your favorite pair of tights, and get thee to the funnery. Once inside the grounds, situated on a hillside amid pine and scrub oak, you can forget the travails that the centuries since Elizabeth I hath wrought. Listen to buxom versa. (There's not much else around here, either) But this is no walk from the Gothic. Herman's is the old workhorse of the Denver scene. Big Head Todd & the Monsters were born here—you can look it up! Big open room with a wide dance floor, good sound system, two bars, and usually plenty of music to go around. Some edgy bands; others might make Fleetwood Mac sound raucous. You're taking your chances, but it's a neat space.

Lion's Lair, 2022 E. Colfax, 303/320-9200: Small. Very small. Get there early (say 10:30 P.M.) if it's a band you have to see. Or get tickets ahead of time. A few seats around a bar, a few booths around the wall, and a "stage" that has bands dipping their tuning pegs into the bartenders' tipping jars. If you think this is an exaggeration, then you would be wrong. An "intimate" feel, as in your drinks are next to their drinks and this stranger is your friend, got it? Great scene. Several tattoo parlors are nearby, and the Satire (just west) serves pretty good Mexican food for those needing some sustenance.

Little Bear, 28075 Hwy. 74 (in Evergreen—40 minutes from downtown Denver), 303/674-9991: A big old roadhouse with a freewheeling attitude, hard-working people from the foothills, and the odd chance that the bras will be flying by night's end make the Bear a worthwhile stop. Some big-name national acts and many local blues and rock outfits call this home. The place feels worn, beaten-up, and rundown. Perfect. Don't overlook the small balcony. If it's not crowded up there, you can watch the bands from almost directly above. And on a slow night, you have the upstairs to yourself. On a busy night, well, you might not make it upstairs.

Good food (okay, for a place like this) too. Order a pitcher of the joint's own red beer and settle in.

Ogden Theatre, 935 E. Colfax Ave., 303/831-9448: Yet another movie theater conversion. Close to downtown, and adjacent to a good Independent Records store outlet (just opened in 2001). Bigger than Bluebird, not as offbeat as the Gothic, but the right size for many acts. A straightforward place. If you like the band, go.

Soiled Dove, 1949 Market St., 303/299-0100: A fun lower downtown club with a sweeping bar, an East Coast feel, and a myriad of rising stars mixed with local acts. The upstairs bar makes a good place to get away, particularly in the summer. From here, your late-night options (Denver still pretty much shuts down at 2 A.M., however) are many throughout the seas of college students and sports fans who swarm these parts.

Some final thoughts: if it's summer, check the music schedule at **The Botanic Gardens,** a beautiful outdoor venue in the round. Kids romping, friends chatting. Bring a bottle of Pinot Gris, sharp cheese, and wheat crackers and they'll let you in for free. Not really—it turns out you have to buy a ticket after all. Anyway, it's a beautiful spot to spread out a blanket, dig into a stocked picnic basket, and relax. And never overlook **Red Rocks** (20 minutes west of Denver). Unbelievable scene, view, atmosphere, lights, sound, and mood. It's what large-venue outdoor music was meant to offer. Sit up top, take it all in. Go early, enjoy the music, and take away an unforgettable mental postcard that is all Denver.

Mark Stevens

wenches tell bawdy tales; toss overripe fruit at shackled heads; gnaw on a fresh-fired turkey drumstick and wash it down with a pint of mead; listen to the sweet melodies of zithers and lutes; and sample the wares—glassware, hats, and jewelry of local artisans. Phone 303/756-1501 for exact dates and more information.

In late June/early July, the **Cherry Creek Arts Festival,** a huge juried event at the Cherry Creek Mall, attracts folks from throughout

the Denver area with quality art and crafts, as well as music, food, and first-class people-watching.

As is true throughout the state, the Fourth of July offers a wide array of activities, highlighted by the fireworks at Coors Field. Take in the evening's Rockies' game, and stick around for the fireworks afterward. For ticket information, phone 303/762-5437.

For current information on annual events in Denver, contact the **Denver Metro Convention**

and Visitors Bureau at 303/892-1112, or visit its website at www.denver.org. The staff publish an exhaustive Denver events guide, which they'll gladly send you. Watch also the entertainment sections of *The Denver Post,* the *Rocky Mountain News,* and *Westword.*

SHOPPING

Downtown Denver is rife with shopping malls, plazas, squares, and "centers." In fact, there are so many so close to one another that sometimes you don't realize you've passed from one to the next.

16th Street Mall

Even if you're the type whose blood runs cold at the very sound of the word "mall" and you find yourself looking for a tavern to duck into whenever shops and boutiques have the nerve

to enter your line of vision, you won't mind Denver's 16th Street Mall. In fact, you'll probably enjoy it. Here, strolling, people-watching, window-shopping, or stopping for junk food or a cup of coffee is much more important than *buying things.* You'll be endlessly entertained by street vendors, jugglers, flirting teenagers, and local businesspeople talking about the Rockies or stocks and commodities—not to mention the down-and-outers that hit you up for spare change every block or so, night or day.

And if you do want to do some shopping, there's every kind of store imaginable, from Walgreen's and Eddie Bauer to bookstores, jewelers, and souvenir shops where you can pick up knickknacks to bring home—T-shirts, mugs, stuffed animals, banners, caps, and mementos from Denver's sports teams, especially the Rockies and Broncos.

THE CAPITOL HILL PEOPLE'S FAIR

In the first weekend of June more than 275,000 people swarm through scores of colorful booths at Civic Center Park, the stretch of lawn between the gold-domed capitol and the majestic Greco-Roman-style courthouse in downtown Denver. An arts-and-crafts fair on a grand and multicultural scale, the Capitol Hill People's Fair offers a perfect opportunity to examine everything from ceramics and paintings to bamboo art and African masks. In addition, you can find a booth representing almost any political, philosophical, or religious viewpoint. You can have your fortune told by tarot-card readers, then walk a few feet to Rocky Mountain Skeptics and learn that it's all bunk anyway. From the Caleb Campaign learn that Jesus loves you, and then talk to the Freedom from Religion Foundation and find He doesn't even exist. You can talk to right-wingers and socialists, yoga teachers and chess experts.

If all that philosophical discussion makes you weary, you might want to relax and enjoy some entertainment. A variety of music, from heavy metal and modern jazz to country and classical, is offered on the six different stages. In addition, there are dance performances, ballet to break

dancing, while clowns juggle machetes, torches, and even watermelons.

And then there are the food booths, where you'll find every imaginable food type and cuisine—Chinese, Japanese, Greek, Turkish, Mexican, Indonesian, and more, not to mention good old-fashioned hamburgers, hot dogs, and popcorn.

Attending the People's Fair is an act of bravery because you never know what Colorado's temperamental Mother Nature might do—despite the meteorologist's predictions. You might enjoy several hours of sunshine, only to be bombarded by rain, hail, and gusty winds. In anticipation of such outbursts, the booths are all covered by canopies, and it's not uncommon to make new friends while weathering a storm. If bad weather's expected, the event's organizers move the fair to the second weekend in June. The fair opens at 10 A.M. and closes at 7 P.M. on Saturday and 6 P.M. on Sunday.

For more information on the Capitol Hill People's Fair, contact CHUN (Capitol Hill United Neighborhoods) at 303/830-1651 or 1490 Lafayette, Denver, C0 80218.

Thomas Owen Meinen

The **Tabor Center** at the mall's north end is where you'll find most of the upscale stores, including Brooks Brothers (suits and menswear), Crabtree and Evelyn (soaps, lotions, and cosmetics), Johnston and Murphy (shoes), Keepsakes (fou-fou throw rugs, scents, lamps, etc.), and Pollyanna (fine lingerie). In addition, check out the Lawrence Street Bridge Market on the third floor (be sure to take the glass elevator near the fountain). This is an almost European-style potpourri of assorted cart vendors and booths—selling everything from hats and jewelry to kites and rubber stamps.

Free shuttle buses run every few minutes from one end of the mall to the other with stops at each block.

Still More Downtown Shopping

In addition to the 16th Street Mall, **Larimer Square** and **Writer Square,** at Larimer and 14th and 15th, have a number of shops and boutiques, including Overland Outfitters and Williams and Sonoma. If you're looking to send word of your travels to folks back home, be sure to check out Avant-Card, which, as its name suggests, stocks an excellent selection of greeting cards—innovative and provocative (postcards, as well). The newest major addition to the 16th Street Mall is **Denver Pavilions,** which opened in spring 1999. This huge complex, between Welton and Glenarm, is home to a Hard Rock Cafe, a Virgin Records store, and many other retail outlets.

Cherry Creek Mall

This is Denver's most upscale shopping complex. Stores include Abercrombie and Fitch, Liz Claiborne, Saks Fifth Avenue, and Neiman-Marcus, as well as the other mall-standard shoe, jewelry, cookie, and frozen yogurt shops (more 100 stores in all). The Cherry Creek Mall is at 3000 1st Avenue.

Tattered Cover Bookstore

Bibliophiles go nuts here, for this is one of the West's truly great bookstores: three stories of floor-to-ceiling books on everything you can imagine, as well as chairs and tables and a won-

derfully friendly and knowledgeable staff who encourage you to hang around and read. A bonus: the Tattered Cover validates your parking in the adjacent garage for up to 1.5 hours. You can find the Tattered Cover (see sidebar on next page) at 2955 E. 1st Ave., 303/322-7727 or 800/833-9327, and at a second location in LoDo at 1828 16th St. and Wynkoop, 303/436-1070; the newer store, though not as sprawling as the original, is both huge and cozy in its own right.

Gart Brothers

Denver has more sporting goods stores per capita than any other city in the world, thanks in large part to Gart Brothers. With stores throughout the Denver area, Gart's offers multistory sports emporiums with gigantic equipment selections in golf, skiing, bow hunting, in-line skating, and everything else you can imagine. With entire floors and rooms devoted to single sports, some Gart stores are so huge directional signs are provided to help you find your way around. Anyone with even the slightest interest in sports owes it to herself to stop by a Gart's. The Gart's closest to downtown is at 10th and Broadway.

SERVICES

The central information number for the **Denver Police Department** is 303/575-3127 (in emergencies dial 911). The number for the **sheriff's office** is 303/375-3451. For general information about the City and County of Denver, phone 303/575-2790. To report accidents and emergencies to the **Colorado State Patrol,** or for nonemergencies, phone 303/239-4501.

In medical emergencies, dial 911. Denver's **University Hospital** is at 4200 E. 9th Ave. at the corner of Colorado, 303/270-8901 in emergencies or 303/399-1211 for general information. **AMI St. Luke's Hospital** is at 601 E. 19th; phone 303/629-2111 in emergencies or 303/839-1000 for general information.

The main branch of the Denver **post office** is at 1823 Stout, 303/297-6168. Two **post offices** are downtown. One is in the basement of the May D and F Building at the corner of 16th and Tremont, and the other is on the first floor of

DENVER'S BEST BOOK AND RECORD STORES

Tattered Cover. Twist & Shout. There are others, to be sure. There are imitators, yes indeed. You can find books and music at Wal-Mart if you insist. But if you treat either books or music with a certain reverence, Denver sports two stores with matching moods for those who thirst for the complete retail experience. And by that I mean breathe it all in. For books, it's Tattered Cover. For music, it's Twist & Shout.

Books

You'll find **Tattered Cover** at 2955 E. 1st Ave. at Milwaukee Street in Cherry Creek North, 303/322-7727, or at 1628 16th St. at Wynkoop Street in lower downtown Denver, 303/436-1070.

Endless? Almost. Can you get lost? Better hope your name's not Amelia. The main Tattered Cover store (the lower downtown is equally expansive, but this one was first) starts in the basement and goes to the third floor. Each floor is large. More than 150,000 titles fill the shelves, which know no gaps. Any one floor or section can draw you into its soothing soul. The atmosphere reeks calm. The staff is omnipresent, deployed at small desks here and there. These desks serve as small headquarters for your search, whether it's common or not. Fear no looks, no attitude. This place built its name on support. The store is the conduit between you and your muses, you and your whims. No judgments are allowed to enter the transaction. The places oozes a sense of wonder. It's your job to open the door and look around. Find a book, pick out a comfy chair. Curl up with a prospective purchase and dive in with your mind. The topper here at the main store is The Fourth Story, an exquisite restaurant with interesting offerings and a great scene. But that's another chapter, dealing with real calories, not the mental ones.

A second Tattered Cover is in lower downtown Denver at the corner of 16th and Wynkoop Streets, just four blocks from Coors Field. In the fully restored Morey Mercantile building, the three-story version here offers the same mood as the original store. The floors creak a bit more, there's more elbow room all the way around, and the weekend lines tend to be a little more forgiving. This store also is home to a children's tree house, a good-sized hall for author and literary events (it has even hosted film screenings and discussions), the ubiquitous coffee shop, and yet another solid newsstand.

This is a store that holds essay contests on censorship and recently battled in court for the right to keep private the details of its customers' purchases. Police had found a Tattered Cover shipping envelope in the trash of a suspected drug dealer and wanted the Tattered Cover to reveal the contents of what was sent. The Tattered Cover put up a fight—

Tabor Center underneath the Westin Hotel at 16th and Lawrence. For zip code information, phone 303/297-6000.

Recycling

The best places to drop off recyclables in Denver are the **King Soopers** grocery stores, which all take aluminum, glass, newspapers, and plastic bottles. There are more than two dozen stores in the Denver metropolitan area. **Albertson's** and **Safeway** stores will take aluminum.

For information, phone the **City of Denver Recycling Hotline,** 303/640-1675.

Child Care

Mile High Child Care Association, 303/861-2602, has locations throughout the metro Denver area, with its main office at 1780 Marion Street. Visit its extensive website at www.mile highchildcare.org. **Mile High United Way Child Care Resource and Referral Service** can provide information on thousands of daycare centers in the Denver area; phone 303/433-8900.

INFORMATION

Downtown within a few blocks of each other are several good sources of different kinds of information. At the **Denver Metro Convention and Visitors Bureau Information Center,** 1668 Larimer, you'll find a helpful and knowledgeable staff and brochures on everything from museums and accommodations to parks, events, and lost—but when you spend some money at the Tattered Cover, you know you're supporting a business with a solid moral center and sense of what free speech is all about.

Music

Twist & Shout, 300 E. Alameda Ave., corner of Alameda and Logan, 303/722-1943, is a few minutes south of downtown Denver just east of Broadway. The vinyl store is across the street at 333 E. Alameda Avenue.

You could miss this place if you weren't looking—stuck between a national video chain (guess which one) and a national bagel chain in a renovated grocery store in central Denver. Like the Tattered Cover, this outfit has moved and expanded a few times, too. And now it feels, you know, just right. Crammed (but not overstuffed) with music new and old. A spiffy boutique (shirts, novelties, gifts, cards, etc.) spills out of one corner. Videos cram the wall along the back. A rack of CD players allows you to listen before you buy. Music magazines are stuffed here and there. The place drips tunes. And the staff is helpful. If reality isn't enough, the store also works hard at an up-to-date website that includes such nifty sections as "Rarities For Sale" and extensive, current reviews. Again, the mood is what's right. Friendly,

open, welcoming, upbeat, eclectic, enthusiastic. The staff will stay out of your way, help or not help as much as you prefer.

Close second option: **Wax Trax,** a knot of shops in the East 600 block of East 13th Avenue in Capitol Hill (a few blocks from the state capitol, an easy walk), 303/444-9829. Different stores for new stuff, vintage vinyl, videos and gifts, used stuff, and retro, Wax Trax is another Denver institution. It's more cool compared to Twist & Shout's overall warmth, but it's an impressive collection, and the store employs a bevy of local musicians. Maybe that's the problem—it seems these folks have other priorities (and it shows). If you're near downtown and can't make it out to Twist & Shout, this is a worthwhile option.

Close third option: **Second Spin,** 1485 S. Colorado Blvd., 303/753-8822. This is the store with the nifty website, www.secondspin.com, which made its debut in 1996. It has other outlets in California and one in Boulder, too, but this is Second Spin's 12,000-square-foot superstore. It's a great place to turn in used CDs for cash (it will take everything) and explore well-organized music sections for hours. A warehouse feel, but lots to look through and uncover. (The website does everything just as well).

Mark Stevens

---

and galleries. Phone 303/892-1112. Hours are Mon.–Fri. 8:30 A.M.–5 P.M., Saturday 9 A.M.–5 P.M. (winter hours are Mon.–Fri. 8 A.M.–5 P.M., Saturday 9 A.M.–1 P.M.).

At the corner of Broadway and 13th Avenue, you'll find the downtown branch of the **Denver Public Library,** open Mon.–Wed. 10 A.M.–9 P.M., Thurs.–Sat. 10 A.M.–5:30 P.M., and Sunday 1–5 P.M. For more information, phone the library at 303/640-8845; the number for the children's library is 303/640-8820. The Denver public library has more than 20 branches; the downtown branch can provide addresses, phone numbers, and hours of the others.

For **road conditions,** phone 303/639-1111 (Denver and the West).

To find out what's happening where, check

out the *Weekend* magazine supplement to *The Denver Post* or pick up a copy of *Westword,* the free weekly, found in racks, cafés, and restaurants all over town.

Bookstores

The best source for books and other publications on Denver and Colorado is the **Tattered Cover,** with two locations. The original store (four floors with 500,000 books in stock!) is near the Cherry Creek Mall at 2955 E. Cherry Creek, 303/322-7727; the newer store, smaller than the original but still huge by most standards, is in LoDo at 16th Street and Wynkoop, 303/436-1070. In addition, on the 16th Street Mall, you'll find several chain stores (B. Dalton, Waldenbooks) and a handful of small newsstands with

THE DENVER AREA

tourist publications, Denver and Colorado magazines, and guidebooks.

TRANSPORTATION
Getting There
Denver International Airport opened in early 1995. The new airport, which replaced Stapleton International, is a still a major controversy in the region, partly because of its *long* distance from downtown (a 30–40 minute drive on I-70), as well as the many low and loud flights over areas in the mountains (Boulder, Ward, Golden), where folks had moved to avoid the trappings of the city. But it's a user-friendly airport and visually arresting—the "peaks" of the main building represent the Rocky Mountains—and it makes travel into and out of Colorado much more convenient. **Denver Airport Shuttle (DASH)** offers rides to and from downtown; 303/342-5454 or 800/525-3177. From the airport, fares are about $15 (shuttle) and $35 (taxi).

The city's Union Station, downtown at the west end of 17th Street, is a stop on the **Amtrak** route between Chicago and Los Angeles. For information, phone 303/893-3911.

Getting Around
Several shuttle and taxi companies offer transportation to and from the airport, as well as to the nearby towns and ski areas. Phone **Super Shuttle Denver** at 303/342-5454 or 800/525-3177, or **People's Choice Transportation** at 800/777-2388.

For taxi service in the Denver area, phone **Yellow Cab**, 303/777-7777, **Metro Taxi Company**, 303/333-3333, or **Zone Cab**, 303/444-8888.

You can rent cars in Denver from all the major chain agencies, most of which have 4WD vehicles available. Denver also has an elaborate and much-used **bus system** (RTD—Regional Transportation District), with service throughout the metro area and to some of the smaller nearby towns, including Boulder. For route and schedule information, phone 303/778-6000.

Once here, you'll find Denver is amazingly easy to get around in. First, you can walk from one end of downtown to the other in about a half hour—and that includes window-shopping along the way. And if you're not up for walking—if your arms are too loaded with packages or the day has taken its toll on your feet—there's always the **Mall Ride,** a free bus that runs from one end of 16th Street Mall to the other. With buses running every few minutes and taking on and letting off passengers at every block, the system will take you from the capitol to the Tabor Center in a matter of minutes (though you'll have to hoof it a block or so from the capitol to the east end of the mall).

Around Denver

Heading South

After slicing south through downtown Denver, rising over railroad tracks and waterways, scooting under overpasses, and passing within yards of the Broncos' Mile-High Stadium, I-25 (which at peak hours is often crowded with commuters) routes down through the city's sprawling southern suburbs and finally out onto the rocky plains, always paralleling the massive Front Range. The 70 miles between Denver and Colorado Springs don't offer a whole lot in terms of scenery and diversions—save for the Rockies' forested shoulders and towering peaks to the west—although the trip is quick and easy; it's not unusual for folks in Colorado Springs to run up to Denver for a day of shopping, or even to meet friends for lunch.

Just south of Denver proper, Littleton, seat of Arapahoe County and once a thriving farming community, shows the effects of urban sprawl, with little to distinguish it from southern Denver—strip malls, office buildings, and quiet, whitewashed suburban housing developments, with nice lawns and fences. Nearly halfway to Colorado Springs is the little town of Castle Rock (pop. 3,900; elev. 6,000 feet), named for the stone outcropping appearing very much like some medieval European castle. Over the centuries, the "castle" served as a landmark for travelers—Native Americans, traders, miners, pioneers, and early settlers. Modern travelers now have another landmark, the recently opened **Larkspur Factory Shops.** Take the Meadows Parkway Exchange from I-25.

About 10 miles south of Castle Rock is the turnoff to Larkspur, a tiny little community where the plains begin to green and gently roll as they rise to meet the steep eastern wall of the Rockies. Although not a year-round tourist destination, for a month or so every summer Larkspur is extremely popular among faire travelers and pilgrims, who don leotards and feathered caps and spend the day here (see Colorado Renaissance Festival under Calendar above).

You'll find a **KOA** campground between Castle Rock and Larkspur—open May through October. Take Exit 174/Tomah Road.

Heading West

As you head west out of Denver on I-70 toward Dillon and Summit County, a number of interesting stops could stretch the 70-mile drive into a full-day (or longer) excursion. From the museums and brewery tour in Golden to the old mining towns of Idaho Springs and Georgetown, from Buffalo Bill's grave and museum to the handful of national forest picnic areas, there are seemingly countless diversions. In fact, one of the best and most fascinating diversions is the pure and simple scenic wonder: as you barrel out of the Denver flats and into the high country of the western slope—where pine and fir encircle mountain meadows and aspen and spruce mingle on ridge tops—the vistas and panoramas get downright *serious.* Take the time to pull over at the turnouts along the way: geology buffs will appreciate the little exhibit at Exit 258, where you can examine closely the layers of rock cut away to build the interstate; near Genesee, you might get lucky and see a herd of buffalo; and if you look really closely, up on the hill to the south just west of Exit 256, you can see the futuristic house that Woody Allen used in *Sleeper* (don't get too excited—the orgasmatron's long gone. . .).

Just off the freeway, at Exit 253, **Chief Hosa,** 303/526-0364, is a pleasant little campground with RV and tent sites nestled in the pines. Not the type of place you'd want to spend your two-week vacation, but ideal for short-term, we'll-be-moving-on-in-the-morning camping.

Golden

Probably best known for the massive Coors brewery, which attracts nearly 400,000 visitors a year, Golden (pop. 15,000, elev. 5,680 feet) is a compact and isolated little town in Clear Creek Canyon in the rocky foothills about a half-hour drive west of Denver. Seat of Jefferson County, Golden is also home to the Colorado School of Mines, the Colorado Railroad Museum, the Buffalo Bill Museum and gravesite, and several other small museums and parks. Central Golden is an Old-Westy little downtown area, with gift shops, taverns, and western-wear stores.

HISTORY

Though officially founded in the summer of 1859 by a group of Bostonians in search of gold, the little camp on Clear Creek had been a popular stopover for miners heading west for some time, and at least one settler, farmer David Wall, called the place home for more than a year. In fact, during the spring of '59, Wall made more than $2,000 selling produce to the hordes of miners flocking to the canyon to make their fortunes off the area's fabulous lodes.

On June 12 of that year, Bostonian George West and crew, calling themselves the Boston Company, built the area's first frame house and dubbed the then-thriving camp Golden City, apparently after miner-cum-merchant Thomas Golden. The group also built a bridge across Clear Creek (at what is now Washington Street), charging tolls to the increasing numbers—from the nearby towns of Black Hawk, Central City, Silver Plume, and Georgetown—dependent on Golden for trade. About this time, journalist Horace Greeley rode a rented mule up into Clear Creek Canyon. Mightily impressed by the mines and bustling enterprises, he returned to the East Coast to write, "Go West, young man, and grow with the country."

By the early 1860s, Golden City could claim 800 year-round residents, as well as saloons, stores, hotels, and a school, and from 1862 to 1867, the town served as the capital of Colorado

Territory. In 1872, the word "City" officially dropped from the town's name.

The 1870s saw the arrival of three important contributors to the development of Golden: the Colorado School of Mines, the railroad, and the Coors-Schueler Brewery. Though originally founded in 1869, the Colorado School of Mines, first called Jarvis College and headed by a missionary bishop of the Church of Colorado, opened its doors to students in 1871, offering degrees in assaying and chemical ore testing. With a 25-acre campus, the school is still home to three of the town's earliest buildings, constructed between 1880 and 1890. Colorado's first railroad—the Colorado Central—began operation in late 1870, and by the early part of the decade had a line to Golden. In fact, within a few short years, Golden became the site of the company's headquarters as well as its western terminus, supplying other nearby camps and towns. Golden's heyday as a railroad center was short-lived, however, as the headquarters moved to Denver in the early 1880s.

The Coors-Schueler Brewery was built in 1873 by Adolph Herman Joseph Coors and by the turn of the century produced 500,000 barrels of beer a year. Prohibition (1919–33) definitely put a damper on the outfit, although management was savvy enough to move into the production of nonalcoholic commodities—"near beer," malted milk, and other milk by-products. By Prohibition's end, the brewery was able to again produce beer, unlike the vast majority of the nation's breweries permanently shut down by the Constitution's ill-fated 18th Amendment.

SIGHTS

Coors Brewery

Tours of the Coors brewery—the largest single brewery in the world—are the reason most visitors come to Golden, and indeed, summer days the town is packed with people who've come to pay their respects to the great "Colorado Kool-Aid" and to see how it's made. The tour's free, too. And at the end—assuming you're of age—you can even sample a couple of glasses of Coors' products: Coors, Coors Lite, the "Silver Bullet," etc. And then there's the gift shop (it's no accident that the gift shop is *after* the free sampling), where you can buy Coors T-shirts, steins, Frisbees, and all kinds of other knickknacks with the Coors logo.

In addition to tours of the brewery, Coors offers brief tours of Golden, with buses routing their ways through town, picking up tourists from parking lots, while drivers point out important historical landmarks before delivering passengers to the brewery's doors.

Note: it'll come as no surprise that Coors has had its share of PR problems over the years, from labor and race issues to unfortunate alliances (James Watt and the Sagebrush Rebellion in the 1970s). However, Coors has become known as one of the most progressive large companies in the country in several areas, most notably in terms of employee relations. A company-sanctioned Diversity Council, which includes Women at Coors, African-Americans at Coors, Hispanics at Coors, and other groups, among them LAGER (Lesbian and Gay Employee Resources), meets

regularly to make recommendations to top management regarding employee relations. In the summer of 1995, at the suggestion of the Diversity Council, Coors wrote into company policy a Domestic Partners Benefits package, which guarantees the same benefits to same-sex partners of employees that it guarantees to spouses.

Tours of the Coors brewery are offered Mon.–Sat. 10 A.M.–4 P.M. To get to Golden from Denver, take U.S. 70 west and then Highway 58 north; you can also take U.S. 6 (6th Avenue) directly west out of Denver. A shuttle bus will take you to the brewery from the parking lot at 13th and Ford. For more information, phone 303/277-BEER (277-2337).

Colorado Railroad Museum

This is an absolute must for train buffs, from old-timers who recall the train in its glory days to those whose childhoods were spent assembling model trains and villages. Nothing fancy or high-tech here (as it should be—in fact, the yard is overgrown with weeds and truly invokes ghosts of a bygone era), but the museum does display plenty to recall the railroad and to teach about its past. From historical photos and original ledgers

welcome to Coors country

© STEPHEN METZGER

locomotive in the yard of the Colorado Railroad Museum

and records to a model train with an impeccably detailed miniature town of Golden (cars, people, the courthouse, even a baseball game in progress); from switch lamps, uniforms, and silver, from dining cars to the cars and locomotives themselves, this is a wonderful testament to the railroad, as well as a lesson in Colorado's (and the West's) history. The gift shop, in addition to selling mugs and other souvenirs, carries an excellent selection of books on the railroad and on Colorado history, as well as authentic historical papers (original schedules, announcements, records, etc.).

The Colorado Railroad Museum is open daily 9 A.M.–5 P.M. (till 6 P.M. during the summer). Admission is $4 for adults, $3.50 for seniors, and $2 for kids; family passes are available for $9. To get there from Denver, take I-70 west to Highway 58, and follow the signs (take Exit 265). If you're heading east on I-70, take Exit 266. For more information, phone 303/279-4591 or 800/279-6263.

Colorado School of Mines

First open to students in 1871, this is the largest and most important school of mineral engineering in the United States. The college's **Geology Museum,** open Mon.–Sat. 9 A.M.–4 P.M. and Sunday 1–4 P.M., displays gems, ore, and minerals from around the world, including pieces from Golden's 19th-century mining boom. It's at the corner of 16th and Maple, 303/273-3815.

The School of Mines is also home to the **National Earthquake Information Center,** recording continental drift and other geological activity around the world. The center's 24-hour-a-day Earthquake Early Alerting Service determines the location and magnitude of temblors around the world (roughly 12,000 a year) and disseminates relevant information to authorities. The center is also responsible for publishing data on seismic activity. Free 30- to 45-minute tours available by appointment Tues.–Thurs.; phone 303/273-8500.

For general information on the Colorado School of Mines, phone 303/273-3300.

Golden Pioneer Museum

Exhibiting local pioneer artifacts from the mid-19th century to the 1930s, this small museum at 923 10th St. displays a wide variety of local and American historical artifacts—in addition to individual rooms (kid's nursery, lady's boudoir, etc.), you'll see an eclectic collection of domestic items and historical military gear (Civil War bayonets and uniforms). Hours are Mon.–Sat. 10 A.M.–4:30 P.M. year-round. To book tours or obtain more information, phone 303/278-7151.

Astor House Hotel Museum

Built in 1867 of local stone, this hotel at the corner of 12th and Arapahoe has been restored and decorated with authentic Victorian furnishings and is now on the National Register of Historic Places. Its emphasis is boardinghouse life in 19th-century Golden. Admission is $3 for adults, $1 for kids. Hours are Tues.–Sat. 10 A.M.–4:30 P.M. (until 3 P.M. in winter). For information, phone 303/278-3557.

Rocky Mountain Quilt Museum

This museum, 1111 Washington Ave., displays more than 100 antique and contemporary quilts and attempts to keep alive this American tradition. Eugiana Mitchell, the museum's primary donor, taught quilting in the Rockies for more than 30 years and began a legacy of instruction that continues to this day. Museum docents also travel, offering lectures and workshops at schools and to community groups.

The museum is open Mon.–Sat. 10 A.M.–4 P.M. Admission is $3. For more information, call 303/277-0377.

Buffalo Bill's Grave and Museum

Even those who are not particularly interested in Buffalo Bill, or who feel the hunter, guide, and entrepreneur did as much to make a circus of the West as he did to open it up, will enjoy the drive up Lookout Mountain to his grave and the memorial museum. First of all, just the drive up is quite impressive, with a view from the top of Golden and of Denver in the distance. Second, you'll be surprised how quickly you'll have risen out of the scrubby foothill fauna and into the fresh-smelling pines.

The grave itself is small and unimposing, though the location is spectacular, and you can easily understand why the outdoorsman would want to be buried here—especially before the view was dominated by the gigantic Coors brewery, only partially obstructed by electrical wires and radio antennae. A small museum displays Cody's saddle, Western rifles, Sitting Bull's bows and arrows, supposedly from the Battle of the Little Big Horn, lots of Plains Native American clothing and gear, and, appropriately enough, barbed wire (one of the great contributors to the conquering of the West) from throughout the area.

In addition, there's a small souvenir and curio shop and a snack bar with homemade fudge. A picnic area, with barbecue pits and restrooms, is near the parking lot. The museum is open daily 9 A.M.–5 P.M. May–Oct., and Tues.–Sun. 9 A.M.–4 P.M. Nov.–April. Admission is $3 for adults, $2 for seniors, and $1 for kids. To get there, take 19th Avenue out of Golden, or Exit 256 from I-70. For more information on the Buffalo Bill Museum, phone 303/526-0747.

Dinosaur Ridge

As early as 1877, bones from allosaurus, stegosaurus, and brontosaurus dinosaurs were discovered on the site of this outdoor geological and paleontological museum. Today, visitors can view fossilized bones of these critters and more than 300 fossilized footprints of iguanodons, preserved in the sandstone.

The site is open year-round for self-guided tours along the one-mile ridge; 17 interpretive signs provide descriptions of the various fossil remains. On selected Saturdays and holidays from early spring through October, Dinosaur Ridge hosts "Open Ridge Days," when docents are available to answer questions. Admission is free. Shuttles are available (walk one way, shuttle back; $3). Guided tours can be arranged for groups ($35 for up to 12). You can also buy or rent cassette tapes describing the ridge's features and history.

Dinosaur Ridge is south of Golden near Morrison off Alameda Parkway (south of I-70). To get there from Denver, go west on I-70 to Highway 470 and go south; then take the north exit from Highway 470, and watch for the signs. From Golden, go south on Highway 93, past I-70 toward Morrison, and watch for the signs.

For information, or to make reservations for group tours, write 16831 W. Alameda Pkwy., Morrison, CO 80465, or phone 303/697-3466.

PARKS AND RECREATION

Golden Gate Canyon State Park

This 8,500-acre park about 15 minutes northwest of Golden offers hiking, fishing, horseback riding, camping (both backcountry and in campgrounds), cross-country skiing, and year-round sightseeing—from fields of wildflowers to deep, pine-forested hillsides and steep, rocky cliffs. Orient yourself at the visitor center, where you'll find exhibits of the park's flora and fauna, as well as naturalists and rangers to answer your questions and suggest the best ways to enjoy the park.

To get to the Golden Gate Canyon State Park, take Washington Avenue north to Golden Gate Canyon Road and turn left (west). From there it's about a 15-mile drive to the park's entrance. For more information, write the park at 3873 Hwy. 46, Golden, CO 80403, or phone 303/582-3707.

Golf

Golden's **Applewood Golf Course** is an 18-hole public course just east of town at 14001 W. 32nd Ave.; phone 303/279-3003 for tee times and information.

Hiking

In addition to the 50-plus miles of marked trails meandering through Golden Gate Canyon State Park, **Jefferson County Open Space** also has its own 14,000-acre park system, with nearly 100 city-, county-, and recreation-district-managed parks, many with excellent hiking and sightseeing possibilities. Check out **Apex Trail**, which takes hikers from Heritage Square in Golden to the **Jefferson County Nature Center** on Lookout Mountain, and from there to **Beaver Brook Trail.** You can also get to Beaver Brook Trail from a trailhead and parking lot a few miles up 19th Avenue en route to the Buffalo Bill Museum (watch for the sign and small parking lot). Up there, chances are good you'll get to see a hang

glider or two, as this is a popular launching site for these crazy sky pilots.

For maps and more information on hiking in the Golden area, phone the administrative offices of Jefferson County Open Space at 303/278-5925.

TOURS

In addition to the tours of the Coors Brewery (see above), the Historical Preservation Board of Golden designed a self-guided walking tour of historic Golden, specifically the town's 12th Street District, which is on the National Register of Historic Places. Included on the tour are the Astor House Hotel Museum (see above) and many residences dating from the 1860s, as well as Colorado's original National Guard Armory (1913), the largest cobblestone building in the country (made from 3,300 wagonloads of stone from Clear Creek).

ACCOMMODATIONS

Golden's accommodations range from state park campgrounds to mom-and-pop-type motels and chain hotels. The **Table Mountain Inn,** 1310 Washington, 303/277-9898, offers comfortable and convenient accommodations in a Southwestern (adobe) setting for $100–150. Just up the street is the **Williamsburg Inn Bed and Breakfast,** 1407 Washington, 303/279-7673. Also very nice. Each of the 10 units goes for about $100. The **Golden Hotel,** 11th and Washington, 303/279-0100, has 62 units downtown, some with whirlpools (about $100). Also in Golden are: **Days Inn,** 15059 W. Colfax, 303/277-0200 ($50–100); and the **Holiday Inn Denver West,** 14707 W. Colfax Blvd., 303/279-7611 ($100–150).

Golden Gate Canyon State Park (see above), 303/582-3707, about 20 minutes from downtown Golden, offers RV and tent sites, with laundry facilities and showers. **Clear Creek Campground,** 303/278-1437, just west of town (take 10th Street from Washington), also has tent and RV sites, showers, and a dump station. Showers at the campground are open to

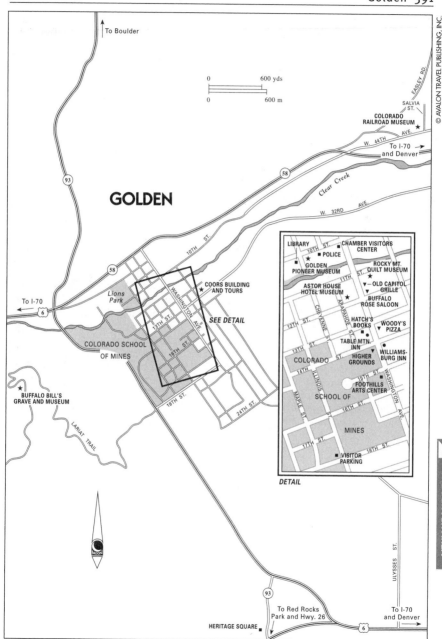

To Boulder

0   600 yds
0   600 m

© AVALON TRAVEL PUBLISHING, INC.

EASLEY RD.

SALVIA ST.

COLORADO RAILROAD MUSEUM ★

W. 44TH AVE.

To I-70 →
and Denver

GOLDEN

Clear Creek

W. 32RD AVE.

To I-70 ←

Lions Park

COORS BUILDING AND TOURS ★

SEE DETAIL

COLORADO SCHOOL OF MINES

★ BUFFALO BILL'S GRAVE AND MUSEUM

LARIAT TRAIL

10TH ST.
13TH ST.
WASHINGTON AVE.
16TH ST.
19TH ST.
24TH ST.

DETAIL

LIBRARY ■
★ ■ POLICE
GOLDEN PIONEER MUSEUM ■
10TH ST.
11TH ST.
CHAMBER VISITORS CENTER ■
★ ROCKY MT. QUILT MUSEUM
▼ — OLD CAPITOL GRILLE
ASTOR HOUSE HOTEL MUSEUM ■
BUFFALO ROSE SALOON ■
12TH ST.
CHEYENNE ST.
ARAPAHOE ST.
HATCH'S BOOKS ■
★ TABLE MTN. INN ■
WOODY'S PIZZA ●
13TH ST.
HIGHER GROUNDS ●
WILLIAMS-BURG INN ●
COLORADO
14TH ST.
FOOTHILLS ARTS CENTER ●
WASHINGTON AVE.
SCHOOL OF
MAPLE ST.
ILLINOIS ST.
15TH ST.
16TH ST.
MINES
17TH ST.
18TH ST.
■ VISITOR PARKING

93

To Red Rocks Park and Hwy. 26

HERITAGE SQUARE ■

To I-70 and Denver

ULYSSES ST.

THE DENVER AREA

the public (small fee). **Scenic Rock RV Park** is an upscale campground five minutes west of Golden at 17700 W. Colfax, 303/279-1625.

FOOD

From Old West saloon-style diners, to Mexican restaurants, to fast-food franchises—Golden's got something for just about every appetite and budget. For starters, try **Higher Grounds,** 803B 14th St., 303/271-0998, offering an enticing range of coffees and pastries, including scones, bagels, and muffins (from 6:30 A.M.). The **Old Capitol Grill,** 1122 Washington, 303/279-6390, is popular among tourists and downtown businessfolk. Open for lunch and dinner daily, with entrées (burgers to steaks) running $7–18. The **Mesa Bar and Grill,** 1310 Washington, 303/277-9898, at the Table Mountain Inn, is popular for lunches and Sunday brunch with a Southwestern flair. Entrées run $8–17. Another good bet is **Woody's Wood-Fired Pizza,** 1305 Washington, 303/277-0443, where you can catch a Rockies or Broncos game or shoot a game of pool while munching on a pizza, calzone, or plate of pasta ($5–7).

The area's most upscale restaurant is probably the **Briarwood Inn,** 1630 8th St., 303/279-3121. Chicken, beef, and other entrées run $10–22. Fast-food freaks can satisfy their cravings at Wendy's, Dairy Queen, and other joints.

ENTERTAINMENT

Visitors to the **Heritage Square Music House** can see a wide range of musical theater—from Victorian-era melodrama to '50s rock 'n' roll—produced by local musicians and actors. Dinner shows include a buffet with salad bar and choice of entrée. For current prices and schedule, or to make reservations, phone 303/279-7800. The **Buffalo Rose,** 1119 Washington, 303/279-5190, is a little downtown bar featuring live music Thurs.–Sat. nights (sometimes other nights). Local and touring acts—some surprisingly well known—both take the stage. Rick Derringer, Edgar Winter, Charlie Musselwhite, and Delbert McClinton have all played the Rose.

Foothills Art Center, at 15th and Washington in downtown Golden, features art galleries with rotating exhibits, an artisans' showcase for local artists, and a gift shop. In addition, the center offers workshops, demonstrations, lectures, poetry readings, and concerts, and each year from late November to Christmas the center is the site of the Holiday Art Market.

For current information on Golden entertainment, check the *Rocky Mountain News, The Denver Post,* and the local paper, the *Golden Transcript.*

CALENDAR

Golden's annual events calendar is virtually booked solid with a variety of things for both visitors and locals to see and do—from free concerts in the downtown park to fireworks displays, parades, bike races, and car, gun, flower, and art shows. Among the highlights: **International Heritage Festival of Folk Arts** (mid-June), **Fourth of July fireworks, Buffalo Bill Days** (late July), and the **GoldenFest** (mid-September). For more information on these and other Golden events and activities, phone the Golden Chamber of Commerce at 303/279-3113. Also be sure to check the local newspaper, the *Golden Transcript,* for current goings-on.

SHOPPING

Golden is particularly proud of its **Heritage Square,** a re-created late 19th-century Western village with boutiques, gift shops, restaurants, and even an Alpine slide and other rides for the kids. Open daily 10 A.M.–6 P.M. (till 9 P.M. Memorial Day through Labor Day). Phone 303/279-2789.

In the downtown you'll find a variety of boutiques, galleries, and specialty shops.

SERVICES

The **Golden Police Department** is at 911 10th St., 303/279-3331. Contact the **Jefferson County Sheriff** at 303/277-0211 and the local offices of the Colorado **State Patrol** at 303/273-1616.

Jefferson County's general hospital, **Lutheran Medical Center,** is at 8300 W. 38th St., Wheatridge (between Golden and west Denver—take the Wadsworth Boulevard exit from I-70); phone the hospital at 303/425-4500 (425-2089 in emergencies).

Golden's main **post office** is at 619 12th St., 303/278-8537.

Recycling

Drop off aluminum, glass, newspaper, and plastics at **Evergreen Disposal,** 15969 S. Golden Rd., 303/278-6000.

INFORMATION

For more information on Golden and Jefferson County, write the **Golden Chamber of Commerce,** P.O. Box 1035, Golden, CO 80402, 303/279-3113, or stop by its offices at the corner of Washington and 10th. For online information, check out the website at www.goldencochamber.org. For books and other publications on the area, stop in at **Hatch's Books,** 807 13th St., 303/279-7095. The Jefferson County **public library,** 303/279-4585, is at 923 10th St., and the **Arthur Lakes Library** (largest map collection in the area), 303/273-3690, is on the campus of the Colorado School of Mines.

For **road conditions** in the Golden area, phone 303/639-1111 (westbound).

TRANSPORTATION

Golden is about a half hour by car from Denver. Get there by heading west on either I-70 or U.S. 6 (West 6th Avenue). Turnoffs are well marked. You can also get to Golden from Denver by bus (Golden's part of the Denver metro Regional Transportation District); phone 303/778-6000. **Golden West Shuttle,** 303/422-1277, provides limousine, taxi, and shuttle service throughout the Golden area.

Idaho Springs, Georgetown, and Silver Plume

Interstate 70 barrels west past the turnoff to Golden and then begins to lift slightly into the sorrel foothills of the Front Range before winding dramatically up into the Rockies' steep and forested canyons, finally rising entirely above the timberline just east of Loveland Pass. From the junction with U.S. 6 (to Golden) to the east side of Eisenhower Tunnel, the road snakes its way through Clear Creek Canyon, where the water, particularly during late-spring runoff, roars riotously toward the plains.

Had you found yourself in this part of Colorado between the early 1870s and 1893, when the silver market crashed, you would have witnessed a canyon teeming with miners, merchants, and railroad workers, and your ears would have buzzed with sounds of men building cabins, mills, and smelters, which they either squeezed into the canyon floor or hung hopefully from cliffsides. Three communities grew out of this mad rush (which eventually produced more than $90 million in silver, gold, copper, and zinc): Georgetown, Idaho Springs, and Silver Plume, which today provide both entertaining and educational tableaux of Colorado's past.

HISTORY

Though a handful of small gold claims were staked in Upper Clear Creek Canyon in the late 1850s, by the mid-'60s silver became the area's most abundant, lucrative, and sought-after ore. Idaho Springs (originally called Jackson's Diggin's, after an early gold miner) was named for the nearby hot springs, which attracted aching and arthritic pioneers. Georgetown was named after George Griffith, another early Clear Creek miner, who came down from Central City around 1860.

Placer mining was the first method of extracting ore from the canyon, and it wasn't long before the few mines played out. By the 1870s, however, lode mining had been developed, and by the middle of the decade Georgetown, home to 5,000 people, was the third-largest city in

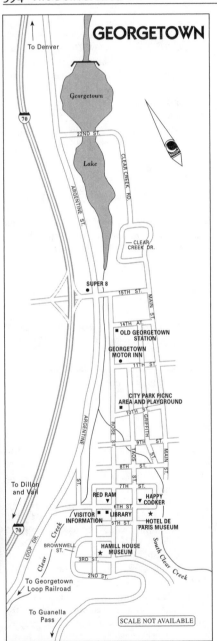

GEORGETOWN

To Denver

Georgetown

70

22ND. ST.

Lake

CLEAR CREEK RD.

CLEAR CREEK DR.

SUPER 8

15TH ST.

MAIN ST.

14TH AT.
OLD GEORGETOWN
STATION
GEORGETOWN
MOTOR INN

11TH ST.

ARGENTINE ST.

CITY PARK PICNC
AREA AND PLAYGROUND

10TH ST.

ROSE ST.

GRIFFITH

9TH ST.

MAIN ST.

TAOS ST.

8TH ST.

ARGENTINE ST.

7TH ST.

RED RAM

HAPPY
COOKER

6TH ST.

To Dillon
and Vail

70

VISITOR
INFORMATION

LIBRARY

5TH ST.

HOTEL DE
PARIS MUSEUM

LOOP DR.

Clear Creek

BROWNWELL
ST.

HAMILL HOUSE
MUSEUM

3RD ST.

South Clear Creek

2ND. ST.

To Georgetown
Loop Railroad

To Guanella
Pass

SCALE NOT AVAILABLE

© AVALON TRAVEL PUBLISHING, INC.

THE DENVER AREA

Colorado; until silver was discovered in Leadville in 1878, Georgetown was the most important silver camp in the state.

The Colorado Central Railroad reached Georgetown in 1877. With the completion a few years later of the Georgetown Loop Railroad, which connected Georgetown and Silver Plume, two miles upstream, silver could be much more easily transported out of the canyon. When silver fell off in 1893, though, many of Clear Creek Canyon's residents left for towns whose economies were not strictly dependent on mining. Many of Georgetown's and Idaho Springs's homes and businesses were abandoned.

Still, a few persistent miners stayed, working away in a labyrinth of tunnels beneath the earth's rocky crust, and in 1910 the Argo Tunnel, connecting Idaho Springs and Central City, was completed. In the 1930s, when gold and silver began once again to command high prices, some of Clear Creek Canyon's mines reopened. Today, Georgetown, Idaho Springs, and Silver Plume rely heavily on tourism to keep their economies stable, as well as on the abundance of nearby recreational opportunities—particularly skiing, cycling, camping, fishing, and hiking.

SIGHTS

Georgetown Historic District

Even if you're just passing through and don't have time for the railroad and mine tours, you'll enjoy a few hours poking around the restored Victorians and gift shops in downtown Georgetown.

Of particular interest in Georgetown are the **Hotel de Paris Museum** and the **Hamill House Museum.** At one time one of the best-known hotels west of the Mississippi—for its elegant design and cuisine, as well as for its controversial builder/owner/proprietor—the Hotel de Paris has been restored with original furnishings that suggest the building's, and area's, colorful past.

Louis du Puy, born in Alençon, France, in 1844, as the wealthy and titled Adolphus Francis Gerard, came to Georgetown in 1869. Injured in a mining accident in 1873, he later bought Georgetown's Delmonico Bakery in

1875 and immediately set about converting it to a hotel to rival those he remembered from his homeland. Known as a fine cook, philosopher, misogynist, and all-around crank, albeit an intelligent and well-educated one, du Puy was rumored to have been a deserter from the French army. As a hotel proprietor, du Puy constantly angered and amused the residents of Clear Creek Canyon, for most of whom he had little or no respect. Nor did du Puy care much for his guests—only those who met his capricious demands were permitted to stay, while others, upon earning his disfavor, would be ordered to leave midstay. When du Puy died in 1900, he willed the hotel to Sophie Galet, about whom history seems to know little, except that she was the widow of a French cabinetmaker, worked for du Puy at the hotel, survived him a scant four months, and was buried beside him as she had requested.

classic Georgetown architecture

© STEPHEN METZGER

The Hotel de Paris Museum is at 409 6th St. in Georgetown; open to visitors daily 11 A.M.–4:30 P.M. from Memorial Day through September, and weekends noon–4 P.M. the rest of the year. Admission is $4 for adults, $3 for seniors over 60, and $2 for ages 6–16. For more information phone 303/569-2311.

The Hamill House, built in 1869 by silver baron and politician William Hamill, is a restored Victorian home, once one of the most elegant in Colorado Territory. With an interior rich with marble, walnut, and glass, as well as gas lighting and central heating, the house is testament to the wealth the Rockies' mines (and miners) brought to their owners.

The Hamill House, in Georgetown at 305 Argentine St., is open daily 10 A.M.–4 P.M. Memorial Day through September, and weekends noon–4 P.M. Oct.–December. Admission is $5 for adults, $4 seniors, and $3 for kids. Phone the Georgetown Society at 303/569-2840 for more information.

Georgetown Loop Railroad

This six-mile tour takes passengers from Georgetown to Silver Plume (and back) via a narrow-gauge steam train that winds through Clear Creek Canyon, up Devil's Gate High Bridge (100 feet high, 300 feet long). Included on the trip is a stop at the Lebanon Mine and Mill, with an optional added tour.

World-famous as an engineering marvel when completed in 1884, the railroad was all but forgotten—in fact, the tracks were completely torn up in 1939—from the turn of the century until 100 years after its inauguration, when the route was restored. Today, round-trip tours begin from either Silver Plume (9:20 A.M.–4 P.M.) or Georgetown (10 A.M.–3:20 P.M.), with a slide show at the Georgetown depot and a gift shop in Silver Plume. Trains run daily late May through October, departing every hour and 20 minutes (allow 2.5 hours for the loop and mine tour, an hour and 10 minutes for just the train ride). Adult rates are around $12.95 ($5 more for the mine tour), $8.50 for kids (mine tour, $3). Reservations recommended.

Note: the Lebanon Mine tour, led by guides from the Colorado Historical Society, takes you 600 feet underground, and it gets cold (44°F) and wet. If you plan to include the mine on your trip, bring warm clothes (hardhats provided). Also, wear comfortable shoes, as the tour includes a quarter-mile hike into the mine—the tunnel actually bores under I-70, which skirts the hillside above the mine. Mine tours are offered Memorial Day through Labor Day only.

To get to the depots, take I-70 Exit 226 (Silver Plume) or Exit 228 (Georgetown). You can also buy tickets at the Old Georgetown Station Visitor Information Center, 1106 Rose St., Georgetown. For more information, phone 303/569-2403 or 800/691-4386. You can also send away for brochures by writing P.O. Box 217, Georgetown, CO 80444, or get information online at www.gtownloop.com.

Georgetown Walking Tours
Guided walking tours of Georgetown's historic district are offered twice a day (10:30 A.M. and 1:30 P.M.) on weekends Memorial Day through Labor Day. The 90-minute tours include the Hamill House, the Hotel de Paris, old firehouses, churches, and private residences (no entry). Tours, sponsored by the nonprofit Historic Georgetown and costing about $5 per person, begin at the Georgetown Community Center, 613 6th Street (be sure to call ahead for availability). You can also arrange private and weekday tours by appointment. For information, phone 800/472-8230.

Georgetown Carriage Tours
You can also tour Georgetown by horse-drawn carriage. **Rutherford Carriage** is a private company offering 45-minute jaunts through historic Georgetown, with custom trips for groups, weddings, and other private parties. For more information and rates, phone 303/569-2675.

Argo Gold Mine, Mill, and Museum
The Argo Mill, in Idaho Springs, was built in 1913 as a processing plant for much of the area's ore, primarily brought down from Central City via the four-mile-long Argo Tunnel. In 1943, the Argo Mine flooded and the mill shut down; today it's on the National Register of Historic Places and open to the public for self-guided tours from late May through mid-October, 10 A.M.–7 P.M. It's at 2350 Riverside Dr.; admission is $9 adults, $5 for ages six and under. For more information, phone 303/567-2421.

Phoenix Mine
A small, family-owned mine first worked in the early 1870s, the Phoenix offers guided public tours during which you can experiment with 19th-century mining tools as well as pan for gold (keep what you find). Open daily 10 A.M.–6 P.M.; group tours by appointment. Admission is $9, $5 for children under 12.

Take Exit 239 at Idaho Springs, go one mile west on the frontage road, and take Trail Creek Road. For more information, or to book group tours, phone 303/567-0422.

Mt. Evans Road/Highway 103
The highest paved road in the country, this breathtaking and sometimes unnerving route climbs out of Clear Creek Canyon, winding through spruce, fir, and pine to Echo Lake. At Echo Lake, the road quickly leaves timber behind and nearly reaches cloud level, clinging to rocky hillsides of glacial moraine and offering stunning views of the Front Range, as well as the dozens of Rockies sub-ranges sprawling to the north, west, and south. Eventually, the road rises to 14,260 feet, where a small lookout station affords one of the most awesome views on the planet.

At the small, alpine Echo Lake, you'll find a picnic area, a Forest Service campground, and the **Echo Lake Lodge,** a restaurant (buffalo burgers, pastas) and gift shop. You can also stop below Echo Lake at two picnic areas: sit streamside at **Chicago Forks** or enjoy great views at **Ponder Point.**

horses in downtown Georgetown

Note: this road is neither for the faint of heart nor large RVs, and weather sometimes keeps it closed anyway. It's 28 miles to Mt. Evans; allow one hour each way. For road conditions, check at the Arapaho National Forest Information Center (see below).

PARKS AND RECREATION

Georgetown, Idaho Springs, and Silver Plume are surrounded by Roosevelt and Arapaho National Forests, whose lands abound with campgrounds, hiking trails, and streams for fishing. Whether you're a cross-country skier, ice climber, mountain biker, or mule trainer, you'll find lots of area to explore.

An excellent source for maps, advice, and general information is the **Arapaho National Forest Information Center** (Clear Creek Ranger Station), at the west end of town at the junction of Highway 103 and I-70 (take Exit 240), 303/567-2901 or 303/893-1474.

If you're just passing through and looking for a nice place to pull off the road, check out the quiet little creekside picnic area in downtown Idaho Springs at the corner of Colorado Boulevard and 23rd Street—no overnight camping. There's also a very nice city park in Georgetown, about a quarter mile east of the central historic district, with picnic benches and a playground.

Walking tours of Idaho Springs are available by calling 303/569-4709.

Downhill Skiing

Whoever coined the term "centrally located" could certainly have been referring to the Clear Creek Canyon area and its relation to Colorado's ski areas. Within an easy hour's drive (weather permitting) lie some of the finest slopes in the country: Winter Park, Arapahoe Basin, Copper Mountain, Vail, and several others. In addition, the mountain roads provide access to some of the state's finest expert-only off-piste skiing. A favorite is **Loveland Pass,** where you can drive up, hoist your skis ashoulder, hike along the ridge top, and ski down to a waiting car. When all that's left of the snow are a few scattered patches and the resorts are closed (as

late as June for Arapahoe Basin), downhill die-hards head to **St. Mary's Glacier,** where you can ski year-round. Take the Fall River Road exit from I-70 (two miles west of Idaho Springs). For more information, phone 303/567-2191.

The nearest lift-serviced downhill skiing is at **Loveland Basin,** a small family-oriented resort 12 miles west of Georgetown near the east entrance to Eisenhower Tunnel. Loveland offers more than 800 acres of skiable terrain, equipment rental and sales, a restaurant, and day care. Though not as large as the resorts just a few miles farther west, the resort charges only $25 for a full-day adult lift ticket—a *huge* bargain in today's world of $60 tickets. For more information on Loveland, write P.O. Box 899, Georgetown, CO 80444, or phone 303/569-3203 or 800/736-3754; see the website at www.skiloveland.com.

Cross-Country Skiing

Arapaho National Forest provides virtually unlimited cross-country skiing opportunities within a few short miles of these little towns and the interstate connecting them. Again, the ranger station (at I-70 Exit 240) is an excellent source for maps and general information. Write P.O. Box 3307, Idaho Springs, CO 80452, or phone 303/567-2901 or 303/893-1474.

Cycling

The steep roads leading into the high country above Clear Creek Canyon are excellent for in-shape riders, and they get surprisingly little auto traffic, considering their proximity to the busy interstate. Colorado touring clubs hold a number of races and rides in the area.

Highway 103, winding south from Idaho Springs (Exit 240), offers a gently rising ride alongside the rippling waters of Chicago Creek. If you turn onto Highway 5 (Mt. Evans Road) at the junction (about 14 miles south of Idaho Springs), you'll be in for one doozy of a ride—the road now rises suddenly toward the treeline, over it, and twists up nearly to the 14,264-foot summit of Mt. Evans. At Summit Lake, you'll find a small picnic area with tables and restrooms.

For information on mountain biking in the area, stop by the Clear Creek ranger station.

Hiking

The Clear Creek area is surrounded by miles and miles of excellent hiking trails and backpacking wonderlands, much of it within the borders of Arapaho National Forest. Among the better designated trails are **Chicago Lakes Trail,** south of Idaho Springs off Highway 5, **Summit Lake Trail,** a 12-mile walk-that-turns-to-climb from Echo Lake Campground to the summit of Mt. Evans, and the **Griffin Monument Trail,** a two-mile hike from downtown Silver Plume to a hillside monument erected to honor a 19th-century English miner.

Fishing

Though Clear Creek looks awfully trouty from the road, fishing has been all but ruined by the century and a half of mining in the area. Locals like to work Chicago Creek, south of Idaho Springs along Highway 103 (respect private property), and the lawn-chair crowd competes for the rainbows regularly stocked in the easily accessible Georgetown Lake, at the east end of town.

White-Water Rafting

Clear Creek Rafting, 303/567-1000 or 800/353-9901, offers a range of trips on several different rivers, including the Arkansas River and Clear Creek near Denver. Rates start at about $35 for a short local jaunt and go to $350 for a three-day trip on the Arkansas. For more information, check out the website: www.clearcreekrafting.com.

ACCOMMODATIONS

You'll find a handful of relatively inexpensive ($50–100) motels along Colorado Boulevard on the east end of Idaho Springs. Among the newest and nicest are the **Heritage Inn,** 303/567-4473, and **H and H Motor Lodge,** 303/567-2838. Just before Colorado Boulevard feeds back onto the freeway, you'll find a couple of other motels, including the **Peoriana Motel,** 303/567-2021.

Indian Springs Resort, 303/567-2191, is a hot springs with a long history (the resort claims

Jesse James, Walt Whitman, Teddy Roosevelt, and Bo Diddley were visitors). Today the resort offers mineral baths, vapor caves, a swimming pool, and the "Club Mud" (a mud puddle touted as capable of cleansing both skin and soul). You can get a room in either the main resort building (130 years old and "rustic"; sink and toilet only) or in the recently built inn or lodge across the street. Rooms run $50–100, which includes access to the hot springs.

In Georgetown, you'll find rooms in the same range at the **Georgetown Super 8,** 1600 Argentine, 303/569-3211, and the **Georgetown Motor Inn,** 1100 Rose St., 303/569-3201.

The **Hardy House Bed and Breakfast,** 605 Brownell, 303/569-3388, has five rooms (each with private bath) in an 1880 Victorian—plus an outdoor hot tub. Rooms run $75–125.

In nearby Empire, you can stay at the **Peck House,** 83 Sunny Ave., 303/569-9870, built in 1862 as a stage stop. Claiming to be Colorado's oldest hotel, the Peck House has been wonderfully restored, and its hillside location (and dirt-road entrance) truly make the visitor feel like a time traveler. The Peck House dining room has won many awards, and it is an especially popular Sunday-brunch spot. Rooms run $50–100; some don't have private baths. Oh, and the Peck House is said to be haunted. . . . Also in Empire, the **Empire House Bed and Breakfast,** 268 E. Park (U.S. 40), 303/569-2557 or 888/569-2557, has five very nice rooms with private baths ($100–150); see the website: www.empirehousebb.com.

Camping and RVing

In the heart of Arapaho National Forest, the Georgetown–Idaho Springs–Silver Plume area is naturally very near to some excellent campgrounds. One particularly nice one is **West Chicago Creek Campground** about nine miles west of town just off Highway 103 (take Exit 240 from I-70). Go south on Highway 103 for six miles, and then follow the signs up a short dirt road to Chicago Creek. Sites are $8 a night.

You'll also find several campgrounds just west of Idaho Springs near the junction of I-70 and U.S. 40. At Exit 232, take U.S. 40 three miles toward Winter Park to the privately owned **Mountain Meadow Campground.** If you'd rather be in the national forest, continue on U.S. 40 for another couple of miles, and almost as soon as you cross back into Arapaho National Forest, you'll find **Mizpah Campground,** where nice shaded sites lie right on Clear Creek, with well water and pit toilets; fee is $8 a night. There are also two Forest Service picnic areas nearby (well marked from the highway): **Clear Creek** and **Big Bend,** both piney, shaded, and cool.

FOOD
Start Me Up
At 2805 Colorado Blvd. at the east end of Idaho Springs, **Marion's of the Rockies,** 303/567-4611, serves breakfast specials daily, as well as biscuits and gravy, eggs, pancakes, and waffles, from 6 A.M.—this is where local contractors scarf down big breakfasts before heading out to their job sites. **Mainstreet, A Restaurant,** at 1518 Miner St., Idaho Springs, is a popular local hangout and down-home kind of place, where waitresses call everyone "Hon." Lots of pancake dishes, including the "Skier's Special" (blueberry), as well as other standard American breakfast fare—prices range $3–6. Mainstreet also serves lunch—sandwiches, burgers, etc.—for $3–8. For lighter fare—espresso and regular coffees, as well as pastries—check out **Java Mountain Roasters,** also in Idaho Springs at the corner of Miner and 15th.

Other Restaurants
A local favorite is **Tommyknocker Brewery and Pub,** 1401 Miner St., 303/567-2688, which occupies a building that has served as a lunch stop on the Colorado Central Railroad and a vintage 1929 bowling alley. Typical brewpub fare—homemade pastas and sausages, miners' stew, Cornish pasties, etc.—runs $6–12. Just down the street, the **Buffalo Restaurant,** 1617 Miner, 303/595-2729, serves a wide range of buffalo-based lunches and dinners (burgers, stew, hot dogs, buffaloaf, fish, chicken, salads, and sandwiches) for $6–15. The relatively new

restaurant has a great feel to it, with huge, high-beamed ceilings, hanging plants, and an overall good-time ambience (though the mounted buffalo heads watching you eat can be a bit disconcerting. . .). The attached **Buffalo Bar** is a favorite nightspot among locals and tipped-off passers-through (particularly skiers heading home to Denver).

Some of the best pizza in the Denver area can be devoured at **Beaujo's Colorado-Style Pizza,** just down the street at 1517 Miner, 303/567-4376. A favorite among Denver-area pizza aficionados, Beaujo's regularly wins rave reviews from local media and readers' polls. Idaho Springs is also home to the excellent and unpretentious **Szechwan Fu,** 1744 Miner St., toward the middle of town, 303/567-9378. Though prices at this little Chinese restaurant top out at $16–18 for dinner specials and seafood (lobster with hot Szechwan sauce), you can order off the south end of the menu and get a huge and satisfying meal for $5–7. The chow and lo mein noodles are excellent, as are the *moo shu* vegetables.

In Georgetown, try the **Red Ram Restaurant and Saloon,** 606 6th St., 303/569-3263. Part Old West saloon and part family restaurant, the Ram serves good food (burgers, salads, pastas) at reasonable rates. The **Happy Cooker,** 412 6th, (across from the Hotel de Paris Museum), 303/569-3166, is a good choice for a hearty breakfast, lunch, or dinner. Daily specials ($4–8) include waffles, soups, lasagna, and homemade bread. Open seven days a week.

INFORMATION
The **Town of Georgetown Visitor Center** is at 404 6th Street. Stop in for more information on dining, lodging, and exploring the area. Before your visit, write P.O. Box 426, Georgetown, CO 80444, or phone 303/569-2555. You can also get information from the **Georgetown Society,** P.O. Box 667, Georgetown, CO 80444, 303/569-2840, and the **Idaho Springs Visitors Information Center,** P.O. Box 97, Idaho Springs, CO 80452, 303/567-4382 or 800/658-7785. You can also stop by the center at the intersection of Colorado Boulevard and Miner Street. For

THE DENVER AREA

books and maps, stop in at **Gingerbread Books,** 435 Miner in Idaho Springs, 303/567-2304.

For excellent Internet information on both Idaho Springs and Georgetown, visit www.clear creekcounty.com.

WEST OF GEORGETOWN

Loveland Pass

Once featured in *National Geographic* magazine as one of America's most harrowing passes for interstate truckers, Loveland is a twisting, turning, switchbacking climb to well above the treeline (at 11,992 feet, it's over *two miles* high). In the late spring of 1973, Eisenhower Tunnel was opened, so motorists traveling between Denver and Summit County no longer had to go up and over the pass, which is especially nasty in winter. The tunnel is the wisest way to go if your main objective is to get where you're going as quickly (and as safely) as possible. But if you've got an extra half hour or so (when the road's clear), and if your brakes are good, take the drive over the pass. The views are astounding, and it's one of the best ways to get a real sense of the Rockies. When snow lingers on the mountainsides, watch for skiers, who drive up the pass, hike along the ridge top, and ski down (recommended for experts only!). Also see the special topic on Eisenhower Tunnel in the Summit County chapter.

Boulder

The Berkeley of Colorado? The Chamonix of the Rockies? A bastion of upscale fitness freaks, politically progressive intellectuals, New Age tofu heads, and the last remnants of 1960s' hippiedom?

Perhaps. Of course it's easy to resort to reductionism when trying to capture the essence of a town and its people in a few words. And it's neither possible nor fair to classify Boulder (pop. 96,727; elev. 5,340 feet) and Boulderites. Sure, in the early 1990s, *Outside* magazine named it the number-one town in the country for outdoor sports, and the city has a disproportionate amount of open-space-designated land. Granted, the state's number-one academic institution—the University of Colorado—is one of the town's major influences. Yes, you do see more Saab Turbos, BMWs, Jeep Wagoneers, and other Yuppie rigs here than you do anywhere east of Marin County, California. True, you're likely to find a copy of *The Teachings of Buddha* sharing space with Gideon's Bible in your motel-room nightstand. And, okay, longhaired, barefoot street musicians still strum Dylan tunes on street corners, their guitar cases open for coins.

But still, Boulder is its own town, completely defying classification. The only generalizations you can safely make about the city are: (1) that it's diverse; and (2) that for a relatively small town a *long* way from the cosmopolitan influences of either coast, it's remarkably tolerant. Tolerant, that is, of just about everything but outsiders. Unfortunately, as the town has grown—housing blanketing once-green pastures, traffic snarled at dozens of intersections—so has an anti-newcomer attitude. You can't blame Boulderites for wanting to preserve their little Eden, but then, it was someone else's paradise long before they came.

HISTORY

In part because the Boulder area was once sacred to several different Native American tribes (predominantly Arapahoe), the line between mythology and history often blurs, creating a folklore that both defines and reflects the town's rare blend of whimsy and stubborn intellectualism. Among the legends of the region is Chief Niwot's (Chief Left Hand's) curse, profoundly proximate to the hearts of thousands of transplanted Boulderites who originally came with no intentions to stay but just to vacation or attend the university. According to the curse, anyone who sets eyes on the area will be so drawn to it that she will be unable to leave, leading eventually to the area's overcrowding and self-destruction (some claim the curse has already proved itself prophetic).

White Settlement

Evidently, Chief Niwot's curse is grounded in history and is linked with his first encounter with white settlers.

In 1858, Captain Thomas Aikens led a small group of settlers up the South Platte River and, after spotting the area through a telescope from the walls of Fort St. Vrain, described it as "right for gold and the valleys. . . rich for grazing." Shortly thereafter, Aikens led a splinter group from the main wagon train and set up camp at what is today Boulder. Also camped in the area was a group of Southern Arapahoe, led by Chief Niwot. According to the WPA guide to Colorado, when the two men first met, Niwot asked Aikens if he remembered when the stars fell. Aikens responded that it was 1832, and Niwot told him he was correct, and that that was the year the whites first came. Then Niwot pointed to a comet in the sky and said:

From then on, the natives in the area pretty much left the white settlers to their own devices, watching from woods as the newcomers planted crops, dug irrigation ditches, carved roads, and built structures with corners.

[its tail pointed] back to when the stars fell as thick as the tears of our women shall fall when you come to drive us away.

Three days later, Niwot, after asking the whites to leave (and being rebuffed), came alone to Aikens's camp and told of a dream he had had: Boulder Creek had overflowed, the Arapahoe had been washed away, and the whites were saved. From then on, the natives in the area pretty much left the white settlers to their own devices, watching from woods as the newcomers planted crops, dug irrigation ditches, carved roads, and built structures with corners.

Boulder City

As early as 1859, Boulder City, then part of Nebraska Territory, was being laid out, with the first 4,044 lots selling for $1,000 each. By 1860, the town claimed 324 residents; in 1861, a federal bill put the town officially in Colorado Territory.

During the 1860s, Boulder's survival depended largely on its proximity to both the plains and the mountains, with crops as well as gold contributing to its economy. Still, though, Boulder was more a trading center for goods than a supply source, and the 1860s weren't really the best of times for the town; eventually many of the area's early settlers became discouraged and left. Things began to look up in the early 1870s, however, when the town began to build schools and the tracks of a couple of railroads (Colorado Central and Boulder Valley) reached town. In 1871, Boulder was incorporated (and "City" dropped from the name), and in 1874, the state legislature approved $15,000 for the construction of the University of Colorado, on the condition that the community match the funds, and work was begun on Old Main, which still stands tall, like the campus patriarch that it is. The first class of freshmen consisted of just 12 students, yet by 1880 the university population was over 3,000.

With the establishment of the university, the school's and the town's history and development became complexly intertwined. At the turn of the 20th century, the campus claimed more than 6,000 students, and the university "Hill" began to develop into the colorful blend of small businesses, university-affiliated buildings, and student housing found there today.

It was also around the turn of the last century that Boulder was first targeted for its tourism potential. In 1898, the Colorado Chautauqua was built at the base of the Flatirons by a group of Texans looking for a place to escape the heat of the summer lowlands. Included were an auditorium, dining hall, community center, and more than 100 cottages. Chautauqua is still

© AVALON TRAVEL PUBLISHING, INC.

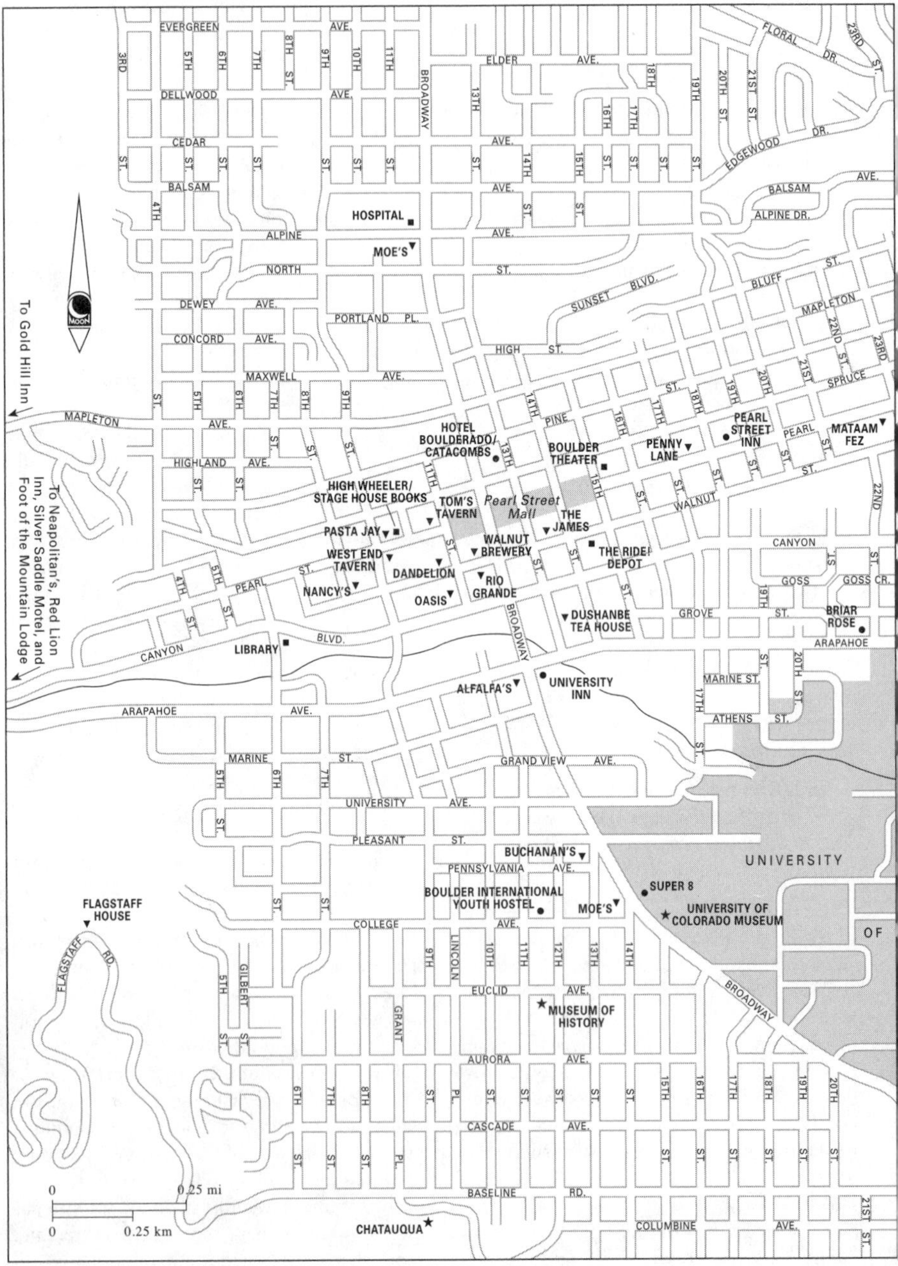

THE DENVER AREA

To Gold Hill Inn

To Neapolitan's, Red Lion Inn, Silver Saddle Motel, and Foot of the Mountain Lodge

EVERGREEN AVE.
DELLWOOD
CEDAR ST.
BALSAM
ELDER AVE.
BROADWAY
13TH
HOSPITAL
MOE'S
ALPINE AVE.
NORTH ST.
SUNSET BLVD.
BLUFF
MAPLETON
ALPINE DR.
BALSAM AVE.
DEWEY AVE.
PORTLAND PL.
CONCORD AVE.
HIGH ST.
MAXWELL AVE.
MAPLETON
HIGHLAND AVE.
SPRUCE
PINE
PEARL
HOTEL BOULDERADO/ CATACOMBS
BOULDER THEATER
PENNY LANE
PEARL STREET INN
MATAAM FEZ
HIGH WHEELER/ STAGE HOUSE BOOKS
TOM'S TAVERN
Pearl Street Mall
WALNUT
PASTA JAY
WALNUT BREWERY
THE JAMES
THE RIDE DEPOT
CANYON
WEST END TAVERN
DANDELION
RIO GRANDE
GOSS
GOSS CR.
NANCY'S
OASIS
DUSHANBE TEA HOUSE
GROVE
BRIAR ROSE
PEARL
CANYON
LIBRARY
BLVD.
ARAPAHOE
ALFALFA'S
UNIVERSITY INN
MARINE ST.
ATHENS ST.
ARAPAHOE AVE.
MARINE ST.
GRAND VIEW AVE.
UNIVERSITY AVE.
PLEASANT ST.
BUCHANAN'S
PENNSYLVANIA AVE.
UNIVERSITY
FLAGSTAFF HOUSE
BOULDER INTERNATIONAL YOUTH HOSTEL
MOE'S
SUPER 8
UNIVERSITY OF COLORADO MUSEUM
OF
COLLEGE AVE.
FLAGSTAFF RD.
GILBERT
GRANT
LINCOLN
EUCLID AVE.
MUSEUM OF HISTORY
BROADWAY
AURORA AVE.
CASCADE AVE.
0   0.25 mi
0   0.25 km
BASELINE RD.
CHATAUQUA
COLUMBINE AVE.

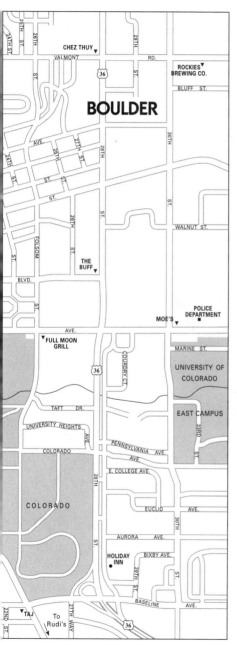

used today for music festivals, conferences, and retreats, and cabins can still be rented by individual parties (see Accommodations, below).

Postmodern Boulder

At the end of World War II, Boulder's population took a significant leap, as the university attracted students on GI loans. By the late 1960s, Boulder began to establish a reputation as one of the counterculture's strongholds, a sort of geographical, political, and spiritual link between Madison and Berkeley. The town was known locally as "the People's Republic of Boulder," and the area nightclubs were hosting some of the best rock and folk bands in the country, thanks primarily to the students. Susan Berman, author of the 1971 book *The Underground Guide to the College of Your Choice,* wrote:

> *For the most part it looks like Berkeley—heavy hip types, mostly freaks. Lots and lots of hair and beards and fringed leather jackets and old jeans, chicks without bras wearing all kinds of good stuff ... Chicks are very liberated ... Entertainment is balling ... Survival is easy. Plenty of drugs, cohabitation, and smiles.*

"I Don't Know Why, They Call Someplace Paradise, Kiss It Good-bye"

Well, the times they have a-changed, and today Boulder's once indisputable "paradise" status is threatened. While plenty of "freaks" still live here, so do lots of Porsche-driving baby boomers seemingly oblivious to the problems outside their city. Indeed, a local joke defines Boulder as "20 square miles surrounded by reality." And while the city's shockingly large homeless population continues to grow, new homes—huge and homogenous—sprawl ever further across the hillsides north and east of town. Predictions are that by the year 2020, nearly a million more people will be living in the area. How to control this inevitable growth? It's a tough question with no easy answer, but a significant number of

Boulder residents seem conscientious enough to make every attempt to preserve what they can of their little piece of heaven.

SIGHTS

Face it. You don't go to Boulder to go to museums. *But,* if you need some time off from mountain biking, hiking, and outdoor sightseeing, or if the afternoon brings with it a storm that makes doing indoor activities more sensible, the town does offer a handful of museums and other attractions worth checking out.

University of Colorado Museum

With three stories of small rooms—some with revolving exhibits—the CU museum features a good display of Southwestern cultures, with Anasazi pottery and Clovis and Sandia points; one wing is devoted to prehistory, with dinosaur fossils and bones, including the skull of a triceratops, and a display of the evolution of the horse, with the hooves and skull of the tiny Eohippus. Kids will love Discovery Corner ("Please Touch"), which teaches them about X-rays, seashells, and starfish. There's also a gigantic bird exhibit. Hours are Mon.–Fri. 9 A.M.–5 P.M., Saturday 9 A.M.–4 P.M., and Sunday 10 A.M.–4 P.M. Admission is free. Phone 303/492-6892 for information. The museum is on the main CU campus just off Broadway. Look for the signs.

Boulder Museum of History

This museum, which occupies an 1899-vintage Victorian home just west of the university, displays items from the town's past—quilts, dolls, china, a huge dollhouse, and other domestic artifacts. On the second floor is a small gift store specializing in books on Boulder's and the state's history. Hours are Tues.–Fri. 11 A.M.–4 P.M. and weekends noon–4 P.M.; group tours offered by appointment. Admission is $3. The museum is at the corner of 12th and Euclid Streets. Adjacent to the museum is Beach Park, lawny, shady, and perfect for picnicking. Phone 303/449-3464 for more information.

University of Colorado Heritage Center

In "Old Main," the University of Colorado's first building, this museum contains a variety of arti-

© STEPHEN METZGER

the Courtyard at the University of Colorado

facts from the area's past, as well as historical photos and photos of well-known CU alumni. Open Tues.–Fri. 10 A.M.–4 P.M. Phone 303/492-6329 for more information.

National Center for Atmospheric Research

Situated on a gorgeous 360-acre site in the Boulder foothills just southeast of the Flatirons Mountains, the National Center for Atmospheric Research (NCAR) was designed by I. M. Pei and is the world's foremost research center for scientists studying weather—"from the tiniest snowflake to the cataclysm of droughts and hurricanes." Known as Mesa Laboratories, it is open to visitors Mon.–Fri. 8 A.M.–5 P.M. and weekends and holidays 9 A.M.–3 P.M. Both guided and self-guided tours are offered (a highly detailed map, with explanatory text, makes the self-guided tour informative and rewarding). View the massive supercomputer system and the 30-foot-high portable automated mesonet (PAM), a weather station that measures wind speed and direction, temperature, humidity, and air pressure. Check out the display of some absolutely stunning photographs of lightning.

To get to NCAR, take Table Mesa Road west from Broadway and follow the signs to the parking lot. Tours are Mon.–Sat. at noon in the summer. Admission is free. For more information, phone 303/497-1174 (recorded tour information) or 303/497-1000 (main office).

Leanin' Tree Museum of Western Art

With the largest privately held collection of Western art in the country, from Native American work to contemporary landscapes and sculptures, this museum also has detailed information about each piece, the artist, and how the work was acquired. Leanin' Tree is one of the largest publishers of Western, wildlife, and regional-interest greeting cards—available in the gift shop. Open Mon.–Fri. 8 A.M.–4 P.M. and weekends 10 A.M.–4 P.M. Admission is free. For more information, phone 303/581-2100.

PARKS AND RECREATION

This is what Boulder's all about. Named the country's number-one sports town by *Outside* magazine, Boulder at times looks like an amusement park for outdoor lovers. No sooner do you cross over into the city limits than the whole landscape comes alive with runners (*not* joggers), cyclists, and overall the most active, healthy-looking people you've seen this side of an Olympic training camp. In fact, many world-class athletes live and train in Boulder. Among them are Norway native Ingrid Kristiansen, who won the 1989 New York Marathon and holds the record for the women's 10,000 meters; and Christian Griffith, a Boulder native and former member of the United States Rock Climbing Team.

And it's not only the people who'll tell you this is one outdoor-oriented town. Pull into any parking lot, or take a look at the cars on the street: skis, bikes, kayaks, sailboards, climbing gear, and every kind of outdoor equipment imaginable is strapped, bungie-corded, or racked atop and stuffed into the backs of 4WD Jeeps, Subarus, and other rigs built for the mountains.

Hiking

Boulderites claim that one of the true beauties of living in the area is the easy access to so many wonderful hiking areas. In fact, many homes in town literally lie within a few yards of trailheads leading into some magnificent country.

Boulder's prime close-to-town hiking is in and around **Chautauqua Park** on the southwest side of town. Newcomers to town will be amazed to find such a place exists within the city limits. At the base of the Flatirons and reached by taking Baseline Road west from town, Chautauqua begins as a sloping meadow, then quickly (within a few hundred yards) gets into some steep, rocky, and piney backcountry that feels miles from nowhere—with several different trails webbing up into the woods. If you'd rather start a bit higher, continue up Baseline (it turns into Flagstaff Mountain Road) into the **Boulder Mountain Parks,** where you'll find more than 33,000 acres of city open space and 100 miles of trails. In fact, it seems a trailhead awaits around every bend in the road—and there are *lots* of those, as the road switchbacks steeply up the mountainside. In addition to the trailheads, picnic tables are scattered along the road, especially at the top, where you'll find 20 or so, along with grills and a shelter (groups can reserve the facility by calling the city **Parks and Recreation Department** at 303/441-3400). A bonus of hiking on Flagstaff Mountain is the views—you look directly down on Boulder, a great way to orient yourself to the city.

A plethora of hiking trails are also in the lower reaches of **Sunshine Canyon** at the west end of Mapleton, and farther up the road on Bald Mountain. Good hiking trails also begin at NCAR. (See National Center for Atmospheric Research, above).

Another hike, albeit a much shorter one than most of those in the Chautauqua or Sunshine Canyon area, is one that begins not far above the Pearl Street Mall. Just west of the mall, where Pearl Street joins Canyon Road, is a small parking lot and trailhead. From there, a short hike takes you up the side of the hill to some redrock outcroppings and an excellent view of Denver and the valley.

When you're ready to head out of town a ways, one of the best places to hike is up by the **Eldora Ski Area.** Take Canyon Road to Nederland, turn south on Highway 119, and turn off at the ski area; follow the paved road to the trailhead. Several great hikes wander into the mountains. You can follow the creek, hike up to **Lost Lake,** or let your soul get lost in the high peaks; whether you just want to get outside and sniff the mountain air or get into serious hiking, this area offers excellent opportunities.

Golden Gate Canyon State Park also offers excellent hiking, as well as fishing and camping. A sprawling park off Highway 119 between Nederland and Blackhawk, Golden Gate Canyon offers a wide range of trails—from simple roadside walks, or strolls to nearby lakes, to serious backcountry challenges, with close to 30 campsites accessible only by foot. For more information, phone the park at 303/582-3707.

This is just a small sampling of available hiking near Boulder; it would take a book-length guide to list everything. Besides, you want to do some exploring on your own, don't you? (For some excellent guides to the area see Suggested Reading in the Resources section).

For maps and more information on hiking in and around Boulder, stop by the **Boulder Mountain Parks Ranger Cottage** at Chautauqua Park (south end of parking lot by main entrance at Grant and Baseline), or phone 303/441-3408. Boulder Mountain Park Trail Maps are $3. You can get information from the **City of Boulder Open Space Operations/Ranger Services** at 1405 S. Foothills Hwy., 303/494-0436. Open Space Trail maps are $5.

Cycling

One of the first things you'll notice about Boulder is that just about everyone rides—mountain bikes, touring bikes, racing bikes. In fact, according to a recent *Colorado Daily* article, seven out of every 10 Boulderites own cycles. And so of course the area's got miles and miles of bike trails, including a wonderful trail system that will take you just about anywhere and everywhere in the city you want to go. Commuters, students, weekend cyclists, and out-of-towners make sure the Boulder Bike Path gets lots of use.

More serious riders head out of town, though—into the canyons or up the switchback roads like the one up Flagstaff Mountain. Following are just a few basic suggestions. For more information, contact the **University of Colorado Bike Office,** 303/492-7384, the **Bike Touring Group of the Colorado Mountain Club,** 303/554-7688, Boulder's **Alternative Transportation Center,** 303/413-7304, or most any bike shop in town. The City of Boulder Bicycle Program also has more information on routes, and can provide you with maps, brochures, and safety manuals; phone 303/441-3216.

East Boulder Trail: This is the longest of the city's off-road trails. Pick it up at the Teller Farm Trailhead on Arapahoe Road between 75th and 95th Streets.

Signs point the way to hiking trails near Eldora Ski area, outside of Boulder.

Flagstaff Mountain: If you're really in shape and want to give your legs the ultimate workout, head up Flagstaff Mountain (from Baseline). This is one rude ride as the road rises by a series of serious switchbacks, but the rewards should be great—not only the knowledge you did it, but the views of Boulder you'll get along the way (assuming you can keep the sweat from your eyes). The four-mile ride rises 900 feet.

Gold Hill-Nederland Loop: Another serious ride is the loop (or any part thereof) winding up out of town via Mapleton Road, over Bald Mountain, through Gold Hill, down into Nederland, and back to town through Boulder Creek Canyon. (Note: a good part of this road is not paved—in fact, it's downright rutty—and you'll need fat tires, not to mention legs of iron, to make it the entire way.)

You can also do this loop the opposite direction; many riders head up Boulder Creek Canyon, where a not-so-steep paved path follows Highway 119 and the creek out of town. After a few miles, the pavement ends, then continues as dirt for a bit longer before joining the highway; if you continue on the curvy road, you need not only be in good shape but constantly vigilant for cars, which are known to drive this road faster than they ought.

Boulder-to-Jamestown Loop: This 34-mile round-trip ride begins at the corner of Broadway and Canyon. Take Broadway eight miles east to Left Hand Canyon Drive. After about six miles, watch for James Canyon Drive, a four-mile stretch that takes you to Jamestown.

Rollins Pass: Originally a section of the Northwestern and Pacific Railway, this route took passengers—en route between Denver and Winter Park—over the Continental Divide from 1903 to 1927, when the Moffat Tunnel was completed. Eventually the tracks were torn out, and today the road is a popular 4WD vehicle pass and one of the premier mountain-bike routes in the state. You can catch the pass at a number of different places (get a map), but the main road runs from Rollins, on Highway 72 south of Nederland, over to Winter Park.

For a complete guide to mountain-bike riding in the Boulder area, stop by any bike shop and pick up the **Boulder Mountain Biking Map.** Also, watch the *Colorado Daily* (CU's newspaper) for regular articles about mountain biking and recommended trails.

Bikes, Rentals, and Equipment: Among Boulder's shops that rent bikes is **Dooby's Bicycle Shop,** 2700 Canyon, 303/546-6438.

Further Reading: If you're serious about biking in the Boulder area and throughout the state, you ought to pick up a copy of Jean and Hartley Alley's *Colorado Cycling Guide* (Pruett Publishing Company, Boulder). This exhaustive book examines back-road and main-route tours around Colorado for both weekend cyclists and serious tourers. Included are more than 30 different trips, with several variations on each one. Learn how to get from Denver's International Airport to Boulder, as well as where to ride in Telluride. The authors also include maps, photos, discussions of difficulty, brief histories of several of the towns along the way, suggestions for accommodations, and contact listings of interest to Colorado cyclists.

Fishing

The lakes and streams around Boulder, including many operated by the city, offer good fishing for both warm- and cold-water species. **Boulder, Viele,** and **Lagerman** Reservoirs are popular for boat and shore fishing, as are **Wonderland** and **Thunderbird** Lakes, **Walden** and **Sawhill** Ponds, and **Barker Meadow Reservoir** in Nederland. Among the streams attracting trout fishermen are the Middle and South Forks of **St. Vrain Creek, Left Hand Creek** between Left Hand Reservoir and Buckingham Park, **North Boulder Creek** between Highway 72 and Boulder Falls, **Middle Boulder Creek** from its headwaters to 28th Street (special restrictions within city limits), and **South Boulder Creek** from its headwaters to Baseline Road (special restrictions between Walker Ranch and South Boulder Road).

You'll also find excellent trout fishing in the streams and lakes of the high country west of town. For more information on fishing in Boulder, phone the Colorado Division of Wildlife, 303/297-1192, City of Boulder Open Space, 303/441-3440, or County of Boulder Open Space, 303/441-3950. For gear, information, local tips, or guided trips, stop in at **Rocky Mountain Anglers,** 1904 Araphoe, 303/447-2400.

Golf

Boulder's 18-hole **Flatirons Golf Course,** at 5706 Arapahoe Ave., is among the more popular public links in the area; phone 303/442-7851 for information and tee times. Five miles north of town on Neva Road, **Lake Valley Golf Club** is another 18-hole course open to the public; phone 303/444-2114.

Other courses in the area include: **Haystack Mountain Golf Course,** 5877 Niwot Rd., 303/530-1400; **Sunset Municipal Golf Course,** 1900 Longs Peak (Longmont), 303/776-3122; and **Twin Peaks Municipal Golf Course,** 1200 Cornell (Longmont), 303/772-1722.

TOURS

From historical walking tours through specific areas of downtown to jeep, mining, railroad, brewery, and national-park tours, you needn't look far in Boulder. Even commercial tours are available: **Celestial Seasonings** tea makers, 4600 Sleepytime Dr., 303/581-1202, is based in

Sunday brunchers at the Chautauqua Dining Hall

Boulder and offers free tours of the production and packaging plants and of the research-and-development lab. Tours begin on the hour Mon.–Sat. 10 A.M.–3 P.M. and Sunday 11 A.M.–3 P.M.

Boulder Historical Tours

Every Sunday from early June through September, groups meet at the Hotel Boulderado at 10 A.M. and 1 P.M. for tours of Boulder's historical districts. The 90-minute tours visit one of seven different areas (the Whittier neighborhood, Mapleton Hill, Columbia Cemetery, Downtown, University of Colorado, University Hill, and Chautauqua) on a rotating basis; $3 per person (groups of 10 or more should make reservations). Twilight tours are also offered twice a month. Wear good, comfortable walking shoes. Phone 303/444-5192 for more information.

Chautauqua Park Historic District

An only-in-Boulder experience is an exploration of Chautauqua Park, which you can do on your own or on a group tour, available by appointment, focusing on the history and architecture of the park. Tours last approximately 45 minutes (some stair climbing) and include information about current programs and activities. Tours can be customized to your group's interests and needs. Cost is $2.50 per person. Phone 303/442-3282, ext. 14.

Scenic Drives from Boulder

If you want to see the Boulder area without having to worry about driving and parking, it may help to have a guide, yet being your own guide can be far more rewarding. And since the area abounds in stunning scenery, with scenic drives lasting from 20 minutes to several days in length, you really owe it to yourself to get out and do a little exploring. Following are but a few of the many routes providing fascinating history and stunning scenery.

One of the more popular day trips is the loop into Estes Park via the north part of the Peak to Peak Highway. Start by heading out Canyon Road through Boulder Creek Canyon. At Nederland, turn north on Highway 72. This road takes you past the old mining town of Ward, along the eastern side of Rocky Mountain National Park (with several access roads to picnic areas and campgrounds along the way), through Allenspark and Ferncliff, Meeker Park, and into Estes Park. In Estes Park, you can either catch U.S. 34 west into Rocky Mountain National Park, or you can loop back through Lyons and into Boulder via U.S. 36 east.

A shorter, but more demanding (at least on your car) tour is a mostly dirt road up through the mining town of Gold Hill and back into Boulder via Nederland and Boulder Creek Canyon. Take Mapleton Avenue west out of town into some of Boulder Open Space lands (you'll pass several trailheads leading up into the hills), and follow it to Bald Mountain and then down into Gold Hill; just west of Gold Hill, you'll come back onto Highway 7 (where you'll turn south), which will take you back down to Nederland. Allow at least 1.5 hours—more if you want to get out and hike, or wander around Gold Hill or Nederland.

Another popular day excursion is the 80-mile round-trip southwest to Black Hawk and Central City. The scenery is stunning along the way, although by the time you get to Central City you'll have met up with hordes of other visitors—mostly tourists taking day jaunts from Denver—and if the point of your trip was to get out and "away from it all," you're probably better off heading elsewhere (on weekends in the summer, traffic can be backed up bumper to bumper a half mile *outside* Central City, while motorists wait to park). If, on the other hand, you're in the mood for wandering through casinos or going on mine tours, then an afternoon in Central City might be just the ticket.

ACCOMMODATIONS

As you'd figure, Boulder offers a full range of lodging options, from bare-bones budget to outrageous opulence. You can camp, stay in a hostel, check into a motel, or go first class by staying in one of the city's luxury hotels. For a complete list of Boulder accommodations, go to www.bouldercoloradousa.com.

Boulder Chautauqua

For no-frills yet uniquely Boulder accommodations, consider a room or cottage at Boulder Chautauqua. Rent by the day, week, month, or season in this quiet, self-contained mini-community at 900 Baseline Rd., right at the base of the Flatirons. The two lodges (13 and 15 rooms) and the 61 cottages are throwbacks to the turn of the 20th century, when the Chautauqua was founded. Maintained by the City of Boulder, the complex features a gorgeous old dining hall, an auditorium, and spacious lawns and hiking areas. Ideal for a quiet getaway or isolated retreat. Lodging includes film viewing and nightly forums on various topics.

Rates for lodge rooms and cottages at the Boulder Chautauqua run $50–100, with three-room cottages topping out at about $130 (minimum of four consecutive nights for the cottages). For a complete brochure, write Colorado Chautauqua Association, Chautauqua Park, Boulder, CO 80302, phone 303/442-3282, or go to www.chautauqua.boulder.net.

Hotel Boulderado

Boulder's most elegant hotel is the Hotel Boulderado, 2115 13th St., 303/442-4344 or 800/433-4344, made famous in song and story (John Prine sings about the pre-restoration days, "at the dark end of the hall"). Built just after the

THE DENVER AREA

turn of the last century and first open for business on New Year's Day 1909, the hotel underwent renovations in the 1980s and today has more than 100 rooms, plus restaurants and convention facilities, while still retaining its early 20th-century feel. Centrally located, the hotel is within easy walking distance of the Pearl Street Mall, The Hill, and the University of Colorado neighborhoods. Doubles are $150–250.

Other Hotels and Motels

Boulder hosts a large number of hotels and motels, some right along the highways, some tucked up in canyons and hidden in trees, others right downtown.

The following all offer good clean rooms in the $100–150 range: **Residence Inn by Marriott,** 3030 Center Green Dr., 303/449-5545; **Holiday Inn Express,** 4777 N. Broadway, 303/442-6600; and **Days Inn,** 5397 S. Boulder Rd., 303/499-4422 or 800/325-2525.

The **Silver Saddle Motel,** 90 W. Arapahoe, 303/442-8022, claims one of the choicest lodging sites in Boulder. On the city's west end, right at the entrance to Boulder Creek Canyon, this unassuming little motel features 32 units ($50–100), some with kitchenettes; fall asleep to the sound of Boulder Creek tumbling by. A few bends downstream, **Foot of the Mountain Motel,** 200 Arapahoe Ave., 303/442-5688, offers 18 quiet, perfectly located log cabin-style rooms on the creek ($50–100).

Another lodge with an ideal location is the **Boulder Mountain Lodge,** 91 Four-Mile Canyon, 303/444-0882, with motel rooms, kitchenettes, bunkhouse rooms, and campsites ($50–100). The motto of **University Inn,** 1632 Broadway, 303/442-3830 or 800/258-7917, is "in the center of things," and that's a pretty decent description of its location. With the university directly to the south and the Pearl Street Mall three blocks to the north, this lodge offers excellent access to libraries, shopping, and biking ($50–100).

If you're just passing through and you don't want to get off the beaten track, try **Super 8,** 970 28th St. (U.S. 36), 303/443-7800 or 800/525-2149, or **Golden Buff Best Western,** 1725 28th St., 303/442-7450 or 800/999-BUFF (999-2833). Both $50–100.

Hostels

The **Boulder International Youth Hostel,** 1107 12th St., 303/442-0522, is on The Hill just a couple of blocks west of campus (under $50). The office for **American Youth Hostels** is in Boulder at 1310 College Ave., 303/442-1166.

Bed-and-Breakfasts

Downtown at 2151 Arapahoe, near both the university and the Pearl Street Mall, the **Briar Rose Bed and Breakfast,** 303/442-3007, has 11 rooms in a secluded old home, and you can either lose yourself in privacy or join other guests around the fire or on the sun porch. Rates are $100–150. See the website at www.briarrosebb.com.

In 1985, a classic downtown Boulder Victorian was restored into the **Pearl Street Inn,** 303/444-5584. This elegant inn, 1820 Pearl, offers private rooms, a restaurant, full bar, and meeting rooms for up to 30 and banquet facilities for 150. Rooms are $100–150 ($190 for the suite). Visit the website at www.pearlstreetinn.com.

Camping and RVing

Boulder is virtually surrounded by campgrounds—or at least national forest lands where you can camp anywhere anyway. In addition, two state parks, **Eldorado Canyon** and **Golden Gate Canyon,** are within short drives of town. And, perhaps most spectacular of all, **Rocky Mountain National Park** is only about 45 minutes away.

Kelly-Dahl Campground is one of many in the nearby Roosevelt National Forest. With 46 units, running water and pit toilets, trailheads leading up onto the Continental Divide, and some of the most stunning vistas on the Front Range, this is a choice little campground. You'll find it three miles south of Nederland on Highway 119—$7 per night. Other Roosevelt National Forest campgrounds include **Camp Dick,** in the Middle St. Vrain Recreation Area; **Olive Ridge,** about 15 miles south of Estes Park on North St. Vrain Creek next to Rocky Mountain

National Park; **Peaceful Valley,** on Highway 72 southwest of Lyon; and **Rainbow Lakes** and **Pawnee,** north on Highway 72 just north of Nederland. For more information on camping in Roosevelt National Forest, stop by the district ranger station in Boulder at 2995 Baseline Rd., Room 16, or phone 303/444-6001.

Golden Gate Canyon State Park, just off Highway 119 south of Nederland, offers camping for all tastes. **Reverend Ridge** touts more than 100 sites with hookups; **Aspen Meadows** has nearly three dozen tent-only sites, with some 30 backcountry sites scattered throughout the park (which features more than 50 miles of hiking trails). In addition, the park offers stream and lake fishing (check out the rainbows in the pond near the visitor center—sorry, no fishing allowed there) and stunning Front Range scenery. For maps and information, phone Golden Gate Canyon State Park at 303/582-3707.

Rocky Mountain National Park offers thousands of square miles for camping, hiking, and backpacking, with entrances on both the west (Grand Lake) and east (Estes Park) sides. (See the section on the park in the North-Central Colorado chapter.)

Closer to town (five miles up Boulder Creek Canyon), **Boulder Mountain Lodge,** 303/444-0882, offers creekside tent and RV sites (in addition to the motel—see above).

FOOD
Start Me Up
The Buff, 1725 28th St. (just behind the Golden Buff Best Western, mentioned above), 303/442-9150, offers a nicely varied menu of inexpensive breakfasts and brunches. Despite its unappealing exterior (it lies tucked into a crowded corner of the motel's parking lot), The Buff strives for the look and feel of a Rocky Mountain lodge on the inside, with antique snowshoes and climbing equipment hanging from the walls and pictures of local climbers from "back in the day." The waitstaff exudes the kind of Western hospitality that attracts locals from all age groups and backgrounds; on a late Sunday morning, you're likely to find a few well-dressed young families

newly arrived from church, several harried but attentive students with their visiting parents, some big-buckled and high-coiffed ranchers from just outside of town, and the occasional lone writer. The Buff serves basic egg breakfasts, Benedict variations, omelettes and frittatas, and a few salads and sandwiches (ask for extra garlic on the Caesar). Potato fans will want to try one of the skillets of spuds mixed with meats and/or cheese and eggs. For the sweet-toothed, the pecan quesadilla is an unusual treat. Open Mon.–Fri. 6:30 A.M.–2 P.M., and weekends 7 A.M.–2 P.M.

Juice and Java
Coffee, schmeared bagels, and juice are the main fare at **Moe's Broadway Bagel,** at three locations: the flagship at 2650 Broadway, 303/444-3252; on The Hill at 1116 13th St., 303/448-9064; and in the mall zone at 3075 Arapahoe, 303/442-4427.

The espresso set heads to **Buchanan's Coffee Pub,** on The Hill just across from the university at 1301 Pennsylvania, 303/440-0222, or **Espresso Roma,** up the street at 1101 13th, 303/442-5011.

For some real local color—of the tie-dyed variety—stop in at **Penny Lane,** 1795 Pearl St., a few blocks east of the mall, 303/443-9516, where, for an only-in-Boulder experience you can check out the "wheatgrass happy hour" (Mon.–Fri. 2–4 P.M.).

Brunchish/Lunchish
Visitors who truly want a taste of Boulder need to have breakfast or lunch at the **Chautauqua Dining Hall,** in the shadows of the Flatirons at Chautauqua Park (900 Baseline Road), 303/440-3776. Eat inside in the high-ceilinged dining room as light slants in onto the polished hardwood floors, or, if you prefer, dine on the porch overlooking the park's lawns, wildflowered meadows, and rocky cliffs. As if that weren't enough, the food comes in generous portions and reflects the range of everything that is Boulder. For breakfast ($5–8) you can have the standard French toast or pancakes, or go with an omelette made with egg whites and nondairy soy cheese. For something lighter, try the fresh

fruit bowl or yogurt and granola. For lunch ($7–10), the Chautauqua specializes in healthful variations of old favorites—turkey burgers, spinach and pasta salads, quiches, and soups. To get there, take Baseline Road west toward the Flatirons and watch for signs to the park. Expect to wait a bit, as the place is popular, but it's hard to imagine a more pleasant spot to wait for a good meal. Open in summer for breakfast, lunch, and dinner daily; open the rest of the year, Sat.–Sun. 7 A.M.–2 P.M. for breakfast and lunch, and Wed.–Sat. 5–9 P.M. for dinner. Call ahead to be sure.

A newer Boulder institution is the **Dushanbe Tea House,** 1770 13th St., between Walnut and Canyon, 303/443-4993. A gift to the people of Boulder from their sister city of Dushanbe, Tajikistan, the Tea House is a traditional *tajik chakhona,* a kind of community gathering place. It was designed and built in Tajikistan, disassembled piece by piece, and then reassembled on its present site next to the Boulder Creek. Ornate tiling and detailed painted borders give it an exotic appearance from the outside, but it's only when you spend time walking around inside—examining the magnificent fountain and the exquisite wood, terra cotta, bronze, and fabric detail—that you fully appreciate the Tea House's beauty and cultural value. Lunch or dinner here can be a real treat. The creative menu includes a number of unusual vegetarian and carnivorous dishes for about $6–12.

If you're really out to impress somebody (or yourself), try lunch at **The Dandelion,** 1011 Walnut, just a block south of the mall, 303/443-6700. This place is fairly expensive ($7–10 for lunch), but worth it; creative soups and salads of mixed local organic greens get coupled with such fare as sashimi, guacamole terrine, grilled vegetables, and sage-roasted chicken with portobello potato cake. The service is attentive and the tablecloths are starched, yet the atmosphere is relaxed and airy; this is the best of what Boulder yuppiedom hath wrought. Worth a try.

For the more budget-minded, the **Walnut Brewery,** 1123 Walnut, 303/447-1345, captures much of the Boulder mystique—and it is an extremely popular gathering spot for locals.

Boulder's first brewpub, the Walnut serves beer made on the premises and a wide range of meals, from typical pub fare (fish and chips, bratwurst, burgers) to full-course dinner entrées, pastas, soups, and salads—a favorite is the duck enchiladas. To wash down the various beers, the Walnut also serves a variety of appetizers, including beer-shrimp boil and crab cakes. Of course the real attraction here is the beer. Varying from light ales and wheat beers to porters and stouts, the brew ranks right up there with the best from other microbreweries. Try a pint of Buffalo Gold, or get a sampler: six tastes for about $5. Dinners run about $9–18.

Speaking of beer, Boulder is home not only to a brewpub but to a microbrewery (do you know the difference?). The **Rockies Brewing Company,** 303/444-8448, home of Boulder Beer, has a tasting room and small restaurant that serves beer-cheese soup, salads, sandwiches, and burgers, Mon.–Fri. 11 A.M.–11 P.M. Take Valmont Road toward the Foothills Parkway and go south on Wilderness Place. The **Oasis Brewery and Restaurant,** downtown at 1095 Canyon, 303/449-0363, is another fine beer emporium popular with the young professional set.

There doesn't seem to be too much debate about where the best hamburgers in town are. **Tom's Tavern,** 1047 Pearl, 303/442-9363, serves a variety of burgers and sandwiches ($4–6) with excellent people-watching window booths and tables.

Later in the Day

For an inexpensive but fully satisfying dinner (or lunch), pasta fans swear by **Pasta Jay's,** on the mall at 1001 Pearl St., 303/444-5800. Fresh pastas (cheese tortellini, potato gnocchi, homemade ravioli) come in alfredo or pesto sauce, or baked in marinara from an old family recipe and smothered in mozzarella cheese. Favorites such as eggplant parmigiana are joined on the menu by such delectables as veggie cannelloni (stuffed with ricotta, spinach, sun-dried tomatoes, and artichoke hearts) and chicken Genovese (chicken breast stuffed with Italian sausage, roasted red peppers, provolone, and mushrooms). Deep-dish entrées are served with a side of pasta and garlic bread for a dinner that leaves you wishing you had more room. For a lighter appetite, the pizzas and sandwiches are great. A friendly staff and informal atmosphere make this a Boulder favorite.

Another popular restaurant is **Rudi's,** 4720 Table Mesa Dr., 303/494-5858, which serves a variety of international dishes made with local organic produce and free-range chicken. Open for lunch Tues.–Fri. 11:30 A.M.–2:30 P.M., for dinner Tues.–Sat. 5–9 P.M., and for brunch Sunday 9 A.M.–2 P.M. Closed Monday.

A little more upscale, the **Full Moon Grill,** 2525 Arapahoe, 303/938-8800, offers a nice range of well-prepared salads, pastas, and meats. Dinners range $10–25 and include such fare as crispy pan-seared duck breast and grilled Chilean sea bass. The excellent wine selection can be discussed with knowledgeable servers, and the atmosphere is cozy and private. Open Tues.–Sun. 5–9 P.M.

The **Boulder Cork,** 3295 30th St., 303/443-9505, is a favorite of locals in the know who are looking for a tasty steak or a hearty chicken or fish dish—and don't mind paying for it. Its many rooms are dimly lit and intimate, even when the place is full (which it often is), and its huge wooden chairs make you feel a little like you're dining in a medieval castle with contemporary decor. One room has a huge colored-glass collage on one wall; another offers a fire burning in the hearth. The Caesar salad is said to be the best in town, and the pepper steak also draws raves. Among the other choices are orange chicken, mahi-mahi, and grilled salmon salad. Entrées run $15 and up. The restaurant is set on the outskirts of town a bit, but it's worth finding. Go out any of the main roads that head east, turn north on 30th and continue just past Valmont.

For Some Cultural Diversity

If you'd like to step out of Boulder and into Morocco for a few hours (and do allow at least two hours), visit the **Mataam Fez,** 2226 Pearl, 303/440-4167. Dinner here is an event—from the authentic decor and cushioned, ground-level seating, to the hand-washing ritual before dinner, to the belly-dancing entertainment during dessert. One fixed price of $28 (wine not included) gets you a five-course feast of soup, traditional salads and appetizer plates, something called *b'stella* that should not be passed up, your choice of a main course, and dessert. The mint tea that accompanies the whole meal and the honey wheat bread offered time and again are downright sensual. Open every night at 6 P.M.

For the best Mexican food in town and margaritas that are so potent there's a house limit, get on over to the **Rio Grande,** 11th and Walnut, 303/444-3690. Excellent food and service at reasonable prices—dinners run $6–8. **Chez Thuy** (shay twee), 2655 28th St., 303/442-1700, offers a surprisingly diverse Vietnamese menu with more than 200 items ($7–29). A few miles south of town, **Rass Kassa's,** at South Broadway and El Dorado Springs Drive, 303/494-2919, prepares mild and spicy vegetarian and meat stews, served with traditional *injera* flatbread—a hearty and fulfilling dining experience.

Fans of Indian cuisine will want to try the **Taj,** 2630 Baseline Rd., 303/494-5216. Don't be fooled by its setting in the Basemar Shopping Center; up above the fray awaits a taste of India in a nice atmosphere with a view of the Flatirons. The tandoori chicken is nicely done, and the *saag paneer* is the best this side of Agra. Try one of the *thali* dishes if you're into variety. Open for lunch buffet Mon.–Fri. 11 A.M.–2 P.M. and Saturday and Sunday 11:30 A.M.–2:30 P.M., also 5–10 P.M. for dinner.

A half hour out of Boulder (but worth the drive) in Nederland, **Neapolitan's,** 303/258-7313, is a small, unassuming Italian restaurant. From the homemade rolls and salad dressings to the huge portions of lasagna, vegetarian combos, and other pasta specials, this fare is guaranteed not to disappoint. Complete dinners and pizzas are $5–13. All food can be ordered to go.

When the Boss is Buying

The **Flagstaff House,** 1138 Flagstaff Rd., 303/442-4640, on Flagstaff Mountain overlooking town, is one of the most famous and elegant restaurants in the entire Boulder-Denver area. Popular for high-class special occasions, it offers more than three dozen main courses

THE DENVER AREA

(including elk, Maine lobster, and pheasant breast) and a huge array of gourmet side dishes and other treats—from rattlesnake appetizers to cappuccino-chocolate mousse dessert. Entrées run $20–35. Those on special diets can call ahead to have the staff cook custom gourmet meals. Reservations requested. Take Baseline Road up past Chautauqua until it turns into Flagstaff Road and watch for the sign on your right. Incredible views.

Just a few miles up Boulder Creek Canyon is the popular and unique **Red Lion Inn,** 38470 Boulder Canyon Rd., 303/442-9368, specializing in wild game (elk, caribou, buffalo, pheasant, and others) and artful presentation—many of the dishes are prepared tableside. Dinners run $15–35, but early-bird specials are offered. Open from 5 P.M. daily.

In Gold Hill, about 10 miles west of and 3,200 feet above town, is the **Gold Hill Inn,** 303/443-6461, which is somewhat of an institution. It's been written up in several national magazines and has achieved a national reputation for huge and delicious dinners. The menu changes nightly, but entrées may include roast duck, paella, or venison.

ENTERTAINMENT

Boulder's a college town, which means it's a young town, which means there's usually a lot going on—from poetry readings to head-banging rock 'n' roll, from gallery openings to outdoor jazz. The best sources for what's happening are *The Colorado Daily,* the newspaper of the University of Colorado (available free around town); *Friday,* the supplement to Friday's *Daily Camera* (Boulder's daily newspaper; available in racks around town); *Westword,* Denver's free weekly alternative paper; as well as the Denver dailies, the *Post* and the *Rocky Mountain News.*

You can count on many clubs in Boulder booking quality acts regularly, and there's certain to be music to suit just about every taste. A favorite is **Tulagi,** on The Hill at 1129 13th St., 303/938-9090. This Boulder institution, having survived since the '60s, has featured hundreds of big-name acts and can always be relied

on for a distinctly Boulder evening, even if it's just a lineup of local college bands. Other clubs and theaters regularly booking live music are **The Catacombs,** 2115 13th St. in the Hotel Boulderado, 303/443-0486; and the **Boulder Theater,** 2030 14th St., 303/444-3600. If you have something a little tamer in mind, check out the Mezzanine at the **Hotel Boulderado,** 303/442-4344, an elegant place to dig some cool jazz—at 13th and Spruce.

Another classic Boulder bar is the **West End Tavern,** 303/444-3535. Now, even if the West End hadn't been named "best neighborhood bar" by both the Boulder *Daily Camera* and *The Denver Post,* this would still be one of the best spots in town to go sip a cold one. On a warm afternoon, it doesn't get much better than sitting up on the roof, with one of Boulder's best views of the Flatirons, and listening to some live music with friends while you work through a Boulder Pale. Just above the Pearl Street Mall, between 9th and 10th Streets, **Buchanan's Coffee Pub,** 1301 Pennsylvania on the Hill, 303/442-0222, features live folk, jazz, and blues most nights of the week.

Those who like to eat and be entertained at the same time can try the **Boulder Dinner Theater,** 5501 Arapahoe, 303/449-6000. Summer stock actors, based around the country, perform well-known and lesser-known plays and musicals. Tickets run $22–28.

Other typically Boulder ways to spend the evening include attending the **Shakespeare Festival** (see Calendar, below), poetry readings, public lectures and workshops, film festivals, and open-mike nights. Even a simple evening stroll down the Pearl Street Mall guarantees surprises and no small amount of entertainment (see Shopping, below).

CALENDAR

Boulder's annual events—much like the town itself—are incredibly diverse, from steeply serious to downright silly.

Kinetic Sculpture Challenge
Another only-in-Boulder attraction, this parade and "race" on Boulder Reservoir in early May

combines equal parts competitiveness, engineering savvy, and silliness. A bizarre array of human-powered vehicles tread and float (and often stall and sink) 'cross land and water before thousands of cheering spectators, many of whom have taken advantage of the bountiful food and drink booths available both at the pre-event parade at the Pearl Street Mall and the race at the lake. For more information, phone 303/444-5600.

Fourth of July

From fireworks to Frisbee, Boulder's Fourth of July events offer something for every taste and mood. One of the country's largest "Ultimate Frisbee" competitions (a noncontact team sport combining a bit of basketball, football, and soccer), usually runs three days around the Fourth; phone 303/443-6343 for more information. More than 50 years old, the annual Independence Day Celebration at Folsom Field features the Boulder Summer Concert Band, a sing-along, and fireworks. You can also see fireworks over Barker Meadow Reservoir in Nederland. **Note:** fireworks displays in the mountains, particularly in forested areas, are always subject to cancellation during fire season. Recent drought years have seen many scheduled displays nixed.

Shakespeare Festival

Founded in 1957, Boulder's Shakespeare Festival generally runs from late June through mid-August and tackles the full range of the bard's work—comedy, history, tragedy—with varying degrees of success. Recent productions have included *As You Like It, King Lear,* and *Richard III.* Part of what makes this festival so special is the theater itself: the Mary Rippon Outdoor Theater on the University of Colorado campus. Surrounded by ivy-covered stone buildings, the amphitheater and stage send even the most cynical playgoer back to 17th-century Stratford-on-Avon. Tickets to the festival range about $15–40. For information and reservations, phone 303/492-0554.

Colorado Music Festival

Very highly regarded—both locally and outside the area—Boulder's classical music festi-

val runs for six weeks, from mid-June to early August. Attracting some of the biggest names in the profession—musicians and conductors—the festival typically includes about two dozen concerts, with music by everyone from Bach, Beethoven, and Shostakovich to Ravel, Bernstein, and Gershwin.

As if the music weren't enough, the concerts are performed in Chautauqua Auditorium, where the shadow-of-the-Flatirons setting, combined with the turn-of-the-20th century structures, makes for the ideal concert locale. Tickets run about $12–40.

For information on the Colorado Music Festival, phone 303/449-1397.

SHOPPING
Pearl Street Mall

Boulder's famous Pearl Street Mall is certainly as much an attraction as it is a place to go shopping, for here's where you can see Boulder at its most crazy, colorful, and cosmopolitan, hip, happy, and unhomogenous. Join the parade of street musicians and jugglers, tourists from Tennessee, kids, families, and local students—everyone's having a good time. And if you get tired of strolling the five-block area, there are several cafés, restaurants, bars, and snack shops—many with sidewalk seating—where you can rest and refuel while the mall continues to buzz around you. Even in the evening after the shops close, street activities continue and the strollers keep strolling.

Among the more interesting shops are **Old Tibet,** 948 Pearl, a small import store with authentic clothing, jewelry, and other items from Tibet and Nepal. In the same building, **Narayan's Gateway to Nepal,** 303/440-0331, specializes in treks and tours to Nepal, Tibet, and India—run by native Nepali.

State of the Arts, a large import and craft store, stocks everything from Grateful Dead T-shirts to African and South American jewelry and clothing. **El Loro Jewelry and Clog Company** is the closest thing I've seen in a long time to a late '60s "head shop" (a true remembrance of things passed), selling incense, jewelry, T-shirts,

THE COLORADO MUSIC FESTIVAL

Every summer for about seven weeks, the Colorado Music Festival (CMF) fills Chautauqua Auditorium in Boulder with fine music and other artistic projects. Inside this century-old, barnlike structure with bare concrete floors, one can hear the rich tones of Mozart, Beethoven, Vivaldi, Mahler, and others. The bare wooden walls inside Chautauqua make for excellent acoustics because, according to former conductor and founding music director Giora Bernstein, the wood is a "live material" and "resonates the sound."

On Thursday and Friday nights, the Colorado Festival Orchestra (CFO) plays; on Sunday night the Festival Chamber Orchestra plays. World-renowned guest artists are often featured with both the philharmonic and chamber orchestras. Tuesday nights are for the Celebrity Series, solo and ensemble performances by CFO musicians and guest artists.

The Colorado Music Festival also offers a special humanities project each year: a series of concerts, lectures, and films focused on a central theme. Projects have included La Belle Epoche—Paris 1885–1914; Stravinsky—The Late Works; World War II through McCarthyism; Music of the Sixties; and Celebration: The Arts of Yamagata, Japan. One series included a tribute to the 50th anniversary of the founding of the United Nations.

The Chautauqua Auditorium sits at the base of a mountain and is elevated just high enough to provide a panoramic view of the town. In front of the hall is a long, lush, sloping lawn, perfect for enjoying the fresh air and sunshine, and maybe even a picnic, before a concert. In addition to the auditorium concerts, the CMF sponsors several free outdoor events, including a Young People's Concert and a Fourth of July Pops Concert.

The CMF is strictly a summer orchestra made up of musicians from all over the world. It has won two awards from the American Society of Composers, Authors, and Publishers, as well as the 1988 Governor's Award for Excellence in the Arts. In 1994, it won *Westword*'s "Best Classical Festival Award." CFO music has also been featured on National Public Radio and on European radio.

Chautauqua Auditorium is at Baseline and 9th. For schedule and ticket information, write 1525 Spruce St., Suite 101, Boulder, CO 80302, phone 303/449-1397. You can also get complete information at the CMF's website: www.coloradomusicfest.org. A bonus of the website is that you can both listen to music and buy CDs by the performers.

Thomas Owen Meinen

and, yes, clogs; my only question is, Where're the black-light posters? Across the street, **Ecology House,** much more than a faddy I-heart-baby-seals, limousine-liberal store, carries *good* books on survival (personal and environmental), posters, T-shirts, jewelry, bumper stickers, and lots of stuff for kids, with 10 percent of each sale going to environmental organizations. **Boulder Arts and Crafts Cooperative** is a large shop with jewelry, pottery, woodcarvings, weavings, stained glass, etc. by local artisans.

A couple of fun novelty shops include **Golden Oldies,** which carries a fine selection of funky vintage men's and women's clothing, from ties and hats to vests and dresses; and **Into the Wind,** 1408 Pearl, which specializes in wind toys—kites, wind chimes, weather vanes, Frisbees. And be sure to check out **Peppercorn,** 1235 Pearl St., which carries a huge array of gourmet kitchenware, as well as zillions of cookbooks and a huge selection of coffee beans.

Rue Morgue Mystery Bookshop carries *only* mystery/murder/detective novels (the name is from a story by Edgar Alan Poe, the grandfather of the mystery novel). Not only does the little shop carry books by mainstream authors (Raymond Chandler, Tony Hillerman, Robert Parker, etc.), but it stocks hundreds of titles by lesser-known writers as well—both new and used books.

If you're looking for food on the mall, you don't have to look far, but you do have to be able to make decisions—because there's a *lot* from which to choose, from Mexican to Chinese, pasta to popcorn. There's also a crepe cart, a vegetarian takeout place, and a pizza-by-the-slice shop. The **Trident Coffee House and Bookstore,** 940 Pearl, 303/443-3133, is an Old World–style coffeehouse serving espressos, other coffees, and pastries. The adjoining bookstore (you can walk between the two without stepping out onto the sidewalk) lends the place a legitimate literary air.

Public restrooms are about mid-mall, at the corner of Pearl and 13th.

The Hill

At 13th and College just west of the campus, the Hill is a collage of cafés, taverns, boutiques, and used-book and record stores. Bordering one of the city's densest concentrations of student housing, The Hill is a way hip hangout: coeds pierced and tattooed linger solo over cappuccinos and Camus; Lycra-shorted frat studs pound beers and trade insider information on papers in their fraternity files; transients hit up passers-by for spare change; freshmen, always walking a few steps ahead, give their parents the grand tour; and the music, incense, and even patchouli oil

waft from open doorways. A must for anyone visiting Boulder.

Particularly impressive are the book and record stores (three of each lie within a few hundred yards). Check out **Albums on the Hill,** 1128 13th St., specializing in rare albums; when you see some of the price tags you'll wish you hadn't donated your Herman's Hermits records to your little sister. While you're at it, wander into **Rock and Roll Posters,** 1091 13th St., or **Art to Go,** 1118 13th, for excellent full-sized rock, film, and celebrity posters and prints. For books of all kinds, as well as University of Colorado mementos, be sure to hit the university bookstore at the corner of College and Broadway.

Buchanan's Coffee Pub, 1301 Pennsylvania, 303/440-0222, is one of the best places in town to cop a cappuccino and read the morning news, while eavesdropping on what the local students are up to (and were the night before). Around the corner, at 1322 College, **Brillig Works Café and Bakery,** 1322 College Ave., 303/443-7461, also serves cappuccino and other gourmet coffees, as well as dynamite baked goods and vegetarian specials—with background music from the Dead to Miles Davis to Brahms.

© STEPHEN METZGER

the Boulder Courthouse, just off the Pearl Street Mall

SERVICES

The **Boulder Police Department** can be reached by calling 303/441-4444 (911 in emergencies). The offices of the **Boulder County Sheriff** are at 1777 6th St., 303/441-4444. **Boulder Community Hospital** is at 1100 Balsam (corner of North Broadway), 303/440-2037 (emergency care) or 303/440-2273 (hospital switchboard). The central **post office** is at 1905 15th, 303/938-1100.

Recycling

Drop off aluminum, glass, newspaper, and plastic at the three **King Soopers** (6550 Lookout Rd., 3600 Table Mesa Rd., and 1650 30th St.) and at both **Safeways** (4800 E. Baseline and 2798 Arapahoe). For information, phone **Recycle Boulder** at 303/441-4234.

INFORMATION

The central office of the **Boulder Convention and Visitors Bureau** is at 2440 Pearl (corner of Folsom), tel. 303/442-2911 or 800/444-0447. Helpful staff will answer questions and point you toward attractions, lodging, dining, etc. Be sure to pick up a copy of *Boulder Magazine,* which runs articles on local issues and personalities, as well as extensive dining and lodging lists. Another useful publication—available free at the Convention and Visitors Bureau offices—is the Boulder Parks and Recreation Department's booklet detailing the city's recreational camps, seminars, workshops, hikes, and clinics. Listed activities include tennis lessons, water-skiing lessons, various adventure outings, and more. For a copy, contact Parks and Recreation Registration, 5660 Sioux Dr., Boulder, CO 80303, 303/413-7200. Additionally, the bureau's website offers extensive information on everything from lodging to walking tours to convention venues. Go to www.bouldercoloradousa.com.

The Boulder **public library** is at 1000 Canyon Dr., 303/441-3111. The historical library is at 1125 Pine, 303/441-3110.

For **road and weather information,** phone or 303/639-1111 (Denver and west). Tune to Boulder's public radio station, KGNU, at 88.5 FM.

Bookstores

With one of the highest per-capita number of bookstores in the West (the phone book lists more than 30), Boulder could, and does, entertain bibliophiles for days on end—it would take you that long to make the rounds from the usual chains, Waldenbooks and B. Dalton, to shops specializing in rare books or politics. **Stage House Books and Prints** would be an excellent place to start. This two-story shop on Pearl, a block above the mall, is a used-book lover's dream. Not only will you find every kind of book imaginable, but there are chairs for plunking down and actually *reading,* while books are literally *everywhere*—strewn on the stairs, cluttered on the countertops, lined and piled up on the floor. Stage House features a special section of first editions and signed books.

Almost directly across the street you'll find the **Rue Morgue Mystery Bookshop,** 946 Pearl St., 303/443-8346.

Naropa University

Offering an educational and intellectual environment alternative to traditional universities, Naropa, at 2130 Arapahoe, is a fully accredited undergraduate and graduate school inspired by a 5th–12th century Buddhist university in India. Though the general tenor and underlying philosophy of the school reflects its Buddhist model, the courses are nonsectarian and wide-ranging, with a general emphasis in arts, humanities, and social sciences. In addition to the classes and seminars available to students, many programs and events—from poetry readings to deep-ecology workshops—open their doors to the public. Gary Snyder is a semiregular faculty member.

For more information, phone 303/444-0202; website www.naropa.edu.

TRANSPORTATION

If you're coming into Boulder via Denver International Airport, you can get here quite easily.

Boulder Supershuttle offers door-to-door service for about $18 each way; phone 303/444-0808.

Getting around in Boulder is quite easy, what with the excellent public transportation system, the fine network of bike trails, and the straightforward way in which the town's laid out. For starters, remember the numbered streets run parallel to the mountains—north to south—as do Broadway, which runs along the west end of Boulder between town and the mountains, and Folsom, running pretty much through the center of town. (U.S. 36 through town is 28th Street.) The main drags running east to west, crossing the numbered streets, are Baseline, Arapahoe, Canyon, Pearl, and Valmont. Iris Avenue, which runs east from Broadway, becomes Diagonal Highway/Highway 119, to Niwot.

In addition, **The Ride!,** Denver's bus system, offers regular service to Boulder ($.60—$.50 for seniors) as well as a depot at 14th and Walnut; phone 303/299-6000 for route and schedule information. The **HOP,** Boulder's shuttle service that connects downtown, the university, and the Hill, runs weekdays 7 A.M.–7 P.M. with buses every 10 minutes. Rides are $.25. For information, phone 303/447-8282.

For 24-hour taxi service, phone **Boulder Yellow Cab** at 303/442-2277.

NEDERLAND

Highway 119 winds west out of Boulder into Boulder Creek Canyon. Just a few miles out of town, you enter Roosevelt National Forest, and at Nederland, 17 miles out of Boulder, the road tees into Highway 72. From there, you can either turn north toward Estes Park and Rocky Mountain National Park or turn south to Central City and Black Hawk.

Nederland (pop. 1,200; elev. 8,236 feet) is a quirky little town in three parts: the funky, one-block old town, with a natural-foods store, gift shop, and a couple of cafés; the restored old town, with restaurants and liquor stores; and a new shopping center with a large grocery store, video store, and Mail Boxes, Etc.

Barker Meadow Reservoir is a stone's throw from town and is a favorite fishing lake (stocked regularly). No camping or boating allowed. Public parking and restrooms can be found in the center of town at the junction of Highway 119 and Highway 72. **Chipeta Park** behind the shopping center has a nice playground and picnic area. Next to the lodge, in an old railroad car, is **Happy Trails Bicycle Shop,** 303/258-3435, where you can buy and rent mountain bikes (call in advance to reserve it and get it adjusted to your height) and get information and maps on cycling in the area.

Accommodations and Food

You can stay in Nederland at the **Best Western Lodge at Nederland,** 303/258-9463 or 800/279-9463, a new log inn right off the highway. Doubles run $50–100. For a great place to get your morning going, stop in at **Acoustic Coffee,** 303/258-3209, a "community coffeehouse" right downtown on 1st Street, the only coffee shop I've seen where you can also pick up a new set of banjo or mandolin strings. Live acoustic (of course!) music some weekend evenings. **Neopolitan's Italian Restaurant,** 303/258-7313, 1 W. 1st St., serves excellent lasagna, pizzas, and sandwiches. Hours are Mon.–Fri. 4–9:30 P.M., Sat.–Sun. noon–9:30 P.M. ("depending on business").

South of Nederland, at Rollinsville, the **Stage Stop Inn Restaurant,** 303/258-3270, is a classic roadhouse catering mostly to locals. Stop in for a burger, chicken sandwich, or homemade soup ($4–8). Play a game of shuffleboard, and check out one of the best jukeboxes around, with everything from Jimi Hendrix to Flatt and Scruggs.

Central City and Black Hawk

Long known as the home of the Central City Opera, attracting well-known performers and discriminating fans since 1932, Central City and Black Hawk underwent a serious makeover in 1991 when they legalized gambling. Though maximum bets stand at only $5, and gaming is limited to blackjack, poker, and slots, the new diversion has divided locals and thrown a bizarre variable at real estate. Property values skyrocketed as soon as the measure passed (summer 1990), casinos went up seemingly overnight (by April 1993, there were 17 casinos in Central City and 21 in Black Hawk).

Whatever the result, gambling is guaranteed to draw even greater numbers of travelers to the region, and the two communities are being forced to rethink local transportation, as well as housing and other sundry business concerns.

HISTORY

When gold was first discovered in Gregory Gulch in 1859, word spread quickly to the gold camps of Auraria and Denver City, where disgruntled miners cursed the "Pikes Peak Hoax." Many of them immediately headed for the hills, and soon the Central City area was teeming with newly hopeful prospectors. Horace Greeley, the New York *Tribune* editor researching a piece on the West's goldfields, visited the camp and was given a tour by a group of miners. Unbeknownst to Greeley, the men had "salted" a placer mine by shooting gold dust into it with a shotgun. Greeley's subsequent report dramatically increased East Coast interest in the area, and soon even more miners poured into the gulch.

Originally, Gregory Gulch was dotted with a number of small camps, including Gregory Point, Mountain City, Black Hawk, and Nevadaville. Soon, though, Central City, named for its location about midway up the gulch, became the hub of the area's action, informally incorporating some of the other camps. Greeley, in addition to writing about the easily ex-

tractable gold, described the camps and the miners themselves:

> *I doubt there is as yet a table or chair in these diggings . . . the entire population sleep in tents or under pine boughs.*

Between 1859 and 1867, the gulch produced $9 million in gold, earning it the nickname, "The richest square mile on earth." During this time, engineers perfected mining techniques, smelters were built in Central City and Black Hawk, and more and more prospectors arrived in the gulch hoping to strike it rich. Central City's mid-1860s population hit 15,000.

From its very beginnings, Central City earned a reputation for being more "cultured" and sophisticated than some of the other mountain mining camps, and its diverse group of miners—Russians, Welshmen, French, Germans, Italians, blacks, among others—lent the little community a cosmopolitan air. In 1861, the Central City Opera House hosted its first production, *Camille,* and throughout the decade the town was well known for its vaudeville and minstrel shows.

The railroad came to Black Hawk in 1872 and extended to Central shortly thereafter, making the community much more accessible. In 1874, a fire swept through Central City, destroying many buildings, including the opera house, although the theater was rebuilt four years later—with four-foot-thick stone walls—and by the late '70s was attracting some of the biggest names in American theater, including Sarah Bernhardt, Lillian Russell, and Edwin Booth.

Like most other Colorado mining towns, Central City and Black Hawk were all but abandoned by the early 20th century once silver was devalued and production in the gold mines had slowed to almost nothing. The opera house was boarded up. Then in 1932, the newly formed Central City Opera Association pulled down the boards, restored the seats and interior, and reopened the opera house. In honor of the old building's history, the first show put on was, again, *Camille.* The Central City Opera remains one of the town's primary draws.

During the 1950s, Central City was known as a wild and woolly anything-goes outpost town, with more than its share of colorful characters. Among those who showed up to raise hell here were Jack Kerouac and gang. In *On the Road,* Kerouac describes his adventures:

> *It was a wonderful night. Central City is two miles high; at first you get drunk on the altitude, then you get tired, and there's a fever in your soul. We approached the lights around the opera house down the narrow dark street; then we took a sharp right and hit some old saloons with swinging doors . . . . Beyond the back door was a view of the mountainsides in the moonlight. I let out a yahoo. The night was on.*

Through the '60s, '70s, and '80s, Central City continued to draw tourists. In addition to the opera, boosters bragged about the museums, mine tours, and the century-old buildings. And with its proximity to Denver, Central City attracted large numbers of travelers. In fact, during this time, traffic was often bumper to bumper through town in the summer, and on particularly busy days (weekends), cars were often backed up well below town. The little streets and sidewalks, meanwhile, swelled with tourists; the gift and souvenir shops, T-shirt shops, and restaurants packing in camera-toting visitors.

And now, with legalized gambling, the atmosphere in the two towns is one of excitement mixed with general chaos, as Bermuda-shorted tourists cash in their coupons for gambling tokens and ninety-nine-cent breakfasts while motorhomes chug away at stoplights—the two communities are situated in a narrow gulch where traffic posed a problem well before legal betting showed up. And though there are a number of pioneer festivals celebrating the area's history, most visitors today seem far more drawn to the tawdry allure of the casinos and a quick jackpot than to the towns' colorful past.

SIGHTS

Gilpin County Historical Museum

Displaying a huge array of authentic items and artifacts from the area's fascinating history, this museum is one of Central City's less touristy attractions. Its rooms represent various eras and themes, including early travel, education, fashion, business, and medicine. In addition, historical photos and miniature reproductions of a Victorian-era mining town combine to give the visitor a very real sense of life in the rough-and-tumble Colorado of the late 19th century.

The museum, at 228 E. High St. (a half block east of Eureka), is open daily 11 A.M.–4 P.M., Memorial Day through Labor Day. Admission is $3 (or $5 for admission to the Thomas Historical House as well—see below). For more information, write P.O. Box 244, Central City, CO 80427, or phone 303/582-5283.

Thomas Historical House

The home of the family of Ben Thomas, who bought it in 1894, the house privides an up-close look at life at the turn of the (last) century, with domestic items and family photographs. Tours are given on the hour, Fri.–Mon. 11 A.M.–4 P.M. Memorial Day through Labor Day. Admission is $3 (or $5 for a combination pass to the Gilpin County Historical Museum). The house is at 209 Eureka Street. Phone 303/582-5283.

Teller House and Opera House Tour

Tours of the Central City Opera House, built in 1873, and adjoining Teller House, at one time one of the West's most luxurious hotels, are offered May through August from late morning to early evening for a small fee. In the bar of the Teller House, you'll see the famous *Face on the Barroom Floor,* painted in 1936 by a Denver journalist.

The tours begin at 120 Eureka St. and take about a half hour. Cost is $3 for adults. During the off season, you can arrange private tours by appointment. For tour information phone 303/292-6500; for opera schedule and ticket information, phone 303/292-6700.

The Gilpin County Historical Mueum in Central City offers a pleasant break from the casinos and other touristy trappings in town.

Central City Cemeteries

One way to escape Central City's shameless appeal to tourism is to continue driving straight through town—Lawrence to Eureka to the dirt road—to the pioneer cemeteries that sprawl over the hilltops west of town. Park and wander among the hundreds of plots. Mostly overgrown, and with some of the headstones broken and/or lying on the ground, the plots offer poignant insights into the area's past; note the young ages at which people died here in the late 19th century. Chances are that even if the city sidewalks are packed, you'll be alone up here.

ACCOMMODATIONS

Lodging in Central City and Black Hawk includes the **Winfield Scott Guest Quarters Bed and Breakfast,** 210 Hooper St., 303/582-3433 ($100–150), and the **Gold Dust Lodge,** 5312 Hwy. 119 (about two miles west of town and offering free shuttle service to casinos), 303/582-5415 ($50–100). In addition, an abundance of large casino-hotels (several new ones each season) offer modern lodging. **Harvey's Wagon Wheel Hotel and Casino,** 321 Gregory, 303/582-0800, has rooms in the $100–150 range.

Camping and RVing

The **Central City KOA** campground is four miles north of Black Hawk on Highway 72; phone 303/582-9979. Campers can also head to **Golden Gate Canyon State Park,** also just north of Black Hawk on Highway 72. In addition to a campground, the 8,500-acre park offers hiking, horseback riding, and cross-country skiing. For information, phone 303/582-3707. (Also see Parks and Recreation under Boulder, above.)

FOOD

The dining scene in Central City and Black Hawk changed considerably when the casinos arrived—essentially, all independent restaurants were offered big bucks to hit the road and make room for the casinos. These days, dining is pretty limited to restaurants in the casinos, many of which offer excellent deals (prime-rib dinners for $3.95!). A note of caution, though: most of the deals are offered simply to get you in the door, and few are those who eat and leave without making a few bets on the way in or out; your $3.95 dinner can wind up costing you $15 or $20 before you can say "craps."

One of the restaurants that has managed to escape much of touristy trappings of the area is the **Black Forest Inn,** 260 Gregory St., 303/279-3333, specializing in Bavarian food and wild game, and which locals regularly cite as the "best in town." Dinners run $8–20.

ENTERTAINMENT

Part of the entertainment in Central City and Black Hawk is simply wandering around the steep streets and into gift shops and saloons—as well as watching all the other folks doing just about the same thing. At the heart of the entertainment scene, though, is the **Central City Opera,** which takes place in the town's 1878 opera house. With productions varying from the classical *(The Magic Flute)* to more modern *(The Merry Widow),* the Central City troupe is the oldest summer opera company in the

country; since its reopening in 1932, it's developed a loyal following, from tourists who simply enjoy the novelty to hard-core opera buffs. The season generally runs mid-July through mid-August. For information and reservations, write Central City Opera House Association, 621 7th St., Suite 1601, Denver, CO 80293, or phone 303/292-6700.

CALENDAR

The highlight of Central City's tourist season is the opera, which runs mid-July to mid-August (see above). In addition, there are a number of other festivals of note, some serious, some silly. The **Jazz Festival** takes place in mid-August, while early June marks the **Lou Bunch Days** "Bed Races" (contestants feel like sheet afterward . . .). For information on annual events in Central City and Black Hawk, contact the Gilpin County Chamber of Commerce, 303/582-5077.

SERVICES

Phone the **Central City Police** at 303/582-5411 and the **Gilpin County Sheriff** at 303/582-5511. The **post office** is on Gregory just east of Spring Street.

Recycling

The closest recycling centers are in **Nederland,** about 25 miles north on Highway 72. The **Boulder County Transfer Station** on County Road 128 East, 303/258-7878, takes aluminum, glass, and newspaper, and the **BF Super Foods,** 60 Lakewood Dr., 303/258-3105, takes aluminum.

INFORMATION

Be sure to stop in at the offices of the **Gilpin County Chamber of Commerce,** 117 Eureka. For information before your visit, write P.O. Box 343, Black Hawk, CO 80422, 303/582-5077, or phone the **Central City Public Relations Office** at 303/582-5251. You can also get information about the area by phoning **Central City Public Information** toll-free at 800/542-2999.

Y'all come back now, hear. . . .

THE DENVER AREA

TRANSPORTATION

Central City and Black Hawk are close to the metro Denver area and easily accessible. From Denver, take I-70 or U.S. 6 about 45 miles west and turn north on Highway 119 (the turnoff is well marked), and continue for about eight miles; allow 45 minutes to one hour. You can also get there from Boulder by going west on Highway 119 and continuing south through Nederland, a distance of about 35 miles; allow 30–45 minutes.

Resources

Suggested Reading

In 1989, when I first started seriously researching this book, there weren't all that many others to recommend. The last few years, however, have brought an explosion of books about the state, nearly all of them interesting and valuable to at least some degree. Shelves in Colorado bookstores are packed with books on the state's history, culture, ecology, economy, and everything else imaginable, from hiking and mountain biking to cooking and bed-and-breakfasting. It would be impossible to list them all. I'd suggest, then, taking a look at the list I have assembled here—these are all top-notch publications—but allowing yourself plenty of time to browse in the bookstores you come across on your trip.

A word on out-of-print books: you'll notice that some of the books I've listed are out of print. Not to worry. Among the many parts of our lives that the Internet has changed is the availability of books. Rare and out-of-print titles are now just a website away, and they're often not as expensive as you might think. Unless you're looking for a signed first edition of *For Whom the Bell Tolls,* or something along those lines, out-of-print books are generally quite reasonable. My favorite site is **Bibliofind.com,** which was recently taken over by **Amazon.com.** Go to Bibliofind's website and type in the title and/or author you're looking for, and you'll get a list of books, with descriptions, conditions (VG = very good, for example), prices, and availability. Books are usually delivered within a couple of days of your ordering them. You can also go straight to Amazon.com, which now also includes out-of-print titles with information on how to get them. As of September 2001, all of the following titles were available from at least one of the above websites.

Finally, I also must add that far and away the best place to find books on Colorado and the West, as well as just about every subject that interests you, is the **Tattered Cover** in Denver. It has two locations: at the Cherry Creek Mall (2955 E. Cherry Creek) and at 16th and

Wynkoop in LoDo (see also Information under Denver). Caution: bibliophiles have been known to enter into these stores virtually to disappear, only to reappear at some later date, their arms laden with books, to find their kids grown and their marriages collapsed.

History

Ambrose, Stephen E. *Undaunted Courage: Meriwether Lewis, Thomas Jefferson, and the Opening of the American West.* New York: Simon and Schuster, 2000. A gorgeously written account of the great expedition westward, with fascinating accounts of the background, encounters along the way, and the unfortunate aftermath. A must-read for anyone interested in the American West.

Bakeless, John, ed. *The Journals of Lewis and Clark.* New York: Mentor Books, 2000. Read firsthand accounts of the first sightings of the Rocky Mountains and the Pacific Ocean, of meetings with the Sioux and other Native Americans. The perfect companion to Ambrose's book.

Buchholtz, C. W. *Rocky Mountain National Park: A History.* Boulder: Colorado Associated University Press, 1983. Exhaustive story of the park area, from the Native Americans who once called this region of the Rockies home to National Park designation in 1915 and the problems of overcrowding in the 1970s and '80s. A refreshing blend of academic research and pleasantly readable writing—full of details, anecdotes, and colorful characters. Out of print.

Bueler, William M. *Roof of the Rockies: A History of Colorado Mountaineering.* Seattle: Mountaineers Books, 2000. Bueler, who had climbed all of Colorado's "14ers" by 1952, divides Colorado climbing into two periods: exploration and modern mountaineering. Very well written and thorough, with maps, charts, and photos.

Burroughs, John Rolfe. *Steamboat in the Rockies.* Fort Collins: The Old Army Press, 1974. The story of Steamboat Springs, from the discovery of the springs in 1839 to the development of the ski resort in the 1970s—as seen through the loving eyes of a 50-year resident of the Steamboat area. Burroughs, who has written extensively on the West—fiction, nonfiction, and poetry—has won several prestigious awards for his writing and draws on both local lore and published reports in the *Routt County Sentinel;* the result is a pleasant blend of homespun folksiness and footnotey history. Out of print.

Collier, Joseph and Grant. *Colorado, Yesterday and Today.* Montrose, CO: Western Reflections, 2000. A look at Colorado's growth and changes through the eye of one of the state's pioneer photographers, Joseph, and his great-grandson, Grant. The contrasting images demonstrate the urgent need for intelligent development and sensitive land management.

Gilliland, Mary Ellen. *Frisco! A Colorful Colorado Community.* Silverthorne: Frisco Historical Society, 1986. A history of Frisco and Summit County, with profiles of major players, contributors, and characters.

Henderson, Junious, ed. *Colorado: Short Studies of its Past and Present.* New York: AMS Press, 1969. A series of academic essays on Colorado—from prehistoric peoples through the gold rush to 20th-century education. Particularly interesting, if only because the subject is otherwise so scantily written about, is Irene Pettit McKeehan's "Colorado in Literature." McKeehan's piece is a scholarly examination of the state's well-known as well as lesser-known writers and writings—from Whitman and Parkman to obscure poets whose works have only recently been rediscovered.

Lee, Mabel Barbee, foreword by Lowell Thomas. *Cripple Creek Days.* Lincoln: University of Nebraska Press, 1984. Well-written and personal narrative account of Cripple Creek, from first word of gold to the early 1900s, and the author's return in midcentury (her father had been one of Cripple Creek's original miners).

Lister, Florence, and Robert Lister. *Those Who Came Before.* Tucson: Southwest Parks and Monuments Association, 1993. A fascinating study of the Native Americans who lived in and/or passed through the Southwest, including Arizona, Colorado, New Mexico, and Utah. The Anasazi, Mogollon, and Hohokam cultures are examined in depth, as are the later Pueblo peoples. Beautiful color and black-and-white photos.

Marks, Paula Mitchell. *And Die in the West.* Norman, OK: University of Oklahoma Press, 1996. An exhaustive sociohistorical examination of the famous gunfight at the OK Corral. Though not specifically about Colorado (the shootout took place in Tombstone, Arizona), this book will be of interest to any fan of the American West (besides, Doc Holliday, one of the fight's participants, is buried in Glenwood Springs, Colorado). Combining the scholar's eye for detail and passion for accuracy with a lively writing style, Marks debunks many of the fictionalized accounts of the gunfight, putting it into a larger context and looking at the conflicting loyalties that led to the showdown.

Marshall, Muriel. *Red Hole in Time.* College Station, TX: A and M University Press, 1988. A poetic and heartfelt study of the geology and history of the remote Escalante Canyon, a sharp crease in the Uncompahgre Plateau. Treated as a microcosm of the settling of the West itself, the story of Escalante is rich in its people, landscapes, and folklore.

428 Moon Handbooks: Colorado

McTighe, James. *Roadside History of Colorado.* Boulder: Johnson Books, 1989. Route-by-route (milepost-by-milepost!) look at the state's history.

Riley, Glenda. *Women and Indians on the Frontier, 1825–1915.* Albuquerque: University of New Mexico Press, 1985. In a refreshingly unique look at the settling of the West, Riley argues that women were less likely to prejudge the natives than were men, and that women both greatly contributed to and were significantly liberated by westward expansion.

Rohrbough, Malcolm J. *Aspen: The History of a Silver Mining Town, 1879–1893.* Boulder: University Press of Colorado, 2000. Detailed and scholarly look at the influences of both mining and the railroad, ending with the collapse of the silver market.

Sprague, Marshall. *Money Mountain.* New York: Ballantine Books, 1971. A detailed and highly readable history of Cripple Creek, from the discovery of gold to the early days of reconstruction.

Ubbelohde, Carl, Maxine Benson, and Duane A. Smith. *A Colorado History.* Boulder: Pruett Publishing Company, 2001 (eighth edition). A nicely readable narrative of the state, from the first cliff dwellers through 20th-century economic challenges. Particularly interesting and well written is the section on frontier Colorado and the Pikes Peak gold rush.

Description and Travel

Abbey, Edward. *Desert Solitaire: A Season in the Wilderness.* New York: Ballantine Books (through arrangement with McGraw-Hill Book Co.), 1991. Abbey's notes and observations as a May-to-September Park Service ranger, spent in virtual solitude in the Southwest desert (actually Arches National Monument in southeastern Utah). Some of the most poetic, emotional, and inspiring writing to come out of the Southwest.

Bryson, Bruce, ed. *The Best Travel Writing of 2000.* New York: Houghton-Mifflin, 2001. Part of the larger series (Best Short Stories, Best Essays), this book includes some two dozen travel pieces by some of the best writers working today, including Tim Cahill, P. J. O'Rourke, Isabel Hilton, and Dave Eggers, with pieces on everything from Italy to Thailand to New York's Central Park. The essays were originally printed in a wide range of publications, including *The New Yorker, Outside,* and *National Geographic Traveler.*

Caughey, Bruce. *The Colorado Guide.* Golden: Fulcrum Press, 2000. An exceptional general guide to Colorado with an emphasis on recreation. Excellent discussions and descriptions of backcountry hiking trails and tips on out-of-the-way lodges and restaurants.

Chronic, Halka. *Roadside Geology of Colorado.* Missoula, MT: Mountain Press Publishing Company, 1986. Part of a popular series, this is an immensely informative book detailing Colorado's fascinating geology along the state's major and minor roads and highways.

Eberhart, Perry. *Guide to the Colorado Ghost Towns and Mining Camps.* Denver: Sage Books, 1959. A difficult-to-find but fascinating and useful book, Perry's guide is fraught with maps, historical photos, and descriptions of the old towns, camps, and characters.

Gregory, Lee. *Colorado Scenic Guide, Northern Region.* Boulder: Johnson Books, 1996. Full of facts, maps, and advice for hikers, jeepers, cross-country skiers, and anyone else who wants to explore Colorado's outdoors. Focuses on areas north of Cañon City, particularly on Colorado Springs and Front Range areas.

Gregory, Lee. *Colorado Scenic Guide, Southern Region.* Boulder: Johnson Books, 1996. Same as above, with most sites concentrated south and west of Cañon City, particularly in the Telluride-Creede-Pagosa Springs areas.

Jones, Tom Lorang, photos by John Fielder. *Colorado's Continental Divide Trail*. Englewood, CO: Westcliff Publishing, 1997. Excellent photos and well-written and highly detailed descriptions of the trail. Indispensable guide for hikers and backpackers.

Work Projects Administration. *The WPA Guide to 1930s Colorado*. Lawrence: University Press of Kansas, 1987 (originally published in 1941 as *Colorado: A Guide to the Highest State*). Reprint from the classic WPA guidebook series, the book is most useful when discussing the state's history (pre-1940). The original, now long out of print, is a wonderful way to get a sense of what Colorado (and traveling) was like between the world wars. Exceptionally thorough discussions of back roads, as well as sites and incidents of relatively minor historical consequence. Out of print.

Recreation

Borneman, Walter R., and Lyndon J. Lampert. *A Climbing Guide to Colorado's Fourteeners*. Boulder: Pruett Publishing Company, 1997. Peak-by-peak discussions of routes, dangers, what to bring. With maps and photos.

Brewer, Robyn. *Colorado Camping*. Emeryville, CA: Avalon Travel Publishing, 2000. Campground-by-campground guide to more than 700 spots in Colorado, with descriptions of campgrounds, number of sites, fees, other activities in the area, etc., as well as contact information.

Cahill, Rick. *Colorado Hot Springs Guide*. Boulder: Pruett Publishing Company, 1986. Dozens of springs around the state are covered, with maps, photos, history, and technicalities, such as water flow. Out of print.

Coello, Dennis. *Bicycle Touring Colorado*. Flagstaff, AZ: Northland Publishing Company, 1989. A look at longer rides around the state, full of suggestions and tips. Lots of first-person anecdotes, lively writing. Out of print.

Fielder, John, and M. John Fayhee. *Along the Colorado Trail*. Englewood, Colorado: Westcliffe Publishing, 1992. A guide to hiking the Colorado Trail.

Gong, Linda, and Gregg Bromka. *Mountain Biking Colorado*. Helena, MT: Falcon Publishing Co., 1998. A thorough look at the best mountain biking in the state, including 66 trails—among them rides to ghost towns, to Mesa Verde, and through Great Sand Dunes. Also includes maps and lists of nearby bike shops.

Lund, Morten, Bob Gillen, and Michael Bartlett, eds. *The Ski Book*. New York: Arbor House, 1982. With a foreword by winter Olympic gold medalist Jean-Claude Killy, this is an anthology of some of the best ski writing of the last century, in addition to other pieces that just seem to fit the mood of the mountains in winter. Essays and articles from *Skiing, Ski, Powder,* and *Sports Illustrated,* as well as pieces by Percy Bysshe Shelley, Robert Frost, Ernest Hemingway, Gay Talese, Thomas Mann, John Updike, Art Buchwald. Out of print.

Ohlrich, Warren. *Aspen Snowmass Trails: A Hiking Guide*. Aspen: Who Press, 1997. An exhaustive account of hiking in the Aspen area, with information on trail length, degrees of difficulty, and views—as well as discussions of backwoods ethics.

Pixler, Paul. *Hiking Trails of Southwestern Colorado*. Boulder: Pruett Publishing Company, 2000. Maps, charts, text descriptions, degrees of difficulty, and time allowances for trails in some of the state's finest and most scenic hiking areas.

Schmidt, Jeremy. *Adventuring in the Rockies: The Sierra Club Travel Guide to the Rocky Mountain Regions of the United States and*

Canada. San Francisco: Sierra Club Books, 1997. Guide to hiking, camping, and sightseeing in the Rockies, with an emphasis on low-impact exploration.

Wheat, Doug. *The Floater's Guide to Colorado.* Billings and Helena, MT: Falcon Publishing Company, 1996. An immeasurably detailed and well-written book exhaustively discussing the state's rivers—fit for kayak, canoe, or raft. Wheat is a biologist and geologist who pioneered many of the rivers covered in the book. *The Denver Post* called it "the American Express card for river running. Don't leave home without it."

Politics and Government

Prucha, Francis Paul. *The Great Father: The United States Government and the American Indian.* Lincoln: University of Nebraska Press, 1984. This huge (1,300 pages) two-volume set is one of the definitive reference works on the delicate and often stormy relationship between Native Americans and those who subdued and govern them.

Wright, James Edward. *The Politics of Populism: Dissent in Colorado.* New Haven: Yale University Press, 1974. Tracing the beginnings of Colorado's progressive politics from the gold rush of the late 1850s through the Populist revolution of the latter part of the century, Wright, a history professor at Dartmouth, argues the state's mining origins were largely what led to its strident support of unionism and other movements that defined 20th-century labor and politics. Out of print.

Biography, Autobiography, and Memoir

Conner, Daniel Ellis. *A Confederate in the Colorado Gold Fields.* Norman: University of Oklahoma Press, 1970. Reworked by editors Donald J. Berthong and Odessa Davenport

from a manuscript written in the late 1860s, this book tells the story of a gold seeker who during the Civil War sympathizes and becomes involved with a group of Colorado Confederates hiding out near Pueblo. Especially interesting are Conner's descriptions of modes of travel (using a gold pan for a snow sled, for example) and of other Colorado pioneers. Out of print.

French, Emily, edited by Janet Lecompte. *Emily: The Diary of a Hard-Worked Woman.* Lincoln: University of Nebraska Press, 1987. An extraordinary collection of diary entries of a 47-year-old laundress, cleaning woman, and nurse, who wrote daily of her life on the Colorado plains and in Denver from January 1 to December 31, 1890. "I got up so early, thinking of the one that now seems to fill all my cravings for a companion, will he be all to me," she writes on June 17, and on November 8: "Another day, oh when will I have my time all to rest, will it ever come, I try to be kind, it does no good."

Hamil, Harold. *Colorado Without Mountains: A High Plains Memoir.* Kansas City, MO: The Lowell Press, 1976. A story of growing up in the "other" Colorado, the cattle ranches east of the Rockies, at a time when the West had been won and the way it was being run was changing dramatically. The author, a former AP reporter and journalism professor, tells his story in short, chatty chapters—one particularly intriguing as well as disturbing anecdote is about the appearance of the Ku Klux Klan at Hamil's high school graduation in 1924.

Iverson, Kristen. *Molly Brown: Unraveling the Myth, the True Story of the Titanic's Most Famous Survivor.* Boulder: Johnson Printing, 2001. A thorough and fascinating study of a fascinating woman, separating fact from fiction. Includes lots of Denver and Colorado history, as well as a foreword by Muffet Brown, Molly's great-granddaughter.

Environment/Ecology

Clow, Deborah, and Donald Snow, eds. *Northern Lights: A Selection of New Writing from the American West.* New York: Vintage Books, 1994. Widely ranging essays, fiction, poetry, and memoirs on the West and its relation to the individual. Pieces by David Quammen, Gretel Ehrlich, Edward Abbey, Simon J. Ortiz, Doug Peacock, and two stunning pieces by Leslie Ryan. Forward by Louise Erdrich. Highly recommended. Out of print.

Katz, Eric, et al, eds. *Beneath the Surface: Critical Essays in the Philosophy of Deep Ecology.* Cambridge, MA: MIT Press, 2000. An important and wide-ranging collection of essays by some of the biggest names in the field. Essays debate the value of deep ecology and make connections to other philosophies, politics, the arts, ecofeminism, and other current issues.

Seed, John, et al. *Thinking Like a Mountain: Toward a Council of All Beings.* Philadelphia and Santa Cruz: New Society Publishers, 1988. An anthology of writings, prose and poetry, most dealing to some degree with the *gaia* concept, of the earth as a spiritual life-force. Includes pieces by Robinson Jeffers, Chief Seattle, Gary Snyder, and others.

Wallace, David Rains, Dwight Holing and Suzanne Methuin. *Guide to National Parks and Preserves and Public Lands and How to Enjoy Them in a Nature Friendly Way.* London: Nature Company/Time Life Books, 2000. An encyclopedic look at exploring the vast amounts of U.S. public lands, with discussions of each national park, and sections on camping, safety, and myriad other topics, including brief biographies of significant "eco-travelers," such as John Muir.

Ethnic Colorado

de Onis, Jose, ed. *The Hispanic Contribution to the State of Colorado.* Boulder: Westview Press, 1976. A collection of essays looking at the many facets making up Hispanic Colorado, from early Spanish contacts and original Spanish and Mexican land grants to Hispanic folklore and close-up examinations of specific regions—including the San Luis Valley, where the Spanish language is more alive than perhaps anywhere else in the state. Out of print.

Native Americana

Black Elk, John Neihardt, and Vine Deloria. *Black Elk Speaks: Being the Life Story of a Holy Man of the Oglala Sioux.* Lincoln, NE: Bison Books, 2000. Told to Neihardt in 1930 by the Sioux warrior and medicine man, the story recounts Black Elk's youth on the plains, his Vision, the coming of the white man, and the battle of Wounded Knee. Though not specifically about Colorado, the book offers a unique insight into Native American life in the late 19th century. A painful yet important book.

Bruchas, Joseph. *Survival This Way: Interviews with American Indian Poets.* Tucson: University of Arizona Press, 1990. Interviews with Joy Harjo, N. Scott Momaday, Simon Ortíz, and 18 others.

Eagle/Walking Turtle. *Indian America: A Traveler's Companion.* Santa Fe: John Muir Publications, 1995. A state-by-state guide to many of the country's Native American tribes, reservations, visitor information centers, art forms, museums, and public festivals. Although there's not a whole lot on Colorado, the book suggests the variety and scope of the hundreds of tribes and their involvements.

Marriot, Alice, and Carol K. Rachlin, eds. *American Indian Mythology.* New York: New American Library, 1968. One of the best available collections of Native American myths, including many from Southwestern tribes. Meet Coyote, Spider Woman, the War Twins, and many others, and watch for the huge difference and fascinating parallels between Native American and Judeo-Christian mythology. The introduction alone is worth the price of admission.

Murphy, James E., and Sharon M. Murphy, eds. *Let My People Know.* Norman: University of Oklahoma Press, 1981. Scholarly study of Native American journalism, from confiscated presses of the mid-19th century to modern journals and newspapers. Out of print.

Witt, Shirley Hill, and Stan Steiner, eds. *The Way, An Anthology of Native American Literature.* New York: Alfred A. Knopf, Inc., 1972. Wonderfully eclectic collection of songs, poetry, oratory, mythology, and contemporary journalism by Native Americans. Includes poetry by Simon Ortíz and N. Scott Momaday, oratory by Tecumseh, and Geronimo's surrender speech to General Cook. Out of print.

Art and Photography

Dallas, Sandra. *Yesterday's Denver.* Miami: E. A. Seemann Publishing Company, 1974. Collection of historical photographs of Denver, from 1859 through World War II. Excellent shots of pioneers, transportation, and architecture, as well as of visiting celebrities, including Billy Sunday, Dwight Eisenhower, and Gary Cooper.

Muench, David, text by David Sumner. *Colorado.* Portland, OR: Graphic Arts Center Publishing Company, 2001. Most readers are familiar with Muench's work—some of the most glorious nature photography of the last century—so suffice it to say that this is Muench at his best, working one of the most gorgeous spots on the planet. Accompanying text, as always, is as informative, eloquent, and inspiring as the photos.

Fiction

Abbey, Edward. *The Monkey Wrench Gang.* New York: Avon Books, 1976. The founding father of modern environmentalism tackles the money-hungry bureaucrats wrecking the Southwest's deserts and rivers.

Hillerman, Tony. *Dance Hall of the Dead; Skinwalker; People of Darkness; The Ghostway; Listening Woman; The Fly on the Wall; The Blessing Way; Thief of Time; Talking God; Coyote Waits; Hunting Badger; The Fallen Man.* Most available in Avon paperback. Hillerman's murder mysteries, most of which take place on the Navajo reservation in the Four Corners area, are universally acclaimed for their authenticity and brilliant depictions of the Southwest. Readers trying to unravel the crimes along with Detective Jim Chee and Lieutenant Joe Leaphorn learn intimate and fascinating details about Indian culture.

Michener, James. *Centennial.* New York: Random House, 1974. A typically Michenerian (that is, l-o-n-g) historical novel of the Colorado plains. Follow professor Lewis Vernor to Greeley and the surrounding area as he researches the geology, prehistory, Native American history, and settlement of the region while on assignment for a major magazine. Meet a colorful cast of characters—some real, some invented—as you absorb the story of this fascinating area.

Momaday, N. Scott. *House Made of Dawn.* New York: Perennial Library, 1977. A young Native American attempts to return to the traditions of his pueblo after fighting in World War II. Beautifully written by one of our great American novelists and poets, the story draws on the mythology, vision, and spirit of the Pueblo peoples.

Shuler, Linda Lay. *She Who Remembers.* New York: William Morrow and Company, 1988.

(Also available in paperback from New American Library.) Imagine *Clan of the Cave Bear* in a Four Corners setting. A historical bodice-ripper (with a strong heroine who's not above a little loincloth-ripping herself). The story of Kwani and her attraction to the Anasazi stud, Kokopelli. Very well researched, providing good background reading on Mesa Verde and the Anasazi people. Ideal vacation reading.

Silko, Leslie Marmon. *Ceremony.* New York: Viking Press, 1977. Powerful story of the spiritual healing of a Navajo veteran of World War II. Blends Native American mythology and storytelling with conventional fictional devices. A must for anyone interested in Southwestern tribes, and especially their literature.

Cookbooks

Graham, Constance, ed. *Creme de Colorado Cookbook.* Junior League of Denver: Denver, 1987. Three hundred pages of Colorado cooking, from the relatively tame (Creamy Banana Coffee Cake) to wild (Minted Grouse Breasts and Gunnison Trapper Game Pie).

McKee, Gwen, ed. *Best of the Best: Selected Recipes from Colorado's Favorite Cookbooks.* Brandon, MS: Quail Ridge Press, 1998.

Odds and Ends

Stegner, Wallace. *The American West as Living Space.* Ann Arbor: University of Michigan Press, 1987. Stegner shares his insights and offers intriguing analyses of why folks are drawn to, live in, and love the West.

Godfrey, Peggy. *Write 'em, Cowboy.* Lake City, Colorado: Peter Carlyle Elliott Publishing, 1993. A collection of "cowboy poetry" that captures in light verse the ranchin', wranglin', cowpokin' life on a Western ranch.

Magazines

Backpacker. Subtitled "The Magazine of Wilderness Travel," this publication mixes hard-hitting stories on environmental issues with destination pieces spotlighting backcountry areas around the world. The magazine also reviews equipment and runs stories on health and safety in the woods. Excellent photo essays, too. Available at most newsracks. For subscription information, write 33 East Minor St., Emmaus, PA 18098.

Powder. A monthly ski magazine for chute-shredders, powderhounds, and cornice-jumpers (including pinheads and snowboarders). Never taking itself too seriously, *Powder* is an excellent blend of intelligent writing, humor, and just the right amount of smugness. Tons of outrageous photos, lots of expert advice. Published seven times a year. P.O. Box 1028, Dana Point, CA 92629; 714/496-5922.

Ski and *Skiing.* The two biggest and most widely read ski magazines in the country, both are Times Mirror publications and run many of the same types of pieces—from annual equipment reviews and instructional articles to exotic travel (from Heavenly Valley to the Himalayas), as well as profiles and reader surveys. Watch *Ski* and *Skiing* for pieces by the country's best ski writers, including Peter Shelton, Andrew Slough, Lito Tejada-Flores. *Ski* and *Skiing* are available at newsstands, grocery stores, and ski shops around the United States.

Trail and Timberline. Monthly publication of the venerable Colorado Mountain Club featuring stories on all aspects of Colorado mountaineering, plus pieces on hiking and climbing around the world. Regular departments include "Book Reviews" and "Outings," which lists upcoming hikes and other CMC-sponsored events. For information, write the club at 2530 W. Alameda Ave., Denver, CO 80219, or phone 303/922-8315.

Newspapers

The Aspen Times. Weekly paper focusing on Aspen's development, real estate, politics, and sports, with a big emphasis on skiing (not surprisingly). Ranges in tone from light-hearted and tongue-in-cheek to stern editorializing. Also includes dining and lodging supplements. Published every Thursday and available throughout the Aspen area at $.35 a copy. For subscriptions, write P.O. Box E, Aspen, CO 81612.

Colorado Daily. University of Colorado (Boulder) paper, emphasizing local and campus news but also with short pieces of national and international interest. Good entertainment listings and reviews, also provocative editorial and op-ed pages. "Colorado Daily Trail Guide" column examines riding and hiking trails in the area and offers advice on what to see and do along the way, as well as what to take along for a safe and enjoyable trip. Available free in newsracks throughout Boulder. Phone 303/443-6272 for subscription information.

Daily Camera. Boulder's daily, with large national and international news and sports sections, and editorials of local and worldwide interest. Good source for what's happenin' in Boulder. Phone 303/442-1202, or write P.O. Box 591, Boulder, CO 80306.

The Denver Post. The best paper in Colorado, in fact one of the best in the West. Progressive editorial slant, in-depth reporting (longer stories than those in the *Rocky Mountain News*), excellent columnists. Printed on recycled paper. Pick one up daily while you're visiting the state for local, national, and international news.

Gazette Telegraph. Daily newspaper of Colorado Springs and Pikes Peak area. For subscription, phone 719/632-5511.

Rocky Mountain News. Founded on April 23, 1859, by William N. Byers, the *News* is Colorado's oldest paper and with *The Denver Post* one of the two largest. Stories shorter and less developed than the *Post*'s, and the editorial slant a bit more conservative.

Westword. This is Denver's controversial news and arts weekly, irreverently written by committed journalists whose aim is to "comfort the afflicted and afflict the comfortable." Particularly good—and eagerly awaited by the entire city—is the annual "Best of Denver" edition, which comes out in late June. Here you'll find the editors' recommendations—as well as those of their readers—for everything from best neighborhood bar and best Mexican restaurant to "Best Ethnic Selection in a Megamarket," and "Best Massage for Those Who Are Embarrassed about Their Bodies" to "Best Gay Rodeo." *Westword* is also one of the best sources for entertainment in and around the Denver area—from comedy clubs to jazz concerts to gallery openings. For information, phone 303/296-7744, or write P.O. Box 5970, Denver, CO 80217.

Internet Resources

Skiing

Colorado Ski Country USA (www.colorado ski.org)
Information on everything from snow conditions (updated twice daily) to lodging to employment opportunities at all of Colorado's ski resorts. Look for complete information about Colorado's ski resorts at their individual websites, listed below.

Arapahoe Basin (www.arapahoebasin.com)
Aspen—Aspen Mountain, Aspen Highlands, Buttermilk, Snowmass (www.skiaspen.com)
Beaver Creek (www.beavercreek.com)
Breckenridge (www.breckenridge.com)
Copper Mountain (www.ski-copper.com)
Cuchara Mountain Resort (www.cuchara.com)
Keystone (www.keystoneresort.com)
Loveland Basin (www.skiloveland.com)
Monarch Ski Area (www.skimonarch.com)
Mt. Crested Butte Ski Area (www.crested butteresort.com)
Powderhorn (www.powderhorn.com)
Purgatory Ski Area (www.ski.purg.com)
Ski Cooper (www.skicooper.com)
SolVista (www.silvercreek-resort.com)
Steamboat Springs Ski Resort (www.steam boat-ski.com)
Sunlight Mountain Resort (www.sunlight mtn.com)
Telluride Ski Area (www.telski.com)
Vail (www.vail.com)
Winter Park Ski Area (www.winterpark-re sort.com)
Wolf Creek Ski Area (www.wolfcreekski.com)

San Juan Hut Systems (www.telluride2 .com/colorado/San-Juan-Hut-System)
A series of Telluride-area backcountry cabins five to six miles apart, linked by cross-country ski trails.

Ski Train (www.skitrain.com)
Departing Denver on weekend mornings, the train takes skiers northwest into the mountains, through Moffat Tunnel, and eventually deposits them at Winter Park Ski Resort. The train leaves the ski area in late afternoon, and is back in Denver by early evening.

10th Mountain Trail Association Hut System (www.huts.org)
The association offers European-style hut-to-hut skiing on 300 miles of trails stretching from Aspen to Vail and throughout much of the White River National Forest. On-trail accommodations are provided at 12 huts and lodges three to eight miles apart.

More Outdoors

Colorado Division of Wildlife (wildlife .state.co.us)
Look here for information on fishing and hunting in Colorado.

Colorado Mountain Club (www.cmc.org)
One of the best sources for information on hiking in Colorado; the website offers an excellent overview of the club, with information on hiking, wilderness preservation, and outdoor literature.

Colorado River Outfitters Association (www.adventuresports.com/croa/welcome.htm)
Here you'll find maps, listings of registered guides, and information on how to select the right river trip.

Colorado Snowmobile Association (www.sled-city.com/states/colorado/index.cfm)
Information on everything from trail conditions and upcoming events to snowmobile parts and accessories, and maps.

Denver Bicycle Touring Club (www.dbtc.org)
The group offers regular rides at all levels of interest and ability, and also publishes maps and a newsletter (with complete listings of events and rides).

Golfing in Colorado (www.golfcolorado.com, www.rockiesgolf.com)
Both these websites offer maps, course reviews, tips, and links to other useful sites.

International Mountain Biking Association (www.imba.com)
An excellent website with links to local chapters and clubs.

Sports

Get information on schedules, tickets, and standings, as well as player profiles and other news at the following sites.

Colorado Rockies (www.rockies.mlb.com)
Denver Broncos (www.denverbroncos.com)
Denver Nuggets (www.nba.com/nuggets)

U.S. Olympic Training Center (www.us olympicteam.com)
This 36-acre training complex in Colorado Springs also serves as headquarters for the U.S. Olympic Committee. Visitors can watch athletes in training here.

Accommodations

Bed and Breakfast Innkeepers of Colorado (www.innsofcolorado.org)
This is a good source for information about the state's bed-and-breakfasts.

Colorado Dude and Guest Ranch Association (www.coloradoranch.com)
Here you'll find what you need to know about Colorado dude ranches.

Historic Hotels (www.historic-hotels.com /colorado)
Look here for information on Colorado's historic inns and hotels.

Hostelling International-American Youth Hostels (www.hiayh.org)
The complete source for information about hostelling in Colorado and around the world.

International Bed and Breakfast Pages (www.ibbp.com)
This website provides information on inns with ratings and reviews from other travelers.

State of Colorado (www.colorado.com/acti vities)
The state's campgrounds are generally safe, comfortable, and well maintained. Look here for information on each one.

Tourist Information

Colorado Tourism Office (www.colorado.com)
Look here for information on fall-color tours, festivals and events, and other things of interest to the traveler.

Denver International Airport (www.fly denver.com)
Complete information on policy, procedures, flight information, weather reports, press releases, etc., plus links to other websites of interest to the traveler.

Road Conditions (www.cotrip.org)
This Colorado Department of Transportation site offers information on real-time road conditions, road closings, road construction, weather links, travel alerts, and much more.

Royal Gorge Route Railway (www.royal gorgeroute.com)
The Royal Gorge Route takes visitors on a diesel train from Cañon City down into Royal Gorge to Parkdale and back.

Useful Contact Information

Emergencies:
Dial 911. Note: when teaching kids, authorities stress memorization as nine-one-one, as opposed to nine-eleven, to keep them from looking for the "11" on the dial.

Aspen Chamber Resort Association and Central Reservations
425 Rio Grande Pl., Aspen, CO 81611, 970/925-1940 or 800/262-7736; www.aspen chamber.org

Boulder Convention and Visitors Bureau
2440 Pearl St., Boulder, CO 80302, 303/442-2911 or 800/444-0447; www.boulder coloradousa.com

Colorado Department of Transportation
Driving Conditions, 303/639-1111 or 303/639-1234; www.cotrip.org

Colorado Division of Parks and Outdoor Recreation
1313 Sherman St. #618, Denver, CO 80203, 303/866-3437. (Also with offices in Grand Junction, Colorado Springs, Littleton, and Fort Collins.); www.parks.state.co.us

Colorado Division of Wildlife
6060 N. Broadway, Denver, CO 80216, 303/297-1192; www.wildlife.state.co.us

Colorado Historical Society
1300 Broadway, Denver, CO 80203, 303/866-3682; www.coloradohistory.org

Colorado Hotel and Lodging Association
999 18th St., Denver, CO 80202, 303/297-8335; www.coloradolodging.com

Colorado Springs Convention and Visitors Bureau
104 S. Cascade Ave., Suite 104, Colorado Springs, CO 80903, 719/635-7506 or 800/368-4748; www.coloradosprings-travel .com

Colorado Tourism Office
1625 Broadway, Ste. 1700, Denver, CO 80202, 800/COLORADO (265-6723); www.colorado.com

Denver Metro Convention and Visitors Bureau
1668 Larimer, Denver, CO 80202, 303/892-1112; www.denver.org

Durango Chamber Resort Association
P.O. Box 2587, Durango, CO 81302, 970/247-0312 or 800/525-8855; www.du-rango.org

National Park Service
12795 W. Alameda Pkwy., Lakewood, CO 80225, 303/969-2000; www.nps.gov

Steamboat Springs Chamber Resort Association
P.O. Box 774408, Steamboat Springs, CO 80477, 970/879-0880 or 800/922-2722; www.steamboat-chamber.com

Summit County Chamber of Commerce
P.O. Box 2010, Frisco, CO 80443, 970/668-2051, or 800/530-3099; www.summit chamber.org

Telluride Visitor Guide
888/605-2578; www.telluride.com

U.S. Bureau of Land Management
2850 Youngfield St., Lakewood, CO 80215, 303/239-3600; www.co.blm.gov

U.S. Fish and Wildlife Service
134 Union Blvd., Denver, CO 80228, 303/236-7904; www.offices.fws.gov/statelinks .html

U.S. Forest Service
P.O. Box 25127, Lakewood, CO 80225, 303/275-5350; www.fs.fed.us/recreation/states /co.shtml

Vail Valley Tourism and Convention Bureau
100 E. Meadow Dr., Vail, CO 81657, 970/476-1000, 970/476-5677, or 800/525-3875; www.visitvailvalley.com

Index

Index

Camping

Cross-Country Skiing

Dinosaurs

Downhill Skiing And Snowboarding

Arapahoe Basin: 342–343
Aspen: 233–235
Beaver Creek: 49–50
Breckenridge: 344–345
Clear Creek Canyon: 397
Crested Butte: 271–272
Cuchara Mountain Resort: 158
Glenwood Springs: 41–42
Grand Mesa: 226
Keystone: 343
Leadville: 253
Monarch Pass: 262
Powderhorn: 220
Purgatory Ski Area: 321–322
SolVista: 93–94
Steamboat Springs: 71–73
Summit County: 341–342
Telluride: 301
Vail: 48–50
Winter Park: 84–85
Wolf Creek Pass Ski Area: 329

Fishing

Historic Sites

Kids' Stuff

Buckskin Joe Frontier Town and Scenic Rail-
    way: 180
Cheyenne Mountain Zoo: 186
Children's Museum of Denver: 362–364
Doo Zoo Children's Museum: 219
Kit Carson County Carousel: 140
Lakeside Amusement Park: 371
North Pole/Santa's Workshop: 199
Six Flags Elitch Gardens: 371

Museums

Rafting/Kayaking

general discussion: 20
Aspen: 240
Buena Vista: 257
Cañon City area: 178
Clear Creek: 398
Craig: 65
Crested Butte: 273
Dolores River: 310
Durango: 320
Estes Park: 105
Fort Collins: 124
Glenwood Springs: 42
Grand Junction: 220
Grand Lake area: 98
Gunnison: 266
Montrose: 285
Salida: 260
Steamboat area: 75
Summit County: 348
Telluride: 303
Vail: 53
Winter Park area 88

Railroads And Railroad Museums

Scenic Drives

Index

Tours

Acknowledgments

This book is now in its fifth edition, and a lot of good people have helped me get it this far. I'm indebted to all of you. Any strengths herein are due to your assistance; faults, errors, and oversights are my own.

I'm especially grateful to Mark Stevens and John Peterson (and their wonderful families) in Denver, for the music, food, and Rockies' games over the years—but most of all for the friendship, for making me feel at home so far away. I'm also indebted to Brian McNeill and Susan Dobra, who researched and wrote the section on Boulder restaurants, and for Brian, who updated my research on food in Denver. Thanks.

Thanks, too, to all the readers of the previous editions of the book who took the time to point out misteaks, tyops, and omis ions, as well as to the many friends, old and new, who suggested a back road, offered a couch to crash on, let me pick their brains over espressos or microbrews, or feigned interest as I passed around photos of my family back in California.

Finally, thanks to my wonderful family—Betsy, Gina, and Hannah—for your unending love and support.

FOGHORN OUTDOORS

guides are for campers, hikers, boaters, anglers, bikers, and golfers of all levels of daring and skill. Each guide focuses on a specific U.S. region and contains site descriptions and ratings, driving directions, facilities and fees information, and easy-to-read maps that leave only the task of deciding where to go.

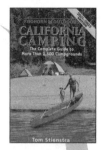

"Foghorn Outdoors has established an ecological conservation standard unmatched by any other publisher."
~**Sierra Club**

WWW.FOGHORN.COM

TRAVEL SMART

guidebooks are accessible, route-based driving guides focusing on regions throughout the United States and Canada. Special interest tours provide the most practical routes for family fun, outdoor activities, or regional history for a trip of anywhere from two to 22 days. Travel Smarts take the guesswork out of planning a trip by recommending only the most interesting places to eat, stay, and visit.

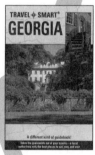

"One of the few travel series that rates sightseeing attractions. That's a handy feature. It helps to have some guidance so that every minute counts."
~*San Diego Union-Tribune*

CiTY·SMaRT™

guides are written by local authors with hometown perspectives who have personally selected the best places to eat, shop, sightsee, and simply hang out. The honest, lively, and opinionated advice is perfect for business travelers looking to relax with the locals or for longtime residents looking for something new to do Saturday night.

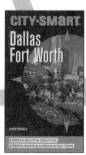

U.S.~METRIC CONVERSION

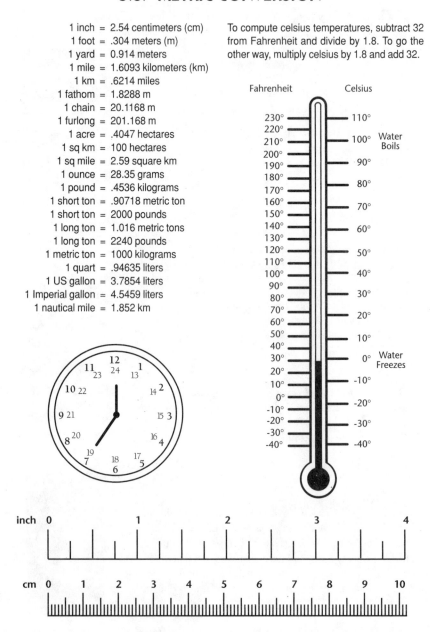

1 inch	= 2.54 centimeters (cm)
1 foot	= .304 meters (m)
1 yard	= 0.914 meters
1 mile	= 1.6093 kilometers (km)
1 km	= .6214 miles
1 fathom	= 1.8288 m
1 chain	= 20.1168 m
1 furlong	= 201.168 m
1 acre	= .4047 hectares
1 sq km	= 100 hectares
1 sq mile	= 2.59 square km
1 ounce	= 28.35 grams
1 pound	= .4536 kilograms
1 short ton	= .90718 metric ton
1 short ton	= 2000 pounds
1 long ton	= 1.016 metric tons
1 long ton	= 2240 pounds
1 metric ton	= 1000 kilograms
1 quart	= .94635 liters
1 US gallon	= 3.7854 liters
1 Imperial gallon	= 4.5459 liters
1 nautical mile	= 1.852 km

To compute celsius temperatures, subtract 32 from Fahrenheit and divide by 1.8. To go the other way, multiply celsius by 1.8 and add 32.